Protect Your Investment with the Best Extended Warranty available.

Savings to 50% off Dealer's Extended Warranty Prices!

Edmunds Teams up with Warranty Gold to offer You the Best Deal on Peace of Mind when Owning, Buying, or Selling Your Vehicle!

http://www.warrantygold.com
1-800-580-9889

Most people have three things in common when they buy a car.

They pay too much.

They waste time.

They hate the experience.

Which is exactly why you should call the Consumers Car Club, a nationwide auto buying service. We offer the quickest and most convenient way to save time and money when you buy a new car or truck. Simple as that. Just tell us the vehicle and options you want (any make or model-foreign or domestic) and we'll get you a lower price than you can get on your own. Guaranteed in writing. We can factory order any domestic vehicle and usually save you even more. No haggling. No hassles. No games.

Don't forget to ask about our loans, leases and extended service contracts. It's a terrific way to save even more money on the purchase of your new car. For more information, call the Consumers Car Club at 1-800-CAR-CLUB (1-800-227-2582).

The Smart New Way to Buy Your Car™

All new cars arranged for sale are subject to price & availability from the selling franchised new car dealer.

"Car dealers take advantage of their knowledge and the customer's lack of knowledge... Edmund's New Car Prices... provides standard costs for cars and optional items."
—Steve Ross, **Successful Car Buying**
(Harrisburg, PA: Stackpole Books, 1990)

"Never pay retail. Buy only at wholesale or below. When buying a car, it is <u>imperative</u> that you know the dealer's cost. Refer to Edmund's ...price guides for current dealer cost information. Armed with this information, you can determine the price that provides the dealer with a <u>minimum</u> 'win' profit."
—Lisa Murr Chapman, **The Savvy Woman's Guide to Cars**
(New York, NY: Bantam Books, 1995)

"How much should you pay for a new car?... Your goal is to buy the car for the lowest price at which the dealer will sell it... To be accurate about profit margins, you should use the most recent edition of Edmund's New Car Prices."
—Dr. Leslie R. Sachs, **How to Buy Your Next Car For a Rock Bottom Price** (New York: Signet, 1986)

"Edmund's publishes a variety of useful guides... buy the guide that deals specifically with the type of car you need.
Wouldn't it be nice if you could know beforehand the dealer's cost for the new vehicle you just fell in love with? Wouldn't it be even nicer if you knew how much to offer him over his costs, a price he would just barely be able to accept?
Well you are in luck. You can find out exactly what the car cost the dealership ...in Edmund's auto books."
—Burke Leon, **The Insider's Guide to Buying A New or Used Car** (Cincinnati, OH: Betterway Books, 1993)

"Obtain a copy of Edmund's New Car Prices... and be certain you have the current copy since they are revised regularly during a year. Edmund's will provide you with the dealer's cost prices for all makes and models along with corresponding prices for the available factory options. These prices will be listed alongside the sticker prices. Match the sticker information of the car you want to buy to the cost prices in Edmund's and add these up... to provide you with a useable answer to "what should I pay for the car?"... It will furnish you with a very reliable figure. This, in turn, will enable you to successfully negotiate with confidence because ultimately you will be able to pay a price that you know is realistic and fair."

—Edward Roop, **Best Deals for New Wheels: How to Save Money When Buying or Leasing a Car** (New York: Berkley Books, 1992)

"Using the percent factor to figure dealer cost is not as accurate as using specific information published in Edmund's New Car Prices."

—Mark Eskeldson, **What Car Dealers Don't Want You to Know** (Fair Oaks, CA: Technews Publishing, 1995)

"If you really want the nitty-gritty, you're going to have to... (get) ...Edmund's New Car Prices. This little book is a gold mine for the curious car buyer... It is an automobile fancier's delight, a straightforward, meaty compendium of raw facts... Buy the book, follow the steps outlined... and you will determine the exact cost of just about any car."

—Demar Sutton, **Don't Get Taken Every Time** (New York: Penguin Books, 1994)

Edmund's **Perfect Partners**

USED CARS: PRICES & RATINGS

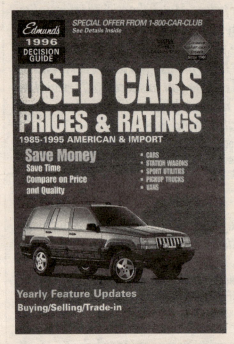

For 30 years, Edmund's has guided smart consumers through the complex used car marketplace. By providing you with the latest wholesale and retail pricing, you are able to determine fair market value before negotiations begin.

Whether buying, selling, or trading, Edmund's *Used Cars: Prices & Ratings* gives all the information you need to get your very best deal.

- √ Prices Most American and Imported Used Cars, Pickup Trucks, Vans, and Sport Utilities
- √ Shows Summary Ratings Graphs for Most Used Vehicles
- √ Listings Cover Models Over Last 10 Years
- √ Price any Vehicle Quickly and Accurately
- √ Adjust Value for Optional Engines, Equipment and Mileage

For information on all Edmund's Automotive Books, call 914-962-6297

1997

Edmund's

NEW TRUCKS
PRICES &
REVIEWS

"THE ORIGINAL CONSUMER PRICE AUTHORITY"

Publisher: Peter Steinlauf

Cover photo: 1997 Dodge Dakota Sport 2WD

Published by:
Edmund Publications Corp.
300 N. Sepulveda, Ste. 2050
El Segundo, CA 90245

ISBN: 0-87759-615-8
ISSN: 1089-8735

Managing Editor:
Christian J. Wardlaw

Automotive Editors:
B. Grant Whitmore
William Badnow

Contributing Editor:
James Flammang

Creative Design:
Debra Katzir
John H. Davis

Cover Design:
Karen Ross

Photography:
Greg Anderson

Information Specialist:
Kathy McManus

© 1997 by Edmund Publications Corporation. All rights reserved. No reproduction in whole or in part may be made without explicit written permission from the publisher.

Printed in Canada

NEW TRUCKS

TABLE OF CONTENTS
SPRING 1997 **VOL S3101-9706**

Automaker Customer
   Assistance Numbers 10
Introduction 11
Understanding
   the Language
   of Auto Buying 14
How to Buy Your Next
   New Automobile 16
Abbreviations 17
Editors' Picks 20
Step-by-Step
   Costing Form 22
Step-by-Step
   Costing Form 416
Specifications 417
Payment Table 419
Step-by-Step
   Costing Form 454
Crash Test Data 455
Leasing Tips 461
Warranties and
   Roadside Assistance 466
Dealer Holdbacks 468
Road Test - Chevrolet K1500
   Extended Cab 480
Road Test - Mazda B4000 SE
   Cab Plus 484
Road Test - Mercury
   Mountaineer AWD 487
Quick Spin - Toyota 4Runner
   Limited 491

ACURA
'96 SLX 23

CHEVROLET
'97 Astro 25
'97 Blazer 31
'97 Chevy Van 40
'97 C/K 1500 Pickup 44
'97 C/K 2500 Pickup 54
'97 C/K 3500 Pickup 60
'97 Express Van 67
'97 S-10 Pickup 71
'97 Suburban 77
'97 Tahoe 83
'97 Venture 89

CHRYSLER
'97 Town & Country 94

DODGE
'97 Caravan 98
'97 Dakota 106
'97 Grand Caravan 123
'97 Ram BR1500 Pickup ... 133
'97 Ram BR2500 Pickup ... 144
'97 Ram BR3500 Pickup ... 154
'97 Ram Van 161
'97 Ram Wagon 161

FORD
'97 Aerostar 170
'97 Club Wagon 175
'97 Econoline 180
'97 Expedition 186
'97 Explorer 190
'97 F150 Pickup 195
'97 F250 Pickup 201
'97 F350 Pickup 209
'97 Ranger 214
'97 Windstar 222
'98 Windstar 226

Special offer from 1-800-CAR-CLUB - details on page 3

GEO
'97 Tracker 231

GMC
'97 Jimmy 235
'97 Safari 244
'97 Savana 250
'97 Sierra 1500 256
'97 Sierra 2500 267
'97 Sierra 3500 273
'97 Sonoma 280
'97 Suburban 288
'97 Yukon 294

HONDA
'97 Odyssey 300
'97 Passport 302

INFINITI
'97 QX4 304

ISUZU
'97 Hombre 306
'97 Rodeo 309
'97 Trooper 312

JEEP
'97 Cherokee 315
'97 Grand Cherokee 321
'97 Wrangler 330

KIA
'97 Sportage 335

LAND ROVER
'97 Defender 90 338
'97 Discovery 340
'97 Range Rover 342

LEXUS
'97 LX 450 345

MAZDA
'97 B-Series Pickup 347
'97 MPV 351

MERCURY
'97 Mountaineer 354
'97 Villager 357

MITSUBISHI
'97 Montero 361

NISSAN
'97 Pathfinder 364
'97 Quest 367
'97 Truck 369

OLDSMOBILE
'97 Bravada 373
'97 Silhouette 376

PLYMOUTH
'97 Voyager/
   Grand Voyager 379

PONTIAC
'97 Trans Sport 386

SUZUKI
'97 Sidekick Sport 392
'97 X-90 394

TOYOTA
'97 4Runner 396
'97 Land Cruiser 400
'97 Previa 402
'97 RAV4 405
'97 T100 407
'97 Tacoma 412

EDMUND'S 1997 NEW TRUCKS

Automobile Manufacturers
Customer Assistance Numbers

Acura	1-800-382-2238
Chevrolet	1-800-222-1020
Chrysler	1-800-992-1997
Dodge	1-800-992-1997
Ford	1-800-392-3673
Geo	1-800-222-1020
GMC	1-800-462-8782
	toll free not available
Honda	1-310-783-2000
Infiniti	1-800-662-6200
Kia	1-800-333-4542
Land Rover	1-800-637-6837
Lexus	1-800-255-3987
Mazda	1-800-222-5500
Mercury	1-800-392-3673
Mitsubishi	1-800-222-0037
Nissan	1-800-647-7261
Oldsmobile	1-800-442-6537
Plymouth	1-800-992-1997
Pontiac	1-800-762-2737
Suzuki	1-800-934-0934
Toyota	1-800-331-4331

INTRODUCTION

Since 1966, Edmund's has been providing consumers with the information they need to get the best price on a new car. This edition of *New Car Prices* continues the tradition of listing most of the cars available on the market today, including pricing data for dealer invoice price and Manufacturer's Suggested Retail Price (MSRP) on each model and its options. We also provide detailed lists of standard equipment for each model, specifications for each model, and helpful articles that will allow you to make an educated decision about your purchase.

What's New For 1997?

New for 1997 is estimated performance data, listed in the same table as the vehicle specifications at the back of the book. We are also featuring Safety Data sections, which tell consumers basic information regarding safety features and crash test data for many models. We've added pages of Frequently Asked Questions that cover a variety of topics related to cars and the buying process. Our advice articles have been revised to reflect new data and information, and we now list option package discounts and net package prices to clear up confusion suffered by buyers who often found the sticker price of a package and the Edmund's price for a package to be the only price discrepancies between our guide and the dealership's claims. This year, we've added detail in the options section to assist the consumer in understanding content, purchase requirements, and when an option can or cannot be ordered in conjunction with other options or trim levels.

How do I use this Guide?

If you're new to Edmund's, or are new to the car buying experience, we should explain how to use this book effectively. Your first step should be to visit a car dealership. Take a pad of paper with you, and write down all pertinent information from the window sticker of the car you like. Then, go home, or go to Mc Donald's, or go have an espresso at the local coffeehouse. Snuggle up with Edmund's *New Car Prices*, and start figuring out how to get the best deal on the car of your dreams.

Read the articles on **dealer holdbacks**, **buying your next new automobile**, and **leasing tips**. Then study the make and model that you're interested in. You'll find a representative photo of the vehicle, followed by a synopsis of what's new for 1997, where applicable. Then, a short review provides our opinion of the car, followed by safety data. An extensive listing of standard equipment for each trim level comes next, telling you what items are included in the base price of the vehicle.

INTRODUCTION

The first paragraph pertains to the base model, and if more than one trim level is available, successive paragraphs will explain what additional features the additional trim levels include over the base model.

Next is the meat of this guide; the pricing data. Each vehicle has base invoice price and base MSRP listed for each trim level, and the destination charge, which is the cost of shipping the vehicle from the factory to the dealer. Don't forget to add the destination charge, which is non-negotiable, when pricing a vehicle. Following the base prices and destination charge is a listing of all the optional equipment available on the vehicle from the factory. Along the left margin you'll find a factory code for each option. The dealer invoice price and the MSRP are listed near the right margin. Some option listings have short descriptions that tell you, for example, what might be included in a particular option package, or what trim level the option is available on, or that you must purchase the power lock group to get the power sunroof.

You'll notice that some imported makes do not have options listings. This is because the automaker includes the most popular accessories as standard equipment on a particular trim level, and any additional items that you might like to add to the vehicle will have to be purchased from and installed by the dealer, or are installed at the port of entry. For example, the Honda Passport LX 2WD comes with power door locks and power windows standard from the factory. Air conditioning is a dealer add-on, and each dealer may price the item differently. Generally, you can haggle about 25% off dealer-installed accessories with little effort.

Supply and Demand

Now that you've priced the vehicle you're interested in, and you've read the articles about how to get the best deal, you're ready to go back to the dealership and buy your new car armed with the knowledge and information that is crucial to getting a good deal. Keep in mind that the laws of supply and demand apply to auto sales as much as they apply to any other material commodity. If a vehicle is in great demand and short supply, don't expect to get much of a discount. On the other hand, inflated inventories and tough competition mean that deals are readily available on models that aren't selling well. If you've got to be the first on your block with a hot new model, you'll pay for the privilege. In fact, dealers sometimes demand profit above the MSRP on ultra hot models, and they expect to get it. Meanwhile, it is not uncommon for older, stale models to sell below invoice thanks to hefty

INTRODUCTION

incentive programs and rebates, particularly at year-end clearance time. All things considered equal, Edmund's feels that a 5% profit to the dealer is fair on a new vehicle. After all, the sales staff have bills to pay just like you do.

Looking for the exact specifications of your dream car? Check the back of this book, where you'll find charts displaying the length of the vehicle, the curb weight of the vehicle, and how much horsepower the base engine makes, among others. New this year are performance estimates for acceleration and braking. This format allows you to easily locate and compare specifications between different models and trim levels.

Write to Us

New Car Prices has even more to offer, from step-by-step costing forms that you can use right at the dealership, to lists of warranty coverage, to pages of crash test data. Edmund's strives to give you precise, accurate information so that you can make your very best deal, and we invite your comments. Please send correspondence to:

Edmund Publications Corporation
300 N. Sepulveda Blvd., Suite 2050
El Segundo, CA 90245
Attn: Automotive Editor
or send e-mail to:
editors@edmund.com

We wish you luck in your hunt for a new vehicle. Use the information contained within to your advantage!

NOTE: All information and prices published herein are gathered from sources which, in the editor's opinion, are considered reliable, but under no circumstances is the reader to assume that this information is official or final. All prices are represented as approximations only, in US dollars, and are rounded to the highest whole dollar amount over 50 cents. Unless otherwise noted, all prices are effective as of 1/15/97, but are subject to change without notice. The publisher does not assume responsibility for errors of omission or interpretation. • The computerized consumer pricing services advertised herein are not operated by nor are they are the responsibility of the publisher. • The publisher assumes no responsibility for claims made by advertisers regarding their products or services.

UNDERSTANDING THE LANGUAGE OF AUTO BUYING

Many consumers are justifiably confused by the language and terms used by automobile manufacturers and dealers. To assist you, here are some basic definitions:

MSRP — Manufacturer's Suggested Retail Price The manufacturer's recommended selling price for a vehicle and each of its optional accessories.

Dealer Invoice The amount that dealers are invoiced or billed by the manufacturer for a vehicle and each of its optional accessories.

Dealer Holdback Many manufacturers provide dealers with a *holdback allowance* (usually 2 or 3% of MSRP) which is eventually credited to the dealer's account. That way, the dealer can end up paying the manufacturer less than the invoiced amount — meaning that they could sell you the vehicle at cost and still make a small profit. Holdback is also known as a 'pack.'

Destination Charge The fee charged for shipping, freight, or delivery of the vehicle to the dealer from the manufacturer or Port of Entry. This charge is passed on to the buyer without any mark-up.

Preparation Charges These are dealer-imposed charges for getting the new car ready to drive away including a full tank of gas, checking and filling the fluid levels, making sure the interior and exterior is clean, etc.

Dealer Charges These are highly profitable extras that dealers try to sell in addition to the vehicle itself. Items such as rustproofing, undercoating and extended warranties fall into this category. Most consumer experts do not recommend the purchase of these extras.

Advertising Fee The amount you are charged to cover the cost of national and local advertising. This fee should be no more than 1-3% of the MSRP.

Manufacturer's Rebate/Dealer Incentives Programs offered by the manufacturers to increase the sales of slow-selling models or to reduce excess inventories. While manufacturer's rebates are passed directly on to the buyer, dealer incentives are passed on only to the dealer — who may or may not elect to pass the savings on to the customer.

Trade-in Value The amount that the dealership will give you for the vehicle you trade in. Generally, this amount will be about 5% below wholesale value of the vehicle. The trade-in value will be deducted from the price of the new vehicle.

Upside-down When you owe more on your car loan than your trade-in is worth, you are *upside-down* on your trade. When this happens, the dealer will add the difference between the trade-in value and what you owe to the price of the new vehicle.

Note: Occasionally there will appear in the "Dealer Invoice" and "MSRP" columns, prices enclosed in parenthesis, example: (90), which indicate a credit or refunded amount is involved.

We don't have hoists and grease pits, but we give incredible service!

"Your Detroit Car and Truck Connection."

Our auto dealership doesn't have a service department but our customers keep coming back, time after time. Why? Because we give them the best prices, support and product knowledge of any dealer in the country!

We're NATIONWIDE AUTO BROKERS.
For nearly thirty years, we have provided our customers with the lowest vehicle prices and best service because *we do the shopping for them*! Once you approve our low, low price (as little as $50-$125 over dealer invoice*) on the domestic or import vehicle of your choice, **NATIONWIDE** can order your domestic vehicle and have it delivered direct to a dealership near you. Factory-authorized service is then handled by the local dealership, and you rest easy knowing you've received a truly remarkable deal!

VISIT OUR INTERNET WEB SITE AT
http://www.car-connect.com

These two numbers could SAVE YOU THOUSANDS OF DOLLARS the next time you BUY A NEW CAR OR TRUCK!

Auto Quote line:
1-800-521-7257
9 am - 7 pm EST Mon.-Fri.

Obtain a printed computer quote on the make and model of your choice. Your quote contains all factory equipment available in an easy to read format. Instructions and pricing (both "**MSRP**" and dealer "**INVOICE**") make it simple to price your own vehicle.
First Quote $11.95, each additional quote $9.95. Add $6.95 for faxes.

Auto Hot Line:
1-900-884-6800
9 am - 5 pm EST Mon.-Fri.

Talk live to one of our sales staff for information on an "**IMMEDIATE QUOTE**", options, rebates, dealer incentives, used vehicle fair market value and plain old good advice!
$2.00 per minute. 6-10 min. avg. per call. You must be 18 or older to use this service.

*Some vehicles may be higher. Some specialty imports and limited production models and vehicles may not be available for delivery to your area or through our pricing service. A message on your printout will advise you of this. You will still be able to use the printout in negotiating the best deal with the dealer of your choice. New car pricing and purchasing services not available where prohibited by law.

NATIONWIDE Auto Brokers
29623 Northwestern Hwy., Southfield, MI 48034 • (810) 354-3400 • FAX (810) 223-1770

HOW TO BUY YOUR NEXT NEW AUTOMOBILE

Every automobile buyer has but one thought in mind — to save money by getting a good deal. Your goal should be to pay no more than 5% over the dealer's true cost, not the 8-12% the dealer wants you to pay. Use the following guide to help you plan your purchase:

Step 1   Know what type of vehicle you need, and study the different models available.

Step 2   Test drive, as extensively as possible, each model you're interested in. Pay special attention to safety features, design, comfort, braking, handling, acceleration, ride quality, ease of entry and exit, etc.

Step 3   Check insurance rates on the models you're interested in, to make sure the premiums fall within your budget.

Step 4   Contact several financial institutions to obtain loan rate information. Later on, you can compare their arrangement with the dealer's financing plan.

Step 5   Find the exact vehicle you want, and copy all the contents of the window sticker onto a pad of paper. Then, use the information in this book to determine actual dealer cost (if ordering the vehicle from the factory, just use the book to determine what the order will cost when you place it):

     a) Total the dealer invoice column for the model and equipment you want using the costing form on the opposite page.

     b) Find the holdback amount on page 512, and subtract this from the invoice amount, along with any applicable customer rebates and dealer incentives. The resulting figure is true dealer cost.

     c) Add 5% fair profit. Keep in mind that hot-selling models that are in high demand and short supply will command additional profit.

     d) Add the destination charge, which is non-negotiable. Also expect non-negotiable advertising fees ranging in value from 1-3% of the sticker price to be added to the total.

Step 6   Shop this price around to several different dealerships. The dealer who meets or comes closest to your target price should get your business. Be sure that the dealer's price quote will be your final cost. Get it in writing!

Step 7   If your present vehicle will be used as a trade-in, negotiate the highest possible value for it. Try not to accept a value that is less that 5% below Edmund's wholesale value for your car (consult Edmund's *Used Cars; Prices and Ratings* book). When trading in your vehicle, you should deduct the trade value from the cost of the new vehicle. If you owe the bank more money than the trade-in is worth to the dealer, you are upside-down on your trade and must add the difference between what you owe and the trade value to the cost of the new vehicle. If you're making a cash down payment, either with or without a trade-in, be sure to deduct this amount from the cost of the new vehicle as well.

Step 8   Add dealer preparation charges, documentation fees, applicable state and/or local sales taxes and, in some areas, license plate charges to the final vehicle cost.

Step 9   When talking to the finance manager as you close the deal, he or she will try to sell you rustproofing, undercoating, protection packages, dealer-added options, and an extended warranty or service contract. Forget about this stuff. Dealers charge a substantial markup on these usually useless items to fatten the profit margin on your deal.

Step 10   Enjoy your new vehicle, knowing that you did everything possible to get the best deal.

ABBREVIATIONS

16V	16-valve	Cu In	Cubic Inch(es)
24V	24-valve	Cust	Custom
32V	32-valve	CVT	Continuously Variable Transmission
2WD	Two-wheel Drive		
3A/4A/5A	3-speed/4-speed/5-speed Automatic Transmission	Cvrs	Covers
		Cyl	Cylinder
		DC	Direct Current
4M/5M/6M	4-speed/5-speed/6-speed Manual Transmission	DFRS	Dual Facing Rear Seats
		DME	Digital Motor Electronics
		DOHC	Dual Overhead Cam Engine
4Sp/5Sp/6Sp	4-speed/5-speed/6-speed Manual Transmission	Dr	Door
		DRLs	Daytime Running Lights
4WD	Four-wheel Drive	Drv	Drive
4WS	Four-wheel Steering	DRW	Dual Rear Wheels
A/S	All-season Tires	Dsl	Diesel Engine
A/T	All-terrain Tires	ECT	Electronically Controlled Transmission
A/C	Air Conditioning		
A/M	Auto-manual Transmission	EEC	Electronic Engine Control
ABS	Anti-lock Braking System	EFI	Electronic Fuel Injection
		ELR	Emergency Locking Retractor Seat Belt
AC	Air Conditioning		
ALR	Automatic Locking Retractor Seat Belt	Eng	Engine
		Equip	Equipment
Amp	Ampere(s)	ETR	Electronically Tuned Radio
AS	All-season Tires		
AT	Automatic Transmission	ETS	Electronically Tuned Stereo
Auto	Automatic		
Aux	Auxiliary	Ext	Extended
Auxl	Auxiliary	FI	Fuel Injection
Avail	Available	Ft	Foot (Feet)
AWD	All-wheel Drive	FWD	Front-wheel Drive
Blk	Black	Gal	Gallon
BSW	Black Sidewall Tires	Grp	Group
BW	Blackwall Tires	GVW	Gross Vehicle Weight
Cptn	Captain	GVWR	Gross Vehicle Weight Rating
Cass	Cassette		
CD	Compact Disc	H4	Horizontally-opposed, Four-cylinder Engine
CFC	Chloroflorocarbon		
CID	Cubic Inch Displacement	H6	Horizontally-opposed, Six-cylinder Engine
Cntry	Country		
Conv	Convertible	Hbk	Hatchback
Cpe	Coupe	HD	Heavy Duty
Ctrl	Control	HO	High Output
Cu Ft	Cubic Foot (Feet)	HP	Horsepower

ABBREVIATIONS

HUD	Heads Up Display	Mus	Music
HVAC	Heating/Ventilation/Air Conditioning	N/A	Not Available or Not Applicable
I4	Inline Type, Four-cylinder Engine	NA	Not Available or Not Applicable
I5	Inline Type, Five-cylinder Engine	Nbk	Notchback
I6	Inline Type, Six-cylinder Engine	N/C	No Charge
		NC	No Charge
Illum	Illuminated	OBD II	On-board Diagnostic System
Incls	Includes	OD	Overdrive
Incld	Included	OHC	Overhead Camshaft Engine
Kw	Kilowatt		
L	Liter	OHV	Overhead Valve Engine
L4	Inline Type, Four-cylinder Engine	Opt	Optional
		OS	Outside
L5	Inline Type, Five-cylinder Engine	OWL	Outline White-letter Tires
		P/U	Pickup Truck
L6	Inline Type, Six-cylinder Engine	Pass	Passenger
		PDL	Power Door Locks
L/R	Left and Right	PEG	Preferred Equipment Group
LB	Longbed		
Lbk	Liftback	PEP	Preferred Equipment Package
Lb/ft	Pounds/Feet (measurement of engine torque)	PGM-FI	Programmed Fuel Injection
Lb(s)	Pound(s)	Pkg	Package
LCD	Liquid Crystal Display	Pkup	Pickup Truck
LD	Light Duty	Prem	Premium
LED	Light Emitting Diode	PS	Power Steering
LH	Left Hand	Psngr	Passenger
Ltd	Limited	PW	Power Windows
Lthr	Leather	Pwr	Power
Lugg	Luggage	Reg	Regular
LWB	Long Wheelbase	Req'd	Required
M+S	Mud and Snow Tires	Req's	Requires
Man	Manual	RH	Right Hand
Max	Maximum	Rpm	Revolutions Per Minute
Med	Medium	RWD	Rear-wheel Drive
Min	Minimum	RWL	Raised White-letter Tires
M m	Millimeter	SB	Shortbed
MPFI	Multi-point Fuel Injection	SBR	Steel-belted Radial Tires
Mpg	Miles Per Gallon	Sdn	Sedan
Mph	Miles Per Hour	SEFI	Sequential Fuel Injection
MPI	Multi-point Fuel Injection	SFI	Sequential Fuel Injection
MT	Manual Transmission		

ABBREVIATIONS

SLA	Short/Long Arm Suspension	TPI	Tuned Port Fuel Injection
Snrf	Sunroof	Trans	Transmission
SOHC	Single Overhead Camshaft Engine	TrbDsl	Turbo-diesel Engine
Spd	Speed	Trbo	Turbocharged Engine
SPFI	Sequential Port Fuel Injection	V6	V-type, Six-cylinder Engine
Spt	Sport	V8	V-type, Eight-cylinder Engine
SRS	Supplemental Restraint System (Airbag)	V10	V-type, Ten-cylinder Engine
SRW	Single Rear Wheels	V12	V-type, Twelve-cylinder Engine
Std	Standard	VTEC	Variable Valve Timing and Lift Electronic Control
Sts	Seats		
Sunscrn	Sunscreen		
SUV	Sport/Utility Vehicle	W/	With
S/W	Station Wagon	W/O	Without
SWB	Short Wheelbase	W/T	Work Truck
Sys	System	WB	Wheelbase
Tach	Tachometer	Wgn	Wagon
TBI	Throttle Body Fuel Injection	Whl(s)	Wheel(s)
		Wndw	Window(s)
TCS	Traction Control System	WS	Wideside
TD	Turbo-diesel Engine	WSW	White Sidewall Tires
Temp	Temperature	X-Cab	Extended Cab Pickup

EDITORS' PICKS FOR 1997

by Christian Wardlaw and B. Grant Whitmore
Automotive Editors, Edmund Publications

Each year, consumers are bombarded with sound and text bites in advertising proclaiming their truck worthy of recommendation by top automotive publications. These accolades are usually culled from top ten lists of this or that published by enthusiast magazines and consumer publications. We didn't want to miss out on the fun this year, or the possibility of some free advertising, so we've compiled our own list of recommended vehicles for 1997.

Edmund's has decided to take a different tack than other buyer's guides and magazines. We've broken the truck market into nine categories. Then, we took into consideration the fact that there are different sorts of buyers in the market. Logical left brainers are more concerned with value and reliability. Creative right brainers are swayed by style and speed. So for each category, we've provided two models worthy of consideration; one for left brainers, and one for right brainers. The exception is the full-size van category. There's nothing emotional about buying a full-size van, so just one choice is provided for this category.

So, instead of giving consumers a list of ten recommended vehicles, Edmund's provides 17 models that you might want to consider. Enjoy our picks for 1997!

EDITORS' PICKS FOR 1997

Size Category	[Left Brain: value/reliability; Right Brain: style/speed]
Compact Pickup	Left Brain: Dodge Dakota SLT Club Cab 4WD Right Brain: GMC Sonoma GT Sportside Regular Cab 2WD
Full-size Pickup	Left Brain: Dodge Ram 3500 Club Cab 4WD Diesel Right Brain: Dodge Ram 1500 Regular Cab 2WD SS/T
Minivan (under $25,000)	Left Brain: Pontiac Trans Sport SE Extended Right Brain: Dodge Caravan SE Sport
Minivan (over $25,000)	Left Brain: Chrysler Town & Country LXi Right Brain: Toyota Previa LE All-Trac
Full-size Van	Left Brain: Ford Club Wagon XLT
Mini-SUV	Left Brain: Honda CR-V Right Brain: Jeep Wrangler Sport 4.0L
Compact SUV (under $25,000)	Left Brain: Jeep Cherokee Sport 4-door 4WD Right Brain: Chevrolet Blazer ZR2 2-door
Compact SUV (over $25,000)	Left Brain: Toyota 4Runner SR5 Right Brain: Land Rover Defender 90
Full-size SUV	Left Brain: Ford Expedition XLT 4WD Right Brain: Toyota Land Cruiser

STEP-BY-STEP COSTING FORM

MAKE: EXTERIOR COLOR:
MODEL: INTERIOR COLOR:
TRIM LEVEL: ENGINE SIZE/TYPE:

ITEMS		MSRP	INVOICE
Basic Vehicle Price:			
Optional Equipment			
1.			
2.			
3.			
4.			
5.			
6.			
7.			
8.			
9.			
10.			
11.			
12.			
13.			
14.			
	TOTAL		
	SUBTRACT Holdback Amount		
	SUBTRACT Rebates and/or Incentives		
	ADD 5% Fair Profit to New Total		
	ADD Destination Charge		
	ADD Advertising Fees (1-3% of MSRP)		
	SUBTRACT Trade-In Value or Cash Down Payment		
	or		
	ADD Difference Between Trade Value and Loan Balance		
	FINAL PRICE		
	ADD Sales Taxes, Documentation/Prep Fees, and License Plates		
	TOTAL COST		

http://edmunds.com

SLX   *ACURA*

SLX (1996)

1996 Acura SLX

What's New for Acura SLX in 1996 — In typical Acura form, the SLX is one of the first luxury badged sport-utes to be released in this country. Based on the successful Isuzu Trooper, the SLX is very similar to its twin.

SLX — Review

Corporate sharing is reaching a fever pitch. Manufacturers are scrambling to fill the holes in their lineups by slapping their badges on vehicles they buy from other makers. Even highly regarded firms like Acura are not above climbing into a cozy relationship with a lesser marque; witness the Acura SLX. Based on Isuzu's competent Trooper, the Acura is a marginally spruced up version of the same truck. This isn't a bad thing since we have always thought the Trooper to be attractive, but it does seem dishonest. Imagine the embarrassment of the SLX owner who thinks they got something special only to find that they are driving an Isuzu?

The SLX has a 3.2-liter dual-overhead-cam engine that produces 190 horsepower. It delivers capable acceleration in a vehicle this large, and this vehicle is definitely large. Markedly wider and taller than most of its competitors, the SLX has a rear cargo capacity capable of hauling several sheets of plywood.

The Acura SLX is priced the same as the top-of-the-line Isuzu Trooper Limited. Offering similar levels of luxury as the Trooper, the SLX has a softer ride that results in improved on-road manners. Off-road capability is equal to the ground-pounding Trooper but large bumps may cause the suspension to bottom out; the price you pay for that luxurious highway ride. Of course, very few SLXs will ever find their way off-road, unless the gravel driveway of the local polo club counts.

We know that luxurious sport-utes of today are like the sports cars so prevalent in the mid-eighties. Designed for function but purchased for prestige, they are seldom driven to their capabilities. With this in mind, the SLX is a fine vehicle delivering the prestige and comfort that Acura owners have come to expect. Infiniti, Mercedes and Lincoln have plans

ACURA SLX

to release luxury sport-utes within a few years; many of them based on vehicles that are already in existence. Who knows, with the rush towards these up-market trucks it may be more exclusive to own the vehicles they are based on.

Safety Data

Driver Airbag: *Standard*
Meets 1999 Side Impact Standards: *No*
Integrated Child Seat(s): *N/A*
Driver Crash Test Grade: *Average*

Passenger Airbag: *Standard*
4-wheel ABS: *Standard*
Insurance Cost: *Unknown*
Passenger Crash Test Grade: *Average*

Standard Equipment

SLX w/o PREMIUM PKG: 3.2 liter 24 valve SOHC EFI V6 engine, 4-speed automatic transmission, speed sensitive power steering, cruise control, anti-lock power 4-wheel disc brakes, driver and front passenger air bags, power windows with driver side express-down feature, air conditioning, power door locks, alarm system, conventional spare tire, P245/70R16 SBR mud and snow tires, 5-spoke aluminum wheels, console, electric rear window defroster, AM/FM ETR stereo radio with cassette and 6 speakers, front and rear stabilizer bars, digital clock, privacy glass, tachometer, 22.5 gallon fuel tank, trip odometer, voltmeter, oil pressure gauge, dual heated power mirrors, rear window wiper/washer, intermittent windshield wipers, leather-wrapped tilt steering wheel, power antenna, skid plates (transmission, transfer case, fuel tank, radiator, exhaust), front and rear wheel flares, front and rear mud guards, rear step bumper, cloth reclining front bucket seats, 60/40 split folding rear seat, cut-pile carpeting, rear air deflector, vinyl spare tire cover, outside spare tire carrier, passenger assist grips, 80 amp battery.

SLX w/PREMIUM PKG (in addition to or instead of SLX w/o PREMIUM PKG equipment): Power moonroof, halogen fog lights, limited slip differential, 6-spoke aluminum alloy wheels with locks, leather seating surfaces, heated front bucket seats with 8-way power driver's seat and 4-way power passenger seat, woodgrain door trim inserts.

Base Prices

Code	Description	Invoice	MSRP
9C326T	4-Dr Sport Utility w/o Premium Pkg	29610	33900
9C327T	4-Dr Sport Utility w/Premium Pkg	33191	38000
	Destination Charge:	420	420

Accessories

NOTE: Acura accessories are dealer installed. Contact an Acura dealer for accessory availability.

CALL NATIONWIDE 1-800-521-7257
FOR A WRITTEN QUOTATION
AS LOW AS $50 OVER INVOICE

See page 15 for details.

ASTRO | CHEVROLET

CODE	DESCRIPTION		INVOICE	MSRP

ASTRO (1997)

1997 Chevrolet Astro LT

What's New for Chevrolet Astro in 1997 — Daytime running lights debut, and LT models can be equipped with leather upholstery. Also optional this year is a HomeLink 3-channel transmitter. Delayed entry/exit lighting is now standard on all Astro passenger vans. Transmission refinements mean smoother shifts, and electronic variable orifice steering eases steering effort at low speeds.

Astro — Review

Models that have been around for a while can still deliver impressive value—and valor. That's true of the long-lived Astro van, a staple in Chevy's lineup since 1985. This hard-working passenger/cargo hauler, sporting a conventionally-boxy shape, has, if anything, mellowed with age.

No, you don't get the curvaceous contours of a Caravan/Voyager or a Windstar. What you do acquire is a highly-practical carrier that can be equipped to suit just about any family, trimmed in any of three levels. Depending on configuration, Astros can seat up to eight passengers and haul as much as three tons.

Out on the road, rolling hour after hour, is where the Astro demonstrates its true worth. Taller than its likely rivals, Astros are admittedly more truck-like in temperament, but deliver a pleasant highway ride with competent handling for long journeys. Seats are a little short, but comfortable, in both the front and center positions. Unfortunately, overly small front foot wells drop the comfort level a notch. A 190-horsepower 4.3-liter V-6 is standard, driving a smooth-shifting four-speed electronically controlled automatic transmission.

Dual airbags and anti-lock brakes are standard. This year, Chevy ups safety equipment levels to include daytime running lights. LT models can be equipped with leather upholstery for 1997. Also optional this year is a HomeLink 3-channel transmitter, while delayed entry/exit lighting is standard on all Astro passenger vans. Transmission refinements mean

CHEVROLET ASTRO

smoother shifts, and electronic variable orifice steering eases steering effort at low speeds. Three new colors are available, and all-wheel drive models get lighter-weight torsion bars and plug-in front differential axle shafts that are easier to service.

You get only one body choice: the extended-length version. The lower-priced rear-drive rendition is the ticket for hauling plenty of weight. All-wheel-drive costs more and delivers improved wet-pavement traction, but slurps up more fuel along the route.

Solid and substantial, Astros remain tempting—if dated—choices, whether in passenger or cargo form. If you need a small van with big van capacity, the Astro should be on your shopping list.

Safety Data

Driver Airbag: *Standard*
Side Airbag: *Not Available*
4-Wheel ABS: *Standard*
Driver Crash Test Grade: *Average*
Passenger Crash Test Grade: *Average*

Passenger Airbag: *Standard*
Meets 1997 Car Side Impact Standards: *No*
Traction Control: *Not Available*
Insurance Cost: *Very Low*
Integrated Child Seat(s): *N/A (Cargo); Opt. (Passenger)*

Standard Equipment

ASTRO CARGO VAN: 4.3-liter Vortec V-6 engine, 4-speed automatic transmission, speed-sensitive power steering, hydraulic power front disc/rear drum anti-lock brakes, 15"x 6" styled steel wheels, P215/75R15 tires, dual front airbags, front air conditioning, side-impact door beams (do not meet 1999 truck standards), trip odometer, Scotchgard fabric protectant, vinyl reclining bucket seats, AM/FM stereo with digital clock, vinyl sunvisors with map bands, headlights-on warning buzzer, intermittent variable wipers, daytime running lights, dual black exterior foldaway mirrors

PASSENGER VAN (in addition to or instead of CARGO VAN equipment): Cloth and carpet door panel trim, cloth headliner, delayed entry interior lighting, vinyl 3-passenger center bench seat, left rear quarter storage compartment, cloth sunvisors with extensions, swing out windows, black center caps for wheels

Base Prices

Code	Description	Invoice	MSRP
CM11005	Astro Cargo Van	17773	19639
CM11006	Astro Passenger Van	18311	20223
CL11005	Astro Cargo Van AWD	20669	22839
CL11006	Passenger Van AWD	20293	22423
Destination Charge:		585	585

Accessories

Code	Description	Invoice	MSRP
1SB	Base Option Package 1SB (Passenger)	355	413
	Manufacturer Discount	(129)	(150)
	Net Price	226	263
	Includes tilt steering wheel, cruise control, and convenience net		
1SC	Base Option Package 1SC (Passenger)	1767	2055
	Includes tilt steering wheel, cruise control, convenience net, power windows, power door locks, deep tinted glass, floor mats, 8-passenger seating with manual lumbar support for front seats, armrests, and map pockets; courtesy and reading lights.		

ASTRO — CHEVROLET

CODE	DESCRIPTION	INVOICE	MSRP
1SF	LS Option Package 1SF (Passenger)	2312	2688
	Manufacturer Discount	(602)	(700)
	Net Price	1710	1988
	Includes LS Decor (tilt steering wheel, cruise control, convenience net, power door locks, floor mats, 8-passenger seating with manual lumbar support for front seats, armrests, and map pockets; reading lights, styled steel wheels, bodyside cladding, swing-out rear door windows, chrome grille, composite headlights, illuminated visor vanity mirrors, sunvisor extensions), deep tinted glass, and power windows		
1SG	LS Option Package 1SG (Passenger)	2862	3328
	Manufacturer Discount	(602)	(700)
	Net Price	2260	2628
	Includes LS Decor (tilt steering wheel, cruise control, convenience net, power door locks, floor mats, 8-passenger seating with manual lumbar support for front seats, armrests, and map pockets; reading lights, styled steel wheels, bodyside cladding, swing-out rear door windows, chrome grille, composite headlights, illuminated visor vanity mirrors, sunvisor extensions), deep tinted glass, power windows, power exterior mirrors, front storage compartment, luggage rack, remote keyless entry and overhead console.		
1SH	LS Option Package 1SH (Passenger)	3282	3816
	Manufacturer Discount	(688)	(800)
	Net Price	2594	3016
	Includes LS Decor (tilt steering wheel, cruise control, convenience net, power door locks, floor mats, 8-passenger seating with manual lumbar support for front seats, armrests, and map pockets; reading lights, bodyside cladding, swing-out rear door windows, chrome grille, composite headlights, illuminated visor vanity mirrors, sunvisor extensions), deep tinted glass, power windows, power exterior mirrors, front storage compartment, luggage rack, remote keyless entry, overhead console, and 6-way power driver's seat		
1SK	LT Option Package (Passenger)	4585	5331
	Manufacturer Discount	(602)	(700)
	Net Price	3983	4631
	Includes LS Decor (tilt steering wheel, cruise control, convenience net, power door locks, floor mats, 8-passenger seating with manual lumbar support for front seats, armrests, and map pockets; reading lights, styled steel wheels, bodyside cladding, swing-out rear door windows, chrome grille, composite headlights, illuminated visor vanity mirrors, sunvisor extensions), LT Decor (deep tinted glass, unique front bucket seats with adjustable headrests, split-folding center bench seat with fold-down center console, overhead console with compass and outside temperature display, power exterior mirrors, power windows, leather-wrapped steering wheel, alloy wheels), power driver's seat, luggage rack		
C69	Air Conditioning — Front and Rear (Passenger)	450	523
YG6	Air Conditioning Delete Credit (Cargo)	(727)	(845)

CHEVROLET ASTRO

CODE	DESCRIPTION	INVOICE	MSRP
PF3	Alloy Wheels (Passenger)	292	340
	With 1SC (Passenger)	213	248
	With 1SF (Passenger)	213	248
	With 1SG (Passenger)	213	248
	INCLUDED in Option Packages 1SH and 1SK		
B74	Bodyside Moldings	104	121
	INCLUDED in Base Option Package 1SC, and in all LS and LT Option Packages, on Passenger Van		
YF5	California Emissions	146	170
TL1	Chrome Grille (Cargo)	99	115
	Includes composite headlights		
V10	Cold Climate Package	40	46
	Includes engine block heater and coolant protection		
ZQ3	Convenience Package ZQ3	329	383
	Includes tilt steering wheel and cruise control		
AJ1	Deep Tinted Glass (Cargo)	46	54
	With ZW3 (Cargo)	92	107
	With ZW6 (Cargo)	225	262
AJ1	Deep Tinted Glass (Passenger)	249	290
	INCLUDED in Option Packages 1SC, 1SF, 1SG, 1SH, and 1SK		
C95	Dome and Reading Lights (Cargo)	28	38
E54	Dutch Doors	313	364
	With 1SH (Passenger)	262	305
	With 1SK (Passenger)	262	305
	With 1SF (Passenger)	262	305
	With 1SG (Passenger)	262	305
	Includes wiper/washer and power release		
B37	Floor Mats (Passenger)	40	47
	With ZP7 (Passenger)	59	69
	With ZP8 (Passenger)	59	69
	INCLUDED in Option Packages 1SC, 1SF, 1SG, 1SH, and 1SK		
ZW6	Glass — Compete Body (Cargo)	316	368
ZW2	Glass — Rear Panel Doors (Cargo)	75	87
	NOT AVAILABLE with Dutch Doors		
ZW3	Glass — Sliding Door & Rear Panel Doors (Cargo)	133	155
	NOT AVAILABLE with Dutch Doors		
A19	Glass — Swing-out Sliding Door (Cargo)	66	77
	REQUIRES Dutch Doors		
A18	Glass — Swing-out Sliding Door & Rear Panel Doors (Cargo)	117	136
	REQUIRES ZW3 Glass or ZW6 Glass; NOT AVAILABLE with Dutch Doors		
UG1	HomeLink Transmitter (Passenger)	92	107
	REQUIRES purchase of an LS or LT Option Package		
NP5	Leather-wrapped Steering Wheel (Passenger)	46	54
	REQUIRES purchase of an LS Option Package		
G80	Locking Differential	217	252

ASTRO — CHEVROLET

CODE	DESCRIPTION	INVOICE	MSRP
V54	Luggage Rack (Passenger)	108	126
	INCLUDED in LS and LT Option Packages 1SG, 1SH, and 1SK.		
NG1	Massachusetts/New York Emissions	146	170
ZQ2	Operating Convenience Package (Cargo)	408	474
	Includes power windows and power door locks		
AU3	Power Door Locks	192	223
	INCLUDED in Operating Convenience Package ZQ2 on Cargo Van; INCLUDED in LS and LT Option Packages on Passenger Van		
AG1	Power Driver's Seat (Passenger)	206	240
	REQUIRES purchase of Base Option Package 1SC, or LS Option Package 1SF or 1SG		
D48	Power Exterior Mirrors (Passenger)	84	98
	REQUIRES LS Option Package 1SF		
AG2	Power Passenger Seat (Passenger)	206	240
	REQUIRES Power Driver's Seat; deletes underseat storage on Passenger Van		
GU6	Rear Axle Ratio — 3.42	NC	NC
GT4	Rear Axle Ratio — 3.73	NC	NC
C36	Rear Heater	176	205
C49	Rear Window Defogger	132	154
	REQUIRES Dutch Doors		
AU0	Remote Keyless Entry	116	135
	REQUIRES Power Door Locks; INCLUDED in LS Option Packages 1SG and 1SH, and in LT Option Package 1SK, on Passenger Van		
AN0	Seat Package	144	168
	Includes inboard and outboard armrests, map pockets, and manual lumbar support; INCLUDED in Base Option Package 1SC, and in LS and LT Option packages, on Passenger Van; INCLUDED with 7-passenger seating (ZP7) on Passenger Van		
ZP7	Seats — 7-passenger Seating (Passenger)	833	969
	With 1SC (Passenger)	349	406
	With 1SF (Passenger)	273	318
	With 1SG (Passenger)	273	318
	With 1SH (Passenger)	273	318
	With 1SK (Passenger)	NC	NC
	Includes center bucket seats		
ZP8	Seats — 8-passenger Seating (Passenger)	340	395
	INCLUDED in Base Option Package 1SC, and in LS and LT Option Packages		
—	Seats — Cloth Upholstery (Passenger)	NC	NC
	INCLUDED in LS and LT Option Packages		
AN5	Seats — Dual Integrated Child Safety (Passenger)	206	240
	REQUIRES Cloth Seats; NOT AVAILABLE with LT Option Package or 7-passenger Seating		
—	Seats — Leather Upholstery (Passenger)	817	950
	REQUIRES purchase of LT Option Package 1SK		
UL5	Stereo — Delete Credit (Cargo)	(164)	(191)
UK6	Stereo — Rear Seat Controls (Passenger)	136	158
	Includes earphone jacks; REQUIRES purchase of an LS or LT Option Package		

CHEVROLET — ASTRO

CODE	DESCRIPTION	INVOICE	MSRP
UL0	Stereo — Uplevel w/cassette	264	307
	AM/FM stereo with cassette player, seek/scan, clock, theft lock, automatic tone control, speed compensated volume; REQUIRES purchase of Base Option Package 1SC, or an LS or LT Option Package, on Passenger Van		
UP0	Stereo — Uplevel w/cassette & CD players	436	507
	AM/FM stereo with cassette and CD players, seek/scan, clock, theft lock, automatic tone control, speed compensated volume; REQUIRES purchase of Base Option Package 1SC, or an LS or LT Option Package, on Passenger Van; REQUIRES purchase of Operating Convenience Package on Cargo Van		
UN0	Stereo — Uplevel w/CD player	350	407
	AM/FM stereo with CD player, seek/scan, clock, theft lock, automatic tone control, speed compensated volume; REQUIRES purchase of Base Option Package 1SC, or an LS or LT Option Package, on Passenger Van; REQUIRES purchase of Operating Convenience Package on Cargo Van		
UM6	Stereo — w/cassette	126	147
	AM/FM stereo with cassette stereo, seek/scan, and clock		
PA6	Styled Steel Wheels	79	92
	INCLUDED in Option Packages 1SC, 1SF, and 1SG on Passenger Van; NOT AVAILABLE with Option Packages 1SH and 1SK on Passenger Van		
PC2	Styled Steel Wheels (w/chrome)	292	340
	With 1SC (Passenger)	213	248
	With 1SF (Passenger)	213	248
	With 1SG (Passenger)	213	248
	With 1SH (Passenger)	NC	NC
	With 1SK (Passenger)	NC	NC
QCM	Tires — P215/75R15	76	88
	All-season outline white-lettered tires		
QCV	Tires — P215/75R15	52	60
	All-season whitewalls; NOT AVAILABLE with Alloy Wheels on Passenger Van		
FE2	Touring Suspension Package (Passenger 2WD)	263	306
	Includes gas shocks, rear stabilizer bar, and P235/65R15 outline white-lettered touring tires; REQUIRES Alloy Wheels		
Z82	Trailering Equipment	266	309
	Includes 8-lead wiring harness and platform trailer hitch		

TO PRICE YOUR TRADE-IN,
PURCHASE EDMUND'S USED CAR PRICES AND RATINGS.

See page 6 for details.

BLAZER — CHEVROLET

BLAZER *(1997)*

1997 Chevrolet Blazer LS 4WD 4-door

What's New for Chevrolet Blazer in 1997 — Those who prefer a liftgate over a tailgate have that option on 1997 4-door Blazers. A power sunroof is a new option for all Blazers, and models equipped with LT decor are equipped with a HomeLink transmitter that will open your garage, among other things. All-wheel drive Blazers get 4-wheel disc brakes, and automatic transmissions are revised for smoother shifting. Early production 4WD 2-door Blazers could be ordered with a ZR2 suspension package, but by the time we got pricing, Chevrolet had canceled the option. Base Blazers get a chrome grille, while LT 4-Door models have body-color grilles in six exterior colors. Two new paint colors round out the changes.

Blazer — Review

Back in 1982, Chevrolet rolled out the S-10 Blazer, the first modern compact sport/utility vehicle. Fifteen years later, the Blazer remains a best-seller in one of the hottest automotive markets. It's not hard to understand the Blazer's appeal.

Powered by a strong 4.3-liter, 190-horsepower, V-6 engine and offering several suspension choices, the Blazer can be tailored to specific needs; with either two-wheel or four-wheel drive, two doors or four. The four-door is the most popular by far; the model of choice with families on the go.

There are accommodations for as many as six passengers, but four would most likely be more comfortable. Lots of cargo space too, with the spare tire mounted underneath the cargo floor on 4-door models. Chevy claims that, with the rear seat folded, a washing machine box will fit into the cargo bay. We tried it with a test vehicle, and they aren't fibbing. Sadly, the Blazer's interior is marred by acres of chintzy plastic and little rear foot room in front of a somewhat low and mushy seat. Adult rear seat riders will complain loudly.

Off-road is not where the Blazer shines, though early in the model year a ZR2 suspension package was optional. Available only on 2-door 4WD models, the ZR2 Blazer had a special chassis with 4 inch wider track, huge 31-inch tires, specially-tuned Bilstein 46mm shocks, drivetrain refinements, an underbody shield package, and LS trim. Chevrolet canceled this

CHEVROLET BLAZER

option late in November of 1996, and we haven't received word on whether it will return or not. Regular Blazers are capable enough for two-track dirt, but serious off-road adventures would be better handled by something with more wheel travel. However, most families don't spend much, if any, time off-road in their sport utes, so this is not a large shortcoming. As a road going hauler, the Blazer is quite capable. An all-wheel drive option is available on 4-door models with LT decor, making the Blazer even more sure-footed.

For 1997, Chevrolet offers an optional liftgate on the 4-door Blazer. Standard is a two-piece hatch and tailgate. The new liftgate features separately opening glass and a rear washer/wiper system with rear defroster. A power sunroof is new to the options list, and LT models have a new HomeLink transmitter that will operate up to three remote-controlled systems as you pull up to your estate. Also new to the LT are body-color grilles in six exterior colors; base models drop their gray grille in favor of chrome. Order all-wheel drive on your Blazer LT and you'll get 4-wheel disc brakes in place of the standard front disc/rear drum setup. Two new exterior colors debut for 1997: Fairway Green Metallic and Medium Beige Mystique Metallic. Finally, transmission improvements result in smoother shifts.

When the current Blazer debuted for the 1995 model year, it won the North American Truck of the Year award. Smart styling, a powerful drivetrain, and reasonable pricing made it a hit with the public. Lately, however, the competition has caught up with the Blazer. A new V-6 engine goes into the more refined Ford Explorer for 1997, and it is more powerful than the Blazer's motor. Jeep updated the Cherokee this year, offering dual airbags and four-wheel drive for less than $20,000. The Blazer isn't the value it used to be. We certainly like this sport ute, however, poor crash test scores prevent us from recommending it.

Safety Data

Driver Airbag: *Standard*
Side Airbag: *Not Available*
4-Wheel ABS: *Standard*
Driver Crash Test Grade: *Average*
Passenger Crash Test Grade: *Very Poor*

Passenger Airbag: *Not Available*
Meets 1999 Side Impact Standards: *No*
Traction Control: *Not Available*
Insurance Cost: *High*
Integrated Child Seat(s): *Not Available*

Standard Equipment

BLAZER 2-DOOR 2WD: Driver's side airbag, air conditioning, side-impact door beams, map pockets in doors, rear seat heating duct, oil pressure gauge, coolant temperature gauge, trip odometer, voltmeter, delayed entry interior lighting, Scotchgard fabric protectant, front bucket seats with manual lumbar support, ETR AM/FM stereo with clock, headlamps-on warning buzzer, intermittent variable windshield wipers, daytime running lights, foldaway black exterior mirrors, steel 15"x 6" argent-painted wheels with bright trim rings, power front disc/rear drum 4-wheel anti-lock brakes, Vortec 4300 V-6 engine, 4-speed electronically controlled automatic transmission

4-DOOR 2WD (in addition to or instead of 2-DOOR 2WD equipment): 60/40 split bench front seat with storage armrest

2-DOOR 4WD (in addition to or instead of 2-DOOR 2WD equipment): Manual shift transfer case, front tow hooks

4-DOOR 4WD (in addition to or instead of 4-DOOR 2WD equipment): Manual shift transfer case, front tow hooks

BLAZER — CHEVROLET

CODE	DESCRIPTION	INVOICE	MSRP

Base Prices

Code	Description	Invoice	MSRP
CS10516	2WD 2-Door	18567	20516
CS10506	2WD 4-Door	20594	22756
CT10516	4WD 2-Door	20015	22116
CT10506	4WD 4-Door	22404	24756
	Destination Charge:	640	640

Accessories

Code	Description	Invoice	MSRP
GU4	3.08 Rear Axle Ratio	NC	NC
	NOT AVAILABLE with Locking Differential, Manual Transmission, Off-road Suspension Package, or Sport Performance Wide Stance Suspension Package		
GU6	3.42 Rear Axle Ratio	NC	NC
	NOT AVAILABLE with Sport Performance Wide Stance Suspension Package		
GT4	3.73 Rear Axle Ratio (4WD)	NC	NC
	REQUIRES Locking Differential or Sport Performance Wide Stance Suspension Package		
C61	4850 lb. GVWR (2-Door 4WD)	NC	NC
	REQUIRES Touring or Off-road Suspension Package		
C4J	4950 lb. GVWR (2-Door 4WD)	NC	NC
	REQUIRES Sport Performance Wide Stance Suspension Package		
M50	5-speed Manual Transmission (2-Door)	(765)	(890)
	REQUIRES 3.42 Rear Axle Ratio, Locking Differential, and Tachometer		
ANL	Air Dam with Fog Lights (2WD)	99	115
	REQUIRES purchase of an LS Decor Option Package		
F46	All Wheel Drive (4-Door 4WD)	228	265
	Includes 4-wheel disc brakes; REQUIRES purchase of LT Decor Option Package and Premium Ride Suspension Package; NOT AVAILABLE with Shield Package		
N60	Argent Aluminum Wheels (2WD)	213	248
	INCLUDED in LS and LT Decor Option Packages		
1SB	Base Decor Option Package 1SB (2-Door 4WD)	1067	1241
	Manufacturer Discount	(602)	(700)
	Net Price	465	541
	Includes tilt steering wheel, cruise control, luggage rack, rear folding seat, ETR AM/FM stereo with cassette player, seek/scan, and digital clock; and electronic shift transfer case		
1SB	Base Decor Option Package 1SB (2WD)	961	1118
	Manufacturer Discount	(602)	(700)
	Net Price	359	418
	Includes tilt steering wheel, cruise control, luggage rack, rear folding seat, ETR AM/FM stereo with cassette player, seek/scan, and digital clock		
1SB	Base Decor Option Package 1SB (4-Door 4WD)	659	766
	Manufacturer Discount	(602)	(700)
	Net Price	57	66
	Includes tilt steering wheel, cruise control, luggage rack, ETR AM/FM stereo with cassette player, seek/scan, and digital clock; and electronic shift transfer case		

CHEVROLET BLAZER

CODE	DESCRIPTION	INVOICE	MSRP
PA3	Bright Aluminum Wheels (4WD)	NC	NC
	REQUIRES purchase of an LS Decor Option Package		
YF5	California Emissions	146	170
N90	Cast Aluminum Wheels (4WD)	241	280
	INCLUDED in LS and LT Decor Option Packages		
V10	Cold Climate Package	77	89
	Includes heavy-duty battery and engine block heater		
ZY7	Custom Two-tone Paint	169	197
	REQUIRES purchase of LS Exterior Appearance-Package or LT Decor Option Package		
NP1	Electronic Shift Transfer Case (4WD)	106	123
	INCLUDED in Option Packages		
UA1	Heavy-duty Battery	48	56
	690 amp Delco Freedom unit; INCLUDED in Cold Weather Package		
Z82	Heavy-duty Trailering Equipment	181	210
	Includes 7-lead wiring harness, weight distributing hitch platform, and heavy-duty flashers; REQUIRES 3.08 or 3.42 Rear Axle Ratio		
UG1	Homelink Transmitter	112	130
	REQUIRES Overhead Console		
G80	Locking Differential	217	252
1SC	LS Decor Option Package 1SC (2-Door 2WD)	2663	3096
	Manufacturer Discount	(1204)	(1400)
	Net Price	1459	1696
	Includes Base Decor Option Package [tilt steering wheel, cruise control, luggage rack, rear folding seat, ETR AM/FM stereo with cassette player, seek/scan, and digital clock), plus LS Decor Upgrade [dark tinted rear window glass, cargo net, power tailgate release, rear window defogger, 2 additional cupholders, rearview mirror map lights, dual auxiliary power outlets, premium cloth seat and door trim, leather-wrapped steering wheel, dual elastic visor map straps, sunshade extenders, dual illuminated visor vanity mirrors, rear window wiper/washer, aluminum wheels] and power door locks, power windows, power exterior mirrors, Z85 Touring Suspension, P235/70R15 BSW all-season tires		
1SC	LS Decor Option Package 1SC (2-Door 4WD)	2768	3219
	Manufacturer Discount	(1204)	(1400)
	Net Price	1564	1819
	Includes Base Decor Option Package [tilt steering wheel, cruise control, luggage rack, rear folding seat, ETR AM/FM stereo with cassette player, seek/scan, and digital clock; and electronic shift transfer case (4WD models)], plus LS Decor Upgrade [dark tinted rear window glass, cargo net, power tailgate release, rear window defogger, 2 additional cupholders, rearview mirror map lights, dual auxiliary power outlets, premium cloth seat and door trim, leather-wrapped steering wheel, dual elastic visor map straps, sunshade extenders, dual illuminated visor vanity mirrors, rear window wiper/washer, aluminum wheels] and power door locks, power windows, power exterior mirrors, Z85 Touring Suspension, P235/70R15 BSW all-season tires		

BLAZER — CHEVROLET

CODE	DESCRIPTION	INVOICE	MSRP
1SC	LS Decor Option Package 1SC (4-Door 2WD)	3187	3706
	Manufacturer Discount	(1204)	(1400)
	Net Price	1983	2306

Includes Base Decor Option Package [tilt steering wheel, cruise control, luggage rack, rear folding seat, ETR AM/FM stereo with cassette player, seek/scan, and digital clock], plus LS Decor Upgrade [dark tinted rear window glass, cargo net, power tailgate release, rear window defogger, 2 additional cupholders, rearview mirror map lights, dual auxiliary power outlets, premium cloth seat and door trim, rear compartment shade, leather-wrapped steering wheel, dual elastic visor map straps, sunshade extenders, dual illuminated visor vanity mirrors, rear window wiper/washer, aluminum wheels] and power door locks, power windows, power exterior mirrors, Z85 Touring Suspension, P235/70R15 BSW all-season tires, body-color bumpers with front bumper rub strip, composite halogen headlamps, dark gray bodyside molding with bright insert, bright wheel opening moldings

CODE	DESCRIPTION	INVOICE	MSRP
1SC	LS Decor Option Package 1SC (4-Door 4WD)	2884	3354
	Manufacturer Discount	(1204)	(1400)
	Net Price	1680	1954

Includes Base Decor Option Package [tilt steering wheel, cruise control, luggage rack, ETR AM/FM stereo with cassette player, seek/scan, and digital clock; and electronic shift transfer case], plus LS Decor Upgrade [dark tinted rear window glass, cargo net, power tailgate release, rear window defogger, 2 additional cupholders, rearview mirror map lights, dual auxiliary power outlets, premium cloth seat and door trim, rear compartment shade, leather-wrapped steering wheel, dual elastic visor map straps, sunshade extenders, dual illuminated visor vanity mirrors, rear window wiper/washer, aluminum wheels] and power door locks, power windows, power exterior mirrors, Z85 Touring Suspension, P235/70R15 BSW all-season tires, body-color bumpers with front bumper rub strip, composite halogen headlamps, dark gray bodyside molding with bright insert, bright wheel opening moldings

CODE	DESCRIPTION	INVOICE	MSRP
1SD	LS Decor Option Package 1SD (2-Door 2WD)	3111	3618
	Manufacturer Discount	(1204)	(1400)
	Net Price	1907	2218

Includes LS Decor Option Package 1SC [tilt steering wheel, cruise control, luggage rack, rear folding seat, ETR AM/FM stereo with cassette player, seek/scan, and digital clock, dark tinted rear window glass, cargo net, power tailgate release, rear window defogger, 2 additional cupholders, rearview mirror map lights, dual auxiliary power outlets, premium cloth seat and door trim, rear compartment shade, leather-wrapped steering wheel, dual elastic visor map straps, sunshade extenders, dual illuminated visor vanity mirrors, rear window wiper/washer, aluminum wheels, power door locks, power windows, power exterior mirrors, Z85 Touring Suspension, P235/70R15 BSW all-season tires] plus overhead console, remote keyless entry, premium cloth reclining high-back bucket seats, and 6-way power driver's seat, body-color bumpers with front bumper rub strip, composite halogen headlamps, dark gray bodyside molding with bright insert, bright wheel opening moldings

CHEVROLET BLAZER

CODE	DESCRIPTION	INVOICE	MSRP
1SD	LS Decor Option Package 1SD (2-Door 4WD)	3217	3741
	Manufacturer Discount	(1204)	(1400)
	Net Price	2013	2341

Includes LS Decor Option Package 1SC [tilt steering wheel, cruise control, luggage rack, rear folding seat, ETR AM/FM stereo with cassette player, seek/scan, and digital clock; and electronic shift transfer case (4WD models), dark tinted rear window glass, cargo net, power tailgate release, rear window defogger, 2 additional cupholders, rearview mirror map lights, dual auxiliary power outlets, premium cloth seat and door trim, leather-wrapped steering wheel, dual elastic visor map straps, sunshade extenders, dual illuminated visor vanity mirrors, rear window wiper/washer, aluminum wheels, power door locks, power windows, power exterior mirrors, Z85 Touring Suspension, P235/70R15 BSW all-season tires] plus overhead console, remote keyless entry, premium cloth reclining high-back bucket seats, and 6-way power driver's seat

1SD	LS Decor Option Package 1SD (4-Door 2WD)	3775	4389
	Manufacturer Discount	(1204)	(1400)
	Net Price	2571	2989

Includes LS Decor Option Package 1SC [tilt steering wheel, cruise control, luggage rack, rear folding seat, ETR AM/FM stereo with cassette player, seek/scan, and digital clock, dark tinted rear window glass, cargo net, power tailgate release, rear window defogger, 2 additional cupholders, rearview mirror map lights, dual auxiliary power outlets, premium cloth seat and door trim, rear compartment shade, leather-wrapped steering wheel, dual elastic visor map straps, sunshade extenders, dual illuminated visor vanity mirrors, rear window wiper/washer, aluminum wheels, power door locks, power windows, power exterior mirrors, Z85 Touring Suspension, P235/70R15 BSW all-season tires] plus overhead console, remote keyless entry, premium cloth reclining high-back bucket seats, and 6-way power driver's seat, body-color bumpers with front bumper rub strip, composite halogen headlamps, dark gray bodyside molding with bright insert, bright wheel opening moldings

1SD	LS Decor Option Package 1SD (4-Door 4WD)	3472	4037
	Manufacturer Discount	(1204)	(1400)
	Net Price	2268	2637

Includes LS Decor Option Package [tilt steering wheel, cruise control, luggage rack, ETR AM/FM stereo with cassette player, seek/scan, and digital clock; and electronic shift transfer case, dark tinted rear window glass, cargo net, power tailgate release, rear window defogger, 2 additional cupholders, rearview mirror map lights, dual auxiliary power outlets, premium cloth seat and door trim, rear compartment shade, leather-wrapped steering wheel, dual elastic visor map straps, sunshade extenders, dual illuminated visor vanity mirrors, rear window wiper/washer, aluminum wheels, power door locks, power windows, power exterior mirrors, Z85 Touring Suspension, P235/70R15 BSW all-season tires] plus overhead console, remote keyless entry, premium cloth reclining high-back bucket seats, and 6-way power driver's seat, body-color bumpers with front bumper rub strip, composite halogen headlamps, dark gray bodyside molding with bright insert, bright wheel opening moldings

BLAZER — CHEVROLET

CODE	DESCRIPTION	INVOICE	MSRP
1SE	LT Decor Option Package (4-Door 4WD)	4725	5494
	Manufacturer Discount	(1204)	(1400)
	Net Price	3521	4094

Includes LS Decor Option Package 1SC [tilt steering wheel, cruise control, luggage rack, electronic shift transfer case, dark tinted rear window glass, cargo net, power tailgate release, rear window defogger, 2 additional cupholders, rearview mirror map lights, dual auxiliary power outlets, rear compartment shade, leather-wrapped steering wheel, dual elastic visor map straps, sunshade extenders, dual illuminated visor vanity mirrors, rear window wiper/washer, aluminum wheels, power door locks, power windows, power exterior mirrors, Z85 Touring Suspension, P235/70R15 BSW all-season tires], plus LT Decor upgrade [composite halogen headlamps, overhead console with reading lamps, outside temperature gauge, compass, and storage area; HomeLink transmitter, remote keyless entry, simulated leather door trim, ultrasoft leather reclining high-back bucket seats with folding seatbacks, power lumbar support, 4-way adjustable headrests and 6-way power driver's seat; tachometer, ETR AM/FM stereo with cassette player, seek/scan, music search and repeat, digital clock, graphic equalizer and speakers

CODE	DESCRIPTION	INVOICE	MSRP
1SE	LT Decor Option Package 1SE (4-Door 2WD)	5126	5961
	Manufacturer Discount	(1204)	(1400)
	Net Price	3922	4561

Includes LS Decor Option Package 1SC [tilt steering wheel, cruise control, luggage rack, rear folding seat, dark tinted rear window glass, cargo net, power tailgate release, rear window defogger, 2 additional cupholders, rearview mirror map lights, dual auxiliary power outlets, rear compartment shade, leather-wrapped steering wheel, dual elastic visor map straps, sunshade extenders, dual illuminated visor vanity mirrors, rear window wiper/washer, aluminum wheels, power door locks, power windows, power exterior mirrors, Z85 Touring Suspension, P235/70R15 BSW all-season tires], plus LT Decor upgrade [composite halogen headlamps, overhead console with reading lamps, outside temperature gauge, compass, and storage area; HomeLink transmitter, remote keyless entry, simulated leather door trim, ultrasoft leather reclining high-back bucket seats with folding seatbacks, power lumbar support, 4-way adjustable headrests and 6-way power driver's seat; air dam with fog lamps, tachometer, ETR AM/FM stereo with cassette player, seek/scan, music search and repeat, digital clock, graphic equalizer and speakers

CODE	DESCRIPTION	INVOICE	MSRP
V54	Luggage Rack	108	126
	INCLUDED in Option Packages		
NG1	Massachusetts/New York Emissions	146	170
ZM6	Off-road Suspension Package (2-Door 4WD)	477	555
	With 1SC (2-Door 4WD)	143	166
	With 1SD (2-Door 4WD)	143	166

Includes special yellow Bilstein shock absorbers, upsized torsion bar, upsized jounce bumpers, full-size spare tire, and stabilizer bar; REQUIRES QEB P235/75R15 OWL tires

CHEVROLET BLAZER

CODE	DESCRIPTION	INVOICE	MSRP
ZQ6	Operating Convenience Package (2-Door)	460	535
	Includes power door locks, power windows, and power exterior mirrors; INCLUDED in LS and LT Decor Option Packages		
P16	Outside Spare Tire Carrier (2-Door 4WD)	137	159
	Includes full-size spare tire and wheel with cover		
DK6	Overhead Console	126	147
	REQUIRES Bucket Seats and LS Decor Option Package 1SC		
QCA	P205/75R15 White-letter Tires (2WD)	104	121
	All-season tread; REQUIRES Smooth Suspension Package		
QBF	P235/70R15 BSW Tires	165	192
	All-season tread; INCLUDED in LS and LT Decor Option Packages; REQUIRES Touring or Premium Ride Suspension Package		
QBG	P235/70R15 OWL Tires	280	325
	With 1SC (4-Door 4WD)	114	133
	With 1SC (4-Door 2WD)	114	133
	With 1SC (2-Door 4WD)	114	133
	With 1SD (4-Door 4WD)	114	133
	With 1SD (4-Door 2WD)	114	133
	With 1SD (2-Door 4WD)	114	133
	With 1SE (4-Door 2WD)	114	133
	With 1SE (4-Door 4WD)	114	133
	All-season tread; REQUIRES Touring or Off-road Suspension Package		
QEB	P235/75R15 OWL Tires (4WD)	288	335
	With 1SC (4-Door 4WD)	123	143
	With 1SC (2-Door 4WD)	123	143
	With 1SD (4-Door 4WD)	123	143
	With 1SE (4-Door 4WD)	123	143
	On/off road tread; REQUIRES Touring or Off-road Suspension Package; REQUIRES Outside Spare Tire Carrier when ordered on 2-Door		
AG1	Power Driver's Seat	206	240
	REQUIRES LS Decor Option Package 1SC and Remote Keyless Entry		
CF5	Power Sunroof	598	695
ZW7	Premium Ride Suspension Package (4-Door)	169	197
	Includes special yellow Bilstein shock absorbers; INCLUDED in LS and LT Decor Option Packages		
UL5	Radio Delete Credit	(194)	(226)
	NOT AVAILABLE with Option Packages		
RYJ	Rear Compartment Shade (2-Door 4WD)	59	69
	REQUIRES Outside Spare Tire and LS Decor Option Package		
RYJ	Rear Compartment Shade (4-Door)	59	69
	INCLUDED in LS and LT Decor Option Packages		
TB4	Rear Liftgate (4-Door)	NC	NC
	REQUIRES purchase of an LS or LT Decor Option Package		
YG4	Rear Seat Delete (All except 4-Door 4WD)	NC	NC
	NOT AVAILABLE with Option Packages		

BLAZER — CHEVROLET

CODE	DESCRIPTION	INVOICE	MSRP
ZM8	Rear Window Convenience Package	277	322
	Includes rear window defogger, power tailgate release, and rear window wiper/washer; INCLUDED in LS and LT Decor Option Packages		
AV5	Reclining High-back Bucket Seats (4-Door)	138	161
	Includes seat separator console; REQUIRES LS Decor Option Package 1SC		
AU0	Remote Keyless Entry	116	135
	REQUIRES LS Decor Option Package 1SC and AG1 Power Driver's Seat		
ZM5	Shield Package (4WD)	108	126
	Includes transfer case skid plate, front differential skid plates, fuel tank skid plate, and steering linkage shields; INCLUDED in Sport Performance Wide Stance Suspension Package; NOT AVAILABLE with All Wheel Drive system		
Z83	Smooth Suspension Package (2-Door)	NC	NC
	With 1SC (2-Door 4WD)	(237)	(275)
	With 1SD (2-Door 4WD)	(237)	(275)
ZQ1	Smooth Suspension Package (4-Door)	NC	NC
	With 1SB (4-Door 4WD)	(237)	(275)
	With 1SB (2WD)	(237)	(275)
	With 1SC (4-Door 2WD)	(237)	(275)
	With 1SC (4-Door 4WD)	(237)	(275)
	With 1SD (4-Door 2WD)	(237)	(275)
	With 1SD (4-Door 4WD)	(237)	(275)
	With 1SE (4-Door 4WD)	(237)	(275)
	With 1SE (4-Door 2WD)	(237)	(275)
5P2	Special Aluminum Wheels (4WD)	NC	NC
	REQUIRES purchase of an LS Decor Option Package on 2-Door models; REQUIRES purchase of LT Decor Option Package on 4-Door models		
AM7	Split Folding Rear Bench Seat (All except 4-Door 4WD)	409	475
	INCLUDED in Option Packages		
UM6	Stereo w/cassette	105	122
	ETR AM/FM stereo with cassette player, seek/scan, and digital clock; NOT AVAILABLE with Option Packages		
U16	Tachometer	51	59
	INCLUDED in LT Decor Option Package		
ZQ3	Tilt Wheel & Cruise Control Package	340	395
	INCLUDED in Option Packages		
Z85	Touring Suspension Package	169	197
	Includes special yellow Bilstein shock absorbers; INCLUDED in LS Decor Packages on 2-Door models		
—	Transfer Case Delete (4WD)	(106)	(123)
	REQUIRES purchase of Option Package 1SB or 1SC, or AM6 60/40 bench seat		
UX1	Uplevel Stereo w/cassette	281	327
	With 1SB (2-Door 4WD)	176	205
	With 1SB (4-Door 4WD)	176	205
	With 1SB (2WD)	176	205

CHEVROLET
BLAZER / CHEVY VAN

CODE	DESCRIPTION	INVOICE	MSRP
	With 1SC (2-Door 4WD)	176	205
	With 1SC (4-Door 2WD)	176	205
	With 1SC (4-Door 4WD)	176	205
	With 1SD (4-Door 4WD)	176	205
	With 1SD (4-Door 2WD)	176	205
	With 1SD (2-Door 4WD)	176	205
	ETR AM/FM stereo with cassette player, seek/scan, music search and repeat, digital clock, graphic equalizer, and 6 speakers; INCLUDED in LT Decor Option Package 1SE		
U1C	Uplevel Stereo w/CD player	283	329
	With 1SE (4-Door 4WD)	107	124
	With 1SE (4-Door 2WD)	107	124
	ETR AM/FM stereo with CD player, seek/scan, digital clock, and 6 speakers; REQUIRES purchase of an LS or LT Decor Option Package		

CHEVY VAN *(1997)*

1997 Chevrolet Chevy Van

What's New for Chevrolet Chevy Van in 1997 — Dual airbags appear on the G3500 model, while daytime running lights and three fresh exterior colors make this van easier to see. (Editor's Note: If you can't see this monster van without DRL's, perhaps you should consider surrendering your driver's license.) Electronic variable orifice steering reduces effort at low speeds for easier parking, and automatic transmissions shift more smoothly.

Chevy Van — Review

Last year, for the first time in 25 years, Chevy dealers received a brand new, completely redesigned, full-size van to sell. Well, sort of. The supply of 1996 models was little more than a trickle as the factory suffered through teething problems. The Chevy Van (the cargo hauler) and the Express (the people hauler) were expected to arrive in dealer showrooms last spring. For 1997, the bugs have been worked out at the plant, and consumers might actually find one

CHEVY VAN — CHEVROLET

of these new vans on a dealer's lot. Equipped with dual airbags and four-wheel anti-lock brakes, Chevrolet is looking forward to stealing some of Ford's thunder in the full-size van market.

Rugged full-frame construction replaces the unibody setup of the previous-generation Chevy Van. Preferred by converters, full-frame construction allows for improved stability, ride and handling. Regular-length models carry 267 cubic feet of cargo, and extended-length vans can haul 317 cubic feet of stuff. Trick rear doors open 180 degrees to make loading and unloading the new van easier. Up to 15 passengers can ride in the extended-length Express, which ought to make this new van a hit with shuttle services. Other seating options include five, eight and twelve passenger arrangements. G3500's can tow up to 10,000 pounds when properly equipped.

For convenience, the full-size spare is stored underneath the cargo floor. A 31-gallon fuel tank keeps this thirsty vehicle from frequent fill-ups, but topping off an empty tank will quickly empty your wallet. Engine choices are sourced from the Chevrolet family of Vortec gasoline motors, and, for the first time, a turbocharged diesel can be installed in Chevy's full-size van. Available are the Vortec 4300 V-6, the 5000, 5700, and 7400 V-8's, and a new 6.5-liter Turbodiesel V-8. Standard side cargo doors are a 60/40 panel arrangement, but a traditional slider is a no-cost option on 135-inch wheelbase vans.

Child safety locks are standard on the rear and side doors of the Express. Passenger assist handles help passengers into and out of the van. Front and rear air conditioning is optional. For 1997, G3500 get dual airbags. Also new are daytime running lights, smoother shifting automatic transmissions, and electronic variable orifice power steering that reduces effort at low speeds, making these vans easier to park.

Exterior styling is an interesting mix of corporate Chevrolet, Astro Van and Lumina Minivan. The high, pillar-mounted taillights are odd, but functional. They can easily be seen if the van is operated with the rear doors open. Low-mounted bumpers and moldings make the Express look taller than it is. An attractively sculpted body side gives the van's smooth, slab-sided flanks a dose of character. Three new colors arrive for 1997, in shades of brown, red, and silver.

Overall, Chevrolet's thoughtful rendition of the traditional full-size van appears to be right on target, giving Ford's Econoline/Club Wagon the first real competition it has faced in years.

Safety Data

Driver Airbag: *Standard (under 9,500 GVWR)*
Side Airbag: *Not Available*
4-Wheel ABS: *Standard*
Driver Crash Test Grade: *Not Available*
Passenger Crash Test Grade: *Not Available*

Passenger Airbag: *Standard (under 9,500 GVWR)*
Meets 1999 Side Impact Standards: *No*
Traction Control: *Not Available*
Insurance Cost: *Not Available*
Integrated Child Seat(s): *Not Available*

Standard Equipment

CHEVY VAN: Vortec 4300 SFI V-6 engine (1500/2500), Vortec 5700 SFI V-8 engine (3500), 4-speed electronic automatic transmission with overdrive (1500/2500), heavy-duty 4-speed automatic transmission with overdrive (3500), power front disc/rear drum 4-wheel anti-lock brakes, variable ratio power steering, brake/transmission shift interlock, P215/75R15N all-season BSW tires (1500), LT225/75R16D all-season BSW tires (2500), LT245/75R16E all-season BSW tires (3500), full-size spare tire (mounted underneath vehicle), argent painted

CHEVROLET
CHEVY VAN

bumpers, dark argent painted grille, argent steel wheels, 60/40 split swing-out side doors, direct control black fold-away outside mirrors, solar-ray tinted glass, intermittent windshield wipers, dual airbags (under 9,500 GVWR), 100-amp alternator (1500/2500), 124-amp alternator (3500), heavy-duty 600 CCA battery, interior power outlet, side window defoggers, front and side cargo door guard beams (do not meet 1999 truck standard), engine temperature gauge, oil pressure gauge, trip odometer, voltmeter gauge, underhood lamp, black vinyl floor covering, cloth headliner, AM/FM stereo with seek/scan and clock, adjustable high back vinyl reclining seats, color-keyed vinyl sunshades, daytime running lights

Base Prices

Code	Description	Invoice	MSRP
CG11405	1500	16688	19072
CG21405	2500	17060	19497
CG21705	2500 Extended	17847	20397
CG31405	3500	18267	20877
CG31705	3500 Extended	19055	21777
Destination Charge:		615	615

Accessories

Code	Description	Invoice	MSRP
1SB	Option Package 1SB	1302	1514
	Includes front air conditioning, convenience group (tilt steering wheel and cruise control), and auxiliary lighting (dome and reading lights, stepwell lights, underhood light)		
C60	Air Conditioning — Front	839	975
	INCLUDED in Option Package 1SB		
C69	Air Conditioning — Front & Rear (G1500/G2500)	1578	1835
	With 1SB	740	860
	Includes rear heater and 124-amp alternator		
C69	Air Conditioning — Front & Rear (G3500)	1530	1779
	With 1SB	691	804
	Includes rear heater		
KW2	Alternator — 124-amp (G1500/G2500)	48	56
	INCLUDED with Front & Rear Air Conditioning		
TR9	Auxiliary Lighting	134	156
	Includes dome and reading lights, stepwell lights, retractable underhood light; INCLUDED in Option Package 1SB		
YF5	California Emissions	146	170
V10	Cold Climate Package	41	48
	Includes engine block heater; NOT AVAILABLE with 6.5-liter Turbodiesel V-8 Engine		
ZQ3	Convenience Package ZQ3	329	383
	Includes tilt steering and cruise control; INCLUDED in Option Package 1SB		
ZR7	Deluxe Front Appearance Package	272	316
	Includes chrome grille, chrome bumpers, and composite headlights		
L65	Engine — 6.5-liter Turbodiesel V-8 (G2500)	3290	3825
	REQUIRES 8,600 lb. GVWR		
L65	Engine — 6.5-liter Turbodiesel V-8 (G3500)	2460	2860
L30	Engine — Vortec 5000 V-8 (G1500/G2500)	426	495
	REQUIRES 3.42 rear axle ratio		

CHEVY VAN — CHEVROLET

CODE	DESCRIPTION	INVOICE	MSRP
L31	Engine — Vortec 5700 V-8 (G1500/G2500)	830	965
L29	Engine — Vortec 7400 V-8 (G3500)	516	600
B31	Floor Covering Delete	NC	NC
	Deletes rear cargo area black vinyl floor covering		
VK3	Front License Plate Bracket	NC	NC
ZW6	Glass Package — Fixed Full Body	267	311
ZW3	Glass Package — Fixed Rear and Side Glass	77	90
ZW2	Glass Package — Fixed Rear Door	43	50
C5Y	GVWR — 7,100 lb. (G1500)	129	150
C6P	GVWR — 8,600 lb. (G2500)	284	330
G80	Locking Differential	217	252
	NOT AVAILABLE with 3.42 Rear Axle Ratio when ordered on G3500		
NG1	Massachusetts/New York Emissions	NC	NC
PNF	Panel Door Trim Delete	NC	NC
ZX1	Passenger Seat Delete	(350)	(407)
	Deletes front passenger seat and passenger airbag		
ZQ2	Power Convenience Package	408	474
	Includes power windows and power door locks		
AG1	Power Driver's Seat	206	240
DE5	Power Exterior Mirrors	97	113
	REQUIRES Power Convenience Package ZQ2 and front air conditioning		
P06	Rally Wheel Trim	52	60
	Includes chrome trim rings and bright center caps		
GU6	Rear Axle Ratio — 3.42	NC	NC
	REQUIRES Locking Differential when ordered on G3500; NOT AVAILABLE on G2500 equipped with 8,600 lb. GVWR		
GT4	Rear Axle Ratio — 3.73	NC	NC
	NOT AVAILABLE with Vortec 5000 V-8 engine; NOT AVAILABLE with Vortec 5700 V-8 engine on G1500 models		
GT5	Rear Axle Ratio — 4.10 (G2500/G3500)	NC	NC
	REQUIRES 8,600 lb. GVWR when ordered on G2500; NOT AVAILABLE with Vortec 5000 V-8 engine		
C36	Rear Heater	176	205
	INCLUDED with Front & Rear Air Conditioning		
YA2	Sliding Side Door	NC	NC
ZX9	Spare Tire Delete Credit (G2500)	(232)	(270)
	REQUIRES XHF tires		
ZX9	Spare Tire Delete Credit (G3500)	(256)	(298)
UL5	Stereo — Delete Credit	(264)	(307)
UM6	Stereo — w/cassette	126	147
	AM/FM stereo with cassette player, seek/scan, and digital clock		
ZX6	Swing-out Rear & Side Glass	117	136
	REQUIRES ZW3 or ZW6 Glass Package		
A18	Swing-out Rear Door Glass	51	59
	REQUIRES ZW2 Glass Package		

CHEVROLET — CHEVY VAN / C/K 1500 PICKUP

CODE	DESCRIPTION	INVOICE	MSRP
XHF	Tires — LT225/75R16E (G2500)	73	85
	All-season blackwall tires; REQUIRES 8,600 lb. GVWR		
XHM	Tires — P235/75R15 (G1500)	108	125
	All-season outline white-lettered tires; REQUIRES 7,100 lb. GVWR		
XHB	Tires — P235/75R15X (G1500)	86	100
	All-season whitewall tires; REQUIRES 7,100 lb. GVWR		
XHA	Tires — P235/75R15X (G1500)	118	160
	All-season blackwall tires; REQUIRES 7,100 lb. GVWR		
Z82	Trailering Equipment	267	310
	Includes heavy-duty platform hitch and 7-lead wiring harness		

C/K 1500 PICKUP *(1997)*

1997 Chevrolet K1500 Silverado

What's New for Chevrolet C/K Pickup in 1997 — Order a truck under 8,600 lbs. GVWR, and you'll get a passenger airbag. The airbag can be deactivated when a rear-facing child safety seat is installed. Low-speed steering effort is reduced this year, and a refined transmission fluid pump results in smoother shifts. An alternative fuel version of the Vortec 5700 is available, but only on a specific model. K1500's get a tighter turning radius, and three new colors debut. The third door option will be more widely available, because it is now a required option on all C/K 1500 shortbed extended cab trucks.

C/K Pickup — Review

General Motors' best-selling vehicles, as truck loyalists know full well, are the full-size pickups: half-, 3/4, and one-tonners with a reputation as reliable workhorses. Ford's similar-sized F-Series grabs the higher sales totals each year, but faithful Chevrolet buyers are seldom swayed. The pickup that feels right at home to a Chevy fan tends to send prickles up the spine

C/K 1500 PICKUP — CHEVROLET

of a Ford fan, and vice versa. Each is likely to declare the other's truck to be harder riding or anemic in acceleration, even if an impartial observer discerns little difference between the two.

This year's big news is the addition of a passenger airbag on all models under 8,600 lbs. GVWR. Those of you carting children in rear-facing safety seats need not worry how you'll load the kiddies into the 1997 C/K. A switch disables the passenger airbag when desirable. Also new this year is Electronic Variable Orifice steering, which reduces low-speed steering effort. Automatic transmissions receive refinements that result in smoother shifts and improved efficiency. The heavy-duty manual transmission offers better shift feel, reduced noise, and quicker response.

Three new paint colors are offered for 1997. The optional third door for extended cab models will be more widely available this year. In November, Chevrolet made the third door a required option on all shortbed extended cab C/K 1500 models. K1500 models benefit from a tighter turning radius, which should improve off-road maneuvering. An alternative fuel version of the Vortec 5700 V-8 is newly available, but to get it consumers must order a C2500 Regular Cab Longbed equipped with 8,600 lb. GVWR, a 3.73 rear axle ratio, and an automatic transmission.

Four-wheel anti-lock braking is standard fare, and models under 8,600 lbs. GVWR have an airbag installed in the steering wheel hub. Correctly fitted, a C/K pickup can tow as much as 10,000 pounds. Long-life engine components extend service intervals up to 100,000 miles on some items. For luxury-oriented truckers, a C/K can be trimmed in leather when the top Silverado trim package is specified.

When selecting a full-size Chevy truck, you have to face the usual bewildering selection of models, which vary by wheelbase, cargo-bed size, cab design, and Sportside or Fleetside bed styling. Don't stop yet: you also have to choose from five engine sizes (including two diesels), and decide whether you want two- or four-wheel drive. Then, you still have the dizzying single-option list to ponder.

We get tired just thinking about all those possibilities, but they come with the territory when you're heading into big-pickup range. Truck customers don't want the same hauler that everybody else is buying—they want one tailored to their own specific needs. Chevrolet provides these customers with myriad possibilities to create that special, one-of-a-kind truck.

Safety Data

Driver Airbag: *Standard*
Side Airbag: *Not Available*
4-Wheel ABS: *Standard*
Driver Crash Test Grade: *Excellent*
Passenger Crash Test Grade: *Not Available*

Passenger Airbag: *Standard*
Meets 1999 Side Impact Standards: *No*
Traction Control: *Not Available*
Insurance Cost: *Low*
Integrated Child Seat(s): *Not Available*

Standard Equipment

BASE C/K 1500 W/T: Dual airbags (models under 8,600 lbs. GVWR), plastic door trim with armrest, full black rubber floor coverings, trip odometer, tachometer, oil pressure gauge, voltmeter, delayed entry lighting, vinyl bench seat, steel side door impact beams (do not meet 1999 standard), AM/FM stereo with digital clock, intermittent variable wipers, daytime running lamps, dual black foldaway exterior mirrors, power front disc/rear drum 4-wheel anti-lock brakes, Vortec 4300 V-6 engine, 5-speed manual transmission with overdrive

CHEVROLET
C/K 1500 PICKUP

CODE	DESCRIPTION	INVOICE	MSRP

C/K 1500 CHEYANNE (in addition to or instead of W/T equipment): Color-keyed rubber floor covering, Scotchgard fabric protectant, 60/40 split front bench seat, rear quarter swing-out windows (Extended Cab model), Vortec 5000 V-8 engine (Extended Cab Longbed models)

Base Prices

Code	Description	Invoice	MSRP
C10703	C1500 Reg. Cab W/T Shortbed	13152	14532
C10903	C1500 Reg. Cab W/T Longbed	13442	14852
C10703	C1500 Fleetside Reg. Cab Shortbed	13950	15942
C10903	C1500 Fleetside Reg. Cab Longbed	14212	16242
C10703	C1500 Sportside Reg. Cab Shortbed	14453	16517
C10753	C1500 Fleetside Ext. Cab Shortbed	15770	18022
C10953	C1500 Fleetside Ext. Cab Longbed	16640	19017
C10753	C1500 Sportside Ext. Cab Shortbed	16273	18597
K10703	K1500 Reg. Cab W/T Shortbed	16500	18232
K10903	K1500 Reg. Cab W/T Longbed	16790	18552
K10703	K1500 Fleetside Reg. Cab Shortbed	16575	18942
K10903	K1500 Fleetside Reg. Cab Longbed	16837	19242
K10703	K1500 Sportside Reg. Cab Shortbed	17078	19517
K10753	K1500 Fleetside Ext. Cab SB	18220	20822
K10953	K1500 Fleetside Ext. Cab LB	19090	21817
K10753	K1500 Sportside Ext. Cab Shortbed	18723	21397
	Destination Charge:	625	625

Accessories

Code	Description	Invoice	MSRP
GU4	3.08 Rear Axle Ratio (C1500)	NC	NC
GU6	3.42 Rear Axle Ratio	NC	NC
	NOT AVAILABLE on K1500 equipped with standard Vortec 4300 V-6 Engine		
GT4	3.73 Rear Axle Ratio	NC	NC
	With L30 (All except X-cab LB)	116	135
	With L31 (All except X-cab LB)	116	135
	With L31 (X-cab LB)	116	135
	With L56 (K1500 X-cab LB)	116	135
	With L56 (K1500 X-cab SB)	116	135
	Includes engine oil cooling		
M30	4-speed Automatic Transmission	834	970
	NOT AVAILABLE with 6.5-liter Turbodiesel V-8 Engine		
L56	6.5-liter Turbodiesel V-8 Engine (K1500 X-cab LB)	3062	3560
	REQUIRES Heavy-duty 4-speed Automatic Transmission (MT1)		
L56	6.5-liter Turbodiesel V-8 Engine (K1500 X-cab SB)	3487	4055
	REQUIRES Heavy-duty 4-speed Automatic Transmission (MT1)		
C60	Air Conditioning	692	805
	INCLUDED in Silverado Equipment Packages and Convenience Package R9A		

C/K 1500 PICKUP — CHEVROLET

CODE	DESCRIPTION	INVOICE	MSRP
N90	Aluminum Wheels (C1500 except W/T)	267	310
	With 1SB (All except W/T)	215	250
	With 1SC (All Reg Cab except W/T)	215	250
	With 1SC (X-cab)	215	250
	With R9B (All Fleetside except W/T)	215	250
	With R9B (Sportside)	215	250
	INCLUDED in Sport Package		
PF4	Aluminum Wheels (K1500 except W/T)	267	310
	With 1SB (All except W/T)	215	250
	With 1SC (All Reg Cab except W/T)	215	250
	With 1SC (X-cab)	215	250
	With R9B (Sportside)	215	250
	With R9B (All Fleetside except W/T)	215	250
	INCLUDED in Sport Package		
V22	Appearance Package (All except W/T)	164	191
	Includes chrome grille, composite headlamps, and dual horns; INCLUDED in Silverado Equipment Packages and Bright Appearance Package R9B		
R9B	Bright Appearance Package (All Fleetside except W/T)	527	613
	Includes bodyside moldings (B85), chrome grille, chrome bumpers, and rally wheels with bright trim rings; REQUIRES Cheyenne Equipment Package 1SA		
R9B	Bright Appearance Package (Sportside)	501	582
	Includes bodyside moldings (B85), chrome grille, chrome bumpers, and rally wheels with bright trim rings; REQUIRES Cheyenne Equipment Package 1SA		
B85	Bright Bodyside Moldings (Fleetside)	92	107
	Includes bright wheel well openings; INCLUDED in Silverado Equipment Packages and Bright Appearance Package R9B; NOT AVAILABLE with Sport Package		
B85	Bright Bodyside Moldings (Sportside)	65	76
	INCLUDED in Silverado Equipment Packages and Bright Appearance Package R9B; NOT AVAILABLE with Sport Package		
YF5	California Emissions	146	170
DF2	Camper Style Stainless Steel Exterior Mirrors (All except W/T)	46	53
	With 1SB (All except W/T)	(39)	(45)
	With 1SC (All Reg Cab except W/T)	(39)	(45)
	With 1SC (X-cab)	(39)	(45)
B30	Carpeted Floor Covering (All Reg Cab except W/T)	30	35
	REQUIRES Cheyenne Equipment Package 1SA		
B30	Carpeted Floor Covering (X-cab)	44	51
	REQUIRES Cheyenne Equipment Package 1SA		
1SA	Cheyenne Equipment Package 1SA (w/ manual transmission) (All except W/T)	(430)	(500)
	With R9B (Sportside)	(602)	(700)
	With R9B (All Fleetside except W/T)	(602)	(700)
	With R9A (All except W/T)	(860)	(1000)
	With R9A (All except W/T) And R9B (Sportside)	(1032)	(1200)
	With R9A (All except W/T) And R9B (All Fleetside except W/T)	(1032)	(1200)
	Includes standard Cheyenne equipment; ATTENTION: this package carries varying manufacturer credits. See above for amounts		

CHEVROLET C/K 1500 PICKUP

CODE	DESCRIPTION	INVOICE	MSRP
1SA	Cheyenne Equipment Package 1SA (w/automatic transmission) (All except W/T)	NC	NC
	With R9A (All except W/T)	(430)	(500)
	With R9B (Sportside)	(172)	(200)
	With R9B (All Fleetside except W/T)	(172)	(200)
	With R9A (All except W/T) And R9B (Sportside)	(602)	(700)
	With R9A (All except W/T) And R9B (All Fleetside except W/T)	(602)	(700)
	Includes standard Cheyenne equipment; ATTENTION: this package carries varying manufacturer credits. See above for amounts		
VG3	Chrome Front Bumper	22	26
	Includes black rub strip; INCLUDED in Silverado Equipment Packages and Bright Appearance Package R9B; NOT AVAILABLE with Sport Package		
N83	Chrome Wheels (C1500)	267	310
	With 1SB (All except W/T)	215	250
	With 1SC (All Reg Cab except W/T)	215	250
	With 1SC (X-cab)	215	250
	With R9B (Sportside)	215	250
	With R9B (All Fleetside except W/T)	215	250
	With BYP (C1500 Reg Cab SB except W/T)	NC	NC
V10	Cold Climate Package	28	33
	Includes engine block heater; NOT AVAILABLE with 6.5-liter Turbodiesel V-8 Engine		
ZQ3	Convenience Group	329	383
	Includes tilt steering column and cruise control; INCLUDED in Silverado Equipment Packages and Convenience Package R9A		
R9A	Convenience Package (All except W/T)	1148	1335
	Includes air conditioning, tilt steering column, cruise control, and AM/FM stereo with cassette player, seek/scan, and digital clock; REQUIRES Cheyenne Equipment Package 1SA		
AJ1	Deep Tinted Glass (All Reg Cab except W/T)	30	35
	REQUIRES Sliding Rear Window		
AJ1	Deep Tinted Glass (X-cab)	92	107
	With C49 (X-cab)	62	72
	Tinting is light if ordered with Rear Window Defogger		
DD7	Electrochromic Rearview Mirror (All except W/T)	125	145
	Includes integrated 8-point compass; REQUIRES Silverado Equipment Package 1SB		
NP1	Electronic Shift Transfer Case (K1500)	129	150
	REQUIRES an Automatic Transmission and Convenience Group ZQ3		
KC4	Engine Oil Cooler	116	135
	INCLUDED with Trailering Special Package, 6.5-liter Turbodiesel V-8 Engine, and 3.73 Rear Axle Ratio; when ordered on K1500 Reg. Cab and K1500 Ext. Cab Shortbed, a Vortec V-8 Engine is required		
B32	Floor Mats — Front (All except W/T)	17	20
	REQUIRES Carpeted Floor Covering; INCLUDED in Silverado Equipment Packages		
B33	Floor Mats — Rear (X-cab)	14	16
	REQUIRES Carpeted Floor Covering and Front Floor Mats; INCLUDED in Silverado Equipment Packages; NOT AVAILABLE when rear seat is deleted		

C/K 1500 PICKUP — CHEVROLET

CODE	DESCRIPTION	INVOICE	MSRP
VK3	Front License Plate Bracket	NC	NC
BG9	Full Rubber Floor Credit (All Reg Cab except W/T)	(30)	(35)
	REQUIRES a Silverado Equipment Package; NOT AVAILABLE with Sport Package		
BG9	Full Rubber Floor Credit (X-cab)	(44)	(51)
	REQUIRES a Silverado Equipment Package		
FG5	Gas Shock Absorbers (C1500)	194	225
	46mm Bilstein shocks; NOT AVAILABLE with Trailering Special Package on Ext. Cab models		
Q4B	GVWR — 6,200 lbs. (X-cab)	NC	NC
	NOT AVAILABLE with Heavy-duty Chassis or 6.5-liter Turbodiesel V-8 Engine		
C5S	GVWR — 6,600 lbs. (K1500 X-cab)	NC	NC
	REQUIRES Heavy-duty Chassis; NOT AVAILABLE with 6.5-liter Turbodiesel V-8 Engine		
C5U	GVWR — 6,800 lbs. (K1500 X-cab LB)	NC	NC
	REQUIRES 6.5-liter Turbodiesel V-8 Engine		
MT1	Heavy-duty 4-speed Automatic Transmission (K1500 X-cab)	834	970
	REQUIRES 6.5-liter Turbodiesel V-8 Engine		
M50	Heavy-duty 5-speed Manual Transmission	NC	NC
	REQUIRES Vortec 5700 V-8 Engine		
TP2	Heavy-duty Auxiliary Battery	115	134
	REQUIRES standard Vortec 4300 V-6 Engine or optional Vortec 5000 V-8 Engine; NOT AVAILABLE with Sport Package		
KNP	Heavy-duty Auxiliary Transmission Cooler	83	96
	INCLUDED with Trailering Special Package and Heavy-duty Automatic Transmission; NOT AVAILABLE with 5-speed Manual Transmission, standard Vortec 4300 V-6 Engine, optional Vortec 5000 V-8 Engine, or 3.08 Rear Axle Ratio		
F44	Heavy-duty Chassis (K1500 X-cab)	198	230
	REQUIRES 6,600 lb. GVWR; INCLUDED with 6.5-liter Turbodiesel V-8 Engine		
F60	Heavy-duty Front Springs (K1500)	54	63
	INCLUDED in Snow Plow Prep Package; NOT AVAILABLE with Off-road Chassis Package or 6.5-liter Turbodiesel V-8 Engine		
F51	Heavy-duty Shock Absorbers	34	40
	INCLUDED with Trailering Special Package and Snow Plow Prep Package; NOT AVAILABLE with Off-road Chassis Package		
K47	High Capacity Air Cleaner	22	25
	NOT AVAILABLE with 6.5-liter Turbodiesel V-8 Engine		
MG5	Light-duty 5-speed Manual Transmission	NC	NC
	NOT AVAILABLE with Vortec 5700 V-8 Engine or 6.5-liter Turbodiesel V-8 Engine		
G80	Locking Differential	217	252
NG1	Massachusetts/New York Emissions	NC	NC
Z71	Off-road Chassis Package (All K1500 except W/T)	232	270
	Includes skid plate; REQUIRES a Silverado Equipment Package and On-off Road Tires; NOT AVAILABLE with Heavy-duty Shock Absorbers		
NZZ	Off-road Skid Plates (K1500)	82	95
	Includes front differential and transfer case shields; INCLUDED in Off-road Chassis Package		

CHEVROLET — C/K 1500 PICKUP

CODE	DESCRIPTION	INVOICE	MSRP
AU3	Power Door Locks (All except W/T)	134	156
	REQUIRES Cheyanne Equipment Group 1SA		
AG9	Power Driver's Seat (X-Cab)	206	240
	REQUIRES Silverado Equipment Package 1SB		
UL5	Radio Delete Credit	(247)	(287)
	REQUIRES W/T Equipment Package 1SW or Cheyanne Equipment Package 1SA		
P06	Rally Wheel Trim	52	60
	INCLUDED in Silverado Equipment Packages and Bright Appearance Package R9B		
EF1	Rear Bumper Delete Credit (All except W/T)	(172)	(200)
	REQUIRES a Silverado Equipment Package; NOT AVAILABLE with Trailering Special Package		
YG4	Rear Seat Delete Credit (X-cab)	(374)	(435)
	NOT AVAILABLE with Silverado Equipment Packages		
VB3	Rear Step Bumper — Chrome (Fleetside)	197	229
	Includes rub strip; REQUIRES Chrome Front Bumper; INCLUDED in Silverado Equipment Packages and Bright Appearance Package R9B		
V43	Rear Step Bumper — Painted (Fleetside)	112	130
	NOT AVAILABLE with Silverado Equipment Packages; INCLUDED in Sport Package		
C49	Rear Window Defogger (X-cab)	132	154
	REQUIRES a Silverado Equipment Package; NOT AVAILABLE with Sliding Rear Window		
AU0	Remote Keyless Entry (All except W/T)	120	140
	REQUIRES Silverado Equipment Package 1SB		
A52	Seat — Cloth Bench (Reg Cab)	NC	NC
	REQUIRES W/T Equipment Package 1SW or Cheyanne Equipment Package 1SA		
AE7	Seat — Cloth Split Reclining Bench (All Reg Cab except W/T)	150	174
	Includes storage armrest and power lumbar support		
A52	Seat — Leather Bench (All Reg Cab except W/T)	860	1000
	REQUIRES Silverado Equipment Package 1SB		
AE7	Seat — Leather Split Reclining Bench (All Reg Cab except W/T)	1010	1174
	Includes storage armrest and power lumbar support; REQUIRES Silverado Equipment Package 1SB		
AE7	Seat — Leather Split Reclining Bench (X-cab)	860	1000
	Includes storage armrest and power lumbar support; REQUIRES Silverado Equipment Package 1SB		
A95	Seats — Cloth Reclining High Back Buckets (All Reg Cab except W/T)	332	386
	Includes power lumbar support; REQUIRES Silverado Equipment Package 1SB		
A95	Seats — Cloth Reclining High Back Buckets (X-cab)	232	270
	Includes power lumbar support; REQUIRES Silverado Equipment Package 1SB		
A95	Seats — Leather Reclining High Back Buckets (All Reg Cab except W/T)	1192	1386
	Without 1SC (All Reg Cab except W/T)	174	202
	Includes power lumbar support; REQUIRES a Silverado Equipment Package		
A95	Seats — Leather Reclining High Back Buckets (X-cab)	1093	1270
	With 1SC (X-cab)	232	270
	Includes power lumbar support; REQUIRES a Silverado Equipment Package		

C/K 1500 PICKUP — CHEVROLET

CODE	DESCRIPTION	INVOICE	MSRP
1SB	Silverado Equipment Package 1SB (All except W/T)	2721	3164
	With MG5	1646	1914
	With M50	1646	1914
	With M30	2076	2414
	With MT1 (K1500 X-cab)	2076	2414

Includes air conditioning, cloth and carpet trimmed door panels, floor carpeting, rubber floor mats, added sound deadening insulation, AM/FM stereo with cassette player, seek/scan, and digital clock; leather-wrapped steering wheel, cloth seats, rear storage tray, power windows, power locks, power mirrors, tilt steering column, cruise control, chrome bumpers, rear step pad, chrome grille, composite headlamps, bright wheel well openings, rally wheels with bright trim rings; ATTENTION: see above for pricing after package discounts

1SC	Silverado Equipment Package 1SC (All Reg Cab except W/T)	3976	4623
	With MG5	2901	3373
	With M50	2901	3373
	With M30	3331	3873
	With MT1 (K1500 X-cab)	3331	3873

Includes air conditioning, cloth and carpet trimmed door panels, floor carpeting, rubber floor mats, added sound deadening insulation, AM/FM stereo with cassette player, seek/scan, and digital clock; leather-wrapped steering wheel, cloth seats, rear storage tray, power windows, power locks, power mirrors, tilt steering column, cruise control, chrome bumpers, rear step pad, chrome grille, composite headlamps, bright wheel well openings, rally wheels with bright trim rings, remote keyless entry, electrochromic rearview mirror with integrated compass, split bench seat, leather seat trim; ATTENTION: see above for pricing after package discounts

1SC	Silverado Equipment Package 1SC (X-cab)	4033	4689
	With MG5	2958	3439
	With M50	2958	3439
	With M30	3338	3939
	With MT1 (K1500 X-cab)	NC	NC

Includes air conditioning, cloth and carpet trimmed door panels, floor carpeting, rubber floor mats, added sound deadening insulation, AM/FM stereo with cassette player, seek/scan, and digital clock; leather-wrapped steering wheel, cloth seats, rear storage tray, power windows, power locks, power mirrors, tilt steering column, cruise control, chrome bumpers, rear step pad, chrome grille, composite headlamps, bright wheel well openings, rally wheels with bright trim rings, remote keyless entry, electrochromic rearview mirror with integrated compass, split bench seat, leather seat trim, power driver's seat; ATTENTION: see above for pricing after package discounts

A28	Sliding Rear Window	97	113
	NOT AVAILABLE with Rear Window Defogger		
VYU	Snow Plow Prep Package (K1500 Reg Cab)	136	158
	With Z71 (All K1500 except W/T)	47	55

Includes Heavy-duty Front Springs and Heavy-duty Shock Absorbers when ordered without Off-road Chassis Package; REQUIRES Engine Oil Cooler when ordered with 3.42 Rear Axle Ratio; NOT AVAILABLE with 6.5-liter Turbodiesel V-8 Engine

CHEVROLET — C/K 1500 PICKUP

CODE	DESCRIPTION	INVOICE	MSRP
BYP	Sport Package (C1500 Reg Cab SB except W/T)	179	208
	Includes body-color bumpers, fog lamps, sport decals, color-keyed exterior mirrors, color-keyed grille, aluminum wheels; REQUIRES a Silverado Equipment Package		
BYP	Sport Package (K1500 Reg Cab SB except W/T)	390	458
	Includes body-color bumpers, fog lamps, sport decals, color-keyed exterior mirrors, color-keyed grille, aluminum wheels; REQUIRES a Silverado Equipment Package		
UN0	Stereo — Premium w/CD player (All except W/T)	163	190
	AM/FM stereo with CD player, seek/scan, digital clock, theft lock, automatic tone control, enhanced performance 6-speaker sound system; REQUIRES a Silverado Equipment Package		
UL0	Stereo — Uplevel w/cassette (All except W/T)	77	40
	AM/FM stereo with cassette player, seek/scan, automatic tone control, theft lock, speed compensated volume, and digital clock; REQUIRES a Silverado Equipment Package		
UP0	Stereo — Uplevel w/CD & cassette players (All except W/T)	249	290
	AM/FM stereo with cassette and CD players, seek/scan, automatic tone control, theft lock, speed compensated volume, and digital clock; REQUIRES a Silverado Equipment Package and an Automatic Transmission		
UM6	Stereo — w/cassette	126	147
	AM/FM stereo with cassette player, seek/scan, and digital clock; REQUIRES W/T Equipment Package or Cheyenne Equipment Package; INCLUDED in Convenience Package R9A		
E24	Third Door (X-cab SB)	361	420
	REQUIRES a Vortec V-8 Engine, Automatic Transmission (M30), and a Silverado Equipment Package; NOT AVAILABLE with Full Rubber Floor Covering or Deluxe Two-tone Paint		
XBN/YBN/ZBN	Tires — LT245/75R16C (K1500)	49	57
	On-off road blackwall tires; includes front, rear, and spare tires		
XBX/YBX/ZBX	Tires — LT245/75R16C (K1500)	157	182
	On-off road outline white-letter tires; includes front, rear and spare tires		
XFN/YFN/ZFN	Tires — P235/75R15 (C1500 except W/T)	108	125
	All-season outline white-letter tires; includes front, rear, and spare tires; NOT AVAILABLE with Sport Package		
XGB/YGB/ZGB	Tires — P245/75R16 (K1500)	108	125
	All-terrain outline white-letter tires; includes front, rear, and spare tires		
XGA/YGA/ZGA	Tires — P245/75R16 (K1500)	NC	NC
	All-terrain blackwall tires; includes front, rear and spare tires		
XGC/YGC/ZGC	Tires — P265/75R16C (K1500 except W/T)	116	135
	On-off road blackwall tires; includes front, rear, and spare tires; INLCUDED in Sport Package; REQUIRES Aluminum Wheels; REQUIRES 3.73 Rear Axle Ratio when ordered without Vortec 5700 V-8 engine		
XGD/YGD/ZGD	Tires — P265/75R16C (K1500 except W/T)	224	260
	On-off road outline white letter tires; includes front, rear, and spare tires; INLCUDED in Sport Package; REQUIRES Aluminum Wheels; REQUIRES 3.73 Rear Axle Ratio when ordered without Vortec 5700 V-8 engine		
V76	Tow Hooks (C1500)	33	38
	NOT AVAILABLE with Sport Package		

C/K 1500 PICKUP — CHEVROLET

CODE	DESCRIPTION	INVOICE	MSRP
Z82	Trailering Special Package (w/3.73 axle ratio)	175	204
	With VYU (K1500 Reg Cab)	141	164
	With Z71 (All K1500 except W/T)	141	164
	Includes trailer hitch and engine oil cooler; includes Heavy-duty Shock Absorbers when ordered without Gas Shock Absorbers or Off-road Chassis Package; REQUIRES a rear step bumper (VB3 or V43) and an Automatic Transmission; NOT AVAILABLE with Gas Shock Absorbers on Ext. Cab models; ATTENTION: if ordering a K1500 with Off-road Chassis Package and Vortec 5000 V-8 Engine, this is the only Trailering Special Package that can be installed		
Z82	Trailering Special Package (w/diesel engine) (X-cab)	175	204
	With VYU (K1500 Reg Cab)	141	164
	With Z71 (All K1500 except W/T)	141	164
	Includes trailer hitch and Heavy-duty Shock Absorbers; REQUIRES a rear step bumper (VB3 or V43)		
Z82	Trailering Special Package (w/gas engine)	292	339
	With VYU (K1500 Reg Cab)	257	299
	With Z71 (All K1500 except W/T)	257	299
	Includes trailer hitch and engine oil cooler; includes Heavy-duty Shock Absorbers when ordered without Gas Shock Absorbers or Off-road Chassis Package; REQUIRES a rear step bumper (VB3 or V43), an Automatic Transmission, and 3.08 or 3.42 Rear Axle Ratio; when ordered on C1500 with standard Vortec 4300 V-6 Engine, the 3.42 Rear Axle Ratio must be selected; NOT AVAILABLE with Gas Shock Absorbers on Ext. Cab models		
ZY2	Two-tone Paint — Conventional (All except W/T)	155	180
	REQUIRES a Silverado Equipment Package		
ZY4	Two-tone Paint — Deluxe (All Fleetside except W/T)	237	275
	REQUIRES a Silverado Equipment Package		
BZY	Under Rail Bedliner (Fleetside)	194	225
L30	Vortec 5000 V-8 Engine (All except X-cab LB)	426	495
	REQUIRES Light-duty 5-speed Manual Transmission (MG5) or 4-speed Automatic Transmission (M30)		
L31	Vortec 5700 V-8 Engine (All except X-cab LB)	1028	1195
	REQUIRES Heavy-duty 5-speed Manual Transmission (M50) or 4-speed Automatic Transmission (M30)		
L31	Vortec 5700 V-8 Engine (X-cab LB)	602	700
	REQUIRES Heavy-duty 5-speed Manual Transmission (M50) or 4-speed Automatic Transmission (M30)		
1SW	W/T Equipment Package 1SW (W/T)	NC	NC
	With MG5	(430)	(500)
	Includes standard W/T equipment; ATTENTION: this package carries a credit when ordered with MG5 5-speed Manual Transmission; see above for amount		

CHEVROLET — C/K 2500 PICKUP

C/K 2500 PICKUP (1997)

Safety Data

Driver Airbag: *Standard under 8,600 GVWR*
Side Airbag: *Not Available*
4-Wheel ABS: *Standard*
Driver Crash Test Grade: *Excellent (w/airbag);*
N/A (w/o airbag)
Passenger Crash Test Grade: *N/A (w/airbag);*
Excellent (w/o airbag)

Passenger Airbag: *Standard under 8,600 GVWR*
Meets 1999 Side Impact Standards: *No*
Traction Control: *Not Available*
Insurance Cost: *Low*
Integrated Child Seat(s): *Not Available*

Standard Equipment

C/K 2500 CHEYANNE: Dual airbags (models under 8,600 lbs. GVWR), plastic door trim with armrest, full color-keyed rubber floor coverings, trip odometer, tachometer, oil pressure gauge, voltmeter, delayed entry lighting, vinyl bench seat, 60/40 split front vinyl bench seat (Extended Cab), steel side door impact beams (do not meet 1999 standard), AM/FM stereo with digital clock, intermittent variable wipers, daytime running lamps, dual black foldaway exterior mirrors, power front disc/rear drum 4-wheel anti-lock brakes, Vortec 5000 V-8 engine, Vortec 5700 V-8 engine (Extended Cab Longbed models), 5-speed manual transmission with overdrive, rear quarter swing-out windows (Extended Cab models)

Base Prices

Code	Description	Invoice	MSRP
CC20903	C2500 Regular Cab Longbed	15242	17419
CC20903	C2500 HD Regular Cab Longbed	15980	18268
CC20753	C2500 Extended Cab Shortbed	17531	20035
CC20953	C2500 HD Extended Cab Longbed	17384	19872
CK20903	K2500 Regular Cab Longbed	18391	21023
CK20753	K2500 Extended Cab Shortbed	20101	22977
CK20953	K2500 Extended Cab Longbed	20213	23105
	Destination Charge:	625	625

Accessories

Code	Description	Invoice	MSRP
L56	6.5-liter Turbodiesel V-8 Engine (Reg Cab)	3062	3560
L65	6.5-liter Turbodiesel V-8 Engine (X-cab)	2460	2860
C60	Air Conditioning	692	805
	INCLUDED in Silverado Equipment Packages and Convenience Package R9A		
V22	Appearance Package	164	191
	Includes dual horns, composite headlamps, and chrome grille; INCLUDED in Silverado Equipment Packages and Bright Appearance Package R9B		
M30/MT1	Automatic Transmission	834	970
TP2	Auxiliary Battery	115	134
	NOT AVAILABLE with Turbodiesel V-8 Engines		
BZY	Bedliner	194	225
	With R9C (4WD)	NC	NC
	With R9C (2WD)	NC	NC

C/K 2500 PICKUP — CHEVROLET

CODE	DESCRIPTION	INVOICE	MSRP
B85	Bodyside Molding (2WD)	92	107
	Includes bright insert; INCLUDED in Silverado Equipment Packages and Bright Appearance Package R9B		
B85	Bodyside Molding (4WD)	65	76
	Includes bright insert; INCLUDED in Silverado Equipment Packages and Bright Appearance Package R9B		
R9B	Bright Appearance Package (2WD)	527	613
	Includes bodyside moldings with bright insert, chrome grille, chrome rear step bumper, chrome front bumper, rally wheel trim; INCLUDED in Silverado Equipment Packages		
YF5	California Emissions	146	170
DF2	Camper-type Exterior Mirrors	46	53
	With 1SB	(39)	(45)
	With 1SC (X-cab)	(39)	(45)
	With 1SC (Reg Cab)	(39)	(45)
1SA	Cheyenne Equipment Package 1SA	NC	NC
	With R9A And R9B (2WD)	(602)	(700)
	With R9B (2WD) And R9C (2WD)	(344)	(400)
	With R9A	(430)	(500)
	With R9B (2WD)	(172)	(200)
	With R9C (2WD)	(172)	(200)
	With R9C (4WD)	(172)	(200)
	Includes vehicle with standard equipment		
V10	Cold Climate Package	28	33
	Includes engine block heater; NOT AVAILABLE with Silverado Equipment Packages or on extended cab model when ordered with Turbodiesel V-8 Engine.		
R9C	Commercial Equipment Package (2WD)	435	506
	Includes bedliner, painted rear step bumper, front tow hooks, sliding rear window (Regular Cab); NOT AVAILABLE with Silverado Equipment Packages or Bright Appearance Package R9B		
R9C	Commercial Equipment Package (4WD)	538	563
	With L56 (Reg Cab)	484	496
	With L65 (X-cab)	484	496
	Includes bedliner, painted rear step bumper, heavy-duty front springs, skid plates, sliding rear window (Regular Cab); NOT AVAILABLE with Silverado Equipment Packages or Bright Appearance Package R9B		
ZQ3	Convenience Group ZQ3	329	383
	Includes tilt steering wheel and cruise control; INCLUDED in Silverado Equipment Packages and Convenience Package R9A		
R9A	Convenience Package	1148	1335
	Includes air conditioning, tilt steering wheel, cruise control, AM/FM stereo with cassette player, seek/scan, and digital clock; INCLUDED in Silverado Equipment Packages		

CHEVROLET C/K 2500 PICKUP

CODE	DESCRIPTION	INVOICE	MSRP
AJ1	Deep Tinted Glass (Reg Cab)	30	35
AJ1	Deep Tinted Glass (X-cab)	92	107
	With C49 (X-cab)	62	72
DD7	Electrochromic Rearview Mirror	125	145
	Includes integrated 8-point compass; REQUIRES purchase of Silverado Equipment Package 1SB		
NP1	Electronic Shift Transfer Case (4WD)	106	123
	REQUIRES purchase of a Silverado Equipment Package or Convenience Group ZQ3 and an automatic transmission		
KC4	Engine Oil Cooler (2WD HD/4WD)	NC	NC
	REQUIRES 3.73 Rear Axle Ratio or Trailering Special Equipment		
KC4	Engine Oil Cooler (2WD Light Duty)	116	135
	NOT AVAILABLE with Turbodiesel V-8 Engines, 3.73 Rear Axle Ratio, or Trailering Special Equipment		
B30	Floor Carpeting (Reg Cab)	30	35
	INCLUDED in Silverado Equipment Packages		
B30	Floor Carpeting (X-cab)	44	51
	INCLUDED in Silverado Equipment Packages		
B32	Floor Mats — Front	17	20
	INCLUDED in Silverado Equipment Packages		
B33	Floor Mats — Rear (X-cab)	14	16
	INCLUDED in Silverado Equipment Packages		
VG3	Front Bumper — Chrome	22	26
	INCLUDED in Silverado Equipment Packages and Bright Appearance Package R9B		
VK3	Front License Plate Bracket	NC	NC
F60	Heavy-duty Front Springs	54	63
	INCLUDED in Snow Plow Prep Package and Commercial Equipment Package		
MW3	Heavy-duty Manual Transmission (2WD HD/4WD)	NC	NC
	Includes deep low and overdrive		
MW3	Heavy-duty Manual Transmission (2WD Light Duty)	84	98
	With L56 (Reg Cab)	NC	NC
	With L65 (X-cab)	NC	NC
	Includes deep low and overdrive		
KNP	Heavy-duty Transmission Cooling	83	96
	With M30/MT1	NC	NC
	With M30/MT1 And Z82 (2WD HD/4WD)	NC	NC
	With M30/MT1 And Z82 (2WD Light Duty)	NC	NC
	REQUIRES purchase of Vortec 5700 V-8 Engine		
K47	High-capacity Air Cleaner	22	25
G80	Locking Differential	217	252
	REQUIRES 3.73 Rear Axle Ratio on 2WD Light Duty models		
NG1	Massachusetts/New York Emissions	NC	NC
ZY2	Paint — Conventional Two-tone	155	180
ZY4	Paint — Deluxe Two-tone	237	275
AU3	Power Door Locks	134	156
	INCLUDED in Silverado Equipment Packages		

C/K 2500 PICKUP — CHEVROLET

CODE	DESCRIPTION	INVOICE	MSRP
AG9	Power Driver's Seat	206	240
	REQUIRES purchase of a Silverado Equipment Package; INCLUDED in Silverado Equipment Package 1SC on extended cab models		
P06	Rally Wheel Trim	52	60
	Includes bright trim rings and chrome center caps; INCLUDED in Silverado Equipment Packages and Bright Appearance Package R9B		
GT4	Rear Axle Ratio — 3.73 (All 2WD except HD)	116	135
VB3	Rear Bumper — Chrome	197	229
	INCLUDED in Silverado Equipment Packages and Bright Appearance Package R9B		
EF1	Rear Bumper — Delete Credit	(172)	(200)
	NOT AVAILABLE with Silverado Equipment Packages or Trailering Special Equipment		
V43	Rear Bumper — Painted	112	130
	With R9C (2WD)	NC	NC
	With R9C (4WD)	NC	NC
	NOT AVAILABLE with Silverado Equipment Packages or Bright Appearance Package R9B		
C49	Rear Window Defogger (X-cab)	132	154
AU0	Remote Keyless Entry	120	140
	REQUIRES purchase of Silverado Equipment Package 1SB; INCLUDED in Silverado Equipment Package 1SC		
U01	Roof Marker Lamps	45	52
BG9	Rubber Floor Covering Credit	(30)	(35)
	REQUIRES purchase of Silverado Equipment Package 1SB		
BG9	Rubber Floor Covering Credit	(44)	(51)
	REQUIRES purchase of Silverado Equipment Package 1SB		
AE7	Seats — Cloth 60/40 Split Bench (Reg Cab)	150	174
A95	Seats — Cloth Reclining High-back Buckets (Reg Cab)	332	386
A95	Seats — Cloth Reclining High-back Buckets (X-cab)	232	270
AE7	Seats — Leather 60/40 Split Bench (Reg Cab)	1010	1174
	REQUIRES purchase of Silverado Equipment Package 1SB		
AE7	Seats — Leather 60/40 Split Bench (X-cab)	860	1000
	REQUIRES purchase of Silverado Equipment Package 1SB		
A52	Seats — Leather Bench	860	1000
	REQUIRES purchase of Silverado Equipment Package 1SB		
A95	Seats — Leather Reclining Bucket Seats (X-cab)	1092	1270
	Without 1SC (X-cab)	232	270
	REQUIRES purchase of a Silverado Equipment Package		
A95	Seats — Leather Reclining High-back Buckets (Reg Cab)	1192	1386
	With 1SC (Reg Cab)	232	270
	REQUIRES purchase of a Silverado Equipment Package		
YG4	Seats — Rear Delete Credit (X-cab)	(374)	(435)
	NOT AVAILABLE with Silverado Equipment Packages		

CHEVROLET — C/K 2500 PICKUP

CODE	DESCRIPTION	INVOICE	MSRP
1SB	Silverado Equipment Package 1SB	2721	3164
	Manufacturer Discount	(645)	(750)
	Net Price	2076	2414

Includes air conditioning, power windows, power door locks, cruise control, full floor carpet, rubber floor mats, additional sound deadening insulation, AM/FM stereo with cassette player, seek/scan, and digital clock; cloth bench seat (60/40 split bench on extended cab), leather-wrapped steering wheel, behind seat storage tray, chrome front bumper with black rub strip, chrome rear bumper with step pad, deluxe chrome grille, composite headlamps, dual note horn, power exterior mirrors, bodyside moldings with bright trim and bright wheel opening moldings (light-duty vehicles), rally wheel trim

1SC	Silverado Equipment Package 1SC (Reg Cab)	3976	4623
	Manufacturer Discount	(645)	(750)
	Net Price	3331	3873

Includes air conditioning, power windows, power door locks, cruise control, full floor carpet, rubber floor mats, additional sound deadening insulation, AM/FM stereo with cassette player, seek/scan, and digital clock; cloth bench seat (60/40 split bench on extended cab), leather-wrapped steering wheel, behind seat storage tray, chrome front bumper with black rub strip, chrome rear bumper with step pad, deluxe chrome grille, composite headlamps, dual note horn, power exterior mirrors, bodyside moldings with bright trim and bright wheel opening moldings (light-duty vehicles), rally wheel trim, remote keyless entry, leather seats, electrochromic rearview mirror with integrated compass

1SC	Silverado Equipment Package 1SC (X-cab)	4033	4689
	Manufacturer Discount	(645)	(750)
	Net Price	3388	3939

Includes air conditioning, power windows, power door locks, cruise control, full floor carpet, rubber floor mats, additional sound deadening insulation, AM/FM stereo with cassette player, seek/scan, and digital clock; cloth bench seat (60/40 split bench on extended cab), leather-wrapped steering wheel, behind seat storage tray, chrome front bumper with black rub strip, chrome rear bumper with step pad, deluxe chrome grille, composite headlamps, dual note horn, power exterior mirrors, bodyside moldings with bright trim and bright wheel opening moldings (light-duty vehicles), rally wheel trim, remote keyless entry, leather seats, electrochromic rearview mirror with integrated compass

NZZ	Skid Plates (4WD)	82	95

INCLUDED in Commercial Equipment Package R9C

A28	Sliding Rear Window	97	113

INCLUDED in Commercial Equipment Package R9C; NOT AVAILABLE with Rear Window Defogger

VYU	Snow Plow Prep Package (4WD)	101	118
	With R9C (4WD)	47	55

Includes heavy-duty front springs; REQUIRES purchase of Commercial Equipment Package or a Turbodiesel V-8 Engine

UL5	Stereo — Delete Credit	(247)	(287)

NOT AVAILABLE with Silverado Equipment Packages

C/K 2500 PICKUP — CHEVROLET

CODE	DESCRIPTION	INVOICE	MSRP
UL0	Stereo — Uplevel w/cassette	174	202
	With 1SB	77	90
	With 1SC (X-cab)	77	90
	With 1SC (Reg Cab)	77	90
	AM/FM stereo with cassette player, seek/scan, automatic tone control, theft lock, and speed compensated volume		
UP0	Stereo — Uplevel w/cassette & CD players	346	402
	With 1SB	249	290
	With 1SC (X-cab)	249	290
	With 1SC (Reg Cab)	249	290
	AM/FM stereo with cassette and CD players, seek/scan, automatic tone control, theft lock, and speed compensated volume		
UN0	Stereo — Uplevel w/CD player	260	302
	With 1SB	163	190
	With 1SC (X-cab)	163	190
	With 1SC (Reg Cab)	163	190
	AM/FM stereo with CD player, seek/scan, automatic tone control, theft lock, and speed compensated volume		
UM6	Stereo — w/cassette	126	147
	AM/FM stereo with cassette player, seek/scan, and digital clock; INCLUDED in Silverado Equipment Packages and in Convenience Package R9A		
XHP/YHR/ZHR	Tires — LT225/75R16D (2WD Light Duty)	47	55
	On/off road tires		
XHP/YHP/ZHP	Tires — LT225/75R16D (2WD Heavy Duty)	(77)	(92)
	All-season tires		
XGK/YGK/ZGK	Tires — LT245/75R16E (2WD HD/4WD)	47	55
	On/off road tires		
XGK/YGK/ZGK	Tires — LT245/75R16E (2WD Light Duty)	240	285
	On/off road tires		
XHH/YHH/ZHH	Tires — LT245/75R16E (2WD Light Duty)	193	230
	All-season tires		
V76	Tow Hooks (2WD)	33	38
	INCLUDED in Commercial Equipment Package		
Z82	Trailering Special Equipment (2WD HD/4WD)	141	164
	Includes trailer hitch; REQUIRES rear step bumper when ordered without a Silverado Equipment Package		
Z82	Trailering Special Equipment (2WD Light Duty)	257	299
	With GT4 (All 2WD except HD)	141	164
	With L56 (Reg Cab)	141	164
	With L65 (X-cab)	141	164
	Includes trailer hitch, and engine oil cooler when ordered with Vortec V-8 Engine; REQUIRES rear step bumper when ordered without a Silverado Equipment Package		
L31	Vortec 5700 V-8 Engine (All except X-cab LB)	602	700
L29	Vortec 7400 V-8 Engine (X-Cab)	516	600

CHEVROLET — C/K 3500 PICKUP

C/K 3500 PICKUP *(1997)*

Safety Data

Driver Airbag: *Not Available*
Side Airbag: *Not Available*
4-Wheel ABS: *Standard*
Driver Crash Test Grade: *Not Available*
Passenger Crash Test Grade: *Not Available*

Passenger Airbag: *Not Available*
Meets 1999 Side Impact Standards: *No*
Traction Control: *Not Available*
Insurance Cost: *Low*
Integrated Child Seat(s): *Not Available*

Standard Equipment

C/K 3500 CHEYANNE: Plastic door trim with armrest, full color-keyed rubber floor coverings (Regular Cab/Extended Cab), black floor coverings (Crew Cab), trip odometer, tachometer, oil pressure gauge, voltmeter, delayed entry lighting, vinyl bench seating, 60/40 split front vinyl bench seat (Extended Cab), steel side door impact beams (do not meet 1999 standard), AM/FM stereo with digital clock, intermittent variable wipers, daytime running lamps, dual black foldaway exterior mirrors, power front disc/rear drum 4-wheel anti-lock brakes, Vortec 5700 V-8 engine, 5-speed manual transmission with deep low and overdrive, rear quarter swing-out windows (Extended Cab models), heavy-duty battery, rear door light switch (Crew Cab)

Base Prices

Code	Description	Invoice	MSRP
CC30903	C3500 Regular Cab Longbed	16102	18407
CC30953	C3500 Extended Cab Longbed	19100	21829
CC30943	C3500 Crew Cab	18841	21537
CK30903	K3500 Regular Cab Longbed	18727	21407
CK30953	K3500 Extended Cab Longbed	21560	24640
CK30943	K3500 Crew Cab	21618	24711
	Destination Charge:	625	625

Accessories

Code	Description	Invoice	MSRP
L65	6.5-liter Turbodiesel V-8 Engine	2460	2860
C60	Air Conditioning	692	805
	INCLUDED in Silverado Equipment Packages and Convenience Package R9A		
V22	Appearance Package	164	191
	Includes dual note horn, chrome grille, and composite headlights; INCLUDED in Silverado Equipment Packages and in Bright Appearacne Package R9B		
MT1	Automatic Transmission	834	970
	Heavy-duty unit with transmission oil cooler		
TP2	Auxiliary Battery	115	134
	NOT AVAILABLE with Turbodiesel V-8 Engine		
BZY	Bedliner	194	225
	INCLUDED in Commercial Equipment Packages		
B85	Bodyside Moldings (2WD Reg Cab)	92	107
	Includes bright insert; INCLUDED in Silverado Equipment Packages and Bright Appearance Package R9B		

C/K 3500 PICKUP — CHEVROLET

CODE	DESCRIPTION	INVOICE	MSRP
B85	Bodyside Moldings (4WD Reg Cab)	65	76
	Includes bright insert; INCLUDED in Silverado Equipment Packages and Bright Appearance Package R9B		
R9B	Bright Appearance Package (2WD Reg Cab)	527	613
	With R05 (Reg Cab)	435	506
	Includes deluxe chrome grille, chrome front bumper with rub strip, chrome rear bumper with step pad, rally wheel trim, bodyside molding with bright insert (N/A with dual rear wheels); INCLUDED in Silverado Equipment Packages		
R9B	Bright Appearance Package (4WD Reg Cab)	501	582
	Includes deluxe chrome grille, chrome front bumper with rub strip, chrome rear bumper with step pad, rally wheel trim, bodyside molding with bright insert (N/A with dual rear wheels); INCLUDED in Silverado Equipment Packages		
R9B	Bright Appearance Package (Crew Cab)	413	480
	Includes deluxe chrome grille, chrome front bumper with rub strip, rally wheel trim, bodyside moldings with bright insert (N/A with dual rear wheels); INCLUDED in Silverado Equipment Packages		
YF5	California Emissions	146	170
DF2	Camper-type Exterior Mirrors	46	53
	With 1SB (Reg Cab/X-cab)	(33)	(45)
	With 1SB (Crew Cab)	(33)	(45)
	With 1SC (X-cab)	(33)	(45)
	With 1SC (Regular Cab)	(33)	(45)
	With 1SC (Crew Cab)	(33)	(45)
B30	Carpeted Floors (Reg Cab)	30	35
B30	Carpeted Floors (X-cab)	44	51
1SA	Cheyenne Equipment Package 1SA (Reg Cab/X-cab)	NC	NC
	With R9A And R9B (2WD Reg Cab)	(602)	(700)
	With R9A And R9B (4WD Reg Cab)	(602)	(700)
	With R9A And R9C (4WD Reg Cab/X-cab)	(602)	(700)
	With R9A And R9C (2WD Reg Cab/X-cab)	(602)	(700)
	With R9B (2WD Reg Cab) And R9C (2WD Reg Cab/X-cab)	(344)	(400)
	With R9B (4WD Reg Cab) And R9C (4WD Reg Cab/X-cab)	(344)	(400)
	With R9B (2WD Reg Cab)	(172)	(200)
	With R9B (4WD Reg Cab)	(172)	(200)
	With R9C (4WD Reg Cab/X-cab)	(172)	(200)
	With R9C (2WD Reg Cab/X-cab)	(172)	(200)
	With R9A	(430)	(500)
	Includes vehicle with standard equipment		
VG3	Chrome Front Bumper	22	26
	INCLUDED in Silverado Equipment Packages and Bright Appearance Package R9B		
V10	Cold Climate Package	28	33
	Includes engine block heater; REQUIRES Cheyanne Equipment Package on Regular Cab models equipped with turbodiesel engine; NOT AVAILABLE on Crew Cab models equipped with turbodiesel engine		
R9C	Commercial Equipment Package (2WD Reg Cab/X-cab)	435	506
	Includes bedliner, painted rear step bumper, front tow hooks, sliding rear window		

CHEVROLET

C/K 3500 PICKUP

CODE	DESCRIPTION	INVOICE	MSRP
R9C	Commercial Equipment Package (4WD Reg Cab/X-cab)	538	626
	With L65	484	563
	Includes bedliner, painted rear step bumper, heavy-duty front springs, skid plates, sliding rear window		
ZQ3	Convenience Group ZQ3	329	383
	Includes tilt steering wheel and cruise control; INCLUDED in Silverado Equipment Packages and Convenience Package R9A		
R9A	Convenience Package R9A	1148	1335
	Includes air conditioning, tilt steering wheel, cruise control, AM/FM stereo with cassette player, seek/scan, and digital clock; INCLUDED in Silverado Equipment Packages		
AJ1	Deep Tinted Glass (Crew Cab)	185	215
	With A28	155	180
AJ1	Deep Tinted Glass (Reg Cab)	30	35
AJ1	Deep Tinted Glass (X-cab)	92	107
	With C49 (X-cab/Crew Cab)	62	72
R05	Dual Rear Wheels (Crew Cab)	737	857
	Includes roof marker lamps and tailgate lamps		
R05	Dual Rear Wheels (Reg Cab)	821	955
	Includes roof marker lamps and tailgate lamps		
R05	Dual Rear Wheels (X-cab)	NC	NC
	Includes roof marker lamps and tailgate lamps		
DD7	Electrochromic Rearview Mirror (Reg Cab/X-cab)	125	145
	Includes 8-point compass; REQUIRES purchase of Silverado Equipment Package 1SB; INCLUDED in Silverado Equipment Package 1SC		
B32	Floor Mats — Front	17	20
	INCLUDED in Silverado Equipment Packages		
B33	Floor Mats — Rear (X-cab)	14	16
	INCLUDED in Silverado Equipment Packages		
VK3	Front License Plate Bracket	NC	NC
F60	Heavy-duty Front Springs (4WD)	54	63
	INCLUDED in Snow Plow Prep Package and Commercial Equipment Package on Regular Cab and Extended Cab models		
K47	High-capacity Air Cleaner	22	25
G80	Locking Differential	217	252
NG1	Massachusetts/New York Emissions	NC	NC
ZY2	Paint — Conventional Two-tone (Reg Cab/X-cab)	155	180
ZY4	Paint — Deluxe Two-tone (Reg Cab/X-cab)	237	275
AU3	Power Door Locks (Crew Cab)	192	223
	INCLUDED in Silverado Equipment Packages		
AU3	Power Door Locks (Reg Cab/X-cab)	134	156
	INCLUDED in Silverado Equipment Packages		
AG9	Power Driver's Seat	206	240
	REQUIRES purchase of a Silverado Equipment Package; INCLUDED in Silverado Equipment Package 1SC on Extended Cab and Crew Cab models		
P06	Rally Wheel Trim	52	60
	INCLUDED in Silverado Equipment Packages and Bright Appearance Package R9B		

C/K 3500 PICKUP — CHEVROLET

CODE	DESCRIPTION	INVOICE	MSRP
HC4	Rear Axle Ratio — 4.56	216	252
	Includes locking differential		
VB3	Rear Step Bumper — Chrome	197	229
	INCLUDED in Silverado Equipment Packages and Bright Appearance Package R9B		
EF1	Rear Step Bumper — Delete Credit	(172)	(200)
V43	Rear Step Bumper — Painted	112	130
	INCLUDED in Commercial Equipment Packages; NOT AVAILABLE with Silverado Equipment Packages		
C49	Rear Window Defogger (X-cab/Crew Cab)	132	154
	NOT AVAILABLE with Sliding Rear Window		
AU0	Remote Keyless Entry	120	140
	REQUIRES purchase of Silverado Equipment Package 1SB; INCLUDED in Silverado Equipment Package 1SC		
U01	Roof Marker Lamps	45	52
BG9	Rubber Floor Credit (Reg Cab)	(30)	(35)
	REQUIRES purchase of a Silverado Equipment Package		
BG9	Rubber Floor Credit (X-cab)	(44)	(51)
	REQUIRES purchase of a Silverado Equipment Package		
AE7	Seats — Cloth 60/40 Split Reclining Bench (Crew Cab)	86	100
	NOT AVAILABLE with Silverado Equipment Package 1SC		
AE7	Seats — Cloth 60/40 Split Reclining Bench (Reg Cab)	150	174
	NOT AVAILABLE with Silverado Equipment Package 1SC		
A95	Seats — Cloth Reclining High-back Buckets (Crew Cab)	364	423
	REQUIRES purchase of Silverado Equipment Package 1SB; NOT AVAILABLE with Silverado Equipment Package 1SC		
A95	Seats — Cloth Reclining High-back Buckets (Reg Cab)	332	386
	REQUIRES purchase of Silverado Equipment Package 1SB; NOT AVAILABLE with Silverado Equipment Package 1SC		
A95	Seats — Cloth Reclining High-back Buckets (X-cab)	232	270
	REQUIRES purchase of Silverado Equipment Package 1SB; NOT AVAILABLE with Silverado Equipment Package 1SC		
AE7	Seats — Leather 60/40 Split Reclining Bench (Crew Cab)	1032	1200
	REQUIRES purchase of Silverado Equipment Package 1SB; INCLUDED in Silverado Equipment Package 1SC		
AE7	Seats — Leather 60/40 Split Reclining Bench (Reg Cab)	1010	1174
	REQUIRES purchase of Silverado Equipment Package 1SB; INCLUDED in Silverado Equipment Package 1SC		
AE7	Seats — Leather 60/40 Split Reclining Bench (X-cab)	860	1000
	REQUIRES purchase of Silverado Equipment Package 1SB; INCLUDED in Silverado Equipment Package 1SC		
A52	Seats — Leather Bench	860	1000
	REQUIRES purchase of Silverado Equipment Package 1SB		

CHEVROLET — C/K 3500 PICKUP

CODE	DESCRIPTION	INVOICE	MSRP
A95	Seats — Leather Reclining High-back Buckets (Crew Cab)	1310	1523
	With 1SC (Crew Cab)	364	423
	REQUIRES purchase of a Silverado Equipment Package		
A95	Seats — Leather Reclining High-back Buckets (Reg Cab)	1192	1386
	With 1SC (Regular Cab)	174	202
	REQUIRES purchase of a Silverado Equipment Package		
A95	Seats — Leather Reclining High-back Buckets (X-cab)	1092	1270
	With 1SC (X-cab)	232	270
	REQUIRES purchase of a Silverado Equipment Package		
YG4	Seats — Rear Seat Delete Credit (X-cab)	(374)	(435)
	NOT AVAILABLE with Silverado Equipment Packages		
1SC	Silverado Equipment Package (Crew Cab)	4625	5378
	Includes air conditioning, power windows, power door locks, tilt steering wheel, cruise control, cloth and carpet door trim, carpeted floors, rubber floor mats, additional sound deadening insulation, electrochromic rearview mirror with 8-point compass, AM/FM stereo with cassette player, seek/scan, and clock; dual illuminated visor vanity mirrors, leather-wrapped steering wheel, chrome front bumper with rub strip, chrome rear bumper with step pad, deluxe chrome grille, dual composite headlights, dual note horn, power exterior mirrors, rally wheel trim, remote keyless entry, power driver's seat, leather seats; NOTE: Package discount unknown at time of publication. Pricing includes any discounts.		
1SB	Silverado Equipment Package (Reg Cab/X-cab)	2076	2414
	With R05 (X-cab)	1991	2315
	With R05 (Reg Cab)	1991	2315
	Includes air conditioning, power windows, power door locks, tilt steering wheel, cruise control, cloth and carpet door trim, carpeted floors, rubber floor mats, additional sound deadening insulation, cloth bench seat (Reg Cab), cloth 60/40 split bench seating (Extended Cab), leather-wrapped steering wheel, behind seat storage tray, chrome front bumper with rub strip, chrome rear bumper with step pad, deluxe chrome grille, dual composite headlights, dual note horn, power exterior mirrors, bodyside moldings with bright trim and bright wheel opening trim (N/A with dual rear wheels), rally wheel trim; NOTE: Package discount unknown at time of publication. Pricing includes any discounts.		
1SC	Silverado Equipment Package (X-cab)	3302	3840
	Includes air conditioning, power windows, power door locks, tilt steering wheel, cruise control, cloth and carpet door trim, carpeted floors, rubber floor mats, additional sound deadening insulation, cloth bench seat, leather-wrapped steering wheel, behind seat storage tray, chrome front bumper with rub strip, chrome rear bumper with step pad, deluxe chrome grille, dual composite headlights, dual note horn, power exterior mirrors, bodyside moldings with bright trim and bright wheel opening trim (N/A with dual rear wheels), rally wheel trim, remote keyless entry, electrochromic rearview mirror with 8-point compass, power driver's seat, leather seats; NOTE: Package discount unknown at time of publication. Pricing includes any discounts.		

C/K 3500 PICKUP — CHEVROLET

CODE	DESCRIPTION	INVOICE	MSRP
1SB	Silverado Equipment Package 1SB (Crew Cab)	3266	3798
	Includes air conditioning, power windows, power door locks, tilt steering wheel, cruise control, cloth and carpet door trim, carpeted floors, rubber floor mats, additional sound deadening insulation, electrochromic rearview mirror with 8-point compass, AM/FM stereo with cassette player, seek/scan, and clock; dual illuminated visor vanity mirrors, leather-wrapped steering wheel, chrome front bumper with rub strip, chrome rear bumper with step pad, deluxe chrome grille, dual composite headlights, dual note horn, power exterior mirrors, rally wheel trim; NOTE: Package discount unknown at time of publication.		
1SC	Silverado Equipment Package 1SC (Regular Cab)	3331	3873
	With R05 (Reg Cab)	3246	3774
	Includes air conditioning, power windows, power door locks, tilt steering wheel, cruise control, cloth and carpet door trim, carpeted floors, rubber floor mats, additional sound deadening insulation, cloth bench seat, leather-wrapped steering wheel, behind seat storage tray, chrome front bumper with rub strip, chrome rear bumper with step pad, deluxe chrome grille, dual composite headlights, dual note horn, power exterior mirrors, bodyside moldings with bright trim and bright wheel opening trim (N/A with dual rear wheels), rally wheel trim, remote keyless entry, electrochromic rearview mirror with 8-point compass, leather seats; NOTE: Package discount unknown at time of publication. Pricing includes any discounts.		
NZZ	Skid Plates (4WD)	82	95
	Includes skid plates for engine, front differential, and transfer case; INCLUDED in Commercial Equipment Package R9C		
A28	Sliding Rear Window	97	113
	INCLUDED in Commercial Equipment Package		
VYU	Snow Plow Prep Package (4WD Reg Cab)	101	118
	With R9C (4WD Reg Cab/X-cab)	47	55
	Includes heavy-duty front springs		
UL5	Stereo — Delete Credit	(247)	(287)
	NOT AVAILABLE with Silverado Equipment Packages		
UL0	Stereo — Uplevel w/cassette	174	202
	With 1SB (Crew Cab)	77	90
	With 1SB (Reg Cab/X-cab)	77	90
	With 1SC (Crew Cab)	77	90
	With 1SC (Regular Cab)	77	90
	With 1SC (X-cab)	77	90
	AM/FM stereo with cassette player, seek/scan, automatic tone control, theft lock, speed compensated volume, and digital clock		
UP0	Stereo — Uplevel w/cassette & CD players	346	402
	With 1SB (Crew Cab)	249	290
	With 1SB (Reg Cab/X-cab)	249	290
	With 1SC (Crew Cab)	249	290
	With 1SC (X-cab)	249	290
	With 1SC (Regular Cab)	249	290
	AM/FM stereo with cassette and CD players, seek/scan, automatic tone control, theft lock, speed compensated volume, and digital clock		

CHEVROLET — C/K 3500 PICKUP

CODE	DESCRIPTION	INVOICE	MSRP
UN0	Stereo — Uplevel w/CD player	260	302
	With 1SB (Crew Cab)	163	190
	With 1SB (Reg Cab/X-cab)	163	190
	With 1SC (Crew Cab)	163	190
	Without 1SC (X-cab)	163	190
	Without 1SC (Regular Cab)	163	190
	AM/FM stereo with CD player, seek/scan, automatic tone control, theft lock, speed compensated volume, and digital clock		
UM6	Stereo — w/cassette	126	147
	AM/FM stereo with cassette player, seek/scan, and digital clock; INCLUDED in Silverado Equipment Packages and Convenience Package R9A		
ZHH	Tire — LT245/75R16E (Spare Only) (X-cab)	39	46
	Blackwall all-season tire		
XYK/YYK/ZYK	Tires — LT215/85R16D (2WD X-cab)	456	531
	Blackwall all-season tires		
XYL/YYL/ZYL	Tires — LT215/85R16D (4WD Reg Cab/4WD Crew Cab)	878	1016
	Blackwall on/off road tires		
XYK/YYK/ZYK	Tires — LT215/85R16D (4WD X-cab)	427	497
	Blackwall all-season tires		
XYL/YYL/ZYL	Tires — LT215/85R16D (4WD X-cab)	596	693
	Blackwall on/off road tires		
XYK/YYK/ZYK	Tires — LT215/85R16D (Reg Cab/2WD Crew Cab)	710	820
	Blackwall all-season tires		
XHP/YHP/ZHP	Tires — LT225/75R16D (2WD X-cab)	29	34
	Blackwall all-season tires		
XHR/YHR/ZHR	Tires — LT225/75R16D (4WD Reg Cab/4WD Crew Cab)	368	428
	Blackwall on/off road tires		
XHR/YHR/ZHR	Tires — LT225/75R16D (4WD X-cab)	66	77
	Blackwall on/off road tires		
XHP/YHP/ZHP	Tires — LT225/75R16D (Reg Cab/2WD Crew Cab)	283	323
	Blackwall all-season tires		
XGK/YGK/ZGK	Tires — LT245/75R16E (4WD)	47	55
	Blackwall on/off road tires		
V76	Tow Hooks (2WD)	33	38
	INCLUDED in Commercial Equipment Package		
Z82	**Trailering Special Equipment**	141	164
	Includes trailer hitch platform; REQUIRES a rear step bumper		
L29	**Vortec 7400 V-8 Engine**	516	600

EXPRESS VAN — CHEVROLET

| CODE | DESCRIPTION | INVOICE | MSRP |

EXPRESS (1997)

1997 Chevrolet G1500 Express LS

What's New for Chevrolet Express in 1997 — Dual airbags appear on the G3500 model, while daytime running lights and three fresh exterior colors make this van easier to see. (Editor's Note: If you can't see this monster van without DRL's, perhaps you should consider surrendering your driver's license.) Electronic variable orifice steering reduces effort at low speeds for easier parking, and automatic transmissions shift more smoothly.

Express — Review

Last year, for the first time in 25 years, Chevy dealers received a brand new, completely redesigned, full-size van to sell. Well, sort of. The supply of 1996 models was little more than a trickle as the factory suffered through teething problems. The Chevy Van (the cargo hauler) and the Express (the people hauler) were expected to arrive in dealer showrooms last spring. For 1997, the bugs have been worked out at the plant, and consumers might actually find one of these new vans on a dealer's lot. Equipped with dual airbags and four-wheel anti-lock brakes, Chevrolet is looking forward to stealing some of Ford's thunder in the full-size van market.

Rugged full-frame construction replaces the unibody setup of the previous-generation Chevy Van. Preferred by converters, full-frame construction allows for improved stability, ride and handling. Regular-length models carry 267 cubic feet of cargo, and extended-length vans can haul 317 cubic feet of stuff. Trick rear doors open 180 degrees to make loading and unloading the new van easier. Up to 15 passengers can ride in the extended-length Express, which ought to make this new van a hit with shuttle services. Other seating options include five, eight and twelve passenger arrangements. G3500's can tow up to 10,000 pounds when properly equipped.

For convenience, the full-size spare is stored underneath the cargo floor. A 31-gallon fuel tank keeps this thirsty vehicle from frequent fill-ups, but topping off an empty tank will quickly empty your wallet. Engine choices are sourced from the Chevrolet family of Vortec

CHEVROLET
EXPRESS VAN

gasoline motors, and, for the first time, a turbocharged diesel can be installed in Chevy's full-size van. Available are the Vortec 4300 V-6, the 5000, 5700, and 7400 V-8's, and a new 6.5-liter Turbodiesel V-8. Standard side cargo doors are a 60/40 panel arrangement, but a traditional slider is a no-cost option on 135-inch wheelbase vans.

Child safety locks are standard on the rear and side doors of the Express. Passenger assist handles help passengers into and out of the van. Front and rear air conditioning is optional. For 1997, G3500 get dual airbags. Also new are daytime running lights, smoother shifting automatic transmissions, and electronic variable orifice power steering that reduces effort at low speeds, making these vans easier to park.

Exterior styling is an interesting mix of corporate Chevrolet, Astro Van and Lumina Minivan. The high, pillar-mounted taillights are odd, but functional. They can easily be seen if the van is operated with the rear doors open. Low-mounted bumpers and moldings make the Express look taller than it is. An attractively sculpted body side gives the van's smooth, slab-sided flanks a dose of character. Three new colors arrive for 1997, in shades of brown, red, and silver.

Overall, Chevrolet's thoughtful rendition of the traditional full-size van appears to be right on target, giving Ford's Econoline/Club Wagon the first real competition it has faced in years.

Safety Data

Driver Airbag: *Standard*
Side Airbag: *Not Available*
4-Wheel ABS: *Standard*
Driver Crash Test Grade: *Not Available*
Passenger Crash Test Grade: *Not Available*

Passenger Airbag: *Standard*
Meets 1999 Side Impact Standards: *No*
Traction Control: *Not Available*
Insurance Cost: *Not Available*
Integrated Child Seat(s): *Not Available*

Standard Equipment

EXPRESS: 4.3-liter V-6 engine (1500), 5.7-liter V-8 engine (2500 & 3500), 4-speed automatic transmission, variable ratio power-assisted steering, power front disc/rear drum 4-wheel anti-lock brakes, dual airbags, front air conditioning, dual cupholders, side window defoggers, front and side cargo door beams (do not meet 1999 truck standards), trip odometer, solar-ray tinted glass, dome interior lighting, headlamps-on warning tone, full-size spare tire/wheel (mounted underneath van), intermittent variable windshield wipers, 100-amp alternator (1500 & 2500), 124-amp alternator (3500), 600 CCA heavy-duty battery, heavy duty springs, AM/FM stereo with seek/scan and clock, adjustable reclining high-back driver and passenger bucket seats with vinyl trim, two rear bench seats with vinyl trim, color-keyed cloth sunshades, composite headlights, painted argent front bumper, painted argent rear bumper with assist step, swing-out side doors, painted dark argent grille, black fold-away direct control outside mirrors, painted argent wheel trim with black center cap, auxiliary power point, Scotchgard fabric protection, illuminated visor vanity mirrors, daytime running lights

Base Prices

CODE	DESCRIPTION	INVOICE	MSRP
CG11406	G1500	19486	22270
CG21406	G2500	21697	24796
CG21706	G2500 Extended	22484	25696
CG31406	G3500	21837	24956
CG31706	G3500 Extended	22624	25856
Destination Charge:		615	615

EXPRESS VAN — CHEVROLET

CODE	DESCRIPTION	INVOICE	MSRP

Accessories

CODE	DESCRIPTION	INVOICE	MSRP
1SB	Base Option Package 1SB	737	857
	Includes convenience package ZQ3 (tilt steering wheel and cruise control) and power convenience package ZQ2 (power windows and power door locks)		
1SC	LS Option Package 1SC	1367	1589
	Includes convenience package ZQ3 (tilt steering wheel and cruise control), power convenience package ZQ2 (power windows and power door locks), LS Decor (chrome bumpers with rear entry assist step, chrome grille, gray bodyside moldings, rally wheel trim, auxiliary lighting package, carpeted floors, cloth seat trim with inboard armrests)		
1SD	LS Option Package 1SD (G2500/G3500)	2714	3156
	Includes convenience package ZQ3 (tilt steering wheel and cruise control), power convenience package ZQ2 (power windows and power door locks), LS Decor (chrome bumpers with rear entry assist step, chrome grille, gray bodyside moldings, rally wheel trim, auxiliary lighting package, carpeted floors, cloth seat trim with inboard armrests), front & rear air conditioning, rear heater, deep tinted glass, remote keyless entry, power exterior mirrors, illuminated visor vanity mirrors, and leather wrapped steering wheel		
1SD	LS Option Package 1SD (G1500)	2762	3212
	Includes convenience package ZQ3 (tilt steering wheel and cruise control), power convenience package ZQ2 (power windows and power door locks), LS Decor (chrome bumpers with rear entry assist step, chrome grille, gray bodyside moldings, rally wheel trim, auxiliary lighting package, carpeted floors, cloth seat trim with inboard armrests), front & rear air conditioning, rear heater, deep tinted glass, remote keyless entry, power exterior mirrors, illuminated visor vanity mirrors, and leather wrapped steering wheel		
C69	Air Conditioning — Front & Rear (G1500)	740	860
	Includes rear heater and 124-amp alternator; INCLUDED in LS Option Package 1SD		
C69	Air Conditioning — Front & Rear (G2500/G3500)	691	804
	Includes rear heater; INCLUDED in LS Option Package 1SD		
KW2	Alternator — 124-amp (G1500)	48	56
	INCLUDED with Front & Rear Air Conditioning		
N90	Aluminum Wheels (G1500)	267	310
	With 1SC	215	250
	With 1SD (G1500)	215	250
TR9	Auxiliary Lighting Package	134	156
	Includes stepwell lights, reading lights, and retractable underhood light		
YF5	California Emissions	146	170
V10	Cold Climate Package	41	48
	Includes engine block heater; NOT AVAILABLE with 6.5-liter Turbodiesel V-8 Engine		
ZQ3	Convenience Package	329	383
	Includes tilt steering wheel and cruise control; INCLUDED in Option Packages		
AJ1	Deep Tinted Glass	327	380
	INCLUDED in LS Option Package 1SD		
L65	Engine — 6.5-liter Turbodiesel V-8 (G2500 (not Extended))	2460	2860

CHEVROLET

EXPRESS VAN

CODE	DESCRIPTION	INVOICE	MSRP
L65	Engine — 6.5-liter Turbodiesel V-8 (G3500)	2460	2860
L30	Engine — Vortec 5000 V-8 (G1500)	426	495
	REQUIRES 3.42 rear axle ratio		
L31	Engine — Vortec 5700 V-8 (G1500)	830	965
L29	Engine — Vortec 7400 V-8 (G3500)	516	600
VK3	Front License Plate Bracket	NC	NC
B30	Full Floor Carpeting	126	147
	INCLUDED in LS Option Packages		
DH6	Illuminated Visor Vanity Mirrors	65	75
	REQUIRES purchase of LS Option Package 1SC		
NP5	Leather-wrapped Steering Wheel	52	60
	INCLUDED in LS Option Package 1SD		
G80	Locking Differential	217	252
	NOT AVAILABLE with 3.42 Rear Axle Ratio on G3500		
NG1	Massachusetts/New York Emissions	NC	NC
U75	Power Antenna	73	85
	INCLUDED with ULO, UNO, and UPO stereos		
ZQ2	Power Convenience Package	408	474
	INCLUDED in Option Packages		

CALL NATIONWIDE 1-800-521-7257

FOR A WRITTEN QUOTATION
AS LOW AS $50 OVER INVOICE

See page 15 for details.

Take Advantage of Warranty Gold!

Savings up to 50% off Dealer's Extended Warranty Prices. Protect and enhance YOUR investment with the best extended warranty available.

Call Toll Free 1-800-580-9889

S-10 (1997)

1997 Chevrolet S-10 LS 4x4

What's New for Chevrolet S-10 in 1997 — Chevy strengthens the 2WD S-10 frame by using tougher components. Refinements to the automatic transmission result in improved efficiency and smoother shifts. 4WD models have lighter-weight plug-in half shafts. Two new colors are available.

S-10 — Review

Like most of today's compact trucks, Chevrolet's S-Series grew more car-like when it was redesigned for 1994. That's the trend, and Chevy has done a good job of transforming its small-scale pickups—without blurring their identity as practical machines. Riding smoother and handling better, they gained plenty in performance potential and overall refinement, ranking closer to their main competition, Ford's similar-size Ranger. Grasp that long manual-transmission gearshift lever and it's easy to imagine you're wielding a big rig, while enjoying the blissful comforts of a compact.

Four-cylinder models need that manual shift to derive top performance, but the two V-6 engine options are strong with either manual or automatic transmissions. For maximum output, the optional 180-horsepower L35 Vortec 4300 V-6 is the engine to select (190 horsepower in 4WD models). The slightly less energetic LF6 Vortec 4300 V-6 is no slouch, nearly matching the L35 in power and torque

Extended cab models can be equipped with a handy access panel that opens wide to allow for easier access to the rear of the cab. Located on the driver's side, the optional third door deletes one of the extended cab's jump seats, but makes it much easier to load cargo, a friend, or your pal Spot into the S-10. Be warned, the third door makes for aggravating rattles on broken pavement.

Two- and four-wheel-drive trucks come in seven models each, with a short or long bed, fleetside box or sportside box, and short or extended wheelbase. Ride comfort varies from car-smooth to strictly firm, depending on the choice of suspensions and tires.

CHEVROLET S-10

Headroom is ample and seats are supportive, but the driver sits low, facing a tall steering wheel and cowl. In theory, three people fit across an S-Series bench seat, but it's hard to conceive of an adult human being slim enough to squeeze into the space allotted. Surprisingly, the extended cab's rear jump seats are comfortable for short trips, as long as only one adult occupies the space behind the front seats.

Full gauges are excellent and easy to read, but the upright dashboard is constructed of cheap and brittle looking plastic. Despite a low-height windshield—not unlike the Ranger's—visibility is super, helped by huge mirrors. A driver's airbag and daytime running lamps are standard. All models have four-wheel anti-lock braking. Off-roaders will want the burly ZR2 package that makes the truck's body wider and taller, featuring special wheel flares, tough suspension components, and aggressive rubber.

For 1997, Chevrolet has strengthened the frame of the 2WD model by using tougher components. Refinements to the automatic transmission result in improved efficiency and smoother shifts. Four-wheel drive models have lighter-weight plug-in half shafts that are easier to service. Two new colors are available; Fairway Green Metallic and Medium Beige Mystique Metallic.

Like many Chevrolets, the S-10 is loaded with value. However, we must take issue with the poor crash test scores of this little pickup, especially in contrast to the good crashworthiness demonstrated by the Ford Ranger. Furthermore, the Ranger can be equipped with dual front airbags, and the new -for-1997 Dodge Dakota offers dual airbags as standard equipment. Chevy doesn't make a passenger airbag available. We genuinely like the S-10, but feel that for safety-minded shoppers, Ford's Ranger and Dodge's Dakota are the better buys in this class.

Safety Data

Driver Airbag: *Standard*
Side Airbag: *Not Available*
4-Wheel ABS: *Standard*
Driver Crash Test Grade: *Average*

Passenger Crash Test Grade: *Poor*

Passenger Airbag: *Not Available*
Meets 1999 Side Impact Standards: *No*
Traction Control: *Not Available*
Insurance Cost: *Very Low (2WD Base); Low (4WD Base/2WD LS); Avg. (4WD LS)*
Integrated Child Seat(s): *Not Available*

Standard Equipment

S-10 BASE 2WD: 2.2-liter inline four-cylinder engine, 5-speed manual transmission with overdrive, power front disc/rear drum 4-wheel anti-lock brakes, power steering, driver's side airbag, passenger side assist handle, side door beams (do not meet 1999 truck standard), Solar-ray tinted glass, glovebox light, color-keyed cloth headliner, oil pressure gauge, temperature gauge, voltmeter, trip odometer, delayed entry interior lights, front floor courtesy lights, engine compartment light, 4 load anchors, Scotchgard fabric protectant, vinyl bench seat with folding seatback, ETR AM/FM stereo with digital clock, day/night rearview mirror, 5-lead trailer wiring harness, headlamps-on warning tone, daytime running lights, dual black exterior mirrors, P205/75R15 tires, 15"x 7" argent steel wheels with black center caps, dark gray front/rear bumpers, dark gray grille

BASE 4WD (in addition to or instead of BASE 2WD equipment): Vortec 4300 V6 engine, Insta-trac shift-on-the-fly four-wheel drive system, 2 front tow hooks

LS REGULAR CAB (in addition to or instead of BASE equipment): Illuminated vanity mirror, soft cloth upper door trim inserts, color-keyed full floor carpeting, dual covered power points,

S-10 CHEVROLET

60/40 custom cloth split bench seat with recliners, center armrest, storage pouch, dual cupholders, color-keyed front and rear step bumpers (2WD), chrome grille, 15"x 7" argent steel wheels with trim rings

LS EXTENDED CAB (in addition to or instead of LS REGULAR CAB equipment): Rear quarter swing-out windows, storage compartment, passenger side easy-entry seat, vinyl folding rear jump seats

Base Prices

CODE	DESCRIPTION	INVOICE	MSRP
CS10603	2WD Fleetside Reg. Cab Shortbed	11447	12113
CS10803	2WD Fleetside Reg. Cab Longbed	11730	12413
CS10603	LS 2WD Fleetside Reg. Cab Shortbed	11270	12453
CS10803	LS 2WD Fleetside Reg. Cab Longbed	11541	12753
CS10653	LS 2WD Fleetside Ext. Cab	13542	14963
CS10603	LS 2WD Reg. Cab Sportside	11677	12903
CS10653	LS 2WD Ext. Cab Sportside	13949	15413
CT10603	4WD Fleetside Reg. Cab Shortbed	15454	16353
CT10803	4WD Fleetside Reg. Cab Longbed	15767	16685
CT10603	LS 4WD Fleetside Reg. Cab Shortbed	15614	17253
CT10803	LS 4WD Fleetside Reg. Cab Longbed	16000	17680
CT10653	LS 4WD Fleetside Extended Cab	17333	19153
CT10603	LS 4WD Reg. Cab Sportside	16021	17703
CT10653	LS 4WD Ext. Cab Sportside	17741	19603
	Destination Charge:	510	510

Accessories

CODE	DESCRIPTION	INVOICE	MSRP
QJJ	31x 10.5R15 BSW On/off Road Tires (LS 4WD)	NC	NC
	REQUIRES Wide Stance Sport Performance Suspension		
M30	4-speed Automatic Transmission	920	1070
	Includes brake/transmission shift interlock		
C60	Air Conditioning	692	805
ANL	Air Dam w/fog lights (LS 2WD)	99	115
	INCLUDED in SS Package		
N60	Argent Aluminum Wheels (2WD)	213	248
	With 1SA (Base)	292	340
	With YC5 (LS 2WD X-Cab/LS 2WD Shortbed)	NC	NC
	INCLUDED in Option Packages 1SH and 1SJ		
PA3	Bright Aluminum Wheels w/gray accent (LS 4WD)	241	280
	With 1SM (LS 4WD X-Cab)	NC	NC
YF5	California Emissions	146	170
B32	Carpeted Front Floor Mats	17	20
	REQUIRES Full Floor Carpeting on Base models		
N90	Cast Aluminum Wheels (LS 4WD)	241	280
	With 1SM (LS 4WD X-Cab)	NC	NC
	With YC5 (LS 4WD X-Cab/LS 4WD Shortbed)	NC	NC

EDMUND'S 1997 NEW TRUCKS — http://edmunds.com

CHEVROLET S-10

CODE	DESCRIPTION	INVOICE	MSRP
V10	Cold Climate Package	77	89
	Includes heavy-duty battery and engine block heater		
ZQ6	Convenience Group (Power Locks & Mirrors) (LS)	460	535
	Includes power door locks and power exterior mirrors		
ZQ3	Convenience Group (Tilt Wheel & Cruise Control)	340	395
	Includes tilt steering column and cruise control		
AJ1	Deep Tinted Rear Glass (Reg. Cab)	61	71
AJ1	Deep Tinted Rear Glass (X-Cab)	92	107
	Includes rear quarter window tint		
NP1	Electronic Shift Transfer Case (LS 4WD)	106	123
	INCLUDED in Option Package 1SM		
B30	Floor Carpeting (Base)	47	55
	REQUIRES Option Package 1SA		
UA1	Heavy-duty Battery	48	56
	INCLUDED in Cold Climate Package		
Z85	Increased Capacity Suspension (2WD Reg. Cab Shortbed/4WD X-cab)	55	64
NP5	Leather-wrapped Steering Wheel (LS)	46	54
	INCLUDED in SS Package		
G80	Locking Differential	217	252
	REQUIRES Vortec 4300 V6 engine; INCLUDED in SS Package		
YC5	LS Exterior Appearance Package (LS 2WD X-Cab/LS 2WD Shortbed)	451	524
	Includes color-keyed bumpers, dark gray bodyside moldings with bright insert, bright wheel opening moldings, and aluminum wheels		
YC5	LS Exterior Appearance Package (LS 4WD X-Cab/LS 4WD Shortbed)	478	556
	Includes color-keyed bumpers, dark gray bodyside moldings with bright insert, bright wheel opening moldings, and aluminum wheels; NOT AVAILABLE with Wide Stance Sport Performance Suspension		
NG1	Massachusetts/New York Emissions	146	170
ZM6	Off-road Suspension (4WD)	560	651
	Includes full-size spare tire		
1SA	Option Package 1SA (Base)	(242)	(281)
	Deletes stereo and rear bumper		
1SB	Option Package 1SB (LS)	NC	NC
	Includes standard LS decor		
1SH	Option Package 1SH (LS 2WD Shortbed)	318	370
	Includes 3.73 rear axle ratio, ETR AM/FM stereo with seek/scan, cassette player, and clock; aluminum wheels		
1SJ	Option Package 1SJ (LS 2WD X-Cab)	1377	1601
	Includes 3.08 rear axle ratio, Vortec 4300 V6 engine, ETR AM/FM stereo with seek/scan, cassette player, and clock; reclining high-back bucket seats, increased capacity suspension, aluminum wheels		
1SM	Option Package 1SM (LS 4WD X-Cab)	879	848
	Includes 3.42 rear axle ratio, ETR AM/FM stereo with seek/scan, cassette player, and clock; reclining high-back bucket seats, increased capacity suspension, P235/70R15 BSW tires, aluminum wheels		
QCA	P205/75R15 OWL All-season Tires	104	126
QCB	P235/55R16 BSW All-season Tires (2WD X-Cab/2WD Reg. Cab Shortbed)	NC	NC

S-10 CHEVROLET

CODE	DESCRIPTION	INVOICE	MSRP
QBF	P235/70R15 BSW All-season Tires (4WD Reg. Cab Longbed)	NC	NC
QBF	P235/70R15 BSW All-season Tires (Reg. Cab Shortbed/4WD X-Cab)	165	192
QEB	P235/75R15 OWL On-off Road Tires (4WD Reg. Cab Longbed)	123	143
QEB	P235/75R15 OWL On/off Road Tires (4WD X-Cab/4WD Reg. Cab Shortbed)	335	390
	REQUIRES Increased Capacity Suspension		
VF6	Rear Step Bumper (Base/LS 2WD Reg. Cab Shortbed)	47	55
	REQUIRES Option Package 1SA or SS Package; rear bumpers are required in some states		
AV5	Reclining High-back Bucket Seats (LS)	83	96
	INCLUDED in Option Packages 1SJ and 1SM		
AU0	Remote Keyless Entry (LS)	120	140
	REQUIRES Convenience Group ZQ6		
ZM5	Shield Package (4WD)	108	126
	INCLUDED with Wide Stance Sport Performance Suspension		
A28	Sliding Rear Window	97	113
Z83	Solid Smooth Ride Suspension (2WD X-cab)	(55)	(64)
5P2	Special Aluminum Wheels (4WD)	241	280
	With 1SA (Base)	292	340
	With 1SM (LS 4WD X-Cab)	NC	NC
ZQ8	Sport Suspension (LS 2WD Reg. Cab SB/LS 2WD X-cab)	605	703
	With B4U (LS 2WD Reg. Cab Fleetside Shortbed)	391	455
	Includes 16"x 8" cast aluminum wheels; REQUIRES V-6 Engine		
ZY7	Sport Two-tone Paint (LS)	169	197
B4U	SS Package (LS 2WD Reg. Cab Fleetside Shortbed)	541	629
	Includes locking differential, air dam with fog lights, cast aluminum wheels with bright center caps, body-color grille, close out panel in lieu of rear step bumper, SS badging, leather-wrapped steering wheel, 3.42 rear axle ratio; REQUIRES L35 Vortec 4300 V-6 High Output Engine, 4-speed Automatic Transmission, Sport Suspension		
UM7	Stereo (Base)	194	226
	ETR AM/FM stereo with seek/scan and digital clock; REQUIRES Option Package 1SA		
UM6	Stereo w/cassette (Base)	299	348
	ETR AM/FM stereo with seek/scan, cassette player, and digital clock; REQUIRES Option Package 1SA		
UM6	Stereo w/cassette (LS)	105	122
	ETR AM/FM stereo with seek/scan, cassette player, and digital clock; INCLUDED in Option Packages 1SH, 1SJ, and 1SM		
U16	Tachometer	51	59
	INCLUDED with Vortec 4300 V-6 High Output Engine		
E24	Third Door (X-cab)	323	375
UX1	Uplevel Stereo w/cassette (Base)	437	508
	ETR AM/FM stereo with seek/scan, cassette player with search and repeat, graphic equalizer, and digital clock		

CHEVROLET S-10

CODE	DESCRIPTION	INVOICE	MSRP
UX1	Uplevel Stereo w/cassette (LS)	243	282
	With 1SH (LS 2WD Shortbed)	138	160
	With 1SJ (LS 2WD X-Cab)	138	160
	With 1SM (LS 4WD X-Cab)	138	160
	ETR AM/FM stereo with seek/scan, cassette player with search and repeat, graphic equalizer, and digital clock		
U1C	Uplevel Stereo w/CD player (LS)	349	406
	With 1SH (LS 2WD Shortbed)	244	284
	With 1SJ (LS 2WD X-Cab)	244	284
	With 1SM (LS 4WD X-Cab)	244	284
	ETR AM/FM stereo with seek/scan, CD player, and digital clock		
LF6	Vortec 4300 V-6 Engine (2WD X-Cab/2WD Shortbed)	851	990
	INCLUDED in Option Package 1SJ		
L35	Vortec 4300 V-6 High Output Engine (2WD)	1074	1249
L35	Vortec 4300 V-6 High Output Engine (4WD)	223	259
ZR2	Wide Stance Sport Performance Suspension (LS 4WD)	1484	1725
	Includes revised frame for wide tread, strengthened front differential gears and drive axles, rear axle with 8.5" ring gear, learger wheel bearings, longer and larger diameter axle shafts, revised rear suspension with multi-leaf springs and rear axle track bar, 28mm front stabilizer bar, 46mm Bilstein gas pressurized shock absorbers, underbody shield package, extra wide wheel flares; REQUIRES 3.73 rear axle ratio (no charge), Reclining High-back Bucket Seats, V-6 Engine, QJJ Tires; NOT AVAILABLE with Sport two-tone paint		

One 15-minute call could save you 15% or more on car insurance.

America's 6th Largest Automobile Insurance Company

1-800-555-2758

SUBURBAN (1997)

1997 Chevrolet K1500 Suburban

What's New for Chevrolet Suburban in 1997 — Dual airbags debut, and a cargo area power lock switch makes locking the vehicle up after unloading cargo more convenient. Electronic Variable Orifice power steering lightens low-speed steering effort, and automatic transmissions are improved. Two new exterior colors are added to the paint roster.

Suburban — Review

In some sections of the country, upmarket folks have been tooling around for several years in mile-long Suburbans, whether or not they have great need for all that expanse behind the driver's seat. Through the suburban reaches of Houston and Dallas, among other spots, the Chevrolet and GMC Suburban have become de facto status-flaunting vehicles.

Yes, those who formerly wheeled around town in a Cadillac or Lincoln or Mercedes, and wouldn't feel quite right in a pickup truck, appear to have twirled their affections toward the biggest passenger vehicles in the General Motors repertoire. Chevrolet, in fact, considers the Suburban *"as suited to the country club as to a roughneck oil field."*

Mechanically, you get the same layout in the smaller Chevrolet Tahoe, but that vehicle is only available with Chevy's Vortec 5700 V-8 engine. Select a Suburban and you can accept that motor, with 255 horsepower. Or, with the 3/4-ton C/K 2500 series you can go all the way, opting for the mammoth Vortec 7400 V-8, whipping out 290 strutting horses and a mean 410 pound-feet of ground-tromping torque. Oh, there's also an optional turbo-diesel. Both the half- and 3/4-ton versions come with either two- or four-wheel drive, and all have four-wheel anti-lock braking.

This season's interior is upgraded with the addition of a driver's airbag. Rear passengers are made more comfortable with the addition of height-adjustable outboard safety belts. Drivers won't need to wrestle the Suburban at low speeds with the introduction of Electronic Variable Orifice power steering. Locking the Suburban after unloading cargo is easier this

CHEVROLET — SUBURBAN

year, because Chevy added a power lock switch to the cargo area. Shifts are smoother from revised transmissions, which also improve efficiency. Two new exterior colors debut: Medium Opal Blue Metallic and Medium Beige Mystique Metallic.

Suburbans seat up to nine occupants and tow as much as five tons, when properly equipped. For families who need plenty of room for youngsters, or for retirees who need loads of power to haul a travel trailer, a Suburban can make good sense. Chevrolet can expect competition from Ford's new Expedition for 1997, but for heavy-duty use and maximum space, Chevrolet and GMC are still the only serious games in town for a mammoth "truck wagon."

Safety Data

Driver Airbag: *Standard*
Side Airbag: *Not Available*
4-Wheel ABS: *Standard*
Driver Crash Test Grade: *Not Available*
Passenger Crash Test Grade: *Not Available*

Passenger Airbag: *Standard*
Meets 1999 Side Impact Standards: *No*
Traction Control: *Not Available*
Insurance Cost: *High*
Integrated Child Seat(s): *Not Available*

Standard Equipment

SUBURBAN C1500/C2500: Dual front airbags, dual in-dash cup holders, steel side-impact door beams, power door locks, molded plastic door trim, full black rubber floor covering, trip odometer, oil pressure gauge, voltmeter, tachometer, delayed entry dome lighting, Scotchgard fabric protectant, front vinyl bench seats, AM/FM stereo with digital clock, simulated leather steering wheel, passenger visor vanity mirror, driver's side visor map strap, intermittent variable windshield wipers, daytime running lights, dual black breakaway mirrors, 7-lead trailer wiring harness, painted silver wheels with black center cap, power front disc/rear drum 4-wheel anti-lock brakes, Vortec 5700 V8 engine, 4-speed electronically controlled automatic transmission

K1500/K2500 (in addition to or instead of C1500/C2500 equipment): Insta-Trac 4WD system

Base Prices

Code	Description	Invoice	MSRP
C10906	C1500	21567	24648
C20906	C2500	22646	25881
K10906	K1500	23843	27249
K20906	K2500	24938	28500
	Destination Charge:	675	675

Accessories

Code	Description	Invoice	MSRP
GU6	3.42 Rear Axle Ratio (1500)	NC	NC
GT4	3.73 Rear Axle Ratio	116	135
	NOT AVAILABLE with Vortec 7400 V8 Engine on 2500 models		
GT5	4.10 Rear Axle Ratio (C2500)	116	135
	With L29 (2500)	NC	NC
GT5	4.10 Rear Axle Ratio (K2500)	NC	NC

SUBURBAN — CHEVROLET

CODE	DESCRIPTION	INVOICE	MSRP
L65	6.5-liter Turbodiesel V8 Engine	2460	2860
	Includes heavy-duty transmission, KNP Heavy-duty Transmission Cooler, and front bumper guards; NOT AVAILABLE with 3.73 Rear Axle Ratio or California Emissions on 1500 models; REQUIRES B71 Wheel Flare Moldings on 2500 models		
AE7	60/40 Split Reclining Front Bench Seat	86	100
	REQUIRES in LS Decor Option Package		
N90	Aluminum Wheels (C1500)	267	310
	INCLUDED in Decor Option Packages; NOT AVAILABLE with 6.5-liter Turbodiesel Engine or QIZ tires		
PF4	Aluminum Wheels (K1500)	267	310
	INCLUDED in Decor Option Packages; NOT AVAILABLE with 6.5-liter Turbodiesel Engine		
YF5	California Emissions (1500)	NC	NC
	With L65	146	170
YF5	California Emissions (2500)	146	170
DF2	Camper Type Mirrors	46	53
	With 1SB (2500)	(39)	(45)
	With 1SB (1500)	(39)	(45)
	With 1SC (1500)	(39)	(45)
	With 1SC (2500)	(39)	(45)
	Stainless steel mirrors; dealer-installed accessory		
V10	Cold Climate Package	28	33
	Includes engine block heater; NOT AVAILABLE with 6.5-liter Turbodiesel Engine		
ZQ3	Convenience Package	329	383
	Includes tilt steering wheel and cruise control; INCLUDED in Decor Option Packages		
ZY2	Conventional Two-tone Paint	155	180
	REQUIRES purchase of a Decor Option Package		
A52	Custom Cloth Bench Seat Credit	(150)	(174)
	REQUIRES LT Decor Option Package		
AJ1	Deep Tinted Glass	262	305
	INCLUDED in Decor Option Packages		
ZY4	Deluxe Two-tone Paint	249	290
	REQUIRES purchase of a Decor Option Package		
NP1	Electronic Shift Transfer Case (K1500/K2500)	106	123
	REQUIRES Convenience Package when ordered on models not equipped with a Decor Option Package		
KC4	Engine Oil Cooling System (1500)	116	135
	INCLUDED in Z82 Trailering Package; NOT AVAILABLE with 3.73 Rear Axle Ratio or 6.5-liter Turbodiesel Engine		
C69	Front & Rear Air Conditioning	1114	1295
	INCLUDED in Decor Option Packages		
C60	Front Air Conditioning	727	845
	INCLUDED in Decor Option Packages		
VK3	Front License Plate Bracket	NC	NC

CHEVROLET SUBURBAN

CODE	DESCRIPTION	INVOICE	MSRP
F60	Heavy-duty Front Springs (K1500/K2500)	54	63
	NOT AVAILABLE with 6.5-liter Turbodiesel Engine on 1500 models		
KNP	Heavy-duty Transmission Cooler (1500)	83	96
	INCLUDED with 6.5-liter Turbodiesel Engine and Z82 Trailering Package		
K47	High Capacity Air Cleaner	22	25
A95	High-back Bucket Seats	327	380
	With 1SC (2500)	241	280
	With 1SC (1500)	241	280
	Includes armrests, roof console, and floor console		
1SB	LS Decor Option Package (1500)	5846	6798

Includes cargo net, tilt steering wheel, cruise control, full floor carpeting with front/rear rubber floor mats, cloth/carpet door trim, cloth rear quarter trim, cloth spare tire cover, ETR AM/FM stereo with auto-reverse cassette player, seek/scan, clock, theft lock, automatic tone control, music search, and enhanced 8 speakers sound system; power windows, 9-passenger seating, custom cloth seat trim, folding center bench seat, driver's power lumbar support, front center storage armrest, leather-wrapped steering wheel, dual illuminated visor vanity mirrors, visor extenders, chrome front bumper with black rub strip and bright trim, deluxe chrome grille, dual composite halogen headlamps, roof-mounted luggage rack, black dual power exterior mirrors, deep tinted glass, electrochromic rear view mirror with integrated compass, cast aluminum wheels, front/rear air conditioning, auxiliary rear heater, rear defogger (when ordered with E55 tailgate, this package includes a rear wiper/washer

1SB	LS Decor Option Package (2500)	5674	6798

Includes cargo net, tilt steering wheel, cruise control, full floor carpeting with front/rear rubber floor mats, cloth/carpet door trim, cloth rear quarter trim, cloth spare tire cover, ETR AM/FM stereo with auto-reverse cassette player, seek/scan, clock, theft lock, automatic tone control, music search, and enhanced 8 speakers sound system; power windows, 9-passenger seating, custom cloth seat trim, folding center bench seat, driver's power lumbar support, front center storage armrest, leather-wrapped steering wheel, dual illuminated visor vanity mirrors, visor extenders, chrome front bumper with black rub strip and bright trim, deluxe chrome grille, dual composite halogen headlamps, roof-mounted luggage rack, black dual power exterior mirrors, deep tinted glass, electrochromic rear view mirror with integrated compass, rally wheel trim, front/rear air conditioning, auxiliary rear heater, rear defogger (when ordered with E55 tailgate, this package includes a rear wiper/washer

1SC	LT Decor Option Package (1500)	7545	8773

Includes LS Decor [cargo net, tilt steering wheel, cruise control, full floor carpeting with front/rear rubber floor mats, cloth/carpet door trim, cloth rear quarter trim, cloth spare tire cover, ETR AM/FM stereo with auto-reverse cassette player, seek/scan, clock, theft lock, automatic tone control, music search, and enhanced 8 speakers sound system; power windows, 9-passenger seating, custom cloth seat trim, folding center bench seat, driver's power lumbar support, front center storage armrest, leather-wrapped steering wheel, dual illuminated visor vanity mirrors, visor extenders, chrome front bumper with black rub strip and bright trim, deluxe chrome grille, dual composite halogen headlamps, roof-mounted luggage rack, black dual power exterior mirrors, deep tinted glass, electrochromic rear view mirror with integrated compass,

SUBURBAN — CHEVROLET

CODE	DESCRIPTION	INVOICE	MSRP
	cast aluminum wheels, front/rear air conditioning, auxiliary rear heater, rear defogger (when ordered with E55 tailgate, this package includes a rear wiper/washer)] plus LT Decor upgrade [front reclining 60/40 split bench seat with leather trim], power driver's seat, and remote keyless entry		
1SC	LT Decor Option Package (2500)	7330	8523
	Includes LS Decor [cargo net, tilt steering wheel, cruise control, full floor carpeting with front/rear rubber floor mats, cloth/carpet door trim, cloth rear quarter trim, cloth spare tire cover, ETR AM/FM stereo with auto-reverse cassette player, seek/scan, clock, theft lock, automatic tone control, music search, and enhanced 8 speakers sound system; power windows, 9-passenger seating, custom cloth seat trim, folding center bench seat, driver's power lumbar support, front center storage armrest, leather-wrapped steering wheel, dual illuminated visor vanity mirrors, visor extenders, chrome front bumper with black rub strip and bright trim, deluxe chrome grille, dual composite halogen headlamps, roof-mounted luggage rack, black dual power exterior mirrors, deep tinted glass, electrochromic rear view mirror with integrated compass, rally wheel trim, front/rear air conditioning, auxiliary rear heater, rear defogger (when ordered with E55 tailgate, this package includes a rear wiper/washer)] plus LT Decor upgrade [front reclining 60/40 split bench seat with leather trim], power driver's seat, and remote keyless entry		
QBN	LT245/75R16C BSW Tires (K1500)	49	57
	On/off road tread; NOT AVAILABLE with 6.5-liter Turbodiesel Engine		
QBX	LT245/75R16C OWL Tires (K1500)	157	182
	On/off road tread; NOT AVAILABLE with 6.5-liter Turbodiesel Engine		
QIZ	LT245/75R16E BSW Tires (2500)	NC	NC
	Standard 2500 tires with all-season tread		
QIZ	LT245/75R16E BSW Tires (C1500)	395	460
	All-season tread; REQUIRES 6.5-liter Turbodiesel Engine		
QIW	LT245/75R16E BSW Tires (K1500)	194	226
	On/off road tread; REQUIRES 6.5-liter Turbodiesel Engine		
QIZ	LT245/75R16E BSW Tires (K1500)	147	171
	All-season tread; REQUIRES 6.5-liter Turbodiesel Engine		
QIW	LT245/75R16E BSW Tires (K2500)	48	55
	On/off road tread		
NG1	Massachusetts/New York Emissions	NC	NC
NZZ	Off-road Skid Plates (K1500/K2500)	194	225
	Includes differential transfer case and fuel tank shields		
QHM	P235/75R15 OWL Tires (C1500)	155	180
	All-season tread; NOT AVAILABLE with 6.5-liter Turbodiesel Engine		
QHA	P235/75R15XL BSW Tires (C1500)	NC	NC
	Standard tires with all-season tread; NOT AVAILABLE with 6.5-liter Turbodiesel Engine		
QGA	P245/75R16 BSW Tires (K1500)	NC	NC
	Standard tires with all-terrain tread; NOT AVAILABLE with 6.5-liter Turbodiesel Engine		
QGB	P245/75R16 OWL Tires (K1500)	120	140
	All-terrain tread; NOT AVAILABLE with 6.5-liter Turbodiesel Engine		

CHEVROLET SUBURBAN

CODE	DESCRIPTION	INVOICE	MSRP
AG9	Power Driver's Seat	206	240
	Includes 6-way adjustment; REQUIRES LS Decor Option Package and AE7 60/40 Split Reclining Front Bench Seat or A95 High-back Bucket Seats		
UL5	Radio Delete	(247)	(287)
	NOT AVAILABLE with Decor Option Packages		
P06	Rally Wheel Trim	52	60
	INCLUDED in Decor Option Packages on 2500 models; REQUIRES 6.5-liter Turbodiesel Engine when ordered on 1500 models equipped with a Decor Option Package		
C36	Rear Auxiliary Heater	176	205
	INCLUDED in Decor Option Packages		
AS3	Rear Center and Third Row Folding Bench Seats	1017	1182
	INCLUDED in Decor Option Packages		
AT5	Rear Center Folding Bench Seat	544	632
	INCLUDED in Decor Option Packages		
E55	Rear Tailgate	NC	NC
	Includes power tailgate release; replaces standard rear panel doors		
C49	Rear Window Defogger	132	154
	INCLUDED in Decor Option Packages and with ZP6 Rear Window Wiper/Washer		
ZP6	Rear Window Wiper/Washer	240	279
	Includes rear window defogger; INCLUDED in Decor Option Packages when E55 Rear Tailgate is ordered; REQUIRES E55 Rear Tailgate		
AU0	Remote Keyless Entry	116	135
	REQUIRES LS Decor Option Package		
U01	Roof Marker Lamps (5)	45	52
	NOT AVAILABLE with California Emissions		
BVE	Running Boards	168	195
	Dealer-installed accessory		
6Y4	Spare Tire Credit (2500)	(243)	(283)
UM6	Stereo w/cassette	126	147
	ETR AM/FM stereo with cassette player, seek/scan, dual rear speakers and digital clock; NOT AVAILABLE with Decor Option Packages		
YG4	Third Row Seat Credit	(875)	(1018)
	With 1SB (2500)	(531)	(618)
	With 1SB (1500)	(531)	(618)
	REQUIRES purchase of a Decor Option Package		
V76	Tow Hooks (C1500/C2500)	33	38
Z82	Trailering Package (1500)	257	299
	With GT4	141	164
	With L65	141	164
	Includes platform hitch, KC4 Engine Oil Cooling System, and KNP Heavy-duty Transmission Cooler		
Z82	Trailering Package (2500)	141	164
	REQUIRES 3.73 Rear Axle Ratio when ordered on models equipped with standard Vortec 5700 V-8 Engine		

SUBURBAN / TAHOE
CHEVROLET

CODE	DESCRIPTION	INVOICE	MSRP
UP0	Uplevel Stereo w/cassette & CD players	172	200
	ETR AM/FM stereo with cassette and CD players, seek/scan, automatic tone control, clock, theft lock, and enhanced performance 8-speaker sound system; REQUIRES purchase of a Decor Option Package		
UN0	Uplevel Stereo w/CD player	86	100
	ETR AM/FM stereo with CD player, seek/scan, automatic tone control, clock, theft lock, and enhanced performance 8-speaker sound system; REQUIRES purchase of a Decor Option Package		
L29	Vortec 7400 V8 Engine (2500)	516	600
B71	Wheel Flare Moldings (K1500)	155	180

TAHOE *(1997)*

1997 Chevrolet Tahoe LT 4x4

What's New for Chevrolet Tahoe in 1997 — A passenger-side airbag is added, and the automatic transmission is improved. Electronic Variable Orifice steering debuts, and cargo areas have a power door lock switch. A new center console comes with high-back bucket seats, and two new paint colors are available.

Tahoe — Review

Compact sport-utility vehicles get most of the attention nowadays, but for folks with big families—or scads of goods to lug around—they're just not spacious enough inside. Chevrolet offers a solution to this problem with the Tahoe, based on the full-size C/K pickup platform but garageable in either 2- or 4-door body styles.

At a glance, the 4-door Tahoe and larger Suburban look nearly identical, but a Tahoe measures 20 inches shorter. Beneath the hood sits a Vortec 5700 V-8, rated 255 horsepower. Two-door Tahoes with LS or LT trim can be equipped with a 6.5-liter turbodiesel V-8 instead of the Vortec 5700.

CHEVROLET — TAHOE

From the driver's seat forward, Tahoes are virtually identical to Chevy's full-size pickups. Space is massive up front. Capable of towing as much as 7,000 pounds, 4-door Tahoes seat either five or six, and an underbody-mounted spare tire helps boost cargo space.

On the Interstate, the Tahoe rides nicely, but the wide body takes some getting used to if you're accustomed to compacts. Turning onto smaller roads, it suddenly feels more like a truck. Easy to control either way, this sizable machine is reasonably maneuverable, if driven with discretion. The V-8 is strong, and the four-speed automatic transmission shifts neatly.

Think about the "entry assist" running boards if your regular riders aren't so nimble. They help. So do the robust grab bars that ease entry into the rear seats. Rear cargo doors are standard, but a lift glass version is available.

New for 1997 is a passenger-side airbag, allowing the Tahoe to match Ford's Expedition in safety features. A new Electronic Variable Orifice steering unit reduces effort in low-speed maneuvering. The automatic transmission is refined for 1997, featuring smoother shifts and increased efficiency. Want to lock the Tahoe after unloading cargo? Now it's easy, with the addition of a power door lock switch in the cargo area. Order high-back bucket seats, and you'll get a new center console that includes a pivoting writing surface, cassette storage, removable coin holder, dual cup holders for rear passengers, and a latched rear storage drawer. Rounding out the improvements for 1997 are two new exterior colors: Medium Opal Blue Metallic and Medium Beige Mystique Metallic.

Because Chevrolet targets customers with an income of $85,000 a year, luxury conveniences are part of upscale Tahoe packages. The typical prospect is an upscale 40-year-old man who currently drives a Chevy Blazer and is attracted to a vehicle's size and power. Those attributes, the Tahoe has in abundance, as does its little-different GMC Yukon counterpart.

With the introduction of the Ford Expedition, Chevrolet loses its dominance of the full-size SUV market. Further complicating matters, the Tahoe is based on a decade-old platform, while the slightly larger, slightly less expensive Expedition is derived from all-new F-Series underpinnings. We recommend investigating the Expedition, unless you're a dyed-in-the-wool Chevy fan.

Safety Data

Driver Airbag: *Standard*
Side Airbag: *Not Available*
4-Wheel ABS: *Standard*
Driver Crash Test Grade: *Not Available*
Passenger Crash Test Grade: *Not Available*

Passenger Airbag: *Standard*
Meets 1999 Side Impact Standards: *No*
Traction Control: *Not Available*
Insurance Cost: *High*
Integrated Child Seat(s): *Not Available*

Standard Equipment

TAHOE 2-DOOR 2WD: Dual front airbags, dual in-dash cup holders, steel side impact door beams, full black rubber floor covering, trip odometer, oil pressure gauge, voltmeter, tachometer, delayed entry dome lighting, front door map pockets, Scotchgard protectant on fabrics, vinyl low back bucket seats, rear 60/40 split folding rear seat, AM/FM stereo with digital clock, simulated leather steering wheel, passenger visor vanity mirror, driver visor map strap, intermittent variable wipers, daytime running lamps, dual black fold-away exterior mirrors, painted silver wheels with black center cap, 4-wheel anti-lock brakes, Vortec 5700 V-8 engine, 4-speed electronically controlled automatic transmission, rear panel doors

2-DOOR 4WD (in addition to or instead of 2-DOOR 2WD equipment): Insta-Trac 4WD system

TAHOE — CHEVROLET

CODE	DESCRIPTION	INVOICE	MSRP

LS 4-DOOR 2WD (in addition to or instead of 2-DOOR 2WD equipment): Air conditioning, power windows, power door locks, rear window defogger, full floor carpet with rubber floor mats, 60/40 custom cloth split front bench seat, AM/FM stereo with cassette player, leather-wrapped steering wheel, sunshade extensions, roof-mounted luggage rack

LS 4-DOOR 4WD (in addition to or instead of LS 4-DOOR 2WD equipment): Insta-Trac 4WD system

Base Prices

Code	Description	Invoice	MSRP
C10516	2-Door 2WD	20569	23507
K10516	2-Door 4WD	22887	26157
C10706	LS 4-Door 2WD	25274	28885
K10706	LS 4-Door 4WD	27549	31485
Destination Charge:		640	640

Accessories

Code	Description	Invoice	MSRP
GU6	3.42 Rear Axle Ratio (2-Door 2WD)	NC	NC
GT4	3.73 Rear Axle Ratio (2-Door 4WD)	116	135
GT4	3.73 Rear Axle Ratio (4-Door)	116	135
L56	6.5-liter Turbodiesel V8 Engine (2-Door 4WD)	2460	2860
	Includes front bumper guards; NOT AVAILABLE with Sport Equipment Package		
C5M	6100 lb. GVWR (2-Door 2WD)	NC	NC
C5P	6250 lb. GVWR (2-Door 4WD)	NC	NC
	NOT AVAILABLE with Turbodiesel Engine		
C5Q	6300 lb. GVWR (4-Door 2WD)	NC	NC
C71	6450 lb. GVWR (2-Door 4WD)	NC	NC
	REQUIRES Turbodiesel Engine		
C5U	6800 lb. GVWR (4-Door 4WD)	NC	NC
C60	Air Conditioning (2-Door)	727	845
	INCLUDED in Decor Option Packages		
N90	Aluminum Wheels (2-Door 2WD)	267	310
	INCLUDED in Decor Option Packages		
PF4	Aluminum Wheels (2-Door 4WD)	267	310
	INCLUDED in Decor Option Packages		
YF5	California Emissions	NC	NC
DF2	Camper Type Exterior Mirrors (2-Door)	45	53
	With 1SB (2-Door)	(39)	(45)
	With 1SC (2-Door)	(39)	(45)
	Stainless steel mirrors; NOT AVAILABLE with Sport Equipment Package		
V10	Cold Climate Package	28	33
	Includes engine block heater; NOT AVAILABLE with Turbodiesel Engine		
ZQ3	Convenience Group (2-Door)	329	383
	Includes tilt wheel and cruise control; INCLUDED in Decor Option Packages		
ZY2	Conventional Two-tone Paint (2-Door)	155	180
	REQUIRES purchase of a Decor Option Package; INCLUDED in Sport Equipment Package		

CHEVROLET — TAHOE

CODE	DESCRIPTION	INVOICE	MSRP
ZY2	Conventional Two-tone Paint (4-Door)	155	180
AJ1	Deep Tinted Glass (2-Door)	185	215
	INCLUDED in Decor Option Packages		
NP1	Electronic Shift Transfer Case (4WD)	106	123
KC4	Engine Oil Cooling System	116	135
	INCLUDED with Turbodiesel Engine, 3.73 Rear Axle Ratio, and Heavy Duty Trailering Package		
VK3	Front License Plate Bracket	NC	NC
KNP	Heavy Duty Auxiliary Transmission Cooling System	83	96
	INCLUDED with Turbodiesel Engine and Heavy Duty Trailering Package; NOT AVAILABLE with 3.08 Rear Axle Ratio on 2-Door 2WD		
F60	Heavy Duty Front Springs (2-Door)	54	63
	NOT AVAILABLE with Turbodiesel Engine		
Z82	Heavy Duty Trailering Equipment	257	299
	With GT4 (2-Door 4WD)	141	164
	With GT4 (4-Door)	141	164
	With L56 (2-Door 4WD)	141	164
	Includes platform hitch, wiring harness, KC4 engine cooling system, and KNP transmission cooling system		
K47	High Capacity Air Cleaner	69	80
	NOT AVAILABLE with Turbodiesel Engine		
A95	High-back Bucket Seats (2-Door)	241	280
	Without 1SB (2-Door)	195	227
	Without 1SC (2-Door)	195	227
	Includes roof console, floor console, and power lumbar adjustment		
A95	High-back Bucket Seats (4-Door)	241	280
	Includes roof console, floor console, and power lumbar adjustment		
G80	Locking Rear Differential (2-Door 2WD)	217	252
	REQUIRES 3.42 Rear Axle Ratio		
G80	Locking Rear Differential (2-Door 4WD)	217	252
G80	Locking Rear Differential (4-Door)	217	252
1SB	LS Decor Option Package (2-Door)	3396	3949
	Includes removable rear compartment security net, air conditioning, power windows, tilt wheel, cruise control, cloth/carpet door trim, full floor carpeting with front/rear rubber floor mats, deep tinted glass, rear window defogger, electrochromic rearview mirror with integrated compass, AM/FM stereo with cassette player, seek/scan, automatic tone control, theft lock, speed compensated volume control, and digital clock; reclining 60/40 split bench seat with storage armrest and power lumbar support, cloth spare tire cover, leather-wrapped steering wheel, dual illuminated visor vanity mirrors, visor extenders, roof-mounted luggage rack, chrome grille, dual composite halogen headlamps, dual power exterior mirrors, aluminum wheels		
1SC	LT Decor Option Package (2-Door)	4579	5324
	Includes LS Decor (removable rear compartment security net, air conditioning, power windows, tilt wheel, cruise control, cloth/carpet door trim, full floor carpeting with front/rear rubber floor mats, deep tinted glass, rear window defogger, electrochromic rearview mirror with integrated compass, AM/FM stereo with cassette player, seek/		

TAHOE — CHEVROLET

CODE	DESCRIPTION	INVOICE	MSRP
	scan, automatic tone control, theft lock, speed compensated volume control, and digital clock; reclining 60/40 split bench seat with storage armrest and power lumbar support, cloth spare tire cover, leather-wrapped steering wheel, dual illuminated visor vanity mirrors, visor extenders, roof-mounted luggage rack, chrome grille, dual composite halogen headlamps, dual power exterior mirrors, aluminum wheels) plus LT Decor upgrade (leather seat trim) plus power driver's seat and remote keyless entry		
1SC	**LT Decor Option Package (4-Door)** .... *Includes LT Decor upgrade (leather seats) plus power driver's seat and remote keyless entry*	1269	1475
QBN	**LT245/75R16C BSW Tires (2-Door 4WD)** .... *On/off road tread*	49	57
QBX	**LT245/75R16C OWL Tires (2-Door 4WD)** .... *On/off road tread*	157	182
NG1	**Massachusetts/New York Emissions**	NC	NC
Z71	**Off-road Chassis Equipment (2-Door 4WD)** .... *Includes skid plate package and Bilstein shock absorbers; REQUIRES purchase of a Decor Option Package and QGC, QGD, QBN, or QBX tires (when ordered in conjunction with Sport Equipment Package, QGC is required)*	344	400
QFN	**P235/75R15 OWL Tires (2WD)** .... *All-season tread*	108	125
QGA	**P245/75R16 BSW Tires (4WD)** .... *All-terrain tread; standard tire on 4WD models; NOT AVAILABLE with Z71 Off-road Chassis Equipment*	NC	NC
QGB	**P245/75R16 OWL Tires (4-Door 4WD)** .... *All-terrain tread*	120	140
QGC	**P265/75R16 BSW Tires (2-Door 4WD)** .... *All-terrain tread; REQUIRES Aluminum Wheels, which are included in Decor Option Packages*	163	190
QGD	**P265/75R16 OWL Tires (2-Door 4WD)** .... *All-terrain tread; REQUIRES Aluminum Wheels, which are included in Decor Option Packages*	271	315
AG9	**Power Driver's Seat** .... *INCLUDED in LT Decor Option Packages*	206	240
UL5	**Radio Delete (2-Door)** .... *Includes instrument panel covers and front fender hole plug*	(247)	(287)
P06	**Rally Wheel Trim (2-Door)** .... *NOT AVAILABLE with Decor Option Packages*	52	60
E55	**Rear Tailgate** .... *Replaces standard panel doors; includes lift glass with drop gate and power release; when ordered with LT Decor Option Package, a rear window wiper/washer is included*	NC	NC
C49	**Rear Window Defogger (2-Door)** .... *INCLUDED in Decor Option Packages and with Rear Window Wiper/Washer; REQUIRES Air Conditioning; to order with E55 Tailgate, you must select the Rear Window Wiper/Washer.*	132	154

CHEVROLET — TAHOE

CODE	DESCRIPTION	INVOICE	MSRP
ZP6	**Rear Window Wiper/Washer (2-Door)**	240	279
	Includes rear defogger; REQUIRES E55 Tailgate; INCLUDED in Decor Option Packages when packages are ordered with E55 Tailgate		
AU0	**Remote Keyless Entry (2-Door)**	116	135
	REQUIRES LS Decor Option Package		
BVE	**Running Boards**	168	195
	Black in color, with 600 lb. weight capacity; Running Boards are dealer-installed		
NZZ	**Skid Plate Package (4WD)**	194	225
	INCLUDED in Z71 Off-road Chassis Equipment for 2-Door models		
BYP	**Sport Equipment Package (2-Door 4WD)**	260	302
	Includes dark argent colored front bumper with rub strip, dark argent colored rear bumper with rub strip and step pad, dark argent colored grille, dark argent colored wheel flares, two-tone paint, Sport decals, black colored front license plate bracket, black exterior mirrors, and black air dam; NOT AVAILABLE with Turbodiesel Engine; REQUIRES purchase of a Decor option package and QGA or QGC tires		
UM6	**Stereo w/cassette (2-Door)**	126	147
	ETR AM/FM stereo with cassette player, seek/scan, and digital clock; NOT AVAILABLE with Decor Option Packages		
V76	**Tow Hooks (4-Door 2WD)**	33	38
UL0	**Uplevel Stereo w/cassette (2-Door)**	174	202
	ETR AM/FM stereo with cassette player, seek/scan, automatic tone control, theft lock, speed compensated volume control, and digital clock; NOT AVAILABLE with Decor Option Packages		
UP0	**Uplevel Stereo w/cassette & CD players (2-Door)**	172	200
	ETR AM/FM stereo with cassette and CD players, seek/scan, automatic tone control, theft lock, speed compensated volume control, and digital clock; REQUIRES purchase of a Decor Option Package		
UP0	**Uplevel Stereo w/cassette & CD players (4-Door)**	172	200
	ETR AM/FM stereo with cassette and CD players, seek/scan, automatic tone control, theft lock, speed compensated volume control, and digital clock		
UN0	**Uplevel Stereo w/CD player (2-Door)**	86	100
	ETR AM/FM stereo with CD player, seek/scan, automatic tone control, theft lock, speed compensated volume control, and digital clock; REQUIRES purchase of a Decor Option Package		
UN0	**Uplevel Stereo w/CD player (4-Door)**	86	100
	ETR AM/FM stereo with CD player, seek/scan, automatic tone control, theft lock, speed compensated volume control, and digital clock		
B71	**Wheel Flare Moldings (2-Door 4WD)**	155	180
	Color-keyed moldings; INCLUDED in Sport Equipment Package		

VENTURE — CHEVROLET

VENTURE *(1997)*

1997 Chevrolet Venture LS Extended

What's New for Chevrolet Venture in 1997 — Complete redesign of Chevy's minivan results in a new name, a left-side sliding door, optional traction control, a powerful standard engine, and a fun-to-drive demeanor. Nice van, except for the big chrome grille.

Venture — Review

If you didn't know Chevrolet produced a minivan other than the Astro, you will soon. The hideous Lumina Minivan has gone to that plastic recycling center in car heaven, replaced by a conservative, steel-bodied family hauler that was developed in concert with GM's European Opel division. The new Venture, as the van is so aptly monikered, is an outstanding entry in the minivan market, featuring an available driver's side sliding door, optional traction control, optional integrated child seats, standard anti-lock brakes, and enough power to make it fun to drive.

Two versions are available on two different wheelbases; base or LS trim on a 112-inch or 120-inch wheelbase. Choose between 3- or 4-door body styles, and all Ventures come equipped with a 180-horsepower 3.4-liter V-6 engine. Designed to satisfy consumers on either side of the Atlantic Ocean, the Venture surprises with a communicative chassis, sharp steering, and nimble handling while providing room inside for up to 7 passengers and a good amount of their belongings.

Like to drink and drive (soda, water, or juice, that is)? The Venture accommodates with cup and drink box holders galore. Don't worry too much about Junior spilling Hawaiian Punch either, because Chevrolet Scotchgards all fabrics at the factory. Several seating configurations are available, with the most user-friendly but least comfortable setup being the multi-configurable modular buckets. Weighing just 38 pounds each, they're easy to install, remove, and re-arrange, but they're mighty uncomfortable for adults. Front buckets are much more soothing for elder backsides.

CHEVROLET

VENTURE

Cool stuff includes optional rear seat audio controls that allow rear passengers to listen to a CD via headphones while front passengers catch NPR on the radio. Also available are rear seat heat and air conditioning controls, a load-leveling suspension complete with auxiliary air hose, and daytime running lamps that illuminate parking lights instead of headlights. Uncool is the toothy chrome eggcrate grille up front that screams "MOMMOBILE." At least there's no fake wood siding, no body cladding, and no gold package.

Our main reservation about the Venture concerns crashworthiness. Recently, the Insurance Institute for Highway Safety conducted 40 mph offset crash tests of the Pontiac Trans Sport, which is essentially a clone of the Venture. The Trans Sport did not fare well in the test. True, there are no federal regulations in place regarding offset crashworthiness, but the Ford Windstar has performed wonderfully in both offset and head-on crash testing. The National Highway and Traffic Safety Administration will be crashing one of the new GM minivans later this year, and we'll update this report at that time.

We like the Venture, in case you hadn't already guessed. Pontiac and Oldsmobile serve up versions of the same van (Oldsmobile's is called Silhouette), and any of the three would make a dandy alternative to Chrysler and import minivans. In the case of the Chevy, though, we'll wait for stylists to offer an LTZ model with body-color grille (yeah, like that's gonna happen).

Safety Data

Driver Airbag: *Standard*
Side Airbag: *Not Available*
4-Wheel ABS: *Standard*
Driver Crash Test Grade: *Not Available*
Passenger Crash Test Grade: *Not Available*

Passenger Airbag: *Standard*
Meets 1997 Car Side Impact Standards: *Yes*
Traction Control: *Optional*
Insurance Cost: *Not Available*
Integrated Child Seat(s): *Optional*

Standard Equipment

VENTURE REGULAR LENGTH: 3.4-liter V-6 engine, 4-speed electronically-controlled automatic transmission, soft ride suspension, power front disc/rear drum 4-wheel anti-lock brakes, dual front airbags, air conditioning, integrated windshield antenna, center console, overhead console, too many cupholders to count, side window defoggers, integrated pollen filter, child safety door lock for sliding door(s), power door locks, power liftgate lock, front door map pockets, front seatback map pockets, Scotchgard fabric protectant, 7-passenger seating, tilt steering wheel, AM/FM stereo with clock, intermittent variable wipers, daytime running lights, dual black power exterior mirrors, P205/70R15 all-season tires, steel wheels with full wheelcovers

BASE 3-DOOR EXTENDED (in addition to or instead of REGULAR LENGTH equipment): Split folding rear bench seats, P215/70R15 all-season tires

LS 4-DOOR EXTENDED (in addition to BASE EXTENDED equipment): Cargo convenience net, cruise control, interior roof rail lighting, custom cloth interior trim, AM/FM stereo with cassette player and automatic tone control, power windows with driver's side express-down feature

VENTURE — CHEVROLET

CODE	DESCRIPTION	INVOICE	MSRP

Base Prices

Code	Description	Invoice	MSRP
1UN06	3-door Regular Wheelbase	18032	19925
1UN16	4-door Regular Length	19488	21534
1UM06	3-door Extended Length	19086	21080
1UM16	4-door Extended Length	20543	22699
	Destination Charge:	570	570

Accessories

Code	Description	Invoice	MSRP
1SD	**LS Option Package 1SD (3-dr Reg Length)**	1156	1344
	Includes cruise control, power windows with driver's express-down feature, 7-passenger seating with split folding rear benches, remote keyless entry, AM/FM stereo with cassette player, seek/scan, clock, automatic tone control, theft lock, and speed compensated volume control; LS Trim (custom cloth interior trim, cargo convenience net, interior roof rail lighting)		
1SH	**LS Option Package 1SH (3-dr Ext Length)**	868	1009
	Includes power windows with driver's express-down feature, remote keyless entry, cruise control, AM/FM stereo with cassette player, seek/scan, clock, automatic tone control, theft lock, and speed compensated volume control; LS Trim (custom cloth interior trim, cargo convenience net, interior roof rail lighting)		
1SJ	**LS Option Package 1SJ (3-dr Ext Length)**	1637	1904
	Includes power windows with driver's express-down feature, remote keyless entry, cruise control, AM/FM stereo with cassette player, seek/scan, clock, automatic tone control, theft lock, and speed compensated volume control; LS Trim (custom cloth interior trim, cargo convenience net, interior roof rail lighting), deep tinted glass, luggage rack, rear window defogger, 6-way power driver's seat, touring tires		
1SB	**Option Package 1SB (3-dr Reg Length)**	194	225
	Includes cruise control		
1SC	**Option Package 1SC (3-dr Reg Length)**	834	970
	Includes cruise control, power windows with driver's express-down feature, 7-passenger seating with split folding rear benches, remote keyless entry		
1SF	**Option Package 1SF (3-dr Ext Length)**	194	225
	Includes cruise control		
1SG	**Option Package 1SG (3-dr Ext Length)**	546	635
	Includes power windows with driver's express-down feature, remote keyless entry, cruise control		
1SL	**Option Package 1SL (4-dr Ext Length)**	770	895
	Includes deep tinted glass, luggage rack, rear window defogger, 6-way power driver's seat, touring tires		
C34	Air Conditioning — Front & Rear	387	450
PH3	Aluminum Wheels	237	275

CHEVROLET VENTURE

CODE	DESCRIPTION	INVOICE	MSRP
YF5	California Emissions	146	170
AJ1	Deep Tinted Glass	211	245
	INCLUDED in Option Packages 1SJ and 1SL		
K05	Engine Block Heater	17	20
VK3	Front License Plate Bracket	NC	NC
V54	Luggage Rack	151	175
	INCLUDED in Option Packages 1SJ and 1SL		
NG1	Massachusetts/New York Emissions	146	170
E58	Power Sliding Right Side Door (Ext Length)	301	350
UK6	Rear Audio Controls	95	110
	Includes headphone jacks		
C49	Rear Window Defogger	146	170
	INCLUDED in Option Packages 1SJ and 1SL		
R7D	Safety & Security System (3-dr Reg Length)	52	60
	REQUIRES purchase of LS Option Package 1SD		
R7D	Safety & Security System (Ext Length)	211	245
	With 1SJ (3-dr Ext Length)	181	210
	With 1SL (4-dr Ext Length)	181	210
	REQUIRES purchase of Option Package 1SH, 1SK, 1SJ, or 1SL		
ABB	Seating — 7-passenger modular buckets (Ext Length)	99	115
ABB	Seating — 7-passenger modular buckets (Reg Length)	387	450
	With 1SD (3-dr Reg Length)	99	115
ABA	Seating — 7-passenger w/split-folding rear benches	288	335
	INCLUDED in Option Packages 1SC and 1SD		
AN5	Seating — Dual Integrated Child Seats	194	225
AG1	Seating — Power Driver's Seat	232	270
	Includes 6-way adjustment; INCLUDED in Option Packages 1SJ and 1SL		
AN2	Seating — Single Integrated Child Seat	108	125
UN7	Stereo — Premium w/cassette & CD players (3-dr)	172	200
	AM/FM stereo with seek/scan, clock, auto-reverse cassette player, remote CD player, theft lock, automatic tone control, speed compensated volume control, front and rear coaxial speakers; REQUIRES purchase of Option Package 1SD, 1SH, or		
UN7	Stereo — Premium w/cassette & CD players (4-dr Ext Length)	172	200
	AM/FM stereo with seek/scan, clock, auto-reverse cassette player, remote CD player, theft lock, automatic tone control, speed compensated volume control, front and rear coaxial speakers		
UN0	Stereo — Uplevel w/CD player (3-dr)	86	100
	AM/FM stereo with seek/scan, clock, CD player, theft lock, automatic tone control, speed compensated volume control; REQUIRES purchase of Option Package 1SD, 1SH, or 1SJ		
UN0	Stereo — Uplevel w/CD player (4-dr Ext Length)	86	100
	AM/FM stereo with seek/scan, clock, CD player, theft lock, automatic tone control, speed compensated volume control		
UM6	Stereo — w/cassette (All except 4-dr Ext Length)	142	165
	AM/FM stereo with seek/scan, clock, and cassette player		
XPK	Tires — P215/70R15 (Reg Length)	33	38
	All-season blackwall tires		

VENTURE — CHEVROLET

CODE	DESCRIPTION	INVOICE	MSRP
P42	Tires — Self-sealing Tires (Ext Length)	129	150
	REQUIRES purchase of Option Package 1SJ or 1SL, or XPU Tires		
XPU	Tires — Touring Tires (Ext Length)	30	35
	INCLUDED in Option Packages 1SJ and 1SL		
FE3	Touring Suspension (3-dr Reg Length)	187	218
	REQUIRES purchase of LS Option Package 1SD		
FE3	Touring Suspension (Ext Length)	185	215
	With 1SJ (3-dr Ext Length)	155	180
	With 1SL (4-dr Ext Length)	155	180
	REQUIRES purchase of Option Package 1SH, 1SK, 1SJ, or 1SL		
NW9	Traction Control	151	175
V92	Trailering Package (3-dr Reg Length)	316	368
	REQUIRES purchase of LS Option Package 1SD		
V92	Trailering Package (Ext Length)	314	365
	With 1SJ (3-dr Ext Length)	284	330
	With 1SL (4-dr Ext Length)	284	330
	REQUIRES purchase of Option Package 1SH, 1SK, 1SJ, or 1SL		

Save hundreds, even thousands, off the sticker price of the new car you want.

Call Autovantage®
your FREE auto-buying service
1-800-201-7703

No purchase required. No fees.

CALL NATIONWIDE 1-800-521-7257
FOR A WRITTEN QUOTATION
AS LOW AS $50 OVER INVOICE

See page 15 for details.

CHRYSLER — TOWN & COUNTRY

TOWN & COUNTRY *(1997)*

1997 Chrysler Town & Country LXi

What's New for Chrysler Town & Country in 1997 — Chrysler's luxury minivans get a few improvements this year, as AWD extended length models are added to the lineup. Also new this year is a sporty SX model, which replaces last year's LX as the regular length Town & Country. Families with kids will love the standard driver's side sliding door on this vehicle.

Town & Country — Review

Elegance and expressiveness, grace and grandeur. These are the words that describe Chrysler's posh rendition of the Dodge/Plymouth minivan.

Oh sure, you get the same fresh shape and interior space in a lower-priced Caravan or Voyager, the same car-like ride/handling qualities, the same practical virtues as a people and cargo hauler. What Chrysler adds to that mix is luxury. Plenty of it—and that's enough to attract a fair share of extra customers to the Chrysler end of the minivan spectrum.

Town & Country customers have three distinct choices now: the LX model, an "ultimate" LXi that promises features ordinarily found only on luxury cars—plus a new short-wheelbase (113.3-inch) SX version. (This minivan was badged the LX last year). The SX is Chrysler's sporty minivan. It offers cast aluminum wheels, touring tires, and a very inexpensive touring and handling package. Properly outfitted, the SX transforms into a quick, little sport van capable of embarrassing most sedan owners.

All-wheel drive, being all the rage right now, is optional on the LX and LXi models of the T&C. Since these minivans only have 5 inches of ground clearance, they aren't meant for serious off-road adventure. They do, however, give drivers the security of knowing that their traction is improved when driving on slippery surfaces. They also make piloting the extended length minivans a little more fun, by evening out the weight distribution and providing some rear-wheel motive power. Chrysler's AWD minivans also replace the standard rear drum brakes with discs.

TOWN & COUNTRY — CHRYSLER

All three minivans feature seven-passenger seating, with an "Easy-Out" rollaway back seat. A 3.8-liter V-6 is standard in the LXi, and optional in its mates, which otherwise come with a 3.3-liter engine. Both engines drive a four-speed automatic transmission, which delivers neat and smooth gearchanges. Minivanners who do lots of highway cruising and Interstate hopping might be happier with the bigger engine, which lets the T&C pass and merge into traffic with greater confidence and briskness.

Extras in the LXi edition include dual zone control heat/air conditioning, eight-way leather trimmed driver and passenger seats, plus a memory for both the seats and outside mirrors. A roof rack is standard on the LXi, and optional on the others. To further humiliate Ford Motor Company, which had the chance to put a left side passenger door on their Windstar and didn't, Chrysler has made this feature standard on all Town & Country models for 1997.

If you want luxury and spaciousness, but you just can't abide the thought of a boxy Volvo wagon or lethargic Audi A6, drop by your local Chrysler store and try the Town & Country on for size.

Safety Data

Driver Airbag: *Standard*
Side Airbag: *Not Available*
4-Wheel ABS: *Standard*
Driver Crash Test Grade: *Average*
Passenger Crash Test Grade: *Good*

Passenger Airbag: *Standard*
Meets 1997 Side Impact Standards: *Yes*
Traction Control: *Standard*
Insurance Cost: *Low*
Integrated Child Seat(s): *Optional*

Standard Equipment

SX: 3.3-liter V-6 engine, 4-speed automatic transmission, power rack-and-pinion steering, anti-lock front disc/rear drum brakes, low-speed traction control, P215/65R16 touring tires, 16" cast aluminum wheels, bright grille, halogen headlamps, fog lights, heated power outside mirrors, speed-sensitive interval windshield wipers, rear window washer/wiper, remote keyless entry, illuminated entry, dual air bags, deluxe quad bucket seating, premium cloth seat trim, overhead console with sun glasses holder/garage door opener/compass/temperature gauge/trip computer, front air conditioning, rear window defroster, power windows, power door locks, speed control, tilt steering, leather-wrapped steering wheel, AM/FM stereo w/cassette, 8 cupholders, floor mats, front and middle map lights, glove box light, liftgate light, dual flood lights, ignition lights, and dual illuminated vanity mirrors.

LX 2WD (in addition to or instead of SX): P215/65R15 tires and 15" wheel covers.

LXi 2WD (in addition to or instead of LX 2WD): 3.8-liter V-6 engine, load leveling suspension, P215/65R16 tires, conventional spare tire, 16" cast aluminum wheels, luggage rack, solar-tinted windshield and front window glass, tinted side and rear window glass, 8-way power driver's and front seat passenger's seat, leather seats, rear air conditioning, power doors with central locking, security system, AM/FM stereo w/cassette/CD player/equalizer/Infinity speakers, auto-dimming rearview mirror, and rear seat map lights.

LX AWD (in addition to or instead of LX 2WD): 3.8-liter V-6 engine, load levelling suspension, AWD system, AWD badging, 4-wheel anti-lock disc brakes, and P215/70R15 A/S tires.

LXi AWD (in addition to or instead of LXi 2WD): AWD system, AWD badging, 4-wheel anti-lock disc brakes, and P215/70R16 touring tires, conventional spare tire.

CHRYSLER TOWN & COUNTRY

CODE	DESCRIPTION	INVOICE	MSRP

Base Prices

NSYP52	SX	24213	26680
NSYP53	LX	24403	26895
NSCP53	LX AWD	28512	31565
NSYS53	LXi	28424	31465
NSC553	LXi AWD	30602	33940
Destination Charge:		580	580

Accessories

CODE	DESCRIPTION	INVOICE	MSRP
WNS	16" Cast Aluminum Wheels (LX)	349	410
	REQUIRES Quick Order Pkg 28R or 29R.		
CYR	7-Passenger Seating w/Child Seats	NC	NC
	Includes deluxe 7-passenger seating with 2 integrated child seats in the second row bench seat. NOT AVAILABLE with FL leather seats. REQUIRES Quick Order Pkg 28H, 29H, 28R, or 29R.		
SER	Automatic Load Leveling Suspension (SX/LX 2WD)	247	290
	REQUIRES Quick Order Pkg 28H, 29H, 28R, or 29R.		
YCF	Border States Emissions	151	170
NAE	California Emissions	151	170
TBB	Conventional Spare Tire (SX/LX)	94	110
	INCLUDED in AAP and AAR towing groups. REQUIRES Quick Order Pkg 28H, 29H, 28R, or 29R.		
NHK	Engine Block Heater	30	35
PH2	Extra Cost Paint: Candy Apple Red (SX/LX)	170	200
PWP	Extra Cost Paint: Golden White Pearl (SX/LXi)	170	200
FL	Leather Seats (SX/LX)	757	890
	NOT AVAILABLE with CYR seating group.		
MWG	Luggage Rack (LX/LXi)	149	175
	REQUIRES Quick Order Pkg 28H, 29H, 28R or 29R.		
28H	Quick Order Pkg 28H (SX)	973	1145
	Manufacturer Discount	(646)	(760)
	Net Price	327	385
	Includes solar screen glass; AM/FM stereo with cassette, equalizer and 10 Infinity speakers; and driver's 8-way power seats		
28R	Quick Order Pkg 28R (LX 2WD)	973	1145
	Manufacturer Discount	(646)	(760)
	Net Price	327	385
	Includes solar glass; AM/FM stereo with cassette, eqaulizer and 10 Infinity speakers; and 8-way power driver's seat.		
29H	Quick Order Pkg 29H (SX)	1249	1470
	Manufacturer Discount	(646)	(760)
	Net Price	603	710
	Includes Quick Order Pkg 29H (solar screen glass; AM/FM stereo with cassette, equalizer and 10 Infinity speakers; and driver's 8-way power seat), and 3.8-liter V-6 engine upgrade.		

TOWN & COUNTRY — CHRYSLER

CODE	DESCRIPTION	INVOICE	MSRP
29R	Quick Order Pkg 29R (LX 2WD)	1249	1470
	Manufacturer Discount	(646)	(760)
	Net Price	603	710
	Includes Quick Order Pkg 28R (solar glass; AM/FM stereo with cassette, equalizer and 10 Infinity speakers; and 8-way power driver's seat), and 3.8-liter V-6 engine upgrade.		
29R	Quick Order Pkg 29R (LX AWD)	973	1145
	Manufacturer Discount	(646)	(760)
	Net Price	327	385
	Includes solar tinted glass; AM/FM stereo with cassette, equalizer, and 10 Infinity speakers; and 8-way power driver's seat.		
AAB	Rear Air Conditioning (LX)	344	405
	REQUIRES 28R or 29R.		
AAH	Security Alarm (SX/LX)	128	150
	REQUIRES Quick Order Pkg 28H, 29H, 28R, or 29R.		
AWS	Smoker's Group	18	20
	Includes cigar lighter and three ashtrays.		
RAZ	Stereo w/Cassette & CD Player (SX/LX)	336	395
	Includes AM/FM stereo with cassette, CD player, equalizer and 10 Infinity speakers. REQUIRES Quick Order Pkg 28H, 29H, 28R, or 29R.		
AAT	Touring & Handling Group (LX 2WD)	399	470
	Includes rear sway bar, touring suspension, P215/65R16 touring tires, upgraded struts and shocks, and 16" cast aluminum wheels.		
AAT	Touring & Handling Group (SX)	51	60
	Includes rear sway bar, touring suspension, P215/65R16 touring tires, upgraded struts and shocks, and 16" cast aluminum wheels.		
AAP	Towing Group II (SX/LX 2WD)	153	180
	With AAT (LX 2WD) And AAT (SX)	234	145
	Includes 15" brakes, P215/65R15 B/W tires, 15" steel wheels, firm ride suspension, and conventional spare tire. REQUIRES Quick Order Pkg 28H, 29H, 28R, or 29R.		
AAR	Towing Group III (LX AWD)	323	380
	Includes firm ride suspension, conventional spare tire, heavy duty brakes, heavy duty radiator, heavy duty transmission oil cooler, and trailer wiring harness. REQUIRES Quick Order Pkg 29R.		
AAR	Towing Group III (SX/LX 2WD)	323	380
	Without AAT (LX 2WD) And AAT (SX)	293	345
	Includes firm ride suspension, conventional spare tire, heavy duty brakes, heavy duty radiator, heavy duty transmission oil cooler, and trailer wiring harness. REQUIRES Quick Order Pkg 28H, 29H, 28R, or 29R.		
AHT	Trailer Tow Group (LXi)	230	270
	Includes heavy duty brakes, heavy duty radiator, heavy duty transmission oil cooler, and trailer wiring harness.		

DODGE CARAVAN

CARAVAN (1997)

1997 Dodge Caravan

What's New for Dodge Caravan in 1997 — Traction control is a new option, so long as you get LE or ES trim, and an enhanced accident response system will automatically unlock the doors and illuminate the interior when an airbag deploys. Appearance and equipment refinements complete the modest changes to this best-in-class minivan.

Caravan — Review

If there is a perfect family vehicle in existence, it is the Dodge Caravan. What's the data say? The average American has two kids and spends a little more than $20,000 on a new car or truck. The Dodge Caravan fits into this scenario better than Velveeta in a grilled cheese sandwich.

We like the Caravan SE, because it is the most flexible trim level and upgrades seating positions from five to seven. You can go with the bare-bones $20,000 edition, or add luxury items like remote keyless entry, CD player with premium sound, and a security alarm. A third way to spec an SE model is with a Sport Option Package, which includes a firmer suspension, alloy wheels, fog lights, and monochromatic trim. Oddly, the 3.8-liter V-6 engine cannot be purchased on an SE model, which means the most sport your Sport can attain uses the 158 horsepower churned out by the 3.3-liter V-6 that comes with the package. Still, a Caravan Sport is the raciest minivan you can buy, short of popping an extra four grand for the ES model and its 3.8-liter V-6.

Step up to LE and ES trim levels, and you buy your ticket to a stronger engine, traction control, trip computer, snazzy trim, and leather seating. Just for fun, let's see what a loaded ES runs...Whoa! $30,000 for a packed Caravan ES! Not much value here, folks. Stick with the SE.

Caravan offers several thoughtful details, but the most important are the easy-out rolling seats and the innovative driver-side sliding door—a feature that makes so much sense, it's amazing that no one tried this before. Easy-out seats are a snap to release and remove, though lifting the seat from the rear of the van may still require two sets of biceps. Optional on

CARAVAN — DODGE

base and SE, and standard on LE and ES, the driver's side sliding door offers the convenience of loading kids and cargo from either side of the Caravan. Also intriguing is the windshield-wiper de-icer, which comes standard on the LE and ES.

Cupholders not only are numerous, they "ratchet down" to a smaller size. Except for an overabundance of climate controls, and an oddly-shaped column gearshift, the attractively curved dashboard is a pleasure to consult. Seats are soft but reasonably supportive, with moderate side bolstering.

Light steering response gives the Caravan an undeniably car-like feel, with an exceptionally smooth ride. Highly maneuverable and easy to control, the minivan delivers just a hint that you could exceed its capabilities, as when rounding a sharp curve. A 150-horsepower 16-valve dual-cam four serves as the base engine, with a 3.0-, 3.3-, or 3.8-liter V-6 optional. The Sport and ES Caravans feature specially tuned shocks and springs.

New for 1997 is the aforementioned traction control system for LE and ES models, and an enhanced accident response system that will automatically unlock the doors and illuminate the interior when an airbag deploys. Other new stuff includes fresh paint colors, new wheel covers for base models, enhanced interior quietness, and liftgate flood lamps. The basic cassette stereo sports refinement, and new software helps the transmission shift more smoothly.

Chrysler notes that the Caravan is 3.6 inches shorter than a Mercury Villager and nearly 15 inches shorter than a Ford Windstar, but offers more cargo space than either rival. The Caravan doesn't feel nearly so massive from the driver's seat, which is one of its many charms. Definitely investigate the Dodge Caravan if a smaller minivan meets your needs.

Safety Data

Driver Airbag: *Standard*
Side Airbag: *Not Available*
4-Wheel ABS: *Opt. (Base); Std. (ES/LE/SE)*
Driver Crash Test Grade: *Good*
Passenger Crash Test Grade: *Good*

Passenger Airbag: *Standard*
Meets 1997 Car Side Impact Standards: *Yes*
Traction Control: *N/A (Base/SE); Opt. (ES/LE)*
Insurance Cost: *Very Low*
Integrated Child Seat(s): *Optional*

Standard Equipment

CARAVAN: 2.4-liter inline four-cylinder engine, 3-speed automatic transmission, dual front airbags, power front disc/rear drum brakes, 14"x 6" steel wheels, P205/75R14 all-season BSW tires, 5-mph front/rear bumpers, 8 cupholders, sliding door child protection locks, dynamic side impact protection, body color fascias with molded accent strip, black liftgate light bar, narrow bodyside accent color moldings, tinted windows, black door handles, liftgate closing assist handle, sliding door closing assist handle, full length carpeting, 4 coat hooks, cloth sunvisors with covered mirrors, front courtesy/reading lights, rear cargo dome light, dual liftgate flood lights, sliding side door hold-open latch, day/night rearview mirror, exterior folding mirrors with manual operation, 12-volt power outlets in dashboard and cargo area, AM/FM stereo with clock and 4 speakers, cloth seat fabric, manual reclining high-back buckets seats with folding armrests, easy-out roller seats, 5-passenger seating with adjustable center bench, instrument panel storage bin, covered center and rear quarter panel storage bins, 14-inch wheel covers, manual quarter vent windows, rear wiper/washer with intermittent and speed-sensitive operation, 2-speed windshield wipers with speed-sensitive variable delay

SE (in addition to or instead of CARAVAN equipment): 4-speed automatic transmission, 15"x 6.5" steel wheels, P215/65R15 all-season BSW tires, four-wheel anti-lock brakes, accent color liftgate moldings, wide accent color bodyside moldings, 2 seatback assist straps, middle passenger vent outlets, dual note horn, cloth door and quarter panel bolsters, power heated

DODGE CARAVAN

| CODE | DESCRIPTION | INVOICE | MSRP |

exterior folding mirrors, AM/FM stereo with cassette player, clock, and 4 speakers; front door trim panel reflectors, 7-passenger seating including middle bench seat with folding armrests and rear folding and adjustable bench seat, deluxe sound insulation, cruise control, tilt steering column, quarter panel cargo net, underseat locking storage drawer, 15-inch deluxe wheel covers

LE (in addition to or instead of SE equipment): Overhead console with compass, thermometer, trip computer, sunglass storage, and garage door opener storage; rear window defroster, windshield wiper de-icer, power door locks, lower bodyside accent color applique, body color liftgate light bar, bodyside accent color paint stripe, body color door handles, front air conditioning, acoustically improved carpeting, front/rear carpeted floor mats, sliding sunvisor extensions, premium cloth door and quarter panel bolsters, remote keyless entry with panic alarm, illuminated entry, and headlight delay timer; front door courtesy lamps, middle seat courtesy/reading lamps, light group (includes instrument panel storage bin light, ash tray light, ignition switch light, glovebox light), premium cloth seat fabric, adjustable front head restraints, folding and reclining middle and rear bench seats, second sliding door on driver's side, premium sound insulation, covered instrument panel storage bin with audio inserts, passenger seatback map pocket, 15-inch premium wheel covers, power front door windows with driver's one-touch down feature, power vented rear quarter windows

ES (in addition to or instead of LE equipment): Heavy load/firm ride suspension, rear sway bar, wide body color bodyside molding, sill moldings, gold liftgate nameplate, tape stripe, side window outline, fog lights, P215/65R16 touring tires, cast aluminum wheels with gold accents

Base Prices

Code	Description	Invoice	MSRP
NSKL52	Base	15687	17235
NSKH52	SE	18054	19925
NSKP52	LE	22709	25215
NSKP52	ES	23228	25805
Destination Charge:		580	580

Accessories

Code	Description	Invoice	MSRP
WNR	Aluminum Wheels (LE)	349	410
	REQUIRES purchase of an Option Package		
BGF	Anti-lock Brakes (Base)	480	565
22T	Base Option Package 22T (Base)	1063	1250
	Manufacturer Discount	(1063)	(1250)
	Net Price	NC	NC
	Includes air conditioning, dual note horn, rear floor silencer pad, under seat storage drawer		
24T	Base Option Package 24T (Base)	1718	2020
	Manufacturer Discount	(731)	(860)
	Net Price	987	1160
	Includes 3.0-liter V6 engine, air conditioning, dual note horn, rear floor silencer pad, under seat storage drawer; NOT AVAILABLE in Calif., Mass., or New York		

CARAVAN — DODGE

CODE	DESCRIPTION	INVOICE	MSRP
28T	Base Option Package 28T (Base)	2033	2390
	Manufacturer Discount	(731)	(860)
	Net Price	1302	1530
	Includes 3.3-liter V6 engine, 4-speed automatic transmission, air conditioning, dual note horn, rear floor silencer pad, under seat storage drawer; AVAILABLE only in Calif., Mass., and New York		
YCF	Border State Emissions	145	170
NAE	Calif./Mass./New York Emissions	145	170
PH2	Candy Apple Red Paint (LE/ES)	170	200
PH2	Candy Apple Red Paint (SE)	170	200
	REQUIRES purchase of a Sport Option Package		
HAA	Climate Group I (Base/SE)	731	860
	Includes front air conditioning; INCLUDED in Option Packages		
AAA	Climate Group II (Base/SE)	383	450
	Includes sunscreen/solar control windows and windshield wiper de-icer; REQUIRES purchase of an Option Package; INCLUDED in Sport Option Packages		
AAC	Convenience/Security Group I (Base)	370	435
	Includes cruise control, tilt steering column, and power exterior mirrors		
AAE	Convenience/Security Group II (Base)	638	750
	Includes cruise control, tilt steering column, power exterior mirrors, and power door locks		
AAE	Convenience/Security Group II (SE)	268	315
	Includes power door locks; REQUIRES purchase of SE Option Package 23B, 24B, 28B, or Sport Option Package 28C; INCLUDED in SE Option Packages 24D, 28D and Sport Option Package 28E		
AAF	Convenience/Security Group III (SE)	582	685
	Includes power door locks, power front door windows, and power rear quarter windows; REQUIRES purchase of SE Option Package 23B, 24B, 28B, or Sport Option Package 28C; INCLUDED in SE Option Packages 24D, 28D and Sport Option Package 28E		
AAG	Convenience/Security Group IV (SE)	200	235
	Includes remote keyless entry, illuminated entry, and headlight-off time delay; REQUIRES purchase of SE Option Package 24D, 28D or Sport Option Package 28E		
AAH	Convenience/Security Group V (LE/ES)	128	150
	REQUIRES purchase of an Option Package		
AAH	Convenience/Security Group V (SE)	327	385
	Includes remote keyless entry, illuminated entry, headlight-off time delay, and security alarm; REQUIRES purchase of SE Option Package 24D, 28D or Sport Option Package 28E		
TBB	Conventional Spare Tire	94	110
	REQUIRES purchase of an Option Package		
GKD	Driver Side Sliding Door (Base/SE)	506	595
	REQUIRES purchase of an Option Package		
NHK	Engine Block Heater	30	35

DODGE CARAVAN

CODE	DESCRIPTION	INVOICE	MSRP
28M	ES Option Package 28M (ES)	1284	1510
	Manufacturer Discount	(646)	(760)
	Net Price	638	750
	Includes low speed traction control, dual-zone air conditioning temperature control, sunscreen and solar control windows, AM/FM stereo with cassette player, equalizer, CD changer controls, and 10 Infinity speakers; power driver's seat with 8-way adjustment, automatic day/night rearview mirror, front passenger assist strap, leather-wrapped steering wheel		
29M	ES Option Package 29M (ES)	1560	1835
	Manufacturer Discount	(646)	(760)
	Net Price	914	1075
	Includes 3.8-liter V6 engine, low speed traction control, dual-zone air conditioning temperature control, sunscreen and solar control windows, AM/FM stereo with cassette player, equalizer, CD changer controls, and 10 Infinity speakers; power driver's seat with 8-way adjustment, automatic day/night rearview mirror, front passenger assist strap, leather-wrapped steering wheel		
PWP	Golden White Pearl Paint (ES)	170	200
28K	LE Option Package 28K (LE)	1012	1190
	Manufacturer Discount	(646)	(760)
	Net Price	366	430
	Includes dual-zone air conditioning temperature control, sunscreen and solar control windows, AM/FM stereo with cassette player, equalizer, CD changer controls, and 10 Infinity speakers; power driver's seat with 8-way adjustment		
29K	LE Option Package 29K (LE)	1288	1515
	Manufacturer Discount	(646)	(760)
	Net Price	642	755
	Includes 3.8-liter V6 engine, dual-zone air conditioning temperature control, sunscreen and solar control windows, AM/FM stereo with cassette player, equalizer, CD changer controls, and 10 Infinity speakers; power driver's seat with 8-way adjustment		
—	Leather Seats (LE/ES)	757	890
	REQUIRES Seating Group II		
SER	Load-leveling Suspension (LE/ES)	247	290
	REQUIRES purchase of an Option Package		
AAP	Loading & Towing Group II (LE/ES)	153	180
	With 28M (ES)	123	145
	With 29M (ES)	123	145
	With AAT (LE)	123	145
	Includes conventional spare tire and heavy load/firm ride suspension; REQUIRES purchase of an Option Package		
AAR	Loading & Towing Group III (ES)	293	345
	Includes conventional spare tire, heavy load/firm ride suspension, 120-amp alternator, 685 CCA battery, heavy duty front disc/rear drum brakes, trailer tow wiring harness, and heavy duty transmission oil cooler; REQUIRES purchase of an Option Package		

CARAVAN — DODGE

CODE	DESCRIPTION	INVOICE	MSRP
AAR	Loading & Towing Group III (LE)	378	445
	With AAT (LE)	349	410
	Includes conventional spare tire, heavy load/firm ride suspension, 120-amp alternator, 685 CCA battery, heavy duty front disc/rear drum brakes, trailer tow wiring harness, and heavy duty transmission oil cooler; REQUIRES purchase of an Option Package		
MWG	Luggage Rack	149	175
	REQUIRES purchase of an Option Package; INCLUDED in Sport Option Packages		
RBN	Premium Stereo w/cassette (SE)	276	325
	AM/FM stereo with cassette player, graphic equalizer, CD changer controls, and 10 Infinity speakers; REQUIRES purchase of SE Option Package 24D, 28D, or Sport Option Package 28E		
RAZ	Premium Stereo w/cassette & CD player (LE/ES)	336	395
	AM/FM stereo with cassette and CD players, graphic equalizer, CD changer controls, and 10 Infinity speakers; REQUIRES purchase of an Option Package		
RAZ	Premium Stereo w/cassette & CD player (SE)	612	720
	AM/FM stereo with cassette and CD players, graphic equalizer, CD changer controls, and 10 Infinity speakers; REQUIRES purchase of SE Option Package 24D, 28D, or Sport Option Package 28E		
GFA	Rear Window Defroster (Base)	196	230
	Without AAC (Base)	166	195
	Without AAE (Base)	166	195
	Includes windshield wiper de-icer		
23B	SE Option Package 23B (SE)	1024	1205
	Manufacturer Discount	(595)	(700)
	Net Price	429	505
	Includes air conditioning, rear window defroster, windshield wiper de-icer, and deluxe 7-passenger seating (includes middle and rear reclining and folding seats with adjustable headrests)		
24A	SE Option Package 24A (SE)	442	520
	Includes 3.0-liter V6 engine and 3-speed automatic transmission; pricing includes credit of $213 invoice and $250 MSRP for 3-speed automatic transmission downgrade; NOT AVAILABLE in Calif., Mass., or New York		
24B	SE Option Package 24B (SE)	1466	1725
	Manufacturer Discount	(595)	(700)
	Net Price	871	1025
	Includes 3.0-liter V6 engine, 3-speed automatic transmission, air conditioning, rear window defroster, windshield wiper de-icer, and deluxe 7-passenger seating (includes middle and rear reclining and folding seats with adjustable headrests); pricing includes credit of $213 invoice and $250 MSRP for the 3-speed automatic transmission downgrade; NOT AVAILABLE in Calif., Mass., or New York		
24D	SE Option Package 24D (SE)	2346	2760
	Manufacturer Discount	(850)	(1000)
	Net Price	1496	1760
	Includes 3.0-liter V6 engine, air conditioning, rear window defroster, windshield wiper de-icer, and deluxe 7-passenger seating (includes		

DODGE CARAVAN

CODE	DESCRIPTION	INVOICE	MSRP
	middle and rear reclining and folding seats with adjustable headrests), power door locks, front/rear floor mats, light group (includes lighting for instrument panel storage bin, ash tray, glove box, and ignition switch), dual illuminated visor vanity mirrors with visor extensions, deluxe sound insulation, power front door windows, power rear quarter vent windows; pricing includes credit of $213 invoice and $250 MSRP for 3-speed automatic transmission downgrade; NOT AVAILABLE in Calif., Mass., or New York		
28B	SE Option Package 28B (SE)	1849	2175
	Manufacturer Discount	(595)	(700)
	Net Price	1254	1475
	Includes 3.3-liter V6 engine, air conditioning, rear window defroster, windshield wiper de-icer, and deluxe 7-passenger seating (includes middle and rear reclining and folding seats with adjustable headrests)		
28D	SE Option Package 28D (SE)	2729	3210
	Manufacturer Discount	(850)	(1000)
	Net Price	1879	2210
	Includes 3.3-liter V6 engine, air conditioning, rear window defroster, windshield wiper de-icer, deluxe 7-passenger seating (includes middle and rear reclining and folding seats with adjustable headrests), power door locks, front/rear floor mats, light group (includes lighting for instrument panel storage bin, ash tray, glove box, and ignition switch), dual illuminated visor vanity mirrors with visor extensions, deluxe sound insulation, power front door windows, power rear quarter vent windows		
CYE	Seating Group I (Base)	298	350
	Includes 7-passenger capacity with middle folding bench seat with armrest; INCLUDED in Base Option Packages		
CYR	Seating Group I (SE/LE/ES)	191	225
	Includes deluxe 7-passenger seating with integrated child safety seats (reclining and folding middle bench seat with adjustable headrests; reclining and folding rear bench with adjustable headrests); REQUIRES purchase of an Option Group Package		
CYK	Seating Group II (Base)	242	285
	Includes integrated child safety seats; REQUIRES purchase of an Option Package		
CYS	Seating Group II (LE/ES)	531	625
	Includes deluxe seating with middle folding/reclining bucket seats; rear folding/reclining bench seat with adjustable headrests; REQUIRES purchase of an Option Package		
CYS	Seating Group II (SE)	531	625
	Includes deluxe seating with middle folding/reclining bucket seats; rear folding/reclining bench seat with adjustable headrests; REQUIRES purchase of SE Option Package 24D, 28D, or Sport Option Package 28E; REQUIRES purchase of Driver Side Sliding Door		

CARAVAN — DODGE

CODE	DESCRIPTION	INVOICE	MSRP
AWS	Smoker's Group	17	20
	Includes cigarette lighter and 3 ash trays		
28C	Sport Option Package 28C (SE)	3158	3715
	Manufacturer Discount	(918)	(1080)
	Net Price	2240	2635

Includes 3.3-liter V6 engine, air conditioning, rear window defroster, windshield wiper de-icer, and deluxe 7-passenger seating (includes middle and rear reclining and folding seats with adjustable headrests), Sport decor group (includes Sport decals, body color door handles, body color fascias, fog lights, body color luggage rack, sunscreen and solar control windows, narrow body color bodyside moldings, leather-wrapped steering wheel, P215/65R16 all-season touring tires, 16-inch cast aluminum wheels, touring and handling group [solid rear sway bar, touring and handling suspension, upgraded front struts and rear shocks)

28E	Sport Option Package 28E (SE)	4038	4750
	Manufacturer Discount	(1173)	(1380)
	Net Price	2865	3370

Includes 3.3-liter V6 engine, air conditioning, rear window defroster, windshield wiper de-icer, and deluxe 7-passenger seating (includes middle and rear reclining and folding seats with adjustable headrests), Sport decor group (includes Sport decals, body color door handles, body color fascias, fog lights, body color luggage rack, sunscreen and solar control windows, narrow body color bodyside moldings, leather-wrapped steering wheel, P215/65R16 all-season touring tires, 16-inch cast aluminum wheels, touring and handling group [solid rear sway bar, touring and handling suspension, upgraded front struts and rear shocks]), power door locks, front/rear floor mats, light group (includes lighting for instrument panel storage bin, ash tray, glove box, and ignition switch), dual illuminated visor vanity mirrors with visor extensions, deluxe sound insulation, power front door windows, power rear quarter vent windows

RAS	Stereo w/cassette (Base)	153	180

AM/FM stereo with cassette player and 4 speakers; REQUIRES purchase of an Option Package

AAT	Touring Handling Package (LE)	349	410

Includes 16-inch cast aluminum wheels and touring and handling group (solid rear sway bar, P215/65R16 all-season touring tires, upgraded front struts and rear shocks); REQUIRES purchase of an Option Package

BNM	Traction Control (LE)	149	175

TO PRICE YOUR TRADE-IN,
PURCHASE EDMUND'S USED CAR PRICES AND RATINGS.

See page 6 for details.

DODGE DAKOTA

DAKOTA (1997)

1997 Dodge Dakota Sport 2WD Regular Cab

What's New for Dodge Dakota in 1997 — The entire truck, that's what. Powertrains are carried over, but everything else is new. Distinctions? Tightest turning circle in class, roomiest cabs, and dual airbags are standard. Faux pas? No third door option, and the passenger airbag cannot be deactivated, so a rear-facing child seat is out of the question unless you cram it into the rear of the Club Cab.

Dakota — Review

Frankly, the Dakota was getting about as stale as Halloween candy on April Fool's Day. The exterior was still ruggedly handsome, but the interior was an ergonomic throwback to 1980. SLT models had horrific fake wood that looked like it had been ripped from a 70s tract home basement. Seat comfort was marginal. The best thing the Dakota had going for it was an optional 5.2-liter V-8 engine and class-leading bed size.

Now that Chrysler is flush with cash, the Dakota has received a complete makeover for 1997. The most obvious difference is the styling of the new truck. Call it mini-Ram, inside and out. The exterior isn't as attractive as the Ram, mostly because the front end doesn't gel right thanks to a multitude of cutlines around the grille and headlight assemblies. From certain angles, the ellipsoidal grille looks tacked on rather than integrated with the lights and front bumper, giving the truck an oddly proportioned appearance.

Inside, user-friendly controls and displays pass the same work-glove ease-of-operation test that the Ram does. Seats are king-of-the-road high, and infinitely more comfortable. Club Cab models will carry up to six people. Dual airbags are standard, but it is important to note that the passenger airbag cannot be switched off. This means that rear-facing child safety seats can never be used in the front seat of a 1997 Dakota. Babies and young children will need to ride on the rear bench of the Club Cab model. Can't afford a Club Cab? Shop for a Ford Ranger or a Mazda B-Series. They've had passenger airbags since 1995, and they offer a switch to turn off the airbag. Kinda makes you wonder what Chrysler was thinking.

DAKOTA — DODGE

| CODE | DESCRIPTION | INVOICE | MSRP |

Here's another mystery. The Club Cab offers no third door option. Seems odd from the company that pioneered the fourth sliding door on minivans and is planning a 4-door full-size Ram Club Cab for 1998. To get this convenience, you've got to buy a Chevy S-10 or GMC Sonoma. Press materials indicate that the new Dakota is equipped with side door guard beams, but makes no mention that these beams pass 1999 side-impact standards for trucks. Why didn't engineers just but the stronger beams in from the get-go, rather than wait a couple of years? Dodge had a chance to build the perfect compact pickup, and blew it.

Still, it's a nice piece of work. Base, Sport, and SLT models are available. Regular cab 2WD models feature a 2.5-liter inline four-cylinder engine that provides 120 horsepower. Club Cab and 4WD models get a 3.9-liter V-6 good for 175 horsepower and 225 lb./ft. of torque. Optional on all models is a 5.2-liter V-8 engine that makes 230 horsepower and 300 lb./ft. of torque at 3,200 rpm. Crammed into a regular cab shortbed with 2WD, the V-8 transforms the Dakota into a storming sport truck.

Overall, the new Dakota is quite satisfying. However, we can't help but think some short-sighted thinking and cost-cutting went into the design because of the lack of several major safety and convenience features. Makes us wonder about the integrity of the stuff that isn't quite so obvious.

Safety Data

Driver Airbag: *Standard*
Side Airbag: *Not Available*
4-Wheel ABS: *Optional*
Driver Crash Test Grade: *Not Available*
Passenger Crash Test Grade: *Not Available*

Passenger Airbag: *Standard*
Meets 1999 Side Impact Standards: *No*
Traction Control: *Not Available*
Insurance Cost: *Not Available*
Integrated Child Seat(s): *Not Available*

Standard Equipment

DAKOTA BASE REGULAR CAB: 2.5-liter inline four-cylinder engine, 5-speed manual transmission, dual front airbags, trip odometer, power rack and pinion steering, 15"x 6" steel wheels, P215/75R15 BSW all-season tires, power front disc/rear drum brakes with rear anti-lock, 600 CCA battery, cigarette lighter, black painted front bumper, black painted rear step bumper, gray front and rear fascias, dark silver painted grille, black windshield molding, 117-amp generator, tinted glass, cab back carpeting, black rubber floor covering, 2 coat hooks, cloth headliner, dual cupholders, cloth sun visors, day/night rearview mirror, dual exterior mirrors, AM/FM stereo with cassette player, 4 speakers, and clock; vinyl bench seat, intermittent windshield wipers

BASE CLUB CAB (in addition to or instead of BASE REGULAR CAB equipment): Sunscreen quarter and rear window glass, front floor carpeting, 2-compartment floor storage module with cupholders and storage trays, easy-entry front passenger seat, cloth 40/20/40 split bench seat with recliners and integral head restraints, center armrest storage console, 60/40 split fold-up rear seat

DODGE DAKOTA

CODE	DESCRIPTION	INVOICE	MSRP

Base Prices

AN1L61	2WD Regular Cab Shortbed	11598	12725
AN1L62	2WD Regular Cab Longbed	12003	13185
AN5L61	4WD Regular Cab Shortbed	15562	17190
AN1L31	2WD Club Cab	14885	16420
AN5L31	4WD Club Cab	17797	19690
Destination Charge:		510	510

Accessories

23W	Base Package 23W (2WD Reg Cab)	469	552
	Includes 3.9-liter V-6 engine; REQUIRES 22-gallon Fuel Tank		
24W	Base Package 24W (2WD Reg Cab)	1277	1502
	Includes 3.9-liter V-6 engine and 4-speed automatic transmission; REQUIRES 22-gallon Fuel Tank		
24W	Base Package 24W (Club Cab/4WD Reg Cab)	808	950
	Includes 4-speed automatic transmission		
21W	Four-cylinder Engine Bonus Discount (2WD Reg Cab)	(595)	(700)
21W	Manual Transmission Bonus Discount (2WD)	(170)	(200)
23E	SLT Package 23E (2WD Reg Cab)	2665	3135
	Manufacturer Discount	(553)	(650)
	Net Price	2112	2485

Includes air conditioning, floor carpeting, SLT Decor (chrome bumpers, chrome grille, heavy-duty sound insulation package, storage tray, jack cover, passenger vanity mirror, 15"x 7" 5-spoke aluminum wheels), premium door panel trim, 22-gallon fuel tank, light group (ash tray light, courtesy light, cargo light, glove box light, auxiliary power outlet, underhood light), cloth 40/20/40 bench seat with center storage armrest, rallye gauge cluster with tachometer, P215/75R15 white letter all season tires, 3.9-liter V-6 engine

23E	SLT Package 23E (4WD Reg Cab)	2389	2811
	Manufacturer Discount	(553)	(650)
	Net Price	1836	2161

Includes air conditioning, floor carpeting, SLT Decor (chrome bumpers, chrome grille, heavy-duty sound insulation package, storage tray, jack cover, passenger vanity mirror, 15"x 7" 5-spoke aluminum wheels), premium door panel trim, 22-gallon fuel tank, light group (ash tray light, courtesy light, cargo light, glove box light, auxiliary power outlet, underhood light), cloth 40/20/40 bench seat with center storage armrest, rallye gauge cluster with tachometer, P235/75R15 outline white-lettered-all-season tires

DAKOTA — DODGE

CODE	DESCRIPTION	INVOICE	MSRP
23F	SLT Package 23F (2WD Club Cab)	1646	1936
	Manufacturer Discount	(850)	(1000)
	Net Price	796	936

Includes air conditioning, SLT Decor (chrome bumpers, chrome grille, heavy-duty sound insulation package, storage tray, jack cover, passenger vanity mirror, 15"x 7" 5-spoke aluminum wheels), premium door panel trim, 22-gallon fuel tank, light group (ash tray light, courtesy light, cargo light, glove box light, auxiliary power outlet, underhood light), rallye gauge cluster with tachometer, P215/75R15 white-lettered-all-season tires

23F	SLT Package 23F (4WD Club Cab)	1801	2119
	Manufacturer Discount	(850)	(1000)
	Net Price	951	1119

Includes air conditioning, SLT Decor (chrome bumpers, chrome grille, heavy-duty sound insulation package, storage tray, jack cover, passenger vanity mirror, 15"x 7" 5-spoke aluminum wheels), premium door panel trim, 22-gallon fuel tank, light group (ash tray light, courtesy light, cargo light, glove box light, auxiliary power outlet, underhood light), rallye gauge cluster with tachometer, P215/75R15 white-lettered-all-season tires

24E	SLT Package 24E (2WD Reg Cab)	3473	4085
	Manufacturer Discount	(553)	(650)
	Net Price	2920	3435

Includes air conditioning, floor carpeting, SLT Decor (chrome bumpers, chrome grille, heavy-duty sound insulation package, storage tray, jack cover, passenger vanity mirror, 15"x 7" 5-spoke aluminum wheels), premium door panel trim, 22-gallon fuel tank, light group (ash tray light, courtesy light, cargo light, glove box light, auxiliary power outlet, underhood light), cloth 40/20/40 bench seat with center storage armrest, rallye gauge cluster with tachometer, P215/75R15 white-lettered-all-season tires, 3.9-liter V-6 engine, 4-speed automatic transmission

24E	SLT Package 24E (4WD Reg Cab)	3197	3761
	Manufacturer Discount	(553)	(650)
	Net Price	2644	3111

Includes air conditioning, floor carpeting, SLT Decor (chrome bumpers, chrome grille, heavy-duty sound insulation package, storage tray, jack cover, passenger vanity mirror, 15"x 7" 5-spoke aluminum wheels), premium door panel trim, 22-gallon fuel tank, light group (ash tray light, courtesy light, cargo light, glove box light, auxiliary power outlet, underhood light), cloth 40/20/40 bench seat with center storage armrest, rallye gauge cluster with tachometer, P235/75R15 outline white-lettered-all-season tires, 4-speed automatic transmission

24F	SLT Package 24F (2WD Club Cab)	2454	2886
	Manufacturer Discount	(850)	(1000)
	Net Price	1604	1886

Includes air conditioning, SLT Decor (chrome bumpers, chrome grille, heavy-duty sound insulation package, storage tray, jack cover, passenger vanity mirror, 15"x 7" 5-spoke aluminum wheels), premium door panel trim, 22-gallon fuel tank, light group (ash tray light, courtesy light, cargo light, glove box light, auxiliary power outlet, underhood light), rallye gauge cluster with tachometer, P215/75R15 white-lettered-all-season tires-all-season tires, 4-speed automatic transmission

DODGE DAKOTA

CODE	DESCRIPTION	INVOICE	MSRP
24F	SLT Package 24F (4WD Club Cab)	2609	3069
	Manufacturer Discount	(850)	(1000)
	Net Price	1759	2069

Includes air conditioning, SLT Decor (chrome bumpers, chrome grille, heavy-duty sound insulation package, storage tray, jack cover, passenger vanity mirror, 15"x 7" 5-spoke aluminum wheels), premium door panel trim, 22-gallon fuel tank, light group (ash tray light, courtesy light, cargo light, glove box light, auxiliary power outlet, underhood light), rallye gauge cluster with tachometer, P215/75R15 white-lettered-all-season tires, 4-speed automatic transmission

25E	SLT Package 25E (2WD Reg Cab)	3164	3722
	Manufacturer Discount	(553)	(650)
	Net Price	2611	3072

Includes air conditioning, floor carpeting, SLT Decor (chrome bumpers, chrome grille, heavy-duty sound insulation package, storage tray, jack cover, passenger vanity mirror, 15"x 7" 5-spoke aluminum wheels), premium door panel trim, 22-gallon fuel tank, light group (ash tray light, courtesy light, cargo light, glove box light, auxiliary power outlet, underhood light), cloth 40/20/40 bench seat with center storage armrest, rallye gauge cluster with tachometer, P215/75R15 white-lettered, 5.2 liter V-8 engine

25E	SLT Package 25E (4WD Reg Cab)	2888	3398
	Manufacturer Discount	(553)	(650)
	Net Price	2335	2748

Includes air conditioning, floor carpeting, SLT Decor (chrome bumpers, chrome grille, heavy-duty sound insulation package, storage tray, jack cover, passenger vanity mirror, 15"x 7" 5-spoke aluminum wheels), premium door panel trim, 22-gallon fuel tank, light group (ash tray light, courtesy light, cargo light, glove box light, auxiliary power outlet, underhood light), cloth 40/20/40 bench seat with center storage armrest, rallye gauge cluster with tachometer, P235/75R15 white-lettered, 5.2 liter V-8 engine

25F	SLT Package 25F (2WD Club Cab)	2145	2523
	Manufacturer Discount	(850)	(1000)
	Net Price	1295	1523

Includes air conditioning, SLT Decor (chrome bumpers, chrome grille, heavy-duty sound insulation package, storage tray, jack cover, passenger vanity mirror, 15"x 7" 5-spoke aluminum wheels), premium door panel trim, 22-gallon fuel tank, light group (ash tray light, courtesy light, cargo light, glove box light, auxiliary power outlet, underhood light), rallye gauge cluster with tachometer, P215/75R15 white-lettered-all-season tires, 5.2-liter V-8 engine

25F	SLT Package 25F (4WD Club Cab)	2300	2706
	Manufacturer Discount	(850)	(1000)
	Net Price	1450	1706

Includes air conditioning, SLT Decor (chrome bumpers, chrome grille, heavy-duty sound insulation package, storage tray, jack cover, passenger vanity mirror, 15"x 7" 5-spoke aluminum wheels), premium door panel trim, 22-gallon fuel tank, light group (ash tray light, courtesy light, cargo light, glove box light, auxiliary power outlet, underhood light), rallye gauge cluster with tachometer, P215/75R15 white-lettered-all-season tires, 5.2-liter V-8 engine

DAKOTA — DODGE

CODE	DESCRIPTION	INVOICE	MSRP
26E	SLT Package 26E (2WD Reg Cab)	3972	4672
	Manufacturer Discount	(553)	(650)
	Net Price	3419	4022

Includes air conditioning, floor carpeting, SLT Decor (chrome bumpers, chrome grille, heavy-duty sound insulation package, storage tray, jack cover, passenger vanity mirror, 15"x 7" 5-spoke aluminum wheels), premium door panel trim, 22-gallon fuel tank, light group (ash tray light, courtesy light, cargo light, glove box light, auxiliary power outlet, underhood light), cloth 40/20/40 bench seat with center storage armrest, rallye gauge cluster with tachometer, P215/75R15 white-lettered-all-season tires, 5.2-liter V-8 engine, 4-speed automatic transmission

26E	SLT Package 26E (4WD Reg Cab)	3696	4348
	Manufacturer Discount	(553)	(650)
	Net Price	3143	3698

Includes air conditioning, floor carpeting, SLT Decor (chrome bumpers, chrome grille, heavy-duty sound insulation package, storage tray, jack cover, passenger vanity mirror, 15"x 7" 5-spoke aluminum wheels), premium door panel trim, 22-gallon fuel tank, light group (ash tray light, courtesy light, cargo light, glove box light, auxiliary power outlet, underhood light), cloth 40/20/40 bench seat with center storage armrest, rallye gauge cluster with tachometer, P235/75R15 outline white-lettered-all-season tires, 5.2-liter V-8 engine, 4-speed automatic transmission

26F	SLT Package 26F (2WD Club Cab)	2953	3473
	Manufacturer Discount	(850)	(1000)
	Net Price	2103	2473

Includes air conditioning, SLT Decor (chrome bumpers, chrome grille, heavy-duty sound insulation package, storage tray, jack cover, passenger vanity mirror, 15"x 7" 5-spoke aluminum wheels), premium door panel trim, 22-gallon fuel tank, light group (ash tray light, courtesy light, cargo light, glove box light, auxiliary power outlet, underhood light), rallye gauge cluster with tachometer, P215/75R15 white-lettered-all-season tires, 5.2-liter V-8 engine, 4-speed automatic

26F	SLT Package 26F (4WD Club Cab)	3108	3656
	Manufacturer Discount	(850)	(1000)
	Net Price	2258	2656

Includes air conditioning, SLT Decor (chrome bumpers, chrome grille, heavy-duty sound insulation package, storage tray, jack cover, passenger vanity mirror, 15"x 7" 5-spoke aluminum wheels), premium door panel trim, 22-gallon fuel tank, light group (ash tray light, courtesy light, cargo light, glove box light, auxiliary power outlet, underhood light), rallye gauge cluster with tachometer, P215/75R15 white-lettered-all-season tires, 5.2-liter V-8 engine, 4-speed automatic

DODGE DAKOTA

Code	Description	Invoice	MSRP
23G	SLT Plus Package 23G (2WD Club Cab)	2797	3291
	Manufacturer Discount	(1403)	(1650)
	Net Price	1394	1641

Includes air conditioning, SLT Decor (chrome bumpers, chrome grille, heavy-duty sound insulation package, storage tray, jack cover, passenger vanity mirror, 15"x 7" 5-spoke aluminum wheels), premium door panel trim, 22-gallon fuel tank, light group (ash tray light, courtesy light, cargo light, glove box light, auxiliary power outlet, underhood light), rallye gauge cluster with tachometer, P215/75R15 white-lettered-all-season tires, cruise control, tilt steering wheel, power windows, power door locks, remote keyless entry, power exterior mirrors, sliding rear window, security group (anti-theft system)

Code	Description	Invoice	MSRP
23G	SLT Plus Package 23G (4WD Club Cab)	2953	3474
	Manufacturer Discount	(1403)	(1650)
	Net Price	1550	1824

Includes air conditioning, SLT Decor (chrome bumpers, chrome grille, heavy-duty sound insulation package, storage tray, jack cover, passenger vanity mirror, 15"x 7" 5-spoke aluminum wheels), premium door panel trim, 22-gallon fuel tank, light group (ash tray light, courtesy light, cargo light, glove box light, auxiliary power outlet, underhood light), rallye gauge cluster with tachometer, 31x10.5 R15 outline white-lettered-all-season tires, cruise control, tilt steering wheel, power windows, power door locks, remote keyless entry, power exterior mirrors, security group (anti-theft system)

Code	Description	Invoice	MSRP
24G	SLT Plus Package 24G (2WD Club Cab)	3605	4241
	Manufacturer Discount	(1403)	(1650)
	Net Price	2202	2591

Includes air conditioning, SLT Decor (chrome bumpers, chrome grille, heavy-duty sound insulation package, storage tray, jack cover, passenger vanity mirror, 15"x 7" 5-spoke aluminum wheels), premium door panel trim, 22-gallon fuel tank, light group (ash tray light, courtesy light, cargo light, glove box light, auxiliary power outlet, underhood light), rallye gauge cluster with tachometer, P215/75R15 white-lettered-all-season tires, cruise control, tilt steering wheel, power windows, power door locks, remote keyless entry, power exterior mirrors, sliding rear window, security group (anti-theft system) 4-speed automatic transmission

Code	Description	Invoice	MSRP
24G	SLT Plus Package 24G (4WD Club Cab)	3761	4424
	Manufacturer Discount	(1403)	(1650)
	Net Price	2358	2774

Includes air conditioning, SLT Decor (chrome bumpers, chrome grille, heavy-duty sound insulation package, storage tray, jack cover, passenger vanity mirror, 15"x 7" 5-spoke aluminum wheels), premium door panel trim, 22-gallon fuel tank, light group (ash tray light, courtesy light, cargo light, glove box light, auxiliary power outlet, underhood light), rallye gauge cluster with tachometer, 31x10.5 R15 outline white-lettered-all-season tires, cruise control, tilt steering wheel, power windows, power door locks, remote keyless entry, power exterior mirrors, security group (anti-theft system), 4-speed automatic transmission

DAKOTA — DODGE

CODE	DESCRIPTION	INVOICE	MSRP
25G	SLT Plus Package 25G (2WD Club Cab)	3296	3878
	Manufacturer Discount	(1403)	(1650)
	Net Price	1893	2228

Includes air conditioning, SLT Decor (chrome bumpers, chrome grille, heavy-duty sound insulation package, storage tray, jack cover, passenger vanity mirror, 15"x 7" 5-spoke aluminum wheels), premium door panel trim, 22-gallon fuel tank, light group (ash tray light, courtesy light, cargo light, glove box light, auxiliary power outlet, underhood light), rallye gauge cluster with tachometer, P215/75R15 white-lettered-all-season tires, cruise control, tilt steering wheel, power windows, power door locks, remote keyless entry, power exterior mirrors, sliding rear window, security group (anti-theft system) 5.2-liter V-8 engine

25G	SLT Plus Package 25G (4WD Club Cab)	3452	4061
	Manufacturer Discount	(1403)	(1650)
	Net Price	2049	2411

Includes air conditioning, SLT Decor (chrome bumpers, chrome grille, heavy-duty sound insulation package, storage tray, jack cover, passenger vanity mirror, 15"x 7" 5-spoke aluminum wheels), premium door panel trim, 22-gallon fuel tank, light group (ash tray light, courtesy light, cargo light, glove box light, auxiliary power outlet, underhood light), rallye gauge cluster with tachometer, 31x10.5 R15 outline white-lettered-all-season tires, cruise control, tilt steering wheel, power windows, power door locks, remote keyless entry, power exterior mirrors, security group (anti-theft system), 5.2-liter V-8 engine

26G	SLT Plus Package 26G (2WD Club Cab)	4104	4828
	Manufacturer Discount	(1403)	(1650)
	Net Price	2701	3178

Includes air conditioning, SLT Decor (chrome bumpers, chrome grille, heavy-duty sound insulation package, storage tray, jack cover, passenger vanity mirror, 15"x 7" 5-spoke aluminum wheels), premium door panel trim, 22-gallon fuel tank, light group (ash tray light, courtesy light, cargo light, glove box light, auxiliary power outlet, underhood light), rallye gauge cluster with tachometer, P215/75R15 white-lettered-all-season tires, cruise control, tilt steering wheel, power windows, power door locks, remote keyless entry, power exterior mirrors, sliding rear window, security group (anti-theft system) 5.2-liter V-8 engine 4-speed automatic transmission

26G	SLT Plus Package 26G (4WD Club Cab)	4260	5011
	Manufacturer Discount	(1403)	(1650)
	Net Price	2857	3361

Includes air conditioning, SLT Decor (chrome bumpers, chrome grille, heavy-duty sound insulation package, storage tray, jack cover, passenger vanity mirror, 15"x 7" 5-spoke aluminum wheels), premium door panel trim, 22-gallon fuel tank, light group (ash tray light, courtesy light, cargo light, glove box light, auxiliary power outlet, underhood light), rallye gauge cluster with tachometer, 31x10.5 R15 outline white-lettered-all-season tires, cruise control, tilt steering wheel, power windows, power door locks, remote keyless entry, power exterior mirrors, security group (anti-theft system), 5.2-liter V-8 engine, 4-speed automatic transmission

DODGE — DAKOTA

CODE	DESCRIPTION	INVOICE	MSRP
23B	Sport Option Package 23B (2WD Reg Cab)	1821	2141
	Manufacturer Discount	(553)	(650)
	Net Price	1268	1491

Includes floor carpeting, premium door panel trim, cloth 40/20/40 bench seat with center storage armrest, Sport Package (body-color front and rear fascias, body-color grille, Sport graphics, 15"x 7" 5-spoke aluminum wheels), rallye gauge cluster with tachometer, P215/75R15 white-lettered-all-season tires, 3.9-liter V-6 engine

24B	Sport Option Package 24B (2WD Reg Cab)	2629	3091
	Manufacturer Discount	(553)	(650)
	Net Price	2076	2441

Includes floor carpeting, premium door panel trim, cloth 40/20/40 bench seat with center storage armrest, Sport Package (body-color front and rear fascias, body-color grille, Sport graphics, 15"x 7" 5-spoke aluminum wheels), rallye gauge cluster with tachometer, P215/75R15 white-lettered-all-season tires, 3.9-liter V-6 engine, 4-speed automatic transmission

25B	Sport Option Package 25B (2WD Reg Cab)	2320	2728
	Manufacturer Discount	(553)	(650)
	Net Price	1767	2078

Includes floor carpeting, premium door panel trim, cloth 40/20/40 bench seat with center storage armrest, Sport Package (body-color front and rear fascias, body-color grille, Sport graphics, 15"x 7" 5-spoke aluminum wheels), rallye gauge cluster with tachometer, P215/75R15 white-lettered-all-season tires, 5.2-liter V-8 engine

26B	Sport Option Package 26B (2WD Reg Cab)	3128	3678
	Manufacturer Discount	(553)	(650)
	Net Price	2575	3028

Includes floor carpeting, premium door panel trim, cloth 40/20/40 bench seat with center storage armrest, Sport Package (body-color front and rear fascias, body-color grille, Sport graphics, 15"x 7" 5-spoke aluminum wheels), rallye gauge cluster with tachometer, P215/75R15 white-lettered-all-season tires, 5.2-liter V-8 engine, 4-speed automatic transmission

21B	Sport Package 21B (2WD Reg Cab)	1335	1570
	Manufacturer Discount	(553)	(650)
	Net Price	782	920

Includes floor carpeting, premium door panel trim, cloth 40/20/40 bench seat with center storage armrest, Sport Package (body-color front and rear fascias, body-color grille, Sport graphics, 15"x 7" 5-spoke aluminum wheels), rallye gauge cluster with tachometer, P215/75R15 white-lettered-all-season tires

23B	Sport Package 23B (2WD Club Cab)	876	1030
	Manufacturer Discount	(850)	(1000)
	Net Price	26	30

Includes premium door panel trim, 22-gallon fuel tank, Sport Package (body-color front and rear fascias, body-color grille, Sport graphics, 15"x 7" 5-spoke aluminum wheels), rallye gauge cluster with tachometer, P215/75R15 white-lettered-all-season tires

DAKOTA — DODGE

CODE	DESCRIPTION	INVOICE	MSRP
23B	Sport Package 23B (4WD Club Cab)	1016	1195
	Manufacturer Discount	(850)	(1000)
	Net Price	166	195
	Includes premium door panel trim, 22-gallon fuel tank, Sport Package (body-color front and rear fascias, body-color grille, Sport graphics, 15"x 7" 5-spoke aluminum wheels), rallye gauge cluster with tachometer, P235/75R15 outline white-lettered-all-season tires		
23B	Sport Package 23B (4WD Reg Cab)	1539	1810
	Manufacturer Discount	(553)	(650)
	Net Price	986	1160
	Includes floor carpeting, premium door panel trim, cloth 40/20/40 bench seat with center storage armrest, Sport Package (body-color front and rear fascias, body-color grille, Sport graphics, 15"x 7" 5-spoke aluminum wheels), rallye gauge cluster with tachometer, P235/75R15 outline white-lettered-all-season tires		
24B	Sport Package 24B (2WD Club Cab)	1684	1980
	Manufacturer Discount	(850)	(1000)
	Net Price	834	980
	Includes premium door panel trim, 22-gallon fuel tank, Sport Package (body-color front and rear fascias, body-color grille, Sport graphics, 15"x 7" 5-spoke aluminum wheels), rallye gauge cluster with tachometer, P215/75R15 white-lettered-all-season tires, 4-speed automatic transmission		
24B	Sport Package 24B (4WD Club Cab)	1824	2145
	Manufacturer Discount	(850)	(1000)
	Net Price	974	1145
	Includes premium door panel trim, 22-gallon fuel tank, Sport Package (body-color front and rear fascias, body-color grille, Sport graphics, 15"x 7" 5-spoke aluminum wheels), rallye gauge cluster with tachometer, P235/75R15 outline white-lettered-all-season tires, 4-speed automatic transmission		
24B	Sport Package 24B (4WD Reg Cab)	2347	2760
	Manufacturer Discount	(553)	(650)
	Net Price	1794	2110
	Includes floor carpeting, premium door panel trim, cloth 40/20/40 bench seat with center storage armrest, Sport Package (body-color front and rear fascias, body-color grille, Sport graphics, 15"x 7" 5-spoke aluminum wheels), rallye gauge cluster with tachometer, P235/75R15 outline white-lettered-all-season tires, 4-speed automatic transmission		
25B	Sport Package 25B (2WD Club Cab)	1375	1617
	Manufacturer Discount	(850)	(1000)
	Net Price	525	617
	Includes premium door panel trim, 22-gallon fuel tank, Sport Package (body-color front and rear fascias, body-color grille, Sport graphics, 15"x 7" 5-spoke aluminum wheels), rallye gauge cluster with tachometer, P215/75R15 white-lettered-all-season tires, 5.2-liter V-8 engine		

DODGE DAKOTA

CODE	DESCRIPTION	INVOICE	MSRP
25B	Sport Package 25B (4WD Club Cab)	1515	1782
	Manufacturer Discount	(850)	(1000)
	Net Price	665	782

Includes premium door panel trim, 22-gallon fuel tank, Sport Package (body-color front and rear fascias, body-color grille, Sport graphics, 15"x 7" 5-spoke aluminum wheels), rallye gauge cluster with tachometer, P235/75R15 outline white-lettered-all-season tires, 5.2-liter V-8 engine

25B	Sport Package 25B (4WD Reg Cab)	2038	2397
	Manufacturer Discount	(553)	(650)
	Net Price	1485	1747

Includes floor carpeting, premium door panel trim, cloth 40/20/40 bench seat with center storage armrest, Sport Package (body-color front and rear fascias, body-color grille, Sport graphics, 15"x 7" 5-spoke aluminum wheels), rallye gauge cluster with tachometer, P235/75R15 outline white-lettered-all-season tires, 5.2-liter V-8 engine

26B	Sport Package 26B (2WD Club Cab)	2183	2567
	Manufacturer Discount	(850)	(1000)
	Net Price	1333	1567

Includes premium door panel trim, 22-gallon fuel tank, Sport Package (body-color front and rear fascias, body-color grille, Sport graphics, 15"x 7" 5-spoke aluminum wheels), rallye gauge cluster with tachometer, P215/75R15 white-lettered-all-season tires, 5.2-liter V-8 engine, 4-speed automatic transmission

26B	Sport Package 26B (4WD Club Cab)	2323	2732
	Manufacturer Discount	(850)	(1000)
	Net Price	1473	1732

Includes premium door panel trim, 22-gallon fuel tank, Sport Package (body-color front and rear fascias, body-color grille, Sport graphics, 15"x 7" 5-spoke aluminum wheels), rallye gauge cluster with tachometer, P235/75R15 outline white-lettered-all-season tires, 5.2-liter V-8 engine, 4-speed automatic transmission

26B	Sport Package 26B (4WD Reg Cab)	2846	3347
	Manufacturer Discount	(553)	(650)
	Net Price	2293	2697

Includes floor carpeting, premium door panel trim, cloth 40/20/40 bench seat with center storage armrest, Sport Package (body-color front and rear fascias, body-color grille, Sport graphics, 15"x 7" 5-spoke aluminum wheels), rallye gauge cluster with tachometer, P235/75R15 outline white-lettered-all-season tires, 5.2-liter V-8 engine, 4-speed automatic transmission

25H	Sport Plus Package 25H (4WD Club Cab)	3457	4067
	Manufacturer Discount	(1403)	(1650)
	Net Price	2054	2417

Includes premium door panel trim, 22-gallon fuel tank, Sport Package (body-color front and rear fascias, body-color grille, Sport graphics, 15"x 7" 5-spoke aluminum wheels), rallye gauge cluster with tachometer, 31x10.5 R15 outline white-lettered-all-season tires, air conditioning, cruise control, tilt steering wheel, fog lights, light group (ash tray light, courtesy light, cargo light, glove box light, auxiliary power outlet, underhood light), power exterior mirrors, cloth and vinyl bucket seats, sliding rear window, 5.2 liter V-8 engine

DAKOTA — DODGE

CODE	DESCRIPTION	INVOICE	MSRP
26H	Sport Plus Package 26H (4WD Club Cab)	4265	5017
	Manufacturer Discount	(1403)	(1650)
	Net Price	2862	3367

Includes premium door panel trim, 22-gallon fuel tank, Sport Package (body-color front and rear fascias, body-color grille, Sport graphics, 15"x 7" 5-spoke aluminum wheels), rallye gauge cluster with tachometer, 31x10.5 R15 outline white-lettered-all-season tires, air conditioning, cruise control, tilt steering wheel, fog lights, light group (ash tray light, courtesy light, cargo light, glove box light, auxiliary power outlet, underhood light), power exterior mirrors, cloth and vinyl high-back bucket seats, sliding rear window, 5.2-liter V-8 engine, 4-speed automatic transmission

CODE	DESCRIPTION	INVOICE	MSRP
NFB	22-gallon Fuel Tank	44	52
	INCLUDED in SLT Packages; INCLUDED in Sport Packages except on Regular Cab models		
HAA	Air Conditioning	677	797
	INCLUDED in Sport Plus, SLT and SLT Plus Packages		
BGK	Anti-lock Brakes	425	500
DSA	Axle — Sure Grip	242	285
	REQUIRES 3.55 or 3.90 Axle Ratio on 2WD models equipped with the V-8 engine and 4WD models equipped with the V-6 engine		
DMC	Axle Ratio — 3.21	NC	NC
	REQUIRES purchase of the V-6 or V-8 engine; NOT AVAILABLE with Calif./Mass./New York Emissions on 4WD models		
DMD	Axle Ratio — 3.55	33	39
	REQUIRES purchase of an SLT Package on 2WD Regular Cab Shortbed		
DMH	Axle Ratio — 3.90	33	39
K17	Bodyside Molding	64	75
	REQUIRES purchase of an SLT Package		
YCF	Border States Emissions	145	170
NAE	Calif./Mass./New York Emissions	145	170
AJK	Convenience Group — Deluxe	332	390
	Includes cruise control and tilt steering wheel; REQUIRES purchase of a Sport or SLT Package; INCLUDED in Sport Plus and SLT Plus Packages; NOT AVAILABLE with four-cylinder engine on 2WD Regular Cab models		
AJP	Convenience Group — Power	476	560
	Includes power windows, power door locks, and remote keyless entry; REQUIRES purchase of a Sport or SLT Package; INCLUDED in SLT Plus Packages and Power Overhead Convenience Group		
AJL	Convenience Group — Power Overhead	655	771
	With 23G (2WD Club Cab)	179	211
	With 23G (4WD Club Cab)	179	211
	With 24G (4WD Club Cab)	179	211
	With 24G (2WD Club Cab)	179	211

DODGE DAKOTA

CODE	DESCRIPTION	INVOICE	MSRP
	With 25G (2WD Club Cab)	179	211
	With 25G (4WD Club Cab)	179	211
	With 26G (4WD Club Cab)	179	211
	With 26G (2WD Club Cab)	179	211
	Includes overhead console with compass, temperature display, reading lamps, garage door opener compartment, and sunglasses holder; automatic dimming day/night rearview mirror, remote keyless entry system, power door locks, and power windows; REQUIRES purchase of a Sport or SLT package		
NHK	Engine Block Heater	29	34
CLA	Floor Mats	26	30
	Front only; REQUIRES purchase of a Sport or SLT Package		
LNJ	Fog Lights	102	120
	REQUIRES purchase of a Sport or SLT Package; INCLUDED in Sport Plus Packages		
ADH	Heavy-duty Electrical Group	102	120
	Includes 136-amp heavy-duty alternator and 750-amp maintenance-free battery; INCLUDED in Heavy-duty Service Group and Snow Plow Prep Group		
ADJ	Heavy-duty Service Group (2WD Club Cab)	200	235
	With 24W (Club Cab/4WD Reg Cab)	248	292
	With 23B (2WD Club Cab)	150	177
	With 23F (2WD Club Cab)	150	177
	With 23G (2WD Club Cab)	150	177
	With 25B (2WD Club Cab)	150	177
	With 25F (2WD Club Cab)	150	177
	With 25G (2WD Club Cab)	150	177
	With 24B (2WD Club Cab)	204	240
	With 24F (2WD Club Cab)	204	240
	With 24G (2WD Club Cab)	204	240
	With 26B (2WD Club Cab)	204	240
	With 26F (2WD Club Cab)	204	240
	With 26G (2WD Club Cab)	204	240
	Includes 136-amp alternator, 750-amp maintenance-free battery, rallye gauge package with tachometer, 22-gallon fuel tank, maximum engine cooling		
ADJ	Heavy-duty Service Group (2WD Reg Cab)	302	355
	With 23W (2WD Reg Cab)	244	287
	With 23B (2WD Reg Cab)	195	229
	With 25B (2WD Reg Cab)	195	229
	With 24B (2WD Reg Cab)	248	292
	With 26B (2WD Reg Cab)	248	292
	With 23E (2WD Reg Cab)	150	177
	With 25E (2WD Reg Cab)	150	177
	With 24E (2WD Reg Cab)	204	240
	With 26E (2WD Reg Cab)	204	240
	Includes 136-amp alternator, 750-amp maintenance-free battery, rallye gauge package with tachometer, 22-gallon fuel tank, maximum engine cooling; REQUIRES purchase of the V-6 or V-8 engine		

DAKOTA — DODGE

CODE	DESCRIPTION	INVOICE	MSRP
ADJ	Heavy-duty Service Group (4WD Club Cab)	200	235
	With 24W (Club Cab/4WD Reg Cab)	248	292
	With 23B (4WD Club Cab)	150	177
	With 23F (4WD Club Cab)	150	177
	With 23G (4WD Club Cab)	150	177
	With 25B (4WD Club Cab)	150	177
	With 25F (4WD Club Cab)	150	177
	With 25G (4WD Club Cab)	150	177
	With 25H (4WD Club Cab)	150	177
	With 24B (4WD Club Cab)	204	240
	With 24F (4WD Club Cab)	204	240
	With 24G (4WD Club Cab)	204	240
	With 26B (4WD Club Cab)	204	240
	With 26F (4WD Club Cab)	204	240
	With 26G (4WD Club Cab)	204	240
	With 26H (4WD Club Cab)	204	240

Includes 136-amp alternator, 750-amp maintenance-free battery, rallye gauge package with tachometer, 22-gallon fuel tank, maximum engine cooling

CODE	DESCRIPTION	INVOICE	MSRP
ADJ	Heavy-duty Service Group (4WD Reg Cab)	248	292
	With 24W (Club Cab/4WD Reg Cab)	302	355
	With 23B (4WD Reg Cab)	200	235
	With 25B (4WD Reg Cab)	200	235
	With 24B (4WD Reg Cab)	251	295
	With 26B (4WD Reg Cab)	251	295
	With 23E (4WD Reg Cab)	150	177
	With 25E (4WD Reg Cab)	150	177
	With 24E (4WD Reg Cab)	204	240
	With 26E (4WD Reg Cab)	204	240

Includes 136-amp alternator, 750-amp maintenance-free battery, rallye gauge package with tachometer, 22-gallon fuel tank, maximum engine cooling

CODE	DESCRIPTION	INVOICE	MSRP
RCK	Infinity Sound System	145	171

REQUIRES purchase of a Sport or SLT Package

CODE	DESCRIPTION	INVOICE	MSRP
ADA	Light Group	104	122

Includes ash tray light, courtesy light, cargo bed light, glovebox light, underhood light, and auxiliary power point; INCLUDED in Sport Plus and all SLT Packages

CODE	DESCRIPTION	INVOICE	MSRP
NMC	Maximum Engine Cooling	48	57
	With 24B (4WD Club Cab)	102	120
	With 24B (2WD Club Cab)	102	120
	With 24B (4WD Reg Cab)	102	120
	Without 24B (2WD Reg Cab)	102	120
	Without 24E (2WD Reg Cab)	102	120
	Without 24E (4WD Reg Cab)	102	120
	Without 24F (2WD Club Cab)	102	120
	Without 24F (4WD Club Cab)	102	120
	Without 24G (4WD Club Cab)	102	120

DODGE DAKOTA

CODE	DESCRIPTION	INVOICE	MSRP
	Without 24G (2WD Club Cab)	102	120
	Without 24W (Club Cab/4WD Reg Cab)	102	120
	Without 24W (2WD Reg Cab)	102	120
	Without 26B (2WD Reg Cab)	102	120
	Without 26B (2WD Club Cab)	102	120
	Without 26B (4WD Club Cab)	102	120
	Without 26B (4WD Reg Cab)	102	120
	Without 26E (2WD Club Cab)	102	120
	Without 26E (4WD Reg Cab)	102	120
	Without 26F (4WD Club Cab)	102	120
	Without 26F (2WD Club Cab)	102	120
	Without 26G (2WD Club Cab)	102	120
	Without 26G (4WD Club Cab)	102	120
	Without 26H (4WD Club Cab)	102	120
	INCLUDED in Heavy-duty Service Group		
Z1C	Payload Package — 1,800 lb. (2WD Reg Cab)	33	39
	REQUIRES purchase of the V-6 or V-8 engine; NOT AVAILABLE with Sport Packages		
Z5B	Payload Package — 1,800 lb. (4WD Club Cab)	11	13
	With 24F (4WD Club Cab)	33	39
	With 26F (4WD Club Cab)	33	39
	With 24G (4WD Club Cab)	33	39
	With 26G (4WD Club Cab)	33	39
	REQUIRES purchase of an SLT Package		
Z1D	Payload Package — 2,000 lb. (2WD Club Cab)	102	120
	Includes P235/75R15-XL BSW all-terrain tires; REQUIRES purchase of an SLT Package		
Z5C	Payload Package — 2,000 lb. (4WD Reg Cab)	11	13
	With 26E (4WD Reg Cab)	44	52
	NOT AVAILABLE with Sport or SLT Packages except SLT Package 26E		
Z1E	Payload Package — 2,600 lb. (2WD Reg Cab)	204	240
	With 23E (2WD Reg Cab)	98	115
	With 24E (2WD Reg Cab)	98	115
	With 25E (2WD Reg Cab)	98	115
	With 26E (2WD Reg Cab)	98	115
	REQUIRES purchase of the V-6 or V-8 engine; NOT AVAILABLE with Sport Packages		
GUR	Power Exterior Fixed Mirrors	119	140
	REQUIRES purchase of a Sport or SLT Package; INCLUDED in Sport Plus and SLT Plus packages		
GT4	Power Exterior Fold-away Mirrors	136	160
	With 23G (4WD Club Cab)	17	20
	With 23G (2WD Club Cab)	17	20
	With 24G (2WD Club Cab)	17	20
	With 24G (4WD Club Cab)	17	20
	With 25H (4WD Club Cab)	17	20

DAKOTA — DODGE

CODE	DESCRIPTION	INVOICE	MSRP
	With 26G (4WD Club Cab)	17	20
	With 26G (2WD Club Cab)	17	20
	With 26H (4WD Club Cab)	17	20
	REQUIRES purchase of a Sport or SLT Package		
GFD	Rear Sliding Window	98	115
	INCLUDED in Sport Plus and SLT Plus Packages		
M5	Seat — Cloth & Vinyl Buckets	170	200
	Includes center console; REQUIRES purchase of a Sport or SLT Package; INCLUDED in Sport Plus Packages		
G1C3	Seat — Deluxe Cloth & Vinyl Bench (Reg Cab)	45	53
	NOT AVAILABLE with Sport and SLT Packages		
AJB	Security Group	128	150
	Includes anti-theft system; REQUIRES Power Convenience Group and purchase of a Sport or SLT Package; INCLUDED in SLT Plus Packages		
RA8	Stereo — Delete Credit	(85)	(100)
	NOT AVAILABLE with Sport and SLT Packages		
RBN	Stereo — Premium w/cassette	255	300
	AM/FM stereo with cassette player, Infinity speakers and graphic equalizer; REQUIRES purchase of a Sport or SLT Package		
RAZ	Stereo — Premium w/CD player	560	659
	AM/FM stereo with CD player, Infinity speakers and graphic equalizer; REQUIRES purchase of a Sport or SLT Package		
RBR	Stereo — Uplevel w/CD player	407	479
	AM/FM stereo w/CD player and Infinity speakers; REQUIRES purchase of a Sport or SLT Package		
JAY	Tachometer	49	58
	REQUIRES purchase of a V-6 or V-8 engine on 2WD Regular Cab models; INCLUDED in Heavy-duty Service Group, Sport Packages, and SLT Packages		
SUA	Tilt Steering Wheel	119	140
	INCLUDED in Sport Plus and SLT Plus Packages; INCLUDED in Deluxe Convenience Group		
AGB	Tire & Handling Package (2WD Club Cab)	194	228
	Includes rear stabilizer bar, 15"x 8" cast aluminum wheels, and P235/70R15 all-season outline white-lettered tires; REQUIRES purchase of a Sport or SLT Package		

**TO PRICE YOUR TRADE-IN,
PURCHASE EDMUND'S USED CAR
PRICES AND RATINGS.**

See page 6 for details.

DODGE DAKOTA

CODE	DESCRIPTION	INVOICE	MSRP
TUT	Tires — 31x10.5 R15 (4WD)	339	399
	All-season outline white-lettered tires; Includes rear stabilizer bar, wheel flares, and 15"x 8" aluminum wheels; REQUIRES purchase of a Sport or SLT Package; NOT AVAILABLE with 3.21 Axle Ratio		
TSH	Tires — P235/70R15 (2WD Reg Cab)	173	203
	All-season outline white-lettered tires; Includes 15"x 8" aluminum wheels; REQUIRES purchase of a V-6 or V-8 engine; NOT AVAILABLE with Payload Packages		
TS1	Tires — P235/75R15 (2WD Club Cab)	162	190
	With 23B (2WD Club Cab)	53	62
	With 23F (2WD Club Cab)	53	62
	With 23G (2WD Club Cab)	53	62
	With 24B (2WD Club Cab)	53	62
	With 24F (2WD Club Cab)	53	62
	With 24G (2WD Club Cab)	53	62
	With 25B (2WD Club Cab)	53	62
	With 25F (2WD Club Cab)	53	62
	With 25G (2WD Club Cab)	53	62
	With 26B (2WD Club Cab)	53	62
	With 26F (2WD Club Cab)	53	62
	With 26G (2WD Club Cab)	53	62
	All-terrain blackwall tires		
TS1	Tires — P235/75R15 (2WD Reg Cab)	53	62
	All-terrain blackwall tires; REQUIRES purchase of a Sport or SLT Package		
TS1	Tires — P235/75R15 (4WD Club Cab)	156	184
	All-season blackwall tires; NOT AVAILABLE with Sport or SLT Packages		
AHC	Trailer Tow Group (All except 2WD Reg Cab Shortbed)	206	242
	Includes Class IV trailer hitch receiver and 4-wire adaptor; REQUIRES Heavy-duty Service Group; REQUIRES purchase of a V-6 or V-8 engine on 2WD Regular Cab Longbed models; NOT AVAILABLE with Valence Panel		
QFA	Two-tone Paint	166	195
ADL	Underbody Protection Group (4WD)	110	129
	Includes front deflector shield and skid plates for fuel tank, transfer case, and front axle		
MBV	Valence Panel	43	51
	REQUIRES purchase of a Sport Package; NOT AVAILABLE with Trailer Tow Group		

For a guaranteed low price on a new vehicle in your area, call

1-800-CAR-CLUB

GRAND CARAVAN — DODGE

| CODE | DESCRIPTION | INVOICE | MSRP |

GRAND CARAVAN *(1997)*

1997 Dodge Grand Caravan ES

What's New for Dodge Grand Caravan in 1997 — After a one year hiatus, all-wheel drive returns to the lineup, available on SE and LE models. Traction control is newly available, and an enhanced accident response system will automatically unlock the doors and illuminate the interior when an airbag deployment is detected. A Sport decor group is newly available on Grand Caravan SE.

Grand Caravan — Review

Who's the minivan champ? Why, Chrysler Corporation is, of course. They pioneered the concept of a 7-passenger box-on-wheels way back in 1984, and have dominated this market since. Last year, the Chrysler minivans received a complete makeover that instantly relegated newcomers Ford Windstar and Honda Odyssey to runner-up status.

Dodge's interpretation of the minivan concept doesn't look much different from Plymouth's. That's because it differs little in design and engineering, but Dodge offers a broader selection of models: base, SE, and top-of-the-line LE. LE models can be ordered with an ES trim package that includes traction control, alloy wheels, special exterior trim, and a firmer suspension. SE models get a new Sport trim package for 1997, which is similar to ES trim with the exception of traction control.

A 2.4-liter four-cylinder engine is standard on base and SE models, but these sizable vans benefit from little extra oomph. Acceleration with the 3.3-liter engine (standard in the LE) is pretty strong from startup, but sometimes unimpressive when merging into an expressway. Many buyers are likely to elect the more potent 3.8-liter V-6 instead. Automatic-transmission shifts are neat and smooth. Engine and tire sounds are virtually absent.

Though tautly suspended, the ride is seldom harsh or jarring, unless you get onto truly rough surfaces. Even then, the seven-passenger minivan behaves itself well. Light steering-wheel response makes handling even more car-like than in the past. Visibility is great, courtesy of more glass and a reduced-height cowl. Dodge claims that 85 percent of controls can be reached "without leaning."

DODGE GRAND CARAVAN

An innovative left-side sliding door has attracted plenty of notice, and with good cause—it's an idea whose time clearly has come. Better yet, its sliding track is hidden at the base of the glass. Also tempting is the available electric windshield-wiper de-icer. A rollaway rear seat is handy, but it still weighs 95 pounds, so removal can be a chore. A new handle for the liftgate makes it easier to close. Outboard seatbelts are height adjustable, in both the front and middle positions. Front-seat occupants enjoy loads of leg, head, and elbow room.

So, how do engineers improve a nearly perfect package for 1997? By offering an all-wheel drive (AWD) model in SE and LE trim. The Grand Caravan AWD includes standard four-wheel disc brakes. All Grand Caravan LE models can be equipped with traction control and automatic load-leveling suspension. Also new is an accident response system designed to unlock the doors and illuminate the interior moments after an airbag deploys. Minor updates include revised automatic transmission software, enhanced interior quietness, more affordable quad-seating for the SE, a refined cassette stereo, a cargo area power outlet, and liftgate flood lamps

This minivan exhibits not a hint of looseness, squeaks, or rattles, feeling tight all over. Ford's Windstar is the strongest challenger, but we think that the Grand Caravan is the superior minivan.

Safety Data

Driver Airbag: *Standard*
Side Airbag: *Not Available*
4-Wheel ABS: *Opt. (Base); Std. (ES/LE/SE)*

Driver Crash Test Grade: *Average*
Passenger Crash Test Grade: *Good*

Passenger Airbag: *Standard*
Meets 1997 Car Side Impact Standards: *Yes*
Traction Control: *N/A (Base/SE/AWD); Opt. (ES 2WD/LE 2WD)*
Insurance Cost: *Very Low (Base/SE); Low (ES/LE)*
Integrated Child Seat(s): *Optional*

Standard Equipment

GRAND CARAVAN: 2.4-liter inline four-cylinder engine, 3-speed automatic transmission, dual front airbags, power rack and pinion steering, power front disc/rear drum brakes, 14"x 6" steel wheels, P205/75R14 all-season BSW tires, 5-mph front/rear bumpers, 8 cupholders, sliding door child protection locks, dynamic side impact protection, body color fascias with molded accent strip, black liftgate light bar, narrow bodyside accent color moldings, tinted windows, black door handles, liftgate closing assist handle, sliding door closing assist handle, full length carpeting, 4 coat hooks, cloth sunvisors with covered mirrors, front courtesy/reading lights, rear cargo dome light, dual liftgate flood lights, sliding side door hold-open latch, day/night rearview mirror, exterior folding mirrors with manual operation, 12-volt power outlets in dashboard and cargo area, AM/FM stereo with clock and 4 speakers, cloth seat fabric, manual reclining high-back buckets seats with folding armrests, easy-out roller seats, 7-passenger seating with center bench and rear folding bench, instrument panel storage bin, covered center and rear quarter panel storage bins, 14-inch wheel covers, manual quarter vent windows, rear wiper/washer with intermittent and speed-sensitive operation, 2-speed windshield wipers with speed-sensitive variable delay

SE (in addition to or instead of GRAND CARAVAN equipment): 4-speed automatic transmission, 15"x 6.5" steel wheels, P215/65R15 all-season BSW tires, four-wheel anti-lock brakes, accent color liftgate moldings, wide accent color bodyside moldings, 2 seatback assist straps, middle passenger vent outlets, dual note horn, cloth door and quarter panel bolsters, power heated exterior folding mirrors, AM/FM stereo with cassette player, clock, and 4 speakers; front door

GRAND CARAVAN — DODGE

trim panel reflectors, middle bench seat with folding armrests, deluxe sound insulation, cruise control, tilt steering column, quarter panel cargo net, underseat locking storage drawer, 15-inch deluxe wheel covers

SE AWD (in addition to or instead of SE equipment): 3.8-liter V6 engine, all-wheel drive, four-wheel disc brakes, load-leveling suspension, P215/70R15 all-season BSW tires, body color liftgate light bar

LE (in addition to or instead of SE equipment): Overhead console with compass, thermometer, trip computer, sunglass storage, and garage door opener storage; rear window defroster, windshield wiper de-icer, power door locks, lower bodyside accent color applique, body color liftgate light bar, bodyside accent color paint stripe, body color door handles, front air conditioning, acoustically improved carpeting, front/rear carpeted floor mats, sliding sunvisor extensions, premium cloth door and quarter panel bolsters, remote keyless entry with panic alarm, illuminated entry, and headlight delay timer; front door courtesy lamps, middle seat courtesy/reading lamps, light group (includes instrument panel storage bin light, ash tray light, ignition switch light, glovebox light), premium cloth seat fabric, adjustable front head restraints, folding and reclining middle and rear bench seats, second sliding door on driver's side, premium sound insulation, covered instrument panel storage bin with audio inserts, passenger seatback map pocket, 15-inch premium wheel covers, power front door windows with driver's one-touch down feature, power vented rear quarter windows

LE AWD (in addition to or instead of LE equipment): 3.8-liter V6 engine, all-wheel drive, four-wheel disc brakes, load-leveling suspension P215/70R15 all-season BSW tires

ES (in addition to or instead of LE equipment): Heavy load/firm ride suspension, rear sway bar, wide body color bodyside molding, sill moldings, gold liftgate nameplate, tape stripe, side window outline, fog lights, P215/65R16 touring tires, cast aluminum wheels with gold accents

ES AWD (in addition to or instead of ES equipment): 3.8-liter V6 engine, all-wheel drive, four-wheel disc brakes, load-leveling suspension P215/70R15 all-season BSW tires

Base Prices

Code	Description	Invoice	MSRP
NSKL53	Base	16910	18580
NSKH53	SE	18824	20755
NSKP53	LE	23356	25905
NSKP53	ES	23876	26495
NSDH53	SE AWD	22978	25475
NSDP53	LE AWD	26142	29070
NSDP53	ES AWD	26608	29600
	Destination Charge:	580	580

Accessories

Code	Description	Invoice	MSRP
WJA	Aluminum Wheels (15-inch) (SE)	353	415
	REQUIRES purchase of an SE or SE AWD Option Package; INCLUDED in Sport Option Packages		
WNR	Aluminum Wheels (16-inch) (LE 2WD/AWD)	349	410
	REQUIRES purchase of an Option Package		
BGF	Anti-lock Brakes (Base)	480	565

DODGE — GRAND CARAVAN

CODE	DESCRIPTION	INVOICE	MSRP
22T	Base Option Package 22T (Base)	765	900
	Manufacturer Discount	(731)	(860)
	Net Price	34	40
	Includes air conditioning, dual note horn, rear floor silencer pad, and under seat storage drawer		
24T	Base Option Package 24T (Base)	1420	1670
	Manufacturer Discount	(731)	(860)
	Net Price	689	810
	Includes 3.0-liter V6 engine, air conditioning, dual note horn, rear floor silencer pad, and under seat storage drawer; NOT AVAILABLE in Calif., Mass., or New York		
28T	Base Option Package 28T (Base)	1802	2120
	Manufacturer Discount	(731)	(860)
	Net Price	1071	1260
	Includes 3.3-liter V6 engine, 4-speed automatic transmission, air conditioning, dual note horn, rear floor silencer pad, and under seat storage drawer; AVAILABLE only in Calif., Mass., and New York		
YCF	Border State Emissions (2WD/AWD)	145	170
	REQUIRES purchase of an Option Package on AWD models		
NAE	Calif./Mass./New York Emissions (2WD/AWD)	145	170
	REQUIRES purchase of an Option Package on AWD models		
PH2	Candy Apple Red Paint (ES 2WD/AWD)	170	200
	REQUIRES purchase of an Option Package		
PH2	Candy Apple Red Paint (LE 2WD/AWD)	170	200
	REQUIRES purchase of an Option Package on AWD models		
PH2	Candy Apple Red Paint (SE)	170	200
	REQUIRES purchase of a Sport Option Package		
HAA	Climate Group I (Base/SE)	731	860
	Includes front air conditioning; INCLUDED in Option Packages		
AAA	Climate Group II (Base/SE 2WD/AWD)	383	450
	Includes sunscreen/solar control glass and windshield wiper de-icer; REQUIRES purchase of a Base, SE, or SE AWD Option Package; INCLUDED in Sport Option Packages		
AAB	Climate Group III (ES 2WD/AWD)	344	405
	Includes rear heater and air conditioning; REQUIRES purchase of an Option Package 23B		
AAB	Climate Group III (LE 2WD/AWD)	400	470
	Includes rear heater and air conditioning; REQUIRES purchase of an Option Package		
AAB	Climate Group III (SE)	961	1130
	With 28C (SE)	523	615
	With 24D (SE)	867	1020
	With 28D (SE)	867	1020
	With 28E (SE)	429	505
	Includes sunscreen/solar control glass, windshield wiper de-icer, rear heater, dual-zone temperature control air conditioning, overhead console without trip computer; REQUIRES purchase of an Option Package; NOT AVAILABLE with SE Option		

GRAND CARAVAN — DODGE

CODE	DESCRIPTION	INVOICE	MSRP
AAB	**Climate Group III (SE AWD)**	867	1020
	Includes sunscreen/solar control windows, windshield wiper de-icer, rear heater, dual-zone temperature control air conditioning, and overhead console without trip computer; REQUIRES purchase of an Option Package		
AAC	**Convenience/Security Group I (Base)**	370	435
	Includes cruise control, tilt steering column, and power exterior mirrors; REQUIRES purchase of a Base Option Package		
AAE	**Convenience/Security Group II (Base)**	638	750
	Includes cruise control, tilt steering column, power exterior mirrors, and power door locks; REQUIRES purchase of a Base Option Package		
AAE	**Convenience/Security Group II (SE)**	268	315
	Includes power door locks; INCLUDED in SE Option Packages 24D, 28D and Sport Option Package 28E		
AAF	**Convenience/Security Group III (SE)**	582	685
	Includes power door locks, power front door windows, power rear quarter vent windows; INCLUDED in SE Option Packages 24D, 28D, and in Sport Option Package 28E		
AAG	**Convenience/Security Group IV (SE 2WD/AWD)**	200	235
	Includes remote keyless entry, illuminated entry, and headlight-off delay feature; REQUIRES purchase of SE Option Package 24D or 28D, Sport Option Package 28E, or SE AWD Option Package 29D		
AAH	**Convenience/Security Group V (LE/ES 2WD/AWD)**	128	150
	Includes security alarm		
AAH	**Convenience/Security Group V (SE)**	327	385
	Includes remote keyless entry, illuminated entry, headlight-off delay feature, and security alarm; REQUIRES purchase of SE Option Package 24D or 28D, Sport Option Package 28E, or SE AWD Option Package 29D		
GKD	**Driver Side Sliding Door (Base/SE)**	506	595
	REQUIRES purchase of an Option Package		
NHK	**Engine Block Heater (2WD/AWD)**	30	35
	REQUIRES purchase of an Option Package on AWD models		
29M	**ES AWD Option Package (ES AWD)**	1135	1335
	Manufacturer Discount	(570)	(670)
	Net Price	565	665
	Includes dual-zone air conditioning temperature control, sunscreen and solar control windows, AM/FM stereo with cassette player, equalizer, CD changer controls, and 10 Infinity speakers; power driver's seat with 8-way adjustment, automatic day/night rearview mirror, front passenger assist strap, leather-wrapped steering wheel		
28M	**ES Option Package 28M (ES)**	1284	1510
	Manufacturer Discount	(646)	(760)
	Net Price	638	750
	Includes dual-zone temperature control air conditioning, sunscreen and solar control windows, AM/FM stereo with cassette player, equalizer, CD changer controls, and 10 Infinity speakers; power driver's seat with 8-way adjustment, automatic day/night rearview mirror, front passenger assist strap, leather-wrapped steering wheel, low-speed traction control		

EDMUND'S 1997 NEW TRUCKS — http://edmunds.com

DODGE GRAND CARAVAN

CODE	DESCRIPTION	INVOICE	MSRP
29M	ES Option Package 29M (ES)	1560	1835
	Manufacturer Discount	(646)	(760)
	Net Price	914	1075
	Includes 3.8-liter V6 engine, dual-zone temperature control air conditioning, sunscreen and solar control windows, AM/FM stereo with cassette player, equalizer, CD changer controls, and 10 Infinity speakers; power driver's seat with 8-way adjustment, automatic day/night rearview mirror, front passenger assist strap, leather-wrapped steering wheel, low-speed traction control		
PWP	Golden White Pearl Paint (ES 2WD/AWD)	170	200
	REQUIRES purchase of an Option Package		
29K	LE AWD Option Package 29K (LE AWD)	1012	1190
	Manufacturer Discount	(646)	(760)
	Net Price	366	430
	Includes dual-zone air conditioning temperature control, sunscreen and solar control windows, AM/FM stereo with cassette player, equalizer, CD changer controls, and 10 Infinity speakers; power driver's seat with 8-way adjustment		
28K	LE Option Package 28K (LE)	1012	1190
	Manufacturer Discount	(646)	(760)
	Net Price	366	430
	Includes dual-zone temperature control air conditioning, sunscreen and solar control windows, AM/FM stereo with cassette player, equalizer, CD changer controls, and 10 Infinity speakers; power driver's seat with 8-way adjustment		
29K	LE Option Package 29K (LE)	1288	1515
	Manufacturer Discount	(646)	(760)
	Net Price	642	755
	Includes 3.8-liter V6 engine, dual-zone temperature control air conditioning, sunscreen and solar control windows, AM/FM stereo with cassette player, equalizer, CD changer controls, and 10 Infinity speakers; power driver's seat with 8-way adjustment		
—	Leather Seats (LE/ES 2WD/AWD)	757	890
	REQUIRES Seating Group II; REQUIRES purchase of an Option Package on ES and AWD models		
SER	Load-leveling Suspension (LE/ES)	247	290
	REQUIRES purchase of an Option Package		
SER	Load-leveling Suspension (SE)	247	290
	REQUIRES purchase of SE Option Package 24D, 28D, or Sport Package 28E		
TBB	Loading & Towing Group I (2WD/AWD)	94	110
	Includes conventional spare tire; REQUIRES purchase of an Option Package		
AAP	Loading & Towing Group II (ES)	123	145
	Includes conventional spare tire, and heavy load/firm ride suspension; REQUIRES purchase of an Option Package		

GRAND CARAVAN — DODGE

CODE	DESCRIPTION	INVOICE	MSRP
AAP	Loading & Towing Group II (LE)	153	180
	With AAT (LE)	123	145
	Includes conventional spare tire, and heavy load/firm ride suspension; REQUIRES purchase of an Option Package		
AAP	Loading & Towing Group II (SE)	153	180
	Includes conventional spare tire and heavy load/firm ride suspension; REQUIRES purchase of an SE Option Package; NOT AVAILABLE with Sport Option Packages		
AAR	Loading & Towing Group III (ES 2WD/AWD)	293	345
	Includes conventional spare tire, heavy load/firm ride suspension, and trailer tow group (includes 120-amp alternator, 685 CCA battery, heavy duty front disc/rear drum brakes, heavy duty radiator, trailer tow wiring harness, heavy duty transmission oil cooler); REQUIRES purchase of an Option Package		
AAR	Loading & Towing Group III (LE 2WD/AWD)	378	445
	With AAT (LE)	349	410
	With AAB (LE 2WD/AWD)	323	380
	Includes conventional spare tire, heavy load/firm ride suspension, and trailer tow group (includes 120-amp alternator, 685 CCA battery, heavy duty front disc/rear drum brakes, heavy duty radiator, trailer tow wiring harness, heavy duty transmission oil cooler); REQUIRES purchase of an Option Package		
AAR	Loading & Towing Group III (SE 2WD/AWD)	378	445
	With AAB (SE)	323	380
	With AAB (SE AWD)	323	380
	Includes conventional spare tire, heavy load/firm ride suspension, 120-amp alternator, 685 CCA battery, heavy duty front disc/rear drum brakes, heavy duty radiator, trailer tow wiring harness, heavy duty transmission oil cooler; REQUIRES purchase of SE Option Package 28D, Sport Option Package 28E, or SE AWD Option Package 29D		
MWG	Luggage Rack (2WD/AWD)	149	175
	REQUIRES purchase of an Option Package; INCLUDED in Sport Option Packages		
RBN	Premium Stereo w/cassette (SE 2WD/AWD)	276	325
	AM/FM stereo with cassette player, equalizer, CD changer controls, and 10 Infinity speakers; REQUIRES purchase of SE Option Package 24D or 28D, Sport Package 28E, or SE AWD Option Package 29D		
RAZ	Premium Stereo w/cassette & CD player (LE/ES 2WD/AWD)	336	395
	AM/FM stereo with cassette and CD player, equalizer, and 10 Infinity speakers; REQUIRES purchase of an Option Package		
RAZ	Premium Stereo w/cassette & CD player (SE 2WD/AWD)	612	720
	AM/FM stereo with cassette and CD player, equalizer, CD changer controls, and 10 Infinity speakers; REQUIRES purchase of SE Option Package 24D or 28D, Sport Package 28E, or SE AWD Option Package 29D		
GFA	Rear Window Defroster (Base)	196	230
	Without AAC (Base)	166	195
	Without AAE (Base)	166	195
	Includes windshield wiper de-icer; REQUIRED in New York State		

DODGE GRAND CARAVAN

CODE	DESCRIPTION	INVOICE	MSRP
29D	SE AWD Option Package 29D (SE AWD)	1904	2240
	Manufacturer Discount	(850)	(1000)
	Net Price	1054	1240
	Includes air conditioning, rear window defroster, windshield wiper de-icer, deluxe 7-passenger seating (includes middle and rear reclining and folding seats with adjustable headrests), power door locks, front/rear floor mats, dual illuminated visor vanity mirrors with visor extensions, deluxe sound insulation, power front door windows, power rear quarter vent windows		
23B	SE Option Package 23B (SE)	1024	1205
	Manufacturer Discount	(595)	(700)
	Net Price	429	505
	Includes air conditioning, rear defroster, windshield wiper de-icer, 7-passenger deluxe seating (includes folding and reclining middle and rear bench seats with adjustable headrests)		
24A	SE Option Package 24A (SE)	442	520
	Includes 3.0-liter V6 engine and 3-speed automatic transmission; pricing includes a credit of $213 invoice and $250 MSRP for the 3-speed transmission downgrade; NOT AVAILABLE in Calif., Mass., or New York		
24B	SE Option Package 24B (SE)	1466	1725
	Manufacturer Discount	(595)	(700)
	Net Price	871	1025
	Includes 3.0-liter V6 engine, 3-speed automatic transmission, air conditioning, rear defroster, windshield wiper de-icer, 7-passenger deluxe seating (includes folding and reclining middle and rear bench seats with adjustable headrests); pricing includes credit of $213 invoice and $250 MSRP for 3-speed automatic transmission downgrade; NOT AVAILABLE in Calif., Mass., or New York		
24D	SE Option Package 24D (SE)	2346	2760
	Manufacturer Discount	(850)	(1000)
	Net Price	1496	1760
	Includes 3.0-liter V6 engine, 3-speed automatic transmission, air conditioning, rear defroster, windshield wiper de-icer, 7-passenger deluxe seating (includes folding and reclining middle and rear bench seats with adjustable headrests), light group (includes lighting for instrument panel storage bin, ash tray, glovebox, and ignition switch), power door locks, front/rear floor mats, dual illuminated visor vanity mirrors with visor extensions, deluxe sound insulation, power front door windows, power rear quarter vent windows; pricing includes credit of $213 invoice and $250 MSRP for 3-speed automatic transmission downgrade; NOT AVAILABLE in Calif., Mass., New York		
28B	SE Option Package 28B (SE)	1849	2175
	Manufacturer Discount	(595)	(700)
	Net Price	1254	1475
	Includes 3.3-liter V6 engine, air conditioning, rear defroster, windshield wiper de-icer, 7-passenger deluxe seating (includes folding and reclining middle and rear bench seats with adjustable headrests)		

GRAND CARAVAN — DODGE

CODE	DESCRIPTION	INVOICE	MSRP
28D	SE Option Package 28D (SE)	2729	3210
	Manufacturer Discount	(850)	(1000)
	Net Price	1879	2210

Includes 3.3-liter V6 engine, air conditioning, rear defroster, windshield wiper de-icer, 7-passenger deluxe seating (includes folding and reclining middle and rear bench seats with adjustable headrests), light group (includes lighting for instrument panel storage bin, ash tray, glovebox, and ignition switch), power door locks, front/rear floor mats, dual illuminated visor vanity mirrors with visor extensions, deluxe sound insulation, power front door windows, power rear quarter vent windows

CYK	Seating Group I (Base)	242	285

Includes integrated child safety seats; REQUIRES purchase of a Base Option Package

CYR	Seating Group I (SE/LE/ES 2WD/AWD)	191	225

Includes integrated child safety seats; REQUIRES purchase of an Option Package

CYS	Seating Group II (LE/ES 2WD/AWD)	531	625

Includes 7-passenger deluxe quad buckets (middle folding and reclining bucket seats with armrests); REQUIRES purchase of an Option Package

CYS	Seating Group II (SE 2WD/AWD)	531	625

Includes 7-passenger deluxe quad buckets (middle folding and reclining bucket seats with armrests); REQUIRES purchase of SE Option Package 24D or 28D, Sport Option Package 28E, or SE AWD Option Package 29D

AWS	Smoker's Group (2WD/AWD)	17	20

Includes cigarette lighter and three ash trays; REQUIRES purchase of an Option Package on AWD models

28C	Sport Option Package 28C (SE)	3158	3715
	Manufacturer Discount	(918)	(1080)
	Net Price	2240	2635

Includes 3.3-liter V6 engine, air conditioning, rear defroster, windshield wiper de-icer, 7-passenger deluxe seating (includes folding and reclining middle and rear bench seats with adjustable headrests), Sport decor group (includes Sport decals, body color door handles, body color fascias, fog lights, body color luggage rack, sunscreen and solar control windows, touring & handling group [solid rear sway bar, touring & handling suspension, upgraded front struts and rear shocks], narrow body color bodyside moldings, leather-wrapped steering wheel, P215/65R16 all-season touring tires, 16-inch cast aluminum wheels

28E	Sport Option Package 28E (SE)	4038	4750
	Manufacturer Discount	(1173)	(1380)
	Net Price	2865	3370

Includes 3.3-liter V6 engine, air conditioning, rear defroster, windshield wiper de-icer, 7-passenger deluxe seating (includes folding and reclining middle and rear bench seats with adjustable headrests), Sport decor group (includes Sport decals, body color door handles, body color fascias, fog lights, body color luggage rack, sunscreen and solar control windows, touring & handling group [solid rear sway bar, touring & handling suspension, upgraded front struts and rear shocks], narrow body color bodyside moldings, leather-wrapped steering wheel, P215/65R16 all-season

DODGE — GRAND CARAVAN

CODE	DESCRIPTION	INVOICE	MSRP
	touring tires, 16-inch cast aluminum wheels), light group (includes lighting for instrument panel storage bin, ash tray, glovebox, and ignition switch), power door locks, front/rear floor mats, dual illuminated visor vanity mirrors with visor extensions, deluxe sound insulation, power front door windows, power rear quarter vent windows		
RAS	Stereo w/cassette (Base)	153	180
	AM/FM stereo with cassette player and 4 speakers; REQUIRES purchase of an Option Package		
AAT	Touring Handling Group (LE)	349	410
	Includes 16-inch cast aluminum wheels and touring & handling group (solid rear sway bar, touring & handling suspension, P215/65R16 all-season touring tires, upgraded front struts and rear shocks); REQUIRES purchase of an Option Package		
BNM	Traction Control (LE)	149	175

For expert advice in selecting/buying/leasing a new car, call
1-900-AUTOPRO
($2.00 per minute)

One 15-minute call could save you 15% or more on car insurance.

GEICO DIRECT

America's 6th Largest Automobile Insurance Company
1-800-555-2758

RAM 1500 *(1997)*

1997 Dodge Ram Club Cab 1500 4WD

What's New for Dodge Ram 1500 in 1997 — No major changes to this popular truck for 1997. Refinements include available leather seating and woodgrain trim on SLT models, optional remote keyless entry, and standard deep-tinted quarter glass on Club Cab models. Newly available is a combination CD/cassette stereo. Items from the 1996 Indy 500 Special Edition are available in a new Sport Package upgrade. Fresh interior and exterior colors sum up the changes this year.

Ram 1500 — Review

The Dodge boys had to know they had a winner when their bold Ram pickup debuted for 1994. Few trucks have turned as many heads, or prompted so much comment. Whether decked out in Sport trim or wearing conventional chrome on its chest-thumping grille, this is macho mentality sculpted in steel.

Under the hood, the goods range from modest to mammoth. For the practical-minded, there's a mild-mannered 3.9-liter V-6; or, a Cummins diesel whose throbbing note and power make a guy want to grab his Stetson and haul on out.

Those who'd like a little more muscle have a pair of V-8s to choose from. Whoa! You're still not satisfied? Like TV's Tim the Tool Man, you want "more power?" Say no more. Just check the option list and you can barrel homeward with an 8.0-liter V-10, blasting out 295 horses, and a locomotive-like 450 pounds-feet of torque. The Magnum V-10 is available only in heavy-duty 2500 and 3500 series pickups.

This year finds four new exterior colors and two new interior colors available, as well as a Sport Plus upgrade for the Sport Appearance Group which includes 17-inch wheels and tires, sport-tuned exhaust, refined suspension, and a 5.9-liter V-8.

One first-season criticism centered on space. Only the regular cab was available, seating three on a bench. Dodge claimed its cab was the most spacious in the industry, but that

DODGE
RAM 1500

was little consolation to potential buyers who needed to carry extra people. Last year, Dodge introduced a Club Cab that seats six adults, even if access to the rear isn't so easy. For 1997, Club Cab models receive standard rear quarter window glass, and 2500 models can be equipped with a Snow Plow Prep Package.

Inside, the Ram is totally truck, as you face a flat, upright dashboard (but a steering wheel that contains an airbag). With any engine, tromping the gas produces a reassuring roar—a reverberation of vitality. Otherwise, it's fairly quiet. Ride and handling are so competent that you almost forget you're in a full-size pickup, though occupants will notice plenty of bumps. Visibility is great, and controls are excellent. Automatic-transmission shifts are firm, but not harsh, and the column-mounted gearshift operates easily. For such a large and bulky vehicle, the Ram is surprisingly agile and reasonably sure-footed, but think twice before making any quick maneuvers.

Ram livability is improved this year. Order SLT trim, and you ca opt for leather seats and woodgrain interior trim. Remote keyless entry is newly optional, and includes illuminated entry lighting. A new combination CD and cassette playing stereo ensures that audiophiles can maximize utilization of their music collection.

More than 800,000 Rams went to customers during the first three years of production. Demand is still strong, and Chrysler recently opened a new plant to keep the supply lines full. Curiosity has tapered off, but when pickup owners think about a new truck, they can hardly help wondering whether a Ram lies in their future.

Safety Data

Driver Airbag: *Standard*
Side Airbag: *Not Available*
4-Wheel ABS: *Optional*
Driver Crash Test Grade: *Excellent*

Passenger Crash Test Grade: *Not Available*

Passenger Airbag: *Not Available*
Meets 1999 Side Impact Standards: *No*
Traction Control: *Not Available*
Insurance Cost: *Low (2WD Reg Cab); Average (Club Cab; 4WD Reg Cab)*
Integrated Child Seat(s): *Not Available*

Standard Equipment

RAM 1500 WS REGULAR CAB: 3.9-liter V-6 engine, 5-speed manual transmission, power front disc brakes, power rear drum anti-lock brakes, driver airbag, dual cupholders, black front bumper, upper front bumper fascia with step pad, dark silver metallic painted grille, tinted glass, black vinyl floor covering, dual vinyl sunvisors, dual black manual exterior mirrors, instrument panel power outlet, vinyl bench seat with folding back and integral headrests, conventional spare tire, black two-spoke steering wheel, headlights-on warning buzzer, black wheel center caps, two-speed intermittent wipers

1500 LT REGULAR CAB (in addition to or instead of WS REGULAR CAB equipment): Digital clock, chrome grille, coat hook, AM/FM stereo with cassette player and 4 speakers

1500 ST CLUB CAB (in addition to or instead of LT REGULAR CAB equipment): 5.2-liter V-8 engine, chrome front bumper with black step pad, bright argent painted rear step bumper with step pad, carpeted floor covering, rear trim panel armrest, cab-mounted cargo light, deluxe cloth 40/20/40 split bench reclining seat, center armrest storage console, easy-entry passenger seat, rear folding bench seat, bright hub caps and trim rings, swing-out deep tinted quarter windows, additional coat hook

RAM 1500 — DODGE

CODE	DESCRIPTION	INVOICE	MSRP

Base Prices

Code	Description	Invoice	MSRP
BR1L61	WS 2WD Regular Cab Shortbed	12871	14075
BR1L62	WS 2WD Regular Cab Longbed	13109	14435
BR1L61	LT 2WD Regular Cab Shortbed	13983	15880
BR1L62	LT 2WD Regular Cab Longbed	14225	16165
BR1L31	ST 2WD Club Cab Shortbed	16288	18550
BR1L32	ST 2WD Club Cab Longbed	16526	18830
BR6L61	LT 4WD Regular Cab Shortbed	16674	19005
BR6L62	LT 4WD Regular Cab Longbed	16963	19345
BR6L31	ST 4WD Club Cab Shortbed	18958	21645
BR6L32	ST 4WD Club Cab Longbed	19239	21975
	Destination Charge:	640	640

Accessories

Code	Description	Invoice	MSRP
HAA	Air Conditioning	677	797
	INCLUDED in Laramie SLT Packages		
BGK	Anti-lock Brakes	425	500
	Includes 4-wheel operation		
AMR	Behind Seat Storage (Reg Cab)	81	95
	Includes floor mounted tray and storage bins; INCLUDED in Laramie SLT Packages and ST Decor Group		
K17	Bodyside Moldings (All except WS)	87	102
	REQUIRES ST Decor Group on Regular Cab models; NOT AVAILABLE with Sport Appearance Group; INCLUDED in Laramie SLT Packages		
YCF	Border States Emissions	145	170
WMC	Bright Wheel Trim Rings (Reg Cab except WS)	51	60
	Includes bright center cap; NOT AVAILABLE with Laramie SLT Packages		
LNC	Cab Clearance Lights	68	80
NAE	Calif./Mass./New York Emissions	145	170
—	California Bonus Discount (2WD Reg Cab)	(677)	(797)
	With 23G (2WD Reg Cab)	(519)	(610)
	With 24G (2WD Reg Cab)	(519)	(610)
	With 26G (2WD Reg Cab)	(519)	(610)
	REQUIRES purchase of an A code or G code Option Package		
—	California Bonus Discount (2WD X-cab)	(677)	(797)
	With 23G (2WD X-cab)	(507)	(597)
	With 24G (2WD X-cab)	(507)	(597)
	With 26G (2WD X-cab)	(507)	(597)
	REQUIRES purchase of an A code or G code Option Package		
LPE	Cargo Bed Light (WS)	32	38
WDB	Chrome Wheels (All except WS)	NC	NC
	REQUIRES Sport Appearance Group		
AJK	Deluxe Convenience Package	332	390
	INCLUDED in Laramie SLT Packages		

DODGE RAM 1500

CODE	DESCRIPTION	INVOICE	MSRP
GPC	Dual Chrome Oversize Exterior Mirrors (All except WS)	41	48
	With 23G (2WD Reg Cab)	(43)	(50)
	With 23G (4WD Reg Cab)	(43)	(50)
	With 23G (4WD X-cab)	(43)	(50)
	With 23G (2WD X-cab)	(43)	(50)
	With 24G (2WD X-cab)	(43)	(50)
	With 24G (4WD Reg Cab)	(43)	(50)
	With 24G (4WD X-cab)	(43)	(50)
	With 24G (2WD Reg Cab)	(43)	(50)
	With 26G (2WD X-cab)	(43)	(50)
	With 26G (2WD Reg Cab)	(43)	(50)
	With 26G (4WD Reg Cab)	(43)	(50)
	With 26G (4WD X-Cab)	(43)	(50)
	Recommended for towing; NOT AVAILABLE with Super Sport Truck Performance Package		
GPP	Dual Power Chrome Exterior Mirrors (All except WS)	84	99
	INCLUDED in Laramie SLT Packages		
NHK	Engine Block Heater	34	40
LNJ	Fog Lights (All except WS)	102	120
	REQUIRES a Laramie SLT Package		
NMC	Heavy-duty Engine Cooling (All except WS)	111	130
	With 23A (2WD Reg Cab)	56	66
	With 23A (4WD Reg Cab)	56	66
	With 23C (2WD X-cab)	56	66
	With 23C (4WD X-cab)	56	66
	With 23G (2WD X-cab)	56	66
	With 23G (2WD Reg Cab)	56	66
	With 23G (4WD Reg Cab)	56	66
	With 23G (4WD X-cab)	56	66
	REQUIRES V-8 engine upgrade		
ADJ	Heavy-duty Service Group (2WD)	290	341
	With 21W (WS)	179	211
	With 22A (2WD Reg Cab)	179	211
	With 22W (WS)	179	211
	With 23A (2WD Reg Cab)	235	277
	With 23C (2WD X-cab)	235	277
	Includes 136 amp alternator, 750 amp battery, heavy-duty engine cooling (V-8 models), auxiliary transmission oil cooler (w/V-8 and automatic transmission)		
ADJ	Heavy-duty Service Group (4WD)	332	390
	With 23C (4WD X-cab)	217	255
	With 23G (4WD Reg Cab)	217	255
	With 23G (4WD X-cab)	217	255
	With 23A (4WD Reg Cab)	217	255
	Includes 136 amp alternator, 750 amp battery, heavy-duty engine cooling, auxiliary transmission oil cooler (w/automatic transmission)		

RAM 1500 — DODGE

CODE	DESCRIPTION	INVOICE	MSRP
GNC	Illuminated Visor Vanity Mirrors (All except WS)	80	94
23G	Laramie SLT Option Package 23G (2WD Reg Cab)	3504	4122
	Manufacturer Discount	(1009)	(1187)
	Net Price	2495	2935

Includes 5.2-liter V-8 engine, air conditioning, cruise control, tilt steering column, light group (ignition key light, map ligts, courtesy lights, underhood light, glovebox light, overhead console with storage, deluxe cloth headliner, passenger assist handle, exterior cargo lamp), power windows, power door locks, P245/75R16 all-season tires, behind seat storage with bins, netting, and floor storage tray; tachometer, chrome bumpers, cast aluminum wheels, SLT Decor (protective bodyside moldings with bright insert, dual horns, carpeted cab back, cloth door trim bolsters with lower carpeted section and map pockets, carpeted front floor mats, cloth sunvisors with covered passenger side vanity mirror, premium cloth seat trim, hood silencer pad, leather-wrapped steering wheel, headlights-on chime instead of buzzer)

CODE	DESCRIPTION	INVOICE	MSRP
23G	Laramie SLT Package 23G (2WD X-cab)	2314	2722
	Manufacturer Discount	(595)	(700)
	Net Price	1719	2022

Includes air conditioning, cruise control, tilt steering column, light group (ignition key light, map ligts, courtesy lights, underhood light, glovebox light, overhead console with storage, deluxe cloth headliner, passenger assist handle, exterior cargo lamp), power windows, power door locks, P245/75R16C all-season tires, behind seat storage with bins, netting, and floor storage tray; tachometer, chrome bumpers, cast aluminum wheels, SLT Decor (protective bodyside moldings with bright insert, dual horns, carpeted cab back, cloth door trim bolsters with lower carpeted section and map pockets, carpeted front floor mats, cloth sunvisors with covered passenger side vanity mirror, premium cloth seat trim, hood silencer pad, leather-wrapped steering wheel, headlights - on chimes instead of buzzer)

CODE	DESCRIPTION	INVOICE	MSRP
23G	Laramie SLT Package 23G (4WD Reg Cab)	3013	3545
	Manufacturer Discount	(1009)	(1187)
	Net Price	2004	2358

Includes air conditioning, cruise control, tilt steering column, light group (ignition key light, map ligts, courtesy lights, underhood light, glovebox light, overhead console with storage, deluxe cloth headliner, passenger assist handle, exterior cargo lamp), power windows, power door locks, P245/75R16C tires, behind seat storage with bins, netting, and floor storage tray; tachometer, chrome bumpers, cast aluminum wheels, SLT Decor (protective bodyside moldings with bright insert, dual horns, carpeted cab back, cloth door trim bolsters with lower carpeted section and map pockets, carpeted front floor mats, cloth sunvisors with covered passenger side vanity mirror, premium cloth seat trim, hood silencer pad, leather wrapped steering wheel, headlights - on chimes instead of buzzer)

DODGE
RAM 1500

CODE	DESCRIPTION	INVOICE	MSRP
23G	Laramie SLT Package 23G (4WD X-cab)	2322	2732
	Manufacturer Discount	(595)	(700)
	Net Price	1727	2032

Includes air conditioning, cruise control, tilt steering column, light group (ignition key light, map ligts, courtesy lights, underhood light, glovebox light, overhead console with storage, deluxe cloth headliner, passenger assist handle, exterior cargo lamp), power windows, power door locks, P245/75R16 tires, behind seat storage with bins, netting, and floor storage tray; tachometer, chrome bumpers, cast aluminum wheels, SLT Decor (protective bodyside moldings with bright insert, dual horns, carpeted cab back, cloth door trim bolsters with lower carpeted section and map pockets, carpeted front floor mats, cloth sunvisors with covered passenger side vanity mirror, premium cloth seat trim, hood silencer pad, leather-wrapped

24G	Laramie SLT Package 24G (2WD Reg Cab)	4312	5072
	Manufacturer Discount	(1009)	(1187)
	Net Price	3303	3885

Includes 5.2-liter V-8 engine, air conditioning, cruise control, tilt steering column, light group (ignition key light, map ligts, courtesy lights, underhood light, glovebox light, overhead console with storage, deluxe cloth headliner, passenger assist handle, exterior cargo lamp), power windows, power door locks, P245/75R16 all-season tires, behind seat storage with bins, netting, and floor storage tray; tachometer, chrome bumpers, cast aluminum wheels, SLT Decor (protective bodyside moldings with bright insert, dual horns, carpeted cab back, cloth door trim bolsters with lower carpeted section and map pockets, carpeted front floor mats, cloth sunvisors with covered passenger side vanity mirror, premium cloth seat trim, hood silencer pad, leather-wrapped steering wheel, headlights-on chime instead of buzzer) plus 4-speed automatic transmission

24G	Laramie SLT Package 24G (2WD X-cab)	3122	3672
	Manufacturer Discount	(595)	(700)
	Net Price	2527	2972

Includes air conditioning, cruise control, tilt steering column, light group (ignition key light, map ligts, courtesy lights, underhood light, glovebox light, overhead console with storage, deluxe cloth headliner, passenger assist handle, exterior cargo lamp), power windows, power door locks, P245/75R16C all-season tires, behind seat storage with bins, netting, and floor storage tray; tachometer, chrome bumpers, cast aluminum wheels, SLT Decor (protective bodyside moldings with bright insert, dual horns, carpeted cab back, cloth door trim bolsters with lower carpeted section and map pockets, carpeted front floor mats, cloth sunvisors with covered passenger side vanity mirror, premium cloth seat trim, hood silencer pad, leather-wrapped steering wheel, headlights-on chime instead of buzzer) plus 4-speed automatic transmission

24G	Laramie SLT Package 24G (4WD Reg Cab)	3821	4495
	Manufacturer Discount	(1009)	(1187)
	Net Price	2812	3308

Includes air conditioning, cruise control, tilt steering column, light group (ignition key light, map ligts, courtesy lights, underhood light, glovebox light, overhead console with storage, deluxe cloth headliner, passenger assist handle, exterior cargo lamp), power

RAM 1500 — DODGE

CODE	DESCRIPTION	INVOICE	MSRP

windows, power door locks, P245/75R16C tires, behind seat storage with bins, netting, and floor storage tray; tachometer, chrome bumpers, cast aluminum wheels, SLT Decor (protective bodyside moldings with bright insert, dual horns, carpeted cab back, cloth door trim bolsters with lower carpeted section and map pockets, carpeted front floor mats, cloth sunvisors with covered passenger side vanity mirror, premium cloth seat trim, hood silencer pad, leather-wrapped steering wheel, headlights-on chime instead of buzzer) plus 4-speed automatic transmission

24G	Laramie SLT Package 24G (4WD X-cab)	3130	3682
	Manufacturer Discount	(595)	(700)
	Net Price	2535	2982

Includes air conditioning, cruise control, tilt steering column, light group (ignition key light, map ligts, courtesy lights, underhood light, glovebox light, overhead console with storage, deluxe cloth headliner, passenger assist handle, exterior cargo lamp), power windows, power door locks, P245/75R16 tires, behind seat storage with bins, netting, and floor storage tray; tachometer, chrome bumpers, cast aluminum wheels, SLT Decor (protective bodyside moldings with bright insert, dual horns, carpeted cab back, cloth door trim bolsters with lower carpeted section and map pockets, carpeted front floor mats, cloth sunvisors with covered passenger side vanity mirror, premium cloth seat trim, hood silencer pad, leather-wrapped steering wheel, headlights-on chime instead of buzzer) plus 4-speed automatic transmission

26G	Laramie SLT Package 26G (2WD Reg Cab)	4541	5342
	Manufacturer Discount	(1238)	(1457)
	Net Price	3303	3885

Includes 5.9-liter V-8 engine, 4-speed automatic transmission, air conditioning, cruise control, tilt steering column, light group (igniton key light, map ligts, courtesy lights, underhood light, glovebox light, overhead console with storage, deluxe cloth headliner, passenger assist handle, exterior cargo lamp), power windows, power door locks, P245/75R16 all-season tires, behind seat storage with bins, netting, and floor storage tray; tachometer, chrome bumpers, cast aluminum wheels, SLT Decor (protective bodyside moldings with bright insert, dual horns, carpeted cab back, cloth door trim bolsters with lower carpeted section and map pockets, carpeted front floor mats, cloth sunvisors with covered passenger side vanity mirror, premium cloth seat trim, hood silencer pad, leather-wrapped steering wheel, headlights-on chime instead of buzzer)

26G	Laramie SLT Package 26G (2WD X-cab)	3352	3942
	Manufacturer Discount	(825)	(970)
	Net Price	2527	2972

Includes air conditioning, cruise control, tilt steering column, light group (ignition key light, map ligts, courtesy lights, underhood light, glovebox light, overhead console with storage, deluxe cloth headliner, passenger assist handle, exterior cargo lamp), power windows, power door locks, P245/75R16C all-season tires, behind seat storage with bins, netting, and floor storage tray; tachometer, chrome bumpers, cast aluminum wheels, SLT Decor (protective bodyside moldings with bright insert, dual horns, carpeted cab back, cloth door trim bolsters with lower carpeted section and map

DODGE RAM 1500

CODE	DESCRIPTION	INVOICE	MSRP

pockets, carpeted front floor mats, cloth sunvisors with covered passenger side vanity mirror, premium cloth seat trim, hood silencer pad, leather-wrapped steering wheel, headlights-on chime instead of buzzer) plus 5.9-liter V-8 engine and 4-speed automatic transmission

26G	Laramie SLT Package 26G (4WD Reg Cab)	4051	4765
	Manufacturer Discount	(1238)	(1457)
	Net Price	2813	3308

Includes air conditioning, cruise control, tilt steering column, light group (ignition key light, map ligts, courtesy lights, underhood light, glovebox light, overhead console with storage, deluxe cloth headliner, passenger assist handle, exterior cargo lamp), power windows, power door locks, P245/75R16C tires, behind seat storage with bins, netting, and floor storage tray; tachometer, chrome bumpers, cast aluminum wheels, SLT Decor (protective bodyside moldings with bright insert, dual horns, carpeted cab back, cloth door trim bolsters with lower carpeted section and map pockets, carpeted front floor mats, cloth sunvisors with covered passenger side vanity mirror, premium cloth seat trim, hood silencer pad, leather-wrapped steering wheel, headlights-on chime instead of buzzer) plus 5.9-liter V-8 engine and 4-speed automatic transmission

26G	Laramie SLT Package 26G (4WD X-Cab)	3360	3952
	Manufacturer Discount	(825)	(970)
	Net Price	2535	2982

Includes air conditioning, cruise control, tilt steering column, light group (ignition key light, map ligts, courtesy lights, underhood light, glovebox light, overhead console with storage, deluxe cloth headliner, passenger assist handle, exterior cargo lamp), power windows, power door locks, P245/75R16 tires, behind seat storage with bins, netting, and floor storage tray; tachometer, chrome bumpers, cast aluminum wheels, SLT Decor (protective bodyside moldings with bright insert, dual horns, carpeted cab back, cloth door trim bolsters with lower carpeted section and map pockets, carpeted front floor mats, cloth sunvisors with covered passenger side vanity mirror, premium cloth seat trim, hood silencer pad, leather-wrapped steering wheel, headlights-on chime instead of buzzer) plus 5.9-liter V-8 engine and 4-speed automatic transmission

AJD	Leather Interior Group (Reg Cab except WS)	1190	1400

Includes leather seating surfaces, 6-way power driver's seat, illuminated visor vanity mirrors, woodgrain interior trim, travel convenience group (automatic day/night rearview mirror, overhead console with compass, overhead temperature readout, overhead reading lamps); REQUIRES a Laramie SLT Package

AJD	Leather Interior Group (X-cab)	1275	1500

Includes leather front seating surfaces, 6-way power driver's seat, illuminated visor vanity mirrors, woodgrain interior trim, travel convenience group (automatic day/night rearview mirror, overhead console with compass, overhead temperature readout, overhead reading lamps); REQUIRES a Laramie SLT Package

RAM 1500 — DODGE

CODE	DESCRIPTION	INVOICE	MSRP
ADA	**Light Group (Reg Cab except WS)**	134	158
	Includes glovebox light, ignition key light with time delay, underhood light, exterior cargo bed light, passenger assist handle, overhead console with storage, overhead map and reading lights, deluxe cloth headliner, 12-volt auxiliary power point; INCLUDED in Laramie SLT Packages		
ADA	**Light Group (X-cab)**	102	120
	Includes glovebox light, ignition key light with time delay, underhood light, passenger assist handle, overhead console with storage, overhead map and reading lights, deluxe cloth headliner, 12-volt auxiliary power point; INCLUDED in Laramie SLT Packages		
21A	**Option Package 21A (Regional) (2WD Reg Cab)**	1009	1187
	Manufacturer Discount	(1455)	(1712)
	Net Price	(446)	(525)
	Includes air conditioning, cruise control, and tilt steering wheel; AVAILABLE only in Louisiana, Oklahoma, and Texas.		
21W	**Option Package 21W (WS)**	NC	NC
	Includes vehicle with standard equipment		
22A	**Option Package 22A (2WD Reg Cab)**	808	950
	Includes 4-speed automatic transmission; NOTE: In LA, OK, and TX, this package includes air conditioning and costs $170 invoice and $200 MSRP after the regional discount.		
22W	**Option Package 22W (WS)**	808	950
	Includes 4-speed automatic transmission		
23A	**Option Package 23A (2WD Reg Cab)**	499	587
	Includes 5.2-liter V-8 engine; NOTE: In LA, OK, and TX, this package has a regional discount that results in an invoice price of $329 and a MSRP of $387.		
23A	**Option Package 23A (4WD Reg Cab)**	NC	NC
	Includes vehicle with standard equipment		
23C	**Option Package 23C (2WD X-cab)**	NC	NC
	Includes vehicle with standard equipment		
23C	**Option Package 23C (4WD X-cab)**	NC	NC
	Includes vehicle with standard equipment		
24A	**Option Package 24A (2WD Reg Cab)**	1307	1537
	Includes 5.2-liter V-8 engine and 4-speed automatic transmission; NOTE: In LA, OK, and TX, this package costs $1,097 invoice and $1,337 MSRP after regional discounts.		
24A	**Option Package 24A (4WD Reg Cab)**	808	950
	Includes 4-speed automatic transmission		
24C	**Option Package 24C (2WD X-cab)**	808	950
	Includes 4-speed automatic transmission		
24C	**Option Package 24C (4WD X-cab)**	808	950
	Includes 4-speed automatic transmission		
26A	**Option Package 26A (2WD Reg Cab)**	1536	1807
	Manufacturer Discount	(230)	(270)
	Net Price	1306	1537
	Includes 5.9-liter V-8 engine and 4-speed automatic transmission		

DODGE RAM 1500

CODE	DESCRIPTION	INVOICE	MSRP
26A	Option Package 26A (4WD Reg Cab)	1038	1220
	Manufacturer Discount	(230)	(270)
	Net Price	808	950
	Includes 5.9-liter V-8 engine and 4-speed automatic transmission		
26C	Option Package 26C (2WD X-cab)	1038	1220
	Manufacturer Discount	(230)	(270)
	Net Price	808	950
	Includes 5.9-liter V-8 engine and 4-speed automatic transmission		
26C	Option Package 26C (4WD X-cab)	1038	1220
	Manufacturer Discount	(230)	(270)
	Net Price	808	950
	Includes 5.9-liter V-8 engine and 4-speed automatic transmission		
—	Optional Ratio Axle (2WD)	43	50
	REQUIRES V-8 engine upgrade on Regular Cab models		
JPS	Power Driver's Seat (All except WS)	272	320
	Includes 6-way adjustment; REQUIRES a Laramie SLT Package; INCLUDED in Leather Interior Group (AJD)		
RA8	Radio Delete Credit (All except WS)	(85)	(100)
MBD	Rear Step Bumper — Painted Black (Reg Cab)	113	133
	NOT AVAILABLE with Laramie SLT Packages		
MBQ	Rear Step Bumper — Painted Body Color (Shortbed except WS)	43	50
	REQUIRES Sport Appearance Group or Super Sport Truck Performance Package		
4XM	Rear Step Bumper Delete (Shortbed except WS)	NC	NC
	REQUIRES Sport Appearance Group or Super Sport Truck Performance Package		
GXD	Remote Keyless Entry (All except WS)	162	190
	REQUIRES a Laramie SLT Package		
CKJ	Rubber Floor Covering (All except WS)	NC	NC
	REQUIRES a Laramie SLT Package or the ST Decor Group on Regular Cab models		
B3	Seat — Deluxe Cloth & Vinyl Bench (Reg Cab)	85	100
	NOT AVAILABLE with Laramie SLT Packages or with ST Decor Group		
T9	Seat — Deluxe Cloth 40/20/40 Split Back Bench (Reg Cab except WS)	222	261
	With AMP (Reg Cab except WS)	NC	NC
	NOT AVAILABLE with Laramie SLT Packages		
TX	Seat — Heavy-duty Vinyl 40/20/40 Split Back Bench (Reg Cab except WS)		222
261	With AMP (Reg Cab except WS)	NC	NC
	NOT AVAILABLE with Laramie SLT Packages		
GFD	Sliding Rear Window	117	138
AGG	Sport Appearance Group (2WD Shortbed except WS)	808	950
	With 23G (2WD Reg Cab)	391	460
	With 23G (2WD X-cab)	391	460
	With 24G (2WD Reg Cab)	391	460
	With 24G (2WD X-cab)	391	460
	With 26G (2WD Reg Cab)	391	460
	With 26G (2WD X-cab)	391	460
	Includes color-keyed front bumper, color-keyed rear valence panel, color-keyed grille, dual electric horns, tachometer, Sport decals, fog lights, cast aluminum wheels, P245/75R16C OWL tires; REQUIRES V-8 engine upgrade		

RAM 1500 — DODGE

CODE	DESCRIPTION	INVOICE	MSRP
AGG	Sport Appearance Group (4WD Shortbed)	1063	1250
	With 23G (4WD X-cab)	519	610
	With 23G (4WD Reg Cab)	519	610
	With 24G (4WD Reg Cab)	519	610
	With 24G (4WD X-cab)	519	610
	With 26G (4WD X-cab)	519	610
	With 26G (4WD Reg Cab)	519	610
	Includes color-keyed front bumper, color-keyed rear valance panel, color-keyed grille, dual electric horns, tachometer, Sport decals, fog lights, cast aluminum wheels, P265/75R16C all-terrain OWL tires		
AMP	ST Decor Group (Reg Cab except WS)	664	781
	Manufacturer Discount	(340)	(400)
	Net Price	324	381
	Includes chrome front bumper with black step pad, carpeted floor covering, deluxe cloth 40/20/40 split bench seat, rear floor storage tray, rear storage bins, bright trim rings; REQUIRES Two-tone Center Band Paint (6C); NOT AVAILABLE with Laramie SLT Packages		
RBN	Stereo — Uplevel w/cassette (All except WS)	281	331
	AM/FM stereo with cassette player, 4 speakers, and graphic equalizer; REQUIRES a Laramie SLT Package		
RAZ	Stereo — Uplevel w/cassette & CD players (All except WS)	587	690
	AM/FM stereo with cassette and CD players, 4 speakers, and graphic equalizer; REQUIRES a Laramie SLT Package		
RBR	Stereo — Uplevel w/CD player (All except WS)	434	510
	AM/FM stereo with CD player, 4 speakers, and graphic equalizer; REQUIRES a Laramie SLT Package		
RAS	Stereo — w/cassette (WS)	340	400
	AM/FM stereo with cassette player and 4 speakers		
AGL	Super Sport Truck Performance Package (2WD Reg Cab Shortbed)	1156	1360
	Includes color-keyed front bumper, color-keyed rear valance panel, color-keyed grille, sport-tuned exhaust with chrome tip, fog lights, dual wide center paint stripes, tachometer, P257/60R17 tires, 17-inch cast aluminum wheels; REQUIRES Laramie SLT Package 26G; NOT AVAILABLE with Sport Appearance Group		
DSA	Sure Grip Axle	242	285
JAY	Tachometer (All except WS)	65	76
	INCLUDED in Laramie SLT Packages		
TYL	Tires — LT245/75R16 All-terrain BSW (4WD)	238	280
	REQUIRES ST Decor Group; NOT AVAILABLE with Laramie SLT Packages		
TYM	Tires — LT245/75R16C All-terrain OWL (4WD)	225	265
	REQUIRES a Laramie SLT Package		
TYW	Tires — P245/75R16C (4WD)	119	140
	INCLUDED in Laramie SLT Packages		
TYF	Tires — P245/75R16C A/S BSW (2WD except WS)	111	130
	INCLUDED in Laramie SLT Packages		
TYG	Tires — P245/75R16C A/S OWL (2WD except WS)	107	126
	REQUIRES a Laramie SLT Package		

DODGE
RAM 1500 / 2500

CODE	DESCRIPTION	INVOICE	MSRP
TXW	Tires — P265/75R16C All-terrain OWL (4WD)	344	405
	REQUIRES a Laramie SLT Package		
AHC	Trailer Towing Package (All except WS)	206	242
	Includes Class IV trailer hitch receiver, adaptor plug, and heavy-duty flashers; REQUIRES a rear bumper and the Heavy-duty Service Group; REQUIRES V-8 engine upgrade		
AWK	Travel Convenience Group (All except WS)	176	207
	Includes automatic day/night rearview mirror, overhead console with compass, overhead temperature readout, and overhead reading lamps; REQUIRES a Laramie SLT Package; INCLUDED in the Leather Interior Group		
6C	Two-tone Center Band Paint (All except WS)	235	276
	With 23G (4WD X-cab)	183	215
	With 23G (4WD Reg Cab)	183	215
	With 23G (2WD X-cab)	183	215
	With 23G (2WD Reg Cab)	183	215
	With 24G (4WD Reg Cab)	183	215
	With 24G (4WD X-cab)	183	215
	With 24G (2WD Reg Cab)	183	215
	With 24G (2WD X-cab)	183	215
	With 26G (4WD X-Cab)	183	215
	With 26G (4WD Reg Cab)	183	215
	With 26G (2WD Reg Cab)	183	215
	With 26G (2WD X-cab)	183	215
	Includes tape stripes		
6D	Two-tone Lower Break Paint (All except WS)	166	195
	NOT AVAILABLE with ST Decor Group		

RAM 2500 (1997)

Safety Data

Driver Airbag: *Standard*
Side Airbag: *Not Available*
4-Wheel ABS: *Optional*
Driver Crash Test Grade: *Excellent*

Passenger Crash Test Grade: *Not Available*

Passenger Airbag: *Not Available*
Meets 1999 Side Impact Standards: *No*
Traction Control: *Not Available*
Insurance Cost: *Avg. (2WD; 4WD Reg Cab); High (4WD Club Cab)*

Integrated Child Seat(s): *Not Available*

Standard Equipment

RAM 2500 REGULAR CAB: Driver's side airbag, 117-amp alternator, 600-amp battery, power front disc/rear drum brakes with rear anti-lock, argent front bumper, headlamps-on warning buzzer, digital clock, cigarette lighter, auxiliary power outlet, 5.9-liter V-8 engine, black rubber floor covering, voltmeter, oil pressure gauge, temperature gauge, trip odometer, tinted glass, chrome grille, day/night rearview mirror, power steering, AM/FM stereo with cassette player

RAM 2500 — DODGE

and 4 speakers, vinyl bench seat with head restraints, dual exterior mirrors, front and rear heavy-duty shocks, LT245/75R16E BSW all-season tires, under-bed spare tire carrier, 5-speed manual transmission, 16"x 6.5" silver painted steel wheels with black center caps, 2-speed deluxe intermittent wipers, shift-on-the-fly 2-speed transfer case (4WD)

2500 EXTENDED CAB (in addition to or instead of REGULAR CAB equipment): 40/20/40 deluxe cloth split front bench seat, deluxe cloth rear bench seat, front stabilizer bar, chrome wheel trim rings and bright center caps

Base Prices

Code	Description	Invoice	MSRP
BR2L62	2WD Heavy Duty Regular Cab	16440	18770
BR2L31	2WD Club Cab Shortbed	18179	20775
BR2L32	2WD Club Cab Longbed	18353	20980
BR7L62	4WD Heavy Duty Regular Cab	19097	21855
BR7L31	4WD Club Cab Shortbed	20777	23785
BR7L32	4WD Club Cab Longbed	20952	23990
	Destination Charge:	640	640

Accessories

Code	Description	Invoice	MSRP
25H	Laramie SLT Option Package 25H (Club Cab)	2186	2572
	Manufacturer Discount	(340)	(400)
	Net Price	1846	2172

Includes power convenience group (power windows, power door locks), air conditioning, tachometer, light group (cloth headliner, passenger assist grip, glove box light, under hood light, overhead console with storage and reading lights, exterior cargo light), deluxe convenience group (tilt steering column and cruise control), chrome wheels, chrome bumpers, Laramie SLT Decor (40/20/40 split front bench seat with premium cloth upholstery, passenger visor vanity mirror, leather-wrapped steering wheel, chrome front bumper, tailgate panel applique, front floor mats, under hood sound deadening insulation, dual horns, full floor carpeting, black bodyside moldings, chrome power exterior mirrors)

Code	Description	Invoice	MSRP
25H	Laramie SLT Option Package 25H (Reg Cab)	2877	3385
	Manufacturer Discount	(680)	(800)
	Net Price	2197	2585

Includes power convenience group (power windows, power door locks), behind seat storage, air conditioning, tachometer, light group (cloth headliner, passenger assist grip, glove box light, under hood light, overhead console with storage and reading lights, exterior cargo light), deluxe convenience group (tilt steering column and cruise control), chrome wheels, chrome bumpers, Laramie SLT Decor (40/20/40 split front bench seat with premium cloth upholstery, passenger visor vanity mirror, chrome front bumper, tailgate panel applique, front floor mats, under hood sound deadening insulation, leather-wrapped steering wheel, dual horns, full floor carpeting, black bodyside moldings, chrome power exterior mirrors)

DODGE RAM 2500

CODE	DESCRIPTION	INVOICE	MSRP
26H	Laramie SLT Option Package 26H (Club Cab)	2994	3522
	Manufacturer Discount	(340)	(400)
	Net Price	2654	3122

Includes power convenience group (power windows, power door locks), air conditioning, tachometer, light group (cloth headliner, passenger assist grip, glove box light, under hood light, overhead console with storage and reading lights, exterior cargo light), deluxe convenience group (tilt steering column and cruise control), chrome wheels, chrome bumpers, Laramie SLT Decor (40/20/40 split front bench seat with premium cloth upholstery, passenger visor vanity mirror, leather-wrapped steering wheel, chrome front bumper, tailgate panel applique, front floor mats, under hood sound deadening insulation, dual horns, full floor carpeting, black bodyside moldings, chrome power exterior mirrors), 4-speed automatic transmission

26H	Laramie SLT Option Package 26H (Reg Cab)	3685	4335
	Manufacturer Discount	(680)	(800)
	Net Price	3005	3535

Includes power convenience group (power windows, power door locks), behind seat storage, air conditioning, tachometer, light group (cloth headliner, passenger assist grip, glove box light, under hood light, overhead console with storage and reading lights, exterior cargo light), deluxe convenience group (tilt steering column and cruise control), chrome wheels, chrome bumpers, Laramie SLT Decor (40/20/40 split front bench seat with premium cloth upholstery, passenger visor vanity mirror, chrome front bumper, tailgate panel applique, front floor mats, under hood sound deadening insulation, leather-wrapped steering wheel, dual horns, full floor carpeting, black bodyside moldings, chrome power exterior mirrors), 4-speed automatic transmission

27H	Laramie SLT Option Package 27H (Club Cab)	3015	3547
	Manufacturer Discount	(340)	(400)
	Net Price	2675	3147

Includes power convenience group (power windows, power door locks), air conditioning, tachometer, light group (cloth headliner, passenger assist grip, glove box light, under hood light, overhead console with storage and reading lights, exterior cargo light), deluxe convenience group (tilt steering column and cruise control), chrome wheels, chrome bumpers, Laramie SLT Decor (40/20/40 split front bench seat with premium cloth upholstery, passenger visor vanity mirror, leather-wrapped steering wheel, chrome front bumper, tailgate panel applique, front floor mats, under hood sound deadening insulation, dual horns, full floor carpeting, black bodyside moldings, chrome power exterior mirrors), heavy-duty service group (HD 750-amp battery, HD 136-amp alternator, HD engine cooling), transfer case skid plate (4WD), 8.0-liter V-10 engine

27H	Laramie SLT Option Package 27H (Reg Cab)	3706	4360
	Manufacturer Discount	(680)	(800)
	Net Price	3026	3560

Includes power convenience group (power windows, power door locks), behind seat storage, air conditioning, tachometer, light group (cloth headliner, passenger assist grip, glove box light, under hood light, overhead console with storage and reading lights, exterior cargo light), deluxe convenience group (tilt steering column and cruise control), chrome wheels, chrome bumpers, Laramie SLT Decor (40/20/40 split front

RAM 2500 — DODGE

CODE	DESCRIPTION	INVOICE	MSRP

bench seat with premium cloth upholstery, passenger visor vanity mirror, chrome front bumper, tailgate panel applique, front floor mats, under hood sound deadening insulation, dual horns, full floor carpeting, black bodyside moldings, chrome power exterior mirrors), transfer case skid plate (4WD), heavy-duty service group (HD 750-amp battery, HD 136-amp alternator, HD engine cooling), 8.0-liter V-10 engine

28H	Laramie SLT Option Package 28H (Club Cab)	3823	4497
	Manufacturer Discount	(340)	(400)
	Net Price	3483	4097

Includes power convenience group (power windows, power door locks), air conditioning, tachometer, light group (cloth headliner, passenger assist grip, glove box light, under hood light, overhead console with storage and reading lights, exterior cargo light), deluxe convenience group (tilt steering column and cruise control), chrome wheels, chrome bumpers, Laramie SLT Decor (40/20/40 split front bench seat with premium cloth upholstery, passenger visor vanity mirror, leather-wrapped steering wheel, chrome front bumper, tailgate panel applique, front floor mats, under hood sound deadening insulation, dual horns, full floor carpeting, black bodyside moldings, chrome power exterior mirrors), heavy-duty service group (HD 750-amp battery, HD 136-amp alternator, HD engine cooling), transfer case skid plate (4WD), 8.0-liter V-10 engine, 4-speed automatic transmission, auxiliary transmission oil cooler

28H	Laramie SLT Option Package 28H (Reg Cab)	4515	5310
	Manufacturer Discount	(680)	(800)
	Net Price	3835	4510

Includes power convenience group (power windows, power door locks), behind seat storage, air conditioning, tachometer, light group (cloth headliner, passenger assist grip, glove box light, under hood light, overhead console with storage and reading lights, exterior cargo light), deluxe convenience group (tilt steering column and cruise control), chrome wheels, chrome bumpers, Laramie SLT Decor (40/20/40 split front bench seat with premium cloth upholstery, passenger visor vanity mirror, chrome front bumper, tailgate panel applique, front floor mats, under hood sound deadening insulation, dual horns, full floor carpeting, black bodyside moldings, chrome power exterior mirrors), transfer case skid plate (4WD), heavy-duty service group (HD 750-amp battery, HD 136-amp alternator, HD engine cooling), auxiliary transmission oil cooler, 8.0-liter V-10 engine, 4-speed automatic transmission

29H	Laramie SLT Option Package 29H (Club Cab Longbed)	5900	6941
	Manufacturer Discount	(340)	(400)
	Net Price	5560	6541

Includes power convenience group (power windows, power door locks), air conditioning, tachometer, light group (cloth headliner, passenger assist grip, glove box light, under hood light, overhead console with storage and reading lights, exterior cargo light), deluxe convenience group (tilt steering column and cruise control), chrome wheels, chrome bumpers, Laramie SLT Decor (40/20/40 split front bench seat with premium cloth upholstery, passenger visor vanity mirror, leather-wrapped steering wheel, chrome front bumper, tailgate panel applique, front floor mats, under

DODGE RAM 2500

CODE	DESCRIPTION	INVOICE	MSRP

hood sound deadening insulation, dual horns, full floor carpeting, black bodyside moldings, chrome power exterior mirrors), heavy-duty service group (HD 750-amp battery, HD 136-amp alternator, HD engine cooling), transfer case skid plate (4WD), 5.9-liter Cummins Turbodiesel engine (includes 1 additional battery, diesel sound insulation, message center with warning lights)

29H	Laramie SLT Option Package 29H (Reg Cab)	6591	7754
	Manufacturer Discount	(680)	(800)
	Net Price	5911	6954

Includes power convenience group (power windows, power door locks), behind seat storage, air conditioning, tachometer, light group (cloth headliner, passenger assist grip, glove box light, under hood light, overhead console with storage and reading lights, exterior cargo light), deluxe convenience group (tilt steering column and cruise control), chrome wheels, chrome bumpers, Laramie SLT Decor (40/20/40 split front bench seat with premium cloth upholstery, passenger visor vanity mirror, chrome front bumper, tailgate panel applique, front floor mats, under hood sound deadening insulation, dual horns, full floor carpeting, black bodyside moldings, chrome power exterior mirrors), transfer case skid plate (4WD), heavy-duty service group (HD 750-amp battery, HD 136-amp alternator, HD engine cooling), 5.9-liter Cummins Turbodiesel engine (with 1 additional HD 750-amp battery, diesel sound insulation, message center with warning lights), engine block heater

2YH	Laramie SLT Option Package 2YH (Club Cab Longbed)	6708	7891
	Manufacturer Discount	(340)	(400)
	Net Price	6368	7491

Includes power convenience group (power windows, power door locks), air conditioning, tachometer, light group (cloth headliner, passenger assist grip, glove box light, under hood light, overhead console with storage and reading lights, exterior cargo light), deluxe convenience group (tilt steering column and cruise control), chrome wheels, chrome bumpers, Laramie SLT Decor (40/20/40 split front bench seat with premium cloth upholstery, passenger visor vanity mirror, leather-wrapped steering wheel, chrome front bumper, tailgate panel applique, front floor mats, under hood sound deadening insulation, dual horns, full floor carpeting, black bodyside moldings, chrome power exterior mirrors), heavy-duty service group (HD 750-amp battery, HD 136-amp alternator, HD engine cooling), transfer case skid plate (4WD), 5.9-liter Cummins Turbodiesel engine (includes 1 additional battery, diesel sound insulation, message center with warning lights), 4-speed automatic transmission, auxiliary transmission oil cooler.

2YH	Laramie SLT Option Package 2YH (Reg Cab)	7399	8704
	Manufacturer Discount	(680)	(800)
	Net Price	6719	7904

Includes power convenience group (power windows, power door locks), behind seat storage, air conditioning, tachometer, light group (cloth headliner, passenger assist grip, glove box light, under hood light, overhead console with storage and reading lights, exterior cargo light), deluxe convenience group (tilt steering column and cruise control), chrome wheels, chrome bumpers, Laramie SLT Decor (40/20/40 split front bench seat with premium cloth upholstery, passenger visor vanity mirror, chrome front bumper, tailgate panel applique, front floor mats, under hood sound deadening

RAM 2500 — DODGE

CODE	DESCRIPTION	INVOICE	MSRP

insulation, dual horns, full floor carpeting, black bodyside moldings, chrome power exterior mirrors), transfer case skid plate (4WD), heavy-duty service group (HD 750-amp battery, HD 136-amp alternator, HD engine cooling), 5.9-liter Cummins Turbodiesel engine (with 1 additional HD 750-amp battery, diesel sound insulation, message center with warning lights), 4-speed automatic transmission, auxiliary transmission oil cooler, engine block heater

Code	Description	Invoice	MSRP
26B	**LT Option Package 26B (Reg Cab)**	808	950
	Includes 4-speed automatic transmission		
26D	**LT Option Package 26D (Club Cab)**	808	950
	Includes 4-speed automatic transmission		
27B	**LT Option Package 27B (Reg Cab)**	829	975
	Includes 8.0-liter V-10 engine		
29B	**LT Option Package 29B (Reg Cab)**	3778	4445
	Includes 5.9-liter Cummins Turbodiesel engine (includes additional 750-amp battery, diesel sound insulation, message center with warning lights), heavy-duty service group (HD 750-amp battery, HD 136-amp alternator, HD engine cooling), engine block heater, tachometer, transfer case skid plate (4WD)		
2YB	**LT Option Package 2YB (Reg Cab)**	4586	5395
	Includes 5.9-liter Cummins Turbodiesel engine (includes additional 750-amp battery, diesel sound insulation, message center with warning lights), heavy-duty service group (HD 750-amp battery, HD 136-amp alternator, HD engine cooling), engine block heater, tachometer, 4-speed automatic transmission, auxiliary transmission oil cooler, trasnfer case skid plate (4WD)		
27D	**ST Option Package 27D (Club Cab)**	829	975
	Includes 8.0-liter V-10 engine, heavy-duty service group (HD 750-amp battery, HD 136-amp alternator, HD engine cooling), transfer case skid plate (4WD)		
28D	**ST Option Package 28D (Club Cab)**	1637	1925
	Includes 8.0-liter V-10 engine, heavy-duty service group (HD 750-amp battery, HD 136-amp alternator, HD engine cooling), transfer case skid plate (4WD), 4-speed automatic transmission, auxiliary transmission oil cooler		
29D	**ST Option Package 29D (Club Cab Longbed)**	3778	4445
	Includes 5.9-liter Cummins Turbodiesel engine (includes 1 additional 750-amp battery, diesel sound insulation, message center with warning lights), heavy-duty service group (HD 750-amp battery, HD 136-amp alternator, HD engine cooling), tachometer, transfer case skid plate (4WD)		
2YD	**ST Option Package 2YD (Club Cab Longbed)**	4586	5395
	Includes 5.9-liter Cummins Turbodiesel engine (includes 1 additional 750-amp battery, diesel sound insulation, message center with warning lights), heavy-duty service group (HD 750-amp battery, HD 136-amp alternator, HD engine cooling), tachometer, transfer case skid plate (4WD), 4-speed automatic transmission, auxiliary transmission oil cooler		
HAA	**Air Conditioning**	677	797
BGK	**Anti-lock Brakes**	425	500
AMR	**Behind Seat Storage (Reg Cab)**	81	95
	INCLUDED in Laramie SLT Option Packages		

DODGE RAM 2500

CODE	DESCRIPTION	INVOICE	MSRP
K17	Bodyside Moldings	87	102
	INCLUDED in Laramie SLT Option Packages		
YCF	Border States Emissions	145	170
LNC	Cab Clearance Lights	68	80
NAE	Calif./Mass./New York Emissions	145	170
AHJ	Camper Special Package	78	92
	Includes auxiliary springs and stabilizer bars; REQUIRES heavy-duty engine cooling		
AJK	Deluxe Convenience Group	332	390
	Includes tilt steering column and cruise control; INCLUDED in Laramie SLT Option Packages		
GNC	Dual Illuminated Visor Vanity Mirrors	80	94
	REQUIRES purchase of a Laramie SLT Option Package		
NHK	Engine Block Heater	34	40
GPC	Exterior Mirrors — Chrome Manual	43	50
	With 25H (Reg Cab)	(43)	(50)
	With 25H (Club Cab)	(43)	(50)
	With 26H (Reg Cab)	(43)	(50)
	With 26H (Club Cab)	(43)	(50)
	With 27H (Reg Cab)	(43)	(50)
	With 27H (Club Cab)	(43)	(50)
	With 28H (Club Cab)	(43)	(50)
	With 28H (Reg Cab)	(43)	(50)
	With 29H (Club Cab Longbed)	(43)	(50)
	With 29H (Reg Cab)	(43)	(50)
	With 2YH (Reg Cab)	(43)	(50)
	With 2YH (Club Cab Longbed)	(43)	(50)
	Sized 7"x 10"		
GPP	Exterior Mirrors — Chrome Power	84	99
	Sized 6"x 9"		
LNJ	Fog Lights	102	120
	REQUIRES purchase of a Laramie SLT Option Package		
MXB	Front Air Dam	21	25
NMC	Heavy-duty Engine Cooling	56	66
	With 26D (Club Cab)	111	130
	With 28D (Club Cab)	111	130
	With 26H (Club Cab)	111	130
	With 28H (Club Cab)	111	130
	With 2YD (Club Cab Longbed)	111	130
	With 2YH (Club Cab Longbed)	111	130
	With 26B (Reg Cab)	111	130
	With 26H (Reg Cab)	111	130
	With 28B (Reg Cab)	111	130
	With 28H (Reg Cab)	111	130
	With 2YB (Reg Cab)	111	130
	With 2YH (Reg Cab)	111	130

RAM 2500 — DODGE

CODE	DESCRIPTION	INVOICE	MSRP
ADJ	Heavy-duty Service Group (2WD Club Cab)	235	277
	With 26D (Club Cab)	290	341
	With 26H (Club Cab)	290	341

Includes heavy-duty engine cooling, 136-amp alternator, 750-amp battery, auxiliary transmission oil cooler (with automatic transmission); INCLUDED in LT, ST, and Laramie SLT Option Packages containing V-10 or Turbodiesel engines Turbodiesel engines

ADJ	Heavy-duty Service Group (2WD Reg Cab)	235	277
	With 26B (Reg Cab)	290	341
	With 26H (Reg Cab)	290	341

Includes heavy-duty engine cooling, 136-amp alternator, 750-amp battery, auxiliary transmission oil cooler (with automatic transmission); INCLUDED in LT, ST, and Laramie SLT Option Packages containing V-10 or Turbodiesel engines

ADJ	Heavy-duty Service Group (4WD Club Cab)	273	321
	With 26D (Club Cab)	332	390
	With 26H (Club Cab)	332	390

Includes heavy-duty engine cooling, 136-amp alternator, 750-amp battery, auxiliary transmission oil cooler (with automatic transmission), transfer case skid plate; INCLUDED in LT, ST, and Laramie SLT Option Packages containing V-10 or Turbodiesel engines

ADJ	Heavy-duty Service Group (4WD Reg Cab)	273	321
	With 26B (Reg Cab)	327	385
	With 26H (Reg Cab)	327	385

Includes heavy-duty engine cooling, 136-amp alternator, 750-amp battery, auxiliary transmission oil cooler (with automatic transmission) transfer case skid plate; INCLUDED in LT, ST, and Laramie SLT Option Packages containing V-10 or

DHG	Heavy-duty Transfer Case (4WD)	85	100
AJD	Leather Interior Group (Club Cab)	1275	1500

Includes leather upholstery, travel convenience group (overhead console with compass, reading lights, and outside temperature display; auto dimming day/night rear view mirror), woodgrain interior trim, dual illuminated visor vanity mirrors, 6-way power driver's seat; REQUIRES purchase of a Laramie SLT Option Package

AJD	Leather Interior Group (Reg Cab)	1190	1400

Includes leather upholstery, travel convenience group (overhead console with compass, reading lights, and outside temperature display; auto dimming day/night rear view mirror), woodgrain interior trim, dual illuminated visor vanity mirrors, 6-way power driver's seat; REQUIRES purchase of a Laramie SLT Option Package

ADA	Light Group (Club Cab)	102	120

Includes cloth headliner, overhead reading lights, passenger assist grip, exterior cargo light, overhead console with storage, glove box light, under hood light; INCLUDED in Laramie SLT Option Packages

ADA	Light Group (Reg Cab)	134	158

Includes cloth headliner, overhead reading lights, passenger assist grip, exterior cargo light, overhead console with storage, glove box light, under hood light; INCLUDED in Laramie SLT Option Packages

DODGE RAM 2500

CODE	DESCRIPTION	INVOICE	MSRP
28B	LT Option Package 28B (Reg Cab)	1637	1925
	Includes 8.0-liter V-10 engine and 4-speed automatic transmission		
6C	Paint — Two-tone Center Band	235	276
	With 25H (Club Cab)	183	215
	With 25H (Reg Cab)	183	215
	With 26H (Reg Cab)	183	215
	With 26H (Club Cab)	183	215
	With 27H (Club Cab)	183	215
	With 27H (Reg Cab)	183	215
	With 28H (Club Cab)	183	215
	With 28H (Reg Cab)	183	215
	With 29H (Club Cab Longbed)	183	215
	With 29H (Reg Cab)	183	215
	With 2YH (Reg Cab)	183	215
	With 2YH (Club Cab Longbed)	183	215
	Includes bodyside moldings and tape stripes		
6D	Paint — Two-tone Lower Break	166	195
	Includes bodyside moldings		
JPS	Power Driver's Seat	272	320
	Includes 6-way adjustment; REQUIRES purchase of a Laramie SLT Option Package		
DM	Rear Axle — Optional Ratio	43	50
MBQ	Rear Step Bumper — Color-keyed (Club Cab Shortbed)	43	50
	REQUIRES Sport Appearance Group		
4XM	Rear Step Bumper — Delete (Club Cab Shortbed)	NC	NC
MBD	Rear Step Bumper — Painted (Reg Cab)	113	133
GXM	Remote Keyless Entry	162	190
	REQUIRES purchase of a Laramie SLT Option Package		
CKJ	Rubber Floor Covering	NC	NC
B3	Seats — Deluxe Cloth & Vinyl Bench (Reg Cab)	85	100
	NOT AVAILABLE with Laramie SLT Option Packages		
T9	Seats — Deluxe Cloth 40/20/40 Split Bench (Reg Cab)	222	261
	NOT AVAILABLE with Laramie SLT Option Package		
TX	Seats — Heavy-duty Vinyl 40/20/40 Split Bench (Club Cab)	NC	NC
TX	Seats — Heavy-duty Vinyl 40/20/40 Split Bench (Reg Cab)	222	261
	With 25H (Reg Cab)	NC	NC
	With 26H (Reg Cab)	NC	NC
	With 27H (Reg Cab)	NC	NC
	With 28H (Reg Cab)	NC	NC
	With 29H (Reg Cab)	NC	NC
	With 2YH (Reg Cab)	NC	NC
GFD	Sliding Rear Window	117	138
AHD	Snow Plow Prep Group (4WD)	156	183
	Manufacturer Discount	(71)	(83)
	Net Price	85	100
	Includes heavy-duty front springs, extra-duty front suspension, heavy-duty transfer case; REQUIRES trailer tow group, heavy-duty service group, and rear bumper		

RAM 2500 — DODGE

CODE	DESCRIPTION	INVOICE	MSRP
AGG	Sport Appearance Group (Club Cab Shortbed)	808	950
	With 25H (Club Cab)	391	460
	With 26H (Club Cab)	391	460
	With 27H (Club Cab)	391	460
	With 28H (Club Cab)	391	460
	Includes color-keyed rear valance panel, fog lights, LT245/75R16 al-season outline white-lettered tires (2WD), LT245/75R16 all-terrain outline white-lettered tires (4WD), color-keyed grille, chrome wheels, tachometer, Sport decals; NOT AVAILABLE with V-10 or Diesel engines		
AMP	ST Decor Group (Reg Cab)	324	381
	Includes deluxe cloth 40/20/40 split bench seat, wheel dress-up package (chrome trim rings and bright center caps), chrome rear step bumper, chrome front bumper, floor carpeting, cab back panel storage		
RA8	Stereo — Delete Credit	(85)	(100)
	NOT AVAILABLE with Laramie SLT Option Packages		
RBN	Stereo — Uplevel w/cassette	281	331
	AM/FM stereo with cassette player and graphic equalizer; REQUIRES purchase of a Laramie SLT Option Package		
RAZ	Stereo — Uplevel w/cassette & CD players	587	690
	AM/FM stereo with cassette and CD players and graphic equalizer; REQUIRES purchase of a Laramie SLT Option Package		
RBR	Stereo — w/CD changer	434	510
	AM/FM stereo with CD changer; REQUIRES purchase of a Laramie SLT Option Package		
DSA	Sure Grip Axle	242	285
JAY	Tachometer	65	76
TYH	Tires — LT245/75R16	119	140
	Blackwall all-terrain tires; REQUIRES purchase of a Laramie SLT Option Package on Regular Cab models		
TYN	Tires — LT245/75R16	106	125
	Outline white-lettered-all-season tires; REQUIRES purchase of a Laramie SLT Option Package		
TYP	Tires — LT245/75R16	225	265
	Outline white-lettered all-terrain tires; REQUIRES purchase of a Laramie SLT Option Package		
AHC	Trailer Tow Group	206	242
	Includes heavy-duty flashers, class IV trailer hitch receiver, adaptor plug; REQUIRES heavy-duty service group and rear bumper		
AWK	Travel Convenience Group	176	207
	Includes overhead console with compass, reading lights, and outside temperature display; automatic dimming day/night rearview mirror; REQUIRES purchase of a Laramie SLT Option Package		
WMC	Wheel Dress-up Package (Reg Cab)	51	60
	Includes chrome trim rings and bright center caps; NOT AVAILABLE with Laramie SLT Option Packages		

DODGE — RAM 3500

RAM 3500 *(1997)*

Safety Data

Driver Airbag: *Standard*
Side Airbag: *Not Available*
4-Wheel ABS: *Optional*
Driver Crash Test Grade: *Excellent*

Passenger Crash Test Grade: *Not Available*

Passenger Airbag: *Not Available*
Meets 1999 Side Impact Standards: *No*
Traction Control: *Not Available*
Insurance Cost: *Avg. (2WD Reg Cab); High (4WD; 2WD Club Cab)*
Integrated Child Seat(s): *Not Available*

Standard Equipment

RAM 3500 REGULAR CAB: Driver's airbag, power front disc/rear drum brakes with rear ABS, argent front bumper, headlights-on warning buzzer, digital clock, cigarette lighter, auxiliary power outlet, 5.9-liter V-8 engine, black rubber floor covering, voltmeter, oil pressure gauge, engine temperature gauge, trip odometer, tinted glass, chrome grille, heavy-duty service group (750-amp HD battery, 136-amp HD alternator, HD engine cooling, skid plates (4WD), auxiliary transmission oil cooler (w/automatic transmission), 10 front/side/rear clearance and identification lights, fender flares, day/night rearview mirror, dual chrome power exterior mirrors, power steering, AM/FM stereo with cassette player and 4 speakers, vinyl bench seat with head restraints, heavy-duty front and rear shocks, LT215/85R16D blackwall all-season tires, underbody spare tire carrier, 5-speed manual transmission, 16"x 6" steel wheels, 2-speed intermittent windshield wipers, heavy-duty 2-speed transfer case with shift-on-the-fly auto-locking front hubs (4WD)

3500 CLUB CAB (in addition to or instead of REGULAR CAB equipment): Deluxe cloth 40/20/40 split bench seat, deluxe cloth rear bench seat, front stabilizer bar

Base Prices

CODE	DESCRIPTION	INVOICE	MSRP
BR3L62	2WD Regular Cab Duallie	17702	20255
BR3L32	2WD Club Cab Duallie	19730	22600
BR8L62	4WD Regular Cab Duallie	19875	22770
BR8L32	4WD Club Cab Duallie	21912	25120
	Destination Charge:	640	640

Accessories

CODE	DESCRIPTION	INVOICE	MSRP
25G	Laramie SLT Option Package 25G (Club Cab)	1828	2151
	Manufacturer Discount	(340)	(400)
	Net Price	1488	1751

Includes Laramie SLT Decor (black bodyside moldings, full floor carpeting, 40/20/40 split bench seat, tailgate applique, front floor mats, chrome front bumper, under hood sound insulation, dual horns, premium cloth upholstery, passenger visor vanity mirror), power convenience group (power windows, power door locks), deluxe convenience group (tilt steering wheel, cruise control), light group (cloth headliner, passenger assist grip, glovebox light, exterior cargo light, overhead console with storage and reading lights, under hood light), air conditioning, tachometer, chrome front and rear bumpers

RAM 3500 — DODGE

CODE	DESCRIPTION	INVOICE	MSRP
25G	Laramie SLT Option Package 25G (Reg Cab)	2728	3209
	Manufacturer Discount	(680)	(800)
	Net Price	2048	2409

Includes Laramie SLT Decor (black bodyside moldings, full floor carpeting, 40/20/40 split bench seat, tailgate applique, front floor mats, chrome front bumper, under hood sound insulation, dual horns, premium cloth upholstery, passenger visor vanity mirror), power convenience group (power windows, power door locks), deluxe convenience group (tilt steering wheel, cruise control), light group (cloth headliner, passenger assist grip, glovebox light, exterior cargo light, overhead console with storage and reading lights, under hood light), behind seat storage, air conditioning, tachometer, wheel dress-up

26G	Laramie SLT Option Package 26G (Club Cab)	2636	3101
	Manufacturer Discount	(340)	(400)
	Net Price	2296	2701

Includes Laramie SLT Decor (black bodyside moldings, full floor carpeting, 40/20/40 split bench seat, tailgate applique, front floor mats, chrome front bumper, under hood sound insulation, dual horns, premium cloth upholstery, passenger visor vanity mirror), power convenience group (power windows, power door locks), deluxe convenience group (tilt steering wheel, cruise control), light group (cloth headliner, passenger assist grip, glovebox light, exterior cargo light, overhead console with storage and reading lights, under hood light), air conditioning, tachometer, chrome front and rear bumpers, 4-speed automatic transmission

26G	Laramie SLT Option Package 26G (Reg Cab)	3536	4159
	Manufacturer Discount	(680)	(800)
	Net Price	2856	3359

Includes Laramie SLT Decor (black bodyside moldings, full floor carpeting, 40/20/40 split bench seat, tailgate applique, front floor mats, chrome front bumper, under hood sound insulation, dual horns, premium cloth upholstery, passenger visor vanity mirror), power convenience group (power windows, power door locks), deluxe convenience group (tilt steering wheel, cruise control), light group (cloth headliner, passenger assist grip, glovebox light, exterior cargo light, overhead console with storage and reading lights, under hood light), behind seat storage, air conditioning, tachometer, wheel dress-up package (chrome wheel skins), chrome front and rear bumpers, 4-speed automatic transmission

27G	Laramie SLT Option Package 27G (Club Cab)	2657	3126
	Manufacturer Discount	(340)	(400)
	Net Price	2317	2726

Includes Laramie SLT Decor (black bodyside moldings, full floor carpeting, 40/20/40 split bench seat, tailgate applique, front floor mats, chrome front bumper, under hood sound insulation, dual horns, premium cloth upholstery, passenger visor vanity mirror), power convenience group (power windows, power door locks), deluxe convenience group (tilt steering wheel, cruise control), light group (cloth headliner, passenger assist grip, glovebox light, exterior cargo light, overhead console with storage and reading lights, under hood light), air conditioning, tachometer, chrome front and rear bumpers, 8.0-liter V-10 engine, 4-speed automatic transmission

DODGE RAM 3500

CODE	DESCRIPTION	INVOICE	MSRP
27G	Laramie SLT Option Package 27G (Reg Cab)	3557	4184
	Manufacturer Discount	(680)	(800)
	Net Price	2877	3384

Includes Laramie SLT Decor (black bodyside moldings, full floor carpeting, 40/20/40 split bench seat, tailgate applique, front floor mats, chrome front bumper, under hood sound insulation, dual horns, premium cloth upholstery, passenger visor vanity mirror), power convenience group (power windows, power door locks), deluxe convenience group (tilt steering wheel, cruise control), light group (cloth headliner, passenger assist grip, glovebox light, exterior cargo light, overhead console with storage and reading lights, under hood light), behind seat storage, air conditioning, tachometer, wheel dress-up package (chrome wheel skins), chrome front and rear bumpers, 8.0-liter V-10 engine

28G	Laramie SLT Option Package 28G (Club Cab)	3465	4076
	Manufacturer Discount	(340)	(400)
	Net Price	3125	3676

Includes Laramie SLT Decor (black bodyside moldings, full floor carpeting, 40/20/40 split bench seat, tailgate applique, front floor mats, chrome front bumper, under hood sound insulation, dual horns, premium cloth upholstery, passenger visor vanity mirror), power convenience group (power windows, power door locks), deluxe convenience group (tilt steering wheel, cruise control), light group (cloth headliner, passenger assist grip, glovebox light, exterior cargo light, overhead console with storage and reading lights, under hood light), air conditioning, tachometer, chrome front and rear bumpers,

28G	Laramie SLT Option Package 28G (Reg Cab)	4365	5134
	Manufacturer Discount	(680)	(800)
	Net Price	3685	4334

Includes Laramie SLT Decor (black bodyside moldings, full floor carpeting, 40/20/40 split bench seat, tailgate applique, front floor mats, chrome front bumper, under hood sound insulation, dual horns, premium cloth upholstery, passenger visor vanity mirror), power convenience group (power windows, power door locks), deluxe convenience group (tilt steering wheel, cruise control), light group (cloth headliner, passenger assist grip, glovebox light, exterior cargo light, overhead console with storage and reading lights, under hood light), behind seat storage, air conditioning, tachometer, wheel dress-up package (chrome wheel skins), chrome front and rear bumpers, 8.0-liter V-10, 4-speed automatic transmission

29G	Laramie SLT Option Package 29G (Club Cab)	5542	6520
	Manufacturer Discount	(340)	(400)
	Net Price	5202	6120

Includes Laramie SLT Decor (black bodyside moldings, full floor carpeting, 40/20/40 split bench seat, tailgate applique, front floor mats, chrome front bumper, under hood sound insulation, dual horns, premium cloth upholstery, passenger visor vanity mirror), power convenience group (power windows, power door locks), deluxe convenience group (tilt steering wheel, cruise control), light group (cloth headliner, passenger assist grip, glovebox light, exterior cargo light, overhead console with storage and reading lights, under hood light), air conditioning, tachometer, chrome

RAM 3500 — DODGE

CODE	DESCRIPTION	INVOICE	MSRP

front and rear bumpers, 5.9-liter Cummins Turbodiesel engine, two 750-amp batteries, diesel sound insulation, engine block heater, message center with warning lights, tachometer

29G Laramie SLT Option Package 29G (Reg Cab) .... 6441 / 7578
Manufacturer Discount .... (680) / (800)
Net Price .... 5761 / 6778

Includes Laramie SLT Decor (black bodyside moldings, full floor carpeting, 40/20/40 split bench seat, tailgate applique, front floor mats, chrome front bumper, under hood sound insulation, dual horns, premium cloth upholstery, passenger visor vanity mirror), power convenience group (power windows, power door locks), deluxe convenience group (tilt steering wheel, cruise control), light group (cloth headliner, passenger assist grip, glovebox light, exterior cargo light, overhead console with storage and reading lights, under hood light), behind seat storage, air conditioning, tachometer, wheel dress-up package (chrome wheel skins), chrome front and rear bumpers, 5.9-liter Cummins Turbodiesel engine, two 750-amp batteries, diesel sound insulation, engine block heater, message center with warning lights, tachometer

2YG Laramie SLT Option Package 2YG (Club Cab) .... 6350 / 7470
Manufacturer Discount .... (340) / (400)
Net Price .... 6010 / 7070

Includes Laramie SLT Decor (black bodyside moldings, full floor carpeting, 40/20/40 split bench seat, tailgate applique, front floor mats, chrome front bumper, under hood sound insulation, dual horns, premium cloth upholstery, passenger visor vanity mirror), power convenience group (power windows, power door locks), deluxe convenience group (tilt steering wheel, cruise control), light group (cloth headliner, passenger assist grip, glovebox light, exterior cargo light, overhead console with storage and reading lights, under hood light), air conditioning, tachometer, chrome front and rear bumpers, 5.9-liter Cummins Turbodiesel engine, 4-speed automatic transmission, two 750-amp batteries, diesel sound insulation, engine block heater, message center with warning lights, tachometer

2YG Laramie SLT Option Package 2YG (Reg Cab) .... 7249 / 8530
Manufacturer Discount .... (680) / (800)
Net Price .... 6569 / 7730

Includes Laramie SLT Decor (black bodyside moldings, full floor carpeting, 40/20/40 split bench seat, tailgate applique, front floor mats, chrome front bumper, under hood sound insulation, dual horns, premium cloth upholstery, passenger visor vanity mirror), power convenience group (power windows, power door locks), deluxe convenience group (tilt steering wheel, cruise control), light group (cloth headliner, passenger assist grip, glovebox light, exterior cargo light, overhead console with storage and reading lights, under hood light), behind seat storage, air conditioning, tachometer, wheel dress-up package (chrome wheel skins), chrome front and rear bumpers, 5.9-liter Cummins Turbodiesel engine, 4-speed automatic transmission, two 750-amp batteries, diesel sound insulation, engine block heater, message center with warning lights, block heater, message center with warning lights, tachometer

26A LT Option Package 26A (Reg Cab) .... 808 / 950
Includes 4-speed automatic transmission

DODGE RAM 3500

CODE	DESCRIPTION	INVOICE	MSRP
27A	**LT Option Package 27A (Reg Cab)**	829	975
	Includes 8.0-liter V-10 engine		
28A	**LT Option Package 28A (Reg Cab)**	1637	1925
	Includes 8.0-liter V-10 engine and 4-speed automatic transmission		
29A	**LT Option Package 29A (Reg Cab)**	3778	4445
	Includes 5.9-liter Cummins Turbodiesel engine, two 750-amp batteries, diesel sound insulation, engine block heater, message center with warning lights, tachometer		
2YA	**LT Option Package 2YA (Reg Cab)**	4586	5395
	Includes 5.9-liter Cummins Turbodiesel engine, 4-speed automatic transmission, two 750-amp batteries, diesel sound insulation, engine block heater, message center with warning lights, tachometer		
26C	**ST Option Package 26C (Club Cab)**	808	950
	Includes 4-speed automatic transmission		
27C	**ST Option Package 27C (Club Cab)**	829	975
	Includes 8.0-liter V-10 engine		
28C	**ST Option Package 28C (Club Cab)**	1637	1925
	Includes 8.0-liter V-10 engine and 4-speed automatic transmission		
29C	**ST Option Package 29C (Club Cab)**	3778	4445
	Includes 5.9-liter Cummins Turbodiesel engine, two 750-amp batteries, diesel sound insulation, engine block heater, message center with warning lights, tachometer		
2YC	**ST Option Package 2YC (Club Cab)**	4586	5395
	Includes 5.9-liter Cummins Turbodiesel engine, 4-speed automatic transmission, two 750-amp batteries, diesel sound insulation, engine block heater, message center with warning lights, tachometer		
HAA	**Air Conditioning**	677	797
	INCLUDED in Laramie SLT Option Packages		
BGK	**Anti-lock Brakes**	425	500
K17	**Bodyside Moldings**	87	102
YCF	**Border States Emissions**	145	170
NAE	**Calif./Mass./New York Emissions**	145	170
AHJ	**Camper Special Package**	78	92
	Includes stabilizer bars and auxiliary springs		
AJK	**Deluxe Convenience Group**	332	390
	Includes tilt steering column and cruise control		
GNC	**Dual Illuminated Visor Vanity Mirrors**	80	94
	REQUIRES purchase of a Laramie SLT Option Package		
NHK	**Engine Block Heater**	34	40
GPC	**Exterior Mirrors — Chrome Manual**	(43)	(50)
	Sized 7"x 10"		
LNJ	**Fog Lights**	102	120
	REQUIRES purchase of a Laramie SLT Option Package		
MXB	**Front Air Dam**	21	25
AJD	**Leather Interior Group (Club Cab)**	1275	1500
	Includes leather upholstery, power driver's seat with 6-way adjustment, woodgrain interior trim, travel convenience group (overhead console with compass, reading		

RAM 3500 — DODGE

CODE	DESCRIPTION	INVOICE	MSRP
	lights, and outside temperature readout; automatic dimming rearview mirror), dual illuminated visor vanity mirrors; REQUIRES purchase of a Laramie SLT Option Package		
AJD	Leather Interior Group (Reg Cab)	1190	1400
	Includes leather upholstery, power driver's seat with 6-way adjustment, woodgrain interior trim, travel convenience group (overhead console with compass, reading lights, and outside temperature readout; automatic dimming rearview mirror), dual illuminated visor vanity mirrors; REQUIRES purchase of a Laramie SLT Option Package		
ADA	Light Group (Club Cab)	102	120
	Includes cloth headliner, passenger assist grip, glove box light, exterior cargo light, overhead console with storage and reading lights, under hood light		
ADA	Light Group (Reg Cab)	134	158
	Includes cloth headliner, passenger assist grip, glove box light, exterior cargo light, overhead console with storage and reading lights, under hood light		
6B	Paint — Two-tone	211	248
	With 25G (Club Cab)	159	187
	With 25G (Reg Cab)	159	187
	With 26G (Club Cab)	159	187
	With 26G (Reg Cab)	159	187
	With 27G (Reg Cab)	159	187
	With 27G (Club Cab)	159	187
	With 28G (Club Cab)	159	187
	With 28G (Reg Cab)	159	187
	With 29G (Reg Cab)	159	187
	With 29G (Club Cab)	159	187
	With 2YG (Reg Cab)	159	187
	With 2YG (Club Cab)	159	187
JPS	Power Driver's Seat	272	320
	REQUIRES purchase of a Laramie SLT Option Package		
DM	Rear Axle — Optional Ratio	43	50
MBD	Rear Step Bumper — Painted (Reg Cab)	113	133
GXM	Remote Keyless Entry	162	190
	REQUIRES purchase of a Laramie SLT Option Package		
CKJ	Rubber Floor Covering	NC	NC
	REQUIRES purchase of ST Decor Group on Regular Cab models; NOT AVAILABLE with Laramie SLT Option Packages on Regular Cab models		
B3	Seats — Deluxe Cloth & Vinyl Bench (Reg Cab)	85	100
T9	Seats — Deluxe Cloth 40/20/40 Split Bench (Reg Cab)	222	261
TX	Seats — Heavy-duty Vinyl 40/20/40 Split Bench (Club Cab)	NC	NC

DODGE — RAM 3500

CODE	DESCRIPTION	INVOICE	MSRP
TX	Seats — Heavy-duty Vinyl 40/20/40 Split Bench (Reg Cab)	222	261
	With 25G (Reg Cab)	NC	NC
	With 26G (Reg Cab)	NC	NC
	With 27G (Reg Cab)	NC	NC
	With 28G (Reg Cab)	NC	NC
	With 29G (Reg Cab)	NC	NC
	With 2YG (Reg Cab)	NC	NC
	With AMP (Reg Cab)	NC	NC
GFD	Sliding Rear Window	117	138
AHD	Snow Plow Prep Group (4WD)	71	83
	Manufacturer Discount	(71)	(83)
	Net Price	NC	NC

Includes extra-duty front suspension and warning light for automatic transmission oil overheat; REQUIRES trailer tow group and rear bumper

AMP	ST Decor Group (Reg Cab)	532	626

Includes deluxe cloth 40/20/40 split bench seat, floor carpeting, chrome bumpers, chrome wheel skins, behind seat storage tray, cab back panel storage; NOT AVAILABLE with Laramie SLT Option Packages

RA8	Stereo — Delete Credit	(85)	(100)

NOT AVAILABLE with Laramie SLT Option Packages

RBN	Stereo — Uplevel w/cassette	281	331

AM/FM stereo with cassette player, graphic equalizer, and clock

RAZ	Stereo — Uplevel w/cassette & CD players	587	690

AM/FM stereo with cassette and CD players, graphic equalizer, and clock; REQUIRES purchase of a Laramie SLT Option

RBR	Stereo — w/CD player	434	510

AM/FM stereo with CD changer; REQUIRES purchase of a Laramie SLT Option Package

DSA	Sure Grip Axle	242	285
JAY	Tachometer	65	76
TVW	Tires — LT215/85R16D (2WD)	167	196

Blackwall all-terrain tires

TV2	Tires — LT215/85R16E (4WD)	167	196

Blackwall all-terrain tires

AHC	Trailer Tow Group	206	242

Includes heavy-duty flashers, class IV trailer hitch receiver, and adaptor plug; REQUIRES a rear bumper

AWK	Travel Convenience Group	176	207

Includes overhead console with compass, reading lights, and outside temperature display; automatic dimming rearview mirror; REQUIRES purchase of a Laramie SLT Option Package

WMG	Wheel Dress-up Package (Reg Cab)	259	305

Includes chrome wheel skins

RAM VAN / RAM WAGON

DODGE

| CODE | DESCRIPTION | INVOICE | MSRP |

RAM VAN / RAM WAGON (1997)

1997 Dodge Ram Wagon

What's New for Dodge Ram Van / Ram Wago in 1997 — New this year are wider cargo doors, upgraded stereo systems, and an improved ignition switch with anti-theft protection. Front quarter vent windows disappear for 1997, and underhood service points feature colored identification.

Ram Van / Ram Wagon — Review

Dodge's full-size vans and wagons haven't changed all that much through nearly three decades of existence. Squint your eyes and focus away from the front end (which was redesigned in 1994), and the latest big Rams could almost be mistaken for 1971 models. Does that matter to their fans? Not in the least. Dodge's brawny haulers have earned an enviable reputation over the years, proving their worth against rivals from Ford and General Motors. Like those makes, Dodge offers a bewildering selection of models, in three capacities with payloads as great as 4,264 pounds—not to mention the dazzlingly long list of options to be considered. Wagons can be equipped to carry as many as 15 passengers.

A driver's airbag is standard, and all Rams have rear-wheel anti-lock braking (four-wheel on the Wagons). Base engine in the 1500 and 2500 series is a 3.9-liter V-6, but most buyers would be better off with a V-8 (standard in the 3500 series). With 295 pound-feet of torque on tap, the 5.2-liter V-8 yields a rewarding combination of strength and economy, but no Ram vehicle ranks miserly at the gas pump.

For demanding applications, whether in cargo-carrying or passenger-seating, the 5.9-liter V-8, packing 330 pound-feet of twisting force, might be a better bet. To compensate for thirsty engine choices, Dodge includes a 35-gallon gas tank on all Ram Vans and Wagons.

New this year are wider cargo doors, upgraded stereo systems, and an improved ignition switch with anti-theft protection (Like theft is a problem here. Ooooh! Can't wait to get my thieving hands on that antique Dodge Van in mint condition...hey! Wait a minute! That's an airbag. This van is new!). Front quarter vent windows disappear for 1997, and underhood service points feature colored identification.

DODGE RAM VAN / RAM WAGON

| CODE | DESCRIPTION | INVOICE | MSRP |

Plenty of RV converters turn out fancied-up variants of the Dodge Ram, but even the stock models can be fitted with a few comforts and conveniences to make driving pleasant, if not exactly posh. Wagons can have a power driver's seat, for instance, and you can even get a CD player with a graphic equalizer and Infinity speakers. An upscale SLT Wagon Package includes cupholders, seat map pockets, and cloth trim panels. Standard gear includes dual side doors, tinted windows, power steering, and a front stabilizer bar.

We find the Ram Van and Wagon to be packed full of value and think that they are a reasonable alternative to the full-size offerings from Ford and Chevy for those on a strict budget. When searching in this market segment, price is often the only thing separating somewhat unequal competitors.

Safety Data

Driver Airbag: *Standard*
Side Airbag: *Not Available*
4-Wheel ABS: *Optional*
Driver Crash Test Grade: *Average*
Passenger Crash Test Grade: *Good*

Passenger Airbag: *Not Available*
Meets 1999 Side Impact Standards: *No*
Traction Control: *Not Available*
Insurance Cost: *Not Available*
Integrated Child Seat(s): *Not Available*

RAM VAN

Standard Equipment

RAM VAN 1500/2500: 3.9-liter V-6 engine, 3-speed automatic transmission, power recirculating ball steering, power front disc/rear drum brakes, rear anti-lock brake system, 15"x 6.5" wheels, hub caps, P235/75R15XL tires, driver airbag, dual hinged right side cargo doors, painted front and rear bumpers, painted dark silver metallic grille, tinted front door glass and windshield, lockable glovebox, black rubber floor covering, hardboard front headliner, woodgrain applique on instrument panel, door sill scuff pads, front sunvisors, dual exterior mirrors, AM/FM stereo with clock and 2 speakers, heavy-duty vinyl bucket seats, conventional spare tire, rear door windows, 2-speed intermittent wipers

3500 (in addition to 1500/2500 equipment): 5.2-liter V-8 engine, 4-speed automatic transmission, larger front and rear brakes, 16"x 6" wheels, LT225/75R16 tires

Base Prices

Code	Description	Invoice	MSRP
AB1L11	1500 SWB	15289	16845
AB1L12	1500 LWB	15344	17505
AB2L11	2500 SWB	15480	17665
AB2L12	2500 LWB	15519	17710
AB2L13	2500 Maxivan	16921	19360
AB3L12	3500 LWB	17720	20300
AB3L13	3500 Maxivan	18209	20875
Destination Charge:		615	615

RAM VAN / RAM WAGON — DODGE

CODE	DESCRIPTION	INVOICE	MSRP

Accessories

CODE	DESCRIPTION	INVOICE	MSRP
HAA	Air Conditioning	825	970
BAZ	Alternator — 136 amp	131	154
	INCLUDED in Trailer Tow Prep Group		
BGK	Anti-lock Brakes	425	500
NHB	Auxiliary Transmission Oil Cooler (1500/2500)	54	64
	REQUIRES Maximum Engine Cooling; INCLUDED in Trailer Tow Prep Group		
GMF	Cargo Door — Single Rear	NC	NC
	NOT AVAILABLE with No Glass Group		
GKF	Cargo Door — Sliding Right Side	NC	NC
MBF	Chrome Bumpers	255	300
24C	Commercial Package 24C (1500/2500)	499	587
	Includes 5.2-liter V-8 engine		
28C	Commercial Package 28C (2500 LWB)	983	1157
	Includes 5.9-liter V-8 engine and 4-speed automatic transmission		
28C	Commercial Package 28C (3500)	230	270
	Includes 5.9-liter V-8 engine		
26C	Commericial Package 26C (1500/2500)	754	887
	Includes 5.2-liter V-8 engine and 4-speed automatic transmission		
AJK	Convenience Group — Deluxe	332	390
	Includes tilt steering wheel and cruise control		
AJP	Convenience Package	591	695
	Includes power windows and door locks		
GAE	Deep Tinted Glass	348	409
	With GHB	102	120
	With GHD	205	241
	REQUIRES purchase of a Window Group		
YCF	Emissions — Border States	145	170
	On 1500 SWB models, this emissions system REQUIRES the 3.55 Rear Axle Ratio on vans not equipped with Commercial Package 24C or 26C		
NAE	Emissions — Calif./Mass./New York	145	170
	On 1500 SWB models, this emissions system REQUIRES the 3.55 Rear Axle Ratio on vans not equipped with Commercial Package 24C or 26C		
NHK	Engine Block Heater	43	50
CUB	Engine Cover Console	130	153
AEA	Exterior Appearance Group	319	375
	Includes chrome bumpers and grille		
Z3B	GVWR — 8,510 lb. (3500 LWB)	344	405
Z3D	GVWR — 9,000 lb. (3500 Maxivan)	221	260
	REQUIRES Commercial Package 28C		
BCQ	Heavy-duty Battery — 750 CCA	48	57
	INCLUDED in Trailer Tow Prep Group		
GXE	Lock Group	7	8
	Includes separate keys for ignition, front doors, and rear doors		
DSA	Locking Differential	242	285
	NOT AVAILABLE with 3.90 Rear Axle Ratio or 9000 lb. GVWR		

DODGE RAM VAN / RAM WAGON

CODE	DESCRIPTION	INVOICE	MSRP
TBW	Matching Spare Wheel (1500/2500)	85	100
	With WJA (1500/2500)	55	65
	With WJM (1500/2500)	85	100
	REQUIRES purchase of Styled Steel Wheels or Chrome Styled Steel Wheels		
NMC	Maximum Engine Cooling (1500/2500)	56	66
	REQUIRES Auxiliary Transmission Oil Cooler; INCLUDED in Trailer Tow Prep Group		
GHA	No Glass Group	(51)	(60)
	Removes rear door glass		
CYA	Passenger Seat Delete	(156)	(184)
GPS	Power Exterior Mirrors — 6 x 9 Painted Black	136	160
DMD	Rear Axle Ratio — 3.55 (1500)	33	39
	NOT AVAILABLE with Commercial Package 26C		
DMD	Rear Axle Ratio — 3.55 (2500)	33	39
	REQUIRES Commercial Package 24C		
DMH	Rear Axle Ratio — 3.90 (1500)	33	39
	REQUIRES Commercial Package 26C		
DMH	Rear Axle Ratio — 3.90 (2500)	33	39
	REQUIRES Commercial Package 26C or 28C		
DMF	Rear Axle Ratio — 4.10 (3500)	33	39
	REQUIRES Locking Differential		
K5	Seats — Cloth & Vinyl Highback Buckets	129	152
	NOT AVAILABLE with Passenger Seat Delete		
N5	Seats — Reclining Cloth & Vinyl Buckets	179	210
	With CYA	89	105
	NOT AVAILABLE with Tradesman Package		
N6	Seats — Vinyl Highback Buckets	57	67
	With CYA	29	34
RAS	Stereo — w/cassette	187	220
RA8	Stereo Delete	(85)	(100)
WJM	Styled Steel Wheels — Chrome (1500/2500)	337	396
WJA	Styled Steel Wheels — Painted (1500/2500)	209	246
SUA	Tilt Steering Wheel	114	134
	INCLUDED in Deluxe Convenience Group		
TWT	Tires — LT225/75R16E (3500 LWB)	143	168
TSD	Tires — P235/75R15 Whitewalls (2500 Maxivan)	78	92
TSF	Tires — P235/75R15XL OWL (1500/2500)	105	123
	Outline white-lettered-all-season tires		
ASF	Tradesman Package (2500 LWB)	1156	1360
	Manufacturer Discount	(310)	(365)
	Net Price	846	995
	Includes ladder rack, cargo area floor mat, and metal partition behind front seats		
AHC	Trailer Tow Prep Group (2500)	327	385
	Includes 136-amp alternator, heavy-duty battery, maximum engine cooling, auxiliary transmission oil cooler, and heavy-duty flashers; REQUIRES Commercial Package 24C, 26C, or 28C		
AHC	Trailer Tow Prep Group (3500)	217	255
	Includes 136-amp alternator, heavy-duty battery, and heavy-duty flashers		

RAM VAN / RAM WAGON — DODGE

CODE	DESCRIPTION	INVOICE	MSRP
GAH	Vented Windows	184	217
	With GHB	51	60
	With GHD	118	139
	With GHJ	118	139
	REQUIRES purchase of a Window Group		
WMC	Wheel Trim Rings (3500)	107	126
GHD	Window Group — Fixed Rear and Side Door Glass	37	43
GHB	Window Group — Fixed Rear Door Glass	NC	NC
GHG	Window Group — Vision Van All Around Glass	127	149
	Includes windows all around, and a larger day/night rearview mirror		
GHJ	Window Group — Vision Van Curb Side Glass	63	74
	Includes windows in rear doors and along right side of van		

RAM WAGON

Standard Equipment

RAM WAGON 1500: 3.9-liter V-6 engine, 3-speed automatic transmission, power recirculating ball steering, power front disc/rear drum brakes with rear anti-lock system, 15"x 6.5" styled steel wheels, P235/75R15XL tires, driver airbag, convenience group (glovebox light, cigarette lighter, underhood light), single rear door with vent window, dual hinged side doors with vent windows, chrome bumpers, tinted windows, lockable glove compartment, front air conditioning, front and rear carpeting, spare tire cover, cloth headliner, woodgrain applique on instrument panel, door sill scuff pads, dual front sunvisors, dual exterior mirrors, AM/FM stereo with cassette player, clock, and 4 speakers; 8-passenger seating, premium vinyl front bucket seats, conventional spare tire, vented glass windows, 2-speed intermittent windshield wipers

2500 (in addition to or instead of 1500 equipment): 5.2-liter V-8 engine, 4-speed automatic transmission

3500 (in addition to or instead of 2500 equipment): Larger front and rear brakes, 16"x 6" steel wheels, LY225/75R16 tires, hub caps and trim rings, deluxe floor mat, 15-passenger seating (Maxiwagon)

Base Prices

AB1L51	1500 SWB	17886	19740
AB2L52	2500 LWB	19164	21940
AB3L52	3500 LWB	20184	23140
AB3L53	3500 Maxiwagon	21723	24950
Destination Charge:		615	615

Accessories

HBB	Air Conditioning — Rear (2500/3500)	650	765
	With AHC (2500/3500 LWB)	604	710
	With AHC (3500 Maxiwagon)	604	710
	Includes rear heater, heavy-duty battery, and heavy-duty alternator; INCLUDED in SLT Option Packages on 3500 models		

DODGE — RAM VAN / RAM WAGON

CODE	DESCRIPTION	INVOICE	MSRP
WJC	Aluminum Wheels (1500/2500)	NC	NC
	REQUIRES purchase of an SLT Option Package		
BGK	Anti-lock Brakes	425	500
NHB	Auxiliary Transmission Oil Cooler (All except 3500 Maxivan)	54	64
	REQUIRES Maximum Engine Cooling; INCLUDED in Trailer Tow Prep Group		
CKZ	Carpet Delete	NC	NC
	Replaces carpet on 1500, 2500 and 3500 models (w/SLT Option Package) with black rubber floor covering		
MBF	Chrome Rear Step Bumper	81	95
AJK	Convenience Group — Deluxe	332	390
	Includes cruise control and tilt steering wheel; INCLUDED in SLT Option Packages		
GAE	Deep Tinted Glass	348	409
	INCLUDED in SLT Option Packages		
YCF	Emissions — Border States	145	170
	On 1500 models without an Option Package, this emissions system REQUIRES the 3.55 Rear Axle Ratio		
NAE	Emissions — Calif./Mass./New York	145	170
	On 1500 models without an Option Package, this emissions system REQUIRES the 3.55 Rear Axle Ratio		
NHK	Engine Block Heater	43	50
CUB	Engine Cover Console Storage	130	153
	INCLUDED in SLT Option Packages		
CKE/CKN	Floor Carpeting (3500)	133	157
Z3B	GVWR — 8,510 lb. (3500 LWB)	344	405
Z3D	GVWR — 9,000 lb. (3500 Maxiwagon)	221	260
	REQUIRES purchase of Value Package 28B or SLT Option Package 28E		
BCQ	Heavy-duty Battery	48	57
	INCLUDED with Rear Air Conditioning and Trailer Tow Prep Group		
RCE	Infinity Sound System	145	171
	INCLUDED in SLT Option Packages		
DSA	Locking Differential	242	285
	NOT AVAILABLE with 3.90 Rear Axle Ratio		
TBW	Matching Spare Wheel (1500/2500)	55	65
	With WJC (1500/2500)	85	100
	With WJM (1500/2500)	85	100
	REQUIRES purchase of an SLT Option Package with Aluminum Wheels		
NMC	Maximum Engine Cooling (All except 3500 Maxivan)	56	66
	REQUIRES Auxiliary Transmission Oil Cooler; INCLUDED in Trailer Tow Prep Group		
6P	Paint — Two-tone Center Band	336	395
	With 26E (1500)	251	295
	With 26E (2500 LWB)	251	295
	With 26E (3500)	251	295
	With 28E (2500 LWB)	251	295
	With 28E (3500)	251	295

RAM VAN / RAM WAGON — DODGE

CODE	DESCRIPTION	INVOICE	MSRP
6L	Paint — Two-tone Lower Break	298	350
	With 26E (1500)	196	230
	With 26E (2500 LWB)	196	230
	With 26E (3500)	196	230
	With 28E (2500 LWB)	196	230
	With 28E (3500)	196	230
CSR	Passenger Assist Handle	31	37
	INCLUDED in SLT Option Packages		
AJP	Power Convenience Group	591	695
	Includes power windows and door locks; INCLUDED in SLT Option Packages		
JPS	Power Driver's Seat	252	296
	REQUIRES purchase of an SLT Option Package		
DMD	Rear Axle Ratio — 3.55 (1500)	33	39
	INCLUDED in Option Packages		
DMH	Rear Axle Ratio — 3.90 (1500)	33	39
	REQUIRES purchase of an Option Package; NOT AVAILABLE with Locking Differential		
DMH	Rear Axle Ratio — 3.90 (2500)	33	39
	NOT AVAILABLE with Locking Differential		
DMF	Rear Axle Ratio — 4.10 (3500)	33	39
	REQUIRES Locking Differential		
GLC	Rear Door — Dual w/Vented Glass	NC	NC
GMC	Rear Door — Single w/Vented Glass	NC	NC
HDA	Rear Heater	179	211
	INCLUDED with Rear Air Conditioning		
GFA	Rear Window Defroster	153	180
	REQUIRED in New York State; REQUIRES Single Rear Door		
K5	Seat Trim — Cloth & Vinyl	72	85
	INCLUDED in SLT Option Packages		
CYH	Seating Downgrade — 12-passenger (3500 Maxiwagon)	(242)	(285)
26E	SLT Option Package 26E (1500)	3100	3647
	Manufacturer Discount	(128)	(150)
	Net Price	2972	3497
	Includes 5.2-liter V-8 engine, 4-speed automatic transmission, SLT Decor (reclining cloth and vinyl front bucket seats, front door armrests, full floor carpeting, engine cover console, extra sound insulation, passenger's illuminated visor vanity mirror, bodyside moldings, dual horns), deluxe convenience group (cruise control, tilt steering wheel), deep tinted glass, power exterior mirrors, Infinity sound system, passenger assist handles, power convenience group (power windows and door locks)		
26E	SLT Option Package 26E (2500 LWB)	2424	2852
	Manufacturer Discount	(170)	(200)
	Net Price	2254	2652
	Includes SLT Decor (reclining cloth and vinyl front bucket seats, front door armrests, full floor carpeting, engine cover console, extra sound insulation, passenger's illuminated visor vanity mirror, bodyside moldings, dual horns), deluxe convenience group (cruise control, tilt steering wheel), deep tinted glass, power exterior mirrors, Infinity sound system, power convenience group (power windows and door locks), chrome wheels, whitewall tires		

DODGE — RAM VAN / RAM WAGON

CODE	DESCRIPTION	INVOICE	MSRP
26E	SLT Option Package 26E (3500)	3005	3535
	Manufacturer Discount	(255)	(300)
	Net Price	2750	3235

Includes SLT Decor (reclining cloth and vinyl front bucket seats, front door armrests, full floor carpeting, engine cover console, extra sound insulation, passenger's illuminated visor vanity mirror, bodyside moldings, dual horns), rear heater and air conditioning, deluxe convenience group (cruise control, tilt steering wheel), deep tinted glass, power exterior mirrors, Infinity sound system, power convenience group (power windows and door locks)

28E	SLT Option Package 28E (2500 LWB)	2654	3122
	Manufacturer Discount	(170)	(200)
	Net Price	2484	2922

Includes 5.9-liter V-8 engine, SLT Decor (reclining cloth and vinyl front bucket seats, front door armrests, full floor carpeting, engine cover console, extra sound insulation, passenger's illuminated visor vanity mirror, bodyside moldings, dual horns), deluxe convenience group (cruise control, tilt steering wheel), deep tinted glass, power exterior mirrors, Infinity sound system, power convenience group (power windows and door locks), chrome wheels, whitewall tires

28E	SLT Option Package 28E (3500)	3235	3805
	Manufacturer Discount	(255)	(300)
	Net Price	2980	3505

Includes 5.9-liter V-8 engine, SLT Decor (reclining cloth and vinyl front bucket seats, front door armrests, full floor carpeting, engine cover console, extra sound insulation, passenger's illuminated visor vanity mirror, bodyside moldings, dual horns), rear heater and air conditioning, deluxe convenience group (cruise control, tilt steering wheel), deep tinted glass, power exterior mirrors, Infinity sound system, power convenience group (power windows and door locks)

RBN	Stereo — Uplevel w/cassette	130	153
	Includes graphic equalizer; REQUIRES purchase of an SLT Option Package		
RBR	Stereo — Uplevel w/CD player	262	308
	Includes graphic equalizer; REQUIRES purchase of an SLT Option Package		
WJM	Styled Steel Chrome Wheels (1500/2500)	128	150
	INCLUDED in SLT Option Packages		
SUA	Tilt Steering Wheel	114	134
	INCLUDED in Deluxe Convenience Group and in SLT Option Packages		
TSC	Tire Downgrade — P235/75R15 Blackwalls (2500)	NC	NC
	REQUIRES purchase of an SLT Option Package		
TSF	Tires — P235/75R15 OWL (1500)	105	123
	Outline white-lettered-all-season tires; REQUIRES purchase of an SLT Option Package		
TSF	Tires — P235/75R15 OWL (2500)	26	31
	Outline white-lettered-all-season tires; REQUIRES purchase of an SLT Option Package		
TSD	Tires — P235/75R15 Whitewalls (1500)	78	92
	REQUIRES purchase of an SLT Option Package		
AHC	Trailer Tow Prep Group (2500/3500 LWB)	196	230
	Includes 136-amp alternator, heavy-duty battery, maximum engine cooling, auxiliary engine oil cooler, and heavy-duty flushers		

RAM VAN / RAM WAGON — DODGE

CODE	DESCRIPTION	INVOICE	MSRP
AHC	Trailer Tow Prep Group (3500 Maxiwagon)	85	100
	Includes 136-amp alternator, heavy-duty battery, and heavy-duty flashers		
26C	Value Option Package 26C (1500)	754	887
	Includes 5.2-liter V-8 engine and 4-speed automatic transmission		
28B	Value Option Package 28B (3500)	230	270
	Includes 5.9-liter V-8 engine		

Take Advantage of Warranty Gold !

Savings up to 50% off Dealer's Extended Warranty Prices. Protect and enhance YOUR investment with the best extended warranty available.

Call Toll Free 1-800-580-9889

For expert advice in selecting/buying/leasing a new car, call

1-900-AUTOPRO

($2.00 per minute)

FORD — AEROSTAR

AEROSTAR VAN *(1997)*

1997 Ford Aerostar XLT

What's New for Ford Aerostar in 1997 — The Aerostar gets Ford's 5-speed swap-shift automatic transmission this year. This aids hill climbing and towing. The Aerostar's seats are restyled, and the sound systems are upgraded.

Aerostar — Review

Ford's Aerostar was the Blue Ovals first entry in the fight against Chrysler Corporations dominance in the minivan market. Unlike the Dodge Caravan and Plymouth Voyager, the Aerostar has never been much like a car, retaining a rear-wheel drive layout and very truck-like handling.

Although the Aerostar didn't succeed in its mission to wrest the minivan sales crown from Chrysler, it did develop a loyal following of consumers who wanted a van smaller than the Club Wagon, but something that was still strong enough to pull a boat or a trailer. In fact, there became so many Aerostar fans that when Ford introduced the Windstar to replace the Aerostar in 1995, there was such an uproar that Ford decided to keep it around for a few more years.

Unfortunately, the Aerostar's time is finally up. Ford is putting it out to pasture with a couple new bells and whistles to get people into the showroom to buy one last time. Changes to this year's model include new interior fabrics, an upgraded sound system, and Ford's slick new 5-speed manual transmission. So, if you are in the market for a minivan but aren't crazy about all of the car-like offerings from Chrysler, GM, and Ford, try out the Aerostar. It may be what you had in mind.

AEROSTAR — FORD

CODE	DESCRIPTION	INVOICE	MSRP

Safety Data:

Driver Airbag: *Standard*
Side Airbag: *Not Available*
4-Wheel ABS: *Optional*
Driver Crash Test Grade: *Good*
Passenger Crash Test Grade: *Good*

Passenger Airbag: *Standard*
Meets 1999 Side Impact Standards: *No*
Traction Control: *Not Available*
Insurance Cost: *Very Low*
Integrated Child Seat(s): *Not Available*

Standard Equipment

AEROSTAR VAN: Medium platinum front and rear bumpers, solar tinted glass, medium platinum grille, aero headlights, LH/RH "A" pillar mirrors (RH Includes convex glass), black flush windshield and rear window surround moldings, dual rear doors, front black aero spoiler, high-mounted stop light, full face wheel covers, front door and fixed rear door windows, driver air bag, cargo lamp, 13 oz. color-keyed front carpet, cigarette lighter, color-keyed coat hook, courtesy light switches (all doors), color-keyed door trim panel, black engine cover, black polyprophylene rear floor liner, headlamp-on warning, white front headliner, 4-gauge mechanical cluster instrumentation, color-keyed instrument panel (Includes black plastic applique, stowage bin, ashtray, lockable glove box, driver side knee bolster), front dome and rear cargo lights, rearview 10" day/night mirror, black plastic scuff plates on front/side doors and front floor, galvanized rear door scuff plates, dual front high back bucket seats with fixed back and color-keyed vinyl seat trim, spare tire carrier, color-keyed locking energy absorbing steering column, color-keyed soft vinyl steering wheel, black rubber step well pad, vinyl covered driver and passenger white sun visor with passenger side mirror, interval wipers, 95 amp alternator, 2650 lb. front axle, 2950 lb. rear axle, 72 AH 650 CCA battery, power brakes with rear wheel anti-lock, dual rear/sliding side doors, 3.0 liter EFI V6 engine, 21 gallon fuel tank, gas shock absorbers, 2325 lb. front springs, 2639 lb. rear springs, front stabilizer bar, power steering, P215/75R14SL BSW AS tires, limited service spare tire, automatic overdrive transmission, 6.0JJ 5-hole wheels.

Base Prices

Code	Description	Invoice	MSRP
A14	Regular Length 2WD 3-Dr Van	15604	17235
	Destination Charge:	580	580

Accessories

Code	Description	Invoice	MSRP
—	Preferred Equipment Pkgs — prices include pkg discounts		
420A	Pkg 420A	NC	NC
	Includes vehicle with standard equipment		
423A	Pkg 423A	1079	1270
	Includes air conditioning, electronic AM/FM stereo with clock and 4 speakers, speed control/tilt steering wheel		
99U	Engine — 3.0 liter EFI V6	STD	STD
44V	Transmission — 4-speed automatic w/overdrive	STD	STD
XAB	Rear Limited Slip Axle — use w/o trailer towing pkg	213	250
	use with trailer towing pkg	NC	NC
422	California Emission System	85	100
428	High Altitude Principal Use Emission System	NC	NC
T86	Tires — P215/75R14SL BSW all-season	STD	STD
211	Seats — dual buckets	STD	STD
212	Seats — dual captain's chairs	534	630
572	Air Conditioning	739	870

FORD AEROSTAR

CODE	DESCRIPTION	INVOICE	MSRP
41H	Engine Block Heater	30	35
153	License Plate Bracket	NC	NC
542	Mirrors — "A" pillar	STD	STD
512	Underbody Space Saver Spare Tire	17	20
52N	Speed Control/Tilt Steering Wheel	314	370
534	Trailer Towing Pkg	238	280
	Includes class I wiring harness, heavy duty turn signal flasher, limited slip axle		
434	Underseat Stowage Bin — right hand side	30	35
175	Window — side door fixed	59	70
—	Audio		
587	electronic AM/FM stereo/clock	238	280
589	electronic AM/FM stereo/clock/cassette - use w/pkg 423A	106	125
	use w/all other pkgs	344	405
58Y	radio delete	(51)	(60)
51A	Conventional Spare Tire — fleet only	89	105

AEROSTAR WAGON (1997)

Standard Equipment

AEROSTAR XLT WAGON - ALL MODELS: 3.0 liter EFI V6 engine (2WD), 4.0 liter EFI V6 engine (4WD), automatic overdrive transmission, power steering, 2650 lb. front axle (2WD), 2950 lb. rear axle (2WD), 2800 lb. front axle (4WD), 2950 lb. rear axle (4WD), 95 amp alternator, 72 AH 650 CCA heavy duty battery, power brakes with rear wheel anti-lock, super cool cooling, 21.0 gallon fuel tank, 2325 lb. front springs (2WD), 2639 lb. rear springs (2WD), 2650 lb. front springs (4WD), 2950 lb. rear springs (4WD), front stabilizer bar, P215/70R14SL BSW all-season tires, limited service spare, 6.0JJ 5-hole wheels.

REGULAR: Color-coordinated front and rear bumpers, solar tinted glass, medium platinum grille with bright surround, aero headlights, dual note horn, LH/RH "A" pillar mirrors (RH Includes convex glass), moldings (Includes black flush windshield, bodyside, liftgate surround), monotone paint, underbody spare tire carrier, front black aero spoiler, high-mounted stop light, full face wheel covers, rear washers/wiper, RH/LH bodyside sliding window with locking feature and liftgate, front interval wipers, driver air bag, front air conditioning, 2 ashtrays, full length color-keyed carpeting, cigarette lighter, coat hooks, Convenience Group (Includes courtesy lamp switches [all doors], cargo lamp), color-keyed door trim panel, front door carpet covered map pockets, carpet-covered engine cover, inside fuel filler release, headlamp-on warning, color-keyed two-piece full length cloth headliner, 4-gauge mechanical cluster instrumentation, color-keyed instrument panel (Includes black plastic appliques, stowage bin, ashtray, glove box, driver side knee bolster), front dome light, stepwell and cargo lights, mini floor consolette with 2 cup holders, day/night 10" rearview mirror, rear color-keyed vinyl-covered quarter trim panels, electronic AM/FM stereo radio with digital clock, color-coordinated plastic scuff plates, dual front captain's chairs (Includes recliners, inboard fold-down armrests, underseat RH storage bin), rear seats (Includes one 2-passenger and one 3-passenger bench seat, cloth seat trim with folding seatback), color-keyed energy-absorbing locking steering column, color-keyed soft vinyl steering wheel, black rubber stepwell pad, three bodyside storage bins with fish net covers, cloth-covered RH/LH color-keyed sun visor with covered illuminated vanity mirror.

EXTENDED (in addition to or instead of REGULAR equipment): Two floor storage bins.

AEROSTAR — FORD

CODE	DESCRIPTION	INVOICE	MSRP
Base Prices			
A11	XLT Regular Length 2WD Wagon	16299	17925
A31	XLT Extended Length 2WD Wagon	18801	20865
A41	XLT Extended Length 4WD Wagon	21517	23950
	Destination Charge:	580	580
Accessories			
—	Preferred Equipment Pkgs — prices include pkg discounts		
402A	Pkg 402A — Regular Length 2WD	NC	NC
	Includes model with standard equipment		
404A	Pkg 404A — Regular Length 2WD	1312	1545
	Includes 7-passenger seating with dual captain's chairs (Includes manual lumbar, map pockets), privacy glass, speed control/tilt steering wheel, convenience group (Includes rear window defroster, power convenience group, electronic AM/FM stereo/clock/cassette), luggage rack		
401A	Pkg 401A — Extended Length 2WD	NC	NC
	Includes model with standard equipment		
403A	Pkg 403A — Extended Length 2WD	1583	1865
	Extended Length 4WD	1312	1545
	Includes pkg 404A contents plus 4.0 liter V6 engine and automatic overdrive transmission		
21C	Seat	136	160
	7-passenger with dual captain's chairs (Includes manual lumbar/map pockets)		
21D	Seat — w/pkg 401A and 402A	658	775
	w/pkg 403A and 404A	522	615
	7-passenger with dual captain's chairs and 2- and 3-passenger seat/bed		
21E	Seat — w/pkg 401A and 402A	706	830
	w/pkg 403A and 404A	570	670
558	Exterior Appearance Group — w/pkg 403A and 404A	126	150
	if luggage rack deleted from 403A and 404A	249	295
	Includes lower two-tone paint, lower tape stripe, luggage rack		
99U	Engine — 3.0 liter EFI V6 - 2WD models	STD	STD
99X	Engine — 4.0 liter EFI V6	357	420
	STANDARD on 4WD models; Includes auxiliary transmission oil cooler		
44V	Transmission — 4-speed automatic w/overdrive	STD	STD
XAB	Rear Limited Slip Axle — use w/o trailer towing pkg	213	250
	use w/trailer towing pkg	NC	NC
422	California Emission System	85	100
428	High Altitude Principal Use Emission System	NC	NC
—	Tires		
T85	P215/70R14SL BSW all-season - Regular 2WD, Extended 4WD	STD	STD
T86	P215/75R14SL BSW all-season - Extended 2WD	STD	STD
51A	Conventional Spare Tire — fleet only	89	105
646	Forged Aluminum Wheels	310	365
87C	Child Safety Seat	192	225

FORD AEROSTAR

CODE	DESCRIPTION	INVOICE	MSRP
21G	Seat Delete — 5-passenger w/dual captain's chairs	(281)	(330)
574	Air Conditioning — high capacity and auxiliary heater	489	575
414	Floor Console	149	175
57Q	Rear Window Defroster — electric	144	170
94B	Convenience Group	769	905
	Includes electric rear window defroster, power convenience group, radio (electronic AM/FM stereo w/clock and cassette)		
924	Privacy Glass	352	415
41H	Engine Block Heater	30	35
153	License Plate Bracket	NC	NC
593	Light Group	136	160
	Includes glove box lamp, under instrument panel lamps, illuminated entry, front map dome lamps		
615	Luggage Rack	123	145
951	Lower Two-Tone Paint Delete	(54)	(65)
542	Mirrors — "A" pillar	STD	STD
963	Bodyside Protection Molding	55	65
903	Power Convenience Group	459	540
	Includes power windows and door locks and electric remote mirrors		
52N	Speed Control/Tilt Steering Wheel	314	370
534	Trailer Towing Pkg	238	280
	Includes class I wiring harness, heavy duty turn signal flasher, limited slip axle		
—	Audio		
587	electronic AM/FM stereo/clock	STD	STD
589	electronic AM/FM stereo/clock/cassette	166	195
588	premium electronic AM/FM stereo/clock/cassette - w/pkg 401A, 402A	251	295
	w/pkg 403A, 404A	85	100
582	premium electronic AM/FM stereo/clock/compact disc - w/pkg 401A, 402A	391	460
	w/pkg 403A, 404A	225	265

For expert advice in selecting/buying/leasing a new car, call 1-900-AUTOPRO

($2.00 per minute)

CLUB WAGON / ECONOLINE (1997)

1997 Ford Econoline Van XL

What's New for Ford Club Wagon/Econoline in 1997 — Ford offers a V-10 engine in its full-size vans; the first offered in this segment. Ford's 5-speed automatic transmission also debuts on the 1997 Club Wagon/Econoline twins, insuring Ford's continued dominance of the full-size van market for year's to come.

Club Wagon/Econoline — Review

Tough and roomy, rugged and reliable, Ford's full-size vans and wagons have a favorable, well-earned reputation that reaches way back to the Sixties. Ford calls the Econoline/Club Wagon group the U.S. industry's only family of body-on-frame vans and passenger wagons, adding that the Econoline leads in sales to aftermarket conversions—the folks who turn no-frills vans into alluring recreational vehicles.

This year, a V10 engine and 5-speed automatic transmission are available. The V-10 makes 265-horespower and an earth-moving 411 lb./ft. of torque. The new transmission adds a gear between first and second, giving the Econoline/Club wagon smoother acceleration when climbing hills or towing gear.

All Econolines and Club Wagons ride a 138-inch wheelbase. Club Wagons have four-wheel anti-lock braking, and the Chateau edition sports such goodies as privacy glass and power mirrors.

Driving a Club Wagon, despite its passenger seating, differs little from piloting a delivery vehicle, so it's not a logical choice for everyday motoring—though quite a few families happily employ their Wagons exactly that way. The virtues of sitting tall with a panoramic view of the road ahead can outweigh many a minor inconvenience—such as the difficulty of squeezing these biggies into urban parking spots and compact garages. Handling is light, seats are acceptably comfortable, and Club Wagons don't ride badly at all, considering the old-fashioned suspension configurations they employ.

FORD — CLUB WAGON

Full size vans fell out of favor with families when the minivan was introduced. Few find their way into suburban driveways anymore. The Ford Club Wagon is one of the best, and can be had at prices that rival Ford's own Windstar. For your money, wouldn't you rather have more space and utility?

CLUB WAGON

Safety Data:

Driver Airbag: *Standard*
Side Airbag: *Not Available*
4-Wheel ABS: *Standard*
Driver Crash Test Grade: *Excellent*
Passenger Crash Test Grade: *Excellent*

Passenger Airbag: *Standard*
Meets 1999 Side Impact Standards: *No*
Traction Control: *N/A*
Insurance Cost: *Very Low*
Integrated Child Seat(s): *N/A*

Standard Equipment

CLUB WAGON - ALL MODELS: 4.2 liter EFI V6 engine (Regular), 5.4 liter EFI V8 engine (HD Regular, Super), 4-speed automatic overdrive transmission (Regular), electric 4-speed automatic transmission (HD Regular, Super), power steering, 95 amp alternator, 3600 lb. twin I-beam front axle (Regular), 3800 lb. rear axle (Regular), 4600 lb. twin I-beam front axle (HD Regular, Super), 6340 lb. rear axle (HD Regular, Super), 72 AH 650 CCA maintenance-free battery, power brakes with 4-wheel anti-lock, 35.0 gallon fuel tank, gas shock absorbers, 3400 lb. front springs (Regular), 3830 lb. rear springs (Regular), 3550 lb. front springs (HD Regular), 5545 lb. rear springs (HD Regular), 3400 lb. front springs (Super), 6195 lb. rear springs (Super), P235/75R15XL BSW all-season tires (Regular), LT225/75R16E BSW all-season tires (HD Regular), LT245/75R16E all-season tires (Super), 6.0J 5-hole wheels (Regular), 7.0K 8-hole wheels (HD Regular, Super).

XL: Light charcoal front bumper, light charcoal rear bumper, solar-tinted glass, tinted swing-out side/fixed rear door and rear quarter glass, light charcoal grille and grille surround, halogen sealed beam headlights, high mount stop light, black sail-mounted tubular neck RH convex mirrors, hub caps, driver and passenger air bags, color-keyed coat hooks, medium graphite cowl trim panels, hinged side cargo door, medium graphite engine cover with map pocket, black full-length floor mat, full-length medium graphite cloth acoustical headliner, dual electric horn, medium dark graphite instrument panel, liquid crystal display odometer, front dome light, rear cargo light, courtesy light switches (all doors), electronic AM/FM stereo radio with digital clock and 4 speakers, color-keyed vinyl dual bucket front seats, rear bench seats, black vinyl steering wheel, black plastic stepwell pads, medium graphite cloth sun visors (w/RH mirror and cover), medium graphite plastic front door trim panels, medium graphite side/rear trim panels, interval windshield wipers, Handling Pkg (HD Regular, Super), Trailer Towing Pkg Class I (HD Regular, Super).

XLT (in addition to or instead of XL equipment): Chrome front/rear bumpers, chrome insert grille and grille surround, halogen aero headlights, wheel covers (Regular), sport wheel covers (HD Regular, Super), air conditioning, color-keyed full-length carpeting, color-keyed cowl trim panels, color-keyed engine cover with map pocket, full-length color-keyed cloth acoustical headliner, color-keyed instrument panel, deluxe insulation package, reading light, illuminated entry light, power door locks, power windows (Includes rear cargo door lock), color-keyed cloth dual captain's chairs, color-keyed cloth sun visors with RH mirror and cover, color-keyed plastic and cloth front door trim panels with carpet insert, color-keyed side/rear trim panels, Handling Pkg, Trailer Towing Pkg Class I, electronic AM/FM stereo radio with digital clock and 6 speakers.

CLUB WAGON — FORD

CODE	DESCRIPTION	INVOICE	MSRP

Base Prices

E11	XL Regular Club Wagon	18143	20780
E31	XL HD Regular Club Wagon	20595	23665
S31	XL Super Club Wagon	22521	25930
E11	XLT Regular Club Wagon	20625	23700
E31	XLT HD Regular Club Wagon	23013	26510
S31	XLT Super Club Wagon	23707	27325
Destination Charge:		615	615

Accessories

— Preferred Equipment Pkgs — prices include pkg discounts

XL

700A Pkg 700A — XL Regular ..... NC NC
Includes vehicle with standard equipment

710A Pkg 710A — XL Heavy Duty Regular ..... NC NC
Includes vehicle with standard equipment

721A Pkg 721A — XL Super 501 590
Includes group 3 (Includes front air conditioning, sport wheel covers), speed control/tilt steering wheel

XL PLUS

702A Pkg 702A — XL and Regular 1309 1540
Includes front air conditioning, deluxe upgrade pkg (Includes XLT full-length carpeting and side/rear cargo door trim panels, cloth bucket seats, aero headlamps, chrome front/rear bumpers), 64B wheel covers

712A Pkg 712A — XL and HD Regular 1297 1525
Includes front air conditioning, deluxe upgrade pkg (Includes XLT full-length carpeting and side/rear cargo door trim panels, cloth bucket seats, aero headlamps and chrome front/rear bumpers)

722A Pkg 722A — XL and Super 951 1120
Includes group 3 (Includes front air conditioning, sport wheel covers), speed control/tilt steering wheel, deluxe upgrade pkg (Includes XLT full-length carpeting and side/rear cargo door trim panels, cloth bucket seats, aero headlamps and chrome front/rear bumpers)

XLT

705A Pkg 705A — XLT Regular 748 880
Includes group 1 (Includes engine cover console, privacy glass), group 2 (Includes power sail-mount mirrors, 589 radio [AM/FM stereo/clock/cassette and 6 speakers], 52N speed control/tilt steering wheel)

713A Pkg 713A — XLT HD Regular 748 880
Includes group 1 (Includes engine cover console, privacy glass), group 2 (Includes power sail-mount mirrors, 589 radio [AM/FM stereo/clock/cassette and 6 speakers], 52N speed control/tilt steering wheel)

FORD CLUB WAGON

CODE	DESCRIPTION	INVOICE	MSRP
723A	Pkg 723A — XLT Super	1160	1365
	Includes speed control/tilt steering wheel, high capacity front and rear air conditioning (Includes auxiliary heater, HD alternator and overhead ducts), 589 radio (electronic AM/FM stereo/clock/cassette and 6 speakers)		
724A	Pkg 724A — XLT Super	2163	2545
	Includes speed control/tilt steering wheel, high capacity front and rear air conditioning (Includes auxiliary heater, HD alternator and overhead ducts), 589 radio (electronic AM/FM stereo/clock/cassette and 6 speakers)		
992	Engine — Regular	STD	STD
	4.2 liter EFI I6		
996	Engine — Regular	714	840
	4.6 liter EFI V8		
99L	Engine — Regular	961	1130
	Heavy Duty/Super	STD	STD
	5.4 liter EFI V8		
99F	Engine — Heavy Duty Regular/Super	3936	4630
	7.3 liter power stroke DI turbo diesel V8		
99S	Engine — Heavy Duty Regular/Super	352	415
	6.8 liter EFI V10		
44U	Transmission — Regular	STD	STD
	electronic automatic overdrive		
44E	Transmission — Regular	NC	NC
	Heavy Duty/Super	STD	STD
	electronic 4-speed automatic		
	Rear Axle		
—	standard axle ratio	STD	STD
—	limited slip axle	213	250
—	limited slip axle w/optional ratio	251	295
—	optional axle ratio upgrade	38	45
422	California Emissions System	145	170
428	High Altitude Principal Use Emissions System	NC	NC
	Tires		
T77	P235/75R15XL BSW all-season - Regular	STD	STD
T7Q	P235/75R15XL OWL all-season - Regular	106	125
T37	LT225/75R16E BS all-season - Heavy Duty Regular	STD	STD
T38	LT245/75R16E BS all-season - Heavy Duty Regular	119	140
	Super	STD	STD
645	Wheels — bright cast aluminum - Regular	263	310
644	Wheels — sport - Heavy Duty Regular	73	85
64F	Wheels — aluminum deep dish - Heavy Duty Regular, Super	263	310
M64	Wheel Delete — from 724A pkg - Heavy Duty Regular, Super	(263)	(310)
216	Seats — XL Regular	STD	STD
	8-passenger (Includes two std buckets, two 3-pass bench)		
21E	Seats — XLT Regular	STD	STD
	8-passenger (Includes dual captain's chairs, two 3-pass bench)		
218	Seats — XL Heavy Duty Regular	STD	STD
	12-passenger (Includes two std buckets, two 3-pass bench, one 4-pass bench)		

CLUB WAGON — FORD

CODE	DESCRIPTION	INVOICE	MSRP
21M	Seats — XLT Heavy Duty Regular	STD	STD
	12-passenger (Includes dual captain's chairs, two 3-pass bench, one 4-pass bench)		
218	Seats — XL Super	(119)	(140)
	12-passenger (Includes two std buckets, two 3-pass bench, one 4-pass bench)		
219	Seats — XL Super	STD	STD
	15-passenger (Includes two std buckets, three 3-pass bench, one 4-pass bench)		
21N	Seats — XLT Super	STD	STD
	15-passenger (Includes dual captain's chairs, three 3-pass bench, one 4-pass bench)		
572	Air Conditioning — front	829	975
574	Air Conditioning — high capacity front and rear		
	w/721A, 702A, 712A, 722A	829	975
	w/705A, 713A, 723A, 724A	702	825
	w/700A, 710A	1658	1950
	Includes auxiliary heater, HD alternator and overhead ducts, light/convenience group		
633	Heavy Duty Alternator — 130 amp	55	65
639	Extra Heavy Duty Alternator	493	580
634	Heavy Duty/Auxiliary Battery	115	135
768	Bumper — rear step, chrome	102	120
769	Bumper — rear step, medium titanium	102	120
77C	Chateau Trim — Regular, Heavy Duty Regular	876	1030
	Includes leather-wrapped steering wheel, 645 bright cast aluminum wheels (Regular), 64F deep dish forged aluminum wheels (Heavy Duty Regular), lower accent two-tone paint, rear door badge, 543 dual black power sail-mounted mirrors, privacy glass, speed control/tilt steering wheel, 589 electronic AM/FM stereo radio/cassette with 6 speakers, deluxe engine cover console, 7-passenger cloth quad captain's chairs with 3-passenger bench seat		
415	Engine Cover Console	128	150
94D	Deluxe Upgrade Pkg	565	665
	Includes XLT full-length carpeting and side/rear cargo door trim panels, cloth bucket seats, aero headlamps and chrome front/rear bumpers		
903	Power Door Locks/Windows	404	475
60S	Sliding Side Cargo Door	NC	NC
924	Privacy Glass	332	390
181	Group 1	459	540
	w/99F power stroke diesel engine (Includes privacy glass)	332	390
	Includes console, engine cover, privacy glass		
432	Group 2	595	700
	Includes power sail-mount mirrors, electronic AM/FM stereo radio/clock/cassette and 6 speakers, speed control/tilt steering wheel		
183	Group 3	902	1060
	Includes front air conditioning, sport wheel covers		
434	Group 4	927	1090
	w/power stroke diesel engine (Includes privacy glass, power sail-mount mirrors, power driver's seat)	799	940
	Includes engine cover console, privacy glass, power sail-mount mirrors, power driver's seat		

FORD — CLUB WAGON / ECONOLINE VAN

CODE	DESCRIPTION	INVOICE	MSRP
684	Handling Pkg	STD	STD
	Includes front stabilizer bar, heavy duty front and rear shock absorbers		
41H	Engine Block Heater	30	35
551	Deluxe Insulation Pkg	47	55
153	License Plate Bracket	NC	NC
593	Light & Convenience Group	128	150
	Includes illuminated entry, headlights-on audible alert, warning chime		
182	Luxury Group	208	245
	Includes illuminated visors, remote keyless entry/panic alarm		
548	Mirrors — bright swing-out recreational	51	60
543	Mirrors — power sail-mount	136	160
—	Paint — clearcoat	144	170
956	Paint — lower accent two-tone	298	350
90P	Power Driver's Seat	330	390
948	Remote Keyless Entry/Panic Alarm	166	195
	REQUIRES 903 power door locks/windows and 593 light/convenience group		
52N	Speed Control/Tilt Steering Wheel	325	385
534	Trailer Towing Pkg — Class I	NC	NC
	Includes trailer wiring harness, handling pkg		
535	Trailer Towing Pkg — Class II, III, IV	128	150
	Regular w/4.6 liter engine	73	85
587	Radio	STD	STD
	electronic AM/FM stereo/clock, 4 speakers (6 speakers on XLT models)		
589	Radio	132	155
	electronic AM/FM stereo/clock/cassette, 4 speakers (6 speakers on XLT models)		

ECONOLINE VAN

Standard Equipment

ECONOLINE VAN - ALL MODELS: 4.2 liter EFI V6 engine (E150, E250, E250 HD), 5.4 liter EFI V8 engine (E350), 4-speed automatic overdrive transmission (E150, E250, E250 HD), electric 4-speed automatic transmission (E350), power steering, 95 amp alternator, 3600 lb. front axle (E150), 3800 lb. rear axle (E150), 4600 lb. front axle (E250, E250 HD, E350), 5400 lb. rear axle (E250, E250 HD), 6340 lb. rear axle (E350), 72 AH 650 CCA maintenance-free battery, power brakes with rear wheel anti-lock, 35.0 gallon fuel tank, gas shock absorbers, 2960 lb. front springs (E150), 2950 lb. rear springs (E150), 3400 lb. front springs (E250), 4265 lb. rear springs (E250), 3550 lb. front springs (E250 HD), 5345 lb. rear springs (E250 HD), 3700 lb. front springs (E350), 6195 lb. rear springs (E350), P225/75R15SL BSW all-season tires (E150), LT225/75R16D BSW all-season tires (E250), LT225/75R16E BSW all-season tires (E250 HD), LT245/75R16E BSW all-season tires (E350), 6.0JJ 5-hole wheels (E150), 7.0K 8-hole wheels (E250, E250 HD, E350).

STD: Light charcoal front/rear bumpers, solar tinted glass, light charcoal grille and grille surround, halogen sealed beam headlights, high-mount stop light, black sail-mounted tubular neck mirrors, wheel trim hub caps, driver side air bag, passenger side air bag (under 8500 GVWR; all models w/RV trim), LH/RH coat hook, medium graphite color cowl trim panels, hinged side cargo door, medium graphite color plastic door trim, medium graphite color engine cover with map pocket, black vinyl front floor mats, front color-keyed hardboard headliner, single horn, (dual w/E350),

ECONOLINE — FORD

medium dark graphite instrument panel, liquid crystal display odometer, front dome light, rear cargo light, courtesy light switches (all doors), electronic AM radio with digital clock and 2 speakers, dual bucket seats with vinyl trim, black vinyl steering wheel, black plastic stepwell pads, medium graphite vinyl sun visors, interval windshield wipers, Handling Package (E150), Trailer Towing Package Class I (E150).

XL (in addition to or instead of STD equipment): Chrome front and rear bumpers, chrome grille and grille surround, halogen aero headlights, wheel covers (E150), sport wheel covers (E250, E350), color-keyed full-length carpeting, color-keyed cowl trim panels, color-keyed plastic and cloth door trim with carpeted insert, color-keyed engine cover with map pocket, front/rear color-keyed acoustical cloth headliner, color-keyed instrument panel, deluxe insulation package, illuminated entry, reading light, power door locks/windows (Includes rear cargo door lock), electronic AM/FM stereo radio with clock and 4 speakers, cloth captain's chairs, RH underseat stowage bin, color-keyed cloth sun visors with mirror on passenger side.

Base Prices

Code	Description	Invoice	MSRP
E14	E150 Regular Cargo Van	16422	18755
E24	E250 Regular Cargo Van	16783	19180
S24	E250 Super Cargo Van	17395	19900
E24	E250 HD Regular Cargo Van	17034	19475
S24	E250 HD Super Cargo Van	17727	20290
E34	E350 Regular Cargo Van	19022	21815
S34	E350 Super Cargo Van	19860	22800
	Destination Charge:	615	615

Accessories

Code	Description	Invoice	MSRP
—	Preferred Equipment Pkgs — prices include pkg discounts		
E150			
740A	Pkg 740A Standard — E150	NC	NC
	Includes vehicle with standard equipment		
741A	Pkg 741A XL — E150	1194	1405
	Includes chrome bumpers, deluxe insulation pkg, light and convenience group, power door locks/windows, wheel covers		
743A	Pkg 743A RV — E150	2205	2595
	Includes pkg 741A XL contents plus air conditioning, heavy duty alternator, four wheel anti-lock braking system, fixed side/rear cargo door glass, handling pkg, optional payload pkg #3, P235/75R15XL BSW all-season tires, heavy duty service pkg, speed control/tilt steering wheel, trailer towing pkg (Class I)		
E250			
750A	Pkg 750A Standard — E250	NC	NC
	Includes vehicle with standard equipment		
751A	Pkg 751A XL — E250	1194	1405
	Includes chrome bumpers, deluxe insulation pkg, light and convenience group, power door locks/windows, sport wheel covers		

FORD ECONOLINE

CODE	DESCRIPTION	INVOICE	MSRP
753A	Pkg 753A RV — E250	2273	2675
	Includes pkg 751A XL contents plus heavy duty alternator, four wheel anti-lock braking system, fixed side/rear cargo door glass, handling pkg, optional payload pkg #2, heavy duty service pkg, speed control, tilt steering wheel, trailer towing pkg (Class I), air conditioning		
E250 Heavy Duty			
755A	Pkg 755A Standard — E250 HD	NC	NC
	Includes vehicle with standard equipment		
756A	Pkg 756A XL — E250 HD	1180	1390
	Includes chrome bumpers, deluxe insulation pkg, light and convenience group, power door locks/windows, sport wheel covers		
758A	Pkg 758A RV — E250 HD	2482	2920
	Includes pkg 756A XL contents plus air conditioning, heavy duty alternator, four wheel anti-lock braking system, fixed side/rear cargo door glass, handling pkg, heavy duty service pkg, speed control/tilt steering wheel, trailer towing pkg (Class I)		
E350			
760A	Pkg 760A Standard — E350	NC	NC
	Includes handling pkg, trailer towing pkg (Class I)		
762A	Pkg 762A XL — E350	1180	1390
	Includes handling pkg, trailer towing pkg Class I, chrome bumpers, deluxe insulation pkg, light and convenience group, power door locks/windows, sport wheel covers		
763A	Pkg 763A RV — E350	2320	2730
	Includes pkg 762A XL contents plus air conditioning, heavy duty alternator, four wheel anti-lock braking system, fixed side/rear cargo door, bright swing-out recreational mirrors, heavy duty service pkg, speed control/tilt steering wheel, trailer towing pkg (Class II/III/IV)		
—	Payload Pkgs — E150		
201	Pkg 201 — Regular Cargo Van	STD	STD
202	Pkg 202 — Regular Cargo Van	85	100
207	Pkg 207 — Regular Cargo Van	NC	NC
—	Payload Pkgs — E250		
201	Pkg 201 — Regular Cargo	STD	STD
	Super Cargo	NC	NC
205	Pkg 205 — Regular Cargo	NC	NC
203	Pkg 203 — HD Super Cargo	STD	STD
	HD Regular Cargo	STD	STD
—	Payload Pkgs — E350		
201	Pkg 201 — Super Cargo	NC	NC
202	Pkg 202 — Regular Cargo	NC	NC
—	Rear Axle		
—	optional axle ratio (upgrade)	38	45
—	limited slip axle	213	250
—	limited slip axle w/optional ratio	251	295
422	California Emission System	145	170
428	High Altitude Principal Use Emission System	NC	NC
572	Air Conditioning	829	975

ECONOLINE — FORD

CODE	DESCRIPTION	INVOICE	MSRP
574	Air Conditioning w/Auxiliary Heater — high capacity	1658	1950
	use w/XL pkgs	1530	1800
948	Remote Keyless Entry/Panic Alarm	144	170
67B	Four Wheel Anti-Lock Braking System	518	610
634	Battery — heavy duty/auxiliary	115	135
764	Bumpers — chrome	115	135
769	Bumper — rear step, argent	102	120
768	Bumper — rear step, chrome - Std	251	295
	XL/RV	136	160
415	Console, Engine Cover	128	150
60S	Door, Sliding Side Cargo	NC	NC
173	Glass, Fixed Rear Cargo Door	51	60
178	Glass, Fixed Side/Rear Cargo Door	85	100
924	Glass, Privacy — use w/side/rear cargo door glass	229	270
	use w/window all around	332	390
179	Glass, Swing-Out Side/Rear Cargo Door	158	185
	use w/RV pkg	73	85
684	Handling Pkg — use w/E150 & E250	68	80
	use w/trailer tow pkg	NC	NC
	use w/HD service pkg	NC	NC
41H	Heater, Engine Block	30	35
551	Insulation Pkg, Deluxe	158	185
153	License Plate Bracket	NC	NC
593	Light & Convenience Group	128	150
548	Mirrors — bright, swing-out recreational	51	60
543	Mirrors — power sail-mount		
	use w/pkgs w/bright swing-out recreational mirrors	85	100
	use w/o pkgs w/bright swing-out recreational mirrors	136	160
—	Paint — clearcoat	144	170
903	Power Door Locks/Windows	404	475
90P	Power Driver's Seat	332	390
52N	Speed Control/Tilt Steering Wheel	328	385
64B	Wheel Covers — E150	85	100
644	Wheel Covers — sport	73	85
645	Wheels — bright cast aluminum	263	310
64F	Wheels — forged aluminum	263	310
—	Audio		
587	electronic AM/FM stereo w/clock	136	160
589	electronic AM/FM stereo w/clock/cassette	267	315
	use w/XL trim	132	155
58R	radio prep pkg	(132)	(155)
58Y	radio credit option	(52)	(61)
633	Alternator — heavy duty, 130 amp	55	65
639	Alternator — super duty	493	580
57L	Auxiliary Heater-Air Conditioning Connector Pkg	55	65
57X	Auxiliary Heater-Air Conditioning Connector Pkg — w/rear AC controls	63	75
961	Auxiliary Idle Control	170	200

FORD ECONOLINE

CODE	DESCRIPTION	INVOICE	MSRP
76X	Bumper — painted black	NC	NC
76W	Bumper — painted white	NC	NC
166	Floor Mats, Full-Length, Delete — XL vans	(51)	(60)
965	Molding, Bodyside — black	115	135
17W	Windows, All-Around	298	350
	use w/RV pkg	213	250
	use with RV Plus pkg	140	165
671	Front GAWR-One Up	12	15
—	Tires — steel radial, all-season		
T76	P225/75R15SL BSW - E150 Regular Cargo	STD	STD
T77	P235/75R15XL BSW - E150 Regular Cargo w/o RV pkg	73	85
	E150 Regular Cargo w/RV pkg	STD	STD
T7Q	P235/75R15XL OWL - E150 Regular Cargo w/o RV pkg	178	210
	E150 Regular Cargo w/RV pkg	106	124
T32	LT225/75R16D BSW - E250 Regular/Super Cargo	STD	STD
T37	LT225/75R16E BSW - E250 Regular/Super Cargo	73	85
	E250 HD Regular/HD Super Cargo	STD	STD
T38	LT245/75R16E BSW - E350 Regular/Super Cargo	STD	STD
516	Spare Tire & Wheel Delete — all models (steel radial, all-season)		
	P225/75R15SL BSW	(115)	(135)
	P235/75R15XL BSW	(128)	(150)
	P235/75R15XL OWL	(148)	(175)
	LT225/75R16D BSW	(213)	(250)
	LT225/75R16E BSW	(229)	(270)
	LT245/75R16E BSW	(255)	(300)
992	Engine — E150, E250	STD	STD
	4.2 liter EFI I6		
996	Engine — E150 w/RV Plus Option Group	NC	NC
	E150 w/o RV Plus Option Group	714	840
	4.6 liter EFI V8		
99L	Engine — E350	STD	STD
	E150, E250	961	1130
	E150/E250 w/RV Plus Option Group	247	290
	5.4 liter EFI V8		
99S	Engine — E350	352	415
	6.8 liter EFI V10		
99F	Engine — E350	3740	4400
	7.3 liter power stroke DI turbo diesel V8		
44U	Transmission — E150, E250	STD	STD
	electronic automatic overdrive		
44E	Transmission — E150, E250	NC	NC
	E350	STD	STD
	electronic 4-speed automatic		
—	Seats		
C	cloth on STD vans	17	20

ECONOLINE — FORD

CODE	DESCRIPTION	INVOICE	MSRP
L	dual captain's chairs w/premium cloth on XL vans	204	240
21Y	captain's chairs, dual w/o trim	107	125
21W	seats not included (manual pedestal)	STD	STD
21Z	seats not included (power pedestal)	133	155
43V	RV Plus Group — E150	1454	1710
	Includes P235/75R15XL OWL all-season tires, bright cast aluminum wheels, 179 swing-out side/fixed rear cargo door glass, power mirrors, 57X auxiliary heater/AC connector pkg, leather-wrapped steering wheel, remote keyless entry/panic alarm, 589 AM/FM stereo cassette radio, 996/44U 4.6 liter engine/4-speed auto overdrive transmission		
53C	Heavy Duty Service Pkg		
	w/E150/250 vans	140	165
	w/E150 vans w/4.6 liter engine	85	100
	w/RV pkg	NC	NC
	w/E350 vans	73	85
	Includes dual electric horns, handling pkg, HD alternator, auxiliary fuel port (except w/ 7.3 liter engine)		
534	Trailer Towing Pkg — Class I	174	205
	w/HD service pkg	47	55
	Includes trailer wiring harness, handling pkg, dual electric horns		
535	Trailer Towing Pkg — Class II/III/IV		
	w/E150 and E250	314	370
	w/E150 w/4.6 liter (STD and XL)	259	305
	w/E350 (STD or XL)	140	165
	w/E150 and E250 w/RV pkgs	140	165
	Includes 534 trailer towing pkg, electric brake controller tap-in capability, Pollak-type trailer plugs and bumper bracket, relay system for backup/B+ running lights, HD alternator		
60Z	Door Trim Panel Delete	(73)	(85)
54X	Mirror Delete	NC	NC

Take Advantage of Warranty Gold!

Savings up to 50% off Dealer's Extended Warranty Prices. Protect and enhance YOUR investment with the best extended warranty available.

Call Toll Free 1-800-580-9889

FORD — EXPEDITION

EXPEDITION *(1997)*

1997 Ford Expedition Eddie Bauer

What's New for Ford Expedition in 1997 — Ford's replacement for the aging Bronco is the all-new Expedition. Based on the hugely successful 1997 F-150 platform, this full-size sport-utility vehicle is poised to do battle with the wildly popular Chevrolet Tahoe and GMC Yukon. Ford has priced the Expedition aggressively and stands poised to steal some sales from GM customers who have been told that they'll have to wait 4 months for their full-size SUV.

Expedition — Review

Here it is folks, the truck you've all been waiting for. After allowing GM to dominate the full-size SUV arena for years, Ford introduces a vehicle that has its sights squarely aimed at the Chevy Tahoe and GMC Yukon. Ford boasts that its Expedition is superior to the GM full-size sport/utes in every way.

Larger than the Tahoe and Yukon, the Expedition can seat nine people with its optional 3rd row bench seat; the Tahoe and Yukon can only seat six. Unlike the Suburban, which may have difficulty fitting into a standard garage, the Expedition can be handled with ease in most parking maneuvers. The Expedition also has the best payload and towing capacity in its class: 2,000-lbs. and 8000-lbs. respectively.

On the road the Expedition is well mannered. It's obvious that this is not a car, but compared to the vehicle it replaces the Expedition rides like a limousine. Interior ergonomics are first rate and will be familiar to anyone who has spent time in the new F-150. From the front seat forward the Expedition is nearly identical to the new pickup. That's a good thing; we love the cab of the 1997 F-150 with its easy-to-use climate and stereo controls, steering wheel mounted cruise control, plenty of cupholders and great storage space.

Ford has put a lot of time and money into making this truck the next sales leader in their already dominant light-truck lineup. We came away impressed and think you will too. The Expedition comes standard with dual airbags, a first in this segment, anti-lock brakes, and fold-flat second row seats; features that we feel are important in this increasingly competitive segment. Our few gripes stem from the powertrain. After driving a few Vortec

EXPEDITION — FORD

powered Suburbans this year, we've become spoiled by the GM engine's gobs of torque and horsepower. The Expedition's power output won't be confused with a Geo Tracker, but it did leave us wondering if we could squeeze one of GM's 5.7-liter powerhouses into the engine bay. One option that we think everyone should investigate is the lighted running boards. The Expedition towers above the ground, and entering and exiting this truck will take its toll on most passengers after a few days.

We think that the Expedition will be turning up in our neighborhood parking lots and driveways very soon. If you're thinking of buying a full-size SUV in the near future, you owe it to yourself to take a look at this truck.

Safety Data

Driver Airbag: *Standard*
Side Airbag: *Not Available*
4-Wheel ABS: *Standard*
Driver Crash Test Grade: *Not Available*
Passenger Crash Test Grade: *Not Available*

Passenger Airbag: *Standard*
Meets 1999 Side Impact Standards: *Yes*
Traction Control: *Not Available*
Insurance Cost: *Not Available*
Integrated Child Seat(s): *Not Available*

Standard Equipment

XLT 2WD: 4.6-liter SEFI V-8 engine, 4-speed automatic transmission, 4-wheel anti-lock disc brakes, P255/70R16 BSW A/S tires, full-size underbody spare tire, speed-sensitive variable assist power steering, 26 gallon fuel tank, front and rear stabilizer bars, chrome front bumper, solar tinted glass, bright grille, aero headlamps, liftgate with flip-up glass, dual fold-away power outside mirrors, color-keyed bodyside molding with bright insert, styled steel wheels, speed sensitive intermittent windshield wipers, rear intermittent windshield wiper/washer/defroster, dual airbags, manual air conditioning, front/rear ashtrays, passenger assist handles, cargo area tie downs, 4 coat hooks, 6 cupholders, carpeted front and rear floor mats, glove box, analog instrument panel, lights (underhood, front door puddle lights, front dome light, cargo area light), passive anti-theft system, power door locks, power windows, premium AM/FM cassette stereo with 4 speakers, rear floor heating ducts, remote keyless entry, 40/60 front seat with driver's lumbar support, 60/40 fold-flat 2nd row seat with center armrest and cupholders, side impact door beams and color-keyed visors with right-hand illuminated mirror.

XLT 4WD (in addition to or instead of XLT 2WD): 30 gallon fuel tank, 2-speed transfer case and Control Trac 4WD.

EDDIE BAUER 2WD (in addition to or instead of XLT 2WD): Fog lamps, rear quarter privacy glass, color-keyed grille surround, autolamp, luggage rack, color-keyed bodyside moldings, wheellip and rocker panel, forged aluminum wheels, floor console with storage bin, rear radio controls, headphone jacks, tissue holder, fan control and 2 cupholders; overhead console with map lights, sunglass holder, garage door opener bin, power rear quarter window switch, electronic display with average fuel economy, and compass; leather captain's chairs with 6-way power adjustments, lumbar support, and map pockets; speed control, leather-wrapped steering wheel, and dual illuminated vanity mirrors.

EDDIE BAUER 4WD (in addition to or instead of Eddie Bauer 2WD): 30 gallon fuel tank, 2-speed transfer case, Command-Trac 4WD, and tow hooks.

FORD EXPEDITION

CODE	DESCRIPTION	INVOICE	MSRP
Base Prices			
U17	XLT 2WD	24057	27520
U17	Eddie Bauer 2WD	27432	31490
U18	XLT 4WD	26267	30120
U18	Eddie Bauer 4WD	29672	34125
	Destination Charge:	640	640
Accessories			
645	16" Chrome Wheels (XLT)	43	50
647	17" Aluminum Wheels	158	185
	INCLUDED in PEP 685A and 687A.		
XH7	3.31 Limited Slip Rear Axle	217	255
XH9	3.53 Limited Slip Rear Axle	217	255
68P	4 Corner Load Leveling Suspension (4WD)	692	815
99L	5.4-liter V-8 Engine	480	565
	INCLUDED in PEP 687A.		
91P	6-Disc CD Changer	404	475
	NOT AVAILABLE with Pkg. 684A.		
422	California Emissions System	144	170
535	Class III Trailer Tow Group (2WD /5.4-liter Engine)	799	940
	REQUIRES 5.4-liter engine.		
535	Class III Trailer Tow Group (2WD w/Base Engine)	748	880
	NOT AVAILABLE with 5.4-liter engine.		
535	Class III Trailer Tow Group (4WD w/5.4-liter Engine)	383	450
	REQUIRES 5.4-liter engine.		
535	Class III Trailer Tow Group (4WD w/Base Engine)	332	390
	NOT AVAILABLE with 5.4-liter engine.		
875	Cloth Third Row Seat	510	600
S	Delete-Captain's Chairs & Center Console (XLT)	(285)	(335)
	This credit is only available with package 685A. Replaced with 60/40 bench seat.		
41H	Engine Block Heater	30	35
	REQUIRES Pkg. 684A or 687A.		
63W	Extreme Weather Group (Eddie Bauer)	68	80
63W	Extreme Weather Group (XLT)	162	190
574	High Capacity Front/Rear Air Conditioning (Eddie Bauer)	599	705
574	High Capacity Front/Rear Air Conditioning (XLT)	642	755
	Includes overhead console.		
186	Illuminated Running boards	370	435
	INCLUDED in PEP 687A.		
1	Leather Captain's Chairs (XLT)	1015	1300
875	Leather Third Row Seat	727	855
XH6	Limited Slip Rear Axle	267	315
	Includes 3.73 limited slip rear axle. INCLUDED in Eddie Bauer PEP 687A.		
43M	Power Moonroof (Eddie Bauer)	659	755

EXPEDITION — FORD

CODE	DESCRIPTION	INVOICE	MSRP
685A	Preferred Equipment Pkg. 685A (XLT)	1505	1770
	Manufacturer Discount	(612)	(720)
	Net Price	893	1050
	Includes Captain's chairs w/floor console, popular equipment goup (6-way power driver's seat, privacy glass, dual illuminated visor vanity mirrors, luggage rack), speed control, forged aluminum wheels.		
687A	Preferred Equipment Pkg. 687A (Eddie Bauer 4WD)	1832	2155
	Manufacturer Discount	(638)	(750)
	Net Price	1194	1405
	Includes 5.4-liter engine, Ford Mach audio system with cassette, P265/70R17 OWL A/T tires, power signal mirrors, illuminated running boards and 17" cast aluminum wheels.		
687A	Preferred Equipmnt Pkg. 687A (Eddie Bauer 2WD)	1279	1505
	Manufacturer Discount	(488)	(575)
	Net Price	791	930
	Includes 5.4-liter engine, Ford Mach audio system with cassette, power signal mirrors, illuminated running boards and 17" cast aluminum wheels.		
916	Premium Sound System (Eddie Bauer)	302	355
	Includes Ford Mach audio system with cassette. INCLUDED in PEP 687A.		
68L	Rear Load Leveling Suspension (2WD)	417	490
413	Skid Plate Pkg.	89	105
525	Speed Control (XLT)	200	235
	INCLUDED in PEP 685A		
T54	Tires-P255/70R16 OWL AT (XLT)	196	230
T5N	Tires-P265/70R17 OWL AT (Eddie Bauer)	128	150
	INCLUDED in PEP 687A.		
T5N	Tires-P265/70R17 OWL AT (XLT)	323	380
53T	Tow Hooks (4WD)	34	40
875	Vinyl Third Row Seat	208	245

One 15-minute call could save you 15% or more on car insurance.

GEICO DIRECT

America's 6th Largest Automobile Insurance Company

1-800-555-2758

FORD EXPLORER

| CODE | DESCRIPTION | INVOICE | MSRP |

EXPLORER *(1997)*

1997 Ford Explorer Sport

What's New for Ford Explorer in 1997 — Ford's best-selling Explorer receives a few appreciated improvements this year. A new SOHC V-6 engine is now available, providing nearly as much power as the 5.0-liter V-8. Also new is a 5-speed automatic transmission, the first ever offered by an American auto manufacturer, which is standard on V-6 models equipped with an automatic.

Explorer — Review

Since its introduction in 1991, the Ford Explorer has resided at the top of the sport utility sales heap. With good reason; the Explorer combined style, comfort and room is one go-anywhere package. The modern day Country Squire, some have called it, after the segment leading station wagon of the 1950s.

We think that there's a good reason for this. Simply stated, the Explorer is a more refined vehicle than the competition at Jeep and General Motors. The interior instills a feeling of quality that is missing from the Grand Cherokee and the Blazer. An organically sweeping dashboard houses radio controls that can actually be operated without a magnifying glass. Materials look and feel rich. Rear seat comfort surpasses Chevy, and entry/exit is easier than Jeep. Explorers offer more cargo capacity than most rivals, and five passengers can ride with ease. Exterior styling is a subjective matter, but we think that the Explorer is one of the most attractive SUVs on the road.

The Explorer's standard 4.0-liter V-6 is the puniest engine found in a domestic sport ute. Acceleration is fine from a standstill, but step on the gas at 50 mph and not much happens. That's not good news when there's a need to pass or merge. Fortunately, Ford has introduced an optional SOHC V-6 that offers nearly as much power as the V-8, for a lot less money. We recommend this engine over the other two engine choices due to its great power and affordable price.

Other changes for 1997 include swapping the 4-speed automatic for a new 5-speed automatic on V-6 models. This 5-speed is the first ever developed for an American passenger vehicle. Ford claims that the additional gear, which occurs between the former 1st and 2nd

EXPLORER — FORD

gears, allows for more precise shifting, allowing the truck to move uphill and off-road more authoritatively. When combined with the optional V-6, this should make the Explorer much more fun to drive.

Unlike the reworked Chevy Blazer, Explorers retain a distinctly truck-like character, which could be a bonus or a demerit. They're tough and solid, and easy to maneuver, though steering is a little slow and ponderous, and the body leans through tight corners. Braking is excellent, and the suspension has a compliant attitude, but Ford's Explorer can bounce around, making occupants regret the Denver omelet they had for breakfast.

Ford has a philosophy of building vehicles that everyone can be happy with. Sure, the Jeep Grand Cherokee feels sportier, and the GMC Jimmy looks cooler, but the Explorer has just the right amount of class and ruggedness to make it America's best-selling off-roader. If you are thinking about buying an SUV, chances are you've already checked out the Explorer. If you haven't, do yourself a favor and find out why there are so many of these trucks on the road.

Safety Data

Driver Airbag: *Standard*
Side Airbag: *Not Available*
4-Wheel ABS: *Standard*
Driver Crash Test Grade: *Good*
Passenger Crash Test Grade: *Good*
Integrated Child Seat(s): *Opt. (4-door)*

Passenger Airbag: *Standard*
Meets 1999 Side Impact Standards: *No*
Traction Control: *Not Available*
Insurance Cost: *Very Low (Eddie Bauer/Limited/Sport/XL 2WD);*
Low (XL 4WD/XLT)

Standard Equipment

XL 2WD: 4.0-liter V-6 engine, 5-speed manual transmission, 17.5 gallon fuel tank (21 gallon fuel tank on 4-door), 4-wheel anti-lock disc brakes, power rack-and-pinion steering, P225/70R15 BSW A/S tires, underbody spare tire carrier, heavy-duty gas shock absorbers, front and rear stabilizer bars, bright front and rear bumpers with black rub strip, body color door handles, solar tinted glass windshield and front windows, flip-open opera windows, bright grille with painted insert, aero headlamps, dual outside mirrors, high-mounted rear stop light, steel wheels, dual intermittent front windshield wipers, dual airbags, manual air conditioning, ashtray and cigarette lighter, 2 coat hooks, front map light, cargo area dome light, lockable glove box, three grab handles, remote hood release, illuminated entry, cargo floor tie-down hooks, 12-volt adapter, AM/FM stereo w/4 speakers, height adjustable front seat belts, sun visors with right-hand vanity mirror, knitted front vinyl seats, and rear split-folding bench seat.

XL 4WD (in addition to or instead of XL 2-DOOR 2WD): Skid plates and Control-Trac 4WD.

SPORT 2WD (in addition to or instead of XL 2-DOOR 2WD): Black front and rear bumpers with rub strip, rear quarter privacy glass including tailgate window, body color grille, dual power outside mirrors, color-keyed bodyside molding, wheellip, deep dish cast aluminum wheels, speed-sensitive dual intermittent windshield wipers, rear window wiper/washer/defroster, cargo area cover, map pockets on doors, power liftgate operation, power equipment group (power windows and door locks with illuminated controls, accessory delay, two-step unlocking system with lock/unlock button in the cargo area), speed control with tilt steering, leather-wrapped steering wheel, and illuminated vanity mirror.

SPORT 4WD (In addition to or instead of SPORT 2WD): Skid plates and Control-Trac 4WD.

FORD EXPLORER

XLT 2WD (in addition to or instead of XL 2WD): Rear quarter privacy glass, 21-gallon fuel tank, power outside mirrors, clor-keyed bodyside moldings, tape stripe, deep dish aluminum wheels, speed sensitive dual intermittent wipers, rear window wiper/washer/defroster, map pockets in front doors, liftgate lock/unlock button, power equipment group (power windows and door locks with illuminated controls, accessory delay, two-step unlocking system with lock/unlock button in the cargo area), premium cloth bucket seats, rear split folding bench, speed control, tilt steering column, leather wrapped steering wheel, and illuminated visor vanity mirrors.

XLT 4WD (in addition to or instead of XLT 2WD): Skid plates and Control Trac 4WD.

XLT AWD (in addition to or instead of XLT 4WD): Requires the purchase of the 5.0-liter V-8 engine and 4-speed automatic transmission.

EDDIE BAUER 2WD (in addition to or instead of XLT 2WD): 4.0-liter SOHC V-6 engine, 5-speed automatic transmission, P255/70R16 OWL tires, bright front and rear bumpers with color coordinated stripe, wheellip, two-tone paint, luggage rack, 16" chrome wheels, cargo cover, floor mats, premium AM/FM stereo, sport cloth front bucket seats, rear split-fold bench seat, and center console.

EDDIE BAUER 4WD (in addition to or instead of EDDIE BAUER 2WD): Skid plates and Control Trac 4WD.

EDDIE BAUER AWD (in addition to or instead of EDDIE BAUER 4WD): Requires the purchase of the 5.0-liter V-8 engine and 4-speed automatic transmission.

LIMITED 2WD (in addition to or instead of EDDIE BAUER 2WD): P235/70R15SL OWL A/T tires, painted bumpers with rub strip, fog lamps, unique body color grille, heated power outside mirrors, running boards, Limited cast aluminum wheels, automatic climate control, deluxe carpeting, rear dome light, electronics group (2 remote keyless entry key fobs, door keypad, seat memory switch), floor console with dual cupholders, ashtray, rear radio and climate controls, message center with fuel and oil life warning messages, eletrochromic rearview mirror and autolamp, overhead front console (includes deluxe map lights, compass and outside temperature gauges), JBL stereo, Leather bucket seats with 6-way power adjustments, power lumbar support, split-folding rear bench seat and deluxe leather wrapped steering wheel.

LIMITED 4WD (in addition to or instead of LIMITED 2WD): Skid plates and Control Trac 4WD.

LIMITED AWD (in addition to or instead of LIMITED 4WD): Requires the purchase of the 5.0-liter V-8 engine, and 4-speed automatic transmission.

Base Prices

Code	Description	Invoice	MSRP
U22	XL 2-Door 2WD	18285	20085
U24	XL 2-Door 4WD	20015	22050
U22	Sport 2WD	19323	21265
U24	Sport 4WD	20934	23095
U32	XL 4-Door 2WD	19517	21485
U34	XL 4-Door 4WD	21206	23405
U32	XLT 2WD	21924	24220
U34	XLT 4WD	23688	26225
U35	XLT 4-Door AWD V-8	23688	26225
U32	Eddie Bauer 2WD	26187	29065
U34	Eddie Bauer 4WD	27952	31070

EXPLORER — FORD

CODE	DESCRIPTION	INVOICE	MSRP
U35	Eddie Bauer AWD V-8	27653	30730
U32	Limited Edition 2WD	29404	32720
U34	Limited Edition 4WD	31414	35005
U35	Limited Edition AWD V-8	31120	34670
	Destination Charge:	525	525

Accessories

CODE	DESCRIPTION	INVOICE	MSRP
XD4	3.73 Limited Slip Axle & Trailer Tow Pkg. (XL/XLT)	263	302
99E	4.0-liter SOHC V-6 Engine (XL/Sport/XLT)	362	425
XD2	4.10 Limited Slip Axle & Trailer Tow Pkg. (Sport/Eddie Bauer)	263	310
44D	5-Speed Automatic Transmission	905	1065
	NOT AVAILABLE with 5.0-liter V-8 engine.		
99P	5.0-liter V-8 Engine Pkg. (Eddie Bauer 2WD)	672	790
	Includes upgraded tires and axle.		
99P	5.0-liter V-8 Engine Pkg. (Eddie Bauer AWD)	969	1140
	NOTE: This engine is required for the Eddie Bauer AWD model. Includes upgraded tires and axle.		
99P	5.0-liter V-8 Engine Pkg. (Limited 2WD)	820	965
	Includes upgraded tires and axle.		
99P	5.0-liter V-8 Engine Pkg. (Limited AWD)	1117	1315
	NOTE: This engine is required for Limited AWD model. Includes upgraded tires and axle.		
99P	5.0-liter V-8 Engine Pkg. (XLT)	1313	1545
	NOTE: This engine is required for the XLT AWD model. Includes upgraded tires and axle.		
91P	6-Disc CD Changer (Sport/XLT/Eddie Bauer/Limited)	314	370
	REQUIRES high series floor console.		
69P	Automatic Ride Control (Limited)	553	650
44U	Automatic Transmission (XLT)	803	1065
	REQUIRES 5.0-liter V-8 engine. NOT AVAILABLE with PEP 945B.		
422	California Emissions	85	100
649	Cast Aluminum Wheels (XLT)	NC	NC
M	Cloth 60/40 Bench Seat (XLT)	8	10
	REQUIRES PEP 941A.		
M	Cloth 60/40 Seats (XL 4-Door)	247	290
J	Cloth Captain's Chairs (XL)	238	280
J	Cloth Captian's Chairs (Sport)	238	280
	INCLUDED in PEP 931A.		
Z	Cloth Sport Bucket Seats w/Power Driver Seat (Sport)	867	1020
	REQUIRES PEP 931A.		
66B	Decor Group (XL)	314	370
	Includes privacy glass and bodyside moldings.		
59B	Electrochromic Mirror and Autolamp (Sport/XLT/Eddie Bauer)	158	185
41H	Engine Block Heater	30	35
167	Floor Mats (Sport)	38	45
	INCLUDED in PEP 934A.		

FORD EXPLORER

CODE	DESCRIPTION	INVOICE	MSRP
86D	Floor Mats/Cargo Cover (XLT)	107	125
916	Ford/JBL Stereo w/Cassette (Sport/XLT/Eddie Bauer/Limited)	706	830
418	High Series Floor Console (XLT/Eddie Bauer)	332	390
	INCLUDED in package 945B and 946A.		
87C	Integrated Child Seat	170	200
F	Leather Sport Bucket Seats (Eddie Bauer)	557	655
F	Leather Sport Bucket Seats (Sport)	557	655
	REQUIRES PEP 934A.		
F	Leather Sport Bucket Seats (XLT)	557	655
	REQUIRES PEP 945A.		
615	Luggage Rack (XL/XLT)	119	140
	INCLUDED in PEP 945B.		
Z	Power Cloth Sport Bucket Seats (XLT)	812	955
	REQUIRES PEP 941A.		
903	Power Equipment Group (2-Door)	583	685
903	Power Equipment Group (4-Door)	867	1020
439	Power Moonroof w/Sunshade (Sport/XLT/Eddie Bauer/Limited)	680	800
931A	Preferred Equipment Pkg. 931A (Sport)	612	720
	Manufacturer Discount	(489)	(575)
	Net Price	123	145
	Includes P235/75R15SL OWL A/T tires, premium stereo, and cloth captain's chairs.		
934B	Preferred Equipment Pkg. 934B (Sport)	3072	3615
	Manufacturer Discount	(1139)	(1340)
	Net Price	1933	2275
	Includes P235/75R15SL OWL A/T tires, premium sound, sport bucket seats w/6-way driver power adjustamnts, 4.0-liter SOHC V-6 engine, luxury group (high series floor consoloee, rear climate and stereo controls), rear reading lamp, electronic compass, outside temperature gauge, 2 remote keyless entry transmitters, keypad, anti-theft, autolock/relock and floor mats.		
945B	Preferred Equipment Pkg. 945B (XLT)	3014	3545
	Manufacturer Discount	(1202)	(1415)
	Net Price	1812	2130
	Includes premium sound with cassette, luggage rack, cloth sport bucket seats with 6-way power adjustments, floor console, luxury group (includes dual cup holders rear climate and stereo controls), fog lamps, floor mats, and cargo area cover.		
946A	Preferred Equipment Pkg. 946A (Eddie Bauer)	2542	2990
	Manufacturer Discount	(998)	(1175)
	Net Price	1544	1815
	Includes luuxury group (dual cup holders, rear climate and radio controls), power leather bucket seats with lumbar support, and premium group (automatic climate control, message center and JBL stereo).		
588	Premium Sound Stereo w/Cassette (XL/Sport/XLT)	178	210
	INCLUDED in PEP 931A, 934A, 941A, and 945A.		
17C	Rear Intermittent Windshield Wiper/Defroster/Washer (XL)	238	280
151	Remote Keyless Entry (XLT/Eddie Bauer)	314	370
	Includes anti-theft system.		

EXPLORER / F-150 PICKUP — FORD

CODE	DESCRIPTION	INVOICE	MSRP
186	Running Boards (4-Door/Std. on Limited)	336	395
52N	Speed Control w/Leather Wrapped Steering Wheel (XL)	328	385
	Includes adjustable tilt steering wheel.		
47P	Sport Appearance Pkg. (Sport)	1696	1995
	Manufacturer Discount	(850)	(1000)
	Net Price	846	995
	REQUIRES 4.0-liter SOHC V-6 engine.		
182	Step Bar (2-Door)	251	295
T7R	Tires-P235/75R15SL OWL A/T (Sport/XLT)	195	230
954	Two-Tone Rocker Panel (XLT)	102	120
516	Voice Activated Cellular Phone (Eddie Bauer/Limited)	587	690

F-150 PICKUP *(1997)*

1997 Ford F-150 XLT SuperCab 4WD

What's New for Ford F-Series in 1997 — Everything is new. New engines, new sheetmetal, and a new suspension compliment dual airbags and class-leading side impact protection in this user-friendly heavy hauler. All SuperCab models get a third door for easy access to the rear compartment. Styling is slightly different depending on what drive system is selected.

F-Series — Review

For nearly two decades, the Ford F-Series has been the best selling pickup truck in the United States. For more than half that period of time, it's been the best selling vehicle, period. Understandably, Ford execs were a bit hesitant to completely overhaul their Golden Child. After all, the F-Series, which hadn't seen substantial engineering improvements

FORD
F-150 PICKUP

since 1980, seemed to be selling just fine as it was. Reality was, though, that deadlines for some stringent truck standards were approaching fast, and the F-Series was getting long in the tooth. The redesign was approved.

Five million development miles later, Ford introduced a radically new F-150 in January 1996. The bold look, passenger car accouterments, overhead cam engines, and short and long arm front suspension of the new pickup are either embraced or shunned by die-hard Ford truckers used to the traditional styling, bare bones interior, rugged pushrod motors and Twin-I-Beam suspension of the 1996 model.

So what about this new truck? Overall length is up for all models, and SuperCabs provide substantial improvements in rear passenger leg and hip room. SuperCab models feature a third door as standard equipment, as more and more full-size pickups are purchased for personal use. Styleside and Flareside cargo boxes will be available for both cab styles. Dual airbags are standard, and the passenger side restraint can be switched off in the event that a rear-facing child safety seat has been installed. The new F-150 meets 1999 side-impact standards for trucks, and a four-wheel anti-lock braking system is optional across the board. New options include leather seats, a six-disc CD changer, and an anti-theft system.

Two engines will initially be available, followed by a third in the fall of 1996. A 4.2-liter V-6 is the standard engine, and it makes 210 horsepower at 5000 rpm and 255 foot-pounds of torque at 3000 rpm. That's more than GM, Dodge or Toyota. The optional 4.6-liter V-8 isn't much more powerful, it just provides its power at more useful revs: 210 horsepower at 4400 rpm and 290 foot-pounds of torque at 3250 rpm. The third engine is a 5.4-liter V-8 which makes 235 horsepower and 330 foot-pounds of torque. Tune up intervals occur every 100,000 miles thanks to platinum-tipped spark plugs. Equipped with the 4.6-liter V-8, the F-150 2WD Regular Cab equipped with an automatic transmission and a 3.55 rear axle ratio will tow up to 7,200 pounds. Sixteen-inch wheels are standard; optional are big 17 x 7.5J rims shod with meaty P265/70R-17SL tires.

Sounds good to us. After driving several F-150s this year, it appears that Ford has taken a path designed to bring more personal use buyers into the Ford fold without alienating truck buyers who work their pickups hard. Styling, always a subjective point, might turn potential buyers off with its free-flowing forms and smooth contours. We, however, like its clean lines and lack of clutter; particularly around the grille. If you are in the market for a full-size pickup, you need to see why the F-150 has been the best selling truck on the market for the last decade.

Safety Data

Driver Airbag: *Standard*
Side Airbag: *Not Available*
4-Wheel ABS: *Std (Lariat); Opt (XL/XLT/Standard)*
Driver Crash Test Grade: *Not Available*
Passenger Crash Test Grade: *Not Available*

Passenger Airbag: *Standard*
Meets 1999 Side Impact Standards: *Yes*
Traction Control: *Not Available*
Insurance Cost: *Very Low (2WD); Low (4WD)*
Integrated Child Seat(s): *Not Available*

Standard Equipment

STANDARD 2WD REGULAR CAB: 4.2-liter V-6 engine, 5-speed manual transmission, power front disc/rear drum brakes, rear anti-lock brakes, P235/70Rx16SL BSW tires, 5-hole argent painted wheels, coil springs, gas shock absorbers, power steering, argent painted front bumper, argent grille, black tailgate handle, black door handles, dual black manually adjustable outside

F-150 PICKUP FORD

| CODE | DESCRIPTION | INVOICE | MSRP |

mirrors, pickup bed cargo hooks, removable tailgate with lock, 4-pin trailer tow wiring, dual air bags, dual cupholders mounted on instrument panel, dome light, voltmeter/oil pressure/temperature/speed/fuel gauges, auxiliary power point, AM/FM stereo w/4 speakers, vinyl bench seat, vinyl sun visors and interval windshield wipers.

STANDARD 4WD REGULAR CAB (in addition to or instead of STANDARD 2WD REGULAR CAB): 2-speed transfer case, shift-on-the-fly 4WD, torsion bar front springs, and argent wheel openings.

STANDARD SUPER CAB (in addition to or instead of STANDARD 2WD REGULAR CAB): Third door and rear quarter flip-out windows.

XL 2WD REGULAR CAB (in addition to or instead of STANDARD 2WD REGULAR CAB): Chrome bumper, chrome grille, cargo box light, dual map lights, cloth bench seat, and cloth sun visors.

XL 4WD REGULAR CAB (in addition to or instead of XL 2WD REGULAR CAB): 2-speed transfer case, shift-on-the-fly 4WD, torsion bar front springs, and argent wheel openings.

XL 4WD SUPER CAB (in addition to or instead of XL REGULAR CAB 4WD): Third door and rear quarter flip-out windows.

XLT 2WD REGULAR CAB (in addition to or instead of XL 2WD REGULAR CAB): Chrome rear step bumper, color-keyed door handles, color-keyed power outside mirrors, color-keyed wheel opening moldings, argent styled wheels with chrome hubs, rear storage tray, passenger grab handles, tachometer, power windows and door locks, cloth split bench seat with armrests and driver's side manual lumbar support, and speed dependant interval wipers.

XLT 4WD REGULAR CAB (in addition to or instead of XLT 2WD REGULAR CAB): 2-speed transfer case, shift-on-the-fly 4WD, torsion bar front springs, and color-keyed wheel openings.

XLT SUPER CAB (in addition to XLT REGULAR CAB): Third door, rear quarter privacy glass, and rear quarter flip-out windows.

LARIAT 2WD REGULAR CAB (in addition to or instead of XLT REGULAR CAB 2WD): Fog lamps, P255/70Rx16SL OWL A/S tires, cast aluminum wheels, floor mats, and leather split bench seat.

LARIAT 4WD REGULAR CAB (in addition to or instead of LARIAT 2WD): 2-speed transfer case, shift-on-the-fly 4WD, torsion bar front springs, and color-keyed wheel openings.

LARIAT SUPERCAB (in addition to or instead of LARIAT REGULAR CAB): 4.6-liter V-8 engine, third door, rear quarter privacy glass, and rear quarter flip-out windows.

Base Prices

Code	Description	Invoice	MSRP
F17	2WD Standard Reg Cab Styleside SWB	13219	14505
X17	2WD Standard SuperCab Styleside SWB	15114	16600
X17	2WD Standard SuperCab Styleside LWB	15367	16945
F17	2WD Standard Reg Cab Styleside LWB	13957	14775
X18	4WD Standard SuperCab Styleside SWB	18486	20490
F18	4WD Standard Reg Cab Styleside SWB	16312	18020
F18	4WD Standard Reg Cab Styleside LWB	16590	18335
X18	4WD Standard SuperCab Styleside LWB	18794	20840

FORD
F-150 PICKUP

CODE	DESCRIPTION	INVOICE	MSRP
F17	2WD XL Reg Cab Styleside SWB	13652	15525
X17	2WD XL SuperCab Styleside SWB	15715	17950
F17	2WD XL Reg Cab Styleside LWB	13890	15805
X17	2WD XL SuperCab Styleside SWB	15959	18240
X18	4WD XL SuperCab Styleside SWB	19185	22025
F18	4WD XL Reg Cab Styleside SWB	16614	19010
F18	4WD XL Reg Cab Styleside LWB	16784	19210
X18	4WD XL SuperCab Styleside LWB	19496	22400
X07	2WD XL SuperCab Flareside	16367	18720
F07	2WD XL Reg Cab Flareside	14510	16535
F08	4WD XL Reg Cab Flareside	17191	19690
X08	4WD XL SuperCab Flareside	19840	22805
F17	2WD XLT Reg Cab Styleside SWB	15933	18210
X17	2WD XLT SuperCab Styleside SWB	18178	20850
F17	2WD XLT Reg Cab Styleside LWB	16223	18550
X17	2WD XLT SuperCab Styleside LWB	18407	21120
F18	4WD XLT Reg Cab Styleside SWB	18449	21170
X18	4WD XLT SuperCab Styleside SWB	21268	24485
F18	4WD XLT Reg Cab Styleside LWB	18628	21820
X18	4WD XLT SuperCab LWB	21509	24770
F07	2WD XLT Reg Cab Flareside	16924	19375
X07	2WD XLT SuperCab Flareside	18827	21615
F08	4WD XLT Reg Cab Flareside	19023	22745
X08	4WD XLT SuperCab Flareside	21863	25185
X17	2WD Lariat SuperCab Styleside SWB	20183	23210
F17	2WD Lariat Reg Cab Styleside SWB	17948	20580
F17	2WD Lariat Reg Cab Styleside LWB	18182	20880
X17	2WD Lariat SuperCab Styleside LWB	20442	23490
F18	4WD Lariat Reg Cab Styleside SWB	20634	23740
X18	4WD Lariat SuperCab Styleside SWB	22810	26335
F18	4WD Lariat Reg Cab Styleside LWB	20808	23945
X18	4WD Lariat SuperCab Styleside LWB	23146	26695
F07	2WD Lariat Reg Cab Flareside	18934	21740
X07	2WD Lariat SuperCab Flareside	20843	23985
F08	4WD Lariat Reg Cab Flareside	21197	24415
X08	4WD Lariat SuperCab Flareside	23502	27115
Destination Charge:		640	640

Accessories

CODE	DESCRIPTION	INVOICE	MSRP
67B	4-Wheel Anti-lock Brakes (Lariat)	NC	NC
67B	4-Wheel Anti-lock Brakes (Standard/XL/XLT)	425	500
992	4.2-liter EFI V-6 Engine (Standard/XL/XLT)	NC	NC

F-150 PICKUP — FORD

CODE	DESCRIPTION	INVOICE	MSRP
996	4.6-liter EFI V-8 Engine (Lariat/4WD Ext Cab)	NC	NC
996	4.6-liter EFI V-8 Engine (Standard/XL/XLT)	540	635
E	40/60 Split Bench (Lariat)	NC	NC
M	40/60 Split Bench (XLT)	NC	NC
55R	4WD Off-road Equipment Group (Lariat 4WD)	633	745
	Includes P265/70R175SL OWL all-terrain tires, 17" cast aluminum wheels, skid plates, heavy duty shock absorbers, X19 3.55 rear axle. NOT AVAILABLE w/ SuperCab 157" WB, lower two-tone paint, 4.2 liter engine/auto transmission or payload pkg #3.		
55R	4WD Off-road Equipment Group (XLT4WD)	973	1145
	Includes P265/70R175SL OWL all-terrain tires, 17" cast aluminum wheels, fog lamps, tachometer, skid plates, heavy duty shock absorbers, off road decal, X19 3.55 rear axle. NOT AVAILABLE w/ SuperCab 157" WB, lower two-tone paint, 4.2 liter engine/auto transmission or payload pkg #3		
—	5.4-liter V8 Engine (Lariat/4WD Ext Cab)	480	565
—	5.4-liter V8 Engine (N/A Lariat/4WD Ext Cab)	1020	1200
572	Air Conditioning	685	806
	INCLUDED IN Pkg 507A and 508A.		
641	Aluminum Wheels (XL/XLT)	340	400
	INCLUDED in PEP 507A or 4WD off-road equipment group.		
422	California Emissions System	85	100
	NOT AVAILABLE with engine block heater.		
F	Captain's Chairs w/ Console (XLT)	417	490
—	Carpeted Floor Mats (All Ext Cab)	26	30
768	Chrome Rear Step Bumper (Standard)	128	150
—	Chrome Rear Step Bumper Credit (XL)	(128)	(150)
	delete from pkg 502A		
535	Class III Trailer Towing Group	378	445
	Includes 7-pin trailer wiring harness, class III frame mounted hitch, super engine cooling, auxiliary automatic transmission oil cooler, 130 amp alternator, heavy duty 78 amp hour battery, heavy duty shock absorbers, 3.55 rear axle ratio. REQUIRES rear step bumper.		
535	Class III Trailer Towing Group Credit	(48)	(56)
	MUST have engine block heater to receive credit.		
535	Class III Trailer Towing Group Credit (w/manual transmission 44M)	(59)	(70)
535	Class III Trailer Towing Group Credit (w/off-road pkg 55R or Lariat)	(38)	(45)
44U	Electronic Automatic Transmission	824	970
215	Electronic Shift Touch-Drive 4WD (4WD)	128	150
	REQUIRES 4.6 liter engine, auto transmission and ABS.		
41H	Engine Block Heater	77	90
	Includes 600 watt element, heavy duty 78 amp hour batter. NOT AVAILABLE with California emissions.		
168	Floor Carpeting (XL)	85	100
—	Leather Captain's Chairs (Lariat)	417	490
	Includes console.		
153	License Plate Bracket	NC	NC

FORD
F-150 PICKUP

CODE	DESCRIPTION	INVOICE	MSRP
XH9	Limited Slip Rear Axle	215	252
	REQUIRES 3.55 axle.		
X19	Optional Axle Ratio Upgrade	37	44
	INCLUDED w/535 trailer tow group and w/55R off-road group.		
769	Painted Rear Step Bumper (Standard)	85	100
202	Payload Pkg #2 (Reg Cab 2WD Styleside)	41	50
	AVAILABLE only on Regular Cab 2WD Styleside w/139" WB. NOT AVAILABLE w/ 3.08 axle ratio. REQUIRES 4.6 liter engine and automatic transmission. Includes P255/70R16SL OWL all-season tires, styled steel wheels, heavy-duty springs and shock absorbers.		
203	Payload Pkg #3 (Standard)	357	420
	AVAILABLE only on Regular Cab 2WD Styleside w/139" WB. NOT AVAILABLE w/ 3.08 axle ratio; REQUIRES 4.6 liter engine and auto transmission. Includes P255/70R16SL OWL all-season tires, styled steel wheels, heavy duty springs and shock absorbers.		
203	Payload Pkg #3 (XL)	293	345
	AVAILABLE only on Regular Cab 2WD Styleside w/139" WB. NOT AVAILABLE w/ 3.08 axle ratio. REQUIRES 4.6 liter engine and auto transmisison. Includes P255/70R16SL OWL all-season tires, styled steel wheels, heavy duty springs and shock absorbers.		
203	Payload Pkg #3 (XLT)	122	144
	AVAILABLE only on Regular Cab 2WD Styleside w/139" WB. NOT AVAILABLE w/ 3.08 axle ratio. REQUIRES 4.6 liter engine and auto transmission. Includes P255/70R16SL OWL all-season tires, styled steel wheels, heavy duty springs and shock absorbers.		
C	Poly-Knit Bench Seat (Standard)	85	100
C	Poly-Knit Bench Seat (XL)	NC	NC
90P	Power Driver's Seat/Autolamp (Standard/XL/XLT)	309	363
	REQUIRES air conditioning, speed control, auto transmission and captain's chairs.		
502A	Preferred Equipment Pkg 502A (XL)	NC	NC
	Includes styled steel wheels and chrome rear step bumper.		
507A	Preferred Equipment Pkg 507A (XLT)	NC	NC
	Includes air conditioning, electronic AM/FM stereo, clock and cassette; speed control, tilt steering wheel, and aluminum wheels.		
508A	Preferred Equipment Pkg 508A (Lariat)	NC	NC
	Includes air conditioning, electronic AM/FM stereo, clock and cassette; speed control, tilt steering wheel, two-tone paint, power driver's seat, and autolamp.		
—	Rear Carpeted Floor Mats (Ext Cab)	17	20
872	Rear Seat (Standard Ext Cab)	352	415
61S	Rear Storage Bin	77	90
904	Remote Keyless Entry/Anti-theft System	217	255
	REQUIRES air conditioning, speed control, and electric shift (4WD models).		
413	Skid Plates (4WD NA w/Reg Cab 120" WB)	136	160
	Includes transfer plates and fuel tank skid plates. INCLUDED in 4WD Off-Road Equipment Group.		

F-150 PICKUP / F-250 PICKUP — FORD

CODE	DESCRIPTION	INVOICE	MSRP
413	Skid Plates (4WD Reg Cab 120" WB)	66	78
	Includes transfer case and fuel tank skid plates. INCLUDED in 4WD Off-Road Equipment Group.		
433	Sliding Rear Window	97	115
—	Spec. Disc. w/Manual Trans. & A/C	(425)	(500)
	REQUIRES air conditioning and manual transmission.		
52N	Speed Control/Tilt Steering Wheel	328	385
	INCLUDED in pkg 507A and 508A.		
589	Stereo w/Cassette	93	110
	Includes clock and 4 speakers. INCLUDED in PEP 507A and 508A.		
91P	Stereo w/Cassette & CD Changer	340	400
	REQUIRES air conditioning and speed control.		
642	Styled Steel Wheels (Std.XL/XLT)	170	200
	NOT AVAILABLE 4WD off-road equipment group.		
T53	Tires — P235/&0R16SL OWL A/S (2WD)	107	125
T5K	Tires — P235/70R16SL BSW (4WD)	111	130
	Includes all-terrain spare.		
T52	Tires — P235/70R16SL BSW A/S (2WD)	NC	NC
T52	Tires — P235/70R16SL BSW A/S (4WD)	NC	NC
T5L	Tires — P235/70R16SL OWL (4WD)	217	255
	Includes all-terrain spare.		
T65	Tires — P255/70R16SL OWL (4WD)	417	490
	REQUIRES 3.55 axle ratio.		
—	Tires — P255/70R16SL OWL (4WD Lariat)	111	130
	all-terrain		
T55	Tires — P255/70R16SL OWL A/S (2WD)	208	245
952	Two-tone Paint (Standard/XL/XLT)	162	190
A	Vinyl Bench Seat (Standard)	NC	NC
A	Vinyl Bench Seat (XL)	(85)	(100)

F-250 PICKUP *(1997)*

Safety Data:

Driver Airbag: *Standard*
Side Airbag: *Not Available*
4-Wheel ABS: *Optional Std, XL, XLT; Standard Lariat*
Driver Crash Test Grade: *Excellent*
Passenger Crash Test Grade: *Excellent*

Passenger Airbag: *Standard*
Meets 1999 Side Impact Standards: *Yes*
Traction Control: *N/A*
Insurance Cost: *Low*
Integrated Child Seat(s): *N/A*

Standard Equipment

F250 PICKUP (Under 8500# GVWR) - ALL MODELS: 4.6 liter EFI V8 engine, 5-speed manual overdrive transmission, 2-speed transfer case (4WD), power steering, 95 amp alternator, 3950# front axle, 5300# rear axle, 58 AH 540 CCA maintenance-free battery with battery saver, power front/rear drum brakes with rear wheel anti-lock (STD, XL, XLT), 4-wheel anti-lock (Lariat), 30.5

FORD F-250 PICKUP

gallon fuel tank (Regular Cab), 24.5 gallon fuel tank (Super Cab), center disconnect shift-on-the-fly 4x4 system (4WD), gas shock absorbers, 3600# front springs (2WD), 3950# front springs (4WD), 4800# rear springs, P255/70R16SL BSW all-season tires (2WD), LT245/75R16D BSW all-season tires (4WD), full service spare tire, 7.0J 7-hole wheels.

STD: Argent painted front bumper, 3 doors (Super Cab), argent grille/headlamp surrounds, black tailgate handle, black door handles, manual black aero mirrors, argent wheel openings (4WD), tie-down hooks, bed rail/tailgate moldings, high-mounted stop light, removable tailgate with lock, front tow hooks (4WD), 4-pin trailer tow wiring, argent styled chrome hub wheels, driver and passenger air bags, back panel cover (Regular Cab), dual cup holder, dome light, vinyl upper door trim with integral armrest, black vinyl floor covering, headliner, instrumentation (Includes voltmeter, oil pressure, temperature, speed, fuel), auxiliary power point, electronic AM/FM stereo radio with 4 speakers, front split back vinyl bench seats, vinyl sun visors, interval wipers.

XL (in addition to or instead of STD equipment): Chrome front bumper, chrome grille and headlamp surrounds (2WD), high-mounted stop lamp with cargo box light, dome light with dual map lights, door map pocket, color-keyed vinyl floor covering, front split back cloth bench seats, split bench rear seat (Super Cab), cloth sun visors with LH strap and RH mirror, color-keyed grille/headlamp surrounds (4WD).

XLT (in addition to or instead of XL equipment): Chrome rear step bumper, color-keyed grille/headlamp surrounds, color-keyed door handles, power chrome aero mirrors (2WD), power color-keyed aero mirrors (4WD), color-keyed bodyside moldings, color-keyed wheel opening moldings (4WD), quarter/side windows privacy glass, rear storage tray (Regular Cab w/o CD changer), carpeted lower door trim, grab handle, color-keyed carpeting, tachometer, power windows, power door locks, power mirrors, cloth split bench front seats (Includes recliners, armrest, driver's side manual lumbar support), LH auxiliary sun visor, speed dependent interval wipers.

LARIAT (in addition to or instead of XLT equipment): Fog lamps (4WD), color-keyed carpet with floor mats, leather split bench front seats (Includes recliners, armrest, driver's side manual lumbar support).

Base Prices

Code	Description	Invoice	MSRP
F27	Regular Cab 2WD Standard	14913	16430
F27	Regular Cab 2WD XL	15344	17518
F27	Regular Cab 2WD XLT	17599	20170
F27	Regular Cab 2WD Lariat	18912	21715
F28	Regular Cab 4WD Standard	17843	19763
F28	Regular Cab 4WD XL	18217	20898
F28	Regular Cab 4WD XLT	20053	23080
F28	Regular Cab 4WD Lariat	21514	24775
X27	Super Cab 2WD Standard	16540	18283
X27	Super Cab 2WD XL	17188	19688
X27	Super Cab 2WD XLT	19592	22515
X27	Super Cab 2WD Lariat	20948	24110
X28	Super Cab 4WD Standard	19387	215118
X28	Super Cab 4WD XL	20087	23098
X28	Super Cab 4WD XLT	22152	25525
X28	Super Cab 4WD Lariat	23587	27215
Destination Charge:		640	640

F-250 PICKUP — FORD

CODE	DESCRIPTION	INVOICE	MSRP

Accessories

CODE	DESCRIPTION	INVOICE	MSRP
—	Preferred Equipment Pkgs — prices include pkg discounts		
510A	Pkg 510A — Standard	NC	NC
	Includes vehicle with standard equipment		
512A	Pkg 512A — XL	NC	NC
	Includes vehicle with chrome rear step bumper		
517A	Pkg 517A — XLT	NC	NC
	Includes air conditioning, 589 radio (electronic AM/FM stereo/clock/cassette and 4 speakers), speed control/tilt steering wheel, chrome styled steel wheels		
518A	Pkg 518A — Lariat	NC	NC
	Includes pkg 517A contents plus lower two-tone paint, power driver's seat/autolamp; REQUIRES auto trans w/captain's chairs		
996	Engine — 4.6 liter EFI V8	STD	STD
99L	Engine — 5.4 liter EFI V8	480	565
44M	Transmission — 5-speed manual overdrive	STD	STD
44U	Transmission — electronic automatic overdrive	824	970
	REQUIRES 4.6 liter engine		
44E	Transmission — electronic automatic overdrive	824	970
	REQUIRES 5.4 liter engine		
—	Rear Axle		
XB6	limited slip, rear	213	250
X26	optional axle ratio (upgrade)	38	45
XB6	limited slip w/optional axle ratio (upgrade)	251	295
422	California Emissions System	144	170
207	Payload Pkg #2 — 2WD Super Cab	41	50
209	Payload Pkg #2 — all models except 2WD Super Cab	41	50
—	Tires		
T54	P255/70R16SL BSW all-season - 2WD	STD	STD
T55	P255/70R16SL OWL all-season - 2WD Lariat	STD	STD
	other 2WD models	107	125
T34	LT245/75R16D BSW all-season - 2WD Lariat	77	90
	other 2WD models	182	215
	4WD models	STD	STD
T3P	LT245/75R16D OWL all-terrain - 4WD	336	395
	XLT Includes fog lamps		
—	Seats		
A	vinyl bench - Standard	STD	STD
	XL	(85)	(100)
C	poly-knit bench - Standard	85	100
	XL	(85)	(100)
M	40/60 split bench - XLT	STD	STD
F	captain's chairs w/console - XLT	417	490
E	40/60 leather split bench - Lariat	STD	STD
X	captain's chairs, leather w/console - Lariat	417	490
67B	4-Wheel ABS — Lariat	STD	STD
	all other models	425	500

FORD F-250 PICKUP

CODE	DESCRIPTION	INVOICE	MSRP
572	Air Conditioning	684	805
769	Bumper — painted rear step - Standard	85	100
768	Bumper — chrome rear step - XL	128	150
535	**Class III Trailer Towing Group**		
	w/4.6 liter engine/auto trans and 4WD	(38)	(45)
	w/engine block heater	(47)	(55)
	w/44M manual trans	(59)	(70)
	Includes 7-pin trailer wiring harness, Class III frame mounted hitch, super engine cooling, auxiliary auto transmission oil cooler, 130 amp alternator, heavy duty 78 amp hr battery, spring upgrades, 3.73 rear axle		
215	Electric Shift 4WD Touch Drive	128	150
	REQUIRES auto trans		
—	Floor Mats — carpeted, color-keyed front - XLT	26	30
—	Floor Mats — carpeted, color-keyed rear - Super Cab	17	20
41H	Engine Block Heater	77	90
	Includes heavy duty battery		
53C	Heavy Duty Service Pkg	178	210
	Includes 130 amp alternator, 78 amp hr battery, super engine cooling, auxiliary auto transmission oil cooler; REQUIRES rear step bumper		
153	License Plate Bracket	NC	NC
68P	Load Leveling Suspension — XL, XLT, Lariat	417	490
	Includes heavy duty shocks; REQUIRES 67B ABS and 53C heavy duty service pkg		
952	Paint — lower two-tone - XLT	162	190
	Paint Delete — lower two-tone - Lariat	NC	NC
90P	Power Driver's Seat/Autolamp — XLT	306	360
	REQUIRES air conditioning and speed control; REQUIRES auto trans w/captain's chairs		
61S	Rear Storage Bin — XLT Regular Cab, Lariat Regular Cab	77	90
904	Remote Keyless Entry/Anti-Theft — XLT, Lariat	217	255
	REQUIRES air conditioning and speed control		
413	Skid Plates — 4WD	136	160
	Includes transfer case and fuel tank skid plates		
52N	Speed Control/Tilt Steering Wheel — Standard, XL	328	385
642	Styled Steel Wheels	STD	STD
643	Chrome Steel Wheels — XL	170	200
433	Sliding Rear Window	97	115
—	**Audio**		
587	electronic AM/FM stereo/clock and 4 speakers	STD	STD
589	electronic AM/FM stereo/clock/cassette and 4 speakers	93	110
91P	CD changer with AM/FM premium stereo/cassette - XLT, Lariat	340	400
	REQUIRES air conditioning and speed control		

F-250 HEAVY DUTY PICKUP *(1997)*

Safety Data:

Driver Airbag: *N/A*
Side Airbag: *N/A*
4-Wheel ABS: *N/A*
Driver Crash Test Grade: *Excellent*
Passenger Crash Test Grade: *Excellent*

Passenger Airbag: *N/A*
Meets 1999 Side Impact Standards: *Yes*
Traction Control: *N/A*
Insurance Cost: *Very Low*
Integrated Child Seat(s): *N/A*

Standard Equipment

F250 HEAVY DUTY PICKUP (Over 8500# GVWR) - ALL MODELS: 5.8 liter EFI V8 engine (Regular Cab, Super Cab), 7.5 liter EFI V8 engine (Crew Cab), heavy duty 5-speed manual overdrive transmission, power steering, 95 amp alternator (130 amp w/diesel engine), 4200# front axle (2WD), 4600# front axle (4WD), 6250# rear axle, 72 AH 650 CCA maintenance-free battery, power brakes with rear wheel anti-lock, 37.2 gallon fuel tank, automatic locking hubs (4WD), heavy duty gas shock absorbers, 2765# front springs (2WD Regular Cab/Crew Cab), 3140# front springs (2WD Super Cab), 3305# front springs (4WD Regular Cab/Crew Cab), 3920# front springs (4WD Super Cab), 6363# rear springs (2WD), 6148# rear springs (4WD), LT235/85R16E BSW all-season tires, 2-speed transfer case (4WD), 7.0K 8-hole wheels.

XL: Chrome front bumper, 4x4 decal, tinted glass, argent grille, aero halogen headlights, wrap-around front parking/turn signal lights, black manual mirrors, bright windshield moldings, high-mounted stop light with cargo box light, removable tailgate with bright release handle, wrap-around taillights, bright hub cabs on argent steel wheels (NA 4WD), carpeted back panel cover (Regular Cab, Crew Cab), cigarette lighter, RH color-keyed coat hook, LH/RH door operated courtesy light, color-keyed door trim panel with black handles and reflectors, black rubber mat floor covering, color-keyed cloth headliner (Super Cab, Crew Cab), inside hood release, dual electric horn, instrument panel (Includes color-keyed with glove box, side window demisters, four air registers), black appliques, instrumentation (Includes voltmeter, oil pressure, temperature, fuel gauges with indicator lights), trip odometer, lights (Includes dome, glove box, ashtray), 12" day/night mirror, power point, electronic AM radio with digital clock and 2 door-mounted speakers, black scuff plates, vinyl bench seats with integral head restraints for outboard seating positions, vinyl rear bench seat (Super Cab), black vinyl steering wheel, color-keyed vinyl sun visors (Includes LH retainer band), vent windows, interval wipers.

XLT (in addition to or instead of XL equipment): Black rub strip, chrome grille, bright headlight/parking light bezels, bright manual mirrors, bright wheellip moldings, black lower bodyside protection molding, brushed applique tailgate, sport wheel covers on black steel wheels, color-keyed carpet, carpet back panel cover, vinyl insert door trim with storage bin and courtesy light/reflector, carpeted door map pocket, color-keyed cloth headliner, power windows, power door locks, electronic AM/FM stereo radio with digital clock and 4 speakers, cloth seats (flight bench with power lumbar on Regular Cab, Crew Cab), rear cloth bench seat (Super Cab, Crew Cab), leather-wrapped steering wheel, color-keyed cloth sun visors (Includes LH retainer band and RH visor mirror).

FORD F-250 HD PICKUP

CODE	DESCRIPTION	INVOICE	MSRP
Base Prices			
F25	Regular Cab 2WD 133" WB XL	15686	17830
F26	Regular Cab 4WD 133" WB XL	18253	20850
X25	Super Cab 2WD 139" WB XL	17403	19850
X25	Super Cab 2WD 155" WB XL	17250	19670
X26	Super Cab 4WD 139" WB XL	20076	22995
X26	Super Cab 4WD 155" WB XL	19924	22815
W25	Crew Cab 2WD 152" WB XL	18997	21725
W26	Crew Cab 4WD 152" WB XL	21666	24865
Destination Charge:		640	640
Accessories			
—	Preferred Equipment Pkgs — prices include pkg discounts		
	Regular Cab		
600A	Pkg 600A — XL	NC	NC
	Includes vehicle with standard equipment		
603A	Pkg 603A — XLT	2133	2510
	Includes air conditioning, power door locks/windows, interior enhancement/light group, speed control/tilt steering wheel, deep dish aluminum wheels, electronic AM/FM stereo/clock/cassette/4 speakers		
	Super Cab		
610A	Pkg 610A — XL	NC	NC
	Includes vehicle with standard XL equipment		
613A	Pkg 613A — XLT	2082	2450
	Includes air conditioning, power door locks/windows, interior enhancement/light group, speed control/tilt steering wheel, deep dish aluminum wheels, electronic AM/FM stereo/cassette/clock/4 speakers		
	Crew Cab		
605A	Pkg 605A — XL	NC	NC
	Includes vehicle with standard XL equipment		
606A	Pkg 606A — XLT	2252	2650
	Includes air conditioning, power door locks/windows, interior enhancement/light group, electronic AM/FM stereo/clock/cassette/4 speakers, speed control/tilt steering wheel, deep dish aluminum wheels		
—	**Engines**		
99H	5.8 liter EFI V8 - w/all models except Crew Cab and 139" Super Cab	STD	STD
99G	7.5 liter EFI V8 - w/Crew Cab and 139" Super Cab	STD	STD
	w/all models except Crew Cab and 139" Super Cab	328	385
99F	7.3 liter powerstroke diesel V8 - w/Crew Cab and 139" Super Cab	3297	3880
	w/all models except Crew Cab and 139" Super Cab	3625	4265
—	**Transmissions**		
44W	5-speed manual overdrive heavy duty	STD	STD
44C	5-speed manual overdrive heavy duty - w/diesel engine	NC	NC
44E	electronic 4-speed automatic	824	970

F-250 HD PICKUP — FORD

CODE	DESCRIPTION	INVOICE	MSRP
—	Rear Axle		
—	limited slip axle	213	250
—	optional axle ratio (upgrade)	38	45
—	limited slip axle and optional axle ratio (upgrade)	251	295
422	California Emissions System	144	170
428	High Altitude Principal Use Emissions System	NC	NC
—	Payload Pkgs		
	Regular Cab		
207	133" WB base payload pkg #1 - 2WD	STD	STD
208	133" WB base payload pkg #1 - 4WD	STD	STD
	Super Cab		
209	155" WB base payload pkg #1 - 2WD	STD	STD
208	155" WB base payload pkg #1 - 4WD	STD	STD
209	139" WB base payload pkg #1 - 2WD	STD	STD
208	139" WB base payload pkg #1 - 4WD	STD	STD
	Crew Cab		
209	152" WB base payload pkg #1 - 2WD	STD	STD
208	152" WB base payload pkg #1 - 4WD	STD	STD
—	Tires		
T35	LT235/85R16E BSW all-season (4)	STD	STD
T3N	LT235/85R16E BSW all-terrain (2, rear only) - 2WD	47	55
T3N	LT235/85R16E BSW all-terrain (4) - 4WD	93	110
512	spare tire & wheel, LT235/85R16E BSW A/S	229	270
515	spare tire & wheel, all-terrain	251	295
513	spare rear wheel - 4WD	115	135
—	Seats		
	Regular Cab		
6	vinyl bench - XL	STD	STD
7	cloth & vinyl bench - XL	85	100
5	cloth flight bench - XLT	STD	STD
R	premium cloth 40/20/40 bench - XLT	447	525
	Super Cab		
6	knitted vinyl bench - XL	STD	STD
7	cloth & vinyl bench - XL	85	100
4	cloth captain's chairs - XL	663	780
	Includes floor console, power lumbar, cloth rear bench seat		
8	cloth bench - XLT	STD	STD
4	cloth captain's chairs - XLT	527	620
	Includes floor console, power lumbar, cloth rear bench seat		
R	premium cloth 40/20/40 bench - XLT	527	620
90P	power driver's seat (40/20/40) - XLT	247	290
	Crew Cab		
5	cloth flight bench - XLT	STD	STD
R	premium cloth 40/20/40 bench	527	620

FORD F-250 HD PICKUP

CODE	DESCRIPTION	INVOICE	MSRP
532	Camper/Trailer Towing Pkg	251	295
	credit w/off-road pkg 55R	(102)	(120)
	credit w/7.3 liter diesel turbo engine	(132)	(155)
	Includes super engine cooling, trailer wiring harness, heavy duty turn signal flasher, handling pkg, heavy duty battery (gas engine only)		
684	Handling Pkg	102	120
	Includes front/rear stabilizer bars		
593	Interior Enhancement/Light Group	68	80
	Includes dual beam dome/map light, headlights on audible alert, map pocket, RH visor vanity mirror, mini-console (Regular Cab only), headliner and insulation pkg		
55R	Off-Road Pkg	255	300
	w/7.3 liter 4WD	182	215
	Includes skid plates, front/rear stabilizer bars, 4x4 off-road decal		
535	Trailer Towing Pkg	251	295
	Includes super engine cooling, trailer wiring harness, heavy duty turn signal flasher, handling pkg, heavy duty battery (gas engine only)		
572	Air Conditioning	684	805
76C	Bumper — argent rear step	85	100
768	Bumper — chrome rear step	128	150
183	Chrome Appearance Pkg	153	180
	Includes chrome grille and bright mirror; NA w/argent rear step bumper		
592	Clearance Lights, Roof	47	55
624	Cooling, Super Engine	85	100
167	Carpeted Floor Mats — XLT	43	50
166	Floor Mat — in lieu of carpet	NC	NC
85D	4x4/Off-Road Decal Delete	NC	NC
651	Fuel Tank — single	(97)	(115)
41H	Heater, Engine Block — w/4.9 or 5.8 liter engine	30	35
	w/7.5 liter engine	55	65
21M	Hubs — manual locking	NC	NC
66D	Pickup Box Delete	(532)	(626)
153	License Plate Bracket	NC	NC
186	Cab Steps — color-keyed	340	400
545	Mirrors — bright low-mount swingaway		
	use w/XL, w/o chrome appearance pkg	38	45
	use w/all other	NC	NC
548	Mirrors — bright swing-out recreational		
	use w/XL, w/o chrome appearance pkg	47	55
	use w/all other	8	10
543	Mirrors — bright electric	85	100
952	Paint — deluxe two-tone	234	276
954	Paint — lower accent two-tone	162	190
168	Floor Carpeting — XL	85	100
879	Rear Bench Seat — vinyl - Super Cab S models	NC	NC
87D	Rear Bench Seat Delete	(352)	(415)
948	Remote Keyless Entry	144	170
52N	Speed Control/Tilt Steering Wheel	328	385

F-250 HD PICKUP / F-350 PICKUP — FORD

CODE	DESCRIPTION	INVOICE	MSRP
674	Suspension Pkg — HD front	59	70
683	Suspension Pkg — HD rear	111	130
152	Tachometer	51	60
535	Trailer Towing Pkg	251	295
644	Wheel Covers — sport	85	100
	credit - delete aluminum wheels from XLT pkg	(255)	(300)
433	Window — sliding rear	97	115
924	Privacy Glass — rear	85	100
961	Auxiliary Idle Control	170	200
—	Audio		
587	electronic AM/FM stereo/clock	128	150
589	electronic AM/FM stereo/clock/cassette	221	260
	w/PEP w/AM/FM stereo	93	110
582	premium electronic AM/FM stereo/clock/compact disc player over cassette	255	300
58Y	radio credit option	(51)	(60)

F-350 PICKUP *(1997)*

Standard Equipment

F350 PICKUP - ALL MODELS: 5.8 liter EFI V8 engine (Regular Cab, Crew Cab), 7.5 liter EFI V8 engine (Super Cab, Chassis Cab), heavy duty 5-speed manual overdrive transmission, 2-speed transfer case (4WD), 95 amp alternator (130 amp w/diesel engine), 4200# front axle (2WD), 5000# front axle (4WD), 6250# rear axle (SRW models), 7400# rear axle (DRW 2WD models except 137"/161" WB Chassis Cab), 8250# rear axle (137"/161" Chassis Cab), 8250# rear axle (4WD Regular Cab), 72 amp 650 CCA maintenance-free battery (dual 78 AH 1500 CCA batteries w/7.3 liter diesel engine), power brakes with rear wheel anti-lock, 37.2 gallon fuel tank (38 gallon w/137"/161" WB Chassis Cab models), LT235/85R16E BSW all-season tires (SRW models), LT215/85R16D BSW all-season tires (DRW models), 7.0K 8-hole wheels (SRW models), 6.0K 8-hole wheels (DRW models).

XL: Chrome front bumper, "4x4" decal (SRW Styleside), tinted glass, argent grille, aero halogen headlights, wrap-around front parking/turn signal lights, roof clearance light (DRW Styleside, Chassis Cab), black manual mirrors, bright recreational swing-out mirror (models over 10,000# GVWR), bright windshield moldings, high-mounted stop light with cargo box light, removable tailgate with bright release handle, wrap-around taillights, cigarette lighter, RH color-keyed coat hook, LH/RH door-operated courtesy lights, color-keyed door trim with black handles and reflector, black rubber mat floor covering, color-keyed cloth headliner (Super Cab, Crew Cab), inside hood release, dual electric horn, color-keyed instrument panel (Includes glove box, side window demisters, four air registers), black appliques, instrumentation (Includes voltmeter, oil pressure, temperature, fuel gauges with indicator lights), trip odometer, lights (Includes dome, glove box, ashtray), 12" day/night mirror, power point, electronic AM radio with digital clock and 2 door-mounted speakers, black scuff plates, vinyl bench seats with integrated head restraints for outboard seating positions, rear vinyl bench seat (Super Cab), black vinyl steering wheel, color-keyed vinyl sun visors (Includes LH retainer band), vent windows, interval wipers.

FORD — F-350 PICKUP

XLT (in addition to or instead of XL equipment): Black rub strip, chrome grille, bright headlight/parking light bezels, bright manual mirrors, brushed applique tailgate (Styleside), color-keyed carpet, carpet back panel cover (Regular Cab/Crew Cab), door trim (Includes vinyl insert, storage bin, courtesy light/reflector), carpeted map pocket, color-keyed cloth headliner, power windows, power door locks, electronic AM/FM stereo with digital clock and 4 speakers, cloth seats (flight bench with power lumbar on Regular Cab/Crew Cab), cloth rear bench seat (Super Cab/Crew Cab), leather-wrapped steering wheel, color-keyed cloth sun visors (Includes LH retainer band and RH visor mirror).

Base Prices

Code	Description	Invoice	MSRP
F35	Regular Cab SRW 2WD 133" WB	16119	18340
F35	Regular Cab DRW 2WD 133" WB	16787	19125
F36	Regular Cab SRW 4WD 133" WB	18768	21455
W35	Crew Cab SRW 2WD 168" WB	19048	21785
W35	Crew Cab DRW 2WD 168" WB	19545	22370
W36	Crew Cab SRW 4WD 168" WB	21717	24925
F37	Regular Chassis Cab DRW 2WD 137" WB	16574	18875
F37	Regular Chassis Cab DRW 2WD 161" WB	16706	19030
F38	Regular Chassis Cab DRW 4WD 137" WB	20179	23115
F38	Regular Chassis Cab DRW 4WD 161" WB	20293	23250
X35	Super Cab DRW 2WD 155" WB	18754	21440
Destination Charge:		640	640

Accessories

Code	Description	Invoice	MSRP
—	Preferred Equipment Pkgs — prices include pkg discounts		
	Regular Cab		
640A	Pkg 640A — XL (SRW) 4WD	NC	NC
	Includes vehicle with standard XL equipment, floor mats		
650A	Pkg 650A — XL (SRW) 2WD	NC	NC
	Includes vehicle with standard XL equipment, floor mats, roof clearance lights		
651A	Pkg 651A — XLT (SRW) 2WD	1811	2130
	Includes air conditioning, power door locks/windows, interior enhancement/light group, speed control/tilt steering wheel, electronic AM/FM stereo/clock/cassette/4 speakers, roof clearance lights, floor mats		
642A	Pkg 642A — XLT (SRW) 4WD	2133	2510
	Includes air conditioning, power door locks/windows, interior enhancement/light group, speed control/tilt steering wheel, forged aluminum deep dish wheels, electronic AM/FM stereo/clock/cassette/4 speakers		
660A	Pkg 660A — XL (SRW)	NC	NC
	Includes vehicle with standard XL equipment, floor mats		
670A	Pkg 670A — XL (DRW) 2WD	NC	NC
	Includes vehicle with standard XL equipment, floor mats, roof clearance lights		
661	Pkg 661A — XLT (SRW)	2252	2650
	Includes air conditioning, power door locks/windows, interior enhancement/light group, speed control/tilt steering wheel, forged aluminum deep dish wheels, electronic AM/FM stereo/clock/cassette/4 speakers		

F-350 PICKUP — FORD

CODE	DESCRIPTION	INVOICE	MSRP
671A	Pkg 671A — XLT (DRW) 2WD	2184	2570
	Includes air conditioning, power door locks/windows, interior enhancement/light group, speed control/tilt steering wheel, electronic AM/FM stereo/clock/cassette/4 speakers, roof clearance lights		
	Regular Chassis Cab		
630A	Pkg 630A — XL (DRW)	NC	NC
	Includes model with standard equipment, floor mats		
632A	Pkg 632A — XLT (DRW)	1674	1970
	Includes air conditioning, power door locks/windows, interior enhancement/light group, speed control/tilt steering wheel, electronic AM/FM stereo/clock/cassette/4 speakers		
617A	Pkg 617A — XL (DRW) 2WD	NC	NC
	Includes vehicle with standard equipment, floor mats		
618A	Pkg 618A — XLT (DRW) 2WD	1759	2070
	Includes air conditioning, power door locks/windows, interior enhancement/light group, speed control/tilt steering wheel, electronic AM/FM stereo/clock/cassette/4 speakers		
—	**Engines**		
99H	5.8 liter EFI V8 - w/all models except 4WD Chassis Cab and 2WD Super Cab	STD	STD
99G	7.5 liter EFI V8 - w/4WD Chassis Cab and 2WD Super Cab	STD	STD
	w/all other models	328	385
99F	7.3 liter powerstroke diesel V8 - w/4WD Chassis Cab and Super Cab	3297	3880
	w/all other models	3625	4265
948	Remote Keyless Entry	144	170
—	**Transmissions**		
44W	5-speed manual overdrive, heavy duty	STD	STD
44C	5-speed manual overdrive, heavy duty - w/diesel engine	NC	NC
44E	electronic 4-speed automatic	824	970
—	**Rear Axles**		
—	limited slip rear axle	213	250
—	optional axle ratio (upgrade)	38	45
—	limited slip axle and optional axle ratio (upgrade)	251	295
422	California Emissions System	144	170
428	High Altitude Principal Use Emissions System	NC	NC
—	**Payload Pkgs**		
	Regular Cab		
202	133" WB base payload pkg #1 - DRW 2WD	STD	STD
201	133" WB base payload pkg #1 - SRW 4WD	STD	STD
	Crew Cab		
202	168" WB base payload pkg #1 - SRW 2WD	STD	STD
203	168" WB base payload pkg #1 - DRW 2WD	STD	STD
201	168" WB base payload pkg #1 - SRW 4WD	STD	STD
	Regular Chassis Cab		
208	137" WB base payload pkg #1 - DRW 2WD	STD	STD
209	137" WB optional payload pkg #2 - DRW 2WD	26	30
208	161" WB base payload pkg #1 - DRW 2WD	STD	STD
209	161" WB optional payload pkg #2 - DRW 2WD	26	30

FORD F-350 PICKUP

CODE	DESCRIPTION	INVOICE	MSRP
204	133" WB base payload pkg #1 - DRW 4WD	STD	STD
204	161" WB base payload pkg #1 - DRW 4WD	STD	STD
	Super Cab		
201	155" WB base payload pkg #1 - DRW 2WD	STD	STD
—	Tires		
	Regular/Crew/Regular Chassis Cab - SRW		
T35	LT235/85R16E BSW all-season (4) - 2WD	STD	STD
	4WD	STD	STD
T3N	LT235/85R16E BSW all-terrain - 2WD (2, rear only)	47	55
	4WD (4)	93	110
	Regular/Crew/Regular Chassis/Super Cab - DRW		
T63	LT215/85R16D BSW all-season (6) - 2WD	STD	STD
T6C	LT215/85R16D BSW all-terrain (6) - 2WD	93	110
TE5	LT235/85R16E BSW all-terrain - 4WD	STD	STD
TEE	LT235/85R16E BSW all-terrain (6)	144	170
	All Models		
512	spare tire and wheel, LT215/85R16D BSW all-season	213	250
—	spare tire and wheel, LT235/85R16E BSW all-season	229	270
513	wheel, spare rear	115	135
515	spare tire and wheel, LT235/85R16E BSW all-terrain - 4WD	251	295
—	Seats		
	Regular Cab		
6	vinyl bench - XL	STD	STD
7	cloth & vinyl bench - XL	85	100
5	cloth flight bench - XLT	STD	STD
R	premium cloth 40/20/40 bench - XLT	447	525
	Crew Cab		
6	vinyl bench - XL	STD	STD
7	cloth bench - XL	85	100
	XLT	STD	STD
5	cloth flight bench - XLT	STD	STD
R	premium cloth 40/20/40 bench - XLT	527	620
	Super Cab		
6	knitted vinyl bench - XL	STD	STD
7	cloth & vinyl bench - XL	85	100
4	cloth captain's chairs - XL	663	780
	Includes floor console, power lumbar, cloth rear bench seat		
8	cloth bench - XLT	STD	STD
	Includes cloth rear bench seat		
4	cloth captain's chairs - XLT	527	620
	Includes floor console, power lumbar, cloth rear bench seat		
R	premium cloth 40/20/40 bench - XLT	527	620
90P	power driver's seat, 40/20/40 - XLT	247	290
87D	Rear Bench Seat Delete	(352)	(415)
879	Rear Bench Seat — vinyl	NC	NC
684	Handling Pkg	102	120
	Includes front/rear stabilizer bars		

F-350 PICKUP — FORD

CODE	DESCRIPTION	INVOICE	MSRP
593	Interior Enhancement/Light Group	68	80
	Includes dual beam dome/map light, headlights on audible alert, map pocket, RH visor vanity mirror, mini-console (Regular Cab only), headliner and insulation pkg (Regular Cab XL only)		
55R	Off-Road Pkg	221	260
	w/7.3 liter 4WD	144	170
	Includes skid plate, front/rear stabilizer bars, 4x4 off-road decal		
572	Air Conditioning	684	805
76C	Bumper — argent rear step	85	100
768	Bumper — chrome rear step	128	150
532	Camper/Trailer Towing Pkg	251	295
	credit w/off-road pkg 55R	(102)	(120)
	credit w/7.3 liter diesel turbo engine	(132)	(155)
	Includes super engine cooling, trailer wiring harness, heavy duty turn signal flasher, handling pkg, 84 amp hour heavy duty battery (w/gas engine only)		
183	Chrome Appearance Pkg	153	180
592	Clearance Lights, Roof	47	55
624	Cooling, Super Engine	85	100
166	Floor Mat — in lieu of carpet	NC	NC
85D	4x4/Off-Road Decal Delete	NC	NC
651	Fuel Tank — single	(97)	(115)
435	Fuel Tap — auxiliary	26	30
41H	Heater, Engine Block — w/5.8 liter engine	30	35
	w/7.5 liter engine	55	65
21M	Hubs — manual locking	NC	NC
153	License Plate Bracket	NC	NC
186	Cab Steps — color-keyed	340	400
167	Floor Mats — carpeted	43	50
545	Mirrors — bright low-mount swingaway		
	use w/XL, w/o chrome appearance pkg	38	45
	use w/all other	NC	NC
548	Mirrors — bright swing-out recreational		
	use w/XL, w/o chrome appearance pkg	47	55
	use w/all other	8	10
543	Mirrors — bright electric	85	100
952	Paint — deluxe two-tone - w/XLT trim	234	275
	w/styleside DRW models	140	165
954	Paint — lower accent two-tone	162	190
52N	Speed Control/Tilt Steering Wheel	328	385
674	Suspension Pkg — heavy duty front	26	30
152	Tachometer	51	60
644	Wheel Covers — sport	85	100
649	Wheels — forged aluminum - w/DRW	493	580
	credit, wheels, forged aluminum (deep dish) - from XLT pkg	(255)	(300)
64F	Wheels — heavy duty forged aluminum - w/SRW	323	380
433	Window — sliding rear	97	115
924	Privacy Glass — rear	85	100

FORD
F-350 PICKUP / RANGER

CODE	DESCRIPTION	INVOICE	MSRP
66D	Pickup Box Delete	(532)	(625)
—	Audio		
587	electronic AM/FM stereo/clock	128	150
589	electronic AM/FM stereo/clock/cassette	221	260
	w/PEP w/AM/FM stereo	93	110
582	premium electronic AM/FM stereo/clock/compact disc player over cassette	255	300
58Y	radio credit option	(51)	(60)

RANGER *(1997)*

1997 Ford Ranger Splash SuperCab 2WD

What's New for Ford Ranger in 1997 — Ford introduces its brand-new 5-speed automatic transmission to the Ranger lineup. Available with the V-6 engines, the 5-speed automatic is designed to improve the Ranger's acceleration, towing and hill climbing ability.

Ranger — Review

Whether it's image or utility that attracts you to a compact truck, Ford stands ready to seduce you into its strong-selling Ranger. Trim levels range from the practical XL through the well-trimmed XLT and STX—all the way to the beguiling little Ranger Splash with its fiberglass Flareside bed, chrome wheels, and lowered suspension.

With the optional 4.0-liter V-6 engine, in particular, acceleration is impressively brisk, whether from a standstill or when merging and passing. The base four cylinder engine can overtax the Ranger when carrying a heavy load. Automatic-transmission upshifts are crisp and barely noticed, with just a slight jolt under hard throttle, and downshifts deliver only slightly more harshness. Push-button four-wheel-drive, if installed, is a snap to use.

RANGER — FORD

Well-controlled overall, with good steering feedback, Rangers handle easily, corner capably (within limits), maneuver neatly, and stay reasonably stable on curves. Occupants aren't likely to complain about the ride, either, though it can grow bouncy around town. Gas mileage isn't the greatest with the big engine and automatic, as expected.

Ranger sports a worldwide industry first for safety protection. An optional passenger side airbag is available, and it can be disabled with the flick of a switch in the event that a car seat is installed in the truck. New for 1997 is a 5-speed automatic transmission; a first for vehicles in this segment. Ford claims that the new 5-speed automatic allows better acceleration, trailering, and hill climbing by their capable Ranger. Ford also shuffles option packages this year in an attempt to make the 70+ options easier, and cheaper, to order.

Seats are firm and supportive, urging you to lean back and enjoy a long haul. Rangers are all truck, with few pretensions toward any other identity, but can be loaded with gadgets like a luxury auto. Fun to drive, sharp looking and well-built, they deliver a solid compact-pickup experience.

Safety Data

Driver Airbag: *Standard*
Side Airbag: *Not Available*
4-Wheel ABS: *Opt. (XLT/STX Splash); (N/A XL)*
Driver Crash Test Grade: *Good*
Passenger Crash Grade: *Good*
Integrated Child Seat: *Not Available*

Passenger Airbag: *Optional*
Meets 1999 Side Impact Standards: *No*
Traction Control: *Not Available*
Insurance Cost: *Avg. (4WD Ext Cab);*
Low (All Other Rangers)

Standard Equipment

XL 2WD REGULAR CAB: 2.3-liter 4-cylinder engine, 5-speed manual transmission, front and rear gas shock absorbers, front stabilizer bar, manual steering, P195/70R14 tires, power brakes with rear anti-lock brakes, painted front and rear bumper, tinted glass, painted grille with painted molding, aero headlamps, dual black manually adjustable outside mirrors, front/rear mud flaps, removable tailgate, cargo box tie-down hoows, argent styled steel wheels with bright hub caps, dual intermittent windshield wipers, driver air bag, ash tray and cigarette lighter, front dome light, glove box, driver's door illuminated entry, 4 gauge analog instrument cluster with trip odometer, vinyl bench seat, and vinyl sun visors.

XL 4WD REGULAR CAB (in addition to or instead of XL 2WD REGULAR CAB): 3.0-liter V-6 engine, rear stabilizer bar, power steering, HD gas shocks, P215/75Rx15 tires, select drive transfer case, automatic locking hubs, AM/FM stereo with integral clock, 60/40 split bench cloth seat, cloth sun visors with passenger's vanity mirror, and tachomter.

XL 2WD SUPER CAB (in addition to or instead of XL 2WD REGULAR CAB): Power steering, color keyed headliner with sound insulation and passenger grab handle.

XL 4WD SUPER CAB (in addition to or instead of XL 2WD SUPER CAB): 3.0-liter V-6 engine, rear stabilizer bar, power steering, HD gas shocks, P215/75Rx15 tires, select drive transfer case, automatic locking hubs AM/FM stereo with integral clock, 60/40 split bench cloth seat, cloth sun visors with passenger's vanity mirror, and tachomter.

FORD RANGER

| CODE | DESCRIPTION | INVOICE | MSRP |

XLT 2WD REGULAR CAB (in addition to or instead of XL 2WD REGULAR CAB): Bright front and rear step bumpers, painted grille with bright molding, full face steel wheels, driver and passenger door map pockets, floor console with dual cupholders, cargo box and map lights, AM/FM stereo with clock, 60/40 split bench seat, and color keyed cloth sun visor with passenger vanity mirror.

XLT 4WD REGULAR CAB (in addition to or instead of XLT 2WD REGULAR CAB): 3.0-liter V-6 engine, rear stabilizer bar, power steering, HD gas shocks, P215/75Rx15 tires, tachomter, select drive transfer case, and automatic locking hubs.

XLT 2WD SUPER CAB (in addition to or instead of XLT 2WD REGULAR CAB): Locking rear storage compartment (when jump seat is deleted), fish net storage, and power steering.

XLT 4WD SUPER CAB (in addition to or instead of XLT 4WD REGULAR CAB): Locking rear storage compartment (when jump seat is deleted), and fish net storage.

SPLASH 2WD REGULAR CAB (in addition to or instead of XLT 2WD REGULAR CAB): Rear stabilizer bar, power steering, color-keyed front and rear step bumper, color-keyed grille with color-keyed molding, dual color-keyed outside power mirrors, and chrome 15" wheels.

SPLASH 4WD REGULAR CAB (in addition to or instead of XLT 4WD REGULAR CAB): Color-keyed front and rear step bumper, color-keyed grille with color-keyed molding, dual color-keyed outside power mirrors, and deep dish aluminum wheels.

SPLASH 2WD SUPER CAB (in addition to or instead of SPLASH 2WD REGULAR CAB): 3.0-liter V-6 engine, locking storage compartment (when rear jump seat is deleted), and fish net storage.

SPLASH 4WD SUPER CAB (in addition to or instead of SPLASH 2WD SUPER CAB): Locking storage compartment (when rear jump seat is deleted), and fish net storage.

STX 4WD REGULAR CAB (in addition to or instead of XLT 4WD REGULAR CAB): 6.0 JJ 5-hole wheels, painted front and rear step bumper, painted grille and molding, and STX tape stripe.

STX 4WD SUPER CAB (in addition to or instead of STX 4WD REGULAR CAB): Locking storage compartment (when rear jump seat is deleted), and fish net storage.

For expert advice in selecting/buying/leasing a new car, call
1-900-AUTOPRO
($2.00 per minute)

RANGER — FORD

CODE	DESCRIPTION	INVOICE	MSRP

Base Prices

CODE	DESCRIPTION	INVOICE	MSRP
R10	XL Reg Cab 2WD SWB	10427	10970
R10	XL Reg Cab 2WD LWB	10782	11355
R14	XL SuperCab 2WD	12972	14315
R11	XL Reg Cab 4WD SWB	15391	16365
R11	XL Reg Cab 4WD LWB	15823	16835
R15	XL Super Cab 4WD	16157	17980
R10	XLT Reg Cab 2WD SWB	11546	12740
R10	XLT Reg Cab 2WD LWB	12013	13270
R14	XLT SuperCab XLT	13460	14915
R11	XLT Reg Cab 4WD SWB	16091	17905
R11	XLT Reg Cab 4WD LWB	16611	18395
R15	XLT SuperCab 4WD	17399	19390
R11	STX Reg Cab SWB	16308	18150
R11	STX Reg Cab LWB	16826	18740
R15	STX SuperCab	17323	19305
R10	Splash Reg Cab 2WD	13398	14845
R11	Splash Reg Cab 4WD	17385	19375
R14	Splash SuperCab 2WD	14833	16475
R15	Splash SuperCab 4WD	18221	20325
	Destination Charge:	510	510

Accessories

CODE	DESCRIPTION	INVOICE	MSRP
99A	2.3-liter Engine Discount (4WD/Ext Cab XLT/Splash)	(425)	(500)
	NOT AVAILABLE with XL 2WD SuperCab.		
99U	3.0-liter V-6 Engine (2WD Reg Cab/2WD XL Ext Cab)	569	670
44T	4-Speed Automatic Transmission	903	1070
67B	4-Wheel Anti-lock Brakes (XLT/STX/Splash)	518	610
99X	4.0-liter V-6 Engine (2WD Ext Cab/N/A 2WD XL Ext Cab)	723	850
99X	4.0-liter V-6 Engine (2WD Reg Cab)	723	850
99X	4.0-liter V-6 Engine (4WD/2WD Splash Ext Cab/N/A w/XL 4WD)	NC	NC
44D	5-Speed Automatic Transmission	939	1105
572	Air Conditioning	684	805
	INCLUDED in PEP 856A, 857A, 867A, and 868A.		
965	Bodyside Molding	102	120
	INCLUDED in PEP 866A.		
422	California Emissions	144	170
646	Chrome Wheels (XLT)	34	40
649	Deep Dish Aluminum Wheels (XL)	298	350
	With 173 (XL 4WD) And 173 (XL 2WD)	213	250
954	Deluxe Two-Tone Paint (XLT/STX)	200	235
41H	Engine Block Heater	26	30
173	Flareside Box (XL 2WD)	506	595
173	Flareside Box (XL 4WD)	399	470

FORD RANGER

CODE	DESCRIPTION	INVOICE	MSRP
173	Flareside Box (XLT)	387	455
595	Fog Lamps	158	185
	INCLUDED in 855A, 868A, 854A, and 857A.		
642	Full Face Steel Wheels	86	100
684	Handling Pkg (2WD V-6/Ext Cab)	NC	NC
	REQUIRES 99U or 99X V-6 engine.		
684	Handling Pkg (2WD XLT Reg Cab)	68	80
	REQUIRES PEP 864A or 867A.		
684	Handling Pkg (XL/XLT Reg Cab 2WD)	97	115
	REQUIRES 4-cyl engine and manual steering. NOT AVAILABLE with 864A or 867A.		
632	Heavy Duty Battery	47	55
428	High Altitude Emissions	NC	NC
XAB	Limited Slip Rear Axle	229	270
21M	Manual Locking Hubs	(68)	(80)
85K	Narrow Tape Stripe (XL/XLT/Splash)	47	55
202	Optional Payload Package	51	60
T85	P215/70Rx14 BSW A/S Tires (2WD)	149	175
	Includes full-size spare, except on XL.		
T80	P225/70Rx14 OWL A/S Tires (2WD)	204	240
	Includes a full size spare. INCLUDED in PEP 864A, 867A, 853A, and 856A.		
T73	P235/60Rx15SL BSW A/S Tires (2WD XL/XLT)	97	115
T7R	P235/75Rx15SL OWL A/T Tires (4WD XL/XLT/STX)	59	70
T7S	P265/75Rx15SL OWL A/T Tires (4WD)	153	180
	With 853A (XLT 4WD Ext Cab) And 854A (STX Ext Cab) And 856A (XLT 4WD Ext Cab) And 857A (STX Ext Cab)	93	110
552	Passenger Side Air Bag	340	400
	INCLUDED in PEP 856A, 857A, 867A, and 868A.		
43H	Pivoting Quarter Windows	43	50
543	Power Outside Mirrors	119	140
	INCLUDED in PEP856A, 857A, 867A, and 868A.		
52H	Power Steering (XL/XLT 2WD Reg Cab)	233	275
	INCLUDED in PEP 864A and 867A.		
903	Power Windows & Lock Group	336	395
	INCLUDED in PEP 856A, 857A, and 868A.		
873	Rear Jump Seat (Ext Cab)	192	225
	INCLUDED in PEP 854A and 857A.		
904	Remote Keyless Entry w/Anti-Theft	223	275
	INCLUDED in PEP 856A, 857A, 867A, and 868A.		
E	Seats—60/40 Cloth Split Bench (XL)	247	290
G	Seats—Cloth Sport Buckets w/Floor Console (XLT/STX/Splash)	306	360
	INCLUDED in PEP 865A, 868A, 854A, and 857A. NOT AVAILABLE with PEP 864A.		
90P	Seats—Power Driver's Seat (XLT/STX/Splash Ext Cab)	178	210
	Includes 6-way power adjustable drivers seat. REQUIRES G sport bucket seat.		
433	Sliding Rear Window	97	115
	INCLUDED in PEP 854A, 857A, 865A, 868A and 866A.		

RANGER — FORD

CODE	DESCRIPTION	INVOICE	MSRP
873A	Speed Control & Tilt Steering	336	395
	INCLUDED in PEP 856A, 857A, 865A, 867A, and 868A.		
866A	Splash Preferred Equipment Package 866A (Splash Reg Cab)	318	375
	Manufacturer Discount	(207)	(245)
	Net Price	111	130
	Includes AM/FM stereo and Splash Group (sliding rear window and bodyside molding protection.)		
855A	Splash Preferred Equipment Pkg 855A (Splash Ext Cab)	510	600
	Manufacturer Discount	(403)	(475)
	Net Price	107	125
	Includes AM/FM stereo with colock and cassette and Splash Group (sliding rear window, rear jump seat, and bodyside protection moldings.)		
644	Sport Wheels	247	290
	Includes full face steel wheels with aluminum coating.		
58Z	Stereo w/CD Player & Clock (XLT/STX/Splash)	192	225
	NOT AVAILABLE with a PEP.		
58Z	Stereo w/CD Player & Clock (XLT/STX/Splash)	73	80
	REQUIRES PEP.		
587	Stereo w/Clock (XL 2WD)	153	180
589	Stereo w/Clock & Cassette (N/A w/XL 2WD)	119	140
	INCLUDED in all PEPs.		
589	Stereo w/Clock & Cassette (XL 2WD)	267	315
588	Stereo, Premium w/Cassette & Clock (XLT/STX/Splash)	63	75
	REQUIRES PEP.		
588	Stereo, Premium w/Cassette & Clock (XLT/STX/Splash)	182	215
	NOT AVAILABLE with PEPs.		
91P	Stereo, Premium w/CD Changer & Clock (XLT/STX/Splash)	498	585
	NOT AVAILABLE with PEPs.		
91P	Stereo, Premium w/CD Changer & Clock (XLT/STX/Splash)	378	445
	REQUIRES PEP.		
857A	STX Luxury Pkg 857A (STX Ext Cab)	3289	3870
	Manufacturer Discount	(1118)	(1315)
	Net Price	2171	2555
	Includes upgraded AM/FM stereo with cassette, clock and premium sound; cloth sport bucket seats, STX Group (speed control, tilt steering wheel, luxury aluminum wheels, P235/75Rx15SL OWL A/T tires, rear jump seat, fog lamps, and sliding rear window), passenger side air bag, and Luxury Group (air conditioning, remote keyless entry anf anti-theft system.)		
868A	STX Luxury Value Pkg 866A (STX Reg Cab)	3097	3645
	Manufacturer Discount	(710)	(835)
	Net Price	2387	2810
	Includes upgraded AM/FM stereo with cassette, clock and premium sound, passenger air bag, Luxury Group (air conditioning, speed control, tilt steering column, remote keyless entry, anti-theft system, power windows, power door locks, and power outside mirrors), cloth sport bucket seats, floor console, and STX Group (speed control and tilt steering.)		

FORD RANGER

CODE	DESCRIPTION	INVOICE	MSRP
854A	STX Preferred Equipment Pkg 854A (STX Ext Cab)	1513	1780
	Manufacturer Discount	(548)	(645)
	Net Price	965	1135

Includes AM/FM stereo with cassette and clock, cloth sport bucket seats, and STX Group (speed control, tilt steering wheel, luxury aluminum wheels, P235/75Rx15SL OWL A/T tires, rear jump seat, fog lamps, and sliding rear window.)

865A	STX Preferred Equipment Pkg 865A (STX Reg Cab)	1322	1555
	Manufacturer Discount	(553)	(650)
	Net Price	769	905

Includes AM/FM stereo with cassette, cloth sport bucket seats and floor console, and STX GROUP (speed control and tilt steering.)

152	Tachometer (2WD)	51	60
	INCLUDED in PEP 856A and 867A.		
85A	Tape Stripe Delete (STX)	NC	NC
856A	XLT Luxury Pkg 865A (XLT 4WD Ext Cab)	2881	3390
	Manufacturer Discount	(1331)	(1330)
	Net Price	1550	2060

Includes AM/FM stereo with cassette and clock, and XLT Group (P225/70Rx15SL OWL A/T tires, deep dish cast aluminum wheels, sliding rear window, rear jump seat, and tape stripe), passenger airbag, and Luxury Group (air conditioning, speed control, tilt steering wheel, remote keyless entry, anti-theft system, power windows, power door locks and power mirrors.)

856A	XLT Luxury Value Pkg 856A (XLT 2WD Ext Cab)	3077	3620
	Manufacturer Discount	(888)	(1045)
	Net Price	2189	2575

Includes AM/FM stereo with cassette and clock, and XLT Group (P225/70Rx14SL OWL A/S tires, deep dish cast aluminum wheels, sliding rear window, rear jump seat, and tape stripe), passenger airbag, and Luxury Group (air conditioning, speed control, tilt steering wheel, tachometer, remote keyless entry, anti-theft system, power windows, power door locks and power mirrors.)

867A	XLT Luxury Value Pkg 867A (XLT 2WD Reg Cab)	3118	3670
	Manufacturer Discount	(1220)	(1435)
	Net Price	1898	2235

Includes upgraded AM/FM stereo with cassette, clock and premium sound; power steering, XLT Group (P225/70Rx14 A/S tires, deep dish aluminum wheels, sliding rear window, and tape stripe), passenger side airbag, and Luxury Group (air conditioning, speed control, tilt steering wheel, tachometer, remote keyless entry with anti-theft, power windows, powerd door locks, and power mirrors.

867A	XLT Luxury Value Pkg 867A (XLT 4WD Reg Cab)	2689	3165
	Manufacturer Discount	(850)	(1000)
	Net Price	1839	2165

Includes upgraded AM/FM stereo with cassette, clock, and premium sound; XLT Group (P225/70Rx15 A/T tires, deep dish aluminum wheels, sliding rear window, and tape stripe), passenger side airbag, and Luxury Group (air conditioning, speed control, tilt steering wheel, tachometer, remote keyless entry with anti-theft, power windows, powerd door locks, and power mirrors.)

RANGER — FORD

CODE	DESCRIPTION	INVOICE	MSRP
853A	XLT Special Value Pkg 853A (XLT 2WD Ext Cab)	872	1025
	Manufacturer Discount	(591)	(695)
	Net Price	281	330
	Includes AM/FM stereo with cassette and clock, and XLT Group (P225/70Rx14SL OWL A/S tires, deep dish cast aluminum wheels, sliding rear window, rear jump seat, and tape stripe.)		
853A	XLT Special Value Pkg 853A (XLT 4WD Ext Cab)	727	855
	Manufacturer Discount	(548)	(645)
	Net Price	179	210
	Includes AM/FM stereo with cassette and clock, and XLT Group (P225/70Rx15SL OWL A/T tires, deep dish cast aluminum wheels, sliding rear window, rear jump seat, and tape stripe.)		
864A	XLT Special Value Pkg 864A (XLT 2WD Reg Cab)	913	1075
	Manufacturer Discount	(642)	(755)
	Net Price	271	320
	Includes AM/FM stereo w/cassette, power steering and XLT Group (P225/70Rx14 tires, cast aluminum deep dish wheels, sliding rear window and tape stripe).		
864A	XLT Special Value Pkg 864A (XLT 4WD Reg Cab)	535	630
	Manufacturer Discount	(383)	(450)
	Net Price	152	180
	Includes AM/FM stereo w/cassette, and XLT Group P225/70Rx15 A/T tires, cast aluminum deep dish wheels, sliding rear window and tape stripe.		

Save hundreds, even thousands, off the sticker price of the new car you want.

Call Autovantage®
your FREE auto-buying service

1-800-201-7703

No purchase required. No fees.

FORD WINDSTAR

WINDSTAR (1997)

1997 Ford Windstar LX

What's New for Ford Windstar in 1997 — Not much is new for the 1997 Ford Windsar. Caught flatfooted by the Chrysler and GM minivans that feature sliding left-side doors, Ford has installed a tip forward driver's seat to give passengers the option of entering from the driver's side. Hmmm, seems like that won't be enough to satisfy the fickle buyers of the minivan market.

Windstar — Review

Until mid-1994, nobody had seriously challenged Chrysler's domination of minivan sales. All previous attempts by domestic and imported manufacturers couldn't match the Chrysler standard for user-friendliness. They were either underpowered, too high off the ground, or the wrong size. When Windstars rolled into Ford showrooms, Chrysler finally had been bested at its own game.

For a while, at least. The Windstar's superiority proved to be short-lived. The totally redesigned Chrysler minivans are best-in-class in terms of style and convenience features; the main reasons people buy minivans in the first place. The Windstar is still a good minivan, but the stiff competition in this segment is forcing Ford to offer sweet lease deals and big incentives.

Not everyone favors the Windstar's styling, but the interior is an ergonomic delight. With room for seven, dual airbags, and a commodious cargo area, the Windstar keeps passengers comfortable. Controls and displays are housed in an attractively swept dashboard, lending a well-crafted tone. The radio is crammed with buttons and tiny lettering; it's time for the new family of Ford radios, complete with big buttons and a volume knob, to debut in this van. Climate controls are mounted low, but are easy to modulate without glancing from the road. An optional center console adds generous amounts of much-needed storage, but cuts access to the rear seats. There's little to complain about, and quite a lot to like. Construction quality is fine and the interior is spacious and attractive. A single body size and style is offered, in cargo van, Base, GL or luxury LX guise, with four-wheel anti-lock brakes.

WINDSTAR — FORD

CODE	DESCRIPTION	INVOICE	MSRP

The Windstar receives few changes for 1997. The most notable is the tip forward driver's seat that is intended to allow passenger access from the left side. To people who feel that it's important to have a left side passenger entry this is a poor substitute. Fortunately for Ford, the Windstar has other features which make up for this missing portal. Namely the awesome horsepower available with the optional 3.8-liter engine. Cranking out 200 horsepower, the 3.8-liter equipped Windstar is the fastest minivan on the market.

If you're searching for a minivan with good towing ability, fast acceleration, gobs of interior space and comfortable seating for seven, the Windstar is definitely worth a look. Especially because your local Ford dealer should be offering deep discounts to keep them competitive with the Caravan and new Chevy Venture.

Safety Data

Driver Airbag: *Standard*
Side Airbag: *Not Available*
4-Wheel ABS: *Standard*
Driver Crash Test Grade: *Good*
Passenger Crash Test Grade: *Excellent*

Passenger Airbag: *Standard*
Meets 1997 Car Side Impact Standards: *Yes*
Traction Control: *Opt. GL/LX*
Insurance Cost: *Average*
Integrated Child Seat(s): *Optional*

Standard Equipment

BASE: 3.0-liter SEFI V-6 engine, 4-speed automatic transmission, power rack-and-pinion steering, 4-wheel anti-lock front disc/rear drum brakes, P205/70R15 tires, 20 gallon fuel tank, gas pressurized shock absorbers, 5-mph body color bumpers, aero headlamps, dual outside mirrors, rocker panels, underbody spare tire carrier, plastic wheel covers, single speed rear window wiper, interval windshield wipers with dual washer jets, dual airbags, front and second row ashtray with lighter, passenger assist handle, full length carpeting, digital clock, 3 coat hooks, courtesy lights at all doors, analog gauges, front and rear dome lights, childproof sliding door locks, manual door locks, AM/FM stereo with 4 speakers, second row seat controls and mini-jacks for headphones, 7-passenger seating, 4-way manually adjustable high back front seats with integrated headrests, 2nd row cloth bench seats with forward folding bench seat, sun visors with covered vanity mirrors, manual door locks and windows and flip-out rear quarter windows.

GL (in addition to or instead of BASE equipment): Underseat storage container under front passenger seat, 2nd row storage bin.

LX (in addition to or instead of GL equipment): 3.8-liter SPI V-6 engine, P215/70R15 BSW tires, 25 gallon gas tank, dual remote outside mirrors, contoured bodyside and liftgate moldings, 15" cast aluminum wheels, accessory delay switch, manual front air conditioning, cargo net, analog gauges including tachometer, light group, illuminated entry, Premium AM/FM cassette stereo, dual cloth low back bucket seats with 6-way power tip forward driver's seat, power lumbar support, and seat back map pockets, 3rd row seat, speed control, 5-way tilt steering wheel, leather wrapped steering wheel, center bin, front door amp pockets, cassette tape storage in the instrument panel, dual illuminated vanity mirrors, and power doors and mirrors.

Base Prices

A51	Base	17063	18415
A51	GL	18389	20340
A51	LX	22750	25925
Destination Charge:		580	580

FORD WINDSTAR

Accessories

CODE	DESCRIPTION	INVOICE	MSRP
87C	2 Child Safety Seats	191	225
652	25-Gallon Fuel Tank (Base/GL)	26	30
994	3.8-liter V-6 Engine (Base/GL)	583	685
67A	All-Speed Traction Control (GL/LX)	310	365
965	Bodyside Molding (GL)	68	80
422	California Emissions	85	100
64D	Cast Aluminum Wheels (GL)	352	415
87C	Child Safety Seats (LX)	(412)	(485)
	Credit only applies with deletion of quad bucket seats of PEP 477A.		
51A	Conventional Spare Tire (GL/LX)	93	110
15A	Electronic Instrument Cluster (LX)	417	490
41H	Engine Block Heater	30	35
414	Floor Console (GL/LX)	119	140
916	Ford JBL Sound System (LX)	433	510
595	Fog Lamps (LX)	93	110
167	Front & Rear Floor Mats	77	90
	INCLUDED in packages 476A and 477A.		
527	Front Air Conditioning (Base/GL)	727	855
	INCLUDED in package 469A and 472A.		
428	High Altitude Emissions	NC	NC
21H	High Back Cloth Bucket Seats (GL)	51	60
21D	High Back Cloth Bucket Seats w/ Seat Bed (GL)	522	615
574	High Capacity Rear AC & Heat (GL/LX)	395	465
94H	Interior Convenience Group (GL)	43	50
2	Leather Seats (LX)	735	865
	REQUIRES quad bucket seats.		
593	Light Group (GL)	43	50
	INCLUDED in package 472A.		
68S	Load Levelling Suspension (LX)	247	290
21Q	Low Back Cloth Quad Bucket Seats (GL)	591	695
21K	Low Back Cloth Quad Bucket Seats (LX)	510	600
615	Luggage Rack (GL/LX)	149	175
	INCLUDED in packages 476A and 477A.		
903	Power Convenience Group (Base/GL)	569	670
	INCLUDED in package 469A and 472A.		
476A	Preferred Equipment Pkg 476A (LX)	570	670
	Manufacturer Discount	(298)	(350)
	Net Price	272	320
	Includes electric rear window defroster, front and rear floor mats, luggage rack and two-tone paint.		

WINDSTAR — FORD

CODE	DESCRIPTION	INVOICE	MSRP
469A	Preferred Equipment Pkg. 469A (Base)	1296	1525
	Manufacturer Discount	(446)	(525)
	Net Price	850	1000
	Includes air conditioning and power convenience group (power windows and accessory delay).		
472A	Preferred Equipment Pkg. 472A (GL)	2642	3110
	Manufacturer Discount	(816)	(960)
	Net Price	1826	2150
	Includes air conditioning, power convenience group (power windows and accessory delay), bodyside molding, electric rear window defroster, light group (map light, glove box light, footwell lamps, and underhood lamp), speed control, tip/slide driver's seat, and tilt steering wheel.		
477A	Preferred Equipment Pkg. 477A (LX)	1582	1860
	Manufacturer Discount	(476)	(560)
	Net Price	1106	1300
	Includes low back quad bucket seats, electric rear window defroster, front and rear floor mats, luggage rack, two-tone paint, privacy glass and remote keyless entry.		
582	Premium Stereo w/Clock/CD player (GL)	420	495
	With 472A (GL)	276	352
582	Premium Stereo w/Clock/CD Player (LX)	144	170
924	Privacy Glass (GL/LX)	352	415
	INCLUDED in package 477A.		
57Q	Rear Window Defroster	144	170
	INCLUDED in pacakges 472A, 476A, and 477A.		
948	Remote Keyless Entry (GL/LX)	149	175
	INCLUDED in pakage 477A.		
94D	Remote Keyless Entry (LX)	289	340
52N	Speed Control/Tilt Steering	314	370
589	Stereo w/Cassette/Clock (Base/GL)	144	170
	INCLUDED in package 472A.		
87S	Tip-Slide Driver's Seat (GL)	128	150
	INCLUDED in package 472A.		
539	Trailer Towing Pkg. (GL/LX)	370	435
	With 574 (GL/LX)	347	410
	With 67A (GL/LX) And 574 (GL/LX)	296	350
	Without 67A (GL/LX)	318	375
95M	Two-Tone Paint	200	235

FORD WINDSTAR

WINDSTAR (1998)

What's New for Ford 98 Windstar in 1998 — Ford widens the driver's door as a stop-gap measure until the 1999 Windstar arrives with a fourth door. Subtle styling revisions and a new Limited model round out the changes for 1998.

Standard Equipment

WINDSTAR 3.0L: 3.0-liter V-6 engine, 4-speed automatic transmission with overdrive, P205/70R15 tires, power rack and pinion steering, gas pressurized shock absorbers, 20-gallon fuel tank, power front disc/rear drum 4-wheel anti-lock brakes, stainless steel antenna, body-color 5-mph bumpers, limo-style front Family Entry System (essentially a fancy name for a big driver's door), tethered fuel cap, solar-tinted glass, body-color grille, dual black foldaway exterior mirrors, full plastic sport wheelcovers, intermittent rear window wiper/washer, interval windshield wipers, dual front airbags, low oil level warning chime, headlights-on warning chime, turn signal on warning chime, second row auxiliary power point, AM/FM stereo with clock and 4 speakers, liftgate courtesy light switch, 5 cupholders, front door window demisters, dual note horn, front and rear dome lights with automatic dim delay, child-proof sliding side door locks, day/night rearview mirror, 7-passenger seating, highback cloth front bucket seats with integral headrests, dual covered vanity mirrors, rear quarter flip-out glass

GL (in addition to or instead of 3.0L equipment): Reclining front seats, reclining 2nd row seat, fore-aft adjustment for 3rd row seat

LX (in addition to or instead of GL equipment): 3.8-liter V-6 engine, P215/70R15 tires, 25-gallon fuel tank, power exterior mirrors, color-keyed bodyside molding, reflective applique for tailgate, 15-inch cast aluminum wheels, power front windows with one-touch down feature and retained accessory power, air conditioning, tachometer, front map lights, glovebox light, footwell lighting, power door locks with backlighting, cargo area lock switch, AM/FM stereo with cassette player, digital clock, and 4 speakers; low-back cloth bucket seats with adjustable headrests, power driver's seat, power lumbar support for driver, seatback map pockets, tip/slide driver's seat, cruise control, tilt leather-wrapped steering wheel, center storage bin, cargo area storage bin, illuminated vanity mirrors, driver's auxiliary sunshade, power rear quarter flip-out glass

LIMITED (in addition to or instead of LX equipment): P225/60R16 tires, front fog lights, chrome grille surround, color-keyed exterior mirrors, remote keyless entry, polished aluminum wheels, high capacity air conditioning, auxiliary heater, overhead console (includes rear seat audio controls, compass, external temperature display, conversation mirror, coin holder sunglasses holder, and garage door opener), rear window defroster, automatic on/off headlights, electrochromic rearview mirror, premium sound system, quad lowback leather bucket seats, power lumbar support for front passenger

Base Prices

Code	Description	Invoice	MSRP
A51	3.0L	17697	19085
A51	GL	18697	20655
A51	LX	23316	25905
A51	Limited	26220	29205
Destination Charge:		580	580

WINDSTAR — FORD

CODE	DESCRIPTION	INVOICE	MSRP

Accessories

CODE	DESCRIPTION	INVOICE	MSRP
994	3.8-liter Engine (GL)	583	685
	INCLUDED in Option Packages		
572	Air Conditioning (3.0L/GL)	727	855
	INCLUDED in Option Packages		
574	Air Conditioning — High Capacity (GL/LX)	404	475
	Includes auxiliary heater; REQUIRES Light Group and Power Convenience Group; INCLUDED in GL Option Package 473A and LX Option Package 477A		
965	Bodyside Moldings (GL)	68	80
	INCLUDED in Option Packages		
422	California Emissions	85	100
64D	Cast Aluminum Wheels (GL/LX)	352	415
	INCLUDED in LX Option Package		
51A	Conventional Spare Tire	93	110
	INCLUDED in Trailer Towing Package		
52N	Cruise Control and Tilt Steering Wheel (3.0L/GL)	319	375
	INCLUDED in GL Option Packages		
41H	Engine Block Heater	30	35
414	Floor Console (GL/LX/Limited)	132	155
	Includes cupholder, auxiliary power point, covered storage bin; REQUIRES High-capacity Air Conditioning and Power Convenience Group		
167	Floor Mats	77	90
	INCLUDED in LX and Limited Option Packages		
652	Fuel Tank — 25 gallon (GL)	26	30
428	High Altitude Emissions	NC	NC
87C	Integrated Child Seats (3.0L)	242	285
87C	Integrated Child Seats (GL/LX) With 477A (LX)	191	225
94H	Interior Convenience Group (GL)	43	50
	Includes covered rear storage bin, covered center dashboard bin, and cargo net		
916	JBL Sound System (Limited)	433	510
916	JBL Sound System (LX)	565	665
	REQUIRES a Premium Stereo		
2	Leather Seat Trim (LX)	735	865
	REQUIRES Quad Bucket Seats		
593	Light Group (3.0L/GL)	63	75
	Includes front map light, glovebox light, footwell lighting; INCLUDED in GL Option Package 473A		
60F	Light Group — Premium (LX)	251	295
	Includes front fog lights, automatic on/off headlights, and electrochromic rearview mirror		
68S	Load Leveling Air Suspension (LX/Limited)	247	290
615	Luggage Rack (GL/LX/Limited)	149	175
	INCLUDED in GL Option Package 473A, LX Option Package 477A, and Limited Option Package 479A		

FORD WINDSTAR

CODE	DESCRIPTION	INVOICE	MSRP
470A	Option Package 470A (3.0L)	1305	1535
	Manufacturer Discount	(446)	(525)
	Net Price	859	1010

Includes air conditioning and power convenience group (power front windows with one-touch down feature and retained accessory power, power rear quarter flip-out glass)

472A	Option Package 472A (GL)	2691	3165
	Manufacturer Discount	(850)	(1000)
	Net Price	1841	2165

Includes tip/slide driver's seat, AM/FM stereo with cassette player, 4 speakers, and digital clock; air conditioning, rear window defroster, power convenience group (power windows with one-touch down feature and retained accessory power, power door locks, power exterior mirrors, power rear quarter vent windows), bodyside moldings, cruise control, tilt steering wheel

473A	Option Package 473A (GL)	3745	4405
	Manufacturer Discount	(1131)	(1330)
	Net Price	2614	3075

Includes tip/slide driver's seat, AM/FM stereo with cassette player, 4 speakers, and digital clock; high capacity air conditioning, auxiliary heater, rear window defroster, power convenience group (power windows with one-touch down feature and retained accessory power, power door locks, power exterior mirrors, power rear quarter vent windows), bodyside moldings, cruise control, tilt steering wheel, 3.8-liter V-6 engine, overhead console (includes rear audio controls, conversation mirror, coin holder, sunglasses holder, garage door opener), privacy glass, light group (includes front map lights, glovebox

477A	Option Package 477A (LX)	2161	2545
	Manufacturer Discount	(821)	(965)
	Net Price	1340	1580

Includes quad low-back bucket seats, power lumbar support for front passenger, rear window defroster, high capacity air conditioning, auxiliary heater, overhead console (includes rear audio controls, conversation mirror, coin holder, sunglasses holder, garage door opener, compass, external temperature display), privacy glass, black luggage rack, floor mats, two-tone paint, remote keyless entry

479A	Option Package 479A (Limited)	578	680
	Manufacturer Discount	(578)	(680)
	Net Price	NC	NC

Includes privacy glass, black luggage rack, and floor mats

41N	Overhead Console (GL)	85	100

Includes garage door opener, conversation mirror, sunglasses storage, coin holder, rear audio controls and headphone jacks; REQUIRES Light Group

41N	Overhead Console (LX)	153	180

Includes garage door opener, conversation mirror, sunglasses storage, coin holder, compass, external temperature display, rear audio controls and headphone jacks; REQUIRES Light Group

WINDSTAR — FORD

CODE	DESCRIPTION	INVOICE	MSRP
903	Power Convenience Group (3.0L/GL)	578	680
	Includes power windows with one-touch down feature and retained accessory power, power door locks, power exterior mirrors, and power quarter vent windows; INCLUDED in Option Packages		
924	Privacy Glass (GL/LX/Limited)	325	415
	INCLUDED in GL Option Package 473A, LX Option Package 477A, and Limited Option Package 479A		
21Q	Quad Bucket Seats (GL)	633	745
	REQUIRES Option Package 473A		
21K	Quad Bucket Seats (LX)	532	625
	INCLUDED in Option Package		
57Q	Rear Window Defroster (3.0L/GL/LX)	144	170
	INCLUDED in GL and LX Option Packages		
948	Remote Keyless Entry (GL/LX)	149	175
	REQUIRES Power Convenience Group; INCLUDED in LX Option Package		
21D	Seat Bed (GL)	522	615
151	Security Group (LX/Limited)	171	200
	Includes trainable transmitter capable of handling up to 3 different programs, perimeter anti-theft system; REQUIRES Remote Keyless Entry on LX models		
588	Stereo — Premium w/cassette (LX)	132	155
	AM/FM stereo with cassette player, digital clock, and 4 premium speakers		
582	Stereo — Premium w/CD player (GL/LX)	420	495
	With 472A (GL)	276	352
	With 473A (GL)	276	352
	With 477A (LX)	144	170
	AM/FM stereo with CD player, digital clock, and 4 premium speakers; REQUIRES Light Group, Cruise Control, and Tilt steering		
582	Stereo — Premium w/CD player (Limited)	144	170
	AM/FM stereo with CD player, digital clock, and 4 premium speakers		
589	Stereo — w/cassette (3.0L/GL)	144	170
	AM/FM stereo with cassette player, 4 speakers, and digital clock; INCLUDED in GL Option Packages		
87S	Tip/slide Driver's Seat (3.0L/GL)	128	150
	INCLUDED in GL Option Packages		
T75	Tires — Self-sealing (GL/LX)	208	245
	P215/70R15 all-season tires; REQUIRES 64D Cast Aluminum Wheels		
67A	Traction Control (GL/LX/Limited)	336	395
	All-speed system; REQUIRES 3.8-liter Engine, Cruise Control, and Tilt Steerig Column on GL models		
539	Trailer Towing Package (GL/LX)	370	435
	With 473A (GL)		
	With 477A (LX)		
	Includes heavy-duty battery, engine oil cooler, power steering cooler, class II wiring harness, conventional spare tire, auxiliary transmission oil cooler; REQUIRES 3.8-liter Engine on GL models		

FORD WINDSTAR

CODE	DESCRIPTION	INVOICE	MSRP
539	Trailer Towing Package (Limited)	347	410
	Includes heavy-duty battery, engine oil cooler, power steering cooler, class II wiring harness, conventional spare tire, auxiliary transmission oil cooler		
95M	Two-tone Paint (LX)	200	235
	INCLUDED in Option Package 477A		
95M	Two-tone Paint Delete (LX)	(115)	(135)
	REQUIRES Option Package 477A		

One 15-minute call could save you 15% or more on car insurance.

GEICO DIRECT

America's 6th Largest Automobile Insurance Company

1-800-555-2758

Save hundreds, even thousands, off the sticker price of the new car you want.

Call Autovantage®
your FREE auto-buying service

1-800-201-7703

No purchase required. No fees.

TRACKER — GEO

TRACKER (1997)

1997 Geo Tracker 4WD

What's New for Geo Tracker in 1997 — After a heavy makeover for 1996, changes for 1997 are limited. Convertibles get a standard fold-and-stow rear bench seat along with an enhanced evaporative emissions system. All Trackers can be painted Sunset Red Metallic or Azurite Blue Metallic for the first time. Prices have been at or near 1996 levels in an effort to make the Tracker more attractive to folks shopping Kia Sportage, Toyota RAV4 and Honda CR-V.

Tracker — Review

To the delight of Chevrolet dealers, Geo introduced a new four-door hardtop variant of the cute little Tracker last year. Also new in 1996 was a revised instrument panel with dual airbags. Four-wheel anti-lock brakes were optional. So equipped, the new Tracker proved quite popular in the burgeoning mini sport ute marketplace.

After a heavy makeover for 1996, changes for 1997 are limited. Convertibles get a standard fold-and-stow rear bench seat along with an enhanced evaporative emissions system. All Trackers can be painted Sunset Red Metallic or Azurite Blue Metallic for the first time. Prices have been at or near 1996 levels in an effort to make the Tracker more attractive to folks shopping Kia Sportage, Toyota RAV4 and Honda CR-V.

Fun-in-the-sun takes on fresh meaning behind the wheel of a snug-but-cozy Tracker convertible, whether its engine is driving two wheels or four. A 16-valve engine powers all Tracker models, sending out 95 horsepower. Naturally, the optional automatic transmission saps much of that strength.

Short and stubby, these friendly little vehicles maneuver easily but handle with a very light, sometimes twitchy touch on both the highway and off-road. They're more solidly built than they appear at first glance—not at all like a toy—and deliver a passably pleasant ride most of the time. Differing little from the Suzuki Sidekick, Trackers look and feel substantial, though during off-road driving, the door frames shudder just enough to let in a fine silt of dust

GEO
TRACKER

that coats every plastic interior trim piece. Front seats are firm but lack leg support, and wear nice-looking upholstery. The rear seat of four-door models is surprisingly comfortable for two adults. Dual cupholders and a storage tray sit in the center console.

Convertibles have an "easy opening" top that folds in two ways: either the front half folds back like a sunroof, or the entire canvas top can be stowed for fully-open motoring. Though improved, putting the top up and down still isn't exactly a quickie operation. Several "expressions packages" feature color-keyed convertible tops and wheels, and a Tracker can be equipped to tow half a ton. LSi editions feature automatic-locking hubs, which are nice to have if you switch often between two- and four-wheel drive.

Four-door models can be equipped with power windows, door locks and mirrors. Child security rear door locks are standard on four-door, and daytime running lights are standard on all Trackers. The 1.6-liter engine provides barely enough power in convertibles; in the four-door the engine is severely overmatched. Interstate cruising requires putting the pedal nearly to the metal just to maintain speed.

Would you want the convertible as your sole vehicle? Probably not, but a soft top Tracker in the garage just might turn sunny summer days into a veritable binge of adventure. Practical-minded folks, on the other hand, might prefer the weather-tight construction of a hardtop model. Sadly, we can't recommend using a Tracker for anything but light duty in the flatlands. The 1.6-liter motor is zippy enough to keep up in city traffic, but a heavy load of passengers or cargo keeps the Tracker's breathless engine wound out tightly on slight inclines or at freeway speeds. With a bigger engine, lightly-equipped Trackers would certainly give the competition a run for the money.

Safety Data

Driver Airbag: Standard
Side Airbag: N/A
4-Wheel ABS: Optional
Driver Crash Test Grade: Poor
Passenger Crash Test Grade: Average

Passenger Airbag: Standard
Meets 1999 Side Impact Standards: No
Traction Control: N/A
Insurance Cost: Average
Integrated Child Seat(s): N/A

Standard Equipment

TRACKER CONVERTIBLE: Dual front airbags, full carpeting, center console with cupholders and storage tray, Scotchgard cloth seat protectant, full-folding rear seat, dual black exterior mirrors, fuel tank shield, vinyl spare tire cover, 1.6-liter inline four-cylinder engine, daytime running lamps, 5-speed manual transmission, P195/75R15 all-season tires (2WD), P205/75R15 all-season tires (4WD), manual locking front hubs (4WD), 2-speed transfer case (4WD), power steering (4WD)

4-DOOR (in addition to or instead of CONVERTIBLE equipment): Rear window defogger, power steering (2WD)

4-DOOR LSi (in addition to or instead of 4-DOOR equipment): Floor mats, body-color exterior mirrors, black bodyside moldings

TRACKER — GEO

CODE	DESCRIPTION	INVOICE	MSRP

Base Prices

Code	Description	Invoice	MSRP
CE10367	2WD Convertible	12771	13415
CE10305	2WD 4-door	13871	14570
CE10305/B2Z	2WD 4-door LSi	14251	14970
CJ10367	4WD Convertible	13756	14450
CJ10305	4WD 4-door	14585	15320
CJ10305/B2Z	4WD 4-door LSi	14956	15710
	Destination Charge:	340	340

Accessories

Code	Description	Invoice	MSRP
1SB	**Base Option Package 1SB (2WD Convertible)**	1374	1544
	Includes air conditioning, AM/FM stereo with seek, clock, and 4 speakers, floor mats, body-color bodyside moldings, power steering		
1SB	**Base Option Package 1SB (4WD Convertible)**	1116	1254
	Includes air conditioning, AM/FM stereo with seek, clock, and 4 speakers, floor mats, body-color bodyside moldings		
1SB	**Base Option Package 1SB (Base 4-door)**	1122	1261
	Includes air conditioning, AM/FM stereo with seek, clock, and 4 speakers, floor mats, body-color bodyside moldings		
1SE	**LSi Option Package 1SE (LSi 4-door)**	1367	1536
	Includes air conditioning, cruise control, AM/FM stereo with cassette player, seek/scan, tone select, clock, theft deterrent, and 4 speakers		
1SF	**LSi Option Package 1SF (2WD LSi 4-door)**	2208	2481
	Includes air conditioning, cruise control, AM/FM stereo with cassette player, seek/scan, tone select, clock, theft deterrent, and 4 speakers; alloy wheels, convenience package (power windows, power door locks, and power exterior mirrors)		
1SF	**LSi Option Package 1SF (4WD LSi 4-door)**	2386	2681
	Includes air conditioning, cruise control, AM/FM stereo with cassette player, seek/scan, tone select, clock, theft deterrent, and 4 speakers; alloy wheels, convenience package (power windows, power door locks, and power exterior mirrors), front auto-locking hubs		
C60	Air Conditioning	743	835
	INCLUDED in Option Packages		
QA4	Alloy Wheels	325	365
	INCLUDED in LSi Option Package 1SF and Expressions Package		
JM4	Anti-lock Brakes	530	595
X6Z	Auto Locking Hubs (4WD 4-door)	178	200
	INCLUDED in LSi Option Package 1SF		
MX0	Automatic Transmission (4-door)	846	950
MX1	Automatic Transmission (Convertible)	556	625
B84	Bodyside Moldings (Base)	76	85
	INCLUDED in Base Option Packages and Expressions Package		
YF5	California Emissions	151	170

GEO TRACKER

CODE	DESCRIPTION	INVOICE	MSRP
Z05	Convenience Package (4-door)	516	580
	INCLUDED in Option Package 1SF		
K34	Cruise Control	156	175
	INCLUDED in LSi Option Packages		
WT3	Expressions Package (Convertible)	222	249
	With 1SB (4WD Convertible)	146	164
	With 1SB (2WD Convertible)	146	164
	Includes bodyside moldings, custom interior fabric, rear fold-and-stow bucket seats, tan top, tan alloy wheels, tan spare tire cover		
B58	Floor Mats (Base 4-door)	31	35
	INCLUDED in Base Option Package		
B37	Floor Mats (Convertible)	25	28
	INCLUDED in Base Option Package		
NG1	Massachusetts/New York Emissions	151	170
N40	Power Steering (2WD Convertible)	258	290
	INCLUDED in Base Option Package		
C25	Rear Window Wiper/Washer (4-door)	111	125
NY7	Skid Plates (4WD)	67	75
	Includes skid plates for front differential and transfer case		
UL1	Stereo (All except LSi)	272	306
	AM/FM stereo with seek, clock, and 4 speakers; INCLUDED in Option Packages		
UL0	Stereo — w/cassette	468	526
	With 1SB (Base 4-door)	196	220
	With 1SB (4WD Convertible)	196	220
	With 1SB (2WD Convertible)	196	220
	AM/FM stereo with cassette player, seek/scan, tone select, clock, theft deterrent, and 4 speakers; INCLUDED in LSi Option Packages		
UP0	Stereo — w/cassette & CD players	743	835
	With 1SB (Base 4-door)	471	529
	With 1SB (4WD Convertible)	471	529
	With 1SB (2WD Convertible)	471	529
	With 1SE (LSi 4-door)	275	309
	With 1SF (4WD LSi 4-door)	275	309
	With 1SF (2WD LSi 4-door)	275	309
	AM/FM stereo with cassette and CD players, seek/scan, tone select, clock, theft deterrent, and 4 speakers		

JIMMY (1997)

1997 GMC Jimmy 4-Door

What's New for GMC Jimmy in 1997 — Highrider off-road package deleted as GMC realigns Jimmy as luxury sport ute. Instead, buyers can opt for a Gold Edition in one of four colors. New options include a power sunroof and HomeLink universal transmitter. In a fit of good taste, Radar Purple and Bright Teal paint colors are replaced by Fairway Green and Smoky Caramel.

Jimmy — Review

GMC has the unenviable job of marketing the Jimmy as a luxury SUV now that the Pontiac-GMC merger is nearly complete and crazed brand managers think GMC products need to be perceived as upscale from Chevrolet. Essentially identical to the Blazer and Oldsmobile Bravada, with no distinguishing characteristics to set it apart from either of these models, Jimmy marketers have their work cut out for them. Tightly sandwiched between the Blazer and Bravada, there is only one way to convince buyers that the Jimmy is the one to buy - slick advertising.

Four-door styling is on the staid side, but two-doors are fastback-profiled with a distinctive side-window treatment. A Jimmy is comfortable, easy to handle, and fun to drive. Upgraded versions can be luxuriously equipped, but each rugged rendition looks and feels tough - a little more truck-like than the similar Blazer. An under-the-floor spare tire on four-doors increases cargo space. Headroom is immense, elbow space excellent. There's room for two in back; maybe three if you enjoy hearing comfort complaints while you drive, but the short seat feels hard and there's no room under front seats for feet. Basically, the back seat should be reserved for kiddies.

Though exceptionally sure-footed most of the time, a Jimmy can feel momentarily unstable and top-heavy in a sharp maneuver - but only if you forget what you're driving. On snowy pavement, you almost have to try to make a four-wheel-drive Jimmy skid. Whether maintaining traction while accelerating, or trying to recapture grip through a turn, 4WD delivers a strong feeling of confidence. Gone this year is the stout Highrider package that included a raised suspension, big fat tires, and wider track.

GMC JIMMY

If you don't care to switch between two- and four-wheel drive, an all-wheel drive Jimmy joined the lineup last year. Four-wheel anti-lock braking helps haul the sport-ute to a prompt halt, and AWD models gain 4-wheel discs for 1997. Drivers face an airbag. A passenger side bag is still not available, despite dismal crash test scores. Acceleration is strong from the standard 4300 Vortec V-6 engine, and the smooth four-speed automatic suffers little lag when downshifting. Engineers have improved the transmission for 1997, making it shift smoother. A manual 'box is available only on two-door models.

Other news for the new year includes a Gold Edition available on green, white, black, or dark red Jimmys. A power sunroof is a new option, and buyers who prefer a liftgate with liftglass over the standard split tailgate can opt for it this year. A HomeLink universal transmitter joins the options list, and a floor shifter is standard when bucket seats are specified. Bilstein gas-pressure shock absorbers are new to the standard equipment list, and AWD models get aluminum wheels. Speed-sensitive volume and automatic tone control are standard on Jimmys equipped with an in-dash CD player.

The hardest duty in Jimmy-shopping is deciding what to include. Suspension choices stretch from smooth to off-road. Expect some bounce from the Luxury Ride suspension, but it's compliant and responds quickly. Sport, comfort and touring decor packages are available. Then there's the huge option list to contend with. Overdo it, and the toll can zip skyward in a hurry, though this GMC represents slightly better value than Oldsmobile's Bravada.

Safety Data

Driver Airbag: *Standard*
Side Airbag: *Not Available*
4-Wheel ABS: *Standard*
Driver Crash Test Grade: *Average*
Passenger Crash Test Grade: *Very Poor*

Passenger Airbag: *Not Available*
Meets 1999 Side Impact Standards: *No*
Traction Control: *Not Available*
Insurance Cost: *High*
Integrated Child Seat(s): *Not Available*

Standard Equipment

JIMMY — BASE 2-DOOR: Vortec 4300 V-6 engine, 4-speed automatic transmission, power front disc/rear drum 4-wheel anti-lock brakes, power recirculating ball steering, front/rear stabilizer bars, 15"x 7" steel wheels, P205/75R15 all-season tires, air conditioning, carpeted floor mats, driver's airbag, floor console with coin tray, dual cupholders, and cassette/CD storage; halogen headlamps, trip odometer, tachometer, intermittent windshield wipers, vinyl high-back reclining bucket seats, side-door guard beams (do not meet 1999 truck standards), swing-out rear quarter glass, trailering harness, deep tint side glass with light tint rear window, daytime running lights, dual manual exterior mirrors, headlights-on warning tone, rear seat heat duct, AM/FM stereo with clock and 4 speakers, passenger visor vanity mirror, illuminated entry, glovebox light, underhood light, electronic shift transfer case (4WD), frame-mounted tow hooks (4WD)

BASE 4-DOOR (in addition to or instead of BASE 2-DOOR equipment): Rear door child safety locks, 60/40 reclining split-bench seat, swing-out rear quarter glass deleted

JIMMY — GMC

CODE	DESCRIPTION	INVOICE	MSRP

Base Prices

Code	Description	Invoice	MSRP
TS10516	2WD 2-door	18678	20639
TS10506	2WD 4-door	20058	22164
TT10516	4WD 2-door	20238	22362
TT10506	4WD 4-door	22048	24362
	Destination Charge:	515	515

Accessories

Code	Description	Invoice	MSRP
M50	5-speed Manual Transmission (2-door)	(765)	(890)
ANL	Air Dam w/Fog Lights (2WD)	99	115
F46	All Wheel Drive Transfer Case (4WD 4-door)	228	265
	REQUIRES purchase of Option Package 1SL and Luxury Ride Suspension; NOT AVAILABLE with Underbody Shield Package		
N60	Aluminum Wheels (2WD)	213	248
	INCLUDED in Option Packages 1SG, 1SK and 1SL		
N90	Aluminum Wheels (4WD)	241	280
	INCLUDED in Option Packages 1SG, 1SK, and 1SL		
PA3	Aluminum Wheels (4WD 4-door)	241	280
	REQUIRES purchase of Option Package 1SL and All Wheel Drive; NOT AVAILABLE with Gold Edition Package		
YF5	California Emissions	146	170
RYJ	Cargo Cover (All except 2WD 2-door)	59	69
	REQUIRES Option Package 1SG and Exterior Spare Tire Carrier on 4WD 2-door models; INCLUDED in Option Packages 1SG, 1SK and 1SL on 4-door models		
V10	Cold Climate Package	77	89
	Includes heavy-duty battery and engine block heater		
ZM8	Driver Convenience Package ZM8	277	322
	Includes rear window defogger, power tailgate or liftgate release, rear wiper/washer; INCLUDED in Option Packages 1SG, 1SK, and 1SL		
ZQ3	Driver Convenience Package ZQ3	340	395
	INCLUDED in Option Packages		
P16	Exterior Spare Tire Carrier (4WD 2-door)	185	215
B94	Gold Edition Package (4-door)	129	150
	Includes gold molding inserts, gold badging, gold aluminum wheel ports; REQUIRES Option Package 1SL; NOT AVAILABLE with Two-tone Paint		
C61	GVWR — 4,850 lbs. (4WD 2-door)	NC	NC
	REQUIRES Euro-ride Suspension or Off-road Suspension		
UA1	Heavy-duty Battery	48	56
	690-amp Delco Freedom battery; INCLUDED in Cold Climate Package		
UG1	HomeLink Universal Transmitter	112	130
	Includes trip computer and garage door opener; REQUIRES Overhead Console		
TB4	Liftgate with Liftglass (4-door)	NC	NC
	INCLUDED in Option Packages 1SK and 1SL		
G80	Locking Differential	217	252

GMC JIMMY

CODE	DESCRIPTION	INVOICE	MSRP
V54	Luggage Rack	108	126
	INCLUDED in Option Packages		
NP2	Manual Transfer Case Credit (4WD)	(106)	(123)
	REQUIRES 5-speed Manual Transmission on 2-door models; REQUIRES AM6 seat downgrade on 4-door models		
NG1	Massachusetts/New York Emissions	146	170
1SF	Option Package 1SF (2-door)	1756	2042
	Manufacturer Discount	(602)	(700)
	Net Price	1154	1342

Includes Power Convenience Package ZQ6 (power door locks, power windows, power mirrors), Driver Convenience Package ZQ3 (tilt steering wheel and cruise control), luggage rack, folding rear seat, AM/FM stereo with cassette player, seek/scan, clock and 4 speakers; Euro-ride Suspension (46mm high-pressure Bilstein shocks, front/rear jounce bumpers, heavy-duty springs), P235/70R15 BSW all-season tires (QBF)

1SG	Option Package 1SG (2-door)	2901	3373
	Manufacturer Discount	(1204)	(1400)
	Net Price	1697	1973

Includes Power Convenience Package ZQ6 (power door locks, power windows, power mirrors), Driver Convenience Package ZQ3 (tilt steering wheel and cruise control), luggage rack, folding rear seat, AM/FM stereo with cassette player, seek/scan, clock and 4 speakers; Euro-ride Suspension (46mm high-pressure Bilstein shocks, front/rear jounce bumpers, heavy-duty springs), P235/70R15 BSW all-season tires (QBF), plus SLS Sport Decor (deep tint rear window glass, cargo area convenience net, power tailgate release, rear window defogger, 2 additional cupholders, reading lamps mounted on rearview mirror, dual auxiliary power outlets in dash, cloth door panels with carpeted lower insert, leather-wrapped steering wheel, sunvisors with elastic straps, sunvisor extensions, dual illuminated visor vanity mirrors, rear window wiper/washer, aluminum wheels, cloth seat trim, split folding rear seat, body-color grille, composite halogen headlights, lower body stripe)

1SJ	Option Package 1SJ (2WD 4-door)	1907	2217
	Manufacturer Discount	(602)	(700)
	Net Price	1305	1517

Includes Power Convenience Package ZQ6 (power door locks, power windows, power window lockout switch, power mirrors), Driver Convenience Package ZQ3 (tilt steering wheel and cruise control), luggage rack, folding rear seat, AM/FM stereo with cassette player, seek/scan, clock and 4 speakers; Luxury-ride Suspension (46mm high-pressure Bilstein shocks, front/rear jounce bumpers), P235/70R15 BSW all-season tires (QBF)

1SJ	Option Package 1SJ (4WD 4-door)	1498	1742
	Manufacturer Discount	(602)	(700)
	Net Price	896	1042

Includes Power Convenience Package ZQ6 (power door locks, power windows, power window lockout switch, power mirrors), Driver Convenience Package ZQ3 (tilt steering wheel and cruise control), luggage rack, AM/FM stereo with cassette player, seek/scan, clock and 4 speakers; Luxury-ride Suspension (46mm high-pressure Bilstein shocks, front/rear jounce bumpers), P235/70R15 BSW all-season tires (QBF)

JIMMY — GMC

CODE	DESCRIPTION	INVOICE	MSRP
1SK	Option Package 1SK (SLE trim) (2WD 4-door)	3526	4100
	Manufacturer Discount	(1204)	(1400)
	Net Price	2322	2700

Includes Power Convenience Package ZQ6 (power door locks, power windows, power lockout switch, power mirrors), Driver Convenience Package ZQ3 (tilt steering wheel and cruise control), luggage rack, folding rear seat, AM/FM stereo with cassette player, seek/scan, clock and 4 speakers; Luxury-ride Suspension (46mm high-pressure Bilstein shocks, front/rear jounce bumpers), P235/70R15 BSW all-season tires (QBF), plus SLS Sport Decor (rear liftgate with liftglass, deep tint rear window glass, cargo area convenience net, retractable cargo compartment shade, power tailgate release, rear window defogger, 2 additional cupholders, reading lamps mounted on rearview mirror, dual auxiliary power outlets in dash, cloth door panels with carpeted lower insert, leather-wrapped steering wheel, sunvisors with elastic straps, sunvisor extensions, dual illuminated visor vanity mirrors, rear window wiper/washer, aluminum wheels, cloth seat trim, manual lumbar adjusters in front seats, split folding rear seat, floor console with shifter, body-color grille, composite halogen headlights, lower body stripe) —— What's the difference between SLS and SLE trim, you ask? Bodyside moldings with chrome insert, and chrome grille trim.

CODE	DESCRIPTION	INVOICE	MSRP
1SK	Option Package 1SK (SLE trim) (4WD 4-door)	3118	3625
	Manufacturer Discount	(1204)	(1400)
	Net Price	1914	2225

Includes Power Convenience Package ZQ6 (power door locks, power windows, power window lockout switch, power mirrors), Driver Convenience Package ZQ3 (tilt steering wheel and cruise control), luggage rack, AM/FM stereo with cassette player, seek/scan, clock and 4 speakers; Luxury-ride Suspension (46mm high-pressure Bilstein shocks, front/rear jounce bumpers), P235/70R15 BSW all-season tires (QBF), plus SLS Sport Decor (rear liftgate with liftglass, deep tint rear window glass, cargo area convenience net, retractable cargo compartment shade, power tailgate release, rear window defogger, 2 additional cupholders, reading lamps mounted on rearview mirror, dual auxiliary power outlets in dash, cloth door panels with carpeted lower insert, leather-wrapped steering wheel, sunvisors with elastic straps, sunvisor extensions, dual illuminated visor vanity mirrors, rear window wiper/washer, aluminum wheels, cloth seat trim, manual lumbar adjusters in front seats, split folding rear seat, floor console with shifter, body-color grille, composite halogen headlights, lower body stripe) —— What's the difference between SLS and SLE trim, you ask? Bodyside moldings with chrome insert, and chrome grille trim.

CODE	DESCRIPTION	INVOICE	MSRP
1SK	Option Package 1SK (SLS trim) (2WD 4-door)	3266	3798
	Manufacturer Discount	(1204)	(1400)
	Net Price	2062	2398

Includes Power Convenience Package ZQ6 (power door locks, power windows, power window lockout switch, power mirrors), Driver Convenience Package ZQ3 (tilt steering wheel and cruise control), luggage rack, folding rear seat, AM/FM stereo with cassette player, seek/scan, clock and 4 speakers; Luxury-ride Suspension (46mm high-pressure Bilstein shocks, front/rear jounce bumpers), P235/70R15 BSW all-

GMC JIMMY

CODE	DESCRIPTION	INVOICE	MSRP

season tires (QBF), plus SLS Sport Decor (rear liftgate with liftglass, deep tint rear window glass, cargo area convenience net, retractable cargo compartment shade, power tailgate release, rear window defogger, 2 additional cupholders, reading lamps mounted on rearview mirror, dual auxiliary power outlets in dash, cloth door panels with carpeted lower insert, leather-wrapped steering wheel, sunvisors with elastic straps, sunvisor extensions, dual illuminated visor vanity mirrors, rear window wiper/washer, aluminum wheels, cloth seat trim, manual lumbar adjusters in front seats, split folding rear seat, floor console with shifter, body-color grille, composite halogen headlights, lower body stripe)

1SK	Option Package 1SK (SLS trim) (4WD 4-door)	2858	3323
	Manufacturer Discount	(1204)	(1400)
	Net Price	1654	1923

Includes Power Convenience Package ZQ6 (power door locks, power windows, power window lockout switch, power mirrors), Driver Convenience Package ZQ3 (tilt steering wheel and cruise control), luggage rack, folding rear seat, AM/FM stereo with cassette player, seek/scan, clock and 4 speakers; Luxury-ride Suspension (46mm high-pressure Bilstein shocks, front/rear jounce bumpers), P235/70R15 BSW all-season tires (QBF), plus SLS Sport Decor (rear liftgate with liftglass, deep tint rear window glass, cargo area convenience net, retractable cargo compartment shade, power tailgate release, rear window defogger, 2 additional cupholders, reading lamps mounted on rearview mirror, dual auxiliary power outlets in dash, cloth door panels with carpeted lower insert, leather-wrapped steering wheel, sunvisors with elastic straps, sunvisor extensions, dual illuminated visor vanity mirrors, rear window wiper/washer, aluminum wheels, cloth seat trim, manual lumbar adjusters in front seats, split folding rear seat, floor console with shifter, body-color grille, composite halogen headlights, lower body stripe)

1SL	Option Package 1SL (SLT trim) (2WD 4-door)	4945	5750
	Manufacturer Discount	(1204)	(1400)
	Net Price	3741	4350

Includes Power Convenience Package ZQ6 (power door locks, power windows, power lockout switch, power mirrors), Driver Convenience Package ZQ3 (tilt steering wheel and cruise control), luggage rack, Luxury-ride Suspension (46mm high-pressure Bilstein shocks, front/rear jounce bumpers), P235/70R15 BSW all-season tires (QBF), SLE Comfort Decor (rear liftgate with liftglass, deep tint rear window glass, cargo area convenience net, retractable cargo compartment shade, power tailgate release, rear window defogger, 2 additional cupholders, dual auxiliary power outlets in dash, carpeted lower door panel insert, leather-wrapped steering wheel, sunvisors with elastic straps, sunvisor extensions, dual illuminated visor vanity mirrors, rear window wiper/washer, aluminum wheels, floor console with shifter, body-color grille, composite halogen headlights, lower body stripe, bodyside moldings with chrome insert, chrome grille trim), plus SLT Touring Decor (overhead console with reading lamps, outside temperature display, compass, and storage areas; remote keyless entry system, simulated leather door trim, ultrasoft leather bucket seats with power lumbar adjustment, adjustable headrests, and 6-way adjustable power driver's seat; ultrasoft leather rear split bench seat) AM/FM stereo with cassette player, equalizer, seek/scan, clock, and 6 speakers

JIMMY — GMC

CODE	DESCRIPTION	INVOICE	MSRP
1SL	Option Package 1SL (SLT trim) (4WD 4-door)	4537	5275
	Manufacturer Discount	(1204)	(1400)
	Net Price	3333	3875

Includes Power Convenience Package ZQ6 (power door locks, power windows, power lockout switch, power mirrors), Driver Convenience Package ZQ3 (tilt steering wheel and cruise control), luggage rack, Luxury-ride Suspension (46mm high-pressure Bilstein shocks, front/rear jounce bumpers), P235/70R15 BSW all-season tires (QBF), SLE Comfort Decor (rear liftgate with liftglass, deep tint rear window glass, cargo area convenience net, retractable cargo compartment shade, power tailgate release, rear window defogger, 2 additional cupholders, dual auxiliary power outlets in dash, carpeted lower door panel insert, leather-wrapped steering wheel, sunvisors with elastic straps, sunvisor extensions, dual illuminated visor vanity mirrors, rear window wiper/washer, aluminum wheels, floor console with shifter, body-color grille, composite halogen headlights, lower body stripe, bodyside moldings with chrome insert, chrome grille trim), plus SLT Touring Decor (overhead console with reading lamps, outside temperature display, compass, and storage areas; remote keyless entry system, simulated leather door trim, ultrasoft leather bucket seats with power lumbar adjustment, adjustable headrests, and 6-way adjustable power driver's seat; ultrasoft leather rear split bench seat) AM/FM stereo with cassette player, equalizer, seek/scan, clock, and 6 speakers

CODE	DESCRIPTION	INVOICE	MSRP
DK6	Overhead Console	126	147

Includes adjustable reading lamps, outside temperature display, compass, and storage areas; REQUIRES Bucket Seats and Option Package 1SG or 1SK; INCLUDED in Option Package 1SL; NOT AVAILABLE with AM6 seat downgrade

ZQ6	Power Convenience Package (2-door)	460	535

Includes power door locks, power windows, and power mirrors; INCLUDED in Option Packages

ZQ6	Power Convenience Package (4-door)	611	710

Includes power door locks, power windows, and power mirrors; INCLUDED in Option Packages

AG1	Power Driver's Seat	323	375

Includes 6-way adjustment and remote keyless entry; INCLUDED in Option Package 1SL

CF5	Power Sunroof	598	695

Includes tilt and slide functions and wind deflector; REQUIRES Overhead Console

GU4	Rear Axle Ratio — 3.08	NC	NC

REQUIRES Smooth Ride Suspension when ordered on 4WD 4-door models; NOT AVAILABLE with Locking Differential or 5-speed Manual Transmission

GU6	Rear Axle Ratio — 3.42	NC	NC

REQUIRES Locking Differential when ordered with 5-speed Manual Transmission

GT4	Rear Axle Ratio — 3.73 (4WD)	NC	NC

REQUIRES Locking Differential; NOT AVAILABLE with 5-speed Manual Transmission

AV5	Seats — Cloth Buckets (4-door)	138	161

Reclining cloth buckets with folding seatbacks, dual manual lumbar adjusters, and center floor console; NOT AVAILABLE with Option Packages 1SK or 1SL

GMC JIMMY

CODE	DESCRIPTION	INVOICE	MSRP
AM6	Seats — Downgrade Credit (4-door)	(138)	(161)
	60/40 reclining bench seat with cloth trim, folding center storage console with dual cupholders; REQUIRES Option Package 1SK; NOT AVAILABLE with Trailering Equipment on 2WD models		
YG4	Seats — Rear Seat Delete (All except 4WD 4-door)	NC	NC
	NOT AVAILABLE with Option Packages		
AM7	Seats — Split Folding Rear Bench (All except 4WD 4-door)	409	475
	INCLUDED in Option Packages		
UL5	Stereo — Delete Credit	(194)	(226)
	NOT AVAILABLE with Option Packages		
UX1	Stereo — Uplevel w/cassette	281	327
	With 1SF (2-door)	176	205
	With 1SG (2-door)	176	205
	With 1SJ (2WD 4-door)	176	205
	With 1SJ (4WD 4-door)	176	205
	With 1SK (4WD 4-door)	176	205
	With 1SK (2WD 4-door)	176	205
	With 1SK (4WD 4-door)	176	205
	With 1SK (2WD 4-door)	176	205
	AM/FM stereo with cassette player, equalizer, seek/scan, clock, and 6 speakers		
U1C	Stereo — Uplevel w/CD player	283	329
	With 1SL (4WD 4-door)	107	124
	With 1SL (2WD 4-door)	107	124
	AM/FM stereo with CD player, clock, and 6 speakers; REQUIRES purchase of an Option Package		
UM6	Stereo — w/cassette	105	122
	AM/FM stereo with cassette player, seek/scan, clock and 4 speakers; INCLUDED in Option Packages except 1SL; NOT AVAILABLE with Option Package 1SL		
Z85	Suspension — Euro-ride	169	197
	Includes 46mm high-pressure Bilstein shocks, front and rear stabilizer bars, front and rear jounce bumpers, and heavy-duty springs; INCLUDED in Option Packages 1SF and 1SG		
ZW7	Suspension — Luxury Ride (4-door)	169	197
	Includes 46mm high-pressure Bilstein shocks, front and rear stabilizer bars, front and rear jounce bumpers; INCLUDED in Option Packages		
ZM6	Suspension — Off-road (4WD 2-door)	189	220
	Includes 46mm high-pressure monotube gas Bilstein shocks, larger torsion bars, larger body mounts, front and rear stabilizer bars, front and rear jounce bumpers, and heavy-duty springs; REQUIRES QEB tires and GVWR of 4,850 lbs.		
ZQ1	Suspension — Smooth Ride (4-door)	NC	NC
	With 1SJ (2WD 4-door)	98	114
	With 1SJ (4WD 4-door)	98	114
	With 1SK (2WD 4-door)	98	114
	With 1SK (2WD 4-door)	98	114
	With 1SK (4WD 4-door)	98	114
	With 1SK (4WD 4-door)	98	114

JIMMY — GMC

CODE	DESCRIPTION	INVOICE	MSRP
	With 1SL (2WD 4-door)	98	114
	With 1SL (4WD 4-door)	98	114
	Includes 32mm front and rear twin-tube gas shocks, front urethane jounce bumpers, front and rear stabilizer bars; REQUIRES QCE or QCA tires		
Z83	Suspension — Solid Smooth Ride (2-door)	NC	NC
	With 1SF (2-door)	98	114
	With 1SG (2-door)	98	114
	Includes 32mm front and rear twin-tube gas shocks, front urethane jounce bumpers, front and rear stabilizer bars, and rear springs with new load ride rate		
QCE	Tires — P205/75R15	NC	NC
	Blackwall all-season tires; REQUIRES Solid Smooth Ride Suspension on 2-door models; REQUIRES Smooth Ride Suspension on 4-door models		
QCA	Tires — P205/75R15 (2WD)	104	121
	White-lettered all-season tires; REQUIRES Solid Smooth Ride Suspension on 2-door models; REQUIRES Smooth Ride Suspension on 4-door models		
QBG	Tires — P235/70R15	278	350
	With 1SF (2-door)	114	133
	With 1SG (2-door)	114	133
	With 1SJ (4WD 4-door)	114	133
	With 1SJ (2WD 4-door)	114	133
	With 1SK (2WD 4-door)	114	133
	With 1SK (4WD 4-door)	114	133
	With 1SK (4WD 4-door)	114	133
	With 1SK (2WD 4-door)	114	133
	With 1SL (2WD 4-door)	114	133
	With 1SL (4WD 4-door)	114	133
	Outline white-lettered all-season tires; REQUIRES Euro-ride Suspension on 2-door models; REQUIRES Euro-ride or Luxury Ride Suspension on 4-door models		
QBF	Tires — P235/70R15	165	192
	Blackwall all-season tires; REQUIRES Euro-ride Suspension on 2-door models; REQUIRES Euro-ride or Luxury Ride Suspension on 4-door models		
QEB	Tires — P235/75R15 (4WD 2-door)	288	335
	With 1SF (2-door)	123	143
	With 1SG (2-door)	123	143
	Outline white-lettered on/off road tires; REQUIRES Euro-ride or Off-road Suspension and Exterior Spare Tire Carrier		
QEB	Tires — P235/75R15 (4WD 4-door)	335	390
	With 1SJ (4WD 4-door)	170	198
	With 1SJ (2WD 4-door)	170	198
	With 1SK (2WD 4-door)	170	198
	With 1SK (4WD 4-door)	170	198
	With 1SK (2WD 4-door)	170	198
	With 1SK (4WD 4-door)	170	198
	With 1SL (2WD 4-door)	170	198
	With 1SL (4WD 4-door)	170	198
	Outline white-lettered on/off road tires; REQUIRES Euro-ride Suspension		

GMC

JIMMY / SAFARI

CODE	DESCRIPTION	INVOICE	MSRP
Z82	Trailering Equipment .... Includes 8-lead wiring harness, trailer hitch platform and heavy-duty flashers; REQUIRES 3.08 or 3.42 Rear Axle Ratio on 2WD models; REQUIRES 3.42 or 3.73 Rear Axle Ratio on 4WD models; NOT AVAILABLE with AM6 seat downgrade on 2WD 4-door	181	210
ZY2	Two-tone Paint (4-door) .... REQUIRES Option Package 1SK with SLE trim, or Option Package 1SL; NOT AVAILABLE with Gold Edition Package	148	172
ZM5	Underbody Shield Package (4WD) .... Includes transfer case, front differential, fuel tank, and steering linkage skid plates; NOT AVAILABLE with All Wheel Drive	108	126

SAFARI *(1997)*

1997 GMC Safari

What's New for GMC Safari in 1997 — Illuminated entry and daytime running lights debut this year, along with a couple of new colors and automatic transmission improvements. SLT models can be equipped with leather seating, and a HomeLink 3-channel transmitter is optional. Speed-sensitive power steering makes parking easier.

Safari — Review

Choosing between a Chevrolet Astro and a GMC Safari is more a matter of image than necessity. Do you want to see Chevrolet's badge every time you approach? Or would it be viscerally satisfying to face those bold "GMC" block letters, with their implication, as brand managers hope, of upscale luxury?

Tangible differences between the two are modest—a fact that's true of most Chevrolet and GMC cousins. Once you've decided that a rear-drive (or all-wheel-drive) General Motors mid-size van is the rational choice, you'll likely be satisfied with either one.

SAFARI — GMC

Because of their traditional-type full-frame construction and rear-drive layout, Safaris are most adept at heavy hauling and burly trailer-towing. Not everyone will relish the truck-like ride over harsh surfaces, but it's not bad at all when the highway smoothes out. Don't expect top-notch fuel mileage, though.

Dual airbags are housed in an artfully styled dashboard, and anti-lock brakes are standard. For added safety and visibility, daytime running lights have been installed this year. Integrated child safety seats are available for the center bench seat, and the sliding door has a child safety lock. Rear seat heat ducts direct warm air to freezing rear passengers. For 1997, SLT models can be equipped with leather seats, and Safaris with SLE or SLT trim offer an optional HomeLink 3-channel transmitter. Illuminated entry lighting is a new standard feature for all Safari passenger vans.

One slick feature sure to be appreciated by the parents of teenagers is the middle radio option. The driver and front passenger can listen to Casey Kasem up front, or nothing at all, while Junior blasts the local alternative music station into his eardrums via a set of headphone jacks that plugs into a separate radio unit in the center row. This option alone is worth the savings in family therapy, don't you think?

GM's 4300 Vortec V-6 is standard, sending 190 horsepower to an electronically-controlled four-speed automatic transmission. Long-life engine coolant and 100,000 mile spark plugs help keep maintenance costs to a minimum. This year brings transmission refinements that result in smoother shifts and improved efficiency, and all-wheel drive models get new plug-in half shafts that improve serviceability and save weight. Speed-sensitive power steering now makes parking the Safari easier.

Safaris come in three trim levels. The FE2 touring suspension option has stiffer shocks, a rear stabilizer bar, and grabby Goodyear rubber for a firmer, controlled ride. Eight-passenger seating is standard in Safaris with SLE or SLT trim, and available in the base SLX rendition. Two new colors are available for 1997, and the remote keyless entry key fob is redesigned.

Whether rear-drive or running full-time all-wheel drive, Safaris serve the muscular tasks that a front-drive minivan just cannot handle—yet convey a family in a fashion that won't produce pangs of pain.

Safety Data

Driver Airbag: Standard
Side Airbag: N/A
4-Wheel ABS: Standard
Driver Crash Test Grade: Average
Passenger Crash Test Grade: Average

Passenger Airbag: Standard
Meets 1997 Car Side Impact Standards: No
Traction Control: N/A
Insurance Cost: Very Low
Integrated Child Seat(s): Optional

Standard Equipment

SAFARI CARGO VAN: 4.3-liter Vortec V-6 engine, 4-speed automatic transmission, speed-sensitive power steering, hydraulic power front disc/rear drum anti-lock brakes, 15"x 6" styled steel wheels, P215/75R15 tires, dual front airbags, front air conditioning, side-impact door beams (do not meet 1999 truck standards), trip odometer, Scotchgard fabric protectant, vinyl reclining bucket seats, AM/FM stereo with seek/scan and digital clock, vinyl sunvisors with map bands, headlights-on warning buzzer, intermittent variable wipers, daytime running lights, dual black exterior foldaway mirrors, adjustable 3-point front seatbelts, brake/transmission shift interlock system, tachometer

GMC SAFARI

CODE	DESCRIPTION	INVOICE	MSRP

PASSENGER VAN (in addition to or instead of CARGO VAN equipment): Cloth and carpet door panel trim, cloth headliner, delayed entry interior lighting, vinyl 3-passenger center bench seat, left rear quarter storage compartment, cloth sunvisors with extensions, swing out windows, black center caps for wheel, rear door child safety locks

Base Prices

Code	Description	Invoice	MSRP
TM11005	Cargo Van SL	17251	19062
TM11006	Passenger Van	17190	19646
TL11005	Cargo Van SL AWD	19242	21262
TL11006	Passenger Van AWD	19115	21846
	Destination Charge:	585	585

Accessories

Code	Description	Invoice	MSRP
1SC	SLE Option Package 1SC (Passenger)	2312	2688
	Manufacturer Discount	(602)	(700)
	Net Price	1710	1988

Includes SLE Decor (floor mats, reading lights, rear dome light, 8-passenger seating, cloth upholstery, front seats with armrests, map pocket, and manual lumbar support; removable rear bench seat, fold-down center console, convenience net, power door locks, tilt steering wheel, cruise control, bodyside cladding and moldings with bright insert, composite headlights, chrome grille trim, swing-out rear door glass, styled steel wheels), power windows, deep tinted glass

1SD	SLE Option Package 1SD (Passenger)	2862	3328
	Manufacturer Discount	(602)	(700)
	Net Price	2260	2628

Includes SLE Decor (floor mats, reading lights, rear dome light, 8-passenger seating, cloth upholstery, front seats with armrests, map pocket, and manual lumbar support; removable rear bench seat, fold-down center console, convenience net, power door locks, tilt steering wheel, cruise control, bodyside cladding and moldings with bright insert, composite headlights, chrome grille trim, swing-out rear door glass, styled steel wheels), power windows, deep tinted glass, power exterior mirrors, overhead console, underseat storage, remote keyless entry, roof rack

1SE	SLE Option Package 1SE (Passenger)	3282	3816
	Manufacturer Discount	(688)	(800)
	Net Price	2594	3016

Includes SLE Decor (floor mats, reading lights, rear dome light, 8-passenger seating, cloth upholstery, front seats with armrests, map pocket, and manual lumbar support; removable rear bench seat, fold-down center console, convenience net, power door locks, tilt steering wheel, cruise control, bodyside cladding and moldings with bright insert, composite headlights, chrome grille trim, swing-out rear door glass, styled steel wheels), power windows, deep tinted glass, power exterior mirrors, overhead console, underseat storage, remote keyless entry, roof rack, power driver's seat, aluminum wheels

SAFARI — GMC

CODE	DESCRIPTION	INVOICE	MSRP
1SF	SLT Option Package 1SF (Passenger)	4585	5331
	Manufacturer Discount	(602)	(700)
	Net Price	3983	4631
	Includes SLE Decor (floor mats, reading lights, rear dome light, 8-passenger seating, cloth upholstery, front seats with armrests, map pocket, and manual lumbar support; removable rear bench seat, fold-down center console, convenience net, power door locks, tilt steering wheel, cruise control, bodyside cladding and moldings with bright insert, composite headlights, chrome grille trim, swing-out rear door glass, styled steel wheels), SLT Decor (power windows, deep tinted glass, power exterior mirrors, overhead console with compass and outside temperature readout, remote keyless entry, aluminum wheels, upgraded cloth trim, leather-wrapped steering wheel, reading lights, map lights, additional cupholders, dual illuminated visor mirrors, aluminum wheels, and deep tinted glass)		
R8K	SLX Appearance Package (Passenger)	582	677
	Manufacturer Discount	(301)	(350)
	Net Price	281	327
	Includes painted steel wheels, bodyside moldings, 8-passenger seating, and rubber floor mats; NOT AVAILABLE with SLE and SLT Option Packages		
1SB	SLX Option Package 1SB (Passenger)	1081	1257
	Manufacturer Discount	(215)	(250)
	Net Price	866	1007
	Includes tilt steering wheel, cruise control, convenience net, power windows and locks, deep tinted glass, and floor mats.		
C69	Air Conditioning — Rear (Passenger)	450	523
	Includes 105-amp generator		
YG6	Air Conditioning Delete Credit (Cargo)	(727)	(845)
B74	Bodyside Moldings	104	121
	INCLUDED in SLE and SLT Option Packages, and in SLX Appearance Package, on Passenger Vans		
YF5	California Emissions	146	170
PC2	Chrome Appearance Package	292	340
	With 1SC (Passenger)	213	248
	With 1SD (Passenger)	213	248
	With 1SE (Passenger)	213	248
	With 1SF (Passenger)	NC	NC
V10	Cold Climate Package	40	46
	Includes engine block heater and coolant protection		
ZQ3	Convenience Package ZQ3 (Cargo)	329	383
	Includes tilt steering wheel and cruise control		
AJ1	Deep Tinted Glass (Cargo)	225	262
	With ZW2 (Cargo)	46	54
	With ZW3 (Cargo)	92	107
	REQUIRES purchase of ZW2, ZW3, or ZW6 Glass Packages		
AJ1	Deep Tinted Glass (Passenger)	249	290
	INCLUDED in Option Packages		

GMC SAFARI

CODE	DESCRIPTION	INVOICE	MSRP
E54	Dutch Rear Doors	313	364
	With 1SC (Passenger)	262	305
	With 1SD (Passenger)	262	305
	With 1SE (Passenger)	262	305
	With 1SF (Passenger)	262	305
	Includes rear window wiper/washer		
B37	Floor Mats (Passenger)	40	47
	With ZP7 (Passenger)	59	69
	With ZP8 (Passenger)	59	69
	INCLUDED in Option Packages and SLX Appearance Package		
ZW2	Glass Package (Cargo)	75	87
	Includes rear panel door windows; NOT AVAILABLE with Dutch Rear Doors		
ZW3	Glass Package (Cargo)	133	155
	Includes sliding door and rear panel door windows		
ZW6	Glass Package (Cargo)	316	368
	Complete body windows		
B94	Gold Package (Passenger)	NC	NC
	Includes gold stripe and gold accented aluminum wheels; REQUIRES Option Package 1SF		
C36	Heater — Rear	176	205
UG1	HomeLink Transmitter (Passenger)	92	107
	3-channel universal garage door opener and transmitter; REQUIRES purchase of Option Package 1SD, 1SE, or 1SF		
NP5	Leather-wrapped Steering Wheel (Passenger)	46	54
	REQUIRES purchase of an SLE Option Package		
G80	Locking Rear Differential	217	252
NG1	Massachusetts/New York Emissions	146	170
ZY2	Paint — Conventional Two-tone (Passenger)	NC	NC
	REQUIRES purchase of an SLE or SLT Option Package		
ZQ2	Power Convenience Package (Cargo)	408	474
	Includes power door locks and power windows		
AU3	Power Door Locks	92	223
	INCLUDED in Power Convenience Package (Cargo) and in all Option Packages (Passenger)		
AG1	Power Driver's Seat (Passenger)	206	240
	REQUIRES purchase of Option Package 1SB, 1SC, or 1SD		
D48	Power Exterior Mirrors (Passenger)	84	98
	REQUIRES purchase of Option Package 1SB or 1SC		
AG2	Power Passenger's Seat (Passenger)	206	240
	REQUIRES Power Driver's Seat		
C95	Reading Lights (Cargo)	28	33
GU6	Rear Axle Ratio — 3.42	NC	NC
GT4	Rear Axle Ratio — 3.73	NC	NC
C49	Rear Window Defogger	132	154
	REQUIRES Dutch Rear Doors; NOT AVAILABLE with Air Conditioning Delete Credit on Cargo Van		

SAFARI — GMC

CODE	DESCRIPTION	INVOICE	MSRP
AU0	Remote Keyless Entry	116	135
	REQUIRES Power Door Locks; INCLUDED in Option Packages 1SD, 1SE, and 1SF on Passenger Van		
FE2	Ride & Handling Suspension (2WD)	263	306
	Includes gas shocks, rear stabilizer bar, and P235/65R15 outline white-lettered tires		
V54	Roof Rack (Passenger)	108	126
	INCLUDED in Option Packages 1SD, 1SE, and 1SF		
AN0	Seat Upgrade Package	144	168
	Includes inboard and outboard armrests, map pockets, and manual lumbar support; REQUIRES Option Package 1SB and 8-passenger seating on Passenger Van; REQUIRES Cloth Seats on Cargo Van		
ZP7	Seating — 7-passenger (Passenger)	833	969
	With 1SC (Passenger)	273	318
	With 1SD (Passenger)	273	318
	With 1SE (Passenger)	273	318
	With 1SF (Passenger)	273	318
	Includes front and middle row bucket seats with inboard/outboard armrests and manual lumbar support, reclining rear bench seat with armrests		
ZP8	Seating — 8-passenger (Passenger)	340	395
	INCLUDED in SLE and SLT Option Packages, and in SLX Appearance Package		
—	Seats — Cloth (Cargo)	NC	NC
—	Seats — Leather (Passenger)	817	950
	REQUIRES purchase of SLT Option Package 1SF		
UL5	Stereo — Delete Credit (Cargo)	(164)	(191)
UK6	Stereo — Rear Headphone Jacks (Passenger)	108	125
	REQUIRES purchase of UL0 stereo and an SLE or SLT Option Package		
UL0	Stereo — Uplevel w/cassette (Passenger)	264	307
	AM/FM stereo with cassette player, seek/scan, digital clock, and 4 front speakers, rear speaker wiring, theft lock, speed compensated volume, automatic tone control; REQUIRES purchase of an Option Package		
UP0	Stereo — Uplevel w/cassette & CD players (Passenger)	436	507
	AM/FM stereo with cassette and CD players, seek/scan, digital clock, and 4 front speakers, rear speaker wiring, theft lock, speed compensated volume, automatic tone control; REQUIRES purchase of an Option Package		
UN0	Stereo — Uplevel w/CD player (Passenger)	350	407
	AM/FM stereo with CD player, seek/scan, digital clock, and 4 front speakers, rear speaker wiring, theft lock, speed compensated volume, automatic tone control; REQUIRES purchase of an Option Package		
UM6	Stereo — w/cassette	126	147
	AM/FM stereo with cassette player, seek/scan, digital clock, and 6 speakers		
A18	Swing-out Rear & Side Window Glass (Cargo)	117	136
	REQUIRES ZW3 or ZW6 Glass Package; NOT AVAILABLE with Dutch Rear Doors		
A19	Swing-out Side Window Glass (Cargo)	66	77
	REQUIRES ZW3 or ZW6 Glass Package and Dutch Rear Doors		
QCM	Tires — P215/75R15	76	88
	Outline white-lettered tires		

GMC — SAFARI / SAVANA

CODE	DESCRIPTION	INVOICE	MSRP
QCV	Tires — P215/75R15	52	60
	Whitewall tires; NOT AVAILABLE with Aluminum Wheels on Passenger Van		
Z82	Trailering Equipment	266	309
	Includes heavy-duty platform hitch and 8-lead wiring harness		
PF3	Wheels — Aluminum (Passenger)	292	340
	With 1SC (Passenger)	213	248
	With 1SD (Passenger)	213	248
	With R8K (Passenger)	213	248
	INCLUDED in Option Packages 1SE and 1SF		
PA6	Wheels — Styled Steel	79	92
	INCLUDED in SLX Appearance Package and SLE Option Packages on Passenger Van; NOT AVAILABLE with SLT Option Package 1SF on Passenger Van		

SAVANA (1997)

1997 GMC Savana Passenger Van

What's New for GMC Savana in 1997 — G3500 models get dual airbags, while daytime running lights are a new standard feature. Speed-sensitive steering reduces effort at low speeds. Chrome-plated wheels are a new option, Remote keyless entry key fobs are redesigned, and automatic transmissions provide better fuel economy and smoother shifts.

Savana — Review

Believe it or not, it had been 25 years since GM redesigned its full-size van lineup when the Savana arrived in small numbers for 1996. The GMC Rally Van and Vandura were introduced in 1971, and sold steadily until recently. Competition and safety regulations forced GM to redo the big vans — heck, since 1971 Ford had re-engineered the Club Wagon and Econoline twice! To distinguish the new design, GMC rebadged the van Savana.

SAVANA — GMC

Savana features flush glass and door handles, hidden door hinges, standard anti-lock brakes and dual airbags. Doors contain side impact guard beams, though they do not meet 1999 safety standards yet. Front foot and leg room is adequate, and front seats offer a wide range of fore and aft travel. Rear heat ducts are standard, but for better warming (and cooling) an optional rear heating and air conditioning unit is available. Front air conditioning is standard. The center console contains two cupholders, an auxiliary power outlet, and storage for items like CDs and cassettes. Five sound systems are offered. Savana is available in base SL or luxury SLE trim levels.

New for 1997 is speed-sensitive power steering that lowers parking effort at low speeds. G3500 models receive dual front airbags, and daytime running lights make this huge hauler even more conspicuous to other motorists. Chrome-plated wheels are newly optional, and remote keyless entry fobs are redesigned for easier use. Automatic transmission refinements result in better fuel economy and smoother shifts.

Buyers may select either a 135-inch or a 155-inch wheelbase. There is a choice of side-entry doors as well; a sliding door or a pair of 60/40 hinged doors. Inside the short-wheelbase Savana you'll find 267 cubic feet of cargo area, while the longer wheelbase model provides a whopping 317 cubic feet of volume. Up to 15 passengers can be seated within, on as many as five bench seats. Hinged rear doors open 180 degrees for easy loading, and do not conceal high-mounted taillights when opened up. Gross vehicle weight ratings of up 9500 pounds are available on either wheelbase.

The base engine is a Vortec 4300 V-6 making 200 horsepower. Optional motors include the new GM family of V-8's, ranging from the popular Vortec 5000 to the monster Vortec 7400. Also available is a turbo-diesel V-8 good for 190 horsepower and 385 stump-pulling pound-feet of torque.

Like most new product in showrooms these days, the Savana's styling is rounded and bulbous, with a front end that mimics the corporate look carried by most of GM's truck family. This design should wear well into the next century.

Safety Data

Driver Airbag: *Standard*
Side Airbag: *Not Available*
4-Wheel ABS: *Standard*
Driver Crash Test Grade: *Not Available*
Passenger Crash Test Grade: *Not Available*

Passenger Airbag: *Standard*
Meets 1999 Side Impact Standards: *No*
Traction Control: *Not Available*
Insurance Cost: *Not Available*
Integrated Child Seat(s): *Not Available*

Standard Equipment

SAVANA CARGO VAN: Vortec 4300 V-6 engine (1500/2500), Vortec 5700 V-8 engine (3500), 4-speed automatic transmission, power front disc/rear drum 4-wheel anti-lock brakes, brake/transmission shift interlock, speed-sensitive power steering, 100-amp alternator (1500/2500), 124-amp alternator (3500), P215/75R15N all-season tires (1500), LT225/75R16D all-season tires (2500), LT245/75R16E all-season tires (3500), full-size spare tire, painted steel wheels with black center caps, gray painted bumpers, gray plastic grille, dual black exterior mirrors, halogen sealed beam headlights, daytime running lights, solar tinted glass, intermittent windshild wipers, dual front airbags, height-adjustable front seatbelts, child security locks on cargo doors, reclining high-back vinyl bucket seats, AM/FM stereo with seek/scan and clock, black vinyl floor covering, underhood light, trip odometer, auxiliary power outlet, headlamps-on warning tone, engine cover console with storage compartment

GMC SAVANA

CODE	DESCRIPTION	INVOICE	MSRP

SAVANA PASSENGER VAN (in addition to or instead of CARGO VAN equipment): Front air conditioning, illuminated entry system, 8-passenger seating (Regular Length), 12-passenger seating (Extended Length), 124-amp alternator (2500), swing-out left side center glass

Base Prices

Code	Description	Invoice	MSRP
TG11405	1500 Reg. Length Cargo Van	16744	19136
TG11406	1500 Regular Length Passenger Van	19542	22334
TG21405	2500 Reg. Length Cargo Van	17116	19561
TG21705	2500 Ext. Length Cargo Van	17903	20461
TG21406	2500 Reg. Length Passenger Van	21753	24860
TG21706	2500 Ext. Length Passenger Van	22540	25760
TG31405	3500 Regular Length Cargo Van	18323	20941
TG31705	3500 Ext. Length Cargo Van	19111	21841
TG31406	3500 Reg. Length Passenger Van	21893	25020
TG31706	3500 Ext. Length Passenger	22680	25920
	Destination Charge:	615	615

Accessories

Code	Description	Invoice	MSRP
1SB	Option Package 1SB (Cargo Van)	1302	1514

Includes air conditioning, tilt steering wheel, cruise control, and auxiliary lighting package (dome and reading lights, stepwell lights, and retractable underhood light)

1SB	Option Package 1SB (Passenger Van)	737	857

Includes Convenience Packages ZQ2 and ZQ3 (tilt steering wheel, cruise control, power windows, power door locks)

1SC	SLE Option Package 1SC (Passenger Van)	1367	1589

Includes bodyside moldings, chrome bumpers, composite headlights, chrome wheel trim rings and center caps, chrome-accented grille, power windows, power door locks, full floor carpeting, floor mats, cloth upholstery, tilt steering wheel, cruise control, auxiliary lighting (dome lights, stepwell lighting, reading lights, and retractable underhood light)

1SD	SLE Option Package 1SD (1500 Passenger Van)	2711	3152

Includes bodyside moldings, chrome bumpers, composite headlights, chrome wheel trim rings and center caps, chrome-accented grille, power windows, power door locks, full floor carpeting, floor mats, cloth upholstery, tilt steering wheel, cruise control, auxiliary lighting (dome lights, stepwell lighting, reading lights, and retractable underhood light), front & rear air conditioning, rear heater, deep tinted glass, remote keyless entry, power exterior mirrors, dual illuminated visor mirrors

1SD	SLE Option Package 1SD (2500/3500 Passenger Van)	2663	3096

Includes bodyside moldings, chrome bumpers, composite headlights, chrome wheel trim rings and center caps, chrome-accented grille, power windows, power door locks, full floor carpeting, floor mats, cloth upholstery, tilt steering wheel, cruise control, auxiliary lighting (dome lights, stepwell lighting, reading lights, and retractable underhood light), front & rear air conditioning, rear heater, deep tinted glass, remote keyless entry, power exterior mirrors, dual illuminated visor mirrors

SAVANA — GMC

CODE	DESCRIPTION	INVOICE	MSRP
C60	Air Conditioning (Cargo Van)	839	975
	INCLUDED in Option Package 1SB and with Front & Rear Air Conditioning		
C69	Air Conditioning — Front & Rear (1500 Passenger Van)	740	860
	Includes rear heater and 124-amp alternator		
C69	Air Conditioning — Front & Rear (1500/2500 Cargo Van)	1578	1835
	With 1SB (Cargo Van)	740	860
	Includes rear heater and 124-amp alternator		
C69	Air Conditioning — Front & Rear (2500/3500 Passenger Van)	691	804
	Includes rear heater		
C69	Air Conditioning — Front & Rear (3500 Cargo Van)	1530	1779
	With 1SB (Cargo Van)	691	804
	Includes rear heater		
KW2	Alternator — 124-amp (1500 Passenger Van)	48	56
	INCLUDED in Front & Rear Air Conditioning		
KW2	Alternator — 124-amp (1500/2500 Cargo Van)	48	56
	INCLUDED in Front & Rear Air Conditioning		
N90	Aluminum Wheels (1500 Passenger Van)	267	310
	With 1SC (Passenger Van)	215	250
	With 1SD (1500 Passenger Van)	215	250
TR9	Auxiliary Lighting Package	134	156
	Includes dome lights, reading lights, stepwell lighting, and a retractable underhood light; INCLUDED in Option Package 1SB on Cargo Van; INCLUDED in Option Packages 1SC and 1SD on Passenger Wagon		
YF5	California Emissions	146	170
—	Cloth Seat Trim	NC	NC
V10	Cold Climate Package	41	48
	Includes engine block heater; INCLUDED with 6.5-liter Turbodiesel V-8 Engine		
ZQ2	Convenience Package ZQ2	408	474
	Includes power windows and power door locks; INCLUDED in Option Packages on Passenger Van		
ZQ3	Convenience Package ZQ3	329	383
	Includes tilt steering wheel and cruise control; INCLUDED in Option Packages on Passenger Van		
AJ1	Deep Tinted Glass (Passenger Van)	327	380
	INCLUDED in Option Package 1SD		
ZR7	Deluxe Front Appearance Package (Cargo Van)	272	316
	Includes chrome bumpers, chrome accented grille, and composite headlights		
PNF	Door Trim Panel Delete Credit (Cargo Van)	(26)	(30)
DH6	Dual Illuminated Visor Vanity Mirrors (Passenger Van)	134	156
	REQUIRES Option Package 1SC		
L65	Engine — 6.5-liter Turbodiesel V-8 (2500 Cargo Van)	3290	3825
	Includes dual engine oil coolers, dual batteries, heavy-duty radiator, additional sound insulation, glow plugs, engine block heater, 2-stage fuel filter, fuel and water separator, dashboard warning light, fuel filter change indicator; REQUIRES 8,600 lb. GVWR		

GMC SAVANA

CODE	DESCRIPTION	INVOICE	MSRP
L65	Engine — 6.5-liter Turbodiesel V-8 (2500 Reg. Length Passenger Van) ...	2460	2860
	Includes dual engine oil coolers, dual batteries, heavy-duty radiator, additional sound insulation, glow plugs, engine block heater, 2-stage fuel filter, fuel and water separator, dashboard warning light, fuel filter change indicator		
L65	Engine — 6.5-liter Turbodiesel V-8 (3500 Cargo Van)	2460	2860
	Includes dual engine oil coolers, dual batteries, heavy-duty radiator, additional sound insulation, glow plugs, engine block heater, 2-stage fuel filter, fuel and water separator, dashboard warning light, fuel filter change indicator		
L65	Engine — 6.5-liter Turbodiesel V-8 (3500 Passenger Van)	2460	2860
	Includes dual engine oil coolers, dual batteries, heavy-duty radiator, additional sound insulation, glow plugs, engine block heater, 2-stage fuel filter, fuel and water separator, dashboard warning light, fuel filter change indicator		
L30	Engine — Vortec 5000 V-8 (1500 Passenger Van)	426	495
	REQUIRES 3.42 Rear Axle Ratio		
L30	Engine — Vortec 5000 V-8 (1500/2500 Cargo Van)	426	495
	REQUIRES 3.42 Rear Axle Ratio		
L31	Engine — Vortec 5700 V-8 (1500 Passenger Van)	830	965
L31	Engine — Vortec 5700 V-8 (1500/2500 Cargo Van)	830	965
L29	Engine — Vortec 7400 V-8 (3500)	516	600
VK3	Front License Plate Bracket	NC	NC
B30	Full Floor Carpeting (Passenger Van)	126	147
	INCLUDED in Option Packages 1SC and 1SD		
ZW3	Glass Package — Fixed Rear and Side Door (Cargo Van)	77	90
	INCLUDED in ZW6 Glass Package		
ZW2	Glass Package — Fixed Rear Door (Cargo Van)	43	50
	INCLUDED in ZW3 and ZW6 Glass Packages		
ZW6	Glass Package — Full Body (Cargo Van)	267	311
	Includes swing-out left side center window		
C5Y	GVWR — 7,100 lb. (1500 Cargo Van)	267	310
C6P	GVWR — 8,600 lb. (2500 Cargo Van)	357	415
	NOT AVAILABLE with Vortec 5000 V-8 Engine		
NP5	Leather-wrapped Steering Wheel (Passenger Van)	52	60
G80	Locking Differential	217	252
	NOT AVAILABLE with 3.42 Rear Axle Ratio on 3500 models		
NG1	Massachusetts/New York Emissions	NC	NC
U75	Power Antenna	73	85
	INCLUDED with Uplevel Stereos on Passenger Van		
AG1	Power Driver's Seat	206	240
	REQUIRES cloth seat trim		
DE5	Power Exterior Mirrors	97	113
	Includes mirror defogger; REQUIRES contents of Convenience Package ZQ2; REQUIRES Air Conditioning on Cargo Van; INCLUDED in Option Package 1SD on Passenger Van		
AG2	Power Passenger's Seat (Passenger Van)	206	240
	REQUIRES Power Driver's Seat		

SAVANA — GMC

CODE	DESCRIPTION	INVOICE	MSRP
GU6	Rear Axle Ratio — 3.42	NC	NC
	NOT AVAILABLE on 2500 Passenger Van or with Locking Differential on 3500 models; REQUIRES Vortec 7400 V-8 engine on 3500 Passenger Van		
GT4	Rear Axle Ratio — 3.73	NC	NC
	NOT AVAILABLE with Vortec 5000 V-8 engine; NOT AVAILABLE with any optional engines on 1500 Cargo Van		
GT5	Rear Axle Ratio — 4.10 (2500/3500)	NC	NC
	REQUIRES 8,600 lb. GVWR on 2500 Cargo Van; NOT AVAILABLE with Vortec 5000 V-8 engine		
C36	Rear Heater	176	205
	INCLUDED with Front & Rear Air Conditioning		
AU0	Remote Keyless Entry (Passenger Van)	116	135
	REQUIRES Option Package 1SD		
ZP3	Seating — 15-passenger Upgrade (3500 Extended Length)	319	371
ZP5	Seating — 5-passenger Downgrade Credit (1500 Passenger Van)	(319)	(371)
ZP8	Seating — 8-passenger Downgrade Credit (2500/3500 Passenger Van)	(319)	(371)
ZX1	Seating — Passenger Seat Delete (Cargo Van)	(350)	(407)
	Deletes front passenger seat and passenger airbag		
YA2	Sliding Side Door	NC	NC
UL5	Stereo — Delete Credit (Cargo Van)	(264)	(307)
UL0	Stereo — Uplevel w/cassette (Passenger Van)	380	442
	AM/FM stereo with auto-reverse cassette player, music search, seek/scan, automatic tone control, clock, power antenna, and 8 speakers; REQUIRES contents of Convenience Group ZQ2		
UP0	Stereo — Uplevel w/cassette & CD players (Passenger Van)	552	642
	AM/FM stereo with auto-reverse cassette player, music search, CD player, seek/scan, automatic tone control, clock, power antenna, and 8 speakers; REQUIRES contents of Convenience Group ZQ2		
UN0	Stereo — Uplevel w/CD player (Passenger Van)	466	542
	AM/FM stereo with CD player, seek/scan, automatic tone control, clock, power antenna, and 8 speakers; REQUIRES contents of Convenience Group ZQ2		
UM6	Stereo — w/cassette	126	147
	AM/FM stereo with cassette player, seek/scan, digital clock, and 8 speakers		
A19	Swing-out Rear & Side Door Glass (Cargo Van)	117	136
	REQUIRES ZW3 or ZW6 Glass Package		
A18	Swing-out Rear Door Glass (Cargo Van)	51	59
	REQUIRES ZW2 Glass Package		
XHF/YHF/ZHF	Tires — LT225/75R16E (2500 Cargo Van)	NC	NC
	All-season blackwall tires; REQUIRES 8,600 lb. GVWR		
XHM/YHM/ZHM	Tires — P235/75R15 (2500 Cargo Van)	245	285
	All-season outline white-lettered tires; REQUIRES 7,100 lb. GVWR		
XHM/YHM/ZHM	Tires — P235/75R15 (1500 Passenger Van)	108	125
	All-season outline white-lettered tires		
XHB/YHB/ZHB	Tires — P235/75R15X (1500 Cargo Van)	223	260
	All-season whitewall tires; REQUIRES 7,100 lb. GVWR		
XHA/YHA/ZHA	Tires — P235/75R15X (1500 Cargo Van)	NC	NC
	All-season blackwall tires; REQUIRES 7,100 lb. GVWR		

GMC

SAVANA / SIERRA 1500

CODE	DESCRIPTION	INVOICE	MSRP
XHB/YHB/ZHB	Tires — P235/75R15X (1500 Passenger Van)	85	100
	All-season whitewall tires		
Z82	Trailering Equipment	267	310
	Includes 8-lead wiring harness and hitch platform		
B31	Vinyl Front Floor Covering (Cargo Van)	NC	NC
P06	Wheel Trim Rings	52	60
	Stainless steel with chrome center caps; INCLUDED in Option Packages 1SC and 1SD on Passenger Van		
N83	Wheels — Chrome Plated (1500 Passenger Van)	267	310
	With 1SC (Passenger Van)	215	250
	With 1SD (1500 Passenger Van)	215	250

SIERRA 1500 *(1997)*

1997 GMC Sierra K1500 Extended Cab SLT

What's New for GMC Sierra 1500 in 1997 — A passenger airbag is added to models with a GVWR under 8,600 pounds, and all models get speed-sensitive steering that reduces low-speed effort. K1500 models have a tighter turning radius for better maneuverability. Automatic transmissions are refined to provide smoother shifts and improved efficiency. Three new paint colors debut.

Sierra 1500 — Review

GM has figured out a way to steal some thunder from the Dodge Ram and the new Ford F-Series. Their entire line of truck engines was refined last year, infused with notable horsepower and torque increases. For good measure, engineers made the rear portion of the extended cab model more accessible via a trick panel that opens wide from the passenger's side to make loading cargo or people much easier.

Every Sierra gasoline engine, from the base V-6 to the king-of-the-hill V-8, benefit from Vortec technology which provide healthy power and torque ratings. For example, the standard

SIERRA 1500 — GMC

4300 V-6 makes an ample 200 horsepower, and the optional 5700 V-8 is a much more satisfying powerplant than Ford's new overhead cam designs. Also available are regular- and heavy-duty turbodiesels sporting 6.5 liters of displacement. All Sierras have four-wheel anti-lock braking.

The side access panel makes the extended cab model a true family vehicle. Loading cargo into the rear of the cab is much easier too. To qualify for the side access panel, you must order a 1500 extended cab shortbed equipped with SLE or SLT trim and a Vortec 5000 or Vortec 5700 engine mated to an automatic transmission. In contrast, Ford provides a third door standard on all extended cab models, making life much easier.

Other comforts aren't forgotten, either. Automakers are constantly trying to make their trucks more car-like, so GM has made rear seat heating ducts standard on the Sierra. Shoulder belts are height adjustable to fit a variety of physiques, and upholstery choices include leather. Heck, you'd hardly know this was a truck, especially with the passenger car tires that give some versions of the Sierra a nicer ride and quieter interior.

Improvements for 1997 include a new passenger airbag on models under 8,600 lbs. GVWR, and the airbag can be deactivated for those times when a rear-facing child safety seat is installed. Speed-sensitive steering that boosts power assist at low speeds to make parking easier has been added. On the open road, this system firms up the steering for improved road feel. All K1500 Sierras get a tighter turning radius this year for better maneuverability, and the automatic transmission shifts more smoothly this year thanks to revised hardware.

Although Chevrolet's own C/K Series garners the greatest amount of publicity, GMC's equivalents are pretty strong sellers themselves, approaching 190,000 units each year. Sierras, in fact, account for close to half of GMC output. Americans continue to clamor for burly pickups, whether for their macho image or for real work. Whether you choose a light-duty two-wheel-drive (C1500) or the massive four-wheel-drive K3500 Club Coupe, on a 155.5-inch wheelbase, GMC gives both Chevrolet and its Ford/Dodge rivals a run for their money.

Safety Data

Driver Airbag: *Standard*
Side Airbag: *Not Available*
4-Wheel ABS: *Standard*
Driver Crash Test Grade: *Excellent*
Passenger Crash Test Grade: *Not Available*

Passenger Airbag: *Standard*
Meets 1999 Side Impact Standards: *No*
Traction Control: *Not Available*
Insurance Cost: *Low (2WD); Average (4WD)*
Integrated Child Seat(s): *Not Available*

Standard Equipment

SIERRA 1500 SPECIAL REGULAR CAB: Vortec 4300 V-6 engine, 5-speed manual transmission, power steering, power front disc/rear drum 4-wheel anti-lock brakes, full-size spare tire, argent painted steel wheels with black center caps, chrome front bumper, light argent grille, daytime running lamps, intermittent windshield wipers, tinted glass, dual black exterior mirrors, headlamps-on warning buzzer, cargo bed light, dual airbags, vinyl front bench seat with folding back, side window defoggers, AM/FM stereo with seek/scan and 4 speakers, digital clock, black vinyl floor covering, vinyl headliner, trip odometer, voltmeter, tachometer, oil pressure gauge, temperature gauge, two dash-mounted auxiliary power outlets, passenger visor vanity mirror, dual cupholders, simulated leather steering wheel trim, side door guard beams (do not meet 1999 truck standard)

SL 1500 REGULAR CAB (in addition to or instead of SPECIAL equipment): Color-keyed vinyl floor covering, cloth headliner, reading lights, courtesy lights, underhood light

GMC SIERRA 1500

| CODE | DESCRIPTION | INVOICE | MSRP |

SL 1500 EXTENDED CAB (in addition to or instead of REGULAR CAB equipment): Vortec 5000 V-8 engine (longbed only), swing-out rear quarter windows, vinyl 60/40 split folding bench seat with easy entry feature, vinyl folding rear bench seat

Base Prices

Code	Description	Invoice	MSRP
C10703	C1500 Special Reg Cab Wideside SB	13215	14602
C10903	C1500 Special Reg Cab Wideside LB	13595	15022
C10703	C1500 Reg Cab Wideside Shortbed	14011	16012
C10903	C1500 Reg Cab Wideside Longbed	14273	16312
C10703	C1500 Reg Cab Sportside Shortbed	14514	16587
C10753	C1500 X-cab Wideside Shortbed	15831	18092
C10753	C1500 X-cab Sportside Shortbed	16334	18667
C10953	C1500 X-cab Wideside Longbed	16702	19087
K10703	K1500 Special Reg Cab Wideside SB	16564	18302
K10903	K1500 Special Reg Cab Wideside LB	16853	18622
K10703	K1500 Reg Cab Wideside Shortbed	16636	19012
K10903	K1500 Reg Cab Wideside Longbed	16898	19312
K10703	K1500 Reg Cab Sportside Shortbed	17139	19587
K10753	K1500 X-cab Wideside Shortbed	18285	20897
K10753	K1500 X-cab Sportside Shortbed	18788	21472
K10953	K1500 X-cab Wideside Longbed	19156	21892
	Destination Charge:	625	625

Accessories

Code	Description	Invoice	MSRP
M30	4-speed Automatic Transmission	834	970
	NOT AVAILABLE with 6.5-liter Turbodiesel V-8 Engine or GT Equipment Package 1SK		
MT1	4-speed Automatic Transmission (X-cab/Reg Cab LB except Special)	834	970
	REQUIRES 6.5-liter Turbodiesel V-8 Engine		
MG5	5-speed Manual Transmission	NC	NC
	NOT AVAILABLE with Vortec 5700 V-8 or 6.5-liter Turbodiesel V-8 engines		
M50	5-speed Manual Transmission (All except Special)	NC	NC
	REQUIRES Vortec 5700 V-8 Engine; NOT AVAILABLE with GT Equipment Package 1SK		
L56	6.5-liter Turbodiesel V-8 Engine (X-cab LB)	3062	3560
	Includes dual batteries, hydraulic brakes, heavy-duty radiator, engine oil cooler, extra sound insulation, engine block heater, instrument panel warning light, fuel filter change signal		
L56	6.5-liter Turbodiesel V-8 Engine (X-cab SB/Reg Cab LB except Special)	3487	4055
	Includes dual batteries, hydraulic brakes, heavy-duty radiator, engine oil cooler, extra sound insulation, engine block heater, instrument panel warning light, fuel filter change signal; NOT AVAILABLE with SL Equipment Package 1SJ or GT Equipment Package 1SK on Regular Cab models		
C60	Air Conditioning	692	805
	REQUIRES SL Equipment Package 1SA or Special Equipment Package 1SL		
BZY	Bedliner (Wideside)	194	225

SIERRA 1500 — GMC

CODE	DESCRIPTION	INVOICE	MSRP
R9Q	Bright Appearance Group (All Wideside except Special)	527	613
	Manufacturer Discount	(172)	(200)
	Net Price	355	413
	Includes Deluxe Front Appearance Package (color-keyed grille, composite headlights, dual horns), chrome front and rear bumpers, bright exterior moldings, and bright trim rings with chrome center caps; INCLUDED in SLE and SLT Equipment Packages; INCLUDED in SL Equipment Package 1SJ; NOT AVAILABLE with GT Equipment Package		
R9Q	Bright Appearance Group (Sportside)	501	582
	Manufacturer Discount	(172)	(200)
	Net Price	329	382
	Includes Deluxe Front Appearance Package (color-keyed grille, composite headlights, dual horns), chrome front and rear bumpers, bright exterior moldings, and bright trim rings with chrome center caps; INCLUDED in SLE and SLT Equipment Packages; INCLUDED in SL Equipment Package 1SJ; NOT AVAILABLE with GT Equipment Package		
B85	Bright Exterior Moldings (Sportside)	65	76
	INCLUDED in SLE and SLT Equipment Packages; INCLUDED in Bright Appearance Group; NOT AVAILABLE with GT Equipment Package 1SK		
B85	Bright Exterior Moldings (Wideside except Special)	92	107
	INCLUDED in SLE and SLT Equipment Packages; INCLUDED in Bright Appearance Group; NOT AVAILABLE with GT Equipment Package 1SK		
YF5	California Emissions	146	170
	NOT AVAILABLE with GT Equipment Package 1SK		
N90	Cast Aluminum Wheels (C1500 except Special)	267	310
	With 1SC (All except Special)	215	250
	With 1SG (X-cab SB)	215	250
	With 1SG (X-cab LB)	215	250
	With R9Q (Sportside)	215	250
	With R9Q (All Wideside except Special)	215	250
	INCLUDED in GT and SLT Equipment Packages		
PF4	Cast Aluminum Wheels (K1500 except Special)	267	310
	With 1SC (All except Special)	215	250
	With 1SG (X-cab LB)	215	250
	With 1SG (X-cab SB)	215	250
	With R9Q (All Wideside except Special)	215	250
	With R9Q (Sportside)	215	250
	INCLUDED in SLT Equipment Packages		
VG3	Chrome Front Bumper (All except Special)	22	26
	Includes black bumper guards when ordered with 6.5-liter Turbodiesel V-8 engine; INCLUDED in SLE and SLT Equipment Packages; INCLUDED in Bright Appearance Group		
N83	Chrome Wheels (C1500 except Special)	267	310
	With 1SC (All except Special)	215	250
	With 1SG (X-cab LB)	215	250
	With 1SG (X-cab SB)	215	250
	With R9Q (All Wideside except Special)	215	250
	With R9Q (Sportside)	215	250
	INCLUDED in GT Equipment Package 1SK; NOT AVAILABLE with SLT Equipment Packages		

GMC SIERRA 1500

CODE	DESCRIPTION	INVOICE	MSRP
V10	Cold Climate Package	28	33
	Includes engine block heater; INCLUDED with 6.5-liter Turbodiesel V-8 Engine		
ZQ3	Convenience Group	329	383
	Includes tilt steering wheel and cruise control; REQUIRES SL Equipment Package 1SA or Special Equipment Package 1SL		
AJ1	Deep Tinted Glass (Reg Cab)	30	35
	REQUIRES Sliding Rear Window		
AJ1	Deep Tinted Glass (X-cab)	92	107
	With C49 (X-cab)	62	72
	Tint is light when ordered with Rear Window Defogger		
V22	Deluxe Front Appearance Package (All except Special)	164	191
	Includes color-keyed grille, composite headlights, and dual horns; INCLUDED with SLE and SLT Equipment Packages; INCLUDED in Bright Appearance Group		
DF2	Dual Stainless Steel Camper-style Exterior Mirrors (All except Special)	46	53
	With 1SC (All except Special)	(39)	(45)
	With 1SD (X-cab)	(39)	(45)
	With 1SD (Reg Cab except Special)	(39)	(45)
	With 1SG (X-cab LB)	(39)	(45)
	With 1SG (X-cab SB)	(39)	(45)
	With 1SG (X-cab LB)	(39)	(45)
	With 1SG (X-cab SB)	(39)	(45)
DD7	Electrochromic Rearview Mirror (All except Special)	125	145
	REQUIRES an SLE or SLT Equipment Package		
NP1	Electronic Shift Transfer Case (K1500)	129	150
	REQUIRES Convenience Group ZQ3 and a 4-speed Automatic Transmission		
KC4	Engine Oil Cooler	116	135
	INCLUDED with 6.5-liter Turbodiesel V-8 Engine and 3.73 Rear Axle Ratio		
—	Enhanced Value Manual Transmission Discount	(430)	(500)
	NOT AVAILABLE with SLE and SLT Image Max Equipment Packages		
VK3	Front License Plate Bracket	NC	NC
B30	Full Floor Carpeting (All Reg Cab except Special)	47	55
	Includes vinyl floor mats; INCLUDED in SLE and SLT Equipment Packages, SL Equipment Package 1SJ, and GT Equipment Package 1SK		
B30	Full Floor Carpeting (X-cab)	75	87
	Includes vinyl floor mats; INCLUDED in SLE and SLT Equipment Packages		
FG5	Gas Shock Absorbers (C1500)	194	225
	46mm Bilstien; INCLUDED in GT Equipment Package 1SK		
1SK	GT Equipment Package 1SK (Cloth Interior)	3178	3695
	(C1500 Reg Cab except Special)		
	Manufacturer Discount	(559)	(650)
	Net Price	2619	3045
	Includes Vortec 5000 V-8 engine, chrome wheels, air conditioning, AM/FM stereo with cassette player, seek/scan, 4 speakers, and digital clock (UM6); Convenience Group (tilt steering wheel and cruise control), full floor carpeting, cloth 40/60 reclining split bench seat, Deluxe Front Appearance Package (color-keyed grille, composite headlights, dual horns), front and rear chrome bumpers, gas shock absorbers, fog lights, GT decals		

SIERRA 1500 — GMC

CODE	DESCRIPTION	INVOICE	MSRP
1SK	GT Equipment Package 1SK (Leather Interior)	4038	4695
	(C1500 Reg Cab except Special)		
	Manufacturer Discount	(559)	(650)
	Net Price	3479	4045
	Includes Vortec 5000 V-8 engine, chrome wheels, air conditioning, AM/FM stereo with cassette player, seek/scan, 4 speakers, and digital clock (UM6); Convenience Group (tilt steering wheel and cruise control), full floor carpeting, leather 40/60 reclining split bench seat, Deluxe Front Appearance Package (color-keyed grille, composite headlights, dual horns), front and rear chrome bumpers, gas shock absorbers, fog lights, GT decals		
C5S	GVWR — 6,600 lbs. (K1500 X-cab)	NC	NC
	REQUIRES Heavy-duty Chassis; NOT AVAILABLE with 6.5-liter Turbodiesel V-8 Engine on Longbed models		
C5U	GVWR — 6,800 lbs. (X-cab LB)	NC	NC
	REQUIRES Heavy-duty Chassis and 6.5-liter Turbodiesel V-8 Engine		
TP2	Heavy-duty Auxiliary Battery	115	134
	600 CCA Delco Freedom battery; NOT AVAILABLE with GT Equipment Package 1SK		
F44	Heavy-duty Chassis (K1500 X-cab)	198	230
	REQUIRES 6,600 or 6,800 lb. GVWR; INCLUDED with 6.5-liter Turbodiesel V-8 Engine		
F60	Heavy-duty Front Springs (K1500)	54	63
	NOT AVAILABLE with 6.5-liter Turbodiesel V-8 Engine or Off-road Chassis Package		
F51	Heavy-duty Shock Absorbers	34	40
	INCLUDED in Trailering Equipment Package and Snow Plow Prep Package; NOT AVAILABLE with Off-road Chassis Package		
KNP	Heavy-duty Transmission Cooler	83	96
	REQUIRES the 4-speed Automatic Transmission (M30); NOT AVAILABLE with GT Equipment Package, 3.08 Rear Axle Ratio, Vortec 4300 V-6 Engine, or Vortec 5000 V-8 Engine		
K47	High Capacity Air Cleaner	22	25
	NOT AVAILABLE with 6.5-liter Turbodiesel V-8 Engine		
G80	Locking Differential	217	252
	NOT AVAILABLE with 3.08 rear axle ratio		
NG1	Massachusetts/New York Emissions	NC	NC
Z71	Off-road Chassis Package (K1500 except Special)	232	270
	Includes skid plates and Bilstien gas shock absorbers; REQUIRES SLE or SLT Equipment Packages; NOT AVAILABLE with Heavy-duty Shock Absorbers or the following combination: Vortec 5000 V-8 engine with 4-speed Automatic Transmission, 3.42 Rear Axle Ratio, and Trailering Equipment Package		
NZZ	Off-road Skid Plate (K1500)	82	95
	Includes transfer case and differential skid plates; INCLUDED in Off-road Chassis Package		
ZY2	Paint — Conventional Two-tone (All except Special)	155	180
	REQUIRES an SLE or SLT Equipment Package		
ZY4	Paint — Deluxe Two-tone (All Wideside except Special)	237	275
	REQUIRES an SLE or SLT Equipment Package; NOT AVAILABLE with Third Door		

GMC SIERRA 1500

CODE	DESCRIPTION	INVOICE	MSRP
AU3	Power Door Locks	134	156
	INCLUDED in SLE and SLT Equipment Packages		
AG9	Power Driver's Seat (X-cab)	206	240
	REQUIRES an SLE Equipment Package; NOT AVAILABLE with vinyl seats		
P06	Rally Wheel Trim	52	60
	Includes bright trim rings and chrome center caps; INCLUDED in SLE and SLT Equipment Packages; INCLUDED in Bright Appearance Group		
GU4	Rear Axle Ratio — 3.08 (C1500)	NC	NC
	NOT AVAILABLE with Locking Differential		
GU6	Rear Axle Ratio — 3.42	NC	NC
GT4	Rear Axle Ratio — 3.73	NC	NC
	With L30 (All except X-cab LB & Special)	116	135
	With L31 (X-cab SB)	116	135
	With L31 (Reg Cab except Special)	116	135
	With L31 (X-cab LB)	116	135
	With L56 (X-cab SB/Reg Cab LB except Special)	116	135
	With L56 (X-cab LB)	116	135
	Includes water to oil cooler; NOT AVAILABLE with GT Equipment Package		
EF1	Rear Bumper Delete Credit (All except Special)	(172)	(200)
	REQUIRES an SLE or SLT Equipment Package		
YG4	Rear Seat Delete Credit (X-cab)	(374)	(435)
	REQUIRES 60/40 Split Reclining Bench Seat; NOT AVAILABLE with SLE or SLT Decor Packages		
VB3	Rear Step Bumper — Chrome (All except Special)	197	229
	REQUIRES Chrome Front Bumper; INCLUDED in SLE, SLT and GT Equipment Packages; INCLUDED in Bright Appearance Group		
V43	Rear Step Bumper — Painted (Wideside except Special)	112	130
	NOT AVAILABLE with SLE, SLT and GT Equipment Packages; NOT AVAILABLE with Bright Appearance Group		
C49	Rear Window Defogger (X-cab)	132	154
	REQUIRES an SLE or SLT Equipment Package; NOT AVAILABLE with Sliding Rear Window		
AU0	Remote Keyless Entry (All except Special)	120	140
	REQUIRES an SLE Equipment Package		
BG9	Rubber Floor Covering — Color-keyed (Reg Cab except Special)	(30)	(35)
	REQUIRES an SLE or SLT Equipment Package		
BG9	Rubber Floor Covering — Color-keyed (X-cab)	(44)	(51)
	REQUIRES an SLE or SLT Equipment Package		
AE7	Seat — 60/40 Reclining Split Bench (Reg Cab)	150	174
	REQUIRES an SLE Equipment Package		
A95	Seats — Reclining Buckets (Reg Cab except Special)	332	386
	Includes floor console, dual adjustable headrests, power lumbar adjustment, and behind seat storage pockets; REQUIRES an SLE or SLT Equipment Package; NOT AVAILABLE with SLT Equipment Package 1SD		

SIERRA 1500 — GMC

CODE	DESCRIPTION	INVOICE	MSRP
A95	Seats — Reclining Buckets (X-cab)	232	270
	Includes floor console, dual adjustable headrests, power lumbar adjustment, and behind seat storage pockets; REQUIRES an SLE or SLT Equipment Package		
1SA	SL Equipment Package 1SA (All except Special)	NC	NC
	Includes vehicle with standard equipment		
1SB	SL Equipment Package 1SB (All except Special)	1148	1335
	Manufacturer Discount	(430)	(500)
	Net Price	718	835
	Includes air conditioning, AM/FM stereo with cassette player, seek/scan, 4 speakers, and digital clock (UM6); Convenience Group (tilt steering wheel and cruise control)		
1SJ	SL Equipment Package 1SJ (All except Special)	1723	2003
	Manufacturer Discount	(602)	(700)
	Net Price	1121	1303
	Includes Vortec 5000 V-8 engine, air conditioning, AM/FM stereo with cassette player, seek/scan, 4 speakers, and digital clock (UM6); Convenience Group (tilt steering wheel and cruise control), full floor carpeting, and Bright Appearance Package R9Q (front and rear chrome bumpers, color-keyed grille, composite headlights, dual horns, bright exterior moldings, chrome trim rings with bright center caps)		
1SC	SLE Equipment Package 1SC (All except Special)	2721	3164
	Manufacturer Discount	(645)	(750)
	Net Price	2076	2414
	Includes Deluxe Front Appearance Package (color-keyed grille, composite headlamps, dual horns), bright trim rings and chrome center caps, chrome front and rear bumpers, air conditioning, Convenience Group (tilt steering wheel and cruise control), full floor carpeting, color-keyed floor mats, power door locks, power windows, power exterior mirrors, AM/FM stereo with cassette player, seek/scan, 4 speakers, and digital clock; leather-wrapped steering wheel, behind seat storage tray, removable underhood lamp, bright bodyside moldings and bright wheel opening moldings (not available on Sportside)		
1SG	SLE Image Max Equipment Package (X-cab SB)	4583	5329
	Manufacturer Discount	(645)	(750)
	Net Price	3938	4579
	Includes Vortec 5700 V-8 engine, 4-speed automatic transmission, Deluxe Front Appearance Package (color-keyed grille, composite headlamps, dual horns), bright trim rings and chrome center caps, chrome front and rear bumpers, air conditioning, Convenience Group (tilt steering wheel and cruise control), full floor carpeting, color-keyed floor mats, power door locks, power windows, power exterior mirrors, AM/FM stereo with cassette player, seek/scan, 4 speakers, and digital clock; leather-wrapped steering wheel, behind seat storage tray, removable underhood lamp, bright bodyside moldings and bright wheel opening moldings (not available on Sportside)		

GMC SIERRA 1500

CODE	DESCRIPTION	INVOICE	MSRP
1SG	SLE Image Max Equipment Package 1SG (X-cab LB)	4157	4834
	Manufacturer Discount	(645)	(750)
	Net Price	3512	4084

Includes Vortec 5700 V-8 engine, 4-speed automatic transmission, Deluxe Front Appearance Package (color-keyed grille, composite headlamps, dual horns), bright trim rings and chrome center caps, chrome front and rear bumpers, air conditioning, Convenience Group (tilt steering wheel and cruise control), full floor carpeting, color-keyed floor mats, power door locks, power windows, power exterior mirrors, AM/FM stereo with cassette player, seek/scan, 4 speakers, and digital clock; leather-wrapped steering wheel, behind seat storage tray, removable underhood lamp, bright bodyside moldings and bright wheel opening moldings (not available on Sportside)

A28	Sliding Rear Window	97	113

NOT AVAILABLE with Rear Window Defogger

1SD	SLT Equipment Package 1SD (Reg Cab except Special)	4143	4818
	Manufacturer Discount	(645)	(750)
	Net Price	3498	4068

Includes Deluxe Front Appearance Package (color-keyed grille, composite headlamps, dual horns), bright trim rings and chrome center caps, chrome front and rear bumpers, air conditioning, Convenience Group (tilt steering wheel and cruise control), full floor carpeting, color-keyed floor mats, power door locks, power windows, power exterior mirrors, leather-wrapped steering wheel, behind seat storage tray, removable underhood lamp, bright bodyside moldings and bright wheel opening moldings (not available on Sportside), plus leather seat trim, AM/FM stereo with auto-reverse cassette player, seek/scan, digital clock, theft lock, automatic tone control, music search feature, and enhanced performance 6-speaker sound system, remote keyless entry, 60/40 split reclining bench seat, 6-way power driver's seat, cast aluminum wheels

1SD	SLT Equipment Package 1SD (X-cab)	4200	4884
	Manufacturer Discount	(645)	(750)
	Net Price	3555	4134

Includes Deluxe Front Appearance Package (color-keyed grille, composite headlamps, dual horns), bright trim rings and chrome center caps, chrome front and rear bumpers, air conditioning, Convenience Group (tilt steering wheel and cruise control), full floor carpeting, color-keyed floor mats, power door locks, power windows, power exterior mirrors, leather-wrapped steering wheel, behind seat storage tray, removable underhood lamp, bright bodyside moldings and bright wheel opening moldings (not available on Sportside), plus leather seat trim, AM/FM stereo with auto-reverse cassette player, seek/scan, digital clock, theft lock, automatic tone control, music search feature, and enhanced performance 6-speaker sound system; remote keyless entry, 60/40 split reclining bench seat, 6-way power driver's seat, cast aluminum wheels

1SG	SLT Image Max Equipment Package (X-cab SB)	6062	7049
	Manufacturer Discount	(645)	(750)
	Net Price	5417	6299

Includes Vortec 5700 V-8 engine, 4-speed automatic transmission, Deluxe Front Appearance Package (color-keyed grille, composite headlamps, dual horns), bright trim rings and chrome center caps, chrome front and rear bumpers, air conditioning,

SIERRA 1500 — GMC

CODE	DESCRIPTION	INVOICE	MSRP
	Convenience Group (tilt steering wheel and cruise control), full floor carpeting, color-keyed floor mats, power door locks, power windows, power exterior mirrors, leather-wrapped steering wheel, behind seat storage tray, removable underhood lamp, bright bodyside moldings and bright wheel opening moldings (not available on Sportside), plus leather seat trim, AM/FM stereo with auto-reverse cassette player, seek/scan, digital clock, theft lock, automatic tone control, music search feature, and enhanced performance 6-speaker sound system; remote keyless entry, 60/40 split reclining bench seat, 6-way power driver's seat, cast aluminum wheels		
1SG	SLT Image Max Equipment Package 1SG (X-cab LB)	5636	6554
	Manufacturer Discount	(645)	(750)
	Net Price	4991	5804
	Includes Vortec 5700 V-8 engine, 4-speed automatic transmission, Deluxe Front Appearance Package (color-keyed grille, composite headlamps, dual horns), bright trim rings and chrome center caps, chrome front and rear bumpers, air conditioning, Convenience Group (tilt steering wheel and cruise control), full floor carpeting, color-keyed floor mats, power door locks, power windows, power exterior mirrors, leather-wrapped steering wheel, behind seat storage tray, removable underhood lamp, bright bodyside moldings and bright wheel opening moldings (not available on Sportside), plus leather seat trim, AM/FM stereo with auto-reverse cassette player, seek/scan, digital clock, theft lock, automatic tone control, music search feature, and enhanced performance 6-speaker sound system; remote keyless entry, 60/40 split reclining bench seat, 6-way power driver's seat, cast aluminum wheels		
VYU	Snow Plow Prep Package (K1500 Reg Cab)	136	158
	With Z71 (K1500 except Special)	47	55
	Includes heavy-duty power steering cooler, heavy-duty shock absorbers, and heavy-duty front springs (when ordered without Off-road Chassis Package); REQUIRES Engine Oil Cooler when ordered with 3.08 Rear Axle Ratio; NOT AVAILABLE with 6.5-liter Turbodiesel V-8 Engine		
1SL	Special Equipment Package 1SL (Special)	NC	NC
	Includes vehicle with standard equipment		
UL5	Stereo — Delete Credit	(247)	(287)
	REQUIRES SL Equipment Package 1SA or Special Equipment Package 1SL		
UL0	Stereo — Uplevel w/cassette (All except Special)	77	90
	AM/FM stereo with auto-reverse cassette player, seek/scan, digital clock, automatic tone control, music search feature, and enhanced performance 6-speaker sound system; REQUIRES an SLE Equipment Package		
UP0	Stereo — Uplevel w/cassette & CD players (All except Special)	249	290
	AM/FM stereo with auto-reverse cassette and CD players, seek/scan, digital clock, automatic tone control, music search feature for cassette player, and enhanced performance 6-speaker sound system; REQUIRES an SLE or SLT Equipment Package and an Automatic Transmission		
UN0	Stereo — Uplevel w/CD player (All except Special)	163	190
	AM/FM stereo with CD player, seek/scan, digital clock, automatic tone control, and enhanced performance 6-speaker sound system; REQUIRES an SLE or SLT Equipment Package		

GMC SIERRA 1500

CODE	DESCRIPTION	INVOICE	MSRP
UM6	Stereo — w/cassette	126	147
	AM/FM stereo with cassette player, seek/scan, digital clock, and 4 speakers; REQUIRES SL Equipment Package 1SA or Special Equipment Package 1SL		
E24	Third Door (X-cab SB)	361	420
	REQUIRES an SLE or SLT Equipment Package, a Vortec V-8 Engine, 4-speed Automatic Transmission (M30), and Full Floor Carpet; NOT AVAILABLE with Deluxe Two-tone Paint		
XBN/YBN/ZBN	Tires — LT245/75R16C (K1500 except Special)	50	57
	Includes front, rear, and spare on/off road blackwall tires		
XBX/YBX/ZBX	Tires — LT245/75R16C (K1500 except Special)	157	182
	Includes front, rear, and spare on/off road outline white letter tires		
XFN/YFN/ZFN	Tires — P235/75R15 (C1500 except Special)	108	125
	Includes front, rear and spare all-season white lettered tires		
XGB/YGB/ZGB	Tires — P245/75R16 (K1500)	108	125
	Includes front, rear, and spare all-terrain outline white lettered tires; NOT AVAILABLE with Off-road Chassis Package		
XGD/YGD/ZGD	Tires — P265/75R16 (K1500 except Special)	224	260
	Includes front, rear, and spare all-terrain outline white lettered tires; REQUIRES 3.73 Rear Axle Ratio when ordered with any engine other than Vortec 5700 V-8, and Cast Aluminum Wheels		
XGC/YGC/ZGC	Tires — P265/75R16 (K1500 except Special)	115	135
	Includes front, rear, and spare all-terrain blackwall tires; REQUIRES 3.73 Rear Axle Ratio when ordered with any engine other than Vortec 5700 V-8, and Cast Aluminum Wheels		
V76	Tow Hooks (C1500)	33	38
	NOT AVAILABLE with GT Equipment Package 1SK		
Z82	Trailering Equipment Package (All except Special)	175	204
	With FG5 (C1500)	141	164
	With VYU (K1500 Reg Cab)	141	164
	With Z71 (K1500 except Special)	141	164
	Includes trailer hitch and heavy-duty shock absorbers (when ordered without Off-road Chassis Package) or gas shock absorbers (when ordered with Off-road Chassis Package); REQUIRES Engine Oil Cooler; REQUIRES chrome front and rear bumpers on Longbed models; NOT AVAILABLE with 5-speed Manual Transmission, GT Equipment Package 1SK, on models equipped with the Vortec 4300 V-6 Engine and 3.08 Rear Axle Ratio, or with the following combination: Vortec 5000 V-8 Engine with 4-speed Automatic Transmission, 3.42 Rear Axle Ratio, and Off-road Chassis Package		
L30	Vortec 5000 V-8 Engine (All except X-cab LB & Special)	426	495
	INCLUDED in SL Equipment Package 1SJ and GT Equipment Package 1SK		
L31	Vortec 5700 V-8 Engine (Reg Cab except Special)	1028	1195
	NOT AVAILABLE with SL Equipment Package 1SJ or GT Equipment Package 1SK		
L31	Vortec 5700 V-8 Engine (X-cab LB)	602	700
L31	Vortec 5700 V-8 Engine (X-cab SB)	1028	1195

SIERRA 2500 — GMC

SIERRA 2500 *(1997)*

Safety Data

Driver Airbag: *Std. (Light Duty); N/A (Heavy Duty)*
Side Airbag: *Not Available*
4-Wheel ABS: *Standard*
Driver Crash Test Grade: *Excellent (w/airbag); N/A(w/o airbag)*
Passenger Crash Test Grade: *N/A (w/airbag); Excellent (w/o airbag)*

Passenger Airbag: *Std. (Light Duty); N/A (Heavy Duty)*
Meets 1999 Side Impact Standards: *No*
Traction Control: *Not Available*
Insurance Cost: *Low (C2500 Reg Cab); Avg. (C2500 X-cab; K2500)*
Integrated Child Seat(s): *Not Available*

Standard Equipment

SIERRA 2500 LIGHT DUTY REGULAR CAB: Vortec 5000 V-8 engine, 5-speed manual transmission, power speed-sensitive steering, power front disc/rear drum 4-wheel anti-lock brakes, chrome front bumper, dual airbags, light argent grille with dark argent air intakes, intermittent windshield wipers, tinted glass, dual exterior mirrors, cargo box light, 8-wire trailering harness, daytime running lights, vinyl floor covering, cloth headliner, AM/FM stereo with seek/scan, clock and 4 speakers; tachometer, trip odometer, headlights-on warning buzzer, dual auxiliary in-dash power outlets, vinyl front bench seat, simulated leather-wrapped steering wheel, silver painted steel styled steel wheels with black center caps

C2500 EXTENDED CAB SHORTBED (in addition to or instead of LIGHT DUTY REGULAR CAB equipment): Swing-out rear quarter windows, vinyl 60/40 split bench seat with folding backrests and easy-entry passenger seat, vinyl folding rear bench seat

C/K 2500 HEAVY DUTY (in addition to or instead of LIGHT DUTY REGULAR CAB and C2500 EXTENDED CAB SHORTBED equipment): Vortec 5700 V-8 engine, front tow hooks (K2500), LT245/75R16E all-season tires

Base Prices

Code	Description	Invoice	MSRP
C20903	C2500 Regular Cab Light Duty	15303	17489
C20903	C2500 Regular Cab Heavy Duty	16046	18338
C20753	C2500 Club Coupe Shortbed	17592	20105
C20953	C2500 Club Coupe Longbed	17450	19942
K20903	K2500 Regular Cab Heavy Duty	18457	21093
K20753	K2500 Club Coupe Shortbed	20167	23048
K20953	K2500 Club Coupe Longbed	20279	23175
Destination Charge:		625	625

GMC SIERRA 2500

CODE	DESCRIPTION	INVOICE	MSRP

Accessories

Code	Description	Invoice	MSRP
1SB	SL Option Package 1SB	1148	1335
	Manufacturer Discount	(430)	(500)
	Net Price	718	835

Includes air conditioning, AM/FM stereo with cassette player, seek/scan, clock, and 4 speakers; convenience package (tilt steering wheel and cruise control)

1SC	SLE Option Package 1SC	2721	3164
	Manufacturer Discount	(645)	(750)
	Net Price	2076	2414

Includes air conditioning, AM/FM stereo with cassette player, seek/scan, clock, and 4 speakers; convenience package (tilt steering wheel and cruise control), SLE Decor (appearance package including color-keyed grille, composite headlights, and dual horns; chrome wheel trim rings and bright center caps, chrome bumpers, floor carpeting, power windows, power door locks, power exterior mirrors, leather-wrapped steering wheel, behind seat storage tray)

1SH	SLE Option Package 1SH (Heavy Duty)	4071	4734
	Manufacturer Discount	(645)	(750)
	Net Price	3426	3984

Includes Vortec 7400 V-8 Engine, heavy-duty automatic transmission, SLE Decor (appearance package including color-keyed grille, composite headlights, and dual horns; chrome wheel trim rings and bright center caps, chrome bumpers, floor carpeting, power windows, power door locks, power exterior mirrors, leather-wrapped steering wheel, behind seat storage tray, air conditioning, tilt steering wheel, cruise control, AM/FM stereo with cassette player, seek/scan, clock, and 4 speakers

1SD	SLT Option Package 1SD (Reg Cab)	3928	4568
	Manufacturer Discount	(645)	(750)
	Net Price	3283	3818

Includes air conditioning, convenience package (tilt steering wheel and cruise control), SLE Decor (appearance package including color-keyed grille, composite headlights, and dual horns; chrome wheel trim rings and bright center caps, chrome bumpers, floor carpeting, power windows, power door locks, power exterior mirrors, leather-wrapped steering wheel, behind seat storage tray), SLT Decor (leather 60/40 split bench seat with folding backrests and center folding storage armrest, power lumbar adjustment, behind seat storage pockets, AM/FM stereo with auto-reverse cassette player, seek/scan, clock, theft lock, automatic tone control, music search feature, and enhanced 6 speaker performance sound system), and remote keyless entry

1SD	SLT Option Package 1SD (X-cab)	3985	4634
	Manufacturer Discount	(645)	(750)
	Net Price	3340	3884

Includes air conditioning, convenience package (tilt steering wheel and cruise control), SLE Decor (appearance package including color-keyed grille, composite headlights, and dual horns; chrome wheel trim rings and bright center caps, chrome bumpers, floor carpeting, power windows, power door locks, power exterior mirrors, leather-wrapped steering wheel, behind seat storage tray), SLT Decor (leather 60/40 split

SIERRA 2500 — GMC

CODE	DESCRIPTION	INVOICE	MSRP
	bench seat with folding backrests and center folding storage armrest, power lumbar adjustment, behind seat storage pockets, leather rear bench seat, AM/FM stereo with auto-reverse cassette player, seek/scan, clock, theft lock, automatic tone control, music search feature, and enhanced 6 speaker performance sound system)		
1SH	SLT Option Package 1SH (Reg Cab Heavy Duty)	5279	6138
	Manufacturer Discount	(645)	(750)
	Net Price	4634	5388
	Includes Vortec 7400 V-8 Engine, heavy-duty automatic transmission, SLE Decor (appearance package including color-keyed grille, composite headlights, and dual horns; chrome wheel trim rings and bright center caps, chrome bumpers, floor carpeting, power windows, power door locks, power exterior mirrors, leather-wrapped steering wheel, behind seat storage tray, air conditioning, tilt steering wheel, cruise control), SLT Decor (leather 60/40 split bench seat with folding backrests and center folding storage armrest, power lumbar adjustment, behind seat storage pockets, leather rear bench seat, AM/FM stereo with auto-reverse cassette player, seek/scan, clock, theft lock, automatic tone control, music search feature, and enhanced 6 speaker performance sound system)		
1SH	SLT Option Package 1SH (X-cab Heavy Duty)	5335	6204
	Manufacturer Discount	(645)	(750)
	Net Price	4690	5454
	Includes Vortec 7400 V-8 Engine, heavy-duty automatic transmission, SLE Decor (appearance package including color-keyed grille, composite headlights, and dual horns; chrome wheel trim rings and bright center caps, chrome bumpers, floor carpeting, power windows, power door locks, power exterior mirrors, leather-wrapped steering wheel, behind seat storage tray, air conditioning, tilt steering wheel, cruise control), SLT Decor (leather 60/40 split bench seat with folding backrests and center folding storage armrest, power lumbar adjustment, behind seat storage pockets, leather rear bench seat, AM/FM stereo with auto-reverse cassette player, seek/scan, clock, theft lock, automatic tone control, music search feature, and enhanced 6 speaker performance sound system)		
C60	Air Conditioning	692	805
	INCLUDED in Option Packages		
R9Q	Appearance Package R9Q (2WD)	527	613
	Manufacturer Discount	(172)	(200)
	Net Price	355	413
	Includes Appearance Package V22 (color-keyed grille, composite headlights, dual horns), chrome bumpers, bright moldings, chrome trim rings, bright center caps		
R9Q	Appearance Package R9Q (4WD)	501	582
	Manufacturer Discount	(172)	(200)
	Net Price	329	382
	Includes Appearance Package V22 (color-keyed grille, composite headlights, dual horns), chrome bumpers, bright moldings, chrome trim rings, bright center caps		
V22	Appearance Package V22	164	191
	Includes color-keyed grille, composite headlights, and dual horns; INCLUDED in SLE and SLT Option Packages, and in Appearance Package R9Q		

GMC SIERRA 2500

CODE	DESCRIPTION	INVOICE	MSRP
MT1	Automatic Transmission (Heavy Duty)	834	970
	Includes transmission oil cooler		
M30	Automatic Transmission (Light Duty)	834	970
BZY	Bedliner	194	225
B85	Bright Bodyside Moldings (2WD)	92	107
	INCLUDED in SLE and SLT Option Packages, and in Appearance Package R9Q		
B85	Bright Bodyside Moldings (4WD)	65	76
	INCLUDED in SLE and SLT Option Packages, and in Appearance Package R9Q		
VB3	Bumper — Chrome Rear Step with Rub Strip	197	229
	REQUIRES front bumper rub strip; INCLUDED in SLE and SLT Option Packages, and in Appearance Package R9Q		
VG3	Bumper — Front Rub Strip	22	26
	Includes front bumper guards when ordered with 6.5-liter Turbodiesel V-8 Engine; INCLUDED in SLE and SLT Option Packages, and in Appearance Package R9Q		
V43	Bumper — Painted Rear Step	112	130
	NOT AVAILABLE with SLE or SLT Option Packages, or with Appearance Package R9Q		
EF1	Bumper — Rear Delete Credit (Light Duty)	(172)	(200)
	NOT AVAILABLE with Trailering Equipment		
YF5	California Emissions	146	170
Z81	Camper Equipment	116	135
	With L56 (Light Duty)	NC	NC
	With L65 (Heavy Duty)	NC	NC
	Includes stainless steel exterior mirrors, auxiliary battery, and special wiring harness; REQUIRES Engine Oil Cooler if ordered with Vortec 5000 or Vortec 5700 V-8 engines and 3.42 Rear Axle; REQUIRES purchase of an SLE or SLT Option Package		
Z81	Camper Equipment	200	233
	With L56 (Light Duty)	85	99
	With L65 (Heavy Duty)	85	99
	Includes stainless steel exterior mirrors, auxiliary battery, and special wiring harness; REQUIRES Engine Oil Cooler if ordered with Vortec 5000 or Vortec 5700 V-8 engines and 3.42 Rear Axle Ratio; NOT AVAILABLE with SLE or SLT Option		
DF2	Camper Type Exterior Mirrors	46	53
	With 1SC	(39)	(45)
	With 1SD (Reg Cab)	(39)	(45)
	With 1SD (X-cab)	(39)	(45)
	With 1SH (Heavy Duty)	(39)	(45)
	With 1SH (X-cab Heavy Duty)	(39)	(45)
	With 1SH (Reg Cab Heavy Duty)	(39)	(45)
	Stainless-steel; INCLUDED in Camper Equipment		
B30	Carpeting (Reg Cab)	47	55
	Includes rubber floor mats; NOT AVAILABLE with SLE or SLT Option Packages		
B30	Carpeting (X-cab)	75	87
	With YG4 (X-cab)	61	71
	Includes rubber floor mats; NOT AVAILABLE with SLE or SLT Option Packages		
V10	Cold Climate Package	28	33
	Includes engine block heater; INCLUDED with 6.5-liter Turbodiesel V-8 Engine		

SIERRA 2500 — GMC

CODE	DESCRIPTION	INVOICE	MSRP
ZQ3	Convenience Package ZQ3	329	383
	Includes tilt steering wheel and cruise control; INCLUDED in Option Packages		
AJ1	Deep Tinted Glass (Reg Cab)	30	35
	REQUIRES Sliding Rear Window		
AJ1	Deep Tinted Glass (X-cab)	92	107
	With C49 (X-cab)	62	72
DD7	Electrochromic Rear View Mirror	125	145
	Includes 8-point compass; REQUIRES purchase of SLE and SLT Option Package		
NP1	Electronic Shift Transfer Case (4WD)	150	129
	REQUIRES Convenience Package ZQ3 and Automatic Transmission		
L65	Engine — 6.5-liter Turbodiesel V-8 (Heavy Duty)	2460	2860
	Includes dual batteries, hydraulic brakes, heavy-duty radiator, engine oil cooler, additional sound insulation, engine block heater, instrument panel warning lights, fuel filter change indicator; REQUIRES Option Package 1SC and Bucket Seats when ordered on Club Coupe Longbed models		
L56	Engine — 6.5-liter Turbodiesel V-8 (Light Duty)	3062	3560
	Includes dual batteries, hydraulic brakes, heavy-duty radiator, engine oil cooler, additional sound insulation, engine block heater, instrument panel warning lights, fuel filter change indicator		
L31	Engine — Vortec 5700 V-8 (Light Duty)	602	700
L29	Engine — Vortec 7400 V-8 Engine (Heavy Duty)	516	600
KC4	Engine Oil Cooler (Light Duty)	116	135
	REQUIRES 3.42 Rear Axle Ratio; INCLUDED with 3.73 Rear Axle Ratio and 6.5-liter Turbodiesel V-8 Engine		
VK3	Front License Plate Bracket	NC	NC
TP2	Heavy-duty Battery	115	134
	INCLUDED with 6.5-liter Turbodiesel V-8 Engine and Camper Equipment		
F60	Heavy-duty Front Springs (4WD)	54	63
	INCLUDED in Snow Plow Prep Package		
K47	High Capacity Air Cleaner	22	25
	NOT AVAILABLE with 6.5-liter Turbodiesel V-8 Engine		
G80	Locking Differential	217	252
	NOT AVAILABLE with 3.42 Rear Axle Ratio		
NG1	Massachusetts/New York Emissions	NC	NC
ZY2	Paint — Conventional Two-tone	155	180
	REQUIRES purchase of an SLE or SLT Option Package		
ZY4	Paint — Deluxe Two-tone	237	275
	REQUIRES purchase of an SLE or SLT Option Package		
AU3	Power Door Locks	134	156
	INCLUDED in SLE and SLT Option Packages		
AG9	Power Driver's Seat (X-cab)	206	240
	REQUIRES purchase of an SLE Option Package and upgraded seats (AE7 or A95)		
P06	Rally Wheel Trim	52	60
	Includes chrome trim rings and bright center caps; INCLUDED in SLE and SLT Option Packages		

GMC SIERRA 2500

CODE	DESCRIPTION	INVOICE	MSRP
GU6	Rear Axle Ratio — 3.42	NC	NC
	NOT AVAILABLE with Locking Differential		
GT4	Rear Axle Ratio — 3.73 (Heavy Duty)	NC	NC
GT4	Rear Axle Ratio — 3.73 (Light Duty)	116	135
GT5	Rear Axle Ratio — 4.10	NC	NC
YG4	Rear Seat Delete Credit (X-cab)	(374)	(435)
	NOT AVAILABLE with SLE or SLT Option Packages		
C49	Rear Window Defogger (X-cab)	132	154
	REQUIRES purchase of an SLE or SLT Option Package; NOT AVAILABLE with Sliding Rear Window		
AU0	Remote Keyless Entry	120	140
	REQUIRES purchase of an SLE Option Package		
U01	Roof Marker Lights	45	52
	NOT AVAILABLE with California Emissions		
BG9	Rubber Floor Covering (Reg Cab)	(30)	(35)
	REQUIRES purchase of an SLE or SLT Option Package		
BG9	Rubber Floor Covering (X-cab)	(44)	(51)
	REQUIRES purchase of an SLE or SLT Option Package		
AE7	Seats — 60/40 Split Reclining Bench Seat (Reg Cab)	150	174
	REQUIRES purchase of an SLE Option Package		
A95	Seats — Cloth Buckets (High-back Reclining) (Reg Cab)	332	386
	Includes inboard armrests and center console; REQUIRES purchase of SLE Option Package 1SC		
A95	Seats — Cloth Buckets (High-back Reclining) (X-cab)	230	270
	Includes inboard armrests and center console; REQUIRES purchase of SLE Option Package 1SC		
NZZ	Skid Plate Package (4WD)	82	95
	Includes skid plates for transfer case and differential		
A28	Sliding Rear Window	97	113
	NOT AVAILABLE with Rear Window Defogger		
VYU	Snow Plow Prep Package (4WD Reg Cab)	101	118
	Includes heavy-duty front springs and power steering cooler		
UL5	Stereo — Delete Credit	(247)	(287)
	NOT AVAILABLE with Option Packages		
UP0	Stereo — Premium w/cassette & CD players	249	290
	AM/FM stereo with CD and auto reverse cassette player, seek/scan, clock, theft lock, automatic tone control, music search feature, and enhanced performance 6 speaker sound system; REQUIRES purchase of an SLE or SLT Option Package		
UL0	Stereo — Uplevel w/cassette	77	90
	AM/FM stereo with auto reverse cassette player, seek/scan, clock, theft lock, automatic tone control, music search feature, and enhanced performance 6 speaker sound system; REQUIRES purchase of an SLE Option Package		
UN0	Stereo — Uplevel w/CD player	163	190
	AM/FM stereo with auto reverse cassette player, seek/scan, clock, theft lock, automatic tone control, music search feature, and enhanced performance 6 speaker sound system; REQUIRES purchase of an SLE or SLT Option Package		

SIERRA 2500 / 3500 — GMC

CODE	DESCRIPTION	INVOICE	MSRP
UM6	Stereo — w/cassette	126	147
	AM/FM stereo with cassette player, seek/scan, clock, and 4 speakers; INCLUDED in Option Packages		
XHR/YHR/ZHR	Tires — LT225/75R16D (Light Duty)	47	55
	On/off road blackwall tires		
XGK/YGK/ZGK	Tires — LT245/75R16E (Heavy Duty)	48	55
	On/off road blackwall tires		
XGK/YGK/ZGK	Tires — LT245/75R16E (Light Duty)	245	285
	On/off road blackwall tires		
XHH/YHH/ZHH	Tires — LT245/75R16E (Light Duty)	198	230
	All-season blackwall tires		
V76	Tow Hooks — Front (2WD)	33	38
Z82	Trailering Equipment (Heavy Duty)	141	164
	Includes trailer hitch		
Z82	Trailering Equipment (Light Duty)	141	164
	Includes trailer hitch; REQUIRES Automatic Transmission; REQUIRES Transmission Oil Cooler with 3.42 Rear Axle Ratio; REQUIRES Rear Step Bumper		
KNP	Transmission Oil Cooler (Light Duty)	83	96
	REQUIRES M30 Automatic Transmission and Vortec 5700 V-8 Engine		

SIERRA 3500 *(1997)*

Safety Data

Driver Airbag: *Not Available*
Side Airbag: *Not Available*
4-Wheel ABS: *Standard*
Driver Crash Test Grade: *Not Available*
Passenger Crash Test Grade: *Excellent*

Passenger Airbag: *Not Available*
Meets 1999 Side Impact Standards: *No*
Traction Control: *Not Available*
Insurance Cost: *Average*
Integrated Child Seat(s): *Not Available*

Standard Equipment

SIERRA 3500 REGULAR CAB: Vortec 5700 V-8 engine, 5-speed manual transmission, speed-sensitive power steering, power front disc/rear drum 4-wheel anti-lock brakes, light argent grille with dark argent air intakes, chrome front bumper, intermittent windshield wipers, tinted glass, dual exterior mirrors, vinyl floor covering, cloth headliner, AM/FM stereo with seek/scan, clock, and 4 speakers; trip odometer, tachometer, daytime running lights, headlights-on warning buzzer, dual in-dash auxiliary power outlets, passenger's visor vanity mirror, vinyl bench seat, simulated leather-wrapped steering wheel, 8-wire trailering harness, silver painted styled steel wheels with black center caps, LT245/75R16E all-season tires, front tow hooks (4WD)

3500 EXTENDED CAB (in addition to or instead of REGULAR CAB equipment): Roof marker lights, 60/40 split bench seat with easy entry passenger seat, folding rear bench seat, LT225/75R16 all-season tires

3500 CREW CAB (in addition to or instead of REGULAR CAB equipment): Black bumper rub strip, black bodyside moldings with bright insert, front seat headrests, fixed rear bench seat with folding back, steel wheels that haven't been styled, wheel flares (4WD)

GMC SIERRA 3500

CODE	DESCRIPTION	INVOICE	MSRP

Base Prices

Code	Description	Invoice	MSRP
C30903	C3500 Regular Cab	16168	18477
C30953	C3500 Club Coupe Duallie	19166	21903
C30943	C3500 Crew Cab	21684	24781
K30903	K3500 Regular Cab	18793	21477
K30953	K3500 Club Coupe Duallie	21625	24714
K30943	K3500 Crew Cab	21684	24781
	Destination Charge:	625	625

Accessories

Code	Description	Invoice	MSRP
1SB	SL Option Package 1SB (Crew Cab)	692	805
	Includes air conditioning		
1SB	SL Option Package 1SB (Reg Cab/X-cab)	1148	1335
	Manufacturer Discount	(430)	(500)
	Net Price	718	835
	Includes air conditioning, AM/FM stereo with cassette player, seek/scan, clock, and 4 speakers; convenience package (tilt steering wheel and cruise control)		
1SC	SL Option Package 1SC (Crew Cab)	1148	1335
	Includes air conditioning, AM/FM stereo with cassette player, seek/scan, clock, and 4 speakers; convenience package (tilt steering wheel and cruise control)		
1SC	SLE Option Package 1SC (Crew Cab)	3266	3798
	Includes air conditioning, AM/FM stereo with cassette player, seek/scan, clock, and 4 speakers; convenience package (tilt steering wheel and cruise control), SLE Decor (appearance package including color-keyed grille, composite headlights, and dual horn; rally wheel trim, chrome bumpers, floor carpeting, power windows, power door locks, power exterior mirrors, leather-wrapped steering wheel, behind seat storage)		
1SC	SLE Option Package 1SC (Reg Cab/X-cab)	2721	3164
	Manufacturer Discount	(645)	(750)
	Net Price	2076	2414
	Includes air conditioning, AM/FM stereo with cassette player, seek/scan, clock, and 4 speakers; convenience package (tilt steering wheel and cruise control), SLE Decor (appearance package including color-keyed grille, composite headlights, and dual horn; rally wheel trim, chrome bumpers, floor carpeting, power windows, power door locks, power exterior mirrors, leather-wrapped steering wheel, behind seat storage)		
1SD	SLT Option Package 1SD (Crew Cab)	4702	5468
	Includes air conditioning, convenience package (tilt steering wheel and cruise control), SLE Decor (appearance package including color-keyed grille, composite headlights, and dual horn; rally wheel trim, chrome bumpers, floor carpeting, power windows, power door locks, power exterior mirrors, leather-wrapped steering wheel, behind seat storage), and SLT Decor (leather 60/40 split bench seat with headrests, center		

SIERRA 3500 — GMC

CODE	DESCRIPTION	INVOICE	MSRP

storage console, power lumbar support, behind seat storage pockets, AM/FM stereo with auto-reverse cassette, seek/scan, clock, theft lock, automatic tone control, music search feature, and enhanced performance 6 speaker sound system, remote keyless entry, power driver's seat)

1SD — SLT Option Package 1SD (Reg Cab) .... 3928 / 4568
Manufacturer Discount .... (645) / (750)
Net Price .... 3283 / 3818

Includes air conditioning, convenience package (tilt steering wheel and cruise control), SLE Decor (appearance package including color-keyed grille, composite headlights, and dual horn; rally wheel trim, chrome bumpers, floor carpeting, power windows, power door locks, power exterior mirrors, leather-wrapped steering wheel, behind seat storage), and SLT Decor (leather 60/40 split bench seat with headrests, center storage console, power lumbar support, behind seat storage pockets, AM/FM stereo with auto-reverse cassette, seek/scan, clock, theft lock, automatic tone control, music search feature, and enhanced performance 6 speaker sound system, remote keyless entry)

1SD — SLT Option Package 1SD (X-cab) .... 3985 / 4634
Manufacturer Discount .... (645) / (750)
Net Price .... 3340 / 3884

Includes air conditioning, convenience package (tilt steering wheel and cruise control), SLE Decor (appearance package including color-keyed grille, composite headlights, and dual horn; rally wheel trim, chrome bumpers, floor carpeting, power windows, power door locks, power exterior mirrors, leather-wrapped steering wheel, behind seat storage), and SLT Decor (leather 60/40 split bench seat with headrests, center storage console, power lumbar support, behind seat storage pockets, AM/FM stereo with auto-reverse cassette, seek/scan, clock, theft lock, automatic tone control, music search feature, and enhanced performance 6 speaker sound system, remote keyless entry, leather rear bench seat, power driver's seat)

C60 — Air Conditioning .... 692 / 805
INCLUDED in Option Packages

R9Q — Appearance Package R9Q (2WD Reg Cab) .... 527 / 613

Includes appearance package V22 (color-keyed grille, composite headlights, dual horns), chrome bumpers, bodyside moldings with bright insert (except Duallie), rally wheels trim (chrome trim rings and bright center caps); INCLUDED in SLE and SLT Option Packages

R9Q — Appearance Package R9Q (4WD Reg Cab) .... 500 / 582
Manufacturer Discount .... (172) / (200)
Net Price .... 328 / 382

Includes appearance package V22 (color-keyed grille, composite headlights, dual horns), chrome bumpers, bodyside moldings with bright insert (except Duallie), rally wheels trim (chrome trim rings and bright center caps); INCLUDED in SLE and SLT Option Packages

V22 — Appearance Package V22 .... 164 / 191

Includes color-keyed grille, composite headlights, and dual horn

GMC SIERRA 3500

CODE	DESCRIPTION	INVOICE	MSRP
MT1	Automatic Transmission	834	970
BZY	Bedliner	194	225
B85	Bodyside Moldings (2WD Reg Cab)	92	107
	INCLUDED in SLE and SLT Option Packages, and in Appearance Package R9Q; NOT AVAILABLE with Dual Rear Wheels		
B85	Bodyside Moldings (4WD Reg Cab)	65	76
	INCLUDED in SLE and SLT Option Packages, and in Appearance Package R9Q; NOT AVAILABLE with Dual Rear Wheels		
VB3	Bumper — Chrome Rear Step with Rub Strip	197	229
	REQUIRES front bumper rub strip; INCLUDED in SLE and SLT Option Package, and in Appearance Package R9Q		
VG3	Bumper — Front Rub Strip (Reg Cab/X-cab)	22	26
	Includes front bumper guards when ordered with 6.5-liter Turbodiesel V-8 Engine; INCLUDED in SLE and SLT Option Packages, and in Appearance Package R9Q		
V43	Bumper — Painted Rear Step	112	130
	NOT AVAILABLE with SLE or SLT Option Packages, or with Appearance Package R9Q		
EF1	Bumper — Rear Delete Credit	(172)	(200)
	NOT AVAILABLE with SLE or SLT Option Packages, or with Trailering Equipment		
YF5	California Emissions	145	170
Z81	Camper Equipment	116	135
	With L65	NC	NC
	Includes special wiring harness, stainless-steel exterior mirrors, and heavy-duty battery; REQUIRES 9,600 lb. GVWR on Crew Cab; REQUIRES purchase of an SLE or SLT Option Package		
Z81	Camper Equipment	200	233
	With L65	85	99
	Includes special wiring harness, stainless-steel exterior mirrors, and heavy-duty battery; REQUIRES 9,600 lb. GVWR on Crew Cab; NOT AVAILABLE with SLE or SLT Option Packages		
DF2	Camper Type Exterior Mirrors	46	53
	With 1SC (Reg Cab/X-cab)	(39)	(45)
	With 1SC (Crew Cab)	(39)	(45)
	With 1SD (Crew Cab)	(39)	(45)
	With 1SD (X-cab)	(39)	(45)
	With 1SD (Reg Cab)	(39)	(45)
	Stainless-steel; INCLUDED with Camper Equipment		
B30	Carpeted Floor Covering (Reg Cab)	47	55
	Includes rubber floor mats; INCLUDED in SLE and SLT Option Packages		
B30	Carpeted Floor Covering (X-cab)	75	87
	Includes rubber floor mats; INCLUDED in SLE and SLT Option Packages		
V10	Cold Climate Package	28	33
	Includes engine block heater; INCLUDED with 6.5-liter Turbodiesel V-8 Engine		
ZQ3	Convenience Package ZQ3	329	383
	Includes tilt steering wheel and cruise control; NOT AVAILABLE with option packages except SL Option Package 1SB on Crew Cab		
AJ1	Deep Tinted Glass (Crew Cab)	183	215
	With C49 (X-cab/Crew Cab)	155	180

SIERRA 3500 — GMC

CODE	DESCRIPTION	INVOICE	MSRP
AJ1	Deep Tinted Glass (Reg Cab)	30	35
	REQUIRES Sliding Rear Window		
AJ1	Deep Tinted Glass (X-cab)	92	107
	With C49 (X-cab/Crew Cab)	62	72
R05	Dual Rear Wheels (Crew Cab)	737	857
	Includes roof marker lights; REQUIRES 10,000 lb. GVWR		
R05	Dual Rear Wheels (Reg Cab)	821	955
	Includes roof marker lights; REQUIRES 10,000 lb. GVWR		
DD7	Electrochromic Rearview Mirror (Reg Cab/X-cab)	125	145
	Includes 8-point compass; REQUIRES purchase of an SLE Option Package		
L65	Engine — 6.5-liter Turbodiesel	2460	2860
	Includes dual batteries, hydraulic brakes, heavy-duty radiator, engine oil cooler, additional sound insulation, engine block heater, instrument panel warning lights; REQUIRES purchase of an SLE Option Package and Bucket Seats when ordered on C3500 Extended Cab		
L29	Engine — Vortec 7400 V-8	516	600
VK3	Front License Plate Bracket	NC	NC
V76	Front Tow Hooks (2WD)	33	38
C7A	GVWR — 10,000 lb. (Reg Cab/Crew Cab)	NC	NC
	REQUIRES Dual Rear Wheels; NOT AVAILABLE with Camper Equipment		
C6Y	GVWR — 9,600 lb. (2WD Crew Cab)	NC	NC
	REQUIRES Camper Equipment; NOT AVAILABLE with Dual Rear Wheels		
TP2	Heavy-duty Battery	115	134
	INCLUDED with 6.5-liter Turbodiesel V-8 Engine and Camper Equipment		
F60	Heavy-duty Front Springs (4WD)	54	63
	INCLUDED in Snow Plow Prep Package		
K47	High Capacity Air Cleaner	22	25
	NOT AVAILABLE with 6.5-liter Turbodiesel V-8 Engine		
G80	Locking Differential	217	252
NG1	Massachusetts/New York Emissions	NC	NC
AU3	Operating Convenience Package (Crew Cab)	192	223
	Includes power door locks		
AU3	Operating Convenience Package (Reg Cab/X-cab)	134	156
	Includes power door locks		
ZY2	Paint — Conventional Two-tone (Reg Cab/X-cab)	155	180
ZY4	Paint — Deluxe Two-tone (Reg Cab/X-cab)	237	275
	REQUIRES purchase of an SLE Option Package		
AG9	Power Driver's Seat (X-cab/Crew Cab)	206	240
	REQUIRES purchase of an SLE Option Package		
P06	Rally Wheel Trim (Reg Cab/X-cab)	52	60
	Includes chrome trim rings and bright center caps; INCLUDED with SLE and SLT Option Packages, and in Appearance Package R9Q		
GT5	Rear Axle Ratio — 4.10	NC	NC
HC4	Rear Axle Ratio — 4.56	NC	NC
	REQUIRES Locking Differential		

GMC — SIERRA 3500

CODE	DESCRIPTION	INVOICE	MSRP
C49	Rear Window Defogger (X-cab/Crew Cab)	132	154
	REQUIRES purchase of an SLE or SLT Option Package; NOT AVAILABLE with Sliding Rear Window		
AU0	Remote Keyless Entry	120	140
	REQUIRES purchase of an SLE Option Package and Operating Convenience Package		
U01	Roof Marker Lights (Reg Cab/Crew Cab)	45	52
	INCLUDED with Dual Rear Wheels; NOT AVAILABLE with California Emissions		
BG9	Rubber Floor Covering (Reg Cab)	(30)	(35)
BG9	Rubber Floor Covering (X-cab)	(44)	(51)
AE7	Seats — 60/40 Split Reclining Bench (Crew Cab)	86	100
	REQUIRES purchase of an SLE Option Package		
AE7	Seats — 60/40 Split Reclining Bench (Reg Cab)	150	174
	REQUIRES purchase of an SLE Option Package		
A95	Seats — Bucket Seats (High-back Reclining) (Crew Cab)	335	390
	Includes power lumbar support, floor storage console, and inboard armrests; REQUIRES purchase of an SLE or SLT Option Package		
A95	Seats — Bucket Seats (High-back Reclining) (Reg Cab)	332	386
	Includes power lumbar support, floor storage console, and inboard armrests; REQUIRES purchase of an SLE Option Package		
A95	Seats — Bucket Seats (High-back Reclining) (X-cab)	230	270
	Includes power lumbar support, floor storage console, and inboard armrests; REQUIRES purchase of an SLE or SLT Option Package; NOTE: This is a required option on Club Coupes ordered with the 6.5-liter Turbodiesel V-8 Engine		
YG4	Seats — Rear Seat Delete Credit (X-cab)	(374)	(435)
	NOT AVAILABLE with SLE or SLT Option Packages		
NZZ	Skid Plate Package (4WD)	82	95
	Includes skid plates for transfer case and differential		
A28	Sliding Rear Window	97	113
	NOT AVAILABLE with Rear Window Defogger		
VYU	Snow Plow Prep Package (4WD Reg Cab)	101	118
	Includes heavy-duty front springs and power steering cooler		
UL5	Stereo — Delete Credit	(247)	(287)
	NOT AVAILABLE with Option Packages except SL Option Package 1SB on Crew Cab		
UP0	Stereo — Premium w/cassette & CD players	249	290
	AM/FM stereo with CD player and auto-reverse cassette player, seek/scan, clock, theft lock, automatic tone control, music search feature, and enhanced performance 6 speaker sound system; REQUIRES purchase of an SLE or SLT Option Package and Automatic Transmission		
UL0	Stereo — Uplevel w/cassette	77	90
	AM/FM stereo with auto-reverse cassette player, seek/scan, clock, theft lock, automatic tone control, music search feature, and enhanced performance 6 speaker sound system; REQUIRES purchase of an SLE Option Package		
UN0	Stereo — Uplevel w/CD player	163	190
	AM/FM stereo with CD player, seek/scan, clock, theft lock, automatic tone control, and enhanced performance 6 speaker sound system; REQUIRES purchase of an SLE or SLT Option Package		

SIERRA 3500 — GMC

CODE	DESCRIPTION	INVOICE	MSRP
UM6	Stereo — w/cassette (Reg Cab/X-cab)	126	147
	AM/FM stereo with cassette player, seek/scan, clock, and 4 speakers; NOT AVAILABLE with option packages except SL Option Package 1SB for Crew Cab		
XYK/YYK/ZYK	Tires — LT215/85R16D (2WD X-cab)	456	531
	Blackwall highway tires; REQUIRES Dual Rear Wheels		
XYL/YYL/ZYL	Tires — LT215/85R16D (4WD Reg Cab)	874	1016
	On/off road blackwall tires; REQUIRES Dual Rear Wheels and HD Front Springs		
XYL/YYL/ZYL	Tires — LT215/85R16D (4WD X-cab)	596	693
	On/off road blackwall tires; REQUIRES Dual Rear Wheels and HD Front Springs		
XYK/YYK/ZYK	Tires — LT215/85R16D (4WD X-cab)	427	497
	Blackwall highway tires; REQUIRES Dual Rear Wheels		
XYK/YYK/ZYK	Tires — LT215/85R16D (Crew Cab)	707	820
	Blackwall highway tires; REQUIRES Dual Rear Wheels		
XYL/YYL/ZYL	Tires — LT215/85R16D (Crew Cab)	876	1016
	On/off road blackwall tires; REQUIRES Dual Rear Wheels and HD Front Springs		
XYK/YYK/ZYK	Tires — LT215/85R16D (Reg Cab)	705	820
	Blackwall highway tires; REQUIRES Dual Rear Wheels		
XHP/YHP/ZHP	Tires — LT225/75R16D (2WD X-cab)	29	34
	All-season blackwall; REQUIRES Dual Rear Wheels		
XHR/YHR/ZHR	Tires — LT225/75R16D (4WD Crew Cab)	344	400
	On/off road blackwall tires; REQUIRES Dual Rear Wheels		
XHP/YHP/ZHP	Tires — LT225/75R16D (Crew Cab)	278	323
	All-season blackwall tires; REQUIRES Dual Rear Wheels		
XHR/YHR/ZHR	Tires — LT225/75R16D (Reg Cab)	344	400
	On/off road blackwall tires; REQUIRES Dual Rear Wheels		
XHP/YHP/ZHP	Tires — LT225/75R16D (Reg Cab)	278	323
	All-season blackwall tires; REQUIRES Dual Rear Wheels		
XHR/YHR/ZHR	Tires — LT225/75R16D (X-cab)	66	77
	On/off road blackwall tires; REQUIRES Dual Rear Wheels		
XGK/YGK/ZGK	Tires — LT245/75R16E (4WD Reg Cab)	48	55
	On/off road blackwall tires; NOT AVAILABLE with Dual Rear Wheels		
Z82	Trailering Equipment	141	164
	Includes trailer hitch and heavy-duty flashers; REQUIRES rear step bumper		

CALL NATIONWIDE 1-800-521-7257
FOR A WRITTEN QUOTATION
AS LOW AS $50 OVER INVOICE

See page 15 for details.

GMC SONOMA

SONOMA (1997)

1997 GMC Sonoma Sport Truck

What's New for GMC Sonoma in 1997 — Nothing much. Changes are limited to availability of the Sport Suspension on extended cab models, engine and transmission improvements, lighter-weight plug-in half shafts for 4WD Sonomas, and console-mounted shifter for trucks equipped with a center console and bucket seats. New colors arrive, and the remote keyless entry key fob is redesigned.

Sonoma — Review

Compact trucks are hot sellers, and GMC's entry into that market delivers hard-to-beat value—even if it doesn't stand at the top of its class in every way. A driver airbag with knee bolster and daytime running lights are standard. All Sonomas are equipped with 4-wheel anti-lock braking, and a handy side access panel is optional on the extended cab.

Sonomas can be fitted to suit just about any requirement, from strict utility to sporty style and performance. Choose from three wheelbases, two cab types, a regular-size or long cargo bed in Fleetside or Sportside configuration, and two- or four-wheel drive. Whew! You still have to consider three trim levels, five suspension systems, three engines (a four or two V-6 choices), and manual or automatic shift.

GMC changes little for 1997. Extended cab models can be equipped with the Sport Suspension for the first time, and powertrains have been improved for better efficiency. Order bucket seats and a center console, and you'll get a floor-mounted shifter rather than one sticking out of the steering column. Remote keyless entry key fobs are redesigned, and Fairway Green and Smoky Caramel replace Radar Purple and Bright Teal on the color chart. Plug-in half-shafts on 4WD models are lighter-weight and easier to service.

With the high-output, 180-horsepower Vortec 4300 V-6 on tap, and the Sport Suspension package, the Sonoma performs as energetically as high-priced sports cars did a decade or so ago. By any definition, that's progress. The Sportside box and sharp 5-spoke alloys nicely complement the top powertrain and suspension, turning the Sonoma into a true factory sport

SONOMA — GMC

truck. For off-roading duties, GMC offers the Highrider, riding three-ply all-terrain tires and sporting a reinforced frame (four inches wider, two inches taller) and toughened suspension. Either Sonoma outperforms the Ranger on or off the pavement, but when it comes to interior fittings, only the Nissan Truck is more archaic.

Inside, Sonomas and Chevrolet S-Series pickups are virtually identical, with a roomy cab marred by an aesthetic disaster of a dashboard, which looks and feels as though it were lifted from some defunct Buick project, and uncomfortable bucket seats. A passenger airbag is unavailable. On extended cab trucks, an optional left side access panel makes loading passengers or cargo into the rear of the cab much easier, but takes the place of one of the fold-out jump seats in the rear.

Ford's Ranger, Dodge's Dakota, and Toyota's Tacoma come across as more refined, and their sticker prices reflect this impression. In compact-truck value per dollar, though, GMC just might deliver all the goods you're seeking.

Safety Data

Driver Airbag: *Standard*
Side Airbag: *Not Available*
4-Wheel ABS: *Standard*
Driver Crash Test Grade: *Average*
Passenger Crash Test Grade: *Poor*

Passenger Airbag: *Not Available*
Meets 1999 Side Impact Standards: *No*
Traction Control: *Not Available*
Insurance Cost: *Average*
Integrated Child Seat(s): *Not Available*

Standard Equipment

SONOMA SL 2WD: 2.2-liter inline 4-cylinder engine, 5-speed manual transmission, power front disc/rear drum 4-wheel anti-lock brakes, variable power recirculating ball steering, front stabilizer bar, 15"x 7" steel wheels, P205/75R15 tires all-season tires, brake/transmission shift interlock system, daytime running lights, driver airbag, AM/FM stereo with seek/scan and clock, trip odometer, intermittent windshield wipers, tinted glass, vinyl bench seat, side-door guard beams (do not meet 1999 truck side-impact standards), 5-wire trailer harness

SL 4WD (in addition to or instead of SL 2WD equipment): 4.3-liter V-6 engine, front tow hooks, P235/70R15 all-season tires

SLS 2WD/4WD (in addition to or instead of SL 2WD/4WD equipment): Body-color grille, body-color bumpers, body stripe, wheel trim rings and center cap, composite headlights, dual illuminated visor vanity mirrors, sunvisor extensions, elastic visor straps, illuminated entry, map lights, auxiliary dash-mounted power outlets, 60/40 cloth reclining split bench seat, center storage armrest, rear jump seats (extended cab), cloth and carpet door trim, floor carpeting, black vinyl floor mats

Base Prices

CODE	DESCRIPTION	INVOICE	MSRP
S10603	2WD SL Reg. Cab Shortbed	10931	11567
S10803	2WD SL Reg. Cab Longbed	11243	11867
S10603	2WD SLS Reg. Cab Shortbed	11506	12714
S10803	2WD SLS Reg. Cab Longbed	11778	13014
S10653	2WD SLS Club Coupe	13226	14614
T10603	4WD SL Reg. Cab Shortbed	15467	16367
T10803	4WD SL Reg. Cab Longbed	15781	16699

GMC SONOMA

CODE	DESCRIPTION	INVOICE	MSRP
T10603	4WD SLS Reg. Cab Shortbed	15850	17514
T10803	4WD SLS Reg. Cab Longbed	16237	17941
T10653	4WD SLS Club Coupe	17570	19414
Destination Charge:		510	510

Accessories

CODE	DESCRIPTION	INVOICE	MSRP
C60	Air Conditioning	692	805
	INCLUDED in Option Packages 1SD, 1SP, 1SQ, 1SR, 1ST, 1SU, 1SW, 1SX, and 1SY		
ANL	Air Dam with Fog Lights (SLS 2WD)	99	115
	INCLUDED in Option Packages 1SS, 1ST, 1SX, and 1SY		
N60	Aluminum Wheels (SL 2WD)	292	340
	15"x 7" size		
N90	Aluminum Wheels (SL 4WD)	292	340
	15"x 7" size		
N60	Aluminum Wheels (SLS 2WD)	213	248
	15"x 7" size; INCLUDED in SLE Comfort Decor and Option Packages 1SM, 1SN, 1SP, 1SQ, and 1SU; NOT AVAILABLE with Sport Suspension Package		
N90	Aluminum Wheels (SLS 4WD)	241	280
	15"x 7" size; INCLUDED in SLE Comfort Decor and Option Packages 1SR and 1SW		
YF5	California Emissions	146	170
V10	Cold Climate Package	77	89
	Includes heavy-duty battery and engine block heater		
ZQ3	Convenience Package ZQ3	340	395
	Includes tilt steering wheel and cruise control		
AJ1	Deep Tinted Glass (Reg Cab)	61	71
	With A28	31	36
AJ1	Deep Tinted Glass (X-cab)	92	107
	With A28	62	72
NP1	Electronic Shift Transfer Case (SLS 4WD)	106	123
LF6	Engine — Vortec 4300 V-6 (2WD)	851	990
	Includes transmission oil cooler with automatic; REQUIRES M50 or M30 Transmission; INCLUDED in Option Packages 1SS and 1SX		
L35	Engine — Vortec 4300 V-6 (High Output) (4WD)	223	259
	Includes transmission oil cooler with automatic		
L35	Engine — Vortec 4300 V-6 (High-Output) (2WD)	1074	1249
	Includes transmission oil cooler with automatic; REQUIRES M50 or M30 Transmission		
B30	Floor Carpeting (SL)	34	40
C5T	GVWR — 4,200 lb. (2WD Reg Cab SB)	NC	NC
	REQUIRES Smooth Ride Suspension Package or Sport Suspension Package		
C3A	GVWR — 4,400 lb. (2WD X-cab)	NC	NC
	REQUIRES Convenience Package ZQ3 or Sport Suspension Package and a V-6 engine		
C5D	GVWR — 4,600 lb. (2WD)	NC	NC
	REQUIRES Heavy-duty Suspension Package; NOT AVAILABLE on Longbed models with V-6 engine		

SONOMA — GMC

CODE	DESCRIPTION	INVOICE	MSRP
C5X	GVWR — 4,650 lb. (4WD Reg Cab SB)	NC	NC
	REQUIRES Convenience Package ZQ3 or Highrider Suspension Package		
C5X	GVWR — 4,650 lb. (4WD X-cab)	NC	NC
	REQUIRES Convenience Package ZQ3 or Highrider Suspension Package		
C5A	GVWR — 4,900 lb. (2WD Reg Cab LB)	NC	NC
	REQUIRES Heavy-duty Suspension Package and a V-6 engine		
C5A	GVWR — 4,900 lb. (4WD X-cab)	NC	NC
	REQUIRES Highrider Suspension Package		
C6F	GVWR — 5,150 lb. (4WD)	NC	NC
	REQUIRES Heavy-duty Suspension Package or Off-road Suspension Package		
UA1	Heavy-duty Battery	48	56
	INCLUDED in Cold Climate Package		
NP5	Leather Wrapped Steering Wheel (SLS)	46	54
G80	Locking Rear Differential	217	252
NG1	Massachusetts/New York Emissions	146	170
ZQ6	Operating Convenience Package	460	535
	Includes power door locks, power windows, power exterior mirrors		
1SB	Option Package 1SB (SL Reg Cab)	(242)	(281)
	This package deletes the stereo and rear bumper from the base truck		
1SD	Option Package 1SD (Regional) (SLS)	692	805
	Manufacturer Discount	(129)	(150)
	Net Price	563	655
	Includes air conditioning; NOTE: This package is only available in AL, AK, CA, DC, FL, GA, HA, LA, MD, MS, NC, OK, SC, TN, TX, VA, WV and parts of DE, IN, KS, KY, MO, NM, and Ohio.		
1SM	Option Package 1SM (SLS 2WD Reg Cab)	213	248
	Manufacturer Discount	(213)	(248)
	Net Price	NC	NC
	Includes aluminum wheels and powertrain bonus discount; NOT AVAILABLE with V-6 Engine		
1SN	Option Package 1SN (X-cab)	318	370
	Manufacturer Discount	(318)	(370)
	Net Price	NC	NC
	Includes aluminum wheels, AM/FM stereo with cassette, seek/scan, 4 speakers, and clock		
1SP	Option Package 1SP (Regional) (SLS 2WD Reg Cab)	906	1053
	Manufacturer Discount	(342)	(398)
	Net Price	564	655
	Includes air conditioning, aluminum wheels, and powertrain bonus discount; NOT AVAILABLE with V-6 Engine; NOTE: This package is only available in AL, AK, CA, DC, FL, GA, HA, LA, MD, MS, NC, OK, SC, TN, TX, VA, WV and parts of DE, IN, KS, KY, MO, NM, and Ohio.		

GMC SONOMA

CODE	DESCRIPTION	INVOICE	MSRP
1SQ	Option Package 1SQ (2WD X-cab)	3122	3630
	Manufacturer Discount	(553)	(643)
	Net Price	2569	2987

Includes aluminum wheels, AM/FM stereo with cassette, seek/scan, 4 speakers, and clock; LF6 Vortec 4300 V-6 Engine, automatic transmission, air conditioning, and convenience package (tilt steering wheel and cruise control)

1SR	Option Package 1SR (4WD X-cab)	1585	1843
	Manufacturer Discount	(523)	(643)
	Net Price	1062	1200

Includes aluminum wheels, AM/FM stereo with cassette, seek/scan, 4 speakers, and clock; automatic transmission, air conditioning, cloth bucket seats with driver's lumbar support, and convenience package (tilt steering wheel and cruise control)

1SS	Option Package 1SS (SLS 2WD Reg Cab SB)	1867	2171
	Manufacturer Discount	(306)	(356)
	Net Price	1561	1815

Includes LF6 Vortec 4300 V-6 Engine, Sport Suspension Package (shortened coil springs, heavy-duty stabilizer bars, bilstein front and rear shocks, urethane jounce bumpers, 16'x 8" aluminum wheels, P235/55R16 all-season tires), AM/FM stereo with cassette, seek/scan, 4 speakers, and clock; cloth bucket seats with driver's lumbar support, and air dam with fog lights

1ST	Option Package 1ST (2WD X-cab)	2899	3371
	Manufacturer Discount	(646)	(751)
	Net Price	2253	2620

Includes AM/FM stereo with cassette, seek/scan, 4 speakers, and clock; LF6 4300 Vortec V-6 Engine, air conditioning, cloth bucket seats with driver's lumbar support, convenience package (tilt steering wheel and cruise control), Sport Suspension Package (shortened coil springs, heavy-duty stabilizer bars, Bilstein front and rear shocks, urethane jounce bumpers, 16'x 8" aluminum wheels, P235/55R16 all-season tires) and air dam with fog lights; NOT AVAILABLE with SLE Comfort Decor

1SU	Option Package 1SU (Regional) (2WD X-cab)	1011	1175
	Manufacturer Discount	(447)	(520)
	Net Price	564	655

Includes air conditioning, AM/FM stereo with cassette, seek/scan, 4 speakers, and clock; and aluminum wheels; NOTE: This package is only available in AL, AK, CA, DC, FL, GA, HA, LA, MD, MS, NC, OK, SC, TN, TX, VA, WV and parts of DE, IN, KS, KY, MO, NM, and Ohio.

1SW	Option Package 1SW (Regional) (4WD X-cab)	1585	1843
	Manufacturer Discount	(682)	(793)
	Net Price	903	1050

Includes air conditioning, AM/FM stereo with cassette, seek/scan, 4 speakers, and clock; aluminum wheels, convenience package (tilt steering wheel and cruise control), and cloth bucket seats with driver's manual lumbar adjustment; NOTE: This package is only available in AL, AK, CA, DC, FL, GA, HA, LA, MD, MS, NC, OK, SC, TN, TX, VA, WV and parts of DE, IN, KS, KY, MO, NM, and Ohio

SONOMA — GMC

CODE	DESCRIPTION	INVOICE	MSRP
1SX	Option Package 1SX (Regional) (SLS 2WD Reg Cab SB)	2559	2976
	Manufacturer Discount	(435)	(506)
	Net Price	2124	2470
	Includes air conditioning, LF6 Vortec 4300 V-6 Engine, Sport Suspension Package (shortened coil springs, heavy-duty stabilizer bars, bilstein front and rear shocks, urethane jounce bumpers, 16'x 8" aluminum wheels, P235/55R16 all-season tires), AM/FM stereo with cassette, seek/scan, 4 speakers, and clock; cloth bucket seats with driver's lumbar support, and air dam with fog lights; NOTE: This package is only available in AL, AK, CA, DC, FL, GA, HA, LA, MD, MS, NC, OK, SC, TN, TX, VA, WV and parts of DE, IN, KS, KY, MO, NM, and Ohio.		
1SY	Option Package 1SY (Regional) (2WD X-cab)	2899	3371
	Manufacturer Discount	(775)	(901)
	Net Price	2124	2470
	Includes air conditioning, AM/FM stereo with cassette, seek/scan, 4 speakers, and clock; convenience package (tilt steering wheel and cruise control), cloth bucket seats with driver's manual lumbar adjustment, LF6 Vortec 4300 V-6 Engine, Sport Suspension Package (shortened coil springs, heavy-duty stabilizer bars, Bilstein front and rear shocks, urethane jounce bumpers, 16'x 8" aluminum wheels, P235/55R16 all-season tires) and air dam with fog lights; NOT AVAILABLE with SLE Comfort Decor; NOTE: This package is only available in AL, AK, CA, DC, FL, GA, HA, LA, MD, MS, NC, OK, SC, TN, TX, VA, WV and parts of DE, IN, KS, KY, MO, NM, and Ohio		
ZY3	Paint — Special Two-tone (SLS)	255	297
	NOT AVAILABLE with Sportside Cargo Box		
LN2	Powertrain Bonus Discount (2WD Reg Cab)	(215)	(250)
	Credit issued to buyers of 2WD Regular Cab Sonomas equipped with the standard 2.2-liter 4-cylinder engine; INCLUDED in Option Packages 1SM and 1SP		
GU4	Rear Axle Ratio — 3.08	NC	NC
	REQUIRES Locking Rear Differential when ordered on 2WD trucks or when ordered with L35 Vortec 4300 V-6 High Output Engine and a manual transmission; REQUIRES Smooth Ride Suspenson Package when ordered on 4WD trucks with an Automatic Transmission; NOT AVAILABLE on trucks equipped with the Locking Rear Differential and an Automatic Transmission. Got all that?		
GU6	Rear Axle Ratio — 3.42	NC	NC
	REQUIRES Automatic Transmission on 2WD trucks; REQUIRES Locking Rear Differential on 4WD trucks equipped with the SLE Comfort Decor, Vortec 4300 V-6 High Output Engine, and a manual transmission		
GT4	Rear Axle Ratio — 3.73	NC	NC
	REQUIRES Locking Rear Differential on 2WD trucks, and 4WD trucks equipped with 5,150 lb. GVWR		
GT5	Rear Axle Ratio — 4.10 (2WD)	NC	NC
	NOT AVAILABLE with Locking Rear Differential		
VF7	Rear Bumper Delete (SL)	NC	NC
	Includes rear valance panel; INCLUDED in Option Package 1SB		

GMC SONOMA

CODE	DESCRIPTION	INVOICE	MSRP
A28	Rear Sliding Window	97	113
AU0	Remote Keyless Entry (SLS)	120	140
	REQUIRES Operating Convenience Package		
AV5	Seats — Cloth Buckets (SLS 2WD)	83	96
	With M30	207	241
	With M50 (2WD)	207	241
	Reclining seats with manual driver's lumbar support; Includes floor console when ordered with M50 Manual Transmission or M30 Automatic Transmission; INCLUDED in Option Packages 1SR, 1SS, 1ST, 1SW, 1SX, and 1SY		
AV5	Seats — Cloth Buckets (SLS 4WD)	207	241
	Reclining seats with manual driver's lumbar support and floor console		
ZM5	Skid Plate Package (4WD)	108	126
	Includes skid plates for transfer case, front differential, fuel tank, and steering linkage; INCLUDED in Highrider Suspension Package		
YC5	SLE Comfort Decor (SLS 2WD)	707	822
	Includes gray painted bumpers with gray rub strips and bright inserts, gray grille with bright trim, gray bodyside moldings, conventional two-tone paint, and aluminum wheels; REQUIRES purchase of an Option Package; NOT AVAILABLE with Option Packages 1SX, 1ST, or 1SY		
E62	Sportside Cargo Box (SLS Reg Cab SB)	407	450
E62	Sportside Cargo Box (X-cab)	407	450
UL5	Stereo — Delete Credit (SL)	(194)	(226)
	INCLUDED in Option Package 1SB		
UX1	Stereo — Uplevel w/cassette	243	282
	AM/FM stereo with cassette player, seek/scan, 4 speakers, and clock		
UM6	Stereo — w/cassette	105	122
	AM/FM stereo with cassette player, seek/scan, 4 speakers, and clock; INCLUDED in Option Packages 1SN, 1SQ, 1SR, 1SS, 1ST, 1SU, 1SW, 1SX and 1SY		
U1C	Stereo — w/CD player (SLS)	349	406
	AM/FM stereo with CD player, seek/scan, 4 speakers, and clock		
Z85	Suspension Package — Heavy-duty (2WD Reg Cab SB)	55	64
	Includes heavy-duty shocks and springs; REQUIRES 4,600 lb. GVWR		
Z85	Suspension Package — Heavy-duty (2WD X-cab)	NC	NC
	Includes heavy-duty shocks and springs; REQUIRES 4,600 lb. GVWR		
Z85	Suspension Package — Heavy-duty (4WD except Reg Cab LB)	220	256
	Includes heavy-duty shocks and springs; REQUIRES 5,150 lb. GVWR and P235/75R15 tires or P235/70R15 tires (QEB or QBF)		
Z85	Suspension Package — Heavy-duty (Reg Cab LB)	NC	NC
	Includes heavy duty shocks and springs; REQUIRES 5,150 lb. GVWR and P235/75R15 tires or P235/70R15 tires (QEB or QBF) on 4WD models; REQUIRES 4,900 lb. GVWR with 2WD 4-cylinder models		
ZR2	Suspension Package — Highrider (4WD X-cab)	1484	1725
	Includes wheel flares, 46mm Bilstein shocks, Skid Plate Package (transfer case, front differential, fuel tank, steering linkage), enhanced chassis, heavy-duty springs, 31x10.5R15 on-off road tires (QJJ); REQUIRES 4,900 lb. GVWR, Cloth Bucket Seats, and 3.73 Rear Axle Ratio; NOT AVAILABLE with Sportside Cargo Box		

SONOMA

CODE	DESCRIPTION	INVOICE	MSRP
ZR2	Suspension Package — Highrider (SLS 4WD Reg Cab SB)	1484	1725
	Includes wheel flares, 46mm Bilstein shocks, Skid Plate Package (transfer case, front differential, fuel tank, steering linkage), enhanced chassis, heavy-duty springs, 31x10.5R15 on-off road tires (QJJ); REQUIRES 4,650 lb. GVWR, Cloth Bucket Seats, and 3.73 Rear Axle Ratio; NOT AVAILABLE with Sportside Cargo Box		
ZM6	Suspension Package — Off-road (4WD Reg Cab SB)	513	596
	Includes Bilstein gas shocks, larger torsion bar, jounce bumpers, stabilizer bar, heavy-duty springs, and P235/75R15 on-off road outline white-lettered tires (QEB); REQUIRES 5,150 lb. GVWR		
ZM6	Suspension Package — Off-road (4WD X-cab)	513	596
	Includes Bilstein gas shocks, larger torsion bar, jounce bumpers, stabilizer bar, heavy-duty springs, and P235/75R15 on-off road outline white-lettered tires (QEB); REQUIRES 5,150 lb. GVWR		
Z83	Suspension Package — Smooth Ride (2WD X-cab)	(55)	(64)
	Includes heavy-duty shocks and P205/75R15 tires (QCE)		
Z83	Suspension Package — Smooth Ride (4WD X-cab)	NC	NC
	Includes heavy-duty shocks and P205/75R15 tires (QCE)		
Z83	Suspension Package — Smooth Ride (Reg Cab SB)	NC	NC
	Includes heavy-duty shocks and P205/75R15 tires (QCE); REQUIRES 4,200 lb. GVWR on 2WD models; REQUIRES 4,650 lb. GVWR on 4WD models		
ZQ8	Suspension Package — Sport (2WD X-cab)	605	703
	Includes shortened coil springs, heavy-duty front and rear stabilizer bars, Bilstein front and rear shocks, urethane jounce bumpers, 16"x 8" aluminum wheels, and P235/55R16 all-season tires (QCB); INCLUDED in Option Packages 1ST and 1SY		
ZQ8	Suspension Package — Sport (SLS 2WD Reg Cab SB)	605	703
	Includes shortened coil springs, heavy-duty front and rear stabilizer bars, Bilstein front and rear shocks, urethane jounce bumpers, 16"x 8" aluminum wheels, and P235/55R16 all-season tires (QCB); INCLUDED in Option Packages 1SS and 1SX		
U16	Tachometer	51	59
	INCLUDED with V-6 engine		
E24	Third Door (X-cab)	323	375
QCA	Tires — P205/75R15 (All except 4WD Reg Cab LB)	104	121
	All-season outline white-lettered tires		
QCE	Tires — P205/75R15 (All except 4WD Reg Cab LB)	NC	NC
	All-season blackwall tires		
QBF	Tires — P235/70R15 (4WD)	NC	NC
	All-season blackwall tires; REQUIRES Heavy-duty Suspension Package		
QEB	Tires — P235/75R15 (4WD)	123	143
	On/off road outline white-lettered tires; REQUIRES Heavy-duty Suspension Package; INCLUDED in Off-road Suspension		
M30	Transmission — Automatic 4-speed	920	1070
	Includes brake/transmission shift interlock		
M50	Transmission — Manual 5-speed (2WD)	NC	NC

GMC SUBURBAN

SUBURBAN (1997)

1997 GMC Suburban

What's New for GMC Suburban in 1997 — GMC has added a passenger side airbag and a power lock switch in the cargo compartment. SLE and SLT trim now includes rear heat and air conditioning, as well as remote keyless entry. Uplevel SLT trim also includes a combination CD and cassette player stereo system. All Suburbans receive speed-sensitive power steering, and 4WD models have a tighter turning circle. Two new colors freshen the dated exterior design this year.

Suburban — Review

Gaze down the side of a Suburban and all you see is steel and more steel, stretching rearward. Hike yourself aboard and you can't help but feel you're in a truck, ready for the long haul—which is exactly what pleases many owners of these biggies. Compact-vehicle fans have a hard time grasping the appeal, but full-size "truck wagons" have been luring more and more upscale motorists.

GMC claims this mammoth combines the comfort of a luxury sedan with the "tenacity and utility of a packhorse." Except for the nearly-identical Chevrolet model, also named Suburban and priced just slightly lower, there was nothing else quite like it on the market, until Ford crashed the party this year with the new Expedition.

For 1997, GMC has added a passenger side airbag and a power lock switch in the cargo compartment. SLE and SLT trim now includes rear heat and air conditioning, as well as remote keyless entry. Uplevel SLT trim also includes a combination CD and cassette player stereo system. All Suburbans receive speed-sensitive power steering, and 4WD models have a tighter turning circle. Two new colors freshen the dated exterior design this year.

Inside, the modern instrument panel holds a selection of white-on-black analog gauges with zone markings and red-orange needles. Climate controls are easy to grasp and use, within easy reach of each occupant. Dual cupholders ease out of a compartment at the center

SUBURBAN — GMC

of the dashboard, but are poorly located so that beverages sit in front of the air vents. Three assist handles help entry/exit. Passenger car tires make less rough-and-tumble Suburbans ride smoothly and quietly.

Despite its pickup truck heritage, the Suburban produces a stable and reasonably comfortable, if not exactly cushiony, ride—at least until you stray away from smooth pavement. We do wish the driver's seat backrest didn't feel reclined when in its most upright position. Gasoline engines tend to guzzle as expected, and if you're planning to carry heavy loads much of the time, or haul a trailer, give the big-block Vortec 7400 V-8 a whirl before deciding to accept the base engine.

The Suburban is one our favorites. It's a no-holds barred, no apologies kind of truck that can carry or tow just about anything you'd want to move without professional assistance. With a strong lineup of engines and more room inside than Expedition, we'd take the Suburban so long as we could live with it occupying the driveway rather than the garage.

Safety Data

Driver Airbag: *Standard*
Side Airbag: *Not Available*
4-Wheel ABS: *Standard*
Driver Crash Test Grade: *Not Available*
Passenger Crash Test Grade: *Not Available*

Passenger Airbag: *Standard*
Meets 1999 Side Impact Standards: *No*
Traction Control: *Not Available*
Insurance Cost: *Avg. (C1500); High (C2500/K1500/2500)*
Integrated Child Seat(s): *Not Available*

Standard Equipment

SUBURBAN: 5.7-liter Vortec V-8 engine, 4-speed automatic transmission, power front disc/rear drum anti-lock brakes, 16"x 6.5" steel wheels (15"x 7" on C1500), P235/75R15XL tires, P245/75R16 tires (K1500), LT245/75R16E tires (2500 models), brake/transmission shift interlock system, dash-mounted power outlets, dual airbags, front tow hooks (K1500/2500), trip odometer, tachometer, intermittent windshield wipers, vinyl bench seats, side door guard beams (do not meet 1999 truck side-impact standards), speed-sensitive power steering, 7-wire trailering harness

Base Prices

Code	Description	Invoice	MSRP
TC10906	C1500	21623	24712
TC20906	C2500	22702	25945
TK10906	K1500	23899	27313
TK20906	K2500	24994	28563
	Destination Charge:	675	675

Accessories

Code	Description	Invoice	MSRP
1SB	SLE Option Package 1SB	5825	6773
	Includes SLE Decor (rear cargo net, tilt steering wheel, cruise control, floor mats, spare tire cover, AM/FM stereo with auto-reverse cassette player, seek/scan, clock, theft lock, automatic tone control, music search feature, and enhanced performance 8 speaker sound system; power windows with driver's express-down feature, 9-		

GMC SUBURBAN

CODE	DESCRIPTION	INVOICE	MSRP
	passenger seating with cloth trim, folding center bench seat, removable rear bench seat, driver's seat power lumbar adjustment, storage armrest, third row cupholders, leather-wrapped steering wheel, dual illuminated visor vanity mirrors, sunvisor extensions, rear window wiper/washer (includes rear defogger with tailgate), color-keyed grille with chrome trim, composite headlights, roof rack, power exterior mirrors, deep tinted glass, electrochromic rearview mirror with integrated compass, chrome trim rings with bright center caps), front and rear air conditioning, rear heater, and remote keyless entry		
1SC	**SLT Option Package 1SC**	7829	9103
	Includes SLE Decor (rear cargo net, tilt steering wheel, cruise control, floor mats, spare tire cover, power windows with driver's express-down feature, driver's seat power lumbar adjustment, storage armrest, third row cupholders, leather-wrapped steering wheel, dual illuminated visor vanity mirrors, sunvisor extensions, rear window wiper/washer (includes rear defogger with tailgate), color-keyed grille with chrome trim, composite headlights, roof rack, power exterior mirrors, deep tinted glass, electrochromic rearview mirror with integrated compass, chrome trim rings with bright center caps), front and rear air conditioning, rear heater, remote keyless entry, plus SLT Decor (reclining front bucket seats, 8-passenger seating, leather upholstery, AM/FM stereo with cassette and CD players, seek/scan, clock, theft lock, automatic tone control, and enhanced performance 8 speaker sound system; (rear seat cupholders, power driver's seat.)		
C60	**Air Conditioning — Front**	727	845
	INCLUDED in SLE and SLT Option Packages		
C69	**Air Conditioning — Front and Rear**	1178	1370
	Includes rear controls and rear vents; INCLUDED in SLE and SLT Option Packages		
N90	**Alloy Wheels (C1500)**	267	310
	With 1SB	215	250
	With 1SC	215	250
	REQUIRES standard or QHA tires; NOT AVAILABLE with Vortec 7400 V-8 Engine or 6.5-liter Turbodiesel V-8 Engine		
PF4	**Alloy Wheels (K1500)**	267	310
	With 1SB	215	250
	With 1SC	215	250
	NOT AVAILABLE with Vortec 7400 V-8 Engine or 6.5-liter Turbodiesel V-8 Engine		
YF5	**California Emissions**	146	170
	NOT AVAILABLE with 6.5-liter Turbodiesel V-8 Engine on 1500 models		
DF2	**Camper-type Exterior Mirrors**	46	53
	With 1SB	(39)	(45)
	With 1SC	(39)	(45)
	Stainless-steel		
V10	**Cold Climate Package**	28	33
	Includes engine block heater; NOT AVAILABLE with 6.5-liter Turbodiesel V-8 Engine		
ZQ3	**Convenience Package ZQ3**	329	383
	Includes tilt steering wheel and cruise control; INCLUDED in SLE and SLT Option Packages		
AJ1	**Deep Tinted Glass**	262	305
	INCLUDED in SLE and SLT Option Packages		

SUBURBAN — GMC

CODE	DESCRIPTION	INVOICE	MSRP
NP1	Electronic Shift Transfer Case (K1500/K2500)	129	150
	REQUIRES tilt steering wheel and cruise control		
L65	Engine — 6.5-liter Turbodiesel V-8	2460	2860
	Includes front bumper guards; REQUIRES Heavy-duty Automatic Transmission; REQUIRES 3.42 Rear Axle Ratio on 1500 models; REQUIRES Wheel Flares on K1500 models; NOT AVAILABLE with California Emissions on 1500 models		
L29	Engine — Vortec 7400 V-8 (2500)	516	600
KC4	Engine Oil Cooling (1500)	116	135
	REQUIRES 3.42 Rear Axle Ratio; NOT AVAILABLE with Vortec 7400 V-8 Engine or 6.5-liter Turbodiesel V-8 Engine		
VK3	Front License Plate Bracket	NC	NC
C3F	GVWR — 7,700 lbs. (C1500)	NC	NC
	REQUIRES 6.5-liter Turbodiesel V-8 Engine		
C51	GVWR — 8,050 lbs. (K1500)	NC	NC
	REQUIRES 6.5-liter Turbodiesel V-8 Engine		
MT1	Heavy-duty Automatic Transmission (1500)	NC	NC
	Includes Heavy-duty Transmission Cooling		
F60	Heavy-duty Front Springs (K1500)	54	63
	NOT AVAILABLE with Vortec 7400 V-8 engine or 6.5-liter Turbodiesel V-8 Engine		
KNP	Heavy-duty Transmission Cooling (1500)	83	96
	INCLUDED with Heavy-duty Automatic Transmission		
K47	High Capacity Air Cleaner	22	25
	NOT AVAILABLE with 6.5-liter Turbodiesel V-8 Engine		
G80	Locking Rear Differential	217	252
NG1	Massachusetts/New York Emissions	NC	NC
ZY2	Paint — Conventional Two-tone	172	200
	REQUIRES purchase of an SLE or SLT Option Package		
ZY4	Paint — Deluxe Two-tone	258	300
	REQUIRES purchase of an SLE or SLT Option Package		
AG9	Power Driver's Seat	206	240
	REQUIRES purchase of SLE Option Package 1SB		
P06	Rally Wheel Trim	52	60
	INCLUDED in SLE and SLT Option Packages		
GU6	Rear Axle Ratio — 3.42 (1500)	NC	NC
GT4	Rear Axle Ratio — 3.73 (C1500/C2500)	116	135
	NOT AVAILABLE with 6.5-liter Turbodiesel V-8 Engine on C1500		
GT4	Rear Axle Ratio — 3.73 (K1500/K2500)	NC	NC
	REQUIRES Vortec 7400 V-8 engine or 6.5-liter Turbodiesel V-8 Engine on K2500		
GT5	Rear Axle Ratio — 4.10 (C2500)	116	135
	With L29 (2500)	NC	NC
	With L65	NC	NC
GT5	Rear Axle Ratio — 4.10 (K2500)	NC	NC
C36	Rear Heater	176	205
	INCLUDED in SLE and SLT Option Packages		

GMC SUBURBAN

CODE	DESCRIPTION	INVOICE	MSRP
YG4	Rear Seat Delete Credit	NC	NC
	With 1SB	(531)	(618)
	With 1SC	(875)	(1018)
E55	Rear Tailgate	NC	NC
	Includes power tailgate release		
C49	Rear Window Defogger	132	154
	INCLUDED in SLE and SLT Option Packages and ZP6 Rear Window Wiper/Washer; NOT AVAILABLE with Rear Tailgate (E55)		
ZP6	Rear Window Wiper/Washer	240	279
	Includes rear window defogger; REQUIRES Rear Tailgate (E55); INCLUDED in SLE and SLT Option Packages		
U01	Roof Marker Lamps	45	52
	NOT AVAILABLE with California Emissions		
BVE	Running Boards	194	225
AE7	Seats — 60/40 Reclining Split Cloth Bench	86	100
	REQUIRES purchase of an SLE or SLT Option Package		
AS3	Seats — Center and Rear Folding Benches	1011	1182
	INCLUDED in SLE and SLT Option Packages		
AT5	Seats — Center Folding Bench	544	632
	INCLUDED in SLE and SLT Option Packages		
A95	Seats — High-back Reclining Buckets	335	390
	Includes overhead and center floor consoles; REQUIRES purchase of SLE Option Package 1SB		
NZZ	Skid Plate Package (K1500/K2500) ...	194	225
	Includes skid plates for transfer case and differential; For whatever obscure reason, if you try to order this package on a K1500 equipped with the standard Vortec 5700 V-8 engine, Trailering Equipment, and a 60/40 Split Reclining Bench Seat, GMC won't let you. Nyah, nyah!		
UP0	Stereo — Uplevel w/cassette and CD players	172	200
	AM/FM stereo with auto-reverse cassette and CD player, seek/scan, clock, theft lock, automatic tone control, music search feature, and enhanced 8 speaker sound system; REQUIRES purchase of SLE Option Package		
UN0	Stereo — Uplevel w/CD player	86	100
	AM/FM stereo with CD player, seek/scan, clock, theft lock, automatic tone control, and enhanced 8 speaker sound system		
UM6	Stereo — w/cassette	126	147
	AM/FM stereo with cassette player, seek/scan, clock, and 4 speakers; NOT AVAILABLE with SLE or SLT Option Packages		
QBN	Tires — LT245/75R16C (K1500)	49	57
	On/off road blackwall tires; NOT AVAILABLE with Vortec 7400 V-8 Engine or 6.5-liter Turbodiesel Engine		
QBX	Tires — LT245/75R16C (K1500)	157	182
	On/off road outline white-lettered tires; NOT AVAILABLE with Vortec 7400 V-8 Engine or 6.5-liter Turbodiesel Engine		
QIZ	Tires — LT245/75R16E (C1500)	396	460
	All-season blackwall tires; REQUIRES 6.5-liter Turbodiesel V-8 Engine		

SUBURBAN — GMC

CODE	DESCRIPTION	INVOICE	MSRP
QIW	Tires — LT245/75R16E (K1500)	194	226
	On/off road blackwall tires; REQUIRES 6.5-liter Turbodiesel V-8 Engine		
QIZ	Tires — LT245/75R16E (K1500)	147	171
	All-season blackwall tires; REQUIRES 6.5-liter Turbodiesel V-8 Engine		
QIW	Tires — LT245/75R16E (K2500)	48	55
	On/off road blackwall tires		
QHM	Tires — P235/75R15 (C1500)	155	180
	All-season outline white-lettered tires; NOT AVAILABLE with Vortec 7400 V-8 Engine or 6.5-liter Turbodiesel Engine		
QGB	Tires — P245/75R16 (K1500)	120	140
	All-terrain outline white-lettered tires; NOT AVAILABLE with Vortec 7400 V-8 Engine or 6.5-liter Turbodiesel Engine		
V76	Tow Hooks (C1500/C2500)	33	38
Z82	Trailering Equipment	141	164
	Includes platform trailer hitch and heavy-duty flashers; REQUIRES Engine Oil Cooling on C1500 and K1500 models; REQUIRES 4.10 Rear Axle Ratio if ordered with the standard Vortec 5700 V-8 engine on C2500 and K2500 models		
B71	Wheel Flares (K1500)	155	180

Take Advantage of Warranty Gold!

Savings up to 50% off Dealer's Extended Warranty Prices. Protect and enhance YOUR investment with the best extended warranty available.

Call Toll Free 1-800-580-9889

For a guaranteed low price on a new vehicle in your area, call

1-800-CAR-CLUB

GMC — YUKON

YUKON (1997)

1997 GMC Yukon 4-Door

What's New for GMC Yukon in 1997 — Dual airbags, speed-sensitive steering, and a tighter turning circle for 4WD models. A power lock switch is added to the cargo compartment, and SLT models have a standard CD/cassette combo stereo. Remote keyless entry is standard on 4-door models, and on SLE and SLT 2-door models. Newly optional on 4-door models is a rear air conditioning unit.

Yukon — Review

Until this year, General Motors had a lock on the mid-size sport/utility market, but couldn't build enough to meet demand because of a serious lack of production capacity. The result? Inflated prices as dealers struggled to keep the Yukon and Tahoe in stock. This year, GM is refurbishing a plant in Arlington, Texas, which used to produce full-size Buick, Chevrolet, and Cadillac sedans, and Yukon/Tahoe production will begin in the Lone Star State sometime this spring.

Unfortunately for GM, the additional plant capacity may be coming a bit too late. Ford released the mid-sized Expedition last fall, and this F-150 pickup-based SUV is more refined but less powerful than the GM twins. Next year, Dodge releases the Adventurer, based on the fresh Dakota platform and sure to be slightly smaller and easier to maneuver than the GM and Ford behemoths. Jeep, too, is expected to get into the game by the end of the millenium, introducing a mid-sized sport-ute called the Grand Wagoneer.

In the size race, the Yukon fits squarely between the Jimmy compact and the big-bruiser Suburban wagons. Squint your eyes, in fact, and the difference between a Yukon and Suburban begins to evaporate, despite the latter's extra 20 inches of steel. Ford's Expedition is a bit larger, and offers 8-passenger seating, which is not available on the Yukon.

Yukon's interior has been borrowed from the full-size Sierra pickup, including new-for-1997 dual airbags. The cargo bay receives a power door lock switch — a sensible addition, and one not available from Ford. Rear passengers can be made more comfortable with the addition of a rear air conditioning unit. Remote keyless entry is made standard on 4-door

YUKON — GMC

models, and 2-door Yukons with SLE or SLT trim. Order the SLT trim on either Yukon, and a stereo featuring both cassette and CD players is part of the package. Speed-sensitive steering makes low-speed parking easier and provides better road feel on the interstate, while 4WD models have a tighter turning circle than last year which should improve off-road maneuverability.

How does the Yukon stack up against the Expedition? The Ford is more refined and comfortable, but we prefer Yukon's dated exterior styling. The Ford is powered by smooth overhead-cam engines, but we prefer the torque and roar of GMC's Vortec 5700 V-8 engine. Neither is easy to climb into, particularly without running boards, but the Expedition has larger rear door openings which make entry/exit to the back seat much easier. The Ford also boasts optional 8-passenger seating. As drivers, however, we believe we'd prefer the Yukon's power over the Expedition's refinement. Naturally, though, you can still expect truck-style ride and handling, but reasonable comfort on the road.

With new competitors arriving annually and increased production capacity, GMC dealers have little reason to gouge customers on Yukon pricing. Just threaten to go down the street and pick up a new Expedition, and the dealer will be eager to play ball.

Safety Data

Driver Airbag: *Standard*
Side Airbag: *Not Available*
4-Wheel ABS: *Standard*
Driver Crash Test Grade: *Not Available*
Passenger Crash Test Grade: *Not Available*

Passenger Airbag: *Standard*
Meets 1999 Side Impact Standards: *No*
Traction Control: *Not Available*
Insurance Cost: *High*
Integrated Child Seat(s): *Not Available*

Standard Equipment

YUKON 2-DOOR: 5.7-liter Vortec V-8 engine, 4-speed automatic transmission, power front disc/rear drum anti-lock brakes, 15"x 7" steel wheels, P235/75R15 tires, power speed-sensitive steering, brake/transmission shift interlock system, auxiliary power outlets in dash, dual front airbags, halogen headlights, tachometer, trip odometer, intermittent windshield wipers, vinyl low-back reclining bucket seats, folding rear bench seat, side door guard beams (do not meet 1999 truck side-impact standards), 7-wire trailering harness, front tow hook (4WD)

4-DOOR (in addition to or instead of 2-DOOR equipment): Air conditioning, AM/FM stereo with cassette player, seek/scan, automatic tone control, digital clock, and 8 speakers; rear cargo net, cargo security shade, electrochromic rearview mirror with integrated compass, deep-tinted windows, power exterior mirrors, alloy wheels, leather-wrapped steering wheel, dual illuminated visor vanity mirrors, power windows, power door locks, child safe rear door locks, rear heat ducts, rear window defogger (includes wiper/washer on models with tailgate), remote keyless entry, roof-mounted luggage rack, custom cloth 60/40 split reclining front bench seat, rear 60/40 split folding bench seat, tilt steering wheel

Base Prices

Code	Description	Invoice	MSRP
TC10516	2-door 2WD	20625	23571
TK10516	2-door 4WD	22943	26221
TC10706	4-door 2WD	25330	28949
TK10706	4-door 4WD	27605	31549
Destination Charge:		640	640

GMC YUKON

CODE	DESCRIPTION	INVOICE	MSRP

Accessories

1SB — **SLE Option Package 1SB (2-door)** 3525 4099
Includes SLE Decor (rear cargo net, air conditioning, power windows with driver's express-down feature, tilt steering wheel, cruise control, front/rear floor mats, deep tinted glass, rear window defogger, electrochromic rearview mirror with integrated compass, AM/FM stereo with cassette player, seek/scan, automatic tone control, theft lock, speed compensated volume, digital clock; 60/40 split reclining cloth bench seat, spare tire cover, leather-wrapped steering wheel, dual illuminated visor vanity mirrors, sunvisor extensions, roff-mounted luggage rack, color-keyed grille with chrome trim, composite halogen headlights, power exterior mirrors, alloy wheels) plus remote keyless entry

1SD — **SLE Option Package 1SD (4-door)** 129 150
Includes remote keyless entry. That's it. They made a whole option package just to include remote keyless entry. Pretty dumb, huh?

1SC — **SLT Option Package 1SC (2-door)** 4967 5776
Includes SLE Decor (rear cargo net, air conditioning, power windows with driver's express-down feature, tilt steering wheel, cruise control, front/rear floor mats, deep tinted glass, rear window defogger, electrochromic rearview mirror with integrated compass, 60/40 split reclining cloth bench seat, spare tire cover, leather-wrapped steering wheel, dual illuminated visor vanity mirrors, sunvisor extensions, roff-mounted luggage rack, color-keyed grille with chrome trim, composite halogen headlights, power exterior mirrors, alloy wheels), remote keyless entry, SLT Decor (reclining high-back bucket seats, overhead console, floor console, power lumbar support, leather upholstery, AM/FM stereo with cassette and CD players, seek/scan, automatic tone control, theft lock, speed compensated volume, digital clock; rear passenger cupholders)

1SE — **SLT Option Package 1SE (4-door)** 1657 1927
Includes remote keyless entry, SLT Decor (reclining high-back bucket seats, overhead console, floor console, power lumbar support, leather upholstery, AM/FM stereo with cassette and CD players, seek/scan, automatic tone control, theft lock, speed compensated volume, digital clock; rear passenger cupholders)

L56 — **6.5-liter Turbodiesel V-8 Engine (4WD 2-door)** 2460 2860
Includes front bumper guards; REQUIRES Heavy-duty Automatic Transmission; NOT AVAILABLE with Sport Equipment Package or California Emissions

C60 — **Air Conditioning (2-door)** 727 845
INCLUDED in SLE and SLT Option Packages

N90 — **Alloy Wheels (2WD 2-door)** 267 310
INCLUDED in SLE and SLT Option Packages

PF4 — **Alloy Wheels (4WD 2-door)** 267 310
INCLUDED in SLE and SLT Option Packages

MT1 — **Automatic Transmission — Heavy-duty (4WD 2-door)** .... NC NC
REQUIRES 6.5-liter Turbodiesel V-8 Engine

YF5 — **California Emissions** 146 170
NOT AVAILABLE with 6.5-liter Turbodiesel V-8 Engine

YUKON — GMC

CODE	DESCRIPTION	INVOICE	MSRP
DF2	Camper-style Exterior Mirrors (2-door)	46	53
	With 1SB (2-door)	(39)	(45)
	With 1SC (2-door)	(39)	(45)
	Stainless-steel; NOT AVAILABLE with Sport Equipment Package		
V10	Cold Climate Package	28	33
	Includes engine block heater; NOT AVAILABLE with 6.5-liter Turbodiesel V-8 Engine		
ZQ3	Convenience Group ZQ3 (2-door)	329	383
	Includes tilt steering wheel and cruise control; INCLUDED in SLE and SLT Option Packages		
AJ1	Deep Tinted Glass (2-door)	185	215
	INCLUDED in SLE and SLT Option Packages		
NP1	Electronic Shift Transfer Case (4WD)	129	150
	REQUIRES tilt steering and cruise control		
KC4	Engine Oil Cooler	116	135
	Included with 6.5-liter Turbodiesel V-8 Engine and 3.73 Rear Axle Ratio		
VK3	Front License Plate Bracket	NC	NC
C71	GVWR — 6,450 lbs. (4WD 2-door)	NC	NC
	REQUIRES 6.5-liter Turbodiesel V-8 Engine		
F60	Heavy-duty Front Springs (2WD 2-door)	54	63
KNP	Heavy-duty Transmission Cooler	83	96
	INCLUDED with Heavy-duty Automatic Transmission; NOT AVAILABLE with 3.08 Rear Axle Ratio		
K47	High Capacity Air Cleaner	22	25
	NOT AVAILABLE with 6.5-liter Turbodiesel V-8 Engine		
G80	Locking Rear Differential	217	252
	NOT AVAILABLE with 3.42 Rear Axle Ratio		
NG1	Massachusetts/New York Emissions	NC	NC
Z71	Off-road Chassis Equipment (4WD 2-door)	344	400
	Includes Skid Plate Package and gas shock absorbers; REQUIRES purchase of a SLE or SLT Option Package and QGC or QGD tires		
ZY2	Paint — Conventional Two-tone (2-door)	172	200
	REQUIRES purchase of a SLE or SLT Option Package; NOT AVAILABLE with Sport Equipment Package		
ZY2	Paint — Conventional Two-tone (4-door)	172	200
AG9	Power Driver's Seat (2-door)	206	240
	REQUIRES purchase of SLE Option Package 1SB; INCLUDED in SLT Option Package 1SC		
AG9	Power Driver's Seat (4-door)	206	240
	INCLUDED in SLT Option Packages		
P06	Rally Wheel Trim (2-door)	52	60
	NOT AVAILABLE with SLE or SLT Option Package		
GU4	Rear Axle Ratio — 3.08 (2WD 2-door)	NC	NC
	NOT AVAILABLE with locking rear differential		
GU6	Rear Axle Ratio — 3.42 ratio	NC	NC
GT4	Rear Axle Ratio — 3.73 (All except 2WD 2-door)	116	135

GMC YUKON

CODE	DESCRIPTION	INVOICE	MSRP
E55	Rear Tailgate	NC	NC
	Includes power tailgate release		
C49	Rear Window Defogger (2-door)	132	154
	INCLUDED in SLE and SLT Option Packages and with Rear Window Wiper/Washer on models equipped with a tailgate		
ZP6	Rear Window Wiper/Washer (2-door)	240	279
	Includes rear window defogger; REQUIRES rear tailgate (E55); INCLUDED in SLE and SLT Option Packages		
ZP6	Rear Window Wiper/Washer (4-door)	NC	NC
	Includes rear window defogger; REQUIRES rear tailgate (E55)		
AU0	Remote Keyless Entry	129	150
	Ha, ha, ha. This is funny. This option is INCLUDED in all the SLE and SLT Option Packages, but cannot be ordered on the base vehicles. So, ah, why is it offered as a separate option? Huh?		
BVE	Running Boards	194	225
NZZ	Skid Plate Package (4WD 2-door)	194	225
	Includes skid plates for differential, transfer case, and fuel tank; INCLUDED in Off-road Chassis Equipment		
NZZ	Skid Plate Package (4WD 4-door)	82	95
	Includes skid plates for differential and transfer case		
BYP	Sport Equipment Package (4WD 2-door)	105	122
	Includes body-color bumpers, wheel flares, and Yukon GT decals; REQUIRES purchase of an SLE or SLT Option Package and QGA or QGC tires; NOT AVAILABLE with 6.5-liter Turbodiesel V-8 Engine or Conventional Two-tone Paint		
UP0	Stereo — Uplevel w/cassette & CD players	172	200
	AM/FM stereo with cassette and CD players, seek/scan, automatic tone control, theft lock, speed compensated volume, digital clock; REQUIRES purchase of an SLE Option Package		
UN0	Stereo — Uplevel w/CD player	86	100
	AM/FM stereo with CD player, seek/scan, automatic tone control, theft lock, speed compensated volume, digital clock; REQUIRES purchase of an SLE Option Package		
UM6	Stereo — w/cassette (2-door)	126	147
	AM/FM stereo with cassette player, seek/scan, and digital clock; NOT AVAILABLE with SLE or SLT Option Packages		
QBN	Tires — LT245/75R16C (4WD 2-door)	49	57
	On/off road blackwall tires		
QBX	Tires — LT245/75R16C (4WD 2-door)	157	182
	On/off road outline white-lettered tires		
QFN	Tires — P235/75R15 (2WD)	120	140
	All-season white-lettered tires		
QGA	Tires — P245/75R16 (4WD)	NC	NC
	All-terrain blackwall tires; NOT AVAILABLE with Off-road Chassis Equipment		
QGB	Tires — P245/75R16 (4WD 4-door)	120	140
	All-terrain outline white-lettered tires		

YUKON — GMC

CODE	DESCRIPTION	INVOICE	MSRP
QGC	Tires — P265/75R16 (4WD 2-door)	163	190
	All-terrain blackwall tires; REQUIRES Alloy Wheels		
QGD	Tires — P265/75R16 (4WD 2-door)	271	315
	All-terrain outline white-lettered tires; REQUIRES Alloy Wheels		
V76	Tow Hooks (2WD)	33	38
Z82	Trailering Equipment	141	164
	Includes trailer hitch platform and heavy-duty flashers; REQUIRES Engine Oil Cooler		
B71	Wheel Flares (4WD 2-door)	155	180
	INCLUDED in Sport Equipment Package		

Save hundreds, even thousands, off the sticker price of the new car _you_ want.

Call Autovantage®
your FREE auto-buying service

1-800-201-7703

No purchase required. No fees.

TO PRICE YOUR TRADE-IN, PURCHASE EDMUND'S USED CAR PRICES AND RATINGS.

See page 6 for details.

HONDA ODYSSEY

ODYSSEY (1997)

1997 Honda Odyssey LX

What's New for Honda Odyssey in 1996 — No changes to the Odyssey. The good news? No price changes.

Odyssey — Review

With its doors open and beckoning, Honda's stylish and competent family hauler resembles a tall station wagon more than a minivan. Why? Because instead of the expected sliding side door—a staple of minivan design from the start—you find that all four side doors swing open, like those in a sedan. They contain roll-down windows, too. Naturally, Honda hopes that this unique attribute will help steal sales away from the competition, but a single special feature isn't enough to ensure success in the ferocious minivan market.

Fortunately for Honda, Odysseys possess other virtues. For starters, you get plenty of room for four or five, with a spacious center section that's exceptionally easy to enter. Either bucket seats or a three-place bench can go there. Not enough? Well, a handy two-passenger bench seat pops out of the cargo floor to expand passenger capacity to seven. That back bench folds flat very easily when cargo is the priority, and an inside-mounted, compact spare tire takes up very little space.

The driver occupies a comfortable position, ahead of a low cowl and steering wheel, and a severely sloped windshield, its base stretched far forward. Small front quarter windows do little for visibility in that direction, but mirrors are very good. An unusual slanted dashboard holds a distinctive speedometer. In addition to a large glovebox and ample console storage box, the Odyssey offers a smaller supplementary glovebox. On the safety front, airbags are installed for both the driver and front passenger. So is all-disc anti-lock braking.

Power comes from a VTEC 140-horsepower, 2.2-liter 16-valve four-cylinder engine, borrowed from the Accord. Adequately brisk performance is accompanied, unfortunately, by an excess of buzziness. If noise is a drawback for you, a V-6 choice is likely to arrive soon. Engines in both the LX and EX editions drive an electronically-controlled four-speed

ODYSSEY — HONDA

automatic transmission, complete with a Grade Logic Control System and controlled by a column-mounted gearshift lever. Both Japanese-built models are well-equipped, priced competitively, and carry on Honda's reputation for solid construction.

Safety Data

Driver Airbag: *Standard*
Meets 1997 Side Impact Standards: *Yes*
Integrated Child Seat(s): *N/A*
Driver Crash Test Grade: *Good*

Passenger Airbag: *Standard*
4-wheel ABS: *Standard*
Insurance Cost: *Low*
Passenger Crash Test Grade: *Good*

Standard Equipment

ODYSSEY - LX: 2.2 liter 140 HP 16 valve engine with second-order balance system, aluminum alloy cylinder head and block with cast iron liners, electronic ignition, multi-point programmed fuel injection, dual air bags (SRS), effort sensitive power rack and pinion steering, electronically controlled 4-speed automatic transmission with locking torque converter and grade logic control system, power assisted 4-wheel disc brakes, anti-lock brakes (ABS), front fender-mounted antenna, dual power mirrors, bodyside molding, multi-reflector halogen headlights, 5-mph impact absorbing body colored bumpers, rear window wiper/washer, front/rear air conditioning, power windows, power door and tailgate locks, 4 x 12.5 watt AM/FM high-power stereo cassette, cruise control, upper and lower glove compartments, front 3-point seat belts with adjustable anchors, second-row 3-point seat belts with center lap belt (7-passenger), third-row 3-point seat belts, adjustable steering column, removable second-row bucket seats, retractable fold-down third-row bench seats, quartz digital clock, beverage holders, dual vanity mirrors, tailgate-open warning light, remote fuel filler door release, rear window defroster with timer, 2-speed intermittent windshield wipers, rear seat heater ducts, low fuel warning light, maintenance interval indicator.

EX (in addition to or instead of LX equipment): 15-inch alloy wheels, power sunroof, body color bodyside molding, driver's seat with power height adjustment, 4 x 20 watt AM/FM high-power stereo cassette with 6 speakers, map lights, remote entry system.

Base Prices

Code	Description	Invoice	MSRP
RA186T	LX 7-Passenger Wagon (auto)	20818	23560
RA184T	LX 6-Passenger Wagon (auto)	21180	23970
RA187T	EX 6-Passenger Wagon (auto)	22577	25550
	Destination Charge:	395	395

Accessories

—	California Emissions	NC	NC

NOTE: Honda accessories are dealer installed. Contact a Honda dealer for accessory availability.

HONDA PASSPORT

PASSPORT (1997)

1997 Honda Passport 4WD LX

What's New for Honda Passport in 1997 — Honda drops the slow-selling DX 4-cylinder Passport.

Passport — Review

Honda issued a notable upgrade in 1996, adding airbags for the driver and front passenger. Also new were roof-mounted speakers that expanded available cargo space in the revised interior, plus an improved stereo system. The new dashboard, did away with the old angular look, replacing it with an organically swept affair complete with more legible gauges and improved ergonomics. Nothing has changed since then,

Passports are spacious for five inside, and V-6 models have a swing-out spare tire that creates even greater elbow room. The rear seat folds flat, resulting in a long cargo floor, but the clamshell tailgate design makes it difficult to access the back of the cargo area easily. They are however, better for watching softball games. Fortunately, the rear glass will open independently making it easier to load small items.

Road noise might be a drawback, though the 3.2-liter V-6 engine is quiet-running and strong with either five-speed manual shift or the available four-speed automatic transmission. The 2.6-liter four-cylinder engine, formerly available on the DX model has been discontinued; partially due to poor sales, and to keep the DX from competing with Honda's new mini sport/ute: the CRV. Passports equipped with automatic transmissions have Power and Winter modes, the latter starting off in third gear to reduce wheel-spin on slippery pavements. Towing capacity is 4,500 pounds with the V-6 engine.

Anyone seeking a capable blend of comfortable highway ride and tempting off-road talents could do well to look for a Honda dealer. However, Isuzu markets a version of the Passport and calls it the Rodeo The Rodeo tends to be a bit less expensive, and comes with a more comprehensive warranty. For those reasons, we suggest you stick with a Rodeo.

PASSPORT
HONDA

| CODE | DESCRIPTION | INVOICE | MSRP |

Safety Data:

Driver Airbag: *Standard*
Side Airbag: *Not Available*
4-Wheel ABS: *Optional*
Driver Crash Test Grade: *Good*
Passenger Crash Test Grade: *Average*

Passenger Airbag: *Standard*
Meets 1999 Side Impact Standards: *No*
Traction Control: *Not Available*
Insurance Cost: *N/A*
Integrated Child Seat(s): *N/A*

Standard Equipment

PASSPORT - LX: 3.2 liter 24 valve MFI V6 engine, 5-speed manual transmission with overdrive, black/charcoal bumpers/air dam, dual mirrors, tinted glass, exterior spare tire carrier, aluminum alloy wheels (4WD), dual airbags, air conditioning (4WD), AM/FM stereo with cassette and 6 speakers, clock, adjustable steering column, power windows, power door locks, cruise control, courtesy door lights, remote tailgate window release with warning light, center console with storage compartment, beverage holder, tachometer, reclining front bucket seats with headrests, split 60/40 fold-down rear seatback, 2-speed windshield wipers, rear window defroster, cargo area light, lockable glove compartment, dual vanity mirrors, child-proof rear door locks, variable assist power steering, anti-lock power 4-wheel disc brakes, 16 x 6.0JJ steel wheels, P225/75R16 all-season/mud and snow tires.

EX (in addition to or instead of LX equipment): 4-speed automatic transmission (2WD), chrome/body color bumpers/air dam, heated body color dual power mirrors, rear window wiper/washer, removable tilt-up moonroof, rear privacy glass, aluminum alloy wheels, 16" alloy wheels, flared wheelwell moldings, splash guards, limited slip differential (4WD), air conditioning, leather-wrapped 4-spoke steering wheel, map lights, 2-speed intermittent windshield wipers, cargo net, 16 x 7.0JJ alloy wheels, P245/70R16 all-season/mud and snow tires.

Base Prices

2WD

9B214V	LX 4-Dr (5-spd)	19043	21470
9B224V	LX 4-Dr (auto)	19904	22440
9B227V	EX 4-Dr (auto)	23222	26180

4WD

9B314V	LX 4-Dr (5-spd)	21598	24350
9B324V	LX 4-Dr (auto)	22619	25500
9B315V	LX 4-Dr w/Wheel Pkg (5-spd)	22042	24850
9B325V	LX 4-Dr w/Wheel Pkg (auto)	23062	26000
9B317V	EX 4-Dr (5-spd)	24730	27880
9B327V	EX 4-Dr (auto)	25750	29030
	Destination Charge:	395	395

Accessories

—	California Emissions	138	150

NOTE: Honda accessories are dealer installed. Contact a Honda dealer for accessory availability.

INFINITI   QX4

| CODE | DESCRIPTION | INVOICE | MSRP |

QX4 (1997)

1997 Infiniti QX4

What's New for Infiniti QX4 in 1997 — A version of Nissan's wonderful four-wheeler is introduced by Infiniti, aiming to compete with the Mercury Mountaineer, Acura SLX, and Land Rover Discovery. Differences between the QX4 and the Pathfinder include the Q's full-time four-wheel drive system, a more luxurious interior, and substantially different sheetmetal.

QX4 — Review

It was only a matter of time. Acura jumped on the luxury SUV bandwagon in early 1996, closely followed by Lexus. Land Rover sales have been shooting up steadily, and even Mercedes-Benz is close to production on its version of an off-road luxury vehicle. It's no surprise, then, that Nissan has decided to release a super-luxury version of its capable Pathfinder as an Infiniti.

Nissan took this same course when they decided to introduce a new entry-level sedan to the Infiniti lineup. Like the I30, which is mechanically identical to the Nissan Maxima, the QX4 has little under the skin to distinguish it from its down-market brethren. The QX4 is powered by the same 3.3-liter V-6 found in the lowly Pathfinder XE, but in the Q it is teamed to a 4-speed electronically controlled automatic transmission. Although we haven't yet driven the QX4, we are happy with how this powertrain has performed in the Pathfinder. The QX4 does have one item that stands out, however, and that is the Q's all-mode four-wheel drive which functions continuously without any input from the driver; a must for those who can't be bothered with locking hubs or shifting gears.

Most drivers won't care that the QX4 is so similar to the Pathfinder. For one thing, the Pathfinder rides on one of the best SUV chassis and suspension systems that we've ever experienced. Although most QX4 driver' won't venture far from civilization, it is nice to know that if they do they will be treated to a stable, sure-footed off-road experience. In addition, we must point out that the QX4's steering and on-road manners are unmatched by any other SUV on the market, even the vaunted Toyota 4Runner.

QX4

The other reason that drivers won't care about the QX4's mechanical similarities to the Pathfinder is because the QX4 doesn't look at all similar to the truck that it's based on. Dramatically different front and rear end styling render this SUV unique among a segment famous for look-alike products. Our staff has had mixed reviews about the QX4's styling, but none of us are would call it conventional. This may be good or bad, depending on the amount of attention that you like to draw to yourself, but at least you can rest assured that you won't see the freeways cluttered with them on your daily commute.

The QX4's interior is quite comfortable, with supportive seats, excellent ergonomics (for a truck), good visibility, and an easy step in. As befits a $36,000 vehicle, the materials are first-rate and the fit and finish is excellent. Additionally, Infiniti has made optioning the vehicle easy; there are only three non-standard equipment items to choose from the order sheet.

We haven't driven the QX4 yet, but we anticipate getting our hands on one soon. Stay tuned and keep your fingers crossed; hopefully we can have a full road test before camping season is upon us.

Safety Data

Driver Airbag: *Standard*
Side Airbag: *Not Available*
4-Wheel ABS: *Standard*
Driver Crash Test Grade: *N/A*
Passenger Crash Test Grade: *N/A*

Passenger Airbag: *Standard*
Meets 1999 Side Impact Standards: *No*
Traction Control: *Not Available*
Insurance Cost: *Not Available*
Integrated Child Seat(s): *Not Available*

Standard Equipment

QX4: 3.3-liter V-6 engine, 4-speed electronically controlled automatic transmission, all-wheel drive, power rack-and-pinion steering, power front disc/rear drum brakes, independent front suspension, multilink rear suspension, front and rear stabilizer bars, 16" aluminum wheels, P245/70R16 tires, full size spare tire, 21 gallon fuel tank, fog lights, roof rack, heated outside mirrors, privacy glass, skid plate, body color running boards, color-keyed grille and bumpers, dual airbags, variable intermittent wipers, liftgate with independent- opening glass, dual illuminated vanity mirrors, overhead console with temperature display, compass, and storage; map lights, leather-wrapped steering wheel, hand brake, and shift knob; tilt steering, cruise control, power windows, power door locks, remote keyless entry, rear window defroster, carpeted floor mats, automatic temperature control, power front bucket seats, amazingly comfortable rear seats, Homelink transmitter, Bose stereo with CD player, cassette, and 6 speakers; power antenna, leather upholstery, wood trim, center console, front and rear cup holders, child-proof rear door locks, cargo area cover, cargo net, and remote fuel filler door release.

Base Prices

Code	Description	Invoice	MSRP
71017	QX4	31666	35550
	Destination Charge:	495	495

Accessories

Code	Description	Invoice	MSRP
X03	Heated Seats	355	400
	INCLUDED in Premium Sports Package.		
J01	Power Sunroof	845	950
	INCLUDED in Premium Sports Package.		
S02	Premium Sport Package	1467	1650
	Includes sunroof, limited slip differential, and heated seats.		

ISUZU — HOMBRE

HOMBRE (1997)

1997 Isuzu Hombre XS

What's New for Isuzu Hombre in 1997 — A Spacecab model debuts, with seating for 5 passengers and your choice of four-cylinder or V-6 power. Other news includes two fresh paint colors and revised graphics.

Hombre — Review

Sporting sheetmetal stamped by General Motors do Brasil, and basic mechanical and structural components of the Chevrolet S-10/GMC Sonoma twins, the Hombre is Isuzu's entry the compact pickup market. Sporting two-wheel drive, a regular cab, and a weak 2.2-liter four cylinder engine upon debut in 1996, the Hombre was not exactly the stuff truck buyers craved.

For 1997, Isuzu introduces a Spacecab model that can be equipped with a 4.3-liter V-6 engine teamed to a four-speed automatic transmission. While this new model may jump-start Hombre sales (this editor has seen two Hombres on the road, both of which were equipped with a large refrigerated box in place of a bed), the two new colors and revised graphics that are new this year likely will not.

At least the Hombre is somewhat of an improvement over the aging Japanese-built pickup the company marketed in 1995. Four-wheel anti-lock brakes and a driver airbag are standard on both models. However, crash test scores, based on the performance of the structurally identical Chevy S-10, are worse than they were for the old Isuzu truck, particularly for the front passenger. Horsepower and torque with the the GM 2.2-liter four-cylinder engine is better than the old truck boasted, and fuel economy has improved. However, front leg room has diminished slightly, payload is down a couple hundred pounds, and the turning circle has widened. This is progress?

Hombre regular cab is available in S and XS trim levels, and options are few. S models are the workhorse Hombres, with vinyl floor covering and options limited to air conditioning, a stereo, and a rear step bumper. XS models are better-equipped, offering custom cloth upholstery, carpeted floors, and a tachometer. All Spacecab models have XS trim.

HOMBRE — ISUZU

Isuzu hasn't been selling many pickups in the past several years. As personal use pickup sales skyrocketed, the company stuck with marketing basic trucks more suited for work than play. First impressions indicate that the Hombre will do little to change Isuzu's fortunes in this segment.

Safety Data

Driver Airbag: *Standard*
Side Airbag: *Not Available*
4-Wheel ABS: *Standard*
Driver Crash Test Grade: Average
Passenger Crash Test Grade: Poor

Passenger Airbag: *Not Available*
Meets 1999 Side Impact Standards: *No*
Traction Control: *Not Available*
Insurance Cost: *High (Reg Cab); N/A (Spacecab)*
Integrated Child Seat(s): *Not Available*

Standard Equipment

HOMBRE S: Variable-assist power steering, power front disc/rear drum anti-lock brakes, independent front suspension with stabilizer bar, on-board diagnostic system, maintenance-free battery, driver airbag, side-guard door beams, collapsible steering column, daytime running lights, halogen headlights, dual manual outside mirrors, inside hood release, double-wall cargo bed with two-tier loading, tie-down loops in cargo bed, tinted glass, 15-inch steel wheels with bolt-on wheelcovers, P205/75R15 all-season radial tires, under-bed spare tire carrier with full size spare tire, detachable tailgate, two-sided galvanized steel body sheet metal (except roof and cargo box front panel), tweed cloth bench seat, Scotchgard protective treatment on seating surfaces, dual padded sun visors, intermittent windshield wipers, 2.2-liter I4 OHV SFI engine, 5-speed manual transmission with overdrive, dual cupholders, door pockets, dashboard utility tray and glove compartment, dome light, analog speedometer, trip odometer, gauges for coolant temperature, voltage and fuel level

XS REGULAR CAB (in addition to or instead of HOMBRE S equipment): Rear step bumper, custom cloth 60/40 split bench seat with folding center armrest, cut-pile carpeting, AM/FM stereo with 4 speakers and digital clock

XS SPACECAB (in addition to or instead of XS REGULAR CAB): Dark gray rear bumper, rear quarter swing-out glass, soft cloth upper door trim, front map light, sunvisor extensions, dual illuminated visor vanity mirrors, dual auxiliary power outlets, rear cupholders, vinyl rear jump seats

XS SPACECAB V-6 (in addition to or instead of XS SPACECAB equipment): 4.3-liter V-6 engine, 4-speed automatic transmission, center console with dual cupholders, storage armrest

Base Prices

CODE	DESCRIPTION	INVOICE	MSRP
P15	S Regular Cab	10370	11272
P25	XS Regular Cab	10646	11699
P55	XS Spacecab	12674	14289
P64	XS Spacecab V-6	14413	16413
	Destination Charge:	485	485

ISUZU — HOMBRE

CODE	DESCRIPTION	INVOICE	MSRP
Accessories			
A1	Air Conditioning	710	835
B2	California Emissions	145	170
C0	Convenience Package (XS Spacecab V6)	387	425
	Includes tilt steering wheel and cruise control		
JHG	Floor Mats (XS)	22	26
C2	Massachusetts/New York Emissions	145	170
P2	Performance Package (4-cyl. models)	55	65
	Includes heavy-duty suspension and 4.10 rear axle		
P2	Performance Package (XS Spacecab V6)	55	65
	Includes heavy-duty suspension and 3.42 rear axle ratio		
P5	Power Package (XS Spacecab V6)	482	530
	Includes power windows, power door locks, and power exterior mirrors		
P1	Preferred Equipment Package (Reg Cab)	1029	1131
	Includes air conditioning, sliding rear window, AM/FM stereo with cassette player, 4 speakers, and digital clock; tachometer and floor mats		
P9	Preferred Equipment Package (XS Spacecab)	815	896
	Includes air conditioning, sliding rear window, AM/FM stereo with cassette player, 4 speakers, and digital clock; tachometer and floor mats		
P6	Preferred Equipment Package (XS Spacecab)	1047	1151
	Includes air conditioning, sliding rear window, AM/FM stereo with CD player, 4 premium speakers, and digital clock; tachometer, floor mats		
I2	Rear Step Bumper (S)	51	60
K8	Sliding Rear Window (XS)	106	125
F2	Stereo (S)	200	235
	AM/FM stereo with 4 speakers and digital clock		
F3	Stereo — w/cassette (XS Reg Cab)	323	380
	AM/FM stereo with cassette player, 4 speakers, and digital clock		
F5	Stereo — w/cassette (XS Spacecab)	123	145
	AM/FM stereo with cassette player, 4 speakers, and digital clock		
T2	Tachometer (XS)	55	65

CALL NATIONWIDE 1-800-521-7257

FOR A WRITTEN QUOTATION AS LOW AS $50 OVER INVOICE

See page 15 for details.

RODEO — ISUZU

RODEO (1997)

1997 Isuzu Rodeo LS

What's New for Isuzu Rodeo in 1997 — All 4WD models get a standard shift-on-the-fly transfer case, and improvments have been to reduce noise, vibration, and harshness.

Rodeo — Review

Isuzu's Rodeo is getting a bit long in the tooth. Only mild updates have accompanied new model years since mid-season 1995, when Isuzu added airbags for the driver and front passenger housed in a redesigned dashboard, roof-mounted speakers that expanded available cargo space in the revised interior, plus an improved stereo system. The new dashboard, designed with assistance from Honda, replaced the old unit with an organically swept affair complete with more legible gauges and improved ergonomics.

This year is no different. Isuzu puts the finishing touches on the first-generation Rodeo with standard shift-on-the-fly operation for 4WD models that can be engaged at speeds up to 62 mph and NVH improvements. Continuing from last year is optional 4-wheel anti-lock brakes and two trim levels; basic S and more luxurious LS.

Rodeos are spacious for five inside, and V-6 models have a swing-out spare tire that creates even greater elbow room. The rear seat folds flat, resulting in a long cargo floor, but the clamshell tailgate design makes it difficult to access the back of the cargo area easily. Fortunately, the rear glass will open independently. Oddly, the only way to get a 60/40 split folding rear seat is to order a top-of-the-line LS model; not very convenient, or sensible. Options include side steps and a brush grille guard.

Road noise might be a drawback, though the 3.2-liter V-6 engine is quiet-running and strong with either five-speed manual shift or the available four-speed automatic transmission. A 2.6-liter four-cylinder engine, delivering 70 fewer horses, powers the two-wheel-drive S edition, which comes only with manual shift. Automatic transmissions have Power and Winter modes, the latter starting off in third gear to reduce wheelspin on slippery pavements. Towing capacity is 4,500 pounds with the V-6 engine, but only a ton with the four-cylinder.

ISUZU RODEO

Anyone seeking a capable blend of comfortable highway ride and tempting off-road talents could do well to look for an Isuzu dealer, though buyers may want to wait for the all-new, completely redesigned 1998 Rodeo. Comparison shoppers beware; Honda markets a version of the Rodeo and calls it the Passport. The Passport tends to be a bit more expensive, and doesn't come with as comprehensive a warranty. For those reasons, we suggest you stick with a Rodeo.

Safety Data

Driver Airbag: Standard
Side Airbag: N/A
4-Wheel ABS: Optional
Driver Crash Test Grade: Good
Passenger Crash Test Grade: Average

Passenger Airbag: Standard
Meets 1999 Side Impact Standards: No
Traction Control: N/A
Insurance Cost: N/A
Integrated Child Seat(s): N/A

Standard Equipment

RODEO S 4-CYLINDER: 2.6-liter inline four-cylinder engine, power recirculating ball steering, power front disc/rear drum brakes, rear wheel ABS, P225/75R15 tires, dual airbags, AM/FM stereo with cassette, 100-watt amplifier, and 4 speakers; tinted glass, cloth front bench seat, cloth folding rear seat, carpeted floor mats, trip odometer, dual exterior mirrors, rear window defogger, cargo tie-down hooks, child safe rear door locks, front and rear tow hooks, 2-speed wipers, auto-locking front hubs with 2-speed transfer case (4WD)

S V-6 (in addition to or instead of 4-CYLINDER equipment): 3.2-liter V-6 engine, 4-wheel disc brakes, carpeted floor mats, tachometer, outside spare tire carrier, center console with padded armrest and storage, reclining bucket seats, rear window wiper/washer, skid plates (4WD)

LS (in addition to or instead of S V-6 equipment): Air conditioning, passenger visor vanity mirror, two additional stereo speakers, roof rack, cargo area net, power exterior mirrors with defoggers, deep tinted glass, map lights, 60/40 split rear seat, velour cloth upholstery, leather-wrapped steering wheel, tilt steering column, cruise control, power windows with driver's express down, power door locks, chrome front bumper, chrome rear bumper end caps, remote tailgate release, two-tone paint, intermittent wipers, alloy wheels

Base Prices

CODE	DESCRIPTION	INVOICE	MSRP
P45	S 2WD (5-spd.)	15606	17340
R45	S 2WD V-6 (5-spd.)	18069	20650
R44	S 2WD V-6 (auto.)	18918	21620
V45	S 4WD V-6 (5-spd.)	19740	22690
V44	S 4WD V-6 (auto.)	20741	23840
R64	2WD LS V-6 (auto.)	22741	25990
V65	LS 4WD V-6 (5-spd.)	23716	27260
V64	LS 4WD V-6 (auto.)	24717	28410
Destination Charge:		445	445

RODEO — ISUZU

Accessories

CODE	DESCRIPTION	INVOICE	MSRP
A3/AQ	Air Conditioning (S)	845	950
	INCLUDED in Preferred Equipment Package		
M3	Alloy Wheels (S 2WD)	356	400
	REQUIRES Preferred Equipment Package; NOT AVAILABLE with Mud Guards		
M2	Alloy Wheels (S 4WD)	712	800
	REQUIRES Preferred Equipment Package; NOT AVAILABLE with Mud Guards		
L3/4	Anti-lock Brakes	712	800
	INCLUDED with Luxury & Security Package		
VP	Appearance Package (S 4-cyl.)	276	349
	Includes bodyside moldings, luggage rack, wheel trim rings, and bodyside striping		
OM	Bodyside Moldings (S)	79	100
	INCLUDED in Appearance Package		
B4	California Emissions	169	180
UCC	Cargo Cover (S)	71	90
	INCLUDED in Preferred Equipment Package		
CMC	Cargo Mat	47	60
ENN	Cargo Net (S)	17	22
	INCLUDED in Preferred Equipment Package		
JAG	Floor Mats (S 4-cyl.)	43	55
GRG	Grille Brush Guard	241	305
PHR	Hood Protector	54	68
KSS	Keyless Security System	181	230
	REQUIRES Preferred Equipment Package on S; INCLUDED in Luxury & Security Package		
E2	Leather Seats (LS)	1063	1195
	INCLUDED in Luxury & Security Package		
L1	Limited Slip Differential (4WD)	249	280
HT	Luggage Rack (S)	154	195
	INCLUDED in Preferred Equipment and Appearance Packages		
P7	Luxury & Security Package (LS)	2469	2875
	Manufacturer Discount	(800)	(1000)
	Net Price	1669	1875
	Includes anti-lock brakes, leather seats, 12-disc CD changer, and keyless security system		
C4	Massachusetts/New York Emissions	169	180
MSG	Mud Guards (S)	32	40
	NOT AVAILABLE with Alloy Wheels		
R1	Outside Spare Tire Carrier (S 4-cyl.)	245	275
P3	Preferred Equipment Package (S)	2358	2650
	Manufacturer Discount	(445)	(500)
	Net Price	1913	2150
	Includes tilt steering column, dual visor vanity mirrors, power tailgate release, air conditioning, intermittent front and rear wipers, 2 additional stereo speakers, cargo net, cargo cover, premium door trim, luggage rack, power exterior mirrors, power windows, power door locks		

ISUZU — RODEO / TROOPER

CODE	DESCRIPTION	INVOICE	MSRP
E6	Rear Wiper/Washer (S 4-cyl.)	178	200
RBS	Running Boards	264	335
BST	Sport Side Steps (4WD)	273	345
FDC	Stereo — 12-disc CD Changer	513	650
	REQUIRES Preferred Equipment Package on S; INCLUDED in Luxury & Security Package		
FSY	Stereo — Deluxe CD Player (S)	395	500
	NOT AVAILABLE with Preferred Equipment Package		
FLY	Stereo — Premium CD Player	434	550
	REQUIRES Preferred Equipment Package on S; INCLUDED in Luxury & Security Package		
H2	Sunroof (LS)	311	350
	Manual flip-up style		

TROOPER (1997)

1997 Isuzu Trooper Limited

What's New for Isuzu Trooper in 1997 — Anti-lock brakes are now standard on all models, and dealers get a wider profit margin to help increase sales. Despite delirious requests by a certain consumer group, Isuzu will not equip the Trooper with training wheels for 1997.

Trooper — Review

Just more than a decade ago, Isuzu introduced the first Trooper. It was a tough truck, sturdy and boxy in style, with two doors and a sparse interior. Powered by a four-cylinder engine, the original Trooper wasn't prepped to win any drag races, but the truck won fans for its off-road prowess and exceptional reliability. Soon, 4-door models joined the lineup, and a GM-sourced V-6 engine became available. As the sport utility market grew, luxury amenities were added to the Trooper, but by the early nineties, it was apparent that Isuzu needed to redesign the Trooper so that it could remain competitive against steadily improving competitors.

TROOPER   ISUZU

| CODE | DESCRIPTION | INVOICE | MSRP |

The Rodeo claimed the entry-level slot for Isuzu in 1991, so the Trooper was moved upscale in 1992. Since then, continual refinements have given the Trooper one of the best blends of style, comfort and utility in the class. Dual airbags are standard equipment. For 1997, all Troopers get 4-wheel anti-lock brakes. Fold the rear seats, and a Trooper can carry 90 cubic feet of cargo, ten more than rival Ford Explorer. Ground clearance measures an impressive 8.5 inches with the manual transmission, and rear seat passengers enjoy as much rear leg room as found in a Mercedes S500 sedan.

A 3.2-liter, 24-valve V-6 powers all Troopers, pumping out 190 horsepower. Three trim levels are available: S, LS, and Limited. We think you'd be better off with either the S or the LS. The S model is our favorite, when equipped with alloy wheels and a preferred equipment package (which includes air conditioning, power windows, mirrors and locks, premium sound, cruise, alloy wheels, and a 60/40 split folding rear seat). Add running boards and remote keyless entry, and you've got a comfortable, luxurious $31,000 cruiser that you won't be afraid to take off-roading.

Many of you may have heard a rumor that the Trooper is dangerous, prone to going around corners on two wheels at moderate speeds. Forget it. Government agencies and private test facilities have debunked the myth. The Trooper is no more tippy than any other sport/utility vehicle on the market. However, keep the following in mind; any vehicle with a short wheelbase and a high center of gravity requires care when cornering or traversing rough terrain. The rules of physics necessarily dictate that such a vehicle is more prone to tipping than a longer wheelbase car or truck with a lower center of gravity, as we discovered during an off-road jaunt in a Nissan Pathfinder last summer.

The Trooper has always been one of our favorites, because it has loads of personality and ability. What it doesn't offer is value. As an alternative to the Chevy Tahoe, Ford Explorer XLT and Jeep Grand Cherokee Laredo, the expensive Trooper makes little sense for most suburbanites whose idea of off-road driving is the dirt parking lot at the sweet corn stand. Buyers in this category might want to investigate the Rodeo. As an alternative to more expensive and competent SUV's, like the Toyota Land Cruiser and Land Rover Discovery, the Trooper makes perfect sense.

Safety Data

Driver Airbag: *Standard*
Side Airbag: *Not Available*
4-Wheel ABS: *Standard*
Driver Crash Test Grade: *Average*
Passenger Crash Test Grade: *Average*

Passenger Airbag: *Standard*
Meets 1999 Side Impact Standards: *No*
Traction Control: *Not Available*
Insurance Cost: *Average*
Integrated Child Seat(s): *Not Available*

Standard Equipment

TROOPER S: 3.2-liter V-6 engine, 5-speed manual transmission or 4-speed automatic transmission with winter mode, 2-speed part-time transfer case, power 4-wheel disc anti-lock brakes, speed-sensitive power steering, tilt steering column, skid plates, tow hooks, rocker panel moldings, overfender moldings with integrated mud flaps, cornering lights, outside spare tire carrier, P245/70R16 tires, chrome wheel trim, 2-speed intermittent wipers, rear step bumper, rear intermittent wiper/washer, rear defogger with timer, dual front airbags, center

ISUZU TROOPER

storage console with dual cupholders, child proof rear door locks, trip odometer, tachometer, digital clock, rear passenger heat ducts, front passenger assist grips, rear armrest, rear underseat storage box, front door map pockets, floor mats, cargo tie-down hooks, cargo net, cargo cover, cargo light, remote fuel door opener, reclining front bucket seats, pop-up front headrests, fabric seat coverings, tilt steering wheel

LS (in addition to or instead of S equipment): Two-tone paint, bronze tinted glass, rear privacy glass, chrome power exterior mirrors with defogger and power folding, diversity antenna, aluminum wheels, variable intermittent wipers, power door locks, rails, foot rests, air conditioning, dual vanity mirrors, front map lights, multi-adjustable front seats with armrests, 60/40 split reclining rear seat, velour upholstery, leather-wrapped steering wheel

LIMITED (in addition to or instead of LS equipment): Limited slip differential, leather-wrapped parking brake grip and shift knob, chrome grille, fog lights, power sunroof, headlight wiper/washers, CD changer, compass, altimeter, outside temperature display, outside barometric pressure display, 6-way power driver's seat, 4-way power passenger's seat, front seat heaters, leather upholstery, remote keyless entry system

Base Prices

Code	Description	Invoice	MSRP
L45	S (5-speed)	23099	26550
L44	S (auto)	24186	27800
M64	LS (auto)	27591	32270
M74	Limited (auto)	32481	37990
	Destination Charge:	445	445

Accessories

Code	Description	Invoice	MSRP
B5	California Emissions	162	180
CDT	CD Changer (S/LS)	487	650
CDR	CD Player (S/LS)	412	550
HP	Hood Protector	53	70
E1	Leather Seats (LS)	1912	2250
	Includes 6-way power adjustment for driver and 4-way power adjustment for passenger. Also includes seat heaters.		
L2	Limited Slip Differential (S/LS)	246	290
M9	Multi-information Display (S)	170	200
	Includes altimeter, compass, temperature, and barometric pressure display.		
C5	New York Emissions	162	180
H3	Power Sunroof (LS)	935	1100
P4	Preferred Equipment Package (S)	2714	3190
	Manufacturer Discount	(743)	(1000)
	Net Price	1971	2190
	Includes air conditioning, power windows, power door locks, cruise control, premium stereo with cassette player and 6 speakers, 60/40 split folding rear seat, dual visor vanity mirrors, dual power exterior mirrors with defoggers, aluminum wheels, anti-theft system with starter disable		
SST	Remote Keyless Entry (S/LS)	188	250
DBV	Running Boards	255	340

CHEROKEE — JEEP

CHEROKEE (1997)

1997 Jeep Cherokee Sport

What's New for Jeep Cherokee in 1997 — A new interior sporting modern instrumentation debuts. Front and rear styling is refined, and the rear liftgate is now stamped from steel. Multi-plex wiring is designed to improve reliability of the electrical system, while a new paint process aims to polish the finish of all Cherokees.

Cherokee — Review

Some things never change much, and the Jeep Cherokee is one of those mainstays. Unlike its posh—and bigger—Grand Cherokee brother, which keeps adding comforts and graceful touches, the ever-practical, affordable Cherokee simply keeps on rolling, looking little different now than it did a dozen years ago. This year, however, the Cherokee benefits from some overdue updates, including a new interior with dramatically improved instrumentation.

Utilitarian and upright it is, but with a compelling personality that even the Grand Cherokee lacks. Cherokee's squared-off edges are a bit rounder for 1997, with revised styling front and rear. Inside, the new interior includes dual airbags, new controls and displays, and a new climate control system that improves air flow and reduces interior noise. Fresh door trim panels, illuminated power mirror and power window switches, and a revised floor console round out the major interior changes. Four adults fit inside the Cherokee in reasonable comfort, with fine head room. Rear leg room is lacking, in a very short seat, and entry to the rear is constricted by a narrow door. Worth noting is the fact that the rear bench folds but doesn't offer a split, meaning you can't haul a toddler and a treadmill simultaneously.

Relatively refined on the road, the compact Cherokee is capable of strutting its stuff when the going gets rough. Acceleration is brisk with the 4.0-liter inline six-cylinder engine, courtesy of 190 horsepower, and we highly recommend this upgrade if you select the SE model. With the 4.0-liter engine, the Cherokee puts the 'sport' into sport utility.

JEEP CHEROKEE

SE and Sport models can have two or four doors, while the step-up Country edition is four-door only. All are available with either two- or four-wheel drive. Command-Trac part-time four-wheel drive allows shift-on-the-fly operation. Selec-Trac is Jeep's full-time four-wheel drive system. Standard gear includes power steering, tinted glass, and power front disc brakes. Four-wheel anti-lock braking is optional (six-cylinder only), as are power windows and door locks, keyless entry system, cruise control, air conditioning, and leather seats.

Other refinements for 1997 include new wiring designed to reduce complexity and improve reliability. The rear liftgate is now stamped from steel and features hidden hinges. This new design is lighter and easier to operate, with a new exterior handle and interior pull-down strap. Bumper end caps and side moldings are better integrated into the Cherokee's design, and front windows are ventless for improved visibility. Larger exterior mirrors make it easier to see out of the Cherokee, while new door seals battle to keep dust and noise from filtering into the cabin. Finally, new robotic spray equipment at the factory makes metallic paint colors look better.

Despite its age, the original compact Jeep sport-utility remains a sensible choice in its field, more capable than most of heading into the woods at a moment's notice. What more can anyone ask of a moderately-priced on/off-roader?

Safety Data

Driver Airbag: *Standard*
Side Airbag: *Not Available*
4-Wheel ABS: *Optional*
Driver Crash Test Grade: *N/A*
Passenger Crash Test Grade: *N/A*

Passenger Airbag: *Standard*
Meets 1999 Side Impact Standards: *No*
Traction Control: *Not Available*
Insurance Cost: *Low (SE); Average (Sport/Country)*
Integrated Child Seat(s): *Not Available*

Standard Equipment

CHEROKEE SE: 2.5-liter inline four-cylinder engine, 5-speed manual transmission, dual front airbags with knee bolsters, trip odometer, front/rear stabilizer bars, power recirculating ball steering, 15"x 7" styled steel wheels, P215/75R15 all-season blackwall tires, power front disc/rear drum brakes, cigarette lighter, black bumper and end caps, black bumper guards, black grille and headlight bezels, black wheel flares, tinted glass, glove box light, 4 cargo tie down loops, full-length floor console (includes cupholders, covered storage, padded armrest), black instrument panel bezel, 3 passenger assist handles, dual black manual folding exterior mirrors, auxiliary power outlet, AM/FM stereo with 2 speakers, high back reclining vinyl bucket seats, compact spare tire, headlights-on warning chime, 2-speed variable-delay intermittent windshield wipers

SPORT (in addition to or instead of SE equipment): 4.0-liter inline six-cylinder engine, tachometer, low fuel warning light, full-face styled steel wheels, P225/75R15 all-terrain outline white-lettered tires, black lower side moldings, spare tire cover, AM/FM stereo with cassette, four speakers, and overhead cargo area light; high back cloth reclining wing bucket seats

COUNTRY (in addition to or instead of SPORT equipment): Luxury aluminum wheels, P225/70R15 all-season outline white-lettered tires, 4-speed automatic transmission, Country Decor Group (includes body-color lower side moldings, body-color wheel flares, body-color bumpers and end caps, body-color bumper guards, body-color headlight bezels, body-color grille with black accents), paint stripe, black roof rack, cloth and carpet trimmed door panels with woodgrain moldings, front/rear door map pockets, front/rear floor mats, woodgrain instrument panel bezel, leather-wrapped steering wheel, light group (includes dual illuminated visor vanity

CHEROKEE — JEEP

CODE	DESCRIPTION	INVOICE	MSRP

mirrors, 2 floor courtesy lights, dual overhead map lights, underhood light, cargo area light, headlights-on delay timer), power equipment group (includes power exterior mirrors, remote keyless entry, power windows with driver's express-down feature, power door locks), low back cloth reclining wing bucket seats with adjustable headrests, rear window wiper/washer

Base Prices

CODE	DESCRIPTION	INVOICE	MSRP
XJTL72	SE 2-door 2WD	14383	15300
XJTL74	SE 4-door 2WD	15349	16340
XJJL72	SE 2-door 4WD	15782	16815
XJJL74	SE 4-door 4WD	16744	17850
XJTL72	Sport 2-door 2WD	16225	17915
XJTL74	Sport 4-door 2WD	17156	18950
XJJL72	Sport 2-door 4WD	17574	19425
XJJL74	Sport 4-door 4WD	18505	20460
XJTL74	Country 4-door 2WD	19756	21905
XJJL74	Country 4-door 4WD	21110	23420
	Destination Charge:	525	525

Accessories

CODE	DESCRIPTION	INVOICE	MSRP
HAA	Air Conditioning	723	850
	Manufacturer Discount	(723)	(850)
	Net Price	0	0
	Guess this is what they mean by no-charge air		
WJW	Aluminum Wheels (SE)	374	440
	ECCO style sparkle silver painted wheels; REQUIRES Conventional Spare Tire		
WJW	Aluminum Wheels (Sport)	208	245
	ECCO style sparkle silver painted wheels; REQUIRES Conventional Spare Tire		
BGK	Anti-lock Brakes	510	600
	NOT AVAILABLE with 2.5-liter inline four-cylinder engine on SE models		
YCF	Border States Emissions	106	125
NAE	Calif./Mass./New York Emissions	106	125
CSC	Cargo Area Cover	64	75
E	Cloth High Back Bucket Seats (SE)	123	145
TBB	Conventional Spare Tire (Country)	179	210
	Includes matching wheel		
TBB	Conventional Spare Tire (SE)	64	75
	With TRL (SE)	102	120
	Includes matching wheel		
TBB	Conventional Spare Tire (Sport)	123	145
	With WJW (Sport)	179	210
	Includes matching wheel		
NHM	Cruise Control	213	250
	INCLUDED in Option Package 26H on Country models		
CLE	Engine Block Heater	34	40
CLE	Floor Mats (SE/Sport)	43	50
	Included in Option Packages 25E and 26E on Sport models		

JEEP CHEROKEE

CODE	DESCRIPTION	INVOICE	MSRP
LNJ	Fog Lights (Sport/Country)	94	110
	REQUIRES Rear Window Defroster on both models; REQUIRES Rear Window Wiper/Washer on Sport model		
L	Leather Low Back Bucket Seats (Country)	710	835
	Includes power driver's seat		
SCG	Leather-wrapped Steering Wheel (SE/Sport)	43	50
	INCLUDED in Option Packages 25E and 26E on Sport models		
ADA	Light Group (SE)	170	200
	With RAS (SE)	136	160
	With RAZ (SE)	136	160
	Includes overhead map lights, cargo area light, floor courtesy lights, underhood light, headlights-on delay timer, dual illuminated visor vanity mirrors		
ADA	Light Group (Sport)	136	160
	Includes overhead map lights, cargo area light, floor courtesy lights, underhood light, headlights-on delay timer, dual illuminated visor vanity mirrors		
23B	Option Package 23B (SE)	361	425
	Manufacturer Discount	(128)	(150)
	Net Price	233	275
	Includes cloth seats, dual power exterior mirrors, rear wiper/washer		
25A	Option Package 25A (SE)	846	995
	Includes 4.0-liter inline six-cylinder engine		
25B	Option Package 25B (SE)	1207	1420
	Manufacturer Discount	(128)	(150)
	Net Price	1079	1270
	Includes cloth seats, dual power exterior mirrors, rear wiper/washer, plus 4.0-liter inline six-cylinder engine		
25E	Option Package 25E (Sport)	1284	1510
	Manufacturer Discount	(1191)	(1400)
	Net Price	93	110
	Includes air conditioning, front & rear floor mats, dual power exterior mirrors, black roof rack, tilt steering column, leather-wrapped steering wheel, rear wiper/washer; NOTE: Discount includes package discount and no-charge air		
26A	Option Package 26A (SE)	1649	1940
	Includes 4.0-liter inline six-cylinder engine and 4-speed automatic transmission		
26B	Option Package 26B (SE)	2010	2365
	Manufacturer Discount	(128)	(150)
	Net Price	1882	2215
	Includes cloth seats, dual power exterior mirrors, rear wiper/washer, plus 4.0-liter inline six-cylinder engine and 4-speed automatic transmission		
26D	Option Package 26D (Sport)	803	945
	Includes 4-speed automatic transmission		
26E	Option Package 26E (Sport)	2087	2455
	Manufacturer Discount	(1191)	(1400)
	Net Price	896	1055
	Includes air conditioning, front & rear floor mats, dual power exterior mirrors, black roof rack, tilt steering column, leather-wrapped steering wheel, rear wiper/washer,		

CHEROKEE — JEEP

CODE	DESCRIPTION	INVOICE	MSRP
	plus 4-speed automatic transmission; NOTE: Discount includes package discount and no charge air		
26H	Option Package 26H (Country)	1054	1240
	Manufacturer Discount	(1382)	(1625)
	Net Price	-328	-385
	Includes air conditioning, cruise control, and tilt steering column; NOTE: Price includes package discount and no-charge air discount. Yep, that's right. This package actually amounts to a credit. Seems the folks at Jeep could make things much less confusing by simply including this stuff as standard equipment and lowering the base price of the Country, doesn't it?		
CUN	Overhead Console (Sport/Country)	200	235
	REQUIRES Power Equipment Group and Light Group on Sport models		
JPS	Power Driver's Seat (Sport/Country)	255	300
AWH	Power Equipment Group (Sport 2-door)	536	630
	With 25E (Sport)	425	500
	With 26E (Sport)	425	500
	Includes power windows with driver's express-down feature, power door locks, remote keyless entry, and power exterior mirrors; REQUIRES Light Group and Rear Window Wiper/Washer		
AWH	Power Equipment Group (Sport 4-door)	684	805
	With 25E (Sport)	574	675
	With 26E (Sport)	574	675
	Includes power windows with driver's express-down feature, power door locks, remote keyless entry, and power exterior mirrors; REQUIRES Light Group and Rear Window Wiper/Washer		
GTZ	Power Exterior Mirrors (SE/Sport)	111	130
	INCLUDED in Option Packages 23B, 25B, 26B, 25E, and 26E		
GTS	Power Heated Exterior Mirrors (Country)	38	45
	REQUIRES Rear Window Defogger		
GTS	Power Heated Exterior Mirrors (SE/Sport)	149	175
	With 23B (SE)	38	45
	With 25B (SE)	38	45
	With 26B (SE)	38	45
	With 25E (Sport)	38	45
	With 26E (Sport)	38	45
	REQUIRES Rear Window Defroster		
RCG	Premium Infinity Sound Package	298	350
	Includes 6 premium Infinity speakers; REQUIRES Stereo w/CD player		
GFA	Rear Window Defroster	140	165
	REQUIRES Rear Window Wiper/Washer on SE and Sport models; REQUIRED in New York State		
JHB	Rear Window Wiper/Washer (SE/Sport)	128	150
	INCLUDED in Option Packages 23B, 25B, 26B, 25E, and 26E		
MWG	Roof Rack (SE/Sport)	119	140
	INCLUDED in Option Packages 25E and 26E on Sport models		
DHP	Selec-Trac Full-time 4WD (Sport 4WD/Country 4WD)	336	395
	REQUIRES 4-speed automatic transmission		

JEEP CHEROKEE

CODE	DESCRIPTION	INVOICE	MSRP
ADL	Skid Plate Group (4WD)	123	145
	INCLUDED in Up Country Suspension Package		
CSA	Spare Tire Cover (SE)	43	50
RAS	Stereo — w/cassette (SE)	255	300
	AM/FM stereo with cassette player and 4 speakers		
RAZ	Stereo — w/CD player (SE)	604	710
	AM/FM stereo with CD player and 4 speakers		
RAZ	Stereo — w/CD player (Sport/Country)	349	410
	AM/FM stereo with CD player and 4 speakers		
GAL	Sunscreen Glass (4-door)	230	270
GAF	Sunscreen Glass (Sport 2-door)	319	375
SUA	Tilt Steering Column	119	140
	INCLUDED in Option Packages 23B, 25B, 26B, 25E, 26E, and 26H		
TRL	Tires — P225/75R15 All-terrain (SE)	268	315
	Includes outline white letters; REQUIRES Conventional Spare Tire		
DSA	Trac-lok Rear Differential	242	285
	REQUIRES Conventional Spare Tire		
AHT	Trailer Towing Group	310	365
	With AWE (Sport 4WD)	208	245
	With AWE (Country 4WD)	208	245
	With AWE (SE 4WD)	208	245
	REQUIRES Conventional Spare Tire and the 4-speed automatic transmission		
AWE	Up Country Suspension Package (Country 4WD)	638	750
	Includes skid plate group, trac-lok rear differential, maximum engine cooling, conventional spare tire, 2 front tow hooks, 1 rear tow hook, off-highway suspension with increased height, P225/75R15 all-terrain outline white-lettered tires		
AWE	Up Country Suspension Package (SE 4WD)	901	1060
	Includes skid plate group, trac-lok rear differential, maximum engine cooling, conventional spare tire, 2 front tow hooks, 1 rear tow hook, off-highway suspension with increased height, P225/75R15 all-terrain outline white-lettered tires		
AWE	Up Country Suspension Package (Sport 4WD)	655	770
	With WJW (Sport)	710	835
	Includes skid plate group, trac-lok rear differential, maximum engine cooling, conventional spare tire, 2 front tow hooks, 1 rear tow hook, off-highway suspension with increased height, P225/75R15 all-terrain outline white-lettered tires		

TO PRICE YOUR TRADE-IN,
PURCHASE EDMUND'S USED CAR PRICES AND RATINGS.

See page 6 for details.

GRAND CHEROKEE *(1997)*

1997 Jeep Grand Cherokee Laredo

What's New for Jeep Grand Cherokee in 1997 — Last year's integrated child safety seat has mysteriously disappeared from press kit and dealer order sheet radar. Other big news is the availability of the optional 5.2-liter V-8 engine in 2WD models, and a six-cylinder that qualifies the JGC as a Transitional Low Emissions Vehicle (TLEV) in California. Refinements have been made to the ABS system, entry-level cassette stereo, and floor carpet fit. In January, a sporty TSi model debuted with monotone paint, special aluminum wheels, and other goodies.

Grand Cherokee — Review

For years, the Ford Explorer has been the best-selling sport utility vehicle in this country, but in 1993 a new challenger called Grand Cherokee arrived to try to wrest the sales crown away from the champ. It was not successful. However, it did outsell every other sport utility on the market, and became the Explorer's biggest threat.

Indeed, this Jeep has the most car-like feel of sport utilities, and is among the most stable on pavement. In fact, with the optional 5.2-liter V8 pumping away under the hood, the Grand Cherokee becomes the Porsche of sport utes. Equipped with a dual airbag system and four-wheel anti-lock disc brakes, Grand Cherokee buyers have long list of equipment to wade through, including three different drive systems (2WD, part-time 4WD, full-time 4WD), four different trim levels (Laredo, TSi, Limited, Orvis), and a host of luxury and convenience items.

The exterior is all hard edges and angles, but is instantly recognizable as a Jeep product and looks rugged. A retro touch we could do without is the location of the spare tire. The Grand Cherokee doesn't have tiny tires, and the cargo area is among the smallest in the class to begin with, so why is the tire in the cargo area? It should be under the cargo floor, mounted under the truck or placed on a rack on the liftgate. Otherwise, we have few quibbles with this sport ute.

JEEP GRAND CHEROKEE

Jeep improved the Grand Cherokee for 1997. Mechanical changes are limited to the availability of the optional 5.2-liter V-8 on 2WD models, and a revised 4.0-liter inline six that allows the JGC to qualify as a Transitional Low Emissions Vehicle in California. According to Jeep, the anti-lock brake system has been refined this year.

Inside, Jeep modified the tilt steering column, extended the rear seat heating ducts, and improved the fit and appearance of the floor carpeting. The entry-level cassette stereo has been upgraded as well. Outside, Jeep adds three new exterior colors, and all Grand Cherokees have a full-body anti-chip coat of primer under the paint. As you can see, Jeep isn't resting on its laurels waiting for the competition to leave the Grand Cherokee in the dust.

In January, the TSi model debuted, sporting specific alloy wheels, monotone paint in a choice of three shades, dark blue pinstriping, leather seats, high powered audio system, and more luxurious interior trimmings.

Unfortunately, just as Jeep caught up to and surpassed the Explorer in comfort and safety features last year, Ford went and squeezed a V-8 under the Explorer's hood. This year, Ford is offering a new overhead cam V-6 engine in the Explorer which puts out 20 more horsepower than the Jeep inline six. The Ford also has more room, a more comfy rear seat, and a lower price tag. Plus, you don't have to load cargo around a big ol' tire in the back. The verdict? For around town family hauling, we prefer the value-packed Explorer XLT. But for speedy fun and off-road prowess, the JGC Laredo V-8 gets our vote.

Safety Data

Driver Airbag: *Standard*
Side Airbag: *Not Available*
4-Wheel ABS: *Standard*
Driver Crash Test Grade: *Average*
Passenger Crash Test Grade: *Good*

Passenger Airbag: *Standard*
Meets 1999 Side Impact Standards: *No*
Traction Control: *Not Available*
Insurance Cost: *High*
Integrated Child Seat(s): *Not Available*

Standard Equipment

LAREDO 2WD: 4.0-liter inline six-cylinder engine, 4-speed automatic transmission, dual front airbags, power recirculating ball steering, 4-wheel disc anti-lock brakes, 15"x 7" aluminum wheels, P215/75R15 all-season BSW tires, air conditioning, cigarette lighter, rear window defroster, power door locks with programmable feature, child protection rear door locks, dynamic side impact protection (does not meet 1999 truck standard), bodyside accent color stripes, dark neutral gray lower bodyside and sill cladding, dual power black fold-away exterior mirrors with backlit interior switches, dark neutral gray front/rear fascias, chrome grille, rear passenger heat ducts, tinted glass, graphic display module (door ajar, liftgate ajar, lamp outage), dual note horn, illuminated entry system, retractable cargo cover, floor console with armrest, front/rear cupholders, black door handles, vinyl door trim panels with storage pockets and reflectors, driver's left foot rest, front/rear floor mats, 3 passenger assist handles with integrated coat hooks, leather-wrapped steering wheel, cloth sunvisors with covered illuminated vanity mirrors, remote keyless entry with panic alarm, ash tray light, cargo area light with switch, ignition switch ring lamp, 2 courtesy footwell lamps, glovebox light, underhood light, reading lights, black roof-mounted luggage rack, ETR AM/FM stereo with cassette player, clock, and 4 speakers; cloth and vinyl seat trim, reclining front low-back bucket seats with adjustable head restraints, 60/40 split-folding rear seat with adjustable head restraints, cruise control, tilt steering column, cargo area net, 4 tie down hooks, covered storage console with audio and coin holders, spare tire cover with storage pocket, quarter panel convenience net, locking glovebox, headlight-on warning chime, power windows with illuminated controls, 2-speed windshield wipers with speed-sensitive intermittent wipe, rear intermittent wiper

GRAND CHEROKEE — JEEP

CODE	DESCRIPTION	INVOICE	MSRP

LAREDO 4WD (in addition to or instead of LAREDO 2WD equipment): Selectrac 4WD system

TSi (in addition to or instead of LAREDO equipment): P225/70R16 outline white-lettered tires, 16" 5-spoke aluminum wheels, tape striping, unique styling cues in body-color fascia and bodyside cladding, body-color grille, perforated leather and vinyl low-back bucket seats with integrated headrests, AM/FM stereo with cassette player, graphic equalizer, 120-watt amp, 8 Infinity Gold speakers, and stationary antenna, leather-wrapped steering wheel with radio controls, woodgrain door panel trim, door courtesy lights

LIMITED 2WD (in addition to or instead of TSi equipment): Automatic temperature control, gold accent striping, body-color lower bodyside and sill molding, body-color exterior mirrors, body-color fascias, body-color grille, fog lights, sunscreen glass for rear doors, quarter windows, and liftgate; automatic on-off headlights, full overhead console with compass, outside temperature, trip computer, 4 map/reading lights (deleted when sunroof is ordered); bright door handles, woodgrain applique on door panels, carpeted lower door panels, sliding visor extensions, front door courtesy lights, memory feature for power seat, exterior mirror, and radio settings; automatic day/night rearview mirror, heated exterior mirrors with automatic day/night feature on left mirror, ETR AM/FM stereo with cassette player, 5-band equalizer, CD controls, 8 Infinity Gold speakers, and 120-watt amplifier; steering wheel-mounted radio controls, leather seating surfaces, power driver/front passenger seats with 10-way adjustment, power recliner, and power lumbar; vehicle theft security alarm, HomeLink universal 3-channel transmitter, vehicle information center (clock, scrolling dot matrix message displays), luxury aluminum wheels with gold or sparkle silver accents, flip-up liftgate window

LIMITED 4WD (in addition to or instead of LIMITED 2WD equipment): Quadratrac 4WD system

Base Prices

Code	Description	Invoice	MSRP
ZJTL74	Laredo 2WD	23155	25545
ZJJL74	Laredo 4WD	24923	27515
ZJTL74	TSi 2WD	25047	27695
ZJJL74	TSi 4WD	26815	29665
ZJTL74	Limited 2WD	28272	31360
ZJJL74	Limited 4WD	30445	33790
	Destination Charge:	525	525

Accessories

Code	Description	Invoice	MSRP
LSA	Anti-theft Security System (Laredo/TSi)	127	149
	INCLUDED in Option Packages 26Y, 28Y, 26S, and 28S		
YCF	Border States Emissions	145	170
NAE	Calif./Mass./New York Emissions	145	170
TBB	Conventional Spare Tire (All except 4WD TSi)	136	160
	Includes matching spare wheel; INCLUDED in Orvis Option Packages		
NHK	Engine Block Heater	34	40
GEP	Flip-up Liftgate Glass (Laredo/TSi)	85	100
	REQUIRES purchase of Option Package 26X or 28X on Laredo; INCLUDED in Option packages 26S and 28S on TSi		
LNJ	Fog Lights (Laredo/TSi)	102	120
	INCLUDED in Option Packages 26S and 28S		

JEEP GRAND CHEROKEE

CODE	DESCRIPTION	INVOICE	MSRP
JPX	**Heated Front Seats (Laredo/TSi)**	213	250
	REQUIRES purchase of Option Package 26Y or 28Y and Leather Trimmed Seats on Laredo		
JPM	**Heated Front Seats (Limited)**	213	250
	Includes 136-amp alternator; INCLUDED in Option Packages 26K, 28K, and Orvis Option Packages		
—	**Highland Grain Leather Seats (Laredo)**	490	576
AFF	**Luxury Group (Laredo/TSi)**	820	965
	Includes electrochromic rearview mirror, power driver/passenger seats with 10-way adjustment and power reclining/lumbar support, vehicle information center, automatic on/off headlamps; REQUIRES purchase of Option Package 26X or 28X; INCLUDED in Option Packages 26S and 28S		
26F	**Option Package 26F (Laredo 2WD)**	2269	2669
	Manufacturer Discount	(978)	(1150)
	Net Price	1291	1519
	Includes overhead console, sunscreen glass, P225/75R15 OWL all-season tires, luxury group (electrochromic rearview mirror, power driver/passenger seats with 10-way adjustment and power reclining/lumbar support, vehicle information center, automatic on/off headlamps), AM/FM stereo with cassette player and Infinity Gold speakers, flip-up liftgate glass, dual power heated exterior mirrors, vehicle theft security system		
26F	**Option Package 26F (Laredo 4WD)**	2269	2669
	Manufacturer Discount	(978)	(1150)
	Net Price	1291	1519
	Includes overhead console, sunscreen glass, P225/75R15 OWL all-season tires, luxury group (electrochromic rearview mirror, power driver/passenger seats with 10-way adjustment and power reclining/lumbar support, vehicle information center, automatic on/off headlamps), AM/FM stereo with cassette player and Infinity Gold speakers, flip-up liftgate glass, dual power heated exterior mirrors, vehicle theft security system		
26K	**Option Package 26K (Limited 2WD)**	1097	1290
	Includes AM/FM stereo with cassette/CD players, and Infinity Gold speakers; heated driver/passenger seats, and power sunroof with mini-overhead console (compass, outside temperature, trip computer, and 2 map lights, and electrochromic rearview mirror		
26K	**Option Package 26K (Limited 4WD)**	1097	1290
	Includes AM/FM stereo with cassette/CD players, and Infinity Gold speakers; heated driver/passenger seats, and power sunroof with mini-overhead console (compass, outside temperature, trip computer, and 2 map lights, and electrochromic rearview mirror		
26S	**Option Package 26S (TSi 2WD)**	2380	2800
	Manufacturer Discount	(978)	(1150)
	Net Price	1402	1650
	Includes overhead console, flip-up liftgate glass, fog lights, deep tinted glass, luxury group (includes auto dimming rearview mirror, auto headlight system, 10-way power front seats, and vehicle information center), dual heated power mirrors, vehicle theft security, conventional spare tire		

GRAND CHEROKEE — JEEP

CODE	DESCRIPTION	INVOICE	MSRP
26S	Option Package 26S (TSi 4WD)	2894	3405
	Manufacturer Discount	(978)	(1150)
	Net Price	1916	2255
	Includes overhead console, flip-up liftgate glass, fog lights, deep tinted glass, luxury group (includes auto dimming rearview mirror, auto headlight system, 10-way power front seats, and vehicle information center), dual heated power mirrors, vehicle theft security system, conventional spare tire, Quadra-trac transfer case		
26X	Option Package 26X (Laredo 2WD)	636	748
	Manufacturer Discount	(595)	(700)
	Net Price	41	48
	Includes overhead console, sunscreen glass, and P225/75R15 OWL all-season tires		
26X	Option Package 26X (Laredo 4WD)	636	748
	Manufacturer Discount	(595)	(700)
	Net Price	41	48
	Includes overhead console, sunscreen glass, and P225/75R15 OWL all-season tires		
28F	Option Package 28F (Laredo 2WD)	3014	3546
	Manufacturer Discount	(978)	(1150)
	Net Price	2036	2396
	Includes 5.2-liter V8 engine, trailer tow prep group (auxiliary transmission oil cooler, special fan drive, special power steering pump, 3.73 axle ratio), overhead console, sunscreen glass, P225/75R15 OWL all-season tires, luxury group (electrochromic rearview mirror, power driver/passenger seats with 10-way adjustment and power reclining/lumbar support, vehicle information center, automatic on/off headlamps), AM/FM stereo with cassette player and Infinity Gold speakers, flip-up liftgate glass, dual power heated exterior mirrors, vehicle theft security system		
28F	Option Package 28F (Laredo 4WD)	3392	3990
	Manufacturer Discount	(978)	(1150)
	Net Price	2414	2840
	Includes 5.2-liter V8 engine, Quadratrac transfer case, trailer tow prep group (auxiliary transmission oil cooler, special fan drive, special power steering pump, 3.73 axle ratio), overhead console, sunscreen glass, P225/75R15 OWL all-season tires, luxury group (electrochromic rearview mirror, power driver/passenger seats with 10-way adjustment and power reclining/lumbar support, vehicle information center, automatic on/off headlamps), AM/FM stereo with cassette player and Infinity Gold speakers, flip-up liftgate glass, dual power heated exterior mirrors, vehicle theft security system		
28G	Option Package 28G (Limited 2WD)	745	877
	Includes 5.2-liter V8 engine and trailer tow prep (auxiliary automatic transmission oil cooler, special fan drive, special power steering pump, 3.73 axle ratio)		
28G	Option Package 28G (Limited 4WD)	745	877
	Includes 5.2-liter V8 engine and trailer tow prep (auxiliary automatic transmission oil cooler, special fan drive, special power steering pump, 3.73 axle ratio)		

JEEP GRAND CHEROKEE

CODE	DESCRIPTION	INVOICE	MSRP
28K	**Option Package 28K (Limited 2WD)**	1842	2167
	Includes 5.2-liter V8 engine, trailer tow prep (auxiliary automatic transmission oil cooler, special fan drive, special power steering pump, 3.73 axle ratio), AM/FM stereo with cassette/CD players, and Infinity Gold speakers; heated driver/passenger seats, and power sunroof with mini-overhead console (compass, outside temperature, trip computer, and 2 map lights)		
28K	**Option Package 28K (Limited 4WD)**	1842	2167
	Includes 5.2-liter V8 engine, trailer tow prep (auxiliary automatic transmission oil cooler, special fan drive, special power steering pump, 3.73 axle ratio), AM/FM stereo with cassette/CD players, and Infinity Gold speakers; heated driver/passenger seats, and power sunroof with mini-overhead console (compass, outside temperature, trip computer, and 2 map lights)		
28S	**Option Package 28S (TSi 2WD)**	3128	3680
	Manufacturer Discount	(978)	(1150)
	Net Price	2150	2530
	Includes overhead console, flip-up liftgate glass, fog lights, deep tinted glass, luxury group (includes auto dimming rearview mirror, auto headlight system, 10-way power front seats, and vehicle information center), dual heated power mirrors, vehicle theft security system, 5.2-liter V-8 engine, trailer tow prep package		
28S	**Option Package 28S (TSi 4WD)**	3128	3680
	Manufacturer Discount	(978)	(1150)
	Net Price	2150	2530
	Includes overhead console, flip-up liftgate glass, fog lights, deep tinted glass, luxury group (includes auto dimming rearview mirror, auto headlight system, 10-way power front seats, and vehicle information center), dual heated power mirrors, vehicle theft security system, conventional spare tire, Quadra-trac transfer case, 5.2-liter V-8 engine, trailer tow prep		
28X	**Option Package 28X (Laredo 2WD)**	1381	1625
	Manufacturer Discount	(595)	(700)
	Net Price	786	925
	Includes 5.2-liter V8 engine, trailer tow prep group (auxiliary transmission oil cooler, special fan drive, special power steering pump, 3.73 axle ratio), overhead console, sunscreen glass, and P225/75R15 OWL all-season tires		
28X	**Option Package 28X (Laredo 4WD)**	1759	2069
	Manufacturer Discount	(595)	(700)
	Net Price	1164	1369
	Includes 5.2-liter V8 engine, Quadratrac transfer case, trailer tow prep group (auxiliary transmission oil cooler, special fan drive, special power steering pump, 3.73 axle ratio), overhead console, sunscreen glass, and P225/75R15 OWL tires		
26L	**Orvis Option Package 26L (Limited 4WD)**	1024	1205
	Includes Orvis Decor Group (Orvis badging and graphics, Orvis leather seating, Orvis front/rear floor mats, aluminum wheels with moss green accents or gold accents), AM/FM stereo with cassette/CD players and Infinity Gold speakers, heated driver/passenger seats, trailer tow prep group (auxiliary automatic transmission oil cooler,		

GRAND CHEROKEE

CODE	DESCRIPTION	INVOICE	MSRP
	special fan drive, special power steering pump, 3.73 axle ratio), and Up Country suspension group (skid plate group, 2 front tow hooks, 1 rear tow hook, P245/70R15 OWL all-terrain tires, high-pressure gas shocks, unique springs with 1-inch higher ride height, conventional spare tire, matching wheel		
28L	**Orvis Option Package 28L (Limited 4WD)**	1670	1965
	Includes 5.2-liter V8 engine, Orvis Decor Group (Orvis badging and graphics, Orvis leather seating, Orvis front/rear floor mats, aluminum wheels with moss green accents or gold accents), AM/FM stereo with cassette/CD players and Infinity Gold speakers, heated driver/passenger seats, trailer tow prep group (auxiliary automatic transmission oil cooler, special fan drive, special power steering pump, 3.73 axle ratio), and Up Country suspension group (skid plate group, 2 front tow hooks, 1 rear tow hook, P245/70R15 OWL all-terrain tires, high-pressure gas shocks, unique springs with 1-inch higher ride height, conventional spare tire, matching wheel		
TRD	**P225/70R16 OWL Tires (Limited)**	NC	NC
	INCLUDED in TSi and Orvis Option Packages		
TRT	**P225/75R15 OWL All-season Tires (Laredo)**	213	250
	INCLUDED in Option Packages		
TRL	**P225/75R15 OWL All-terrain Tires (Laredo)**	266	313
	With 26F (Laredo 2WD)	57	67
	With 26F (Laredo 4WD)	57	67
	With 26X (Laredo 2WD)	57	67
	With 26X (Laredo 4WD)	57	67
	With 28F (Laredo 2WD)	57	67
	With 28F (Laredo 4WD)	57	67
	With 28X (Laredo 2WD)	57	67
	With 28X (Laredo 4WD)	57	67
	NOT AVAILABLE with Up Country Suspension Group		
GWA	**Power Sunroof (TSi/Limited)**	646	760
	Includes mini-overhead console (compass, outside temperature, trip computer, and 2 map lights), and electrochromic rearview mirror; INCLUDED in Option Packages 26K and 28K		
AR3	**Premium Stereo w/cassette (Laredo)**	561	660
	AM/FM stereo with cassette player and Infinity Gold speakers; INCLUDED in Option Packages 26F and 28F		
ARD	**Premium Stereo w/cassette & CD player (Laredo)**	799	940
	With 26F (Laredo 2WD)	238	280
	With 26F (Laredo 4WD)	238	280
	With 28F (Laredo 4WD)	238	280
	With 28F (Laredo 2WD)	238	280
	AM/FM stereo with cassette/CD players and Infinity Gold speakers		
ARD	**Premium Stereo w/cassette & CD player (TSi/Limited)**	238	280
	AM/FM stereo with cassette/CD players and Infinity Gold speakers; INCLUDED in Option Packages 26K, 28K, and Orvis Option Packages		
DHR	**Quadratrac Transfer Case (Laredo 4WD/TSi 4WD)**	377	444
	INCLUDED in Option Packages 28X, 28F, 26S, and 28S; REQUIRES Conventional Spare Tire		

JEEP — GRAND CHEROKEE

CODE	DESCRIPTION	INVOICE	MSRP
DHP	Selectrac Transfer Case (TSi 4WD/Limited 4WD)	NC	NC
	NOT AVAILABLE with Option Package 28S, 28G, 28K, or 28L		
AWN	Skid Plate/Tow Hook Group (4WD)	169	199
	NOT AVAILABLE with Up Country Suspension Group; INCLUDED in Orvis Option Packages		
GEG	Sunscreen Glass (Laredo/TSi)	230	270
	INCLUDED in Option Packages		
DSA	Trac-lok Rear Differential	242	285
	Includes 3.73 rear axle ratio		
AHT	Trailer Tow Group III (Laredo)	306	360
	Includes maximum trailer weight of 5,000 lbs., maximum tongue weight of 750 lbs., maximum trailer length of 25 ft., frame-mounted equalizer hitch receptacle, 7 pin bargman outlet with 7 to 4 pin con, 3.73 axle ratio; NOT AVAILABLE with Option Packages 28X or 28F		
AHT	Trailer Tow Group III (Limited)	306	360
	With 26L (Limited 4WD)	219	258
	Includes maximum trailer weight of 5,000 lbs., maximum tongue weight of 750 lbs., maximum trailer length of 25 ft., frame-mounted equalizer hitch receptacle, 7 pin bargman outlet with 7 to 4 pin con, 3.73 axle ratio; NOT AVAILABLE with Option Packages 28G, 28K, or 28L		
AHT	Trailer Tow Group III (TSi)	306	360
	Includes maximum trailer weight of 5,000 lbs., maximum tongue weight of 750 lbs., maximum trailer length of 25 ft., frame-mounted equalizer hitch receptacle, 7 pin bargman outlet with 7 to 4 pin con, 3.73 axle ratio; NOT AVAILABLE with Option Package 28S		
AHX	Trailer Tow Group IV (Laredo)	208	245
	Includes maximum trailer weight of 6,700 lbs. (6,500 on 4WD models), maximum tongue weight of 750 lbs., maximum trailer length of 25 ft., frame-mounted equalizer hitch receptacle, 7 pin bargman outlet with 7 to 4 pin con, 3.73 axle ratio; NOT AVAILABLE with Option Packages 28X of 28F		
AHX	Trailer Tow Group IV (Limited)	208	245
	Includes maximum trailer weight of 6,700 lbs. (6,500 on 4WD models), maximum tongue weight of 750 lbs., maximum trailer length of 25 ft., frame-mounted equalizer hitch receptacle, 7 pin bargman outlet with 7 to 4 pin con, 3.73 axle ratio; REQUIRES Option Package 28G, 28K, or 28L		
AHX	Trailer Tow Group IV (TSi)	208	245
	Includes maximum trailer weight of 6,700 lbs. (6,500 on 4WD models), maximum tongue weight of 750 lbs., maximum trailer length of 25 ft., frame-mounted equalizer hitch receptacle, 7 pin bargman outlet with 7 to 4 pin con, 3.73 axle ratio; NOT AVAILABLE with Option Package 26S		
AHC	Trailer Tow Prep Group	89	105
	Includes auxiliary automatic transmission oil cooler, special fan drive, special power steering pump, 3.73 rear axle ratio; INCLUDED in Option Packages containing 5.2-liter V8 engine and in Orvis Option Packages		

GRAND CHEROKEE — JEEP

CODE	DESCRIPTION	INVOICE	MSRP
AWE	Up Country Suspension Group (Laredo 4WD)	700	824
	With 26F (Laredo 4WD)	491	578
	With 26X (Laredo 4WD)	491	578
	With 28F (Laredo 4WD)	491	578
	With 28X (Laredo 4WD)	491	578
	Includes skid plate group, 2 front tow hooks, 1 rear tow hook (n/a when trailer tow is ordered), P245/70R15 OWL all-terrain tires, high-pressure gas shocks, unique springs with 1-inch higher ride height, conventional spare tire, matching spare wheel		
AWM	Up Country Suspension Group (Limited 4WD)	332	390
	Includes (skid plate group, 2 front tow hooks, 1 rear tow hook, P245/70R15 OWL all-terrain tires, high-pressure gas shocks, unique springs with 1-inch higher ride height, conventional spare tire, matching spare wheel)		
AWM	Up Country Suspension Group (TSi 4WD)	196	230
	Includes (skid plates, tow hooks, high pressure gas shock absorbers, P225/70R16 outline white-lettered tires, conventional spare tire and matching spare wheel, raised ride height)		
RAZ	Uplevel Stereo w/cassette & CD player (Laredo)	476	560
	AM/FM stereo with cassette and CD player; NOT AVAILABLE with Option Packages 26F and 28F		

TO PRICE YOUR TRADE-IN,
PURCHASE EDMUND'S USED CAR PRICES AND RATINGS.

See page 6 for details.

Take Advantage of Warranty Gold!

Savings up to 50% off Dealer's Extended Warranty Prices. Protect and enhance YOUR investment with the best extended warranty available.

Call Toll Free 1-800-580-9889

JEEP WRANGLER

WRANGLER (1997)

1997 Jeep Wrangler Sahara

What's New for Jeep Wrangler in 1997 — Jeep has totally redesigned the original sport-ute. A Quadra-coil suspension improves on and off-road manners; while dual airbags and optional anti-lock brakes increase the Wrangler's ability to keep occupants safe. Round, retro-style headlights add a nostalgic touch to this venerable ground-pounder. Fortunately, none of these refinements soften the Wrangler's tough exterior. A restyled interior includes integrated air vents, a glovebox, and car-like stereo controls and accessory switches.

Wrangler — Review

We were a little concerned when we heard that Jeep was giving its bad-boy mud-machine an overhaul. Luckily, the Wrangler hasn't received the leather interior, cellular phone makeover that has recently emasculated so much of the sport-utility segment. No, the Wrangler remains the drive-me-hard-through-the-slop beast of yesterday; with a few appreciated improvements.

Jeep Wranglers have long been the standard for those valiant explorers who truly wish to go where no one has gone before. If anything, the go-anywhere ability of the Wrangler has been improved by the Quadra-coil suspension which allows an additional seven inches of articulation over the old leaf spring set-up; thus resulting in increased approach and departure angles. Jeep boasts that the Quadra-coil suspension, as well as improved shocks and tires, also greatly improves the Wrangler's on-road manners.

The Wrangler receives minor adjustments to the engine. Reduced engine noise and vibration, as well as improved responsiveness, were the goals of the minor driveline makeover. Nobody, however, will mistake this vehicle for a smooth-running family sedan; the Wrangler is very much a truck. A five-speed manual transmission remains standard and a three-speed automatic is available for those who find it too tedious to depress a clutch pedal.

The interior of the Wrangler is where most people will notice changes. Gone is the flat, no-frills dashboard and instrument panel. An ergonomically superior command center with integrated HVAC and stereo controls will ease driver anxiety when trying to adjust the

WRANGLER

temperature or volume while driving. A lockable glovebox replaces what was once an open hole in the dash. If all this sounds a little too citified, don't be alarmed. There is a bounce-bar tacked onto the dash that reminds you of this Jeep's intended purpose.

We feel that Jeep has done a great job improving the Wrangler. Gone are some of the nagging complaints we had about safety, wind noise and engine roar; what remains is a solid truck with hard-core capabilities and rugged good looks. This is obviously not the truck for everybody; but those willing to put up with a cloth interior and a little road noise will be rewarded with an amazingly fun vehicle. Hey, they even brought back those snazzy round headlights...what's not to like?

Safety Data

Driver Airbag: *Standard*
Side Airbag: *Not Available*
4-Wheel ABS: *N/A (SE); Opt. (Sport/Sahara)*
Driver Crash Test Grade: *N/A*
Passenger Crash Test Grade: *N/A*

Passenger Airbag: *Standard*
Meets 1999 Side Impact Standards: *No*
Traction Control: *Not Available*
Insurance Cost: *Avg. (SE/Sport); High (Sahara)*
Integrated Child Seat(s): *Not Available*

Standard Equipment

WRANGLER SE: 2.5-liter inline four-cylinder engine, 5-speed manual transmission, command-trac transfer case, dual front airbags, manual recirculating ball steering, power front disc/rear drum brakes, 15"x 6" argent styled steel wheels with black center caps, P205/75R15 BSW all-terrain Goodyear Wrangler tires, passenger assist handle, black front bumper, heater, half steel doors with side curtains, stainless steel exhaust system, black front/rear fender flares, front mud guards, body color grille, chrome headlight bezels, tethered fuel cap, dual horns, tinted windshield, halogen sealed-beam headlights, front floor carpeting, 4 cargo tie-down loops, front door map pockets, mini-console with cupholder and storage tray, side and rear sport bar padding, driver's side fotwell courtesy lamp, dual balck swing-away exterior mirrors, manual day/night rearview mirror, vinyl seat coverings, reclining front high-back bucket seats with passenger side easy-entry feature, fuel tank and transfer case skid plates, locking glovebox, compact spare tire, soft folding top with soft windows, headlights-on warning chime, 2-speed wipers

SPORT (in addition to or instead of SE equipment): 4.0-liter inline six-cylinder engine, power steering, 15"x 7" full-face 5-spoke argent steel wheels with argent center caps, P215/75R15 BSW all-terrain tires, black rear bumper, front/rear end caps, digital clock, rear carpeting, cargo floor carpeting, cargo net, full sport bar padding, ETR AM/FM stereo with 2 speakers, rear fold and tumble bench seat

SAHARA (in addition to or instead of SPORT equipment): Black bodyside steps, convenience group (includes engine compartment light, passenger's side footwell courtesy light, full console with lockable storage, dual cupholders, coin holder, storage tray), body color fender flares with sill moldings and front/rear mud guards, spare tire cover with Sahara logo, extra capacity fuel tank, front fog lights, heavy-duty electrical package (includes 117-amp generator, 600-amp battery), carpeted cowl side and door openings, carpeted front floor mats, ETR AM/FM stereo with cassette player, seek, 4 speakers, and dome lamp; Trailcloth seating surfaces, high-pressure gas-charged shock absorbers, tilt steering column, leather-wrapped steering wheel, seatback map pockets, conventional spare tire, cast aluminum spare wheel, 2 front tow hooks, 5-spoke cast aluminum wheels, 2-speed intermittent wipers

JEEP WRANGLER

CODE	DESCRIPTION	INVOICE	MSRP

Base Prices

TJJL77	SE	12927	13470
TJJL77	Sport	15483	17140
TJJL77	Sahara	17305	19210
	Destination Charge:	525	525

Accessories

Code	Description	Invoice	MSRP
AAS	30-inch Tire & Wheel Package (Sport)	667	785
	With 24D (Sport)	570	670
	With 25D (Sport)	570	670
	Includes High-pressure Gas-charged Shock Absorbers; NOT AVAILABLE with optional TMW or TRN tires, or with 5-spoke Aluminum Wheels		
AAS	30-inch Wheel & Tire Package (Sahara)	302	355
	Deletes spare tire cover		
WJ1	5-spoke Aluminum Wheels (Sport)	225	265
	REQUIRES Conventional Spare Tire and optional TMW or TRN tires		
WJ5	5-spoke Steel Wheels (SE)	196	230
	15"x 7" argent full-face wheels with argent center caps; REQUIRES optional TMW or TRN tires		
JKC	Add-A-Trunk Lockable Storage	106	125
	REQUIRES rear seat on SE models		
HAA	Air Conditioning	761	895
	REQUIRES Power Steering on SE		
BGK	Anti-lock Brakes (Sport/Sahara)	509	599
MRJ	Black Bodyside Steps (SE/Sport)	62	73
YCF	Border States Emissions	145	170
NAE	Calif./Mass./New York Emissions	145	170
ADC	Convenience Group (SE/Sport)	140	165
	Includes passenger's footwell courtesy light, engine compartment light, full console with dual cupholders and locking storage; INCLUDED in Sport Option Packages 24D and 25D		
TBB	Conventional Spare Tire (Sahara)	173	204
	Includes matching cast aluminum spare wheel		
TBB	Conventional Spare Tire (SE/Sport)	98	115
	INCLUDED in Sport Option Packages 24D and 25D		
DRK	Dana 44 Rear Axle (Sport/Sahara)	506	595
	REQUIRES Conventional Spare Tire; NOT AVAILABLE with Anti-lock Brakes; INCLUDES Trac-loc Differential		
NHK	Engine Block Heater	30	35
NF1	Extra Capacity Fuel Tank (SE/Sport)	55	65
	19-gallon capacity; INCLUDED in Sport Option Packages 24D and 25D		
LNJ	Fog Lights (Sport)	102	120
	REQUIRES Heavy-duty Electrical Group or Air Conditioning		

WRANGLER — JEEP

CODE	DESCRIPTION	INVOICE	MSRP
CLC	Front Floor Mats (SE/Sport)	26	30
XEA	Front Tow Hooks (SE/Sport)	34	40
GCF	Full Hard Doors	106	125
	INCLUDED with Hard Top		
—	Hard Top (Sahara)	785	923
	Includes sunscreen glass for rear quarter windows and liftgate		
—	Hard Top (SE/Sport)	642	755
ADH	Heavy-duty Electrical Group (SE/Sport)	115	135
	With GFA (SE/Sport)	0	0
	With HAA	0	0
	Includes 117-amp alternator and 600-amp battery		
SDU	High-pressure Gas-charged Shock Absorbers (SE/Sport)	77	90
	REQUIRES optional TMW or TRN tires on SE models		
SCG	Leather-wrapped Steering Wheel (SE/Sport)	43	50
TMW	P215/75R15 OWL All-terrain Tires (SE)	234	275
	REQUIRES 5-spoke full-face steel wheels		
TMW	P215/75R15 OWL All-terrain Tires (Sport)	196	230
	With 24D (Sport)	99	117
	With 25D (Sport)	99	117
	NOT AVAILABLE with 30-inch Tire & Wheel Package		
TRN	P225/75R15 OWL All-terrain Tires (SE)	394	463
	REQUIRES 5-spoke full-face steel wheels		
TRN	P225/75R15 OWL All-terrain Tires (Sport)	356	419
	With 24D (Sport)	262	308
	With 25D (Sport)	262	308
	NOT AVAILABLE with 30-inch Wheel & Tire Package		
SBA	Power Steering (SE)	255	300
	INCLUDED in Option Packages 22B and 23B		
—	Pueblo Cloth Seats (SE)	599	705
	With 22B (SE)	94	110
	With 23B (SE)	94	110
—	Pueblo Cloth Seats (Sport)	94	110
—	Rear Seat (SE)	503	592
	Includes fold and tumble vinyl rear seat; INCLUDED in Option Packages 22B and 23B		
RCD	Rear Soundbar (Sport)	208	245
	Includes full padded sport bar, rear soundbar with 2 speakers, and dome light		
GFA	Rear Window Defroster (SE/Sport)	139	164
	REQUIRES Hard Top and Air Conditioning or Heavy-duty Electrical Group		
24G	Sahara Option Package 25G (Sahara)	530	624
	Includes 3-speed automatic transmission		
22A	SE Option Package 22A (SE)	530	624
	Includes 3-speed automatic transmission		
22B	SE Option Package 22B (SE)	1292	1520
	Includes 3-speed automatic transmission, rear fold and tumble vinyl bench seat, black rear bumper, power steering		
23B	SE Option Package 23B (SE)	761	895
	Includes rear fold and tumble vinyl bench seat, black rear bumper, power steering		

JEEP WRANGLER

CODE	DESCRIPTION	INVOICE	MSRP
AAX	**Sound Group (SE)**	455	535
	Includes AM/FM stereo with 2 speakers, full sport bar padding, rear soundbar with 2 speakers, dome light; INCLUDED with RAS stereo		
CSA	**Spare Tire Cover (SE/Sport)**	43	50
	NOT AVAILABLE with Conventional Spare Tire; NOT AVAILABLE with optional TMW or TRN tires on SE; NOT AVAILABLE with Sport Option Packages 24D or 25D		
24C	**Sport Option Package 24C (Sport)**	530	624
	Includes 3-speed automatic transmission		
24D	**Sport Option Package 24D (Sport)**	990	1165
	Includes 3-speed automatic transmission, convenience group (passenger's footwell courtesy light, engine compartment light, full console with dual cupholders and locking storage), 19-gallon fuel tank, tilt steering column, intermittent wipers, conventional spare tire		
25D	**Sport Option Package 25D (Sport)**	459	540
	Includes convenience group (passenger's footwell courtesy light, engine compartment light, full console with dual cupholders and locking storage), 19-gallon fuel tank, tilt steering column, intermittent wipers, conventional spare tire		
RAL	**Stereo (SE)**	230	270
	AM/FM stereo with 2 speakers		
RAS	**Stereo w/cassette & soundbar (SE)**	606	713
	Includes AM/FM stereo with cassette and 2 speakers, full sport bar padding, rear soundbar with 2 speakers, and dome light		
RAS	**Stereo w/cassette & soundbar (Sport)**	361	425
	AM/FM stereo with cassette player and 2 speakers, full padded sport bar, rear soundbar with 2 speakers, and dome light		
GAF	**Sunscreen Glass (SE/Sport)**	143	168
	Includes sunscreen glass for rear quarter windows and liftgate; REQUIRES Hard Top		
SUA	**Tilt Steering Column (SE/Sport)**	166	195
	Includes intermittent wipers; INCLUDED in Sport Option Packages 24D and 25D		
DSA	**Trac-lok Differential (SE)**	242	285
	REQUIRES Conventional Spare Tire; NOT AVAILABLE with Option Packages 22A or 22B		
DSA	**Trac-lok Differential (Sport/Sahara)**	242	285
	REQUIRES Conventional Spare Tire; REQUIRES Anti-lock Brakes in high-altitude regions (don't ask us, that's what the dealer order sheet says)		

TO PRICE YOUR TRADE-IN,
PURCHASE EDMUND'S USED CAR PRICES AND RATINGS.

See page 6 for details.

SPORTAGE — KIA

SPORTAGE *(1997)*

1997 Kia Sportage

What's New for Kia Sportage in 1997 — An automatic transmission is offered on 2WD models, and the EX trim level is available in 2WD for the first time. Power door locks, a theft deterrent system, and a spare tire carrier are standard on all Sportages for 1997. A new option is a CD player. Sportage gets a new grille. A tan interior can be combined with black paint. Base 2WD models lose their standard alloy wheels.

Sportage — Review

Many residents of the Midwest and along the East Coast don't know what the heck a Kia is. Kia's are built near Seoul, South Korea, and are currently sold in western and southeastern U.S. markets. The company builds an inexpensive compact sedan, called the Sephia, and a wonderfully affordable sport utility called the Sportage.

Part-owned by Ford and Mazda, Kia relies heavily on resources from both companies as it struggles to its feet in a tough marketplace. The Sportage is the product of a collaboration between Kia, Ford, Mazda and suspension-tuning guru Lotus. Designed from the start as a sport utility, the Sportage sports tough ladder frame construction, shift-on-the-fly four-wheel-drive, and a Mazda-based powerplant.

Two trim levels are available: base and EX. Base models are well-trimmed, including power windows, tinted glass, split-folding seats, a remote fuel door release, power mirrors and a rear defroster. Power door locks, a theft deterrent system, and a spare tire carrier are newly standard for 1997. The EX adds cruise control, rear wiper and a remote liftgate release. Optional are a roof rack, air conditioning, premium stereo, CD player, leather interior, an automatic transmission and a limited slip differential.

A wide variety of colors are available on the Sportage's smoothly-styled flanks; few of which appear to have originated from the minds of the folks currently in charge of painting Matchbox cars. The look is rugged yet cute; perfect for family duty in the 'burbs. Off-road, we found the Sportage confidence-inspiring, but it didn't feel as tight as a Toyota RAV4.

KIA SPORTAGE

For most owners, that won't matter. Few SUV's actually leave the pavement, and on the pavement is where the Sportage shines. Lotus engineers worked wonders here, and the Sportage is stable and comfortable. The seating position is high and upright, visibility is outstanding, and the layout of the dashboard and controls is top-notch. Rear seat riders enjoy lots of room and support, afforded by "stadium style" elevated seating. From the driver's seat, the Sportage looks and feels much more substantial than its low price would lead you to believe. Our only quibble with the Sportage's interior was the lack of storage space, though this year's standard spare tire carrier certainly helps.

Kia hopes the younger families and active singles that will be buying the Sportage will find its affordability a welcome trade for some cargo room. With a loaded 4WD EX topping out at around $21,000, we think they've got little to worry about.

Safety Data

Driver Airbag: *Standard*
Side Airbag: *Not Available*
4-Wheel ABS: *Not Available*
Driver Crash Test Grade: *Not Available*
Passenger Crash Test Grade: *Not Available*

Passenger Airbag: *Not Available*
Meets 1999 Side Impact Standards: *No*
Traction Control: *Not Available*
Insurance Cost: *Low*
Integrated Child Seat(s): *Not Available*

Standard Equipment

SPORTAGE: 2.0-liter DOHC 16-valve inline 4-cylinder engine, power ball-and-nut steering, power front disc/rear drum brakes with rear anti-lock, alloy wheels (4WD), body-color bumpers, dual black power exterior mirrors, intermittent windshield wipers, tinted glass, full-size spare tire carrier, cloth reclining front bucket seats with adjustable headrests and driver's manually-adjustable lumbar support, split folding rear seatback, rear seat headrests, front door map pockets, dual cupholders, digital clock, tachometer, passenger visor vanity mirror, theft deterrent system, power windows, power door locks, remote fuel filler door release, rear window defroster, driver airbag, driver knee airbag, steel side door guard beams (do not meet 1999 truck standard), child-safe rear door locks, day/night rearview mirror, part-time 4WD with automatic locking hubs (4WD models)

EX (in addition to or instead of BASE equipment): Cruise control, body-color exterior mirrors, alloy wheels, rear window wiper/washer, roof rack

Base Prices

Code	Description	Invoice	MSRP
42221	4-door 2WD (5-spd.)	13177	14495
42222	4-door 2WD (auto.)	14087	15495
42421	4-door 4WD (5-spd.)	14410	15995
42422	4-door 4WD (auto.)	15320	16995
42241	4-door 2WD EX (5-spd.)	13865	15390
42242	4-door EX 2WD (auto.)	14775	16390
42441	4-door EX 4WD (5-spd.)	14835	16615
42442	4-door EX 4WD (auto.)	15745	17615
Destination Charge:		425	425

SPORTAGE — KIA

CODE	DESCRIPTION	INVOICE	MSRP
Accessories			
AC	Air Conditioning	763	900
AW	Alloy Wheels (Base 2WD)	242	340
CA	California Emissions	70	70
CF	Carpeted Floor Mats	45	64
LE	Leather Package (EX)	865	1000
	Includes leather seats, leather door inserts, and leather-wrapped steering wheel		
SP	Rear Spoiler	143	189
RR	Roof Rack (Base)	142	185
SG	Sport Appearance Graphic	60	95
RP	Stereo — Premium w/cassette	305	400
CD	Stereo — Premium w/CD player	430	545

For a guaranteed low price on a new vehicle in your area, call

1-800-CAR-CLUB

Take Advantage of Warranty Gold!

Savings up to 50% off Dealer's Extended Warranty Prices. Protect and enhance YOUR investment with the best extended warranty available.

Call Toll Free 1-800-580-9889

LAND ROVER — DEFENDER 90

DEFENDER 90 *(1997)*

1997 Defender 90

What's New for Land Rover Defender 90 in 1997 — After a one year hiatus, Defender 90 returns in convertible and hardtop bodystyles. A 4.0-liter V-8 engine is standard, mated to a ZF 4-speed automatic transmission. A redesigned center console includes cupholders, and hardtops have new interior trim. Convertibles get improved top sealing, while all Defender 90s are treated to fresh paint colors.

Defender 90 — Review

When launched as a 1994 model, the Defender 90 was the only convertible-topped sport-utility vehicle with a V-8 engine. Macho, go-anywhere looks aren't an illusion, as the off-road talents of this high-priced fantasy machine, operating with permanent four-wheel drive, rank among the finest. Occupants are surrounded by a "Safari" roll cage setup, over a spartan and uncomfortable interior. Don't try to roll down the soft-top's windows, which slide open for ventilation and can be removed if desired.

In late 1995, a limited production run of hardtop Defender 90s debuted, able to seat six passengers in slightly more sophisticated interior fittings. No 1996 models were produced, thanks to emissions regulations and the limited production nature of the Defender 90. With the transplantation of the powertrain from the Discovery, the Defender 90 returns for an encore performance for 1997, in both convertible and hardtop bodystyles.

Long-travel coil springs front and rear help produce an acceptable ride over a variety of terrain. A removable fastback soft top is standard on the convertible. Optional configurations include a Bimini half-top and surrey-style roof—or no top at all. Hardtops feature an aluminum roof and four center-facing rear jump seats. Convertibles come with a rear bench seat. A swing-away spare tire adds to interior space, and passengers ride on weather-resistant twill-effect upholstery.

Propulsion comes from a 4.0-liter aluminum V-8 that yields 182 horsepower, driving a ZF 4-speed automatic transmission. Riding a compact 92.9-inch wheelbase, the Defender wears aluminum body panels with minimal front and rear overhangs. Neither airbags nor

DEFENDER 90 — LAND ROVER

anti-lock brakes are available, and the brief option list only includes an air conditioning and special Beluga Black paint.

Land Rovers aren't known for silence or for sedate behavior, on or off the road. Gears are noisy, and road sounds are likely to assault passenger ears. Standing more than 6-1/2 feet tall, the sharply-profiled body can't help but lean over when undertaking sharp curves and corners.

A high price means the Defender 90 cannot qualify as a value leader among sport-utilities, but you do get the heritage that comes from the company that built the first jungle-trotting Land Rovers, nearly half a century ago.

Safety Data

Driver Airbag: *Not Available*
Side Airbag: *Not Available*
4-Wheel ABS: *Not Available*
Driver Crash Test Grade: *Not Available*
Passenger Crash Test Grade: *Not Available*

Passenger Airbag: *Not Available*
Meets 1999 Side Impact Standards: *No*
Traction Control: *Not Available*
Insurance Cost: *Not Available*
Integrated Child Seat(s): *Not Available*

Standard Equipment

DEFENDER 90 CONVERTIBLE: 4.0-liter aluminum V-8 engine, permanent 4WD, 2-speed transfer case with manual locking center differential, ZF 4-speed automatic transmission, 4-wheel long-travel coil spring suspension, front/rear sway bars, 4-wheel power disc brakes, internal/external custome Safari Cage system, P265/75R16 B.F. Goodrich all-season tires, 5-spoke alloy wheels with bright silver finish, element-repellent Tweed vinyl upholstery, reclining front bucket seats with integrated headrests, removable rear bench seat, lockable center cubby bin with integral audio system and cupholders, premium high-powered AM/FM cassette audio system with 4 weather-resistant speakers, mast-mounted antenna, swing-away rear-mounted spare tire carrier, half doors with removable sliding windows, door and seatback storage pockets, dual exterior mirrors, 2-speed intermittent front wipers, quartz halogen headlights, tachometer, class III trailer tow hitch receiver, flexible black wheel flares with integrated black bumpers

HARDTOP (in addition to or instead of CONVERTIBLE equipment): Aluminum top with roll-up front and sliding rear windows, one-piece side and rear doors, pop-up sunroof, four inward facing rear seats, full carpeting, full interior trim

Base Prices

		Invoice	MSRP
—	Convertible	28700	32000
—	Hardtop	30300	34000
Destination Charge:		625	625

Accessories

		Invoice	MSRP
—	Air Conditioning	1050	1200
—	California Emissions	100	100
—	Paint — Beluga Black	250	300

LAND ROVER — DISCOVERY

| CODE | DESCRIPTION | INVOICE | MSRP |

DISCOVERY *(1997)*

1997 Land Rover Discovery

What's New for Land Rover Discovery in 1997 — A diversity antenna is added, and all interiors are trimmed with polished burled walnut. The sunroof has darker tinting, the airbag system benefits from simplified operation, and engine management is improved. Three new exterior colors debut: Oxford Blue; Rioja Red; Charleston Green.

Discovery — Review

Introduced in April 1994, this compact 4X4 builds on a couple of Land Rover legends. Designed for go-anywhere capability, the Discovery exhibits excellent off-road ability. Built in England, the Discovery also exhibits a distressing tendency toward reliability problems. We receive lots of horror stories regarding Discovery reliability via e-mail, and Automobile magazine wrapped up a long-term test with a very troublesome 1995 model recently. Just one body style is available: a five-door wagon with permanent four-wheel-drive. An automatic transmission is optional. This year, three trim levels are available; the SD, SE and SE7.

Beneath the hood of all models sits an aluminum 4.0-liter, 182-horsepower V-8 engine. Acceleration isn't bad, but is accompanied by gear noise and other aural annoyances. Worse, this powerplant is rated for 13 mpg city/17 mpg highway, and that's with a light foot. Sizable ground clearance (8.1 inches) is a bonus while off-roading, but contributes to the Discovery's tendency to lean through curves and corners, and also makes it harder to climb inside. Though firm, the sport-utility's suspension delivers a suitable ride, via 16-inch Michelin or Goodyear tires. New exterior colors help differentiate the 1997 Discovery from those that preceded it.

The driver sits high — three feet above the road surface. Rear passengers sit higher still, for a superior view. Seating is available for seven, in the form of center-facing, stowable rear seats that come standard on the SE7, but this is a five-passenger vehicle in SD and SE trim. Though roomy enough, the Discovery holds fewer luxury fittings than might be expected in this price league. Only a handful of options are available, including leather upholstery. The spare

DISCOVERY — LAND ROVER

tire resides outside. The driver and front passenger have adjustable lumbar supports, and enjoy the benefits of dual-temperature control air conditioning. A full-size glovebox and four cupholders are included.

Changes for 1997 are minimal. A diversity antenna is added, and all interiors are trimmed with polished burled walnut. The sunroof has darker tinting, the airbag system benefits from simplified operation, and engine management is improved.

Legendary off-road capabilities help make the aluminum-bodied Discovery an attractive choice, augmented by safety equipment. If you expect to drive mainly around the suburbs rather than through the woods, the Discovery's high center of gravity and short wheelbase could be a drawback. The fact that a Discovery can ford a stream up to 19.7 inches deep isn't exactly a benefit when its primary duties involve driving to the office or the mall. In urban America, the Discovery is all about prestige, and it doesn't come cheaply or conveniently. We recommend the Discovery for off-road use, but most consumers will want a different truck to haul the Little Leaguers in.

Safety Data

Driver Airbag: *Standard*
Side Airbag: *Not Available*
4-Wheel ABS: *Standard*
Driver Crash Test Grade: *Good*
Passenger Crash Test Grade: *Good*

Passenger Airbag: *Standard*
Meets 1999 Side Impact Standards: *No*
Traction Control: *Not Available*
Insurance Cost: *High (5-spd); Very High (auto)*
Integrated Child Seat(s): *Not Available*

Standard Equipment

DISCOVERY SD: 4.0-liter aluminum V-8 engine, permanent 4WD, 2-speed transfer gearbox with manually locking center differential, long-travel single-rate front and dual-rate rear coil-spring suspension, dual-acting hydraulic dampers front and rear, front/rear sway bars, cloth upholstery, reclining front bucket seats with integrated adjustable lumbar support, cruise control, dual-zone climate control system, leather-wrapped steering wheel, burled walnut wood trim on dashboard, dual front airbags, four-wheel anti-lock disc brakes, remote keyless entry, security system featuring engine immobilization, illuminated entry, cargo cover, rear door child safety locks, power window and sunroof lockout switch, locking fuel cap, power windows with one-touch down feature on front windows, power-off delay logic for windows and sunroof, central locking, dual cupholders, center console storage bin, front/rear door map pockets, overhead net storage, roof-mounted storage bins, front seatback storage pockets, illuminated driver/passenger visor vanity mirrors, auto-dimming rearview mirror, 60/40 split-folding rear seat, dual power heated exterior mirrors, rear window defroster, variable intermittent wipers, rear window wiper/washer, quartz halogen headlights with power washers, tachometer, class III trailer tow hitch receiver, P235/70HR16 Michelin or Goodyear all-season tires, alloy wheels, full-size spare tire mounted on rear door, premium audio system with four speakers, amplified subwoofer system, and A-pillar tweeters; CD changer prewiring, diversity power antenna

SE (in addition to or instead of SD equipment): Heated power leather seats, burled walnut trim on door panels and gear shift, unique alloy wheels, dual sunroofs, front fog lights, HomeLink transmitter

SE7 (in addition to or instead of SE equipment): Rear jump seats, rear air conditioning, hydraulic rear step

LAND ROVER — DISCOVERY

CODE	DESCRIPTION	INVOICE	MSRP

Base Prices

SDVZ	SD w/Cloth Interior (5-spd)	28480	32000
SDVZ	SD w/Cloth Interior (auto)	28480	32000
SDVZ	SD w/Leather Interior (auto)	30260	34000
SDVZ	SE (auto)	32040	36000
SDVZ	SE7 (5-spd)	34265	38500
SDVZ	SE7 (auto)	34265	38500
Destination Charge:		625	625

Accessories

—	California Emissions	100	100
—	CD Changer w/6 disc capacity	525	625
—	Leather Power Seat Package (SD w/Cloth (auto))	1780	2000
—	Paint — Beluga Black Clearcoat	250	300
—	Rear Jump Seats — Cloth (SD w/Cloth)	735	875
—	Rear Jump Seats — Leather (SD w/Leather & SE)	819	975

RANGE ROVER *(1997)*

1997 Land Rover Range Rover 4.6 HSE

What's New for Land Rover Range Rover in 1997 — 4.0 SE gets three new exterior colors (Oxford Blue, Rioja Red, and White Gold, all matched to Saddle leather interior), a HomeLink transmitter, and jeweled wheel center caps. The 4.6 HSE gets three new exterior colors (British Racing Green, Monza Red, AA Yellow), one new interior color (Lightstone with contrasting piping), and a leather shift handle.

RANGE ROVER — LAND ROVER

Range Rover — Review

Virtually unbeatable in both snob appeal and off-road talent, the Range Rover comes in two trim levels: 4.0 SE and 4.6 HSE. Both are the benefactors of new colors and fresh finishing touches for 1997.

In the 4.0 SE, an update of Land Rover's 4.0-liter aluminum V-8 engine works in concert with a ZF four-speed automatic transmission, offering normal, sport, and manual shift programs. The 4.6 HSE comes equipped with a significantly stronger 4.6-liter V-8 engine. Electronic traction control augments the permanent four-wheel-drive system. All-disc, all-terrain anti-lock braking is standard. So is a CD changer. This Range Rover 4.0 SE can tow 6,500 pounds on the highway, or 7,700 pounds in low range. Under the sheetmetal is a ladder-type chassis, plus an electronic air suspension system and beam axles. Rear trailing arms are made of lightweight composite material.

The Range Rover is loaded with standard equipment. That means leather and burled walnut in the interior, automatic climate control for the driver and front passenger (with micro-pollen filtration), 10-way adjustable heated front seats with memory preset, sunroof, 120-watt stereo—well, you get the idea. Dual airbags protect driver and passenger.

In addition to a stronger engine, the 4.6 HSE adds Pirelli 255/55HR18 tires, five-spoke 18-inch alloy wheels, mud flaps, a leather shifter, and a chrome exhaust.

With a 4.0 SE priced well past fifty thou', the Range Rover obviously isn't for everyone. The Land Rover company calls it the "world's most advanced sport utility," aimed at "discerning drivers and sportsmen." We won't argue with that description. Given a choice, we'd prefer something on the order of a Lexus LS400 for ordinary highway driving. Still, if a taste of off-roading lies in your future, and a run-of-the-mill sport-utility vehicle doesn't turn you on, what better way to blast into the bush than in a Range Rover? It's not a drive, it's an experience.

Safety Data

Driver Airbag: *Standard*
Side Airbag: *Not Available*
4-Wheel ABS: *Standard*
Driver Crash Test Grade: *Not Available*
Passenger Crash Test Grade: *Not Available*

Passenger Airbag: *Standard*
Meets 1999 Side Impact Standards: *No*
Traction Control: *Standard*
Insurance Cost: *Not Available*
Integrated Child Seat(s): *Not Available*

Standard Equipment

4.0 SE: 4.0-liter aluminum V-8 engine, one-piece serpentine belt system, permanent 4WD, viscous coupling unit on center differential, 2-speed transfer gearbox with electronically-controlled range change, ZF 4-speed automatic transmission with Normal, Sport, and Manual shift programs; electronic air suspension system with air springs, shock absorbers, and height sensors at each wheel; front sway bar, P225/65HR16 Michelin tires, 5-spoke 16"x 8" alloy wheels, cruise control, tilt and slide glass sunroof, 10-way power adjustable heated front seats with lumbar support, 2-position preset memory feature for front seats, remote-activated memory for seats and mirrors when unlocking vehicle, one-touch open and close for windows and sunroof, automatic dual-zone climate control system with micro-pollen air filtration system, programmable defrost function with ice warning indicator, premium 120-watt audio system with 11 active speakers and 6-disc CD changer, steering wheel stereo controls, dual diversity antenna system, HomeLink transmitter, security system with perimetric and volumetric functions, engine immobilization feature, key-activated all-close feature for windows and sunroof, cargo cover, dual front airbags, traction control, four-wheel anti-lock disc brakes, automatic dimming rearview mirror, tilt and telescopic steering wheel, computer message center and vehicle

LAND ROVER — RANGE ROVER

condition displays, ignition-off delay logic for window and sunroof operation, front and rear puddle lamps, power windows, dual illuminated visor vanity mirrors, remote central locking, center console with cubby box and cupholders, remote fuel door release, dual power heated mirrors with right side dip feature when reversing, heated windshield and rear window, variable front wipers with heated washer jets, rear window wiper/washer with automatic activation when reversing with front wipers on, with heated headlight power washers and wipers, class III trailer tow hitch receiver, front spoiler with integrated fog lights, leather-wrapped steering wheel, burled walnut interior trim, leather upholstery

4.6 HSE (in addition to or instead of 4.0 SE equipment): 4.6-liter aluminum V-8 engine, P255/55HR18 Pirelli tires, five-spoke 18"x 8" alloy wheels, leather shift handle, body-flush mud flaps, chrome exhaust tip

Base Prices

Code	Description	Invoice	MSRP
SXLA	4.0 SE	49125	55500
SXLA	4.6 HSE	55750	63000
	Destination Charge:	625	625

Accessories

Code	Description	Invoice	MSRP
416	Beluga Black Paint (4.0 SE)	250	300
—	California Emissions	100	100
—	Kensington Interior Package (4.6 HSE)	2675	3000

One 15-minute call could save you 15% or more on car insurance.

America's 6th Largest Automobile Insurance Company

1-800-555-2758

LX 450 *(1997)*

1997 Lexus LX450

What's New for Lexus LX 450 in 1997 — There are no changes to the 1997 LX450.

LX 450 — Review

Japanese automakers are being very cautious these days. High production costs are softening sales across the board, and executives across the Pacific are frantically searching for ways to cut costs. Decontenting is one way to do this. Badge engineering is the other. Lexus chose the latter method when making the decision to offer a sport utility vehicle.

The Toyota Land Cruiser, legendary desert runner and jungle jumper, was donated to the Lexus team of plastic surgeons. They grafted a new grille, new headlamps, new alloy wheels, and bodyside cladding onto Toyota's big SUV. Inside, they added leather and wood. Underneath the sheetmetal, suspension tuning was reworked to provide a better ride on the pavement. Standard equipment levels were raised to include automatic climate controls, rear seat heater, and an amazing 195-watt audio system powering seven loudspeakers. Topping things off, a LX450 badge was added to the tailgate.

The rest of Land Cruiser remains intact on the LX450. The familiar 4.5-liter inline six produces 212 horsepower and 275 lb-ft. of torque. Four-wheel anti-lock disc brakes are standard, and the LX450 can tow 5,000 pounds when properly equipped. All-wheel drive is permanently engaged, and an optional manual differential lock system provides outstanding traction, for the two LX450 owners who will actually go way off-road in truly lousy weather. Dual airbags and adjustable front seat belts come standard, as well as a handy first-aid kit.

You'll pay a $7,000 premium over the Land Cruiser to get into a LX450, which is less than you'd spend optioning the Toyota up to Lexus standards. Factory options on the LX450 include a CD changer, moonroof, and differential locks. Incredibly, floor mats and wheel locks are optional. Talk about nickel-and-diming; these items should be included as standard equipment.

LEXUS
LX 450

| CODE | DESCRIPTION | INVOICE | MSRP |

Land Rover sales have been skyrocketing, and luxury marques from the United States and Japan have definitely noticed. However, at $47,000, the only reason to purchase a LX450 is for status value, or to save a few thousand over the cost of a Range Rover 4.0 SE. Most luxury SUV intenders will find the value inherent in the GMC Yukon SLE, Chevy Suburban LT, and upcoming Ford Expedition and Lincoln Navigator twins more attractive than nice leather and wood inserted into a tough Toyota.

Safety Data

Driver Airbag: *Standard*
Side Airbag: *Not Available*
4-Wheel ABS: *Standard*
Driver Crash Test Grade: *Good*
Passenger Crash Test Grade: *Good*

Passenger Airbag: *Standard*
Meets 1999 Side Impact Standards: *No*
Traction Control: *Not Available*
Insurance Cost: *N/A*
Integrated Child Seat(s): *Not Available*

Standard Equipment

LX 450: 4.5 liter 24 valve EFI inline 6 cylinder engine, 4-speed ECT automatic transmission with overdrive, power steering, anti-lock power 4-wheel disc brakes, power door locks, tachometer, cruise control, leather-wrapped tilt steering wheel, electric rear window defroster, power windows with driver's side express-down feature, driver and front passenger air bags, front and rear stabilizer bars, P275/70R16 SBR tires, conventional spare tire, alloy wheels, console, tool kit, automatic air conditioning, variable intermittent windshield wipers, intermittent rear window wiper/washer, privacy glass, anti-theft system, keyless remote entry system, voltmeter, oil pressure gauge, remote fuel filler door release, skid plates (transfer case, fuel tank), dual power mirrors, illuminated passenger visor vanity mirror, lower bodyside moldings, AM/FM ETR stereo radio with cassette and 7 speakers, front and rear tow hooks, power reclining front bucket seats, fold-down middle seat, split fold-down removable rear seat, leather seating and door trim panels, full-time 4WD with locking center differential, 25 gallon fuel tank, color-keyed bumpers.

Base Prices

9600	Sport Utility (auto)	41595	48450
	Destination Charge:	495	495

Accessories

WL	Wheel Locks	35	50
SR	Power Moonroof — glass	1040	1300
	incls tilt/slide and shade		
CF	Floor Mats — carpeted, front and rear	68	112
CD	CD Auto Changer — 6-disc, console-mounted	840	1050
DL	Front & Rear Locking Differentials	720	900
2D	Convenience Pkg	646	1039
	incls running boards, cargo compartment mat, luggage rack, trailer towing hitch		

B-SERIES PICKUP *(1997)*

1997 Mazda B4000 SE 2WD

What's New for Mazda B-Series Pickup in 1997 — The lineup is trimmed, leaving just B2300 and B4000 models available. SE-5 designation returns to bolster marketing efforts. B4000 pickups can be equipped with a new 5-speed automatic transmission.

B-Series Pickup — Review

Kinship of Mazda's B-Series with Ford's Ranger is evident both on the surface and beneath. That's because both compact pickups are built at the same New Jersey factory, from the same design, and employ virtually identical powertrains and four-wheel-drive setups. Both are competent and attractive, differing only in detail and pricing structure.

Four-wheel anti-lock brakes are standard on all 4WD models. SE models equipped with the SE-5 Plus package also include this safety feature. A rear-wheel system is standard on all other B-Series trucks. All B-Series models come standard with a driver's side airbag. A passenger's side airbag is available as part of the SE-5 Plus option package, and the airbag can be deactivated for those times when small children must ride in the front seat.

Horsepower of the 2.3-liter four-cylinder engine that powers B2300 models measures 112. Those who like to flex their truck's muscle are likely to be attracted to the B4000 end of the scale. Its 4.0-liter V-6 delivers 160 horsepower, plus a 220 pound-feet torque wallop—just right for heavy hauling and easy merging/passing on the highway. For 1997, this engine can be mated to a 5-speed automatic transmission and can tow up to 5,900 pounds when properly equipped.

Two cab configurations are available with either two- or four-wheel drive. Two trim levels are marketed, down from three in 1996: base and sporty SE. The slow-selling luxury-oriented LE trim level is dropped this year. Your ticket to the options list is the SE trim level. Base models can only be equipped with air conditioning, power steering, an automatic transmission, and a bedliner.

A B2300 pickup looks truly basic inside, but carries full gauges (without graduations) and simple climate controls. In base form, a Mazda with a simple vinyl bench seat looks to be

MAZDA B-SERIES PICKUP

all truck—pristine and practical, almost like a cargo hauler out of the 1940s. Add such amenities as air conditioning and power steering, though, and you get a comfortable-driving, highly functional machine for only a moderate financial outlay.

Select any Mazda truck, and you get rugged construction, good looks and with the B4000, a spirited powertrain. Best of all, Mazda offers one of the best comprehensive truck warranties in the business. It's hard to go wrong with a Mazda B-Series pickup.

Safety Data

Driver Airbag: *Standard*
Side Airbag: *Not Available*
4-Wheel ABS: *N/A (Base); Opt. (SE 2WD); Std. (4WD)*
Driver Crash Test Grade: *Good*
Passenger Crash Test Grade: *Good*

Passenger Airbag: *N/A (B2300); Opt. (B4000 SE)*
Meets 1999 Side Impact Standards: *No*
Traction Control: *Not Available*
Insurance Cost: *Very Low (Reg Cab 2WD); Low (X-cab 2WD); Average (4WD)*
Integrated Child Seat(s): *Not Available*

Standard Equipment

BASE: 2.3-liter inline four-cylinder engine (B2300), 4.0-liter V-6 engine (B4000), power front disc/rear drum brakes, rear anti-lock brakes (2WD), four-wheel anti-lock brakes (4WD), manual steering (Regular Cab 2WD), power steering (Cab Plus and 4WD), P195/70R14 tires (2WD), P215/75R15 tires (4WD), 14"x 5.5" styled steel wheels (2WD), 15"x 6" styled steel wheels (4WD), black front bumper, black rear step bumper, tinted glass, black grille, single note horn, dual black paddle-type exterior mirrors, black front/rear mud flaps, black tailgate handle, four cargo box tie down hooks, rear tow hook (4WD), black wheel flares (4WD), black wheel hub covers, 2-speed intermittent wipers, driver's airbag, passenger assist handle, headlights-on alert, door ajar alert, cigarette lighter, coat hook, vinyl door trim panels, rubber floor covering, cloth headliner, illuminated entry system, tachometer (4WD), trip odometer, day/night rearview mirror, auxiliary 12-volt power outlet, AM/FM stereo with clock and four speakers, vinyl bench seat (Regular Cab), 60/40 cloth split reclining bench seat with center storage armrest (Cab Plus), rear jump seats (Cab Plus), vinyl sunvisors (Regular Cab), cloth sunvisors (Cab Plus), fixed quarter windows (Cab Plus)

SE (in addition to or instead of BASE equipment): P225/70R14 tires (2WD), P235/75R15 tires (4WD Cab Plus), 14"x 6" full face steel wheels (2WD), 15"x 7" full face steel wheels (4WD Cab Plus), chrome front bumper, chrome rear step bumper, medium silver grille with chrome accent, dual note horn, dual black aerohead exterior mirrors, chrome cab outline molding (Cab Plus), SE tape designation, chrome tailgate handle, SE tape striping, overhead map lights, perforated vinyl door trim insert with lower carpeted portion, front door map pockets, full floor carpeting, tachometer (2WD), cargo box light, 60/40 cloth split reclining bench seat with center storage armrest (Regular Cab), rear storage net (Cab Plus), cloth sunvisors (Regular Cab)

Base Prices

CODE	DESCRIPTION	INVOICE	MSRP
CR12A	B2300 2WD Base Reg Cab Shortbed	10036	10870
CR12A	B2300 2WD SE Reg Cab Shortbed	11381	12750
CR13X	B4000 4WD Base Reg Cab Shortbed	15170	16265
CR12A	B2300 2WD SE Cab Plus	13452	15070

B-SERIES PICKUP — MAZDA

CODE	DESCRIPTION	INVOICE	MSRP
CR16X	B4000 2WD SE Cab Plus	14026	15715
CR17X	B4000 4WD Base Cab Plus	16196	18150
CR17X	B4000 4WD SE Cab Plus	17385	19485
	Destination Charge:	510	510

Accessories

CODE	DESCRIPTION	INVOICE	MSRP
AC1	Air Conditioning (Base)	660	805
AT1	Automatic Transmission (B2300 Reg Cab)	857	1045
AT1	Automatic Transmission (B4000 SE X-cab)	886	1080
BLN	Bedliner (Base)	165	275
CE1	California/Massachusetts Emissions	82	100
FLM	Carpeted Floor Mats (SE)	56	80
CD2	CD Changer w/6-disc capacity (SE X-cab)	365	445
	REQUIRES SE-5 Plus Group		
HA1	High Altitude Emissions	NC	NC
PS1	Power Steering (B2300 Base 2WD Reg Cab)	226	275
1SG	SE Group (SE 2WD Reg Cab)	836	1020
	Manufacturer Discount	(455)	(555)
	Net Price	381	465
	Includes power steering, alloy wheels, sliding rear window, AM/FM stereo with cassette player		
1SG	SE Group (SE 2WD X-cab)	734	895
	Manufacturer Discount	(406)	(495)
	Net Price	328	400
	Includes alloy wheels, sliding rear window, swing-out rear quarter windows, retractable cargo cover, AM/FM stereo with cassette player		
1SG	SE Group (SE 4WD X-cab)	595	725
	Manufacturer Discount	(365)	(445)
	Net Price	230	280
	Includes alloy wheels, sliding rear window, swing-out rear quarter windows, retractable cargo cover, AM/FM stereo with cassette player		
SE-5	SE-5 Group (SE 2WD Reg Cab)	1722	2100
	Manufacturer Discount	(619)	(775)
	Net Price	1103	1325
	Includes power steering, alloy wheels, sliding rear window, AM/FM stereo with cassette player, bedliner, air conditioning		
SE-5	SE-5 Group (SE 2WD X-cab)	1620	1975
	Manufacturer Discount	(570)	(695)
	Net Price	1050	1280
	Includes alloy wheels, sliding rear window, swing-out rear quarter windows, retractable cargo cover, AM/FM stereo with cassette player, bedliner, air conditioning		
SE-5	SE-5 Group (SE 4WD X-cab)	1805	1480
	Manufacturer Discount	(529)	(645)
	Net Price	1276	835
	Includes alloy wheels, sliding rear window, swing-out rear quarter windows, retractable cargo cover, AM/FM stereo with cassette player, bedliner, air conditioning		

MAZDA B-SERIES PICKUP

CODE	DESCRIPTION	INVOICE	MSRP
SEP	SE-5 Plus Group (B4000 SE 2WD X-cab)	3497	4265
	Manufacturer Discount	(857)	(1045)
	Net Price	2640	3220

Includes alloy wheels, sliding rear window, swing-out rear quarter windows, retractable cargo cover, AM/FM stereo with cassette player, bedliner, air conditioning, passenger's side airbag, 4-wheel anti-lock brakes, power windows, power door locks, power exterior mirrors, cruise control, tilt steering wheel, premium sound system, remote keyless entry, anti-theft system

SEP	SE-5 Plus Group (B4000 SE 4WD X-cab)	3358	4095
	Manufacturer Discount	(1078)	(1315)
	Net Price	2280	2780

Includes alloy wheels, sliding rear window, swing-out rear quarter windows, retractable cargo cover, AM/FM stereo with cassette player, bedliner, air conditioning, passenger's side airbag, power windows, power door locks, power exterior mirrors, cruise control, tilt steering wheel, premium sound system, remote keyless entry, anti-theft alarm

SB2	Sport Seats (SE X-cab)	295	360
	REQUIRES SE-5 Group or SE-5 Plus Group		
CD1	Stereo — w/CD player (SE)	70	85
1PP	Towing/Payload Package (B4000 SE 2WD X-cab)	271	330
	Includes heavy-duty springs, heavy-duty shocks, rear stabilizer bar, performance axle ratio, limited slip differential, increased payload capacity		
1PP	Towing/Payload Package (B4000 SE 4WD X-cab)	361	440
	Includes heavy-duty springs, heavy-duty shocks, rear stabilizer bar, performance axle ratio, limited slip differential, increased payload capacity, P265/75R15 all-terrain outline white-lettered tires		

Save hundreds, even thousands, off the sticker price of the new car _you_ want.

Call Autovantage®
your FREE auto-buying service

1-800-201-7703

No purchase required. No fees.

MPV (1997)

1997 Mazda MPV All Sport

What's New for Mazda MPV in 1997 — Four-wheel ABS is standard across the board, and all but the LX 2WD model are dressed in dorky All-Sport exterior trim.

MPV — Review

Mazda's MPV lineup, streamlined to three models last year, has been revised again. Two trim levels remain: well-equipped LX, and luxury ES. Last year's value-leader DX trim level has been dropped. Upper-level minivans can have shift-on-the-fly four-wheel-drive. Four-wheel disc anti-lock brakes are standard on all models. The ES edition contains such pleasantries as leather seating surfaces, and automatic load leveling.

Like Honda's Odyssey, the longer-lived Mazda minivan does without a sliding entry door, matching the Odyssey by providing rear doors on both sides. Mazda promises sedan-like comfort and ride qualities for up to eight passengers in the MPV. Front MacPherson struts and front/rear stabilizer bars help keep the minivan comfortable and on-course. Bucket seats hold the front occupants, while three each can fit on the middle and back seat. Optional on LX and standard on ES models are quad captain's chairs. Center-section leg room is less than great, but most riders aren't likely to complain. When fewer passengers are aboard, cargo space can reach 110 cubic feet.

Acceleration with the 155-horsepower, 18-valve, 3.0-liter V-6 engine is sufficient. Four-wheel drive cuts into potential performance, because of its sizable extra weight. Gas mileage also dips considerably with 4WD vans. A four-speed automatic, with electronic controls, is the sole transmission choice. With 4WD, a dashboard switch can lock the center differential, for peak low-speed traction.

Inside and out—especially up front—MPVs offer a distinctive appearance, not quite like most minivans. Styling was revised for 1996, and the MPV now sports a protruding, ungainly countenance in an effort to make it look more like a sport utility. For 1997, all MPV models except the 2WD LX are dressed in All-Sport trim, which consists of a grille guard, fender

MAZDA MPV

flares, rear bumper guard, stone guard, roof rack, special graphics, and alloy wheels. A contemporary instrument panel contains dual airbags. Visibility is terrific from the airy cabin.

The 1997 MPV is the equivalent of an Arch Deluxe that's been sitting under the heating lamp too long. There's more to it, but it's old, loaded with fat, and costs more than many competitors. We liked the old MPV plenty for its crisp, clean looks and fun rear-wheel drive personality. This heavier, bulbous, SUV-wannabe model leaves us cold. And with base stickers approaching $23,500 with destination charges, we can't recommend the MPV over most other minivans on the market.

Safety Data

Driver Airbag: *Standard*
Side Airbag: *Not Available*
4-Wheel ABS: *Standard*
Driver Crash Test Grade: *Not Available*
Passenger Crash Test Grade: *Not Available*

Passenger Airbag: *Standard*
Meets 1997 Car Side Impact Standards: *No*
Traction Control: *Not Available*
Insurance Cost: *High*
Integrated Child Seat(s): *Not Available*

Standard Equipment

MPV LX 2WD: 3.0-liter SOHC 16-valve V-6 engine, 4-speed electronically-controlled automatic transmission with overdrive, engine-rpm-sensing power rack and pinion steering, power 4-wheel disc anti-lock brakes, 15-inch steel wheels with full wheel covers, P195/75R15 tires, dual power exterior mirrors, variable intermittent windshield wipers, intermittent rear window wiper/washer, bodyside moldings, tinted glass, dual front airbags, 8-passenger seating, reclining front bucket seats with adjustable headrests, second row reclining seat with fore/aft adjustment, easy-fold flip forward and removable third row seat, velour upholstery, tilt steering wheel, rear window defogger, AM/FM stereo with full-logic auto-reverse cassette deck and four speakers, digital clock, power door locks, cruise control, power windows, map pockets on front door panels, child safety locks for rear doors, remote fuel door release, tachometer, rear heat vents

LX 4WD (in addition to or instead of LX 2WD equipment): Multi-mode four-wheel drive system, lockable center differential, All-Sport Appearance Package (includes stone guard, grille guard, fender flares, rear bumper guard, roof rack, P225/70R15 tires, polished 5-spoke alloy wheels), special two-tone paint, 4-seasons Package (includes rear heater, large capacity windshield washer tank, heavy-duty battery), larger cooling fan, full-size spare tire

ES 2WD (in addition to or instead of LX 2WD equipment): All-Sport Appearance Package (includes stone guard, grille guard, fender flares, rear bumper buard, roof roack, P215/65R15 tires, polished 5-spoke alloy wheels), special two-tone paint, Load Leveling Package (includes automatic load leveling system, transmission oil cooler, larger cooling fan, full-size spare tire), 7-passenger seating with quad captain's chairs and 3 passenger third row seat, leather seating surfaces, leather-wrapped steering wheel

ES 4WD (in addition to or instead of ES 2WD equipment): Multi-mode four-wheel drive system, lockable center differential, 4-seasons Package (includes rear heater, large capacity windshield washer tank, heavy-duty battery)

MPV

CODE	DESCRIPTION	INVOICE	MSRP

Base Prices

LV522	LX 2WD	20935	23095
LV523	LX 4WD	24379	26895
LV522	ES 2WD	23804	26395
LV523	ES 4WD	26179	28895
Destination Charge:		480	480

Accessories

Code	Description	Invoice	MSRP
1CO	4-Seasons Package (2WD)	298	350
	Includes heavy duty battery, large capacity washer fluid tank, and rear heater		
1AP	All-Sport Package (LX 2WD)	748	880
	Includes grille guard, stone guard, fender flares, rear bumper guard, roof rack, All-Sport graphics, polished alloy wheels, P215/65R15 all-season tires		
1WP	Alloy Wheel Package (LX 2WD)	421	495
	Includes lace design alloy wheels and P215/65R15 all-season tires		
CDP	CD Player	298	350
1ES	ES Preferred Equipment Group 1 (ES)	1913	2250
	Manufacturer Discount	(727)	(855)
	Net Price	1186	1395
	Includes front and rear air conditioning, remote keyless entry, rear privacy glass, floor mats		
1TP	Load Leveling Package (LX 2WD)	506	595
	Includes automatic load leveling, transmission oil cooler, high capacity cooling fan, and full-size spare tire		
1TP	Load Leveling Package (LX 4WD)	421	495
	Includes automatic load leveling and transmission oil cooler		
1LX	LX Preferred Equipment Group 1 (LX)	1318	1550
	Manufacturer Discount	(642)	(755)
	Net Price	676	795
	Includes air conditioning, remote keyless entry, rear privacy glass, floor mats		
2LX	LX Preferred Equipment Group 2 (LX)	1913	2250
	Manufacturer Discount	(642)	(755)
	Net Price	1271	1495
	Includes front and rear air conditioning, remote keyless entry, rear privacy glass, floor mats		
MR1	Power Sunroof (ES)	1020	1200
QC1	Quad Captain's Chairs (LX)	340	400
JCP	Two-tone Paint (LX 2WD)	298	350

MERCURY — MOUNTAINEER

| CODE | DESCRIPTION | INVOICE | MSRP |

MOUNTAINEER *(1997)*

1997 Mercury Mountaineer

What's New for Mercury Mountaineer in 1997 — The all-new Mercury Mountaineer is yet another entrant into the booming luxury sport/utility market. Based on the wildly successful Ford Explorer, the Mountaineer is intended to appeal to outdoor sophisticates rather than true roughnecks. Distinguishing characteristics of the Mountaineer include four-wheel anti-lock brakes, a pushrod V-8 engine and optional all-wheel drive.

Mountaineer — Review

We have received a vast number of requests for information about the Mercury Mountaineer since the first rumors of its existence began circulating in the press last winter. Well folks, here it is; the Ford Explorer, er, we mean Mercury Mountaineer. That's right, the truck you have all been waiting for is nothing more than a Ford Explorer with a big chrome grill, bodyside cladding, two-tone paint and a discus-size Mercury badge on the liftgate. Sorry to burst your bubble, gang.

This isn't anything new for Mercury; their entire lineup consists of slightly dressed-up versions of cars you can buy at Blue Oval dealerships. What is new, however, is the fact that this is the first truck Lincoln-Mercury has ever sold in the U.S.; not counting the Villager minivan. The fact that Mercury is selling a rebadged Explorer only means that it will have considerable success in the market. You see, the Ford Explorer has been far and away the best-selling sport/utility vehicle ever sold in the United States. Why then, did Ford decide to share a piece of its pie with its cousins at Mercury? Probably because Mercury has been losing sales of near-luxury cars since the luxury SUV boom began. It seems that the Grand Marquis just can't keep up with vehicles like the Grand Cherokee.

With half the world already owning Explorers, to whom does Mercury intend to sell this truck? Well, it appears that they have their sights set on women and upscale families. Jim Engelhardt, vice-president of Ford light-truck development says, "We know that women are particularly concerned about safety and security, so the Mountaineer includes many important features that are not always found on compact sport/utility vehicles." These

MOUNTAINEER — MERCURY

features include: dual airbags, anti-lock brakes, fog lamps and dual rear bumper reflectors. For those living in inclement climates, or those who actually intend to make use of the vehicle's off-road capabilities, there is a full-time all-wheel drive model available. The Mountaineer differs from most trucks with four-wheel drive systems because no driver input is needed to engage the front axle, it provides power at all times regardless of road or weather conditions. Families with children will be happy to know that they can order a Mountaineer with an integrated child seat. However, to get the child seat they must also order the leather interior. Does that make sense? Who wants kids climbing all over their leather interior? I bet the designer who came up with that option requirement never had to pick up four toddlers in cleats after a pee-wee soccer match.

The Mountaineer promises to be a big hit. Like the Explorer it is based on, the Mountaineer has plenty of space for hauling people and their stuff through the suburban jungle. The Mercury SUV's abundant standard features provide a great deal of comfort, and the larger-than-average engine is a bonus when passing at freeway speeds. We think, however, that people will buy the Mountaineer for reasons far less tangible than those listed. People will buy the Mountaineer not on the basis of how it serves its master, but how it impresses the neighbors. That's the name of the game with sport/utility vehicles these days; so why not?

Safety Data

Driver Airbag: *Standard*
Side Airbag: *Not Available*
4-Wheel ABS: *Standard*
Driver Crash Test Grade: *Good*
Passenger Crash Test Grade: *Good*

Passenger Airbag: *Standard*
Meets 1999 Side Impact Standards: *Unknown*
Traction Control: *Not Available*
Insurance Cost: *Low*
Integrated Child Seat(s): *Optional*

Standard Equipment

MOUNTAINEER 2WD: 5.0-liter V-8 engine, 4-speed automatic transmisison, 3.73 limted slip differential, heavy duty gas-charged shock absorbers, front and rear stabilizer bars, power rack and pinion steering, P235/75R15 OWL tires, anti-lock brakes, dual air bags, manual air conditioning, cigarette lighter and ashtray, front map/rear dome light, cargo area dome light, front door map pockets, lockable glove box, grab handles, four gauge instrument cluster, light group, cagro floor tie-down hooks, power windows and door locks, power outside mirrors, premium AM/FM stereo with cassette, premium cloth captain's chairs, floor console, speed control, leather-wrapped steering wheel, leather head rests, dual illuminated visor vanity mirrors, tilt steering, fog lamps, tinted glass, privacy glass, two-tone paint, cast aluminum wheels, speed sensitive dual intermittent windshield wipers, and rear windo intermittent wipers.

MOUNTAINEER AWD (in addition or to or instead of MOUNTAINEER 2WD): Full-time AWD transfer case and skid plates.

Base Prices

U52	2WD	24591	27240
U52	4WD	26351	29240
Destination Charge:		525	525

MERCURY MOUNTAINEER

Code	Description	Invoice	MSRP
Accessories			
422	California Emissions System	85	100
655	Cargo Cover	68	80
Z	Cloth Sport Bucket Seats	812	955
	Includes power 6-way adjuster and power lumbar support.		
59B	Electrochromic Mirror/Autolamp	158	185
	REQUIRES 151 electronics group and 41N overhead console. NOT AVAILABLE with package 650A		
151	Electronics Group	314	370
	Includes remote keyless entry and anti-theft.		
41H	Engine Block Heater	30	35
167	Floor Mats	38	45
	NOT AVAILABLE with Preferred Equipment Packages 650A or 655A.		
153	Front License Plate Bracket	NC	NC
428	High Altiitude Principal Use Emissions System	NC	NC
418	High Series Floor Console	332	390
	Includes rear heater and audio controls, front and rear cupholders. REQUIRES 6-way power seat and 151 electronics; NOT AVAILABLE with Pkg 650A.		
87C	Integrated Child Seat	170	200
	REQUIRES leather seat trim.		
916	JBL Audio System	706	830
	Includes cassette. REQUIRES 151 electronics group, 418 high series floor console and 6-way power seat.		
615	Luggage Rack	119	140
	NOT AVAILABLE with Pkg 650A.		
91P	Multi-Disc CD Changer	314	370
	NOT AVAILABLE with Pkg 650A.		
41N	Overhead Storage Console	149	175
	Includes outside temperature gauge, compass, reading light and storage bin. REQUIRES 6-way power seats, 418 high series floor console and 151 electronic group.		
439	Power Moonroof w/Shade	680	800
	Includes 41N overhead console. REQUIRES 151 electronics group, 418 high series floor console, 615 luggage rack and 6-way power seat; NOT AVAILABLE with Pkg 650A.		
655A	Preferred Equipment Package 655A	1118	1315
	Includes Preferred Equipment Package 650A plus retractable cargo cover, cloth sport bucket seats (includes power 6-way adjustment with power lumbar support) overhead storage console, electronics group and high series floor console.		
650A	Preferred Equipment Pkg 650A	195	230
	Includes floor mats, luggage rack and running boards.		
186	Running Boards	336	395
F	Sport Bucket Leather Seats	532	625
	NOT AVAILABLE with package 650A.		

VILLAGER — MERCURY

CODE	DESCRIPTION	INVOICE	MSRP

VILLAGER *(1997)*

1997 Mercury Villager Nautica

What's New for Mercury Villager Passenger Wagon in 1997 — For 1997, the Villager offers a few more luxury items to distinguish this vehicle from the Nissan Quest. Quad captain's chairs are a nice alternative to the middle-row bench, and the addition of rear radio controls and rear air conditioning should also make rear seat passengers happy.

Villager Passenger Wagon — Review

Mercury entered the minivan market in 1993, as part of a joint venture with Nissan. Designed in California and built at the same factory in Ohio, Mercury Villagers and Nissan Quests share plenty of sleek styling touches and on-the-road traits. Wheelbases are similar to the first-generation, short-bodied Dodge Caravan, but the Villager measures nearly a foot longer overall. Three models grace showrooms: GS and LS wagons, a glitzy Nautica edition (attractively trimmed to remind occupants of the sea, or overpriced clothing, depending on your orientation).

Car-like characteristics were a priority when the Villager and Quest were created, and the result is impressive. Even though you're sitting taller than in a passenger car, behind a rather high steering wheel, it's easy enough to forget that this is a minivan. The driver's seat is supportive and comfortable, and there's plenty of space up front. Standard gauges are smallish but easy to read (optional digital instruments are not). You get fairly nimble handling, plus a smooth, quiet ride from the absorbent suspension. Only one powertrain is available—Nissan's 151-horsepower, 3.0-liter V-6 hooked to a four-speed automatic transmission—but that's a smoothie, too.

Four-wheel anti-lock braking is standard on the LS and Nautica versions; optional on the GS. Villagers offer ample space for five, and many are fitted to seat seven, in a flexible interior configuration. The far rear seat on seven-passenger models slides forward and back on a set of tracks, and center seats lift out. Be warned, though: those "removable" seats aren't lightweights. A full load of storage bins and cubbyholes augments the Villager's practical appeal.

MERCURY VILLAGER

Villager blends comfort and convenience into one tidy package. A family of five could easily live with this minivan. For larger broods or folks who regularly tote seven passengers and cargo, we think you ought to shop the bigger Windstar or Grand Caravan.

Safety Data

Driver Airbag: *Standard*
Side Airbag: *Not Available*
4-Wheel ABS: *Std (LS), Nautica;Opt (GS)*
Driver Crash Test Grade: *Good*
Passenger Crash Test Grade: *Average*

Passenger Airbag: *Standard*
Meets 1997 Car Side Impact Standards: *Yes*
Traction Control: *Not Available*
Insurance Cost: *Low*
Integrated Child Seat(s): *Optional*

Standard Equipment

GS: 3.9 liter V-6 engine, 4-speed automatic transmission, rack-and-pinion steering, front disc/rear drum brakes, MacPherson strut front suspension, Hotchkiss rear suspension, front stabilizer bar, P205/75R15 tires, mini spare, high capacity radiator, cornering lamps, 7 cupholders, rear window wiper/washer, front and rear floor mats, underseat storage box, front and rear dome lamps, solar glass, halogen headlamps, dual visor mirrors, dual air bags, AM/FM stereo with 4 speakers, and 7 passenger seatting.

LS (in addition to or instead of GS): Anti-lock brakes, air conditioning, cargo net, rear window defroster, privacy glass, light group, power door locks, power windows, and power outside mirrors.

NAUTICA (in addition to or instead of LS): Leather seats, 4 captain's chairs, extra pluch floor mats, unique grille, color keyed sideview mirrors, Nautica Appearance Pkg, and Nautica badges.

Base Prices

Code	Description	Invoice	MSRP
V11	GS	18299	20215
V11	LS	22585	25085
V11	Nautica	24174	26915
	Destination Charge:	580	580

Accessories

Code	Description	Invoice	MSRP
21A	7-Passenger Seating (GS)	281	330
	With 691A (GS) And 692A (GS)	NC	NC
904	Alarm System	85	100
	REQUIRES anti-lock brakes (GS) and 948 remote keyless entry.		
64U	Aluminum Wheels (GS)	336	395
67B	Anti-Lock Brakes (GS)	503	590
573	Automatic Temperature Control (LS)	548	645
	With 574 (GS)	153	180
422	California Emissions	85	100
18N	Cargo Net (GS)	26	30
64J	Deluxe Aluminum Wheels (GS)	34	40
	REQUIRES PEP 692A.		

VILLAGER — MERCURY

CODE	DESCRIPTION	INVOICE	MSRP
64J	Deluxe Aluminum Wheels (LS)	336	395
15A	Electronic Instrumentation (LS)	208	245
	Includes trip computer, digital speedometer, tachometer, outside temperature gauge, and 2 trip meters. REQUIRES 573 automatic temperature control.		
17F	Flip-Open Tailgate	97	115
	INCLUDED in PEP 692A, 696A, and 697A.		
572	Front Air Conditioning (GS)	727	855
	INCLUDED in GS PEPs.		
694	Handling Suspension	73	85
	Includes firm ride suspension, rear stabilizer bar, P215/70R15 SBR performance tires, and aluminum wheels.		
54H	Heated Mirrors (LS)	43	50
428	High Altitude Emissions	NC	NC
412	Illuminated Vanity Mirrors (GS)	21	25
97C	Integrated Child Seats	204	240
52R	Leather-Wrapped Steering Wheel (LS)	272	320
	Inlcudes steering wheel mounted speed control.		
593	Light Group (GS)	140	165
	Includes overhead map lights, front door step lights, liftgate window, under dash lights, and power vent windows. REQUIRES PEP 692A.		
615	Luggage Rack (GS)	149	175
951	Monotone Paint (LS)	(115)	(135)
90P	Power Driver's Seat	336	395
	INCLUDED in PEP 692A, 696A, and 697A.		
60B	Power Group (GS)	569	670
	Includes power windows, power door locks, and power outside mirrors. INCLUDED in PEP 691A and 692A.		
539	Power Moonroof (LS)	659	775
90F	Power Passenger's Seat (LS)	166	195
	REQUIRES power driver's seat. INCLUDED in PEP 696A.		
691A	Preferred Equipment Pkg 691A (GS)	1359	1600
	Includes front air conditioning, power group (power locks, windows, and mirrors), speed control, electric rear window defroster, and quad seating.		
692A	Preferred Equipment Pkg 692A (GS)	2891	3400
	Includes 8-way power driver's seat, remote keyless entry, privacy glass, anti-lock brakes, rear air conditioning, luggage rack, underseat storage, aluminum wheels, flip-open liftgate window, front air conditioning, power group (power locks, windows, and mirrors), speed control, electric rear window defroster, and quad seating.		
696A	Preferred Equipment Pkg 696A (LS)	1639	1930
	Includes deluxe aluminum wheels, leather quad captain's chairs, 8-way power driver's seat, 4-way power passenger seat, illuminated vanity mirrors, rear air conditioning, remote keyless entry, heated power mirrors, flip-open liftgate window,		

MERCURY VILLAGER

CODE	DESCRIPTION	INVOICE	MSRP
	leather-wrapped steering wheel, and steering wheel radio controls.		
697A	Preferred Equipment Pkg 697A (Nautica)	1275	1500
	Includes 8-way power driver's seat, 4-way power passenger's seat, illuminated vanity mirrors, remote keyless entry, heated power mirrors, flip-open liftgate window, leather-wrapped steering wheel, automatic temperature control, rear air conditioning, electronic instrument cluster, and steering wheel mounted radio controls.		
588	Premium Stereo w/Cassette & CD Player (LS/Nautica)	735	865
	Includes SuperSound AM/FM stereo, cassette, CD player, 4 premium speakers and sub-woofer. REQUIRES PEP 696A (LS).		
924	Privacy Glass	325	415
	REQUIRES 57Q rear window defroster.		
21H	Quad Captain's Chairs (GS)	603	710
21H	Quad Captain's Chairs (LS)	531	625
574	Rear Air Conditioning (GS)	395	465
57Q	Rear Window Defroster	144	170
948	Remote Keyless Entry	149	175
	REQUIRES PEP 691A or 692A (GS).		
52N	Speed Control	191	225
91X	Stereo w/Cassette (GS)	263	310
	REQUIRES PEP 692A.		
91P	Stereo w/Cassette & CD Player (GS)	578	680
91P	Stereo w/Cassette & CD Player (LS/Nautica)	315	370
	REQUIRES PEP 696A or 697A.		
534	Trailer Tow Prep Pkg	213	250
	Includes heavy duty battery, and conventional spare tire.		
952	Two-Tone Paint (GS)	251	295
434	Underseat Storage Bin (GS)	26	30

Save hundreds, even thousands, off the sticker price of the new truck you want.

Call Autovantage®
your FREE auto-buying service

1-800-201-7703

No purchase required. No fees.

MONTERO (1997)

1997 Mitsubishi Montero SR

What's New for Mitsubishi Montero in 1997 — Refinements result in a better SUV this year. A passenger airbag has been installed, optional side steps make it easier to clamber aboard, and split-fold second row seats increase versatility. New colors, new seat fabrics and better audio systems round out the package.

Montero — Review

Marketed since 1983, Mitsubishi's compact sport-utility ranks as an old-timer in its field, though the current four-door version has only been around since '89. Straight-up styling surrounds a spacious interior for five, but climbing aboard a Montero isn't so easy. Optional for 1996 are side steps that make this task much more manageable. These sizable sport-utes stand rather tall—more than six feet from ground to roof—a profile that doesn't exactly help when it's time to undertake a sharp corner. Though refined and well-built, with seating for seven, Monteros hardly rank as bargain-priced, either, despite their extensive equipment lists.

Mitsubishi has seen fit to make some substantial refinements to its premium SUV. A passenger airbag has been added, as well as new seat fabrics. Backlit gauges marked with white numerals are more legible, and the compass has been redesigned. The second-row seat is now a split-fold affair, offering more utility in an already versatile vehicle. New audio systems also debut. Outside, new colors compliment the newly optional side steps and hard shell spare tire cover.

Beneath the hood of an LS edition sits a smooth 24-valve, 3.0-liter V-6. Either five-speed manual shift or an automatic transmission is available. For more demanding tasks, Mitsubishi continues to offer a stronger dual-cam 3.5-liter engine, whipping up 214 horsepower, but only in the costly SR model, which comes solely with the four-speed automatic transmission. Electronically-controlled automatics feature three-mode operation: Power, Normal, and Hold (which avoids first-gear operation on ice, snow, or muddy surfaces).

MITSUBISHI MONTERO

Active Trac four-wheel-drive can be shifted "on the fly," or set up to operate all the time. All-disc brakes are standard, but only the SR has Multi-Mode anti-lock braking (optional in the LS version). A power sunroof, too, is either standard or optional, depending on the model. Prior Monteros could tow as much as 4,000 pounds, but the current peak rating is 5,000. A variable shock-absorber system, optional on the SR, has three settings: hard, medium, and soft.

The Montero is an interesting blend of gee-whiz gadgetry, luxurious conveniences, go-anywhere capability, and unique styling. While it is true that all this cool stuff comes at a premium, buyers considering other luxury sport utility vehicles will want to drop by the Mitsubishi dealer and consider this one as well.

Safety Data

Driver Airbag: Standard
Meets 1999 Side Impact Standards: No
Driver Crash Test Grade: N/A
Passenger Crash Test Grade: N/A

Passenger Airbag: Standard
4-Wheel ABS: Optional
Insurance Cost: High

Standard Equipment

Base Prices

Code	Description	Invoice	MSRP
MP45-N	LS	25094	29360
MP45-W	SR	31542	37780
Destination Charge:		445	445

Accessories

Code	Description	Invoice	MSRP
AB	Anti-lock Brakes (LS)	950	1159
KD	Cargo Storage Kit	153	235
C4	CD Auto Changer	605	865
CW	Chrome Wheels (SR)	760	927
C3	Compact Disc (LS)	310	442
FK	Fog Lights	152	230
LP	Leather & Wood Package (SR)	1360	1659
RR	Luggage Rack (LS)	160	246
PI	Power Sunroof (LS)	720	878
RB	Side Step	247	353
HI	Trailer Hitch	118	181
VA	Value Package	1774	1774

includes air conditioning, alloy wheels, wheel locks, roof rack, remote keyless entry, CD changer, tire cover, side steps, floor mats, cargo mats, cargo cover/net

MONTERO — MITSUBISHI

CODE	DESCRIPTION	INVOICE	MSRP

Base Prices

MP45-N	LS	25094	29360
MP45-W	SR	31542	37780
Destination Charge:		445	445

Accessories

AB	Anti-lock Brakes (LS)	950	1159
KD	Cargo Storage Kit	153	235
C4	CD Auto Changer	605	865
CW	Chrome Wheels (SR)	760	927
C3	Compact Disc (LS)	310	442
FK	Fog Lights	152	230
LP	Leather & Wood Package (SR)	1360	1659
RR	Luggage Rack (LS)	160	246
PI	Power Sunroof (LS)	720	878
RB	Side Step	247	353
HI	Trailer Hitch	118	181
VA	Value Package	1774	1774

includes air conditioning, alloy wheels, wheel locks, roof rack, remote keyless entry, CD changer, tire cover, side steps, floor mats, cargo mats, cargo cover/net

Take Advantage of Warranty Gold!

Savings up to 50% off Dealer's Extended Warranty Prices. Protect and enhance YOUR investment with the best extended warranty available.

Call Toll Free   1-800-580-9889

NISSAN — PATHFINDER

PATHFINDER (1997)

1997 Nissan Pathfinder LE

What's New for Nissan Pathfinder in 1997 — Changes to the 1997 Nissan Pathfinder include: storage pockets added at all doors, a new exterior color and an available Bose sound system.

Pathfinder — Review

The Nissan Pathfinder has largely been overshadowed by the recently redesigned Toyota 4Runner. We think that's too bad. Yes, the 4Runner is a good truck, but it is certainly not the only import SUV on the market. By taking a long, hard look at the Pathfinder, some buyers may be rewarded with a truck that doesn't look like anything else on the road.

The Pathfinder sports one of the friendliest interiors of any SUV we have tested this year. Ample passenger space fore and aft, a large cargo area with convenient tie-down hooks, standard dual air bags, a killer sound system, comfortable seats, and a great view are just a few of the reasons we like this truck so much. One thing we don't like, however, are the narrow rear doors, and the tubular running boards. The combination means that passengers exiting from the rear of the truck will undoubtedly have their pants dirtied by the ineffectual running boards as they try to squeeze out of the tight portal.

With Nissan's 1996 redesign came a larger, gutsier version of their familiar V-6 engine. Though not the engine of choice for speed-freaks, it moves the Pathfinder along highways and two-track roads with ease. Speaking of two-track roads, the Nissan has lost none of its sporting personality when it acquired its much-heralded car-like ride. Just ask our managing editor, who took the Pathfinder on a day-long jaunt up to the Continental Divide.

Do yourself a favor, and drop by a Nissan dealer for a test drive. They'll give you a cool set of binoculars, and you might just find yourself driving home in the perfect alternative to the Toyota 4Runner or Ford Explorer.

PATHFINDER — NISSAN

CODE	DESCRIPTION	INVOICE	MSRP

Safety Data

Driver Airbag: *Standard*
Side Airbag: *Not Available*
4-Wheel ABS: *Standard*
Driver Crash Test Grade: *Not Available*
Passenger Crash Test Grade: *Not Available*

Passenger Airbag: *Standard*
Meets 1999 Side Impact Standards: *Unknown*
Traction Control: *Not Available*
Insurance Cost: *High*
Integrated Child Seat(s): *Not Available*

Standard Equipment

XE: 3.3-liter SOHC V6 engine, shift-on-the-fly four-wheel drive (4WD), power assisted rack and pinion steering, power vented front disc/rear drum brakes, strut-type front suspension with stabilizer bar, 5-link coil-spring rear suspension with stabilizer bar, automatic locking front hubs (4WD), four-wheel anti-lock braking system (ABS), P235/70R15 all-season radial tires, under-body full size spare tire, flush-mounted halogen headlights, green-tinted glass, dual outside mirrors, chromed steel wheels (6 spoke), black grille and upper bumper, rear wiper/washer, reclining front bucket seats with adjustable head restraints, 60/40 split fold-down rear seat bench with adjustable head restraints, reclining rear seatbacks, large center console with armrest, cloth seat trim, concealed storage bin, driver and passenger seat back pockets, front and rear passenger-assist grips, front and rear door map pockets, remote fuel-filler door release, tilt steering column, four 20-oz cupholders, 2-speed variable intermittent windshield wipers, rear window intermittent wiper, rear window defroster with timer, remote hood release, cargo area courtesy lamp, center console with CD and cellular phone compartment, lockable glove box, map lamps and sunglass storage, rear heater ducts (4WD), analog tachometer and trip odometer, coolant temperature gauge, fuel gauge and warning lamps; 160-watt AM/FM stereo with digital clock, integrated compact disc player and six speakers, fixed rod-type antenna, diversity antenna system, dual air bags, steel side-door guard beams, 3-point front seat belt system with height adjustable front shoulder belts, and child-safety rear door locks and child seat anchor.

SE (in addition to or instead of XE equipment): P265/70R15 all-season radial tires, privacy glass on rear door, quarter windows and liftgate; dual heated power remote-controlled mirrors, black integrated fender flare/mud flaps, 6-spoke aluminum alloy wheels, chrome grille and upper bumper, roof-mounted luggage rack, rear window wind deflector, black tubular steel step rail, fog lamps, multi-adjustable driver's seat with seat cushion tilt, seatback recline and adjustable lumbar support; rear seat fold-down center armrest, power windows with driver-side one-touch auto-down feature, power door locks, cruise control, rear cargo area convenience net, remote keyless entry and vehicle security system, automatic power antenna.

LE (in addition to or instead of SE equipment): Limited-slip rear differential (4WD), body-color molded mud flaps, lace spoke aluminum alloy wheels, body-color lower bumper, polished running board, leather seating surfaces (with heated front seats on 4WD), automatic CFC-free air conditioning, illuminated driver and passenger mirrors, and integrated HOMELINK transmitter.

CALL NATIONWIDE 1-800-521-7257
FOR A WRITTEN QUOTATION
AS LOW AS $50 OVER INVOICE

See page 15 for details.

NISSAN — PATHFINDER

CODE	DESCRIPTION	INVOICE	MSRP

Base Prices

Code	Description	Invoice	MSRP
09257	XE 2WD (5-spd)	20619	22899
09217	XE 2WD (auto)	21520	23899
09657	XE 4WD (5-spd)	22420	24889
09617	XE 4WD (auto)	23321	25899
19817	SE 4WD (5-spd)	25167	27949
09717	SE 4WD (auto)	26068	28949
19317	LE 2WD	27418	30449
19817	LE 4WD	29580	32849
	Destination Charge:	420	420

Accessories

Code	Description	Invoice	MSRP
A01	Air Conditioning (SE)	1030	1199
	Includes automatic climate controls.		
A01	Air Conditioning (XE)	858	999
H95	Cassette Player (XE/SE)	287	389
G02	Convenience Pkg (XE)	1288	1499
	Includes power windows, power door locks, security system, remote keyless entry, cruise control, cargo area cover, cargo net, luggage rack, and power mirrors. REQUIRES A01 air conditioning.		
X03	Leather Pkg (SE)	1288	1499
	Includes heated seats, leather-wrapped steering wheel & shift knob, outside temperature meter, and digital compass. REQUIRES A01 air conditioning.		
509	Luxury Pkg (LE)	1116	1299
	Includes power sunroof and power front seats.		
T07	Off-Road Pkg (SE)	214	249
	Includes limited-slip differential, black grille, and black bumpers. REQUIRES J01 sunroof or J02 sunroof/Bose stereo pkg.		
K92	Rear Wind Deflector (XE)	68	89
	INCLUDED in V01 sport pkg.		
U06	Spare Tire Pkg (XE/SE)	257	299
	REQUIRES V01 sport pkg (XE) or T07 off-road pkg (SE).		
V01	Sport Pkg (XE 2WD)	428	499
	Includes black fender flares, halogen fog lamps, and rear window air deflector.		
V01	Sport Pkg (XE 4WD)	601	699
	Includes black fender flares, halogen fog lamps, limited slip differential, and rear window air deflector.		
J01	Sunroof Pkg (SE)	858	999
	Includes power sunroof, HomeLink transmitter, and illuminated vanity mirrors.		
J02	Sunroof/Bose Stereo Pkg (SE)	1331	1549
	Includes power sunroof, HomeLink transmitter, premium Bose stereo with AM/FM cassette, CD player, 8 speakers, and power antenna.		
L95	Wood Trim (XE/SE)	212	299

QUEST — NISSAN

QUEST (1997)

1997 Nissan Quest XE

What's New for Nissan Quest in 1997 — A few new colors are the only changes to the 1997 Quest.

Quest — Review

Nissan claims that its Quest is the top-selling import-brand minivan. Actually, they're made in Ohio, in XE and luxury GXE trim, along with the closely related—but not identical—Mercury Villager. After last year's makeover, the Quest receives few changes for 1997.

Versatile passenger space is the Quest's stock in trade. With seven-passenger Quest Trac Flexible Seating in an XE model, you can get 20 different combinations. In a GXE with captain's chairs, the total possibilities reach an even two dozen. Second row seats can fold down into a table, or be removed completely. The third-row seat also folds into a table, folds further for more cargo space, or slides forward on integrated tracks—all the way to the driver's seat.

Exceptionally smooth and quiet on the road, the Quest delivers more than adequate acceleration when merging or passing, courtesy of the 151-horsepower, 3.0-liter V-6 engine. The column-shifted four-speed automatic transmission changes gears neatly, without a hint of harshness, helped by electronic controls. You also get a smooth, comfortable highway ride and undeniably car-like handling—more so than most. Visibility is great, too, from upright but comfortable seating that's tempting for a long trek. Gauges are small, but acceptable, and controls are pleasing to operate.

Air conditioning and a tachometer are standard fare, while the GXE adds anti-lock braking (including rear disc brakes), a roof rack, and a host of powered conveniences. Distinctive in shape, enjoyable on the road, Quests are solidly assembled and perform admirably. Except for the upright seating position, it's easy to forget that you're inside a minivan, not a plain sedan.

NISSAN QUEST

| CODE | DESCRIPTION | INVOICE | MSRP |

Safety Data

Driver Airbag: *Standard*
Side Airbag: *Not Available*
4-Wheel ABS: *Std (GXE)Opt (XE)*
Driver Crash Test Grade: *Good*
Passenger Crash Test Grade: *Average*

Passenger Airbag: *Standard*
Meets 1997 Car Side Impact Standards: *Yes*
Traction Control: *Not Available*
Insurance Cost: *Low*
Integrated Child Seat(s): *Optional*

Standard Equipment

XE: 3.0-liter V-6 engine, 4-speed automatic transmission, rack-and-pinion steering, front disc/rear drum brakes, independent front suspension, leaf spring rear suspension, front stabilizer bar, 205/75R15 tires, 15" wheel covers, variable intermittent headlights, cornering lamps, manual outside mirrors, rear window defroster, rear windshield wiper, front door map pockets, dual air bags, vanity mirrors, tilt steering, tachometer, air conditioning, AM/FM stereo with cassette, diversity antenna, reclining bucket seats, seatback tray tables, liftgate light.

GXE (in addition to or instead of XE): 4-wheel anti-lock brakes, luggage rack, privacy glass, power heated outside mirrors, 15" aluminum wheels, power windows, power door locks, remote keyless entry, security system, retained accessory power, leather-wrapped steering wheel, cruise control, illuminated vanity mirrors, power antenna, power driver's seat, lockable underseat storage tray, and cargo net.

Base Prices

Code	Description	Invoice	MSRP
10316	XE	18913	21249
10416	GXE	23186	26049
	Destination Charge:	420	420

Accessories

Code	Description	Invoice	MSRP
B07	Anti-Lock Brakes (XE)	428	499
F05	Convenience Pkg (XE)	558	649
	Includes cruise control, cargo net, rear radio controls, luggage rack, vanity mirrors, remote keyless entry, security system, and lockable underseat storage.		
R03	Handling Pkg	472	549
R03	Handling Pkg (GXE)	472	549
	Includes P215/70R15 tires, conventional spare tire, performance shock absorbers, performance springs, rear stabilizer bar, and trailer wiring harness. REQUIRES V01 luxury pkg.		
K09	Integrated Child Seat	170	199
	REQUIRES A04 rear air conditioning, F05 convenience pkg, and 502 power pkg (XE). NOT AVAILABLE with X03 leather seats (GXE).		
X03	Leather Pkg (GXE)	1116	1299
	Includes power passenger's seat.		
V01	Luxury Pkg (GXE)	1074	1249
	Includes automatic temperature control, moonroof, and 6-disc CD changer.		
502	Power & Glass Pkg (XE)	1074	1249
	Includes power front windows, power door locks, power heated outside mirrors, and retained accessory power.		

QUEST / TRUCK — NISSAN

CODE	DESCRIPTION	INVOICE	MSRP
G06	Quad Seating Group (XE)	514	599
A04	Rear Air Conditioning (XE)	558	694
	REQUIRES 502 power pkg and F05 convenience pkg.		
T09	Touring Pkg (XE)	858	999
	Includes 5-spoke alloy wheels, trailer wiring harness, conventional spare tire, leather-wrapped steering wheel, and 6-disc CD changer. REQUIRES A04 air conditioning, F05 convenience pkg, and 502 power pkg.		
E10	Two-Tone Paint	257	299

TRUCK *(1997)*

1997 Nissan Truck 2WD XE

What's New for Nissan Truck in 1997 — Truck faces no changes in light of the 1998 model due for release this fall.

Truck— Review

While other makes play games with names, Nissan calls its compact truck exactly what it is: a Truck. Nothing fancy here, just good dollars-and-cents value and a down-to-business demeanor. A new two-wheel-drive SE edition rounds out the seven model lineup. XE Trucks continue to rank as one of the best values on the compact truck market.

Rear-wheel anti-lock braking is included on all models, but four-wheel ABS is not available. A newly standard airbag should improve the 1997 Truck's average crash test score for the driver. Passengers still ride without airbag protection. Front suspensions contain torsion bar springs and a stabilizer, while back ends hold traditional leaf springs.

Option packages have been shuffled somewhat for 1997. Many items that were formerly optional on XE Trucks have been moved to the standard equipment list of the more plush SE model. XE Value Packages can be had in a variety of configurations; with or without chrome trim, air conditioning, or bodyside graphics.

NISSAN TRUCK

Acceleration is acceptable with manual shift and the 2.4-liter four-cylinder engine. The stronger 3.0-liter V-6 was dropped last year thanks to new emission regulations that it couldn't meet. The four is somewhat coarse, and the din easily finds its way inside the cab. Either five-speed manual shift or an electronically controlled automatic transmission is available. Five-speed 4x4s have a clutch interlock "cancel" control, letting you start off in first gear without pushing down the clutch—a feature that can keep the truck from rolling back down a slope.

Payload and towing capacities lag some compact-pickup rivals, and the lack of car-like qualities puts Nissan a step behind the leaders. Even so, these solid machines aren't lacking in temptations—especially when considering the starting price for the Standard model. Moving up to an SE King Cab boosts the ante considerably. Nissan's role in the small-truck race might change when an all-new Truck arrives, in for 1998.

Safety Data

Driver Airbag: *Standard*
Meets 1999 Side Impact Standards: *No*
Integrated Child Seat(s): *N/A*
Driver Crash Test Grade: *No Data*

Passenger Airbag: *N/A*
4-wheel ABS: *N/A*
Insurance Cost: *High*
Passenger Crash Test Grade: *Good*

Standard Equipment

2WD TRUCK - STANDARD: 2.4-liter SOHC 12-valve 4-cylinder engine, 5-speed manual transmission, 1400 lb. payload, independent front suspension, front stabilizer bar, speedometer, odometer, coolant temperature gauge, 5J x 14 steel wheels, P195/75R14 tires, halogen headlamps, tinted glass, double wall cargo bed with removable tailgate, inside cargo hooks, argent grille and exterior trim, driver side air bag, steel side door guard beams, power vented front disc/rear drum brakes with rear anti-lock, 3-passenger vinyl bench seat with headrests, vinyl floor, side window defoggers, headlamp-on warning chimes, day/night rearview mirror, heater/defroster with 4-speed fan, lighted locking glove box.

XE (in addition to or instead of STANDARD equipment): Power steering, dual black mirrors, sport steering wheel, full carpeting, sliding rear window, argent rear bumper, map pocket, center console (King Cab), reclining front bucket seats (King Cab), rear fold-up jump seats (King Cab), cloth seat trim.

SE KING CAB (in addition to or instead of XE KING CAB equipment): 6JJ14 alloy wheels, P215/70R14 tires, chrome grille/bumpers/trim, dual chrome power mirrors, under rail bedliner, unique SE bodyside graphics, upgraded moquette cloth bucket seats, 12 ounce cut-pile carpeting, driver's side height/lumbar adjustments, cloth covered "see-through" headrests, cloth door inserts with dual map pockets, air conditioning, cruise control, AM/FM cassette stereo with 4 speakers and 100 watt peak amplifier, diversity antenna system, leather-wrapped 4-spoke steering wheel, tilt steering column, variable intermittent wipers, visor vanity mirror, privacy glass, power windows, power door locks, flip-up sunroof.

4WD TRUCK - XE: 6JJ x 15 titanium finish wheels, P235/75R15 tires, halogen headlamps, tinted glass, front/rear mud guards with 4x4 designation on rear mud guards, triple skid plates, double wall cargo bed with removable tailgate, inside cargo hooks, dual outside rearview mirrors, argent grille, exterior trim and rear bumper, fender flares, 3-passenger bench seat with head rests, woven cloth seats, reclining front bucket seats with head rests (King Cab), full carpeting, 4-spoke sport steering wheel, full door trim with driver's side map pocket, rear fold-up jump seats (King Cab), carpeted black panel trim (King Cab), console with dual integrated cup holders (King Cab), side window defoggers, headlamp-on warning chime, day/night

TRUCK NISSAN

rearview mirror, heater/defroster with 4-speed fan, one-piece sliding rear window, single tone horn, glove box light and lock, 2.4-liter SOHC 12 valve 4 cylinder 134 HP engine, 5-speed manual transmission, power vented front disc/rear drum brakes, power recirculating ball steering, sequential multi-point fuel injection, independent front suspension, front stabilizer bar, manual locking front hubs, driver side air bag, steel side door guard beams, rear anti-lock brakes, energy absorbing steering column, safety door locks, speedometer.

SE KING CAB (in addition to or instead of XE KING CAB equipment): 7JJ x 15 alloy wheels, front towing hook, unique bodyside graphics, chrome front/rear step bumpers, chrome grille and trim, dual power chrome mirrors, bedliner (under rail), 6-way sport bucket seats with upgraded moquette cloth, driver's seat lumbar support, driver's seat cushion height adjustment, cloth covered "see-through" head rests, full door trim with large console formed armrests and carpeted lower panel, 12 ounce cut-pile carpeting, air conditioning, cruise control, AM/FM cassette stereo with 4 speakers and 100 watt peak amplifier, diversity antenna system, leather-wrapped 4-spoke steering wheel, tilt steering column, variable intermittent wipers, dual map pockets, lockable glove box with lamp, map lamps, visor vanity mirror, privacy glass, power windows and door locks, flip-up sunroof, automatic front locking hubs, limited slip differential, tachometer, trip odometer, digital clock.

Base Prices

Code	Description	Invoice	MSRP
33056	2WD Standard (5-spd)	10587	10999
33556	2WD XE Regular Cab (5-spd)	12377	12999
33516	2WD XE Regular Cab (auto)	13330	13999
53556	2WD XE King Cab (5-spd)	13495	14649
53516	2WD XE King Cab (auto)	14416	15649
53256	2WD SE King Cab (5-spd)	15528	17049
53216	2WD SE King Cab (auto)	16439	18049
33756	4WD XE Regular Cab (5-spd)	14921	16199
53756	4WD XE King Cab (5-spd)	16439	18049
53356	4WD SE King Cab (5-spd)	18008	19999
	Destination Charge:	470	470

Accessories

Code	Description	Invoice	MSRP
A01	Air Conditioning — XE	858	999
	std on SE		
C01	California Emissions	130	150
G01	Convenience Package — XE	256	298
	incls variable intermittent wipers, locking glove box with lamp, console with dual integrated cup holders (King Cab only), visor vanity mirror, low fuel warning lamp, map lights (King Cab only); req's W03 chrome package; std on SE		
H01	Radio — Standard	428	499
	incls AM/FM cassette stereo		
J08	Privacy Glass — XE King Cab	85	99
	req's value truck pkg (except T03/T09)		
N05	Driver Comfort Package — XE	343	399
	incls cruise control, tilt steering column; req's value truck pkg (except T03/T09); std on SE		

NISSAN TRUCK

CODE	DESCRIPTION	INVOICE	MSRP
P06	Power Steering — Standard	274	319
	std on XE and SE models		
W03	Chrome Package — XE	428	499
	incls chrome grille, chrome mirrors, chrome front/rear bumpers, chrome door handles, chrome windshield molding, chrome side-marker bezels, full wheel covers, bodyside graphics; incld in value truck pkg (except T04/T10)		
T01/T07	Value Truck Package — XE	855	995
	incls convenience pkg, chrome pkg, P215/70R14 tires, non-CFC air conditioning, AM/FM cassette stereo with 2 speakers (4 speakers on King Cab), tachometer, trip odometer, digital clock, alloy wheels; std on SE		
L93	Under Rail Bedliner — port installed	140	299
	std on SE		
L94	Over Rail Bedliner	140	299
	not available on SE		
F92	Floor Mats	43	59
H92	CD Player	349	469
	req's value pkg; not available on Standard		
H93	CD Player — 3-disc - port installed	511	669
	req's value pkg on XE Regular or King Cab		

CALL NATIONWIDE 1-800-521-7257
FOR A WRITTEN QUOTATION
AS LOW AS $50 OVER INVOICE

See page 15 for details.

BRAVADA — OLDSMOBILE

BRAVADA *(1997)*

1997 Oldsmobile Bravada

What's New for Oldsmobile Bravada in 1997 — Bravada drops the split-tailgate arrangement at the rear in favor of a top-hinged liftgate with separately lifting glass. So, tailgate parties aren't as convenient, but loading cargo sure is easier. Also new to the options list is a power tilt and slide sunroof. Included with the hole in the roof are a mini-overhead console, a pop-up wind deflector, and a sun shade. Rear disc brakes replace the former drums, combining with the front discs to provide better stopping ability.

Bravada — Review

After a one year hiatus, the Oldsmobile Bravada returned for the 1996 model year, based on the same platform that serves as the basis for the Chevrolet Blazer and the GMC Jimmy. We said we doubted Oldsmobile would find 20,000 buyers for the Bravada in 1996, partly because of myriad choices in the luxo-SUV market, and partly because we didn't think the Bravada was worth the price of admission over similarly-equipped Chevy Blazers and GMC Jimmys. By August 31, 1996, Olds had sold 6,650 Bravadas, falling short of sales goals by half.

That's too bad, because the Bravada is a great truck. No tacky fender flares and no dopey two-tone paint schemes here. The interior is swathed in leather, and offers one of the most comfortable driver's seats we've encountered in an SUV. The sound system is outstanding. Controls are easy to see and use, though they look and feel somewhat cheap. Bravada's Smart-trak all-wheel drive system makes off-roading carefree. This year, the split rear tailgate is gone, replaced by a liftgate with separately opening rear glass. Best of all, this is one speedy, fun-to-drive truck that can easily swallow a full-size dryer. Truly, the Bravada is what a luxury sport/utility is all about.

OLDSMOBILE — BRAVADA

The Bravada comes loaded with nearly every conceivable luxury option; appropriate since this is Oldsmobile's entry into the quickly expanding luxury sport ute arena. This market niche is quickly filling to capacity, with luxury SUV's from Acura, Lexus, Mercury, and Infiniti reaching showrooms recently.

Is the Bravada worth the price of admission over the Blazer and the Jimmy? Well, the front seats are exclusive to Oldsmobile, and the Smart-trak all-wheel drive system is standard on the Olds (it's optional on the Chevy and GMC). In fact, most of the standard equipment on the Bravada is available on the Chevy or the GMC, with an end result that is less expensive than the Oldsmobile.

Just eight options are available on the Bravada. Buyers can order a heavy-duty 5000-pound towing package, an engine block heater, a CD player that replaces the cassette deck, white-letter tires, and a gold-trim package. New this year is a power tilt and slide sunroof. Cloth seats are a no-charge replacement for the standard leather hides. Olds says the Bravada has a "two-fold mission: keep the driver moving in the face of adverse weather or road conditions and deliver all occupants in comfort and style to the destination of their choice."

Styling is pretty much identical to the Chevy Blazer and GMC Jimmy. The Bravada gets a unique grille and headlamp treatment, bumper trim, and body cladding. The overall effect distances the Olds far enough away from its corporate siblings to make it look and feel unique in a world populated by look-alike Jeep Grand Cherokees and Ford Explorers. A 4.3-liter Vortec V-6 engine that makes 190 horsepower propels the Bravada's four wheels. Though strong, we find the V-6 a strange choice when the Jeep and the Ford can be equipped with a V-8 engine. The Explorer-based Mercury Mountaineer also has all-wheel drive, like the Bravada, along with standard V-8 power. Rear disc brakes debut for 1997, replacing rear drums and combining with the front discs to make stopping distances shorter.

The original Bravada, which competed in a market populated by few luxury-oriented SUV's, never sold very well. It was based on ancient technology, and buyers saw through the first-generation Bravada quicker than they did the ill-fated Cadillac Cimarron. Oldsmobile has come up with quite an enticing package with the second-generation Bravada. However, the luxury market is becoming saturated with very good trucks, which will inevitably push demand for any particular model down. We also think that aging, affluent Boomers are going to tire of climbing in and out of these things in time, depositing their aching legs and backs into the seats of the Cadillacs, BMWs and Acuras that they're currently trading in like baseball cards for the more rugged, outdoorsy, SUV image. Finally, the lack of a passenger airbag, combined with very poor front passenger crash test scores, makes the Bravada a gamble of sorts. Currently, not many are taking a chance on Oldsmobile's luxury SUV.

Safety Data

Driver Airbag: *Standard*
Side Airbag: *Not Available*
4-Wheel ABS: *Standard*
Driver Crash Test Grade: *Average*
Passenger Crash Test Grade: *Very Poor*

Passenger Airbag: *Standard*
Meets 1999 Side Impact Standards: *No*
Traction Control: *Not Available*
Integrated Child Seat(s): *Not Available*

BRAVADA — OLDSMOBILE

Standard Equipment

BRAVADA: 4.3-liter Vortec V-6 engine, electronically-controlled automatic transmission with overdrive, brake/transmission shift interlock, full-time all-wheel drive, variable ratio power steering, high-pressure gas-assisted front/rear shock absorbers, locking rear differential, P235/70R15 BSW tires, 15-inch aluminum wheels, body-color front bumper with argent air intakes, body-color rear bumper with rubber step pads, lower bodyside, rocker panel, and wheel opening moldings; roof-mounted luggage carrier, 2 front tow hooks, fog lights, composite halogen headlamps, daytime running lights, rear liftgate with liftglass, dual power breakaway exterior mirrors, solar-treated windshield, deep tinted glass (rear doors, rear quarter windows, rear window), pulse wiper system, rear liftglass wiper/washer, driver's side airbag, reclining front bucket seats with 6-way power adjustment, dual power lumbar adjustment, manual recliners, and adjustable headrests; split-folding rear bench seat, leather seat trim, door map pockets, seatback map pockets, center console with storage armrest and dual cupholders, floor-mounted shifter, overhead console (trip computer, compass, outside temperature readout, front/rear reading lights, storage, universal garage door opener), air conditioning, flo-thru ventilation, side window defoggers, rear window defogger, power windows with driver's express-down, remote keyless entry, cruise control, tilt steering column, ETR AM/FM stereo with auto-reverse cassette player, seek/scan, graphic equalizer, digital clock, and 6-speaker Dimensional Sound; analog gauges with tachometer and trip odometer, overhead console lighting, glovebox light, underhood light, 2 auxiliary electrical outlets, headlamps-on warning chime, turn signal on warning chime, dual covered and illuminated visor vanity mirrors, front/rear floor mats, retractable cargo area cover, convenience net, rear storage area with toolkit

Base Prices

Code	Description	Invoice	MSRP
V06/R7A	Bravada	27408	30285
	Destination Charge:	515	515

Accessories

Code	Description	Invoice	MSRP
YF5	California Emissions	146	170
AN3	Cloth Trim	NC	NC
K05	Engine Block Heater	28	33
B94	Gold Package	43	50
	Includes gold exterior emblems, beige accent stripe, and gold-tinted aluminum wheel trim		
Z82	Heavy-duty Towing Package	181	210
	Includes weight distributing platform hitch, 8-wire electrical harness, heavy duty hazard warning flasher		
NG1	Massachustts/New York Emissions	146	170
QBG	P235/70R15 OWL Tires	114	133
CF5	Power Sunroof	598	695
	Includes mini-overhead console, sunshade, and wind deflector		
—	Regional Discount	62	975
	This discount applies only to California, Oregon, Washington, and Idaho		
U1C	Stereo w/CD Player	107	124
	ETR AM/FM stereo with CD player, 6 speakers, digtal clock		

OLDSMOBILE — SILHOUETTE

| CODE | DESCRIPTION | INVOICE | MSRP |

SILHOUETTE (1997)

1997 Oldsmobile Silhouette

What's New for Oldsmobile Silhouette in 1997 — Completely redesigned, the new Silhouette comes in several trim levels and two sizes, each with a healthy load of standard equipment.

Silhouette — Review

After years of unsuccessfully peddling a plastic four-wheeled version of the Dustbuster found in your hall closet, Oldsmobile goes back to the drawing board and brings this fresh, conservative, all steel, fun-to-drive minivan to market. Available in three trim levels and three bodystyles, the new Silhouette is indeed one minivan consumers need to consider.

Why is this Oldsmobile so good? You name the convenience, and Olds has thought of it. Want a sliding driver's side door? You can get one here. Wish that passenger's side sliding door was power operated? Oldsmobile has you covered. Want leather? A CD player? Separate audio controls for rear passengers? Traction control? A powerful V-6 engine? Easy to unload seats that can be configured in a variety of ways? It's all here, depending on the body style and trim level you select.

Silhouette is available in three bodystyles; regular length 3-door and extended length 3- or 4-door. Base, GL, and GLS trim levels are available. All Silhouettes are front-wheel drive, and are powered by a 180-horsepower 3.4-liter V-6 mated to an electronically-controlled 4-speed automatic transmission. Dual airbags and anti-lock brakes are standard.

Base models come with air conditioning, tilt steering wheel, cruise control, power door locks, power windows, and fog lights. However, if you want to get traction control, alloy wheels, or integrated child seats, your ticket to ride is the...

...GL trim level, which adds remote keyless entry, theft deterrent system, power sliding right side door, power seats, and deep tinted glass to the base model's equipment list. Next up is the GLS, which adds a touring suspension package, rear climate controls, traction control, alloy wheels, and rear audio controls to the GL standard equipment roster. Leather is only available on the GLS.

SILHOUETTE — OLDSMOBILE

| CODE | DESCRIPTION | INVOICE | MSRP |

We've driven the Silhouette's corporate twin, the Pontiac Trans Sport, and came away quite impressed. Based on that drive, we expect the Oldsmobile Silhouette to be smooth, powerful, and fun-to-drive with excellent road feel provided by sharp steering and easily modulated brakes. Our complaints are limited to uncomfortable rear seating and a noticeable amount of cheap-looking plastic inside the cabin.

Some of you may have seen a recent Dateline NBC expose in which several minivans were crashed into a deformable offset barrier at 40 mph. While there is no standard regarding offset crash protection in the United States, and the Silhouette does meet all current federal safety standards, this test showed that GM's new minivans did not do a good job of protecting the driver in such an accident. General Motors responded that the test represented a tiny percentage of real world crashes.

While we like the new Oldsmobile Silhouette, and find its exterior styling to be the most attractive of the three new GM minivans, we wonder just how crashworthy this new model really is.

Safety Data

Driver Airbag: *Standard*
Side Airbag: *Not Available*
4-Wheel ABS: *Standard*
Driver Crash Test Grade: *Not Available*
Passenger Crash Test Grade: *Not Available*

Passenger Airbag: *Standard*
Meets 1997 Car Side Impact Standards: *No*
Traction Control: *N/A (Base); Opt. (GL); Std. (GLS)*
Insurance Cost: *Not Available*
Integrated Child Seat(s): *N/A (Base/GLS); Opt. (GL)*

Standard Equipment

SILHOUETTE: 3.4-liter V-6 engine, 4-speed automatic transmission, dual front airbags, front air conditioning with air filtration system, integrated windshield antenna, battery rundown protection, power 4-wheel anti-lock front disc/rear drum brakes, power rack and pinion steering, brake/transmission shift interlock, headlamps-on warning chime, turn signal on warning chime, center console with storage bin, cruise control, daytime running lights, front side window defoggers, rear window defogger, power programmable automatic door locks, child security door lock for sliding door, front/rear floor mats, fog lights, tachometer, trip odometer, lighting package (overhead map lights, two rear dome lamps with override switch, third row reading lights, second row reading lights), roof rack, front door map pockets, front seatback map pockets, day/night rearview mirror, body-color bodyside moldings, body-color rocker panel moldings with integrated splash guards, 2 12-volt auxiliary power outlets, purse net between front seats, AM/FM stereo with auto-reverse cassette player, seek/scan, digital clock, and coaxial speaker system; height-adjustable 3-point front safety belts, 3-point outboard rear safety belts, reclining bucket seats with manual lumbar adjustment and folding armrests, second row 60/40 split bench seat, third row 50/50 split bench seat, tilt steering wheel, underseat storage drawer, P205/70R15 blackwall all-season tires (regular length), P215/70R15 blackwall all-season tires (extended length), dual visor vanity mirrors, 15-inch bolt-on wheelcovers, solar-treated windshield, power windows with driver's auto-down feature, pulse wiper system, rear window wiper/washer, dual power exterior mirrors, power quarter vent windows, passenger assist grips, rear cargo tie downs

GL (in addition to or instead of BASE equipment): Overhead console with storage for sunglasses and garage door opener, compass, outside temperature readout, and driver information center; cargo area convenience net, power sliding right side door, remote keyless entry, illuminated entry feature, theft deterrent system, 6-way power driver and front passenger seats, deep tinted glass

OLDSMOBILE — SILHOUETTE

CODE	DESCRIPTION	INVOICE	MSRP

GLS (in addition to or instead of GL equipment): Rear air conditioning and heater, rear seat audio controls, illuminated visor vanity mirrors, second row captain's chairs, touring suspension package (P215/70R15 touring tires, automatic leveling, air inflation kit), steering wheel radio controls, traction control system, aluminum wheels

Base Prices

Code	Description	Invoice	MSRP
N06UV + R7A	3-door Regular Length	19616	21675
M06UV + R7B	3-door Extended Length	20367	22505
M06UV + R7C	GL 3-door Extended Length	21743	24025
M16UV + R7D	GL 4-door Extended Length	22240	24575
M06UV + R7E	GLS 3-door Extended Length	23245	25685
M16UV + R7F	GLS 4-door Extended Length	23743	26235
Destination Charge:		570	570

Accessories

Code	Description	Invoice	MSRP
PH3	Aluminum Wheels (GL)	245	285
YF5	California Emissions	146	170
WJ7	Custom Leather Trim (GLS)	748	870
AJ1	Deep Tinted Glass (Base)	211	245
K05	Engine Block Heater	15	18
AN2	Integrated Child Seat — Single (GL)	108	125
AN5	Integrated Child Seats — Dual (GL)	194	225
NG1	Massachusetts/New York Emissions	146	170
CF5	Power Sunroof (GL 3-door/GLS 3-door)	598	695
R8P	Rear Convenience Package (GL)	452	525
	Includes rear air conditioning, rear heater, and rear audio controls		
UN7	Stereo — w/cassette and CD players (GL/GLS)	172	200
UN0	Stereo — w/CD player (GL/GLS)	86	100
FE3	Touring Suspension (GL)	232	270
	Includes automatic leveling control, P215/70R15 touring tires, and air inflation kit		
V92	Towing Package (Base/GL)	305	355
	Includes engine oil cooler, transmission cooler, 5-wire electrical harness, automatic leveling, inflation kit, touring suspension P215/70R15 touring tires		
V92	Towing Package (GLS)	73	85
	Includes engine oil cooler, transmission cooler, 5-wire electrical harness		
NW9	Traction Control System (GL)	151	175

VOYAGER / GRAND VOYAGER — PLYMOUTH

| CODE | DESCRIPTION | INVOICE | MSRP |

VOYAGER / GRAND VOYAGER *(1997)*

1997 Plymouth Voyager SE Rallye

What's New for Plymouth Voyager/Grand Voyager in 1997 — For 1997, the Plymouth minivans receive a cornucopia of changes. This year brings new wheel covers, improved anti-lock braking systems, an accident response system that unlocks the doors and turns on the interior lights if the air bags deploy, better radios, a quieter interior, and more optional equipment for Base and SE models.

Voyager/Grand Voyager — Review

In the past, Plymouth renderings of Chrysler Corporation's popular front-drive minivans have been virtual clones of the Dodge Caravan. In engineering and design, that's also true of this latest iteration, introduced last year as an early '96 model. In an assertive marketing move, however, Plymouth is pushing value pricing, aiming squarely at entry-level buyers who are shopping for their first minivans. Instead of the three-model lineup that Dodge shoppers face, Plymouth offers only two Voyagers: the base model and a step-up SE.

Even a base-model Voyager is loaded with style and features, though anti-lock braking is an option here. Sleek, lengthened, freshly-rounded bodies surround roomier-than-ever interiors, claiming more cargo space than the competition. Views to the ground and all around have improved, as a result of increasing the minivan's glass area by 30 percent and lowering the cowl. An "Easy Out" roller rear seat makes it easier to modify the passenger/cargo layout to suit specific needs.

Leading the list of appealing innovations is the optional driver-side sliding door—a boon to suburbanites who might want to load their minivans from either side. Two out of three buyers are expected to choose this option. Snowbelt-dwellers who've endured frosted windshields might also like the new optional electric windshield-wiper de-icer.

Anyone who appreciated the prior Voyager's car-like characteristics will be even more pleased by the latest edition, with its light steering response and super-smooth ride. This is an easy minivan to control, with a body that stays reasonably flat through curves—but threatens to lean just a little too much if pushed overly hard.

PLYMOUTH
VOYAGER / GRAND VOYAGER

| CODE | DESCRIPTION | INVOICE | MSRP |

The base engine is a 16-valve dual-cam four, whipping out 50 more horsepower than the old four-cylinder. That's an impressive output hike, but many buyers are likely to choose the 3.0- or 3.3-liter V-6 anyway. Sport-minded customers can select the Voyager Rallye or the Grand Voyager Rallye, which is new for 1997.

Soft seats are amply supportive, and cupholders "ratchet down" to smaller size. Climate controls are a little too complex, and the column-mounted gearshift is oddly-shaped, but the dashboard exhibits an alluring curvature. Inside and out, the latest Voyager and Grand Voyager look poised to retain their league-leading position in the minivan race.

Safety Data

Driver Airbag: *Standard*
Side Airbag: *Not Available*
4-Wheel ABS: *Opt (Base)/Std (SE)*
Driver Crash Test Grade: *Average*
Passenger Crash Test Grade: *Good*

Passenger Airbag: *Standard*
Meets 1997 Car Side Impact Standards: *Yes*
Traction Control: *Not Available*
Insurance Cost: *Very Low*
Integrated Child Seat(s): *Optional*

Standard Equipment

BASE: 2.4-liter 16-valve 4-cylinder engine, 3-speed automatic transmission, power rack-and-pinion steering, front disc/rear drum brakes, independent front suspension, leaf-spring rear suspension, P205/75R14 A/S tires, 14" wheel covers, rear quarter window vents, halogen headlamps, tinted windows, speed sensitive variable windshield wipers, dual outside mirrors, rear window wiper/washer, AM/FM stereo w/4 speakers, front/rear dome lights, cargo light, and driver and passenger vanity mirrors.

SE (in addition to or instead of BASE): 4-speed automatic transmission, anti-lock brakes, P215/65R15 A/S tires, 15" wheel covers, power outside mirrors, tilt steering, cruise control, AM/FM stereo w/cassette and 4 speakers, tachometer, cargo net, under seat lockable storage, and rear floor silencer pad.

Base Prices

NSHL52	Voyager Base	15687	17235
HH52	Voyager SE	18054	19925
NSHL53	Grand Voyager Base	16910	18580
NSHHL53	Grand Voyager SE	18824	20755
Destination Charge:		580	580

Accessories

WJA	15" Aluminum Wheels (Grand Voyager SE)	353	415
	REQUIRES Quick Order Pkg 24B, 28B, 28C, 24D, 28D, or 28L.		
CYE	7-Passenger Seating (Voyager)	289	350
	INCLUDED in Quick Order Pkg 22T, 24T and 28T.		
HAA	Air Conditioning	731	860
	REQUIRES Quick Order Pkg 22S, 23A, or 24A.		
BGF	Anti-Lock Brakes (Base)	480	565
YCF	Border States Emissions	145	170
NAE	CA/NY/MA Emissions	145	170

VOYAGER / GRAND VOYAGER — PLYMOUTH

CODE	DESCRIPTION	INVOICE	MSRP
AAC	**Convenience Group 1 (Base)**	370	435
	Includes power steering, speed control, and tilt steering. NOT AVAILABLE with Quick Order Pkg 22S.		
AAE	**Convenience Group 2 (Base)**	638	750
	Includes power steering, power mirrors, speed control, tilt steering and power locks. NOT AVAILABLE with Quick Order Pkg 22S.		
AAE	**Convenience Group 2 (SE)**	268	315
	Includes power steering, power mirrors, speed control, tilt steering and power locks. NOT AVAILABLE with Quick Order Pkg 23A or 24A.		
AAF	**Convenience Group 3 (SE)**	582	685
	Includes power door locks and windows. INCLUDED in Quick Order Pkg 24D, 28D, 28E, 28L, and 28N.		
AAG	**Convenience Group 4 (SE)**	200	235
	Includes remote keyless entry and headlight delay. REQUIRES Quick Order Pkg 24D, 28D, 28E, 28L, or 28N.		
AAH	**Convenience Group 5 (SE)**	327	385
	Includes remote keyless entry, headlight delay, security system, and illuminated entry. REQUIRES Quick Order Pkg 24D, 28D, 28E, 28L, or 28N.		
TBB	**Conventional Spare Tire**	94	110
	INCLUDED in AAP and AAR towing groups. NOT AVAILABLE with Quick Order Pkg 22S, 23A, or 24A.		
GKD	**Driver's Side Sliding Door**	506	595
	NOT AVAILABLE with Quick Order Pkg 22S, 23A, or 24A.		
NHK	**Engine Block Heater**	30	35
CYK	**Integrated Child Seats (Base)**	242	285
	Includes two integrated child seats in the 2nd row bench. NOT AVAILABLE with Quick Order Pkg 22S.		
CYR	**Integrated Child Seats (SE)**	191	225
	Includes two integrated child seats in the 2nd row bench. NOT AVAILABLE with Quick Order Pkg 23A or 24A.		
SER	**Load Leveling Suspension (Grand Voyager SE)**	247	290
	REQUIRES Quick Order Pkg 24D, 28D, 28E, 28L, and 28N.		
MWG	**Luggage Rack**	149	175
	INCLUDED in Quick Order PKg 28C, 28E and 28N. NOT AVAILABLE with Quick Order Pkg 22S, 23A, or 24A.		
28C	**Rallye Order Pkg 28C (Voyager SE)**	2772	3260
	Manufacturer Discount	(876)	(1030)
	Net Price	1896	2230
	Includes air conditioning, rear window defroster, deluxe 7-passenger seating, 3.3-liter V-6 engine, and rallye decor group (decals, body color door handles, tinted glass, body color grille, luggage rack, and 15" aluminum wheels.)		
RBN	**Premium Stereo w/Cassette (SE)**	276	325
	Includes AM/FM stereo with cassette, CD changer controls, equalizer and 10 speakers. REQUIRES Quick Order Pkg 24D, 28D, 28E, 28L, or 28N.		
RAZ	**Premium Stereo w/CD Player & Cassette (SE)**	612	720
	Includes AM/FM stereo with cassette, CD player, equalizer and 10 speakers. REQUIRES Quick Order Pkg 24D, 28D, 28E, 28L, or 28N.		

PLYMOUTH — VOYAGER / GRAND VOYAGER

CODE	DESCRIPTION	INVOICE	MSRP
CYS	Quad Command Seating (SE)	531	625

Includes front and middle row captain's chairs. INCLUDED in Quick Order Pkg 28L and 28N. REQUIRES driver's side sliding door. NOT AVAILABLE with Quick Order Pkg 23A, 24A, 23B, 24B, 28B, or 28C.

22S	Quick Order Pkg 22S (Base)	NC	NC

Includes vehicle with standard equipment.

22T	Quick Order Pkg 22T (Grand Voyager)	765	900
	Manufacturer Discount	(731)	(860)
	Net Price	34	40

Includes air conditioning, rear floor silencer pad, and under seat storage drawer.

22T	Quick Order Pkg 22T (Voyager)	1063	1250
	Manufacturer Discount	(731)	(860)
	Net Price	332	390

Includes air conditioning, rear floor silencer pad, 7-passenger seating, and underseat storage drawer.

23A	Quick Order Pkg 23A (SE)	NC	NC

Includes vehicle with standard equipment.

23B	Quick Order Pkg 23B (Grand Voyager SE)	1024	1205
	Manufacturer Discount	(595)	(700)
	Net Price	429	505

Includes air conditioning, rear window defroster, and deluxe 7-passenger seating.

23B	Quick Order Pkg 23B (Voyager SE)	1024	1205
	Manufacturer Discount	(595)	(700)
	Net Price	429	505

Includes air conditioning, rear window defroster, and deluxe 7-passenger seating.

24A	Quick Order Pkg 24A (Grand Voyager SE)	442	520

Includes 3.0-liter V-6 engine and 3-speed automatic transmission.

24A	Quick Order Pkg 24A (Voyager SE)	442	520

Includes 3.0-liter V-6 engine and 3-speed automatic transmission.

24B	Quick Order Pkg 24B (Grand Voyager SE)	1466	1725
	Manufacturer Discount	(595)	(700)
	Net Price	871	1025

Includes 3.0-liter V-6 engine, 3-speed automatic transmission, air conditioning, rear window defroster, and deluxe 7-passenger seating.

24B	Quick Order Pkg 24B (Voyager SE)	1466	1725
	Manufacturer Discount	(595)	(700)
	Net Price	871	1025

Includes air conditioning, rear window defroster, deluxe 7-passenger seating, 3.0-liter V-6 engine, and 3-speed automatic transmission.

24D	Quick Order Pkg 24D (Grand Voyager SE)	2346	2760
	Manufacturer Discount	(850)	(1000)
	Net Price	1496	1760

Includes 3.0-liter V-6 engine, 3-speed automatic transmission, floor mats, illuminated vanity mirrors, sun visor extensions, deluxe sound insulation, power door locks, power windows, and light group.

VOYAGER / GRAND VOYAGER — PLYMOUTH

CODE	DESCRIPTION	INVOICE	MSRP
24D	Quick Order Pkg 24D (Voyager SE)	2346	2760
	Manufacturer Discount	(850)	(1000)
	Net Price	1496	1760
	Includes air conditioning, rear window defroster, deluxe 7-passenger seating, 3.0-liter V-6 engine, power door locks, power windows, floor mats, illuminated vanity mirrors, light group, deluxe sound insulation and sun visor extensions.		
24T	Quick Order Pkg 24T (Grand Voyager)	1420	1670
	Manufacturer Discount	(731)	(860)
	Net Price	689	810
	Includes 3.0-liter V-6 engine, air conditioning, rear floor silencer pad, and under seat storage drawer.		
24T	Quick Order Pkg 24T (Voyager)	1718	2020
	Manufacturer Discount	(731)	(860)
	Net Price	987	1160
	Includes air conditioning, rear floor silencer pad, under seat storage drawer, and 3.0-liter V-6 engine.		
28B	Quick Order Pkg 28B (Voyager SE)	1781	2095
	Manufacturer Discount	(595)	(700)
	Net Price	1186	1395
	Includes air conditioning, rear window defroster, deluxe 7-passenger seating, and 3.3-liter V-6 engine.		
28D	Quick Order Pkg 28D (Grand Voyager SE)	2661	3130
	Manufacturer Discount	(850)	(1000)
	Net Price	1811	2130
	Includes 3.3-liter V-6 engine, 4-speed automatic transmission, floor mats, illuminated vanity mirrors, sun visor extensions, deluxe sound insulation, power door locks, power windows, and light group.		
28D	Quick Order Pkg 28D (Voyager SE)	2661	3130
	Manufacturer Discount	(850)	(1000)
	Net Price	1811	2130
	Includes air conditioning, rear window defroster, deluxe 7-passenger seating, 3.3-liter V-6 engine, 4-speed automatic transmission, power door locks, power windows, floor mats, illuminated vanity mirrors, light group, deluxe sound insulation and sun visor extensions.		
28L	Quick Order Pkg 28L (Grand Voyager SE)	4225	4970
	Manufacturer Discount	(850)	(1000)
	Net Price	3375	3970
	Includes air conditioning, rear window defroster, light group, power windows, power door locks, floor mats, illuminated vanity mirrors, sun visor extensions, deluxe sound insulation, overhead console with trip computer, driver's side sliding door, 8-way power driver's seat, 7-passenger quad seating.		

PLYMOUTH — VOYAGER / GRAND VOYAGER

CODE	DESCRIPTION	INVOICE	MSRP
28L	Quick Order Pkg 28L (Voyager SE)	4225	4970
	Manufacturer Discount	(850)	(1000)
	Net Price	3375	3970

Includes air conditioning, rear window defroster, light group, power door locks, power windows, front and rear floor mats, illuminated vanity mirrors, sun visor extensions, overhead console with trip computer, driver's side sliding door, 8-way power driver's seat, 7-passenger deluxe quad seating.

28T	Quick Order Pkg 28T (Grand Voyager)	1735	2040
	Manufacturer Discount	(731)	(860)
	Net Price	1004	1180

Includes 3.3-liter V-6 engine, air conditioning, rear floor silencer pad, and under seat storage drawer.

28T	Quick Order Pkg 28T (Voyager)	2033	2390
	Manufacturer Discount	(731)	(860)
	Net Price	1302	1530

Includes air conditioning, rear floor silencer pad, under seat storage drawer, and 3.3-liter V-6 engine.

28C	Rallye Order Pkg 28C (Grand Voyager SE)	2772	3260
	Manufacturer Discount	(876)	(1030)
	Net Price	1896	2230

Includes 3.0-liter V-6 engine, 3-speed automatic transmission, air conditioning, rear window defroster, rallye decor group (rallye decals, body color door handles, tinted glass, luggage rack and 15" aluminum wheels), and deluxe 7-passenger seating.

28N	Rallye Order Pkg 28N (Grand Voyager SE)	5215	6135
	Manufacturer Discount	(1131)	(1330)
	Net Price	4084	4805

Includes air conditioning, rear window defroster, light group, power windows, power door locks, floor mats, illuminated vanity mirrors, sun visor extensions, deluxe sound insulation, overhead console with trip computer, driver's side sliding door, 8-way power driver's seat, 7-passenger quad seating, and rallye decor group (rallye decals, body color grille, body color door handles, tinted glass, luggage rack, and 15" aluminum wheels).

28N	Rallye Order Pkg 28N (Voyager SE)	5215	6135
	Manufacturer Discount	(1131)	(1330)
	Net Price	4084	4805

Includes air conditioning, rear window defroster, light group, power door locks, power windows, front and rear floor mats, illuminated vanity mirrors, sun visor extensions, overhead console with trip computer, driver's side sliding door, 8-way power driver's seat, 7-passenger deluxe quad seating, and rallye decor group (rallye decals, body color door handles, tinted windows, body color grille, luggage rack, and 15" aluminum wheels).

VOYAGER / GRAND VOYAGER — PLYMOUTH

CODE	DESCRIPTION	INVOICE	MSRP
28E	Rallye Pkg 28E (Grand Voyager SE)	3651	4295
	Manufacturer Discount	(1131)	(1330)
	Net Price	2520	2965
	Includes 3.0-liter V-6 engine, 3-speed automatic transmission, air conditioning, rear window defroster, power door locks, power windows, floor mats, illuminated vanity mirrors, deluxe sound insulation, light group, sun visor extensions, and deluxe 7-passenger seating.		
28E	Rallye Pkg 28E (Voyager SE)	3651	4295
	Manufacturer Discount	(1131)	(1330)
	Net Price	2520	2965
	Includes air conditioning, rear window defroster, deluxe 7-passenger seating, 3.3-liter V-6 engine, power door locks, power windows, illuminated vanity mirrors, deluxe sound insulation, floor mats, sun visor extensions, and rallye decor group (decals, body color door handles, tinted glass, body color grille, luggage rack, and 15" aluminum wheels.)		
AAB	Rear Air Conditioning (Grand Voyager SE)	961	1130
	With 28C (Grand Voyager SE)	578	680
	With 24D (Grand Voyager SE) And 28D (Grand Voyager SE)	867	1020
	With 28E (Grand Voyager SE)	485	570
	With 28L (Grand Voyager SE)	799	940
	With 28N (Grand Voyager SE)	417	440
	Includes tinted glass and overhead console. REQUIRES Quick Order Pkg 24D, 28D, 28E, 28L, or 28N.		
GFA	Rear Window Defroster (Base)	166	195
	With AAC (Base) And AAE (Base)	196	230
	NOT AVAILABLE with Quick Order Pkg 22S.		
AWS	Smoker's Group	17	20
	Includes cigar lighter and three ashtrays.		
RAS	Stereo w/Cassette (Base)	153	180
	NOT AVAILABLE with Quick Order Pkg 22S.		
AAA	Tinted Glass	383	450
	INCLUDED in Quick Order Pkg 28C, 28E and 28N. NOT AVAILABLE with Quick Order Pkg 22S, 23A, or 24A.		
AAP	Towing Group 2 (SE)	153	180
	INCLUDES firm ride suspension, conventional spare tire, P215/65R15 A/S tires, and 15" wheel covers. NOT AVAILABLE with Quick Order Pkg 23A or 24A.		
AAR	Towing Group 3 (Grand Voyager SE)	323	380
	INCLUDES 120 amp alternator, heavy-duty battery, heavy-duty brakes, heavy-duty radiator, heavy-duty transmission oil cooler, trailer tow wiring harness, firm ride suspension, conventional spare tire, P215/65R15 A/S tires, and 15" wheel covers.		

PONTIAC — TRANS SPORT

| CODE | DESCRIPTION | INVOICE | MSRP |

TRANS SPORT (1997)

1997 Pontiac Trans Sport Montana Extended Wheelbase

What's New for Pontiac Trans Sport in 1997 — After years of taking it in the chin, Pontiac redesigns the Trans Sport and lands one squarely in Chrysler's face. This van is good looking, loaded with features, and fun to drive. Wait. Did we say fun to drive?

Trans Sport — Review

The difference is like night and day. Pontiac's new Trans Sport is so much better than the previous version that there really is no comparison. So forget about the bullet-nosed, plastic-bodied, Dustbuster Trans Sport of yesteryear. Pontiac is rewriting Chrysler's book on minivans.

How so? For starters, the Trans Sport features a standard 3.4-liter, 180-horsepower V-6 engine. That's substantially more power than Chrysler offers with its top-of-the-line motor. Available, just like on the Chrysler vans, is a driver's-side sliding door. Buyers needing 8-passenger seating can select the Trans Sport, the only minivan on the market offering this configuration. Chrysler vans feature roll-away bench seats, but they're heavy suckers to unload. The Trans Sport can be equipped with modular seats that weight just 38 pounds each, and are a breeze to remove.

This is one safe van, on paper. Traction control is optional, while dual airbags and anti-lock brakes are standard. Daytime running lights operate the parking lamps rather than the headlights. If GM provided a similar arrangement on all DRL-equipped models, we bet the negative criticism for them wouldn't be nearly as severe or widespread. The new Trans Sport meets 1998 side impact standards, too. Be warned, however, that the Trans Sport fared very poorly in offset crash testing conducted by the Insurance Institute for Highway Safety. (There are no federal standards governing offset crashworthiness.)

The sliding door on the right side of the van can be equipped to open automatically with the push of a button. The ventilation system features a replaceable pollen filter, which is good news for allergy sufferers. Optional rear audio controls allow rear passengers to listen to a

TRANS SPORT — PONTIAC

CD, cassette, or stereo via headphones while front passengers listen to their choice of any of the three mediums simultaneously.

Around town, the Trans Sport feels downright spunky, with good throttle response and car-like handling. Braking is excellent for a 4,000-pound vehicle. Visibility is uncompromised, thanks in part to the huge exterior mirrors that effectively eliminate blind spots. Front seats are quite comfortable, and most controls are easy to see and use. If it weren't for the expansive windshield and high driving position, drivers might not realize the Trans Sport was a van.

Pontiac is pushing the Montana package, making Trans Sports so equipped the focal point of the lineup. Product planners claim that the Montana bridges the gap between sport utility and minivan. Ummm, we don't think so. It takes more than body-cladding, white-letter tires, alloy wheels, fog lights, and traction control to match an SUV when it comes to capability. Image is another matter, and the Montana does blur the line between minivan and sport/utility in terms of styling, but nobody will mistake this Pontiac for a Jeep Grand Cherokee.

Sounds good, for a minivan. There are problems, however. Chief among them are seriously uncomfortable modular seats that provide little in the way of thigh and leg support. When sitting in one of the rear chairs, adult passengers will grow cranky quickly. The automatic sliding door is designed to reverse direction when it determines that an object is blocking its closure path. Be warned; the door doesn't behave like an elevator door. It can almost knock unsuspecting adults over before reversing. Teach children that they are strong enough to push the door back, and not to be afraid of getting closed in if the door doesn't stop immediately. Other flaws include difficult-to-reach center console storage, lack of a power lock switch in the cargo area, and excessive amounts of cheap-looking plastic inside.

Basically, we like the Trans Sport for its standard and optional array of features, combined with a pleasantly surprising fun-to-drive demeanor. So long as adult passengers drive or call shotgun, Pontiac's new people mover should find immediate acceptance from the buying public, though we question crashworthiness until the feds run one of these into a solid barrier later this year.

Safety Data

Driver Airbag: *Standard*
Side Airbag: *Not Available*
4-Wheel ABS: *Standard*
Driver Crash Test Grade: *Not Available*

Passenger Airbag: *Standard*
Meets 1997 Car Side Impact Standards: *Yes*
Traction Control: *Optional*
Insurance Cost: *Not Available*

Standard Equipment

TRANS SPORT SE SWB: 3.4-liter V-6 engine, 4-speed automatic transmission, integrated windshield antenna, daytime running lights with automatic light control, solar-coated heat-repelling windshield, flip-out side windows, tinted glass, composite halogen headlamps, fog lights, dual power fold-and-stow exterior mirrors with blue tint, lower aero rocker panel moldings, wide bodyside moldings, P205/70R15 all-season tires, 15-inch styled bolt-on wheel covers, wet-arm controlled-cycle windshield wipers, rear window wiper, quiet package acoustical insulation, dual front airbags, front air conditioning, child security door lock, power door locks, cloth seat fabric, tachometer, trip odometer, door ajar indicator, theater dimming interior lighting, glovebox light, liftgate security lights, under hood light, front and rear floor mats, day/night rearview mirror, dual covered visor vanity mirrors, pollen filter, auxiliary power outlets front and rear, AM/FM stereo with clock, front reclining bucket seats with manual lumbar adjustment, rotating headrest, and inboard armrests; 7-passenger seating with solid bench seats in second and third rows, integrated headrests, 4-way manual driver's seat adjustment,

PONTIAC — TRANS SPORT

tilt steering wheel, cup and mug holder tray, front seatback pockets, front underseat storage drawer (passenger side), mini-cargo nets in cargo bay, second row storage pockets, rear quarter covered storage with cupholder, under dash storage with coin holder and removable audio storage, battery rundown protection, power front disc/rear drum anti-lock brakes, brake/transmission shift interlock feature, long-life engine coolant, stainless steel exhaust system, power rack and pinion steering

TRANS SPORT SE EXTENDED 3-DOOR (in addition to or instead of SWB equipment): P215/70R15 all-season tires, 7-passenger seating with split-folding modular bench seating in second and third rows

TRANS SPORT SE EXTENDED 4-DOOR (in addition to or instead of EXTENDED 3-DOOR equipment): Rear window defogger, deep tinted glass, power windows with driver's side express-down feature, remote keyless entry, AM/FM stereo with cassette player, power rear quarter windows, driver's side sliding door

Base Prices

Code	Description	Invoice	MSRP
N06V	SE SWB 3-door	18534	20479
M06V	SE Extended 3-door	19402	21439
M16V	SE Extended 4-door	21149	23369
	Destination Charge:	570	570

Accessories

Code	Description	Invoice	MSRP
C34	Air Conditioning — Front & Rear (Extended)	409	460
	With G67	401	450
	With WX4 (Extended)	401	450
	Includes rear seat saddlebag storage; REQUIRES Deep Tinted Glass		
PH3	Alloy Wheels	231	259
	REQUIRES Touring Tires; INCLUDED in Montana Package		
G67	Automatic Level Control	160	180
	Includes rear saddlebag storage; REQUIRES Touring Tires; INCLUDED in Montana Package		
YF5	California Emissions	151	170
AJ1	Deep Tinted Glass (SWB/Ext. 3-dr.)	218	245
	INCLUDED in Option Packages 1SC and 1SD		
K05	Engine Block Heater	18	20
AN5	Integrated Child Seat — Dual	200	225
	REQUIRES modular seating		
AN2	Integrated Child Seat — Single	111	125
	REQUIRES modular seating		
V54	Luggage Rack	156	175
	INCLUDED in Montana Package and Option Package 1SD		
NG1	Massachusetts/New York Emissions	151	170

TRANS SPORT — PONTIAC

CODE	DESCRIPTION	INVOICE	MSRP
WX4	Montana Package (Extended)	1036	1164
	With 1SD (Ext. 3-dr.)	880	989
	With 1SD (Ext. 4-dr.)	880	989
	Includes specific two-tone paint scheme with charcoal lower accent paint, 7-passenger seating with rear split-folding bench seats, luggage rack, rear seat saddlebag storage, cast aluminum wheels, 15-inch raised white-letter self-sealing tires, traction control, automatic load leveling		
WX4	Montana Package (SWB)	1368	1537
	With 1SD (SWB)	914	1027
	Includes specific two-tone paint scheme with charcoal lower accent paint, 7-passenger seating with rear split-folding bench seats, luggage rack, rear seat saddlebag storage, cast aluminum wheels, 15-inch raised white-letter self-sealing tires, traction control, automatic load leveling		
1SB	Option Package 1SB (SWB/Ext. 3-dr.)	409	460
	Includes convenience net, cruise control, AM/FM stereo with cassette player		
1SC	Option Package 1SC (SWB/Ext. 3-dr.)	1255	1410
	Includes convenience net, cruise control, AM/FM stereo with cassette player, deep tinted glass, rear window defogger, remote keyless entry, power windows, power rear quarter windows, perimeter lighting		
1SD	Option Package 1SD (Ext. 3-dr.)	1883	2116
	Includes convenience net, cruise control, AM/FM stereo with cassette player, deep tinted glass, rear window defogger, remote keyless entry, power windows, power rear quarter windows, perimeter lighting, dual illuminated visor vanity mirrors, overhead console, power driver's seat, luggage rack		
1SD	Option Package 1SD (Ext. 4-dr.)	628	706
	Includes dual illuminated visor vanity mirrors, overhead console, power driver's seat, luggage rack		
1SD	Option Package 1SD (SWB)	2181	2451
	Includes convenience net, cruise control, AM/FM stereo with cassette player, deep tinted glass, rear window defogger, remote keyless entry, power windows, power rear quarter windows, perimeter lighting, dual illuminated visor vanity mirrors, overhead console, 7-passenger seating with rear split bench seats, power driver's seat, luggage rack		
D84	Paint — Two-tone	111	125
	NOT AVAILABLE with Montana Package		
AG1	Power Driver's Seat	240	270
	INCLUDED in Option Package 1SD		
AG9	Power Passenger's Seat	271	305
E58	Power Sliding Door (Ext. 3-dr.)	356	400
	With 1SC (SWB/Ext. 3-dr.)	312	350
	With 1SD (Ext. 3-dr.)	312	350
	Includes power rear quarter windows; REQUIRES remote keyless entry		
E58	Power Sliding Door (Ext. 4-dr.)	312	350
	REQUIRES remote keyless entry		

PONTIAC — TRANS SPORT

CODE	DESCRIPTION	INVOICE	MSRP
CF5	Power Sunroof (Ext. 3-dr.)	619	695
	With 1SD (Ext. 3-dr.)	463	520
	REQUIRES purchase of Option Package 1SD, front & rear Air Conditioning, and Power Sliding Door		
A31	Power Windows (SWB/Ext. 3-dr.)	245	275
	Includes driver's express-down feature; INCLUDED in Option Packages 1SC and 1SD		
C36	Rear Heater (Extended)	158	177
	With C34 (Extended)	149	167
	With G67	149	167
	With WX4 (Extended)	149	167
	Includes rear seat saddlebag storage; REQUIRES Deep Tinted Glass		
C49	Rear Window Defogger (SWB/Ext. 3-dr.)	160	180
	INCLUDED in Option Packages 1SC and 1SD		
AU0	Remote Keyless Entry (SWB/Ext. 3-dr.)	134	150
	INCLUDED in Safety & Security Package, and in Option Packages 1SC and 1SD		
R6A	Safety & Security Package	187	210
	With P42	53	60
	With WX4 (SWB)	53	60
	With WX4 (Extended)	53	60
	Includes self-sealing tires, content theft-deterrent alarm system, remote keyless entry system with panic button		
ABB	Seating — 7 passenger with cloth rear modular buckets (Extended)	102	115
ABD	Seating — 7-passenger with cloth middle row captain's chairs (Extended)	236	265
ABD	Seating — 7-passenger with cloth middle row captain's chairs (SWB)	534	600
	With 1SD (SWB)	236	265
	With WX4 (SWB)	236	265
ABB	Seating — 7-passenger with cloth rear modular buckets (SWB)	401	450
	With 1SD (SWB)	102	115
	With WX4 (SWB)	102	115
ABA	Seating — 7-passenger with cloth split rear benches (SWB)	298	335
ZP8	Seating — 8-passenger cloth (Extended)	236	265
ZP8	Seating — 8-passenger cloth (SWB)	534	600
	With 1SD (SWB)	236	265
	With WX4 (SWB)	236	265
WJ7	Seating — Leather Upholstery	939	1055
	Includes steering wheel radio controls; REQUIRES seating with captain's chairs		
UZ5	Stereo — Premium Speakers	45	50
	Extended range coaxial speakers		
UM1	Stereo — Premium w/cassette & CD players	476	535
	With WJ7	312	350
	AM/FM stereo with cassette deck and dual playback CD player, equalizer, and rear seat audio controls		
UK3	Stereo — Steering Wheel Controls	165	185
	Includes leather-wrapped steering wheel; INCLUDED with Leather Seating		

TRANS SPORT — PONTIAC

CODE	DESCRIPTION	INVOICE	MSRP
UT6	Stereo — Uplevel w/cassette	298	335
	With WJ7	134	150
	AM/FM stereo with cassette player, equalizer, and rear seat audio controls		
UP3	Stereo — Uplevel w/CD player	387	435
	With WJ7	223	250
	AM/FM stereo with CD player, equalizer, and rear seat audio controls		
UN6	Stereo — w/cassette (SWB/Ext. 3-dr.)	174	195
	AM/FM stereo with cassette player; INCLUDED in Option Packages		
U1C	Stereo — w/CD player	89	100
	AM/FM stereo with CD player		
XPU	Tires — P215/70R15 Touring (Extended)	31	35
XPU	Tires — P215/70R15 Touring (SWB)	65	73
P42	Tires — Self Sealing Touring	134	150
	INCLUDED in Montana Package and Safety & Security Package		
V92	Towing Package	134	150
	Includes wiring harness, heavy-duty cooling, and heavy-duty flashers; REQUIRES Automatic Load Leveling		
NW9	Traction Control	156	175
	REQUIRES Automatic Load Leveling; INCLUDED in Montana Package		

CALL NATIONWIDE 1-800-521-7257

FOR A WRITTEN QUOTATION
AS LOW AS $50 OVER INVOICE

See page 15 for details.

SUZUKI — SIDEKICK SPORT

SIDEKICK SPORT *(1997)*

1997 Suzuki Sidekick Sport 4-Door

What's New for Suzuki Sidekick Sport in 1997 — A JS Sport 2WD model is added to the Sidekick lineup mid-year. It has a DOHC engine that makes 120-horsepower at 6500 rpm. There are no changes to the rest of the Sidekick line.

Sidekick — Review

Even folks who find it easy to fault small sport-utes run the risk of falling for a Sidekick. Neither a true truck nor a car, this mini SUV has created a niche that other manufacturers are rushing to capitalize on. The Geo Tracker that's sold by Chevrolet dealers is basically identical, and the Kia Sportage is a new competitor. Toyota introduced the RAV4 to do battle with the Sidekick, and Honda is rushing to bring their CRV over from Japan to do the same. Suzuki aims the Sidekick squarely at teens and twenty-somethings, but older adventurers are likely to find it irresistible, too.

The Sport model is offered only with the four-door body style in JS, JX and JLX trim. Hallmarks of the Sport include a twin-cam engine good for 120 horsepower, and a track that has been increased by two inches for increased stability and response. Sixteen-inch tires and wheels, a shiny grille, and a two-tone paint scheme set the Sport model apart from garden-variety Sidekicks.

Four-wheel anti-lock brakes are optional; standard on Sidekick Sport. Exclusive to the Sport is a 100-watt Alpine stereo system, cruise control (on the JLX only), security alarm system, power windows and locks, split-fold rear seat, remote fuel door release, cloth door trim, power remote mirrors, rear window wiper/washer and overhead map lights. The Sport also gets unique paint colors from which to select.

Frankly, we think that the Sport's two-tone paint and chrome-ringed grille make the Sidekick look like a little freckle-faced kid wearing an Armani suit. Still, it has more character than many more mundane mini-SUVs.

SIDEKICK SPORT — SUZUKI

Safety Data:

Driver Airbag: *Standard*
Side Airbag: *Not Available*
4-Wheel ABS: *Optional*
Driver Crash Test Grade: *Poor*
Passenger Crash Test Grade: *Average*

Passenger Airbag: *Standard*
Meets 1999 Side Impact Standards: *No*
Traction Control: *Not Available*
Insurance Cost: *High*
Integrated Child Seat(s): *N/A*

Standard Equipment

SIDEKICK SPORT - 2WD JS: 1.8 liter DOHC 16 valve 4 cylinder engine with electronic multi-point fuel injection, 5-speed manual transmission, power steering, 4-wheel power assisted brakes, stainless steel exhaust, power/normal switch (automatic trans only), daytime running lights, power dual OS mirrors, tinted glass, color-keyed front and rear bumpers, sport trim, spare tire carrier with full-size spare, intermittent windshield wipers with washers, electric rear window defogger, air conditioning, tachometer, tripmeter, dual air bags, rear door child safety locks, AM/FM stereo radio with cassette and 4 speakers, security alarm system, power windows, power door locks, reclining front bucket seats, cloth seat trim, split fold-down rear seat, dual cup holders, passenger vanity mirror, remote fuel filler door release, full carpeting, overhead map lights, three-point front/rear seat belts, P215/65R16 all-season SBR tires, full-size spare tire, styled steel wheels.

4WD JX (in addition to or instead of 2WD JS equipment): Manual front hubs, two-speed transfer case.

4WD JLX (in addition to or instead of 4WD JX equipment): 4-wheel anti-lock brakes, automatic front hubs, 5-spoke aluminum alloy wheels, spare tire cover with wheel lock, electric rear window wiper with washer, cruise control, remote fuel filler door release, aluminum alloy wheels.

Base Prices

		Invoice	MSRP
—	4WD JX 4-Dr Hardtop (5-spd)	16106	17699
—	4WD JX 4-Dr Hardtop (auto)	17016	18699
—	4WD JLX 4-Dr Hardtop (5-spd)	17471	19199
—	4WD JLX 4-Dr Hardtop (auto)	18381	20199
Destination Charge:		420	420

Accessories

NOTE: Suzuki accessories are dealer installed. Contact a Suzuki dealer for accessory availability.

TO PRICE YOUR TRADE-IN,
PURCHASE EDMUND'S USED CAR
PRICES AND RATINGS.

See page 6 for details.

SUZUKI
X-90 (1997)

1997 Suzuki X-90

What's New for Suzuki X-90 in 1997 — No changes for Suzuki's wild-looking X-90.

X-90 — Review

Suzuki's cool new X-90 sport/ute takes the place of the now defunct Samurai in the maker's lineup. Larger, more powerful, and more sophisticated than the Samurai ever dreamed of being, the X-90 is aimed squarely at young singles with disposable income and no responsibilities.

The X-90 is an amalgam of two-seater sports coupe, convertible and four-wheel drive sport utility. The two-seat cockpit sits beneath a T-top roof, just forward of an 8.4 cubic foot conventional trunk, and on top of a two- or four-wheel drive chassis. Body on frame construction is motivated by a 95-horsepower four cylinder engine. An automatic transmission is available in place of the standard five-speed manual gear changer.

The only part of this formula that seems wrong is the 1.6-liter engine. Its power output seems to be a bit on the meager side for a vehicle with such sporting pretensions. The Sidekick Sport's 120-horsepower, 1.8-liter engine should at least be an option on the heavier four-wheel drive model.

Dual airbags, four-wheel anti-lock brakes and daytime running lights are standard. All X-90's come equipped with power windows and locks, power steering, alloy wheels, and intermittent wipers. Order four-wheel drive and you'll get cruise control, a security alarm and an Alpine stereo.

Suzuki's taking a chance here, creating a new niche in the SUV market. We think that the X-90 will find limited success in climates and terrains where its four-wheel drive will have some relevancy, and in places where style-conscious buyers don't find what they want in the slightly more versatile Geo Tracker, Jeep Wrangler, and Suzuki's own Sidekick convertible. The X-90's T-top roof is easier to operate than the soft tops of any of those vehicles, but this new Suzuki won't carry more than two people; the others will carry four.

X-90 SUZUKI

CODE	DESCRIPTION	INVOICE	MSRP

Safety Data

Driver Airbag: *Standard*
Side Airbag: *Not Available*
4-Wheel ABS: *Optional*
Driver Crash Test Grade: *Not Tested*
Passenger Crash Test Grade: *Not Tested*

Passenger Airbag: *Standard*
Meets 1999 Side Impact Standards: *No*
Traction Control: *Not Available*
Insurance Cost: *Low*
Integrated Child Seat(s): *N/A*

Standard Equipment

X-90 - 2WD: 1.6 liter SOHC 16 valve 4 cylinder engine with electronic multi-point fuel injection, 5-speed manual transmission, power steering, 4-wheel power assisted brakes, stainless steel exhaust, power/normal switch (automatic trans only), T-top, daytime running lights, integrated halogen headlamps, rear spoiler with stop lamp, aluminum alloy wheels, dual OS mirrors, intermittent windshield wipers with washers, electric rear window defogger, tinted glass, color-keyed front and rear bumpers, locking fuel filler door, tachometer, tripmeter, dual air bags, power windows, power door locks, full cloth bucket seats, center console with dual cup holders, deluxe door trim with cloth inserts, full carpeting, three-point seat belts, P195/65R15 all-season SBR tires, 15 x 5.5 aluminum wheels, compact spare tire, front stabilizer bar.

4WD (in addition to or instead of 2WD equipment): Automatic front hubs, two-speed transfer case, AM/FM stereo radio with cassette and 4 speakers, security alarm system.

Base Prices

Code	Description	Invoice	MSRP
LCC664V	2WD 2-Dr Sport Utility (5-spd)	12407	13199
LCC694V	2WD 2-Dr Sport Utility (auto)	13300	14149
LAC664V	4WD 2-Dr Sport Utility (5-spd)	13577	14599
LAC694V	4WD 2-Dr Sport Utility (auto)	14460	15549
	Destination Charge:	420	420

Accessories

	Description	Invoice	MSRP
—	Anti-Lock Brakes — 2WD	540	600
—	Anti-Lock Brakes — 4WD	700	800
	incls cruise control on 4WD		

NOTE: Suzuki accessories are dealer installed. Contact a Suzuki dealer for accessory availability.

CALL NATIONWIDE 1-800-521-7257

FOR A WRITTEN QUOTATION
AS LOW AS $50 OVER INVOICE

See page 15 for details.

TOYOTA

4RUNNER (1997)

1997 Toyota 4Runner Limited 4WD

What's New for Toyota 4Runner in 1997 — After last year's redesign, Toyota's hot-selling 4Runner receives minor changes. The most noticeable is the addition of the 2WD Limited to the model lineup. SR5 models receive new interior fabrics.

4Runner — Review

The Toyota 4Runner was redesigned last year, and has been selling like hot cakes ever since. Its aggressive styling, ample interior space, powerful engine choices, and serious off-road ability make it a must-have for anyone who is shopping for a mid-size SUV.

The 4Runner boasts a large interior that comfortably holds five adults. The cargo area accommodates enough stuff to make sure that nothing gets left behind during those week long camping trips. The seats are supportive without being pinchy, and the outward views are outstanding from any seat in the truck. As is typical of Toyota, the interior is an ergonomic masterpiece, with all of the controls falling easily to hand. There are big cupholders that will hold 20-ozs of your favorite beverage, and a large center console that will gladly accept the tapes, CDs, and various other pieces of garbage that accumulate in one's vehicle.

The best news about the 4Runner is the power found under the hood. The inline 4-cylinder engine that is found in the Base model produces almost as much power as the base 6-cylinder engine found in the Ford Explorer. Step up to the V-6 found in the SR5 and Limited models, and be rewarded with 183-horsepower and 217 lb./ft. of torque; enough to haul 5,000 pounds. Unlike many upper-end SUVs, it is possible to get a manual transmission on all but the top-of-the-line Limited model. Those of us that like to row our own gears, or who are interested in saving a little money, will certainly appreciate that.

Despite providing dual air bags in its 1996 redesign, the 4Runner receives only average scores for the driver and passenger for crash tests conducted by the National Highway Traffic and Safety Institute. We are glad to report, though, that SR5 and Limited models are automatically equipped with anti-lock brakes, and that Base models can be ordered with them.

4RUNNER — TOYOTA

Consumers have had a long running love affair with Toyota for years now, and the 4Runner is no exception. Great reliability, outstanding ergonomics, and good performance on- and off-road make it a hard vehicle to pass up. Beware, though, Toyota dealers know that they have a winner with the 4Runner and are offering no discounts on this very popular vehicle. Thus, if you expect to get a good deal on a 4Runner, you'll be waiting for quite a while.

Safety Data

Driver Airbag: *Standard*
Side Airbag: *Not Available*
4-Wheel ABS: *Opt (Base)/Std (Limited/SR5)*
Driver Crash Test Grade: *Average*
Passenger Crash Test Grade: *Average*

Passenger Airbag: *Standard*
Meets 1999 Side Impact Standards: *No*
Traction Control: *Not Available*
Insurance Cost: *High*
Integrated Child Seat(s): *Not Available*

Standard Equipment

BASE: 2.7-liter 16-valve 4-cylinder engine, front disc/rear drum brakes, power assisted rack-and-pinion steering, 15" styled steel wheels, P225/75R15 mud and snow tires, full size spare tire, 4-wheel shift-on-the-fly (4WD), skid plates on front suspension, skid plates on fuel tank and transfer case (4WD), AM/FM stereo with 4 seakers, dual air bags, tinted glass, power rear windows, tachometer, center console with storage bin, front cup holders, bucket seats, split fold rear seats, and remote fuel door release.

SR5: (in addition to or instead of BASE): 3.4-liter DOHC V-6 engine, 4-wheel anti-lock brakes, variable speed windshield wipers, rear window wiper/washer, rear window defogger, privacy glass, power outside mirrors, power antenna, power door locks, deluxe AM/FM stereo with cassette and 4 speakers, tilt steering, digital clock, rear cup holders, passenger's side vanity mirror, and front map lights.

LIMITED (in addition to or instead of SR5): P265/70R16 tires, 16" aluminum wheels, touch-drive 4WD selector, color-keyed fender flares, premium stereo with cassette and 6 speakers, cruise control, leather sport seats, steering wheel, and shift knob.

Base Prices

Code	Description	Invoice	MSRP
8641	2WD (5-spd)	17412	19888
8640	2WD (auto)	18199	20788
8657	4WD (5-spd)	19249	21988
8658	4WD (auto)	20038	22888
8642	SR5 V-6 2WD (auto)	21499	24558
8665	SR5 V-6 4WD (5-spd)	22480	25678
8664	SR5 V-6 4WD (auto)	23267	26578
8668	Limited V-6 (auto)	19536	33738
	Destination Charge:	420	420

TOYOTA 4RUNNER

CODE	DESCRIPTION	INVOICE	MSRP

Accessories

CODE	DESCRIPTION	INVOICE	MSRP
AA	16" Alloy Wheels w/Differential Locks (SR5 4WD)	1092	1355
	NOT AVAILABLE with other tire and wheel pkgs, or A1 and AG preferred equipment groups.		
SV	16" Steel Wheels (Base)	480	600
	Includes P265/70 mud and snow tires, 12.5" front brakes, and 4.556 rear axle differential.		
AC	Air Conditioning (Base/SR5)	788	985
	INCLUDED in UP upgrade pkg, A1, and AG preferred equipment groups.		
CK	All Weather Guard (Base/SR5/2WD Limted)	59	70
	Includes heavy duty battery, heavy duty starter, heavy duty wiper motor, and large washer fluid reservoir. REQUIRES RH rear heater and RW rear wiper (Base).		
AW	Aluminum Wheels (Base/SR5)	824	1030
	Includes P265/70 mud and snow tires, 12.5" brakes, and 4.1 rear differential. REQUIRES AB anti-lock brakes (Base).		
AY	Aluminum Wheels (Base/SR5)	332	415
	NOT AVAILABLE with SP sports pkg, A1, or AG preferred equipment groups.		
AB	Anti-Lock Brakes (Base)	507	590
CA	California Emissions	29	34
CQ	Convenience Pkg (Base)	577	705
	Includes tilt steering, intermittent windshield wiper, rear window wiper, digital clock, rear window defogger, front map lights.		
CL	Cruise Control (Base/SR5)	232	290
	INCLUDED in UP upgrade package, and LA leather trim pkg.		
EX	Deluxe Stereo w/Cassette (Base)	169	225
	INCLUDED in UP upgrade pkg.		
DL	Differential Locks (4WD Base/SR5)	268	325
LA	Leather Trim (SR5)	1228	1535
	Includes sport seats, cruise control, leather seats, and leather-wrapped steering wheel and shift knob.		
PX	Metallic Paint	NC	NC
PO	Power Pkg 1 (Base)	735	920
	Includes power outside mirrors, power door locks, and power lighting pkg. INCLUDED in UP upgrade pkg and PP power pkg.		
PP	Power Pkg 2 (Base)	736	920
	Includes power outside mirrors, power door locks, and power lighting pkg. Includes upgrade pkg.		
PP	Power Pkg 2 (SR5)	432	540
	Includes alloy wheels, power windws, power door locks, power antenna, air conditioning, premium stereo with cassette, and 6 speakers.		
A1	Preferred Equipment Group 1 (SR5)	2190	2750
	Includes P265/70R16 tires, aluminum alloy wheels, 12.5" disc brakes, 4.1 rear differential, power antenna, power door locks, air conditioning, and premium stereo with cassette.		

4RUNNER — TOYOTA

CODE	DESCRIPTION	INVOICE	MSRP
AG	**Preferred Equipment Group 2 (SR5)**	1698	2135
	Includes aluminum wheels, power windows, power door locks, power antenna, air conditioning, and premium stereo with casssette.		
DC	**Premium 3-in-1 Combo (Limited)**	709	945
	Includes stereo with CD player and cassette.		
DC	**Premium 3-in-1 Combo (SR5)**	855	1140
	Includes stereo with CD player and cassette.		
CE	**Premium Stereo w/Cassette (SR5)**	146	195
	Includes premium stereo with cassette and 6 speakers.		
PG	**Privacy Glass (Base)**	236	295
RH	**Rear Heater (Base/SR5)**	132	165
RW	**Rear Wiper & Defroster (Base)**	292	365
	INCLUDED in CQ convenience pkg.		
SP	**Sport Package (SR5 4WD)**	1464	1820
	Includes P265/70R16 mud and snow tires, aluminum alloy wheels, black out sport trim, black bumpers and grille, sport seats, fabric door trim, leather-wrapped steering wheel and shift lever, cruise control, 12.5 front brakes, and 4.1 rear differential ratio.		
SR	**Sun Roof (SR5/Limited)**	732	915
TW	**Tilt Steering (Base)**	201	235
	Includes vairable intermitent windshield wipers. INCLUDED in CQ convenience pkg.		
UP	**Upgrade Pkg (Base)**	1925	2420
	Includes air conditioning, power pkg 2 (aluminum alloy wheels, power windows, power door locks, power antennas, and premium cassette with 6-speakers), cruise control, and carpeted floor mats.		

Save hundreds, even thousands, off the sticker price of the new truck you want.

Call Autovantage®
your FREE auto-buying service

1-800-201-7703

No purchase required. No fees.

TOYOTA — LAND CRUISER

LAND CRUISER (1997)

1997 Toyota Land Cruiser

What's New for Toyota Land Cruiser in 1997 — The Black Package is discontinued, but black paint becomes an available color choice.

T100 — Review

Long before Explorers and Troopers—and years ahead of the first Blazers and Broncos—Toyota joined the slowly-blossoming sport-utility arena with the first Land Cruiser, rival mainly to Jeeps and Land Rovers. That was 1960, when the first canvas-topped "Landcruisers" cost less than $3000. Today, Toyota offers a descendant of that vehicle under the same name that is more powerful and a lot more expensive.

Only one model is for sale, a four-wheel-drive wagon powered by a 4.5-liter, 24-valve six-cylinder engine that cranks out 212 horsepower. Revamping for 1995 added airbags for both the driver and front passenger. Those front occupants also enjoy the benefit of height-adjustable seatbelts. Four-wheel anti-lock braking is installed on all Land Cruisers, working with all-disc binders. The Black Package is dropped for 1997, but vampires and other creatures of the night can still opt for black paint..

For peak traction in difficult spots at low speeds, an exclusive front and rear locking differential is available. That makes Land Cruiser the only sport-utility on sale in the U.S. with three locking units, to amplify the effect of the standard permanent four-wheel-drive system. In fully-locked mode, all four wheels are driven in unison, with equal torque distribution. A second-gear-start feature boosts traction on slippery surfaces. Land Cruisers seat seven and can tow a 5,000-pound trailer.

For its stout sticker price, at least you get a lot of equipment, including air conditioning, power locks and windows, cruise control, and more. Traditionally, potential shoppers have faced long waiting lists to get a Land Cruiser, undaunted by the prospect of a stiff ride or quickly-depleting fuel tank. These capable machines attract the kind of customer who might

LAND CRUISER — TOYOTA

otherwise pay big bucks for a Land Rover or Range Rover, whether or not any plans for off-roading lay ahead. Any of them would look good decorating a driveway in an affluent neighborhood—especially to passersby who can appreciate the heritage that accompanies such a purchase.

Safety Data

Driver Airbag: Standard
Side Airbag: Not Available
4-Wheel ABS: Optional
Driver Crash Test Grade: Good
Passenger Crash Test Grade: Good

Passenger Airbag: Not Available
Meets 1999 Side Impact Standards: No
Traction Control: Not Available
Insurance Cost: High SR5
Integrated Child Seat(s): N/A

Standard Equipment

LAND CRUISER: 4.5 liter 6 cylinder EFI 24-valve engine, heavy duty cooling system, dual air bags, power steering, power 4-wheel disc anti-lock brakes, 4-speed automatic transmission with overdrive, heavy duty transmission fluid cooler, cruise control, air conditioning, power door locks, front and rear stabilizer bars, front and rear mud guards, center console, privacy glass, styled steel wheels, P275/70R16 steel belted radial tires, full-size spare tire, tachometer, fender flares, power antenna, AM/FM ETR stereo radio with cassette, tilt steering wheel, rear window defroster, rear heater ducts, power windows, digital clock, heavy duty battery, chrome grille, cloth reclining front bucket seats, rear fold-down bench seat, variable intermittent windshield wipers, intermittent rear window wiper, front and rear tow hooks, skid plates for fuel tank and transfer case, trip odometer, map pockets, locking center differential, dual power outside mirrors, remote fuel filler door release, chrome front bumper.

Base Prices

Code	Description	Invoice	MSRP
6154	4WD Wagon (auto)	35319	41068
	Destination Charge:	420	420

Accessories

Code	Description	Invoice	MSRP
AW	Aluminum Wheels	420	525
	incls five P275/70R16 tires, five aluminum wheels		
TX	Two-Tone Pkg	228	285
SR	Power Moonroof	948	1185
TH	Third Seat	1212	1515
	incls split folding rear third seat, rear 3-point seat belts, child protector rear hatch lock, rear quarter sliding windows, rear assist grips, fabric headrests, privacy glass		
DC	Radio — premium 3-in-1 combo	709	945
	incls AM/FM ETR radio/cassette/CD player with programmable equalization		
LA	Leather Pkg	3455	4280
	incls leather faced seats and door trim, leather-wrapped steering wheel, leather headrests, leather transmission lever and transfer case knob, leather-covered center console, third seat package, power driver and front passenger seats		
DL	Differential Locks	681	825
	incls lockable front and rear differentials, viscous coupling transfer case, full floating axle		
BX	Black Paint	NC	NC

TOYOTA — PREVIA

PREVIA (1997)

1997 Toyota Previa LE S/C

What's New for Toyota Previa in 1997 — This is the last year for the Previa as we know it. It leaves us this year with lower NVH levels, 2 new colors, new wheel covers, and larger brakes on models NOT equipped with ABS. Does that make sense?

Previa — Review

What runs on supercharged power, has available all-wheel drive, met 1997 passenger car side-impact standards six years early, is as reliable as a Retriever, and boasts one of the most uniquely attractive shapes on the road? A high-profile sports car? A concept vehicle from the early 90s? Give up? It's the Toyota Previa minivan. That's right. A minivan. And in addition to all of these fine attributes, the Previa adds dual airbags, comfortable seating for seven, optional anti-lock brakes, and up to 152.3 cubic feet of cargo capacity.

Toyota minivans come only with a supercharged engine this year; a wise move by product planners since the old base four-cylinder engine was a wheezemeister when it came to traversing anything with an incline. Previas are sold in DX or step-up LE trim, either rear-drive or with permanent All-Trac four-wheel drive.

Acceleration with the 161-horsepower, 2.4-liter supercharged engine is strong. However, it tends to be noisy, and gas mileage isn't the greatest. Worse yet, premium fuel is recommended. A four-speed automatic is the only transmission choice. The engine is mounted amidships, below the floor, but major service points are accessible from under the front hood. Although this is the Previa's last year, Toyota has tried to quiet down some of the engine racket with the addition of more sound deadening material.

Seven people sit in reasonable comfort, with a fair amount of cargo space out back. Either or both sides of the split rear seat folds outward against the bodysides for extra cargo-hauling capacity, while the two-passenger center seat can be removed completely. Swivel-recline captain's chairs can be installed instead, and two-wheel-drive LE Previas can have dual power moonroofs—that's right, a pair of openings to the sky. Standard LE fittings include power door locks and windows, as well as dual air conditioners.

PREVIA — TOYOTA

CODE	DESCRIPTION	INVOICE	MSRP

Unlike some competitors, Previas exhibit a distinctively rounded profile—one of the first minivans to go with curvaceous lines rather than a boxy shape. Previas aren't exactly cheap, and lack a V-6 engine option, but like other Toyotas, they provoke relatively few complaints from owners. Unfortunately, people haven't been buying the Previa fast enough to suit Toyota, so this will be its last year.

Safety Data

Driver Airbag: *Standard*
Side Airbag: *Not Available*
4-Wheel ABS: *Optional*
Driver Crash Test Grade: *Good*
Passenger Crash Test Grade: *Average*

Passenger Airbag: *Standard*
Meets 1997 Car Side Impact Standards: *Yes*
Traction Control: *Not Available*
Insurance Cost: *Average; Low (2WD DX)*
Integrated Child Seat(s): *N/A*

Standard Equipment

PREVIA DX S/C: Carpeting, cloth seats, chrome front grille, tilt steering column, full wheel covers, assist grips, right sliding side door, rear door pull strap, intermittent wipers, front stabilizer bar, driver and passenger air bags, clock, power steering, 2.4 liter 4 cylinder EFI engine with supercharger and intercooler, 4-speed ECT automatic overdrive transmission, deluxe AM/FM ETR radio with 6 speakers, right visor vanity mirror, manual OS mirrors, swing-out side windows, adjustable front armrests, trip odometer, protective lower bodyside cladding, halogen headlights with automatic off, map pockets, power front disc/rear drum brakes, diagnostic warning lights, P215/65R15 SBR all-season BW tires, full-size spare tire, remote fuel filler door release, electric rear window defroster, reclining front bucket seats, 2-passenger removable 2nd row bench seat, 3-passenger split fold-down 3rd row bench seat.

LE S/C (in addition to or instead of DX S/C equipment): Cruise control, dual air conditioning, dual power mirrors, power windows, dual illuminated visor vanity mirrors, power door locks, power 4-wheel disc brakes, deluxe AM/FM ETR radio with cassette and 6 speakers, courtesy lights.

Base Prices

Code	Description	Invoice	MSRP
5124	2WD DX S/C (auto)	21847	24808
5134	2WD LE S/C (auto)	25772	29438
5144	ALL TRAC DX S/C (auto)	24879	28418
5154	ALL TRAC LE S/C (auto)	28749	32838
	Destination Charge:	420	420

Accessories

Code	Description	Invoice	MSRP
VP	Value Pkg #1 — DX	1588	1765
	incls Power Pkg, privacy glass, cruise control, air conditioning, deluxe AM/FM ETR with cassette and 6 speakers		
VP	Value Pkg #1 — LE	284	315
	incls anti-lock brakes, privacy glass		
VF	Value Pkg #2 — LE	572	635
	incls Value Pkg #1, map pockets, 4-way adjustable headrests, cup holders, cloth captain chairs, armrests		
VQ	Value Pkg #3 — LE	1049	1165
	incls Value Pkg #1, leather captain chairs, armrests		

TOYOTA PREVIA

CODE	DESCRIPTION	INVOICE	MSRP
PO	Power Pkg — DX	620	775
	incls power windows, power door locks, power OS mirrors		
LA	Leather Trim Pkg — LE	1520	1900
	incls map pockets, armrests, leather seats		
PN	Security Pkg — DX	796	995
	incls Power Pkg, anti-theft device		
PN	Security Pkg — LE	176	220
	incls anti-theft device		
CL	Cruise Control — DX	244	305
AC	Air Conditioning — dual - DX	1388	1735
EX	Radio — DX	169	225
	incls deluxe AM/FM ETR with cassette and 6 speakers		
CE	Radio — LE	210	280
	incls premium AM/FM ETR with cassette, 7 speakers, programmable equalization; req's Value Pkg and privacy glass		
DC	Radio — LE	949	1265
	incls premium 3-in-1 combo, AM/FM ETR radio with cassette and compact disc, 9 speakers, programmable equalization; req's Value Pkg and privacy glass		
CA	California Emissions	NC	NC
AB	Anti-Lock Brakes — power 4-wheel disc - DX	634	745
	LE	507	590
	DX req's cruise control, Value Pkg #1		
PG	Privacy Glass	340	425
AW	Aluminum Wheels — LE	348	435
SR	Dual Moonroofs — LE 2WD	1288	1610
	incls sunshade, rear spoiler		
CC	Seats — cloth captains chairs - LE	696	870
	incls map pockets, armrests, cup holders, 4-way adjustable headrests		

For expert advice in selecting/buying/leasing a new car, call

1-900-AUTOPRO

($2.00 per minute)

RAV4 *(1997)*

1997 Toyota RAV4 4-Door

What's New for Toyota RAV4 in 1997 — New fabric debuts on the 2-door RAV, and a sunroof is finally available on the 4-door. Improvements have also been made by using sound deadening material in the dash area, reducing engine noise in the passenger compartment.

RAV4 — Review

We've seen quite a few RAV4's around since their introduction last year. Many, many 20-somethings seem to be taken with its zippy engine, available all-wheel drive, cute styling and durable construction. We can't blame them, buying a Toyota is never a bad idea if you want a car that will last a long time.

Buying a RAV4 is also not a bad idea if you want a car that offers off-road capability, comfortable room for four adults (in 4-door variety), and a lot of cargo space. Despite its diminutive-seeming exterior shape, the RAV4 4-door really offers a lot of usable space. Rear seat passengers will be pleased to note that the outward views are great in every direction, thanks to the slightly elevated rear seat. Indeed, after riding in a RAV4, we were surprised to feel that it offered more passenger comfort than a similarly priced Jeep Cherokee. (Much of that has to do with the Cherokee's uncomfortably low and mushy back seat.) The same cannot be said for the 2-door RAV, however, which has minimal back seat room and only 10 cubic feet of behind-the-seat storage space.

The RAV's powerplant puts out 120-ponies through either the front or all wheels, depending on which model you order. When combined with the 5-speed manual transmission this mini-ute moves along surprisingly quickly; put on an automatic, though, and the fun is lost. The RAV also handles well, largely due to its Toyota Camry underpinnings. Unlike most SUVs which are truck-based, the RAV is built around the previous-generation Camry chassis. This gives the RAV stability in heavy cornering that is just not present in competitors like the Geo Tracker or Suzuki Sidekick.

Although the RAV4 is a fun, dependable little truck, we just aren't convinced that it's the best value in the marketplace. Jeep's venerable Cherokee offers gobs more engine in a

TOYOTA RAV4

more mature package, and the outstanding Subaru Impreza Outback Sport has all of the RAVs visual excitement, all-wheel drive, and standard anti-lock brakes in a package that is much more fun to drive; both can be had for about the same price as a fully loaded RAV4. So, if you're in the market for small vehicle that will get you to the ski slopes and back, choose carefully. There are a number of cars and trucks that are built just for you.

Safety Data

Driver Airbag: *Standard*
Side Airbag: *Not Available*
4-Wheel ABS: *Optional*
Driver Crash Test Grade: *Not Tested*
Passenger Crash Test Grade: *Not Tested*

Passenger Airbag: *Standard*
Meets 1999 Side Impact Standards: *Yes*
Traction Control: *Not Available*
Insurance Cost: *High*
Integrated Child Seat(s): *Not Available*

Standard Equipment

RAV4: 2.0-liter DOHC 16-valve 4-cylinder engine, power assisted rack-and-pinion steering, front disc/rear drum brakes, independent front suspension, double-wishbone rear suspension, P215/70R16 tires, dual air bags, halogen headlamps, rear window wiper, rear window defogger, and reclining front and rear seats.

Base Prices

Code	Description	Invoice	MSRP
4413	2-Dr 2WD (5-spd)	13779	15118
4412	2WD 2-Door (auto)	14738	16168
4417	2WD 4-Door (5-spd)	14417	15818
4416	2WD 4-Door (auto)	15375	16868
4423	4WD 2-Door (5-spd)	14801	16518
4427	4WD 4-Door (5-spd)	15428	17218
4426	4WD 4-Door (auto)	16368	18268
	Destination Charge:	420	420

Accessories

Code	Description	Invoice	MSRP
AC	Air Conditioning	788	985
CK	All Weather Pkg	59	70
	Includes heavy duty battery, starter, and windshield washer tank; heavy duty front heater, and rear seat heater duct.		
AW	Aluminum Wheels	548	685
AB	Anti-Lock Brakes	507	590
CA	California Emissions	29	34
CL	Cruise Control	232	290
ER	Deluxe Stereo	143	190
EX	Deluxe Stereo w/Cassette	311	415
LD	Limited-Slip Differential (4WD)	309	375
TW	Tilt Steering	145	170
SR	Twin Moonroof (2-Door)	732	915
UT	Upgrade Pkg	849	1050
	Includes power locks, power windows, power mirrors, and tilt steering.		

T100 PICKUP — TOYOTA

T100 *(1997)*

1997 Toyota T100 SR5 Xtracab 4WD

What's New for Toyota T100 in 1997 — Two new colors debut and the optional wheel and tire packages are larger this year. Standard models get radio pre-wiring, mid-level models get fabric door trim panels, and SR5 models get chrome wheel arches.

T100 — Review

When launched as a 1993 model, Toyota's larger-than-before pickup came only with a regular cab that seated three—and that center person suffered a shortage of usable space. During 1995, an extended Xtracab version joined the T100 line, in either DX or SR5 trim. So did a new, more powerful 3.4-liter V-6 engine that yielded 190 horsepower, bringing towing capacity up to 5,200 pounds.

Cargo space is minimal in a regular-cab T100, but much more practical in the Xtracab, which measures 21.7 inches longer and includes forward-facing 50/50 rear jump seats for three. Unlike some extended-cab trucks whose auxiliary seats are bolt-upright, the T100's recline 15 degrees.

Toyota claims that its biggest pickup can beat some full-size domestic rivals with V-8 engines in the acceleration department. Even before the arrival of the more powerful engine, a V-6 pickup moved out quickly enough with manual shift, though an automatic sapped its vigor somewhat. As expected, 4x4s are slower, due largely to their increased weight. Two-wheel-drive models ride more comfortably, too, but any T100 with an empty cargo bed can turn into a unwieldy handful on the highway, its rear axle unable to remain planted in place. Only the standard 2WD, regular cab half-ton pickup comes with a 2.7-liter four-cylinder engine, which delivers 150 horsepower and 177 lb./ft. of torque.

Ranking in size between Dodge's mid-size Dakota and any of the domestically-built full-size pickups, the T100 can be ordered in two trim levels; Standard, or SR5 with chrome trim, sliding rear window, tilt steering, and a tachometer. SR5 is available only on Xtracab models. This year the T100 gets higher standard equipment content and a few new colors.

TOYOTA

T100 PICKUP

A driver's airbag is installed in all models, but four-wheel anti-lock braking is optional only with the V-6 engine. Naturally, T100 owners get the benefit of Toyota's reputation for refinement and excellent assembly quality, as well as high levels of customer satisfaction.

Safety Data

Driver Airbag: *Standard*
Side Airbag: *Not Available*
4-Wheel ABS: *Optional*
Driver Crash Test Grade: *Not Tested*
Passenger Crash Test Grade: *Not Tested*

Passenger Airbag: *Standard*
Meets 1999 Side Impact Standards: *No*
Traction Control: *Not Available*
Insurance Cost: *Very High*
Integrated Child Seat(s): *N/A*

T100 2WD

Standard Equipment

T100 - STD REGULAR CAB: 2.7 liter inline twin-cam DOHC 16 valve EFI 4 cylinder engine, 5-speed manual transmission, power assisted ventilated front disc brakes, power assisted rear drum brakes, power rack and pinion steering, double-walled bed with 2-tier loading and stake pockets, black outside driver side mirror, 15" styled steel wheels with P215/75R15 all-season SBR tires, vinyl bench seat with outboard headrests and vinyl door trim, gauges (speedometer, odometer, fuel level and coolant temperature), driver side air bag.

DX XTRACAB (in addition to or instead of STD REGULAR CAB equipment): 3.4 liter four-cam DOHC 24 valve EFI V6 engine, dual black outside mirrors with passenger side convex mirror, front and rear mud guards, P235/75R15 SBR tires, full wheel covers, tilt-out rear quarter windows, 60/40 fully split cloth bench seat with center armrest and cloth door trim, forward-facing rear jump seats, dual rear quarter storage compartment, digital quartz clock, dual cup holder, full carpeting, driver side footrest, tachometer, tripmeter, voltmeter, oil pressure gauge.

SR5 XTRACAB (in addition to or instead of DX XTRACAB equipment): Sliding rear window with privacy glass, variable intermittent windshield wipers, tilt steering wheel, chrome pkg (incls chrome front bumper, grille and door handle trim), deluxe ETR radio with 4 speakers.

Base Prices

Code	Description	Invoice	MSRP
8711	2WD Std Regular Cab (5-spd)	13568	14638
8710	2WD Std Regular Cab (auto)	14402	15538
8723	2WD DX Xtracab (5-spd)	16620	18548
8722	2WD DX Xtracab (auto)	17427	19448
8725	2WD SR5 Xtracab (5-spd)	17826	20008
8724	2WD SR5 Xtracab (auto)	18626	20908
	Destination Charge:	420	420

Accessories

Code	Description	Invoice	MSRP
CA	California Emissions — Xtracab	29	34
PX	Metallic Paint	NC	NC
CH	Chrome Pkg — Standard, DX	128	160
	incls chrome front bumper, grille, door handles; std on SR5		

T100 PICKUP — TOYOTA

CODE	DESCRIPTION	INVOICE	MSRP
CQ	Convenience Pkg — DX	414	505
	incls tilt wheel, sliding rear window, variable intermittent wiper with timer, privacy glass		
PO	Power Pkg — Xtracab	528	660
	incls power door locks/windows, dual chrome outside rearview mirrors		
CL	Cruise Control — Xtracab	248	310
TU	Tire Upgrade — Standard	100	125
	incls P235/75R15 tires		
BG	Upgrade Pkg — Standard	530	650
	incls tilt wheel, variable intermittent wiper with timer, full wheel covers, carpeting, fabric bench seat with armrest, digital clock, dual mirrors, day/night mirror		
AL	Aluminum Wheels — DX	484	605
	SR5	428	535
	incls P235/75R15 tires with 6JJ aluminum wheels, aluminum center wheel cap, chrome wheel arch molding		
AB	Anti-Lock Brake System — Xtracab	507	590
TX	Two-Tone Paint — Xtracab	292	365
FW	Full Wheel Covers — Standard	72	90
	std on Xtracab		
FS	Sport Seat Pkg — SR5	264	330
ST	Styled Steel Wheels — Xtracab	88	110
	incls P235/75R15 tires and 6JJ wheels with center wheel cap		
EX	Radio — DX	454	605
	SR5	169	225
	incls deluxe AM/FM radio with cassette and 4 speakers		
CE	Radio — SR5	315	420
	incls premium AM/FM radio with cassette and 4 speakers		
ER	Radio — DX	285	380
	incls deluxe AM/FM radio with 4 speakers; std on SR5		
RA	Radio — Standard, DX	184	245
	incls AM/FM ETR radio with 2 speakers		
TW	Tilt Wheel — DX	198	235
	incls variable intermittent wiper with timer; std on SR5		
CK	All-Weather Guard Pkg — Standard	110	130
	incls heavy duty battery, starter, heater, anti-chip paint		
WR	Sliding Rear Window — Standard	120	150
	DX	216	270
VP	Value Pkg — DX	500	556
	incls chrome pkg, chrome rear step bumper, tilt wheel, variable intermittent wiper with timer, sliding rear window, gray privacy glass, air conditioner, carpet floor mats, bodyside molding		
VP	Value Pkg — SR5	401	446
	incls power pkg, cruise control, air conditioner, carpet floor mats, bodyside molding, chrome rear step bumper		

TOYOTA — T100 PICKUP

| CODE | DESCRIPTION | INVOICE | MSRP |

T100 4WD

Standard Equipment

T100 - DX: 3.4 liter four-cam DOHC 24 valve EFI V6 engine, 5-speed manual transmission, power recirculating ball steering, power assisted ventilated front disc brakes, power assisted rear drum brakes, 4WDemand transfer case, double-walled bed with 2-tier loading and stake pockets, dual black outside mirrors with passenger side convex mirror, front and rear mud guards, 15" styled steel wheels with P235/75R15 SBR tires, 60/40 fully split cloth bench seat with center armrest and cloth door trim, forward-facing rear jump seats, dual rear quarter storage compartment, digital quartz clock, dual cup holder, full carpeting, driver side footrest, gauges (speedometer, odometer, fuel level and coolant temperature, tachometer, trip meter, voltmeter, oil pressure).

SR5 (in addition to or instead of DX equipment): Sliding rear window with privacy glass, variable intermittent windshield wipers, tilt steering wheel, chrome pkg (incls chrome front bumper, grille and door handle trim), deluxe ETR radio with 4 speakers.

Base Prices

Code	Description	Invoice	MSRP
8823	4WD DX Xtracab (5-spd)	19795	22348
8822	4WD DX Xtracab (auto)	20591	23248
8825	4WD SR5 Xtracab (5-spd)	21071	23928
8824	4WD SR5 Xtracab (auto)	21864	24828
	Destination Charge:	420	420

Accessories

Code	Description	Invoice	MSRP
CA	California Emissions	29	34
PX	Metallic Paint	NC	NC
CH	Chrome Pkg — DX	128	160
	incls chrome front bumper, grille and door handles; std on SR5		
CQ	Convenience Pkg — DX	414	505
	incls tilt wheel, sliding rear window, variable intermittent wiper with timer; std on SR5		
PO	Power Pkg	528	660
	incls power door locks/windows, dual chrome outside rearview mirrors		
CL	Cruise Control — DX	248	310
	SR5	316	395
ST	Styled Wheels — DX	260	325
	SR5	228	285
	incls P265/70R16 tires and 7JJ styled wheels		
AW	Aluminum Wheels — DX	660	825
	SR5	572	715
	incls P265/70R16 tires with 7JJ aluminum wheels, aluminum center wheel cap, chrome wheel arch molding		
CW	Chrome Wheels — DX	264	330
	SR5	176	220
	incls chrome wheels, P235/75R15 tires, chrome wheel arch molding		
FS	Sport Seat Pkg — SR5	264	330

T100 PICKUP — TOYOTA

CODE	DESCRIPTION	INVOICE	MSRP
EX	Radio — DX	454	605
	SR5	169	225
	incls deluxe AM/FM radio with cassette and 4 speakers		
CE	Radio — SR5	315	420
	incls premium AM/FM radio with cassette and 6 speakers		
ER	Radio — DX	285	380
	incls deluxe AM/FM radio with 4 speakers; std on SR5		
WR	Sliding Rear Window — DX	216	270
	incls sliding rear window, privacy glass (DX); std on SR5		
TX	Two-Tone Paint	292	365
AB	Anti-Lock Brake System	507	590
TW	Tilt Wheel — DX	198	235
	std on SR5		
VP	Value Pkg — DX	500	556
	incls chrome pkg, chrome rear step bumper, tilt wheel, variable intermittent wiper with timer, sliding rear window, gray privacy glass, air conditioning, carpet floor mats, bodyside molding		
VP	Value Pkg — SR5	401	446
	incls power pkg, cruise control, air conditioning, carpet floor mats, bodyside molding, chrome rear step bumper		

One 15-minute call could save you 15% or more on car insurance.

America's 6th Largest Automobile Insurance Company

1-800-555-2758

TOYOTA — TACOMA

TACOMA (1997)

1997 Toyota Tacoma SR5 Xtracab 2WD

What's New for Toyota Tacoma in 1997 — The 1997 Tacoma receives several new value packages that make optioning the truck easier. A locking rear-wheel differential is now available on all 4WD models. Bucket seats can be had on any Xtracab Tacomas this year; not just the SR5. Two-wheel drive models have new headlamps and a new grille that make the vehicle look more like the T100.

Tacoma — Review

Toyota's sixth-generation compact pickup debuted in April, as a 1995.5 model, with an actual model name: Tacoma. It's supposed to suggest the rugged outdoors, as well as strength and adventure. Any of three potent new engines goes under the hood, and the pickup rides an all-new chassis. Toyota aimed at aggressive styling, inside and out, and Tacomas sport an excellent selection of interior fittings. Regular and extended Xtracab bodies are available, with either two- or four-wheel drive. A deep-sculpted grille/hood/fender structure imparts a sporty personality to the truck, to attract customers who select their 4x4s on non-utilitarian grounds.

Two-wheel-drive Tacomas get a 2.4-liter four-cylinder base engine, rated 142 horsepower (26 more than the prior generation). Tacoma 4x4s earn a 150-horsepower, 2.7-liter four. Toyota claims that its four-cylinder engines are comparable to V-6s from competitors. But if those won't suffice, consider the latest V-6 option: a dual-overhead-cam, 24-valve unit that whips out 190 horses and 220 pound-feet of torque. With V-6 power, borrowed from the bigger T100, this compact pickup can tow up to 5,000 pounds and soundly whip any factory sport truck in the stoplight drag race. In contrast, the V-6 engine available in the prior-generation pickup delivered only 150 horsepower and 180 pound-feet.

All Tacomas have front coil springs instead of the former torsion bars, but 4x4s feature longer suspension travel than before, to improve ride/handling qualities, whether on- or off-road. Track width has been increased, too, for a more stable ride. Rack-and-pinion steering replaces the old recirculating-ball layout, for better feel and response. Manual-shift trucks

TACOMA — TOYOTA

feature reverse-gear synchronization, to reduce gear noise when shifting into reverse. Four-wheel anti-lock braking is an option, but all pickups contain an airbag for the driver. In top-of-the-line SR5 Xtracab pickups, a One-Touch Hi-4 switch is available for easy, pushbutton engagement of four-wheel-drive. By redesigning and lowering the floor by 1.6 inches, Toyota makes 4x4s easier to enter.

Tacomas are produced at the NUMMI joint-venture facility in Fremont, California, having been designed in that state. Options include cruise control, air conditioning, a sliding rear window, tilt steering wheel, and moonroof. We like the Tacoma, but question the value it represents. These new Toyota trucks don't come cheap. Guess that's the price you pay for the peace of mind a Toyota provides.

Safety Data

Driver Airbag: *Standard*
Side Airbag: *Not Available*
4-Wheel ABS: *Optional*
Driver Crash Test Grade: *Poor*
Passenger Crash Test Grade: *Average*

Passenger Airbag: *Not Available*
Meets 1999 Side Impact Standards: *Unknown*
Traction Control: *Not Available*
Insurance Cost: *Average*
Integrated Child Seat(s): *Not Available*

Standard Equipment

BASE: 2.4-liter 4-cylinder engine, 2.7-liter 4-cylinder engine (4WD models), or 3.4-liter V-6 engine (V-6 models), rack-and-pinion steering (power assisted on 4WD and V6 models), front disc/rear drum brakes, independent coil spring front suspension, front stabilizer bar, leaf spring rear suspension, front and rear mud guards (4WD models), front tow hooks (4WD models), flush halogen headlamps, tinted glass, 2-speed windshield wipers, black outside mirrors, flip-out rear quarter windows (Xtracab models), tie down hooks, black painted bumper, full wheel covers (2WD Models), styled steel wheels (4WD models), driver's air bag, vinyl sun visors, fabric bench seat, dual cup holders, passenger assist grip, and cloth door trim.

SR5 (in addition to or instead of BASE): On-demand 4-wheel drive transfer case, chrome package, privacy glass, variable intermittent wipers, sliding rear window, 15" aluminum wheels, passenger's vanity mirror, tilt steering, and tachomter.

CALL NATIONWIDE 1-800-521-7257
FOR A WRITTEN QUOTATION
AS LOW AS $50 OVER INVOICE

See page 15 for details.

TOYOTA TACOMA

CODE	DESCRIPTION	INVOICE	MSRP

Base Prices

CODE	DESCRIPTION	INVOICE	MSRP
7113	2WD Xtracab (5-spd)	13077	14368
7103	Reg Cab (5-spd)	11181	12198
7114	2WD Xtracab (auto)	13674	15088
7104	2WD Reg Cab (auto)	11840	12918
7513	4WD Xtracab (5-spd)	16594	18518
7503	4WD Reg Cab (5-spd)	15303	17078
7514	4WD Xtracab (auto)	17399	19418
7504	4WD Reg Cab (auto)	16019	17978
7523	4DW Reg Cab V6 (5-spd)	16315	18208
7153	2WD Xtracab V6 (5-spd)	14228	15698
7154	2WD Xtracab V6 (auto)	15044	16598
7553	4WD Xtracab V6 5M	17570	19608
7554	4WD Xtracab V6 (auto)	18376	20508
7557	SR5 4WD Xtracab (5-spd)	20115	22448
7558	SR5 4WD Xtracab (auto)	20922	23348
	Destination Charge:	420	420

Accessories

CODE	DESCRIPTION	INVOICE	MSRP
—	4WD Selector Switch (SR5)	107	130
AC	Air Conditioning	788	985
	Included in value pkg.		
CK	All Weather Guard	59	70
	Includes heavy duty starter, windshield wipers, battery, and rain-channel windshield.		
AW	Aluminum Wheels (4-cyl 4WD)	832	1040
	Includes uplevel tires and gas shocks.		
AL	Aluminum Wheels (4-cyl 4WD)	400	500
	Includes 225/75R15 tires and shocks.		
AW	Aluminum Wheels (Reg Cab 4-cyl 2WD)	480	600
AW	Aluminum Wheels (SR5 4WD)	432	540
AL	Aluminum Wheels (V6 4WD)	364	455
AW	Aluminum Wheels (V6 4WD N/A SR5)	796	995
AW	Aluminum Wheels (Xtracab 2WD)	336	420
BA	Anti-Lock Brakes	507	590
BU	Bucket Seats (2WD Reg Cab)	184	230
BU	Bucket Seats w/Center Console (4WD Reg Cab)	232	290
BU	Bucket Seats w/Console (4WD Xtracab)	48	60
CA	California Emissions (V6)	29	34
CH	Chrome Pkg (Base Reg Cab 2WD)	304	380
	Includes chrome grille, front and rear step bumpers, and door handles.		
CH	Chrome Pkg (Base Xtracab 2WD)	188	235
	Includes chrome grille, front and rear step bumpers, and door handles.		

TACOMA — TOYOTA

CODE	DESCRIPTION	INVOICE	MSRP
CQ	Convenience Pkg (Base)	549	670
	Includes tilt steering wheel, cruise control, tachometer, trip meter, and digital clock.		
CL	Cruise Control (Base)	232	290
CL	Cruise Control (SR5)	332	415
	Includes leather-wrapped steering wheel and lighting pkg.		
PX	Metallic Paint	NC	NC
—	On-Demand 4-Wheel Drive System (Base 4WD)	190	230
PA	Power Antenna (SR5 4WD)	88	110
PO	Power Pkg (Base)	376	470
	Includes power windows, power door locks, and chrome power mirrors. REQUIRES CL cruise control and TW tilt steering wheel.		
PO	Power Pkg (SR5)	474	530
	Includes power windows, power door locks, power antenna, lighting pkg, and chrome power mirrors. REQUIRES CL cruise control and TW tilt steering wheel.		
P5	Power Steering (4-cyl 2WD)	257	300
RR	Radio Prep Pkg (Base)	150	200
DL	Rear Locking Differential (4-cyl 4WD)	268	325
	Includes on-demand 4-wheel drive.		
DL	Rear Locking Differential (V6 4WD)	458	555
WR	Sliding Rear Window (Reg Cab)	120	150
WR	Sliding Rear Window (Xtracab)	216	270
RA	Stereo w/2 Speakers (Base)	146	195
EX	Stereo w/Cassette (Base)	424	565
SR	Sunroof (Xtracab)	312	390
TA	Tachometer (Base)	64	80
	Includes trip meter.		
TW	Tilt Steering Wheel	312	390

For expert advice in selecting/buying/leasing a new car, call

1-900-AUTOPRO

($2.00 per minute)

STEP-BY-STEP COSTING FORM

MAKE: EXTERIOR COLOR:
MODEL: INTERIOR COLOR:
TRIM LEVEL: ENGINE SIZE/TYPE:

ITEMS	MSRP	INVOICE
Basic Vehicle Price:		
Optional Equipment		
1.		
2.		
3.		
4.		
5.		
6.		
7.		
8.		
9.		
10.		
11.		
12.		
13.		
14.		
TOTAL		
SUBTRACT Holdback Amount		
SUBTRACT Rebates and/or Incentives		
ADD 5% Fair Profit to New Total		
ADD Destination Charge		
ADD Advertising Fees (1-3% of MSRP)		
SUBTRACT Trade-In Value or Cash Down Payment		
or		
ADD Difference Between Trade Value and Loan Balance		
FINAL PRICE		
ADD Sales Taxes, Documentation/Prep Fees, and License Plates		
TOTAL COST		

Specifications and EPA Mileage Ratings

1997 New Trucks

Contents

Acura	418	Land Rover	444
Chevrolet	418	Lexus	445
Chrysler	424	Mazda	445
Dodge	424	Mercury	446
Ford	429	Mitsubishi	446
Geo	434	Nissan	446
GMC	434	Oldsmobile	448
Honda	440	Plymouth	448
Infiniti	440	Pontiac	449
Isuzu	441	Suzuki	449
Jeep	442	Toyota	450
Kia	444		

SPECIFICATIONS & EPA MILEAGE RATINGS

	ACURA SLX	ACURA SLX Premium	CHEVROLET Astro 2WD	CHEVROLET Astro AWD	CHEVROLET Blazer 2WD 2-Door	CHEVROLET Blazer 2WD 4-Door	CHEVROLET Blazer 4WD 2-Door	CHEVROLET Blazer 4WD 4-Door
Acceleration (0-60/sec)	12	12	10.1	10.4	NA	NA	9.1	9.3
Braking Dist. (60-0/ft)	144	144	148	151	147	147	147	147
Turning Circle (in.)	38.1	38.1	39.5	40.5	36.6	38.5	36.9	39.5
Length (in.)	183.5	183.5	189.8	189.8	174.7	181.2	174.7	181.2
Width (in.)	72.4	72.4	77.5	77.5	67.8	67.8	67.8	67.8
Height (in.)	72.2	72.2	76	76	66	65.9	66.9	66.9
Curb Weight (lbs.)	3946	4640	4197	NA	3515	3685	3874	4046
Wheelbase (in.)	108.7	108.7	111	111	100.5	107	100.5	107
Front Head Room (in.)	39.4	39.4	39.2	39.2	39.6	39.6	39.6	39.6
Rear Head Room (in.)	39.8	39.8	38.7	NA	38.2	38.2	38.2	38.2
Front Leg Room (in.)	40.8	40.8	41.6	41.6	42.4	42.4	42.4	42.4
Rear Leg Room (in.)	39.1	39.1	38.5	NA	36.3	36.3	36.3	36.3
Maximum Seating	5	5	8	2	5	6	5	6
Max Cargo Capacity (cu ft.)	85.3	85.3	170.4	170.4	66.9	74.1	66.9	74.1
Maximum Payload (lbs.)	870	870	1753	1673	935	1165	911	1254
Number of Cylinders	6	6	6	6	6	6	6	6
Displacement (liters)	3.2	3.2	4.3	4.3	4.3	4.3	4.3	4.3
Horsepower @ RPM	200@5000	200@5000	190@4400	190@4400	190@4400	190@4400	190@4400	190@4400
Torque @ RPM	228@3500	228@3500	250@2800	250@2800	250@2800	250@2800	250@2800	250@2800
Fuel Capacity	24	24	25	25	19	18	19	18
Towing Capacity	5000	5000	5500	5000	5500	5500	5000	5000
EPA City (mpg) - Manual	NA	NA	NA	NA	18	NA	18	NA
EPA Hwy (mpg) - Manual	NA	NA	NA	NA	24	NA	24	NA
EPA City (mpg) - Auto	16	15	16	15	17	17	17	17
EPA Hwy (mpg) - Auto	19	18	20	19	22	22	22	22

	C/K 1500 Series Pickup 2WD Reg Cab SB	C/K 1500 Series Pickup 2WD Reg Cab LB	C/K 1500 Series Pickup 2WD X-cab SB	C/K 1500 Series Pickup 2WD X-cab LB	C/K 1500 Series Pickup 4WD Reg Cab SB	C/K 1500 Series Pickup 4WD Reg Cab LB	C/K 1500 Series Pickup 4WD X-cab SB	C/K 1500 Series Pickup 4WD X-cab LB	C/K 2500 Series Pickup 2WD Reg Cab LB	C/K 2500 Series Pickup 2WD HD Reg Cab LB
Acceleration (0-60/sec)	NA	NA	9.3	9.3	NA	NA	NA	NA	NA	NA
Braking Dist. (60-0/ft)	144	144	147	147	NA	NA	NA	NA	NA	NA
Turning Circle (in.)	39.8	39.8	46.6	46.6	40.7	40.7	47.6	47.6	43.7	43.4
Length (in.)	194.5	213.4	217.5	236.6	194.5	213.4	218	236.6	213.4	213.4
Width (in.)	76.8	76.8	76.8	76.8	76.8	76.8	76.8	76.8	76.8	76.8
Height (in.)	70.8	70	70.6	70.1	72.7	72.5	72.6	73.2	75.5	75.5
Curb Weight (lbs.)	3869	4021	4160	4407	4275	4426	4533	4825	4269	4269
Wheelbase (in.)	117.5	131.5	141.5	155.5	117.5	131.5	141.5	155.5	131.5	131.5
Front Head Room (in.)	39.9	39.9	39.9	39.9	39.9	39.9	39.9	39.9	39.9	39.9
Rear Head Room (in.)	NA	NA	37.5	37.5	NA	NA	37.5	37.5	NA	NA
Front Leg Room (in.)	41.7	41.7	41.7	41.7	41.7	41.7	41.7	41.7	41.7	41.7
Rear Leg Room (in.)	NA	NA	34.8	34.8	NA	NA	34.8	34.8	NA	NA
Maximum Seating	3	3	6	6	3	3	6	6	3	3
Max Cargo Capacity (cu ft.)	NA	NA	NA	NA	NA	NA	NA	NA	NA	NA
Maximum Payload (lbs.)	2231	2079	2040	1793	1825	1674	2067	1975	2931	4331
Number of Cylinders	6	6	6	8	6	6	6	8	8	8
Displacement (liters)	4.3	4.3	4.3	5	4.3	4.3	4.3	5	5	5
Horsepower @ RPM	200@4400	200@4400	200@4400	230@4600	200@4400	200@4400	200@4400	230@4600	230@4600	230@4600
Torque @ RPM	255@2800	255@2800	255@2800	285@2800	255@2800	255@2800	255@2800	285@2800	285@2800	285@2800
Fuel Capacity	25	34	25	34	25	34	25	34	34	34
Towing Capacity	7500	7500	7500	7500	7500	7500	7500	7500	8500	8500
EPA City (mpg) - Manual	NA	NA	NA	NA	NA	NA	NA	NA	NA	NA
EPA Hwy (mpg) - Manual	NA	NA	NA	NA	NA	NA	NA	NA	NA	NA
EPA City (mpg) - Auto	NA	NA	NA	NA	NA	NA	NA	NA	NA	NA
EPA Hwy (mpg) - Auto	NA	NA	NA	NA	NA	NA	NA	NA	NA	NA

SPECIFICATIONS & EPA MILEAGE RATINGS

SPECIFICATIONS & EPA MILEAGE RATINGS

	C/K 2500 Series Pickup 2WD X-cab SB	C/K 2500 Series Pickup 2WD HD X-cab LB	C/K 2500 Series Pickup 4WD Reg Cab LB	C/K 2500 Series Pickup 4WD X-cab SB	C/K 2500 Series Pickup 4WD X-cab LB	C/K 3500 Series Pickup 2WD Reg Cab LB	C/K 3500 Series Pickup 2WD X-cab LB	C/K 3500 Series Pickup 2WD Crew Cab	C/K 3500 Series Pickup 4WD Reg Cab LB	C/K 3500 Series Pickup 4WD X-cab LB
Acceleration (0-60/sec)	NA	NA	NA	NA	NA	NA	NA	NA	NA	NA
Braking Dist. (60-0/ft)	NA	NA	NA	NA	NA	NA	NA	173	NA	NA
Turning Circle (in.)	46.6	50.5	44.7	48.5	51.9	43.4	50.2	53.8	44.7	51.9
Length (in.)	217.9	236.6	213.4	217.9	236.6	213.4	236.6	250.9	213.4	236.6
Width (in.)	76.8	76.8	76.8	76.8	76.8	76.8	76.8	76.8	76.8	76.8
Height (in.)	71.2	75.5	75.8	74.3	75.8	72.6	72.6	73.9	74	74
Curb Weight (lbs.)	4400	4961	4640	5339	5339	4798	5338	5475	5181	5778
Wheelbase (in.)	141.5	155.5	131.5	141.5	155.5	131.5	155.5	168.5	131.5	155.5
Front Head Room (in.)	39.9	39.9	39.9	39.9	39.9	39.9	39.9	39.9	39.9	39.9
Rear Head Room (in.)	37.5	37.5	NA	37.5	37.5	NA	37.5	40.8	NA	37.5
Front Leg Room (in.)	41.7	41.7	41.7	41.7	41.7	41.7	41.7	41.7	41.7	41.7
Rear Leg Room (in.)	34.8	34.8	NA	34.8	34.8	NA	34.8	37.9	NA	34.8
Maximum Seating	6	6	3	6	6	3	6	6	3	6
Max Cargo Capacity (cu ft.)	NA	NA	NA	NA	NA	NA	NA	NA	NA	NA
Maximum Payload (lbs.)	2800	3639	3960	3261	3261	4202	4662	3525	4019	4222
Number of Cylinders	8	8	8	8	8	8	8	8	8	8
Displacement (liters)	5	5.7	5	5	5.7	5.7	5.7	5.7	5.7	5.7
Horsepower @ RPM	230@4600	255@4600	230@4600	230@4600	255@4600	255@4600	255@4600	255@4600	255@4600	255@4600
Torque @ RPM	285@2800	330@2800	285@2800	285@2800	330@2800	330@2800	330@2800	330@2800	330@2800	330@2800
Fuel Capacity	25	34	34	25	34	34	34	34	34	34
Towing Capacity	8500	8500	8000	8000	8000	10000	10000	10000	10000	10000
EPA City (mpg) - Manual	NA	NA	NA	NA	NA	NA	NA	NA	NA	NA
EPA Hwy (mpg) - Manual	NA	NA	NA	NA	NA	NA	NA	NA	NA	NA
EPA City (mpg) - Auto	NA	NA	NA	NA	NA	NA	NA	NA	NA	NA
EPA Hwy (mpg) - Auto	NA	NA	NA	NA	NA	NA	NA	NA	NA	NA

SPECIFICATIONS & EPA MILEAGE RATINGS

	C/K 3500 Series Pickup 4WD Crew Cab	Chevy Van 1500	Chevy Van 2500	Chevy Van 2500 Extended	Chevy Van 3500	Chevy Van 3500 Extended	Express G1500	Express G2500	Express G2500 Extended	Express G3500
Acceleration (0-60/sec)	NA	NA	NA	NA	NA	NA	NA	NA	NA	NA
Braking Dist. (60-0/ft)	173	NA	NA	NA	NA	NA	NA	NA	NA	NA
Turning Circle (in.)	55.7	45.1	47.4	53.4	47.5	53.5	45.1	47.4	53.4	47.5
Length (in.)	250.9	218.7	218.7	238.7	218.7	238.7	218.7	218.7	238.7	218.7
Width (in.)	76.8	79.2	79.2	79.2	79.2	79.2	79.2	79.2	79.2	79.2
Height (in.)	74.5	80.7	82.7	81.3	83.3	82.1	80.7	82.7	81.3	83.3
Curb Weight (lbs.)	5827	4654	4829	4983	5434	5609	5075	5803	6008	5937
Wheelbase (in.)	168.5	135	135	155	135	155	135	135	155	135
Front Head Room (in.)	39.9	39	40.6	40.6	40.6	40.6	40.6	40.6	40.6	40.6
Rear Head Room (in.)	40.8	NA	NA	NA	NA	NA	38.2	38.2	38.2	38.2
Front Leg Room (in.)	41.7	41.2	41.2	41.2	41.2	41.2	41.2	41.2	41.2	41.2
Rear Leg Room (in.)	37.9	NA	NA	NA	NA	NA	38.5	35.4	36.2	35.4
Maximum Seating	6	2	2	2	2	2	8	12	12	12
Max Cargo Capacity (cu ft.)	NA	267	267	317	267	317	267	267	317	267
Maximum Payload (lbs.)	3373	1446	2471	2317	4066	3891	2025	2798	2592	3563
Number of Cylinders	8	6	6	6	8	8	6	8	8	8
Displacement (liters)	5.7	4.3	4.3	5.7	5.7	5.7	4.3	5.7	5.7	5.7
Horsepower @ RPM	255@4600	200@4400	200@4400	200@4400	250@4600	250@4600	200@4400	250@4600	250@4600	250@4600
Torque @ RPM	330@2800	250@2800	250@2800	250@2800	330@2800	330@2800	250@2800	330@2800	330@2800	330@2800
Fuel Capacity	34	31	31	31	31	31	31	31	31	31
Towing Capacity	10000	6000	8000	8000	10000	10000	6000	8000	8000	10000
EPA City (mpg) - Manual	NA	NA	NA	NA	NA	NA	NA	NA	NA	NA
EPA Hwy (mpg) - Manual	NA	NA	NA	NA	NA	NA	NA	NA	NA	NA
EPA City (mpg) - Auto	NA	15	15	15	13	13	15	13	13	13
EPA Hwy (mpg) - Auto	NA	19	19	19	18	18	19	18	18	18

SPECIFICATIONS & EPA MILEAGE RATINGS

	Express G3500 Extended	S-10 2WD Reg Cab SB	S-10 2WD Reg Cab LB	S-10 2WD X-cab	S-10 4WD Reg Cab SB	S-10 4WD Reg Cab LB	S-10 4WD X-cab	Suburban C1500	Suburban C2500	Suburban K1500
Acceleration (0-60/sec)	NA	NA	NA	NA	9.2	9.3	9.3	9.9	NA	NA	10.3
Braking Dist. (60-0/ft)	NA	NA	NA	NA	160	NA	NA	NA	157	157	165
Turning Circle (in.)	53.5	NA	NA	NA	NA	NA	NA	NA	43.7	43.4	44.7
Length (in.)	238.7	188.6	204.6	203.3	188.6	204.6	203.3	219.5	219.5	219.5
Width (in.)	79.2	67.9	67.9	67.9	67.9	67.9	67.9	76.7	76.7	76.7
Height (in.)	82.1	63.2	63.2	63.3	63.9	65	63.9	71.3	73.6	73
Curb Weight (lbs.)	6142	NA	NA	NA	NA	NA	NA	4802	5243	5234
Wheelbase (in.)	155	108.3	117.9	122.9	108.3	117.9	122.9	131.5	131.5	131.5
Front Head Room (in.)	40.6	39.5	39.5	39.6	39.5	39.5	39.6	39.9	39.9	39.9
Rear Head Room (in.)	38.2	NA	NA	NA	NA	NA	NA	37.9	37.9	37.9
Front Leg Room (in.)	41.2	42.4	42.4	42.4	42.4	42.4	42.4	41.3	41.3	41.3
Rear Leg Room (in.)	36.2	NA	NA	NA	NA	NA	NA	27.1	27.1	27.1
Maximum Seating	15	3	3	5	3	3	5	9	9	9
Max Cargo Capacity (cu ft.)	317	NA	NA	NA	NA	NA	NA	149.5	149.5	149.5
Maximum Payload (lbs.)	3358	NA	NA	NA	NA	NA	NA	2898	3357	2816
Number of Cylinders	8	4	4	4	6	6	6	8	8	8
Displacement (liters)	5.7	2.2	2.2	2.2	4.3	4.3	4.3	5.7	5.7	5.7
Horsepower @ RPM	250@4600	118@5200	118@5200	118@5200	180@4400	180@4400	180@4400	255@4600	255@4600	255@4600
Torque @ RPM	330@2800	130@2800	130@2800	130@2800	240@2800	240@2800	240@2800	330@2800	330@2800	330@2800
Fuel Capacity	31	19	19	19	19	19	19	42	42	42
Towing Capacity	10000	6000	6000	6000	5500	5500	5500	6500	10000	6000
EPA City (mpg) - Manual	NA	23	23	23	17	17	17	NA	NA	NA
EPA Hwy (mpg) - Manual	NA	30	30	30	22	22	22	NA	NA	NA
EPA City (mpg) - Auto	13	20	20	20	16	16	16	13	13	13
EPA Hwy (mpg) - Auto	18	27	27	27	21	21	21	18	17	18

SPECIFICATIONS & EPA MILEAGE RATINGS

	Suburban K2500	Tahoe 2-Door 2WD	Tahoe 2-Door 4WD	Tahoe 4-Door 2WD	Tahoe 4-Door 4WD	Venture 3-Door Reg Length	Venture 3-Door Reg Length	Venture 3-Door Ext Length	Venture 4-Door Ext Length	
Acceleration (0-60/sec)	9.9	NA	9.5	8.7	9.6	9.9	9.9	10.9	10.9	
Braking Dist. (60-0/ft)	157	NA	156	153	166	143	143	143	143	
Turning Circle (in.)	45	38.1	39.8	39.8	40.7	37.4	37.4	39.7	39.7	
Length (in.)	219.5	188	188	199.6	199.6	186.9	186.9	200.9	200.9	
Width (in.)	76.7	77.1	77.1	76.8	76.8	72	72	72	72	
Height (in.)	74.6	71.4	73	72.8	75	67.4	67.4	68.1	68.1	
Curb Weight (lbs.)	5687	4453	4807	4423	4807	3671	3671	3792	3792	
Wheelbase (in.)	131.5	111.5	111.5	117.5	117.5	112	112	120	120	
Front Head Room (in.)	39.9	39.9	39.9	39.9	39.9	39.9	39.9	39.9	39.9	
Rear Head Room (in.)	37.9	37.8	37.8	38.9	38.9	38.8	38.8	38.9	38.9	
Front Leg Room (in.)	41.3	41.7	41.7	41.7	41.7	39.9	39.9	39.9	39.9	
Rear Leg Room (in.)	27.1	36.4	36.4	36.7	36.7	34	34	36.7	36.7	
Maximum Seating	9	6	6	6	6	7	7	7	7	
Max Cargo Capacity (cu ft.)	149.5	99.4	99.4	124.5	124.5	126.6	126.6	148.3	155.9	
Maximum Payload (lbs.)	2913	1647	1443	1877	1993	1422	1422	1301	1301	
Number of Cylinders	8	8	8	8	8	6	6	6	6	
Displacement (liters)	5.7	5.7	5.7	5.7	5.7	3.4	3.4	3.4	3.4	
Horsepower @ RPM	255@4600	255@4600	255@4600	255@4600	255@4600	180@5200	180@5200	180@5200	180@5200	
Torque @ RPM	330@2800	330@2800	330@2800	330@2800	330@2800	205@4000	205@4000	205@4000	205@4000	
Fuel Capacity	42	30	30	30	30	20	20	25	25	
Towing Capacity	10000	7000	7000	7000	7000	3500	3500	3500	3500	
EPA City (mpg) - Manual	NA	NA	NA	NA	NA	NA	NA	NA	NA	
EPA Hwy (mpg) - Manual	NA	NA	NA	NA	NA	NA	NA	NA	NA	
EPA City (mpg) - Auto	13	14	14	14	14	NA	NA	NA	NA	
EPA Hwy (mpg) - Auto	17	17	17	17	17	NA	NA	NA	NA	

SPECIFICATIONS & EPA MILEAGE RATINGS

CHRYSLER / DODGE

	Town & Country SX	Town & Country LX	Town & Country LX AWD	Town & Country LXi	Town & Country LXi AWD	Caravan Base/SE	Caravan LE/ES	Dakota 2WD Reg Cab SB
Acceleration (0-60/sec)	NA	NA	10.5	NA	9.8	NA	10.8	10.8	8.4
Braking Dist. (60-0/ft)	NA	NA	NA	NA	NA	146	146	149
Turning Circle (in.)	37.6	39.5	39.5	39.5	39.5	37.6	37.6	36
Length (in.)	186.4	199.7	199.7	199.7	199.7	186.3	186.3	195.8
Width (in.)	76.8	76.8	76.8	76.8	76.8	76.8	76.8	71.5
Height (in.)	68.5	68.5	68.5	68.5	68.5	68.5	68.5	65.6
Curb Weight (lbs.)	3877	3991	4257	4161	4447	3544	3872	3273
Wheelbase (in.)	113.3	119.3	119.3	119.3	119.3	113.3	113.3	111.9
Front Head Room (in.)	39.8	39.8	39.8	39.8	39.8	39.8	39.8	40
Rear Head Room (in.)	40.5	40	40	41.2	40	38.1	38.1	NA
Front Leg Room (in.)	41.2	41.2	41.2	41.2	41.2	41.2	41.2	41.9
Rear Leg Room (in.)	35	73.2	37.2	40	37.2	35.8	35.8	NA
Maximum Seating	7	7	7	7	7	7	7	3
Max Cargo Capacity (cu ft.)	138.5	162.9	162.9	162.9	162.9	142.9	142.9	NA
Maximum Payload (lbs.)	NA	NA	NA	NA	NA	NA	NA	2600
Number of Cylinders	6	6	6	6	6	4	6	4
Displacement (liters)	3.3	3.3	3.8	3.8	3.8	2.4	3.3	2.5
Horsepower @ RPM	158@4850	158@4850	166@4300	166@4300	166@4300	150@5200	158@4850	120@5200
Torque @ RPM	203@3250	203@3250	227@3100	227@3100	227@3100	167@4000	203@3250	145@3250
Fuel Capacity	20	20	20	20	20	20	20	15
Towing Capacity	3500	3500	3500	3500	3500	3500	3500	6700
EPA City (mpg) - Manual	NA	NA	NA	NA	NA	NA	NA	21
EPA Hwy (mpg) - Manual	NA	NA	NA	NA	NA	NA	NA	25
EPA City (mpg) - Auto	17	17	16	17	16	20	18	NA
EPA Hwy (mpg) - Auto	24	24	22	22	22	25	24	NA

SPECIFICATIONS & EPA MILEAGE RATINGS

	Dakota 2WD Reg Cab LB	Dakota 4WD Reg Cab SB	Dakota 2WD Club Cab	Dakota 4WD Club Cab	Grand Caravan Base/SE	Grand Caravan LE/ES	Grand Caravan AWD	Ram 1500 WS 2WD Reg Cab SB	Ram 1500 WS 2WD Reg Cab LB	Ram 1500 LT 2WD Reg Cab SB
Acceleration (0-60/sec)	8.4	NA	9	12.6	12.1	10.7	NA	10.6	10.6	9
Braking Dist. (60-0/ft)	149	NA	154	165	150	135	NA	145	145	148
Turning Circle (in.)	39.4	35.8	41.2	41	39.5	39.5	39.5	40.6	45.2	40.6
Length (in.)	215.1	195.8	214.8	214.8	199.6	199.6	199.7	204.1	224.1	204.1
Width (in.)	71.5	71.5	71.5	71.5	76.8	76.8	76.8	79.4	79.4	79.4
Height (in.)	65.3	68	65.6	68.5	68.5	68.5	68.7	71.9	71.8	71.9
Curb Weight (lbs.)	3353	3767	3762	4018	3791	3955	4146	4009	4132	4028
Wheelbase (in.)	123.9	112	131	131	119.3	119.3	119.3	118.7	134.7	118.7
Front Head Room (in.)	40	40	40	40	39.8	39.8	39.8	40.2	40.2	40.2
Rear Head Room (in.)	NA	NA	38	38	38.5	38.5	38.5	NA	NA	NA
Front Leg Room (in.)	41.9	41.9	41.9	41.9	41.2	41.2	41.2	41	41	41
Rear Leg Room (in.)	NA	NA	22.1	22.1	39.8	39.8	39.8	NA	NA	NA
Maximum Seating	3	3	6	6	7	7	7	3	3	3
Max Cargo Capacity (cu ft.)	NA	NA	NA	NA	168.5	168.5	168.5	NA	NA	NA
Maximum Payload (lbs.)	2600	2000	2000	1800	NA	NA	NA	2001	1698	2372
Number of Cylinders	4	6	6	6	4	6	6	6	6	6
Displacement (liters)	2.5	3.9	3.9	3.9	2.4	3.3	3.8	3.9	3.9	3.9
Horsepower @ RPM	120@5200	175@4800	175@4800	175@4800	150@5200	158@4850	166@4300	175@4800	175@4800	175@4800
Torque @ RPM	145@3250	225@3200	225@3200	225@3200	167@4000	203@3250	227@3100	230@3200	230@3200	230@3200
Fuel Capacity	15	15	15	15	20	20	20	26	35	26
Towing Capacity	6700	6500	6400	6200	3500	3500	3500	3600	3600	8100
EPA City (mpg) - Manual	21	15	16	15	NA	NA	NA	16	16	16
EPA Hwy (mpg) - Manual	25	19	22	19	NA	NA	NA	20	20	20
EPA City (mpg) - Auto	NA	15	16	15	18	18	16	14	14	14
EPA Hwy (mpg) - Auto	NA	18	20	18	25	24	22	18	18	18

SPECIFICATIONS & EPA MILEAGE RATINGS

	Ram 1500 LT 2WD Reg Cab LB	Ram 1500 ST 2WD Club Cab SB	Ram 1500 ST 2WD Club Cab LB	Ram 1500 LT 4WD Reg Cab LB	Ram 1500 LT 4WD Reg Cab LB	Ram 1500 ST 4WD Club Cab SB	Ram 1500 ST 4WD Club Cab LB	Ram 2500 2WD HD Reg Cab	Ram 2500 2WD Club Cab SB	Ram 2500 2WD Club Cab LB
Acceleration (0-60/sec)	9	10	10	NA	NA	10.2	10.2	NA	NA	NA
Braking Dist. (60-0/ft)	148	152	152	NA	NA	178	178	NA	NA	NA
Turning Circle (in.)	45.2	46.9	51.6	40.6	45.2	46.3	51	45.4	46.9	51.8
Length (in.)	204.1	224	244	204.1	204.1	224	244	204.1	224	244
Width (in.)	79.4	79.4	79.4	79.4	79.4	79.4	79.4	79.4	79.4	79.4
Height (in.)	71.8	71.6	71.5	74.7	74.6	74.6	74.5	72.1	72.9	72.8
Curb Weight (lbs.)	4339	4575	4658	4525	4682	4960	5039	4765	4983	5103
Wheelbase (in.)	134.7	138.7	154.7	118.7	134.7	138.7	154.7	134.7	138.7	154.7
Front Head Room (in.)	40.2	40.2	40.2	40.2	40.2	40.2	40.2	40.2	40.2	40.2
Rear Head Room (in.)	NA	39.4	39.4	NA	NA	39.4	39.4	NA	39.4	39.4
Front Leg Room (in.)	41	41	41	41	41	41	41	41	41	41
Rear Leg Room (in.)	NA	31.6	31.6	NA	NA	31.6	31.6	NA	31.6	31.6
Maximum Seating	3	6	6	3	3	6	6	3	6	6
Max Cargo Capacity (cu ft.)	NA	NA	NA	NA	NA	NA	NA	NA	NA	NA
Maximum Payload (lbs.)	2069	1825	1742	1875	1712	1440	1361	4043	3817	3697
Number of Cylinders	6	8	8	8	8	8	8	8	8	8
Displacement (liters)	3.9	5.2	5.2	5.2	5.2	5.2	5.2	5.9	5.9	5.9
Horsepower @ RPM	175@4800	220@4400	220@4400	220@4400	220@4400	220@4400	220@4400	235@4000	235@4000	235@4000
Torque @ RPM	230@3200	300@3200	300@3200	300@3200	300@3200	300@3200	300@3200	330@3000	330@3000	330@3000
Fuel Capacity	35	26	35	26	35	26	35	26	26	35
Towing Capacity	8100	8100	8100	7800	7800	7800	7800	13600	13600	13600
EPA City (mpg) - Manual	16	14	14	13	13	13	13	NA	NA	NA
EPA Hwy (mpg) - Manual	20	19	19	17	17	17	17	NA	NA	NA
EPA City (mpg) - Auto	14	13	13	12	12	12	12	NA	NA	NA
EPA Hwy (mpg) - Auto	18	17	17	16	16	16	16	NA	NA	NA

SPECIFICATIONS & EPA MILEAGE RATINGS

	Ram 2500 4WD HD Reg Cab	Ram 2500 4WD Club Cab SB	Ram 2500 4WD Club Cab LB	Ram 3500 2WD Reg Cab DRW	Ram 3500 2WD Club Cab DRW	Ram 3500 4WD Reg Cab DRW	Ram 3500 4WD Club Cab DRW	Ram Van 1500 SWB	Ram Van 1500 LWB	Ram Van 2500 SWB
Acceleration (0-60/sec)	8.2	NA	NA	NA	NA	NA	NA	9.7	9.7	9.7
Braking Dist. (60-0/ft)	168	NA	NA	NA	NA	NA	NA	167	167	167
Turning Circle (in.)	45	46.7	51.3	46.4	51.9	46.4	51.3	40.5	46.2	40.5
Length (in.)	224.1	224	244	224.1	244	224.1	244	187.2	205.2	187.2
Width (in.)	79.4	79.4	79.4	93.5	93.5	93.5	93.5	79.8	79.8	79.8
Height (in.)	75.1	77.2	77.1	73	72.8	77.4	77.2	79.5	79.9	79.9
Curb Weight (lbs.)	5219	5239	5359	5254	5583	5612	5940	3799	3992	3829
Wheelbase (in.)	134.7	138.7	154.7	134.7	154.7	134.7	154.7	109.6	127.6	109.6
Front Head Room (in.)	40.2	40.2	40.2	40.2	40.2	40.2	40.2	40.5	40.5	40.5
Rear Head Room (in.)	NA	39.4	39.4	NA	39.4	NA	39.4	NA	NA	NA
Front Leg Room (in.)	41	41	41	41	41	41	41	39	39	39
Rear Leg Room (in.)	NA	31.6	31.6	NA	31.6	NA	31.6	NA	NA	NA
Maximum Seating	3	6	6	3	6	3	6	2	2	2
Max Cargo Capacity (cu ft.)	NA	NA	NA	NA	NA	NA	NA	206.6	247	206.6
Maximum Payload (lbs.)	3581	3561	3441	5246	4917	4888	5060	2211	2018	2517
Number of Cylinders	8	8	8	8	8	8	8	6	6	6
Displacement (liters)	5.9	5.9	5.9	5.9	5.9	5.9	5.9	3.9	3.9	3.9
Horsepower @ RPM	235@4000	235@4000	235@4000	235@4000	235@4000	235@4000	235@4000	175@4800	175@4800	175@4800
Torque @ RPM	330@3000	330@3000	330@3000	330@3000	330@3000	330@3000	330@3000	225@3200	225@3200	225@3200
Fuel Capacity	35	26	35	35	35	35	35	35	35	35
Towing Capacity	13200	13200	13200	13200	13200	12800	12800	NA	NA	NA
EPA City (mpg) - Manual	NA	NA	NA	NA	NA	NA	NA	NA	NA	NA
EPA Hwy (mpg) - Manual	NA	NA	NA	NA	NA	NA	NA	NA	NA	NA
EPA City (mpg) - Auto	NA	NA	NA	NA	NA	NA	NA	15	15	15
EPA Hwy (mpg) - Auto	NA	NA	NA	NA	NA	NA	NA	17	17	17

SPECIFICATIONS & EPA MILEAGE RATINGS

	Ram Van 2500 LWB	Ram Van 2500 Maxivan	Ram Van 3500 LWB	Ram Van 3500 Maxivan	Ram Wagon 1500 SWB	Ram Wagon 2500 LWB	Ram Wagon 3500 LWB	Ram Wagon 3500 Maxiwagon
Acceleration (0-60/sec)	9.7	NA	NA	NA	9.7	9.7	NA	NA
Braking Dist. (60-0/ft)	167	NA	NA	NA	167	167	NA	NA
Turning Circle (in.)	46.2	46.2	52.4	52.4	40.5	46.2	52.4	52.4
Length (in.)	205.2	231.2	205.2	231.2	187.2	205.2	205.2	231.2
Width (in.)	79.8	79.8	79.8	79.8	79.8	79.8	79.8	79.8
Height (in.)	79.9	79.9	79.9	79.9	79.5	79.5	79.5	79.9
Curb Weight (lbs.)	4032	4234	4414	4633	4339	4790	5047	5247
Wheelbase (in.)	127.6	127.6	127.6	127.6	109.6	127.6	127.6	127.6
Front Head Room (in.)	40.5	40.5	40.5	40.5	40.5	40.5	40.5	40.5
Rear Head Room (in.)	NA	NA	NA	NA	37	36.7	36.7	36.4
Front Leg Room (in.)	39	39	39	39	39	39	39	39
Rear Leg Room (in.)	NA	NA	NA	NA	40.5	40.3	40.3	40.4
Maximum Seating	2	2	2	2	8	12	12	15
Max Cargo Capacity (cu ft.)	246.7	304.5	246.7	304.5	206.6	246.7	246.7	304.5
Maximum Payload (lbs.)	2368	2166	3186	3877	1611	1610	2453	3263
Number of Cylinders	6	6	8	8	6	8	8	8
Displacement (liters)	3.9	3.9	5.2	5.2	3.9	5.2	5.2	5.2
Horsepower @ RPM	175@4800	175@4800	225@4400	225@4400	175@4800	225@4400	225@4400	225@4400
Torque @ RPM	225@3200	225@3200	295@3200	295@3200	225@3200	295@3200	295@3200	295@3200
Fuel Capacity	35	35	35	35	35	35	35	35
Towing Capacity	NA	NA	NA	NA	NA	NA	NA	NA
EPA City (mpg) - Manual	NA	NA	NA	NA	NA	NA	NA	NA
EPA Hwy (mpg) - Manual	NA	NA	NA	NA	NA	NA	NA	NA
EPA City (mpg) - Auto	15	15	13	13	15	12	12	12
EPA Hwy (mpg) - Auto	17	17	17	17	17	14	16	16

SPECIFICATIONS & EPA MILEAGE RATINGS — FORD

	97 F-Series 2WD X-cab SWB	97 F-Series 2WD Reg Cab SWB	97 F-Series 2WD X-cab LWB	97 F-Series 2WD Reg Cab LWB	97 F-Series 4WD X-cab SWB	97 F-Series 4WD Reg Cab SWB	97 F-Series 4WD X-cab LWB	97 F-Series 4WD Reg Cab LWB	97 F-Series 2WD X-cab Flareside
Acceleration (0-60/sec)	10	NA	10	NA	NA	NA	NA	NA	10
Braking Dist. (60-0/ft)	149	NA	149	NA	NA	NA	NA	NA	148
Turning Circle (in.)	45.9	40.5	51.3	45.9	45.8	40.4	51.2	40.4	45.9
Length (in.)	220.8	202.2	239.4	220.8	222.3	203.7	240.9	222.3	239.4
Width (in.)	78.4	78.4	78.4	78.4	79.5	79.5	79.5	79.5	79.1
Height (in.)	72.8	72.7	72.5	72.4	75.4	75.4	75.1	75.1	72.8
Curb Weight (lbs.)	4045	3850	4200	3960	4478	4235	4606	4339	4196
Wheelbase (in.)	138.5	119.9	157.1	138.5	138.8	120.2	157.4	138.8	138.5
Front Head Room (in.)	40.8	40.8	40.8	40.8	40.8	40.8	40.8	40.8	40.8
Rear Head Room (in.)	37.8	NA	37.8	NA	37.8	NA	37.8	NA	37.8
Front Leg Room (in.)	40.9	40.9	40.9	40.9	40.9	40.9	40.9	40.9	40.9
Rear Leg Room (in.)	32.2	NA	32.2	NA	32.2	NA	32.2	NA	32.2
Maximum Seating	6	3	6	3	6	3	6	3	6
Max Cargo Capacity (cu ft.)	39.2	NA	39.2	NA	39.2	NA	39.2	NA	32.2
Maximum Payload (lbs.)	1955	1700	1800	2435	1520	1765	1390	1660	1795
Number of Cylinders	6	6	6	6	8	6	8	6	6
Displacement (liters)	4.2	4.2	4.2	4.2	4.6	4.2	4.6	4.2	4.2
Horsepower @ RPM	210@	210@	210@	210@	210@	210@	210@	210@	210@
Torque @ RPM	255@	255@	255@	255@	290@	255@	290@	255@	255@
Fuel Capacity	25	25	30	30	24.5	24.5	30	30	25
Towing Capacity	7000	7200	7200	7200	6600	6800	6600	6800	7000
EPA City (mpg) - Manual	NA	NA	NA	NA	NA	NA	NA	NA	NA
EPA Hwy (mpg) - Manual	NA	NA	NA	NA	NA	NA	NA	NA	NA
EPA City (mpg) - Auto	NA	NA	NA	NA	NA	NA	NA	NA	NA
EPA Hwy (mpg) - Auto	NA	NA	NA	NA	NA	NA	NA	NA	NA

SPECIFICATIONS & EPA MILEAGE RATINGS

	97 F-Series 2WD Reg Cab Flare	97 F-Series 4WD Reg Cab Flare	97 F-Series 4WD X-cab Flareside	Aerostar Wagon 2WD Regular	Aerostar Wagon 2WD Extended	Aerostar Wagon AWD Extended	Club Wagon Super	Econoline E150 Regular	Econoline E250 Regular	Econoline E250 Regular HD
Acceleration (0-60/sec)	NA	9	NA	NA	10.2	10.2	NA	11.1	11.1	11.1
Braking Dist. (60-0/ft)	NA	162	NA	NA	161	161	162	162	162	162
Turning Circle (in.)	40.5	40.4	45.8	39.8	39.8	39.8	47.8	46.7	45.6	46.5
Length (in.)	205.9	207.4	226	174.9	190.3	190.3	231.8	211.8	211.8	211.8
Width (in.)	79.1	79.5	79.5	71.7	71.7	71.7	79.5	79.3	79.3	79.3
Height (in.)	72.7	75.4	75.5	72.3	72.6	72.8	83.4	80.7	83.4	83.4
Curb Weight (lbs.)	3922	4308	4624	3481	3558	3558	4972	4680	5076	5080
Wheelbase (in.)	119.9	120.2	138.8	118.9	118.9	118.9	138	138	138	138
Front Head Room (in.)	40.8	40.8	40.8	39.5	39.5	39.5	41.5	41.5	41.5	41.5
Rear Head Room (in.)	NA	NA	37.8	38.1	38.1	38.1	NA	NA	NA	NA
Front Leg Room (in.)	40.9	40.9	40.9	41.4	41.4	41.4	39.5	39.5	39.5	39.5
Rear Leg Room (in.)	NA	NA	32.2	37.5	38.8	38.8	NA	NA	NA	NA
Maximum Seating	3	3	6	7	7	7	15	2	2	2
Max Cargo Capacity (cu ft.)	NA	NA	39.2	141.4	170	170	299.8	260.8	260.8	260.8
Maximum Payload (lbs.)	1620	1690	1365	1860	1860	1860	3920	2140	1240	3470
Number of Cylinders	6	6	8	6	6	6	8	6	8	8
Displacement (liters)	4.2	4.2	4.6	3	4	4	5.4	4.2	5.4	5.4
Horsepower @ RPM	210@	210@	210@	135@4600	155@4000	155@4000	235@4250	200@4800	235@4250	235@4250
Torque @ RPM	255@	255@	290@	160@2800	230@2400	230@2400	335@3000	250@2800	335@3000	335@3000
Fuel Capacity	25	24.5	24.5	21	21	21	35	35	35	35
Towing Capacity	7200	6800	6600	3900	4400	4400	10000	10000	10000	10000
EPA City (mpg) - Manual	NA	NA	NA	NA	NA	NA	NA	NA	NA	NA
EPA Hwy (mpg) - Manual	NA	NA	NA	NA	NA	NA	NA	NA	NA	NA
EPA City (mpg) - Auto	NA	NA	NA	17	16	16	14	14	14	14
EPA Hwy (mpg) - Auto	NA	NA	NA	23	22	22	18	18	18	18

SPECIFICATIONS & EPA MILEAGE RATINGS

	Econoline E250 Super	Econoline E250 Super HD	Econoline E350 Regular	Econoline E350 Super	Expedition XLT 2WD	Expedition XLT 4WD	Explorer 2WD 2-Door	Explorer 4WD 2-Door	Explorer 2WD 4-Door	Explorer 4WD 4-Door
Acceleration (0-60/sec)	NA	NA	NA	NA	NA	NA	10.6	10.6	9.5	10.6
Braking Dist. (60-0/ft)	162	162	162	162	NA	NA	146	146	146	146
Turning Circle (in.)	48	48	46.5	48	40.4	40.5	34.6	34.6	37.3	37.3
Length (in.)	231.8	231.8	211.8	231.8	204.6	204.6	178.6	178.6	188.5	188.5
Width (in.)	79.3	79.3	79.3	79.3	78.6	78.6	70.2	70.2	70.2	70.2
Height (in.)	83.4	83.4	84.1	84.1	74.4	76.4	67.8	67.8	67.5	66.8
Curb Weight (lbs.)	5215	5250	5215	5380	4850	4850	3981	3981	4189	4189
Wheelbase (in.)	138	138	138	138	119	119	101.7	101.7	111.5	111.5
Front Head Room (in.)	41.5	41.5	41.5	41.5	39.8	39.8	39.9	39.9	39.9	39.9
Rear Head Room (in.)	NA	NA	NA	NA	39.8	39.8	39.1	39.1	39.3	39.3
Front Leg Room (in.)	39.5	39.5	39.5	39.5	40.9	40.9	42.4	42.4	42.4	42.4
Rear Leg Room (in.)	NA	NA	NA	NA	38.9	38.9	36.5	36.6	37.7	37.7
Maximum Seating	2	2	2	2	9	9	4	4	6	6
Max Cargo Capacity (cu ft.)	299.8	299.8	260.8	299.8	NA	NA	69.4	69.4	81.6	81.6
Maximum Payload (lbs.)	2085	3300	4185	4185	2000	2000	750	750	900	900
Number of Cylinders	8	8	8	8	8	8	6	6	6	6
Displacement (liters)	5.4	5.4	5.4	5.4	4.6	4.6	4	4	4	4
Horsepower @ RPM	235@4250	235@4250	235@4250	235@4250	215@4400	215@4400	160@4400	160@4400	160@4400	160@4400
Torque @ RPM	335@3000	335@3000	335@3000	335@3000	290@3250	290@3250	225@2800	225@2800	225@2800	225@2800
Fuel Capacity	35	35	35	35	26	30	17.5	17.5	21	21
Towing Capacity	10000	10000	10000	10000	8000	8000	5100	5100	6700	5100
EPA City (mpg) - Manual	NA	NA	14	14	NA	NA	18	17	17	17
EPA Hwy (mpg) - Manual	NA	NA	16	16	NA	NA	21	21	21	21
EPA City (mpg) - Auto	14	14	14	14	14	14	17	15	15	15
EPA Hwy (mpg) - Auto	18	18	18	18	20	18	20	20	20	20

SPECIFICATIONS & EPA MILEAGE RATINGS

	Explorer AWD 4-Door	F350 Pickup 2WD Crew Cab	F350 Pickup 4WD Crew Cab	F350 Pickup 2WD Crew Cab DRW	F350 Pickup 2WD Ext Cab DRW	F350 Pickup 2WD Reg Cab	F350 Pickup 2WD Reg Cab DRW	F350 Pickup 4WD Reg Cab	Ranger 2WD X-cab	Ranger 2WD Reg Cab SB
Acceleration (0-60/sec)	NA	NA	NA	NA	NA	NA	NA	NA	8.8	9.5
Braking Dist. (60-0/ft)	NA	NA	NA	NA	NA	NA	NA	NA	140	144
Turning Circle (in.)	37.3	NA	59	59	50.4	43.9	43.9	43.9	41.6	36.5
Length (in.)	188.5	248.7	248.7	248.7	225.3	213.3	213.3	213.3	201.4	184.3
Width (in.)	70.2	79	79	94.5	95.4	79	95.4	79	69.4	69.4
Height (in.)	67.5	71	74	71	74	71	71	71	64.1	64
Curb Weight (lbs.)	NA	5215	5660	5380	5345	4480	4900	5135	3300	2970
Wheelbase (in.)	111.5	168.4	168.4	168.4	155	133	133	133	125.2	107.9
Front Head Room (in.)	39.8	40.2	40.2	39.9	39.9	40.3	40.3	40.3	39.3	39.1
Rear Head Room (in.)	39.9	39.6	39.6	39.6	37.6	NA	NA	NA	NA	NA
Front Leg Room (in.)	39.3	41.1	41.1	41.1	41	41.1	41.1	41.1	42.4	42.4
Rear Leg Room (in.)	37.7	37.9	37.9	37.9	28.8	NA	NA	NA	NA	NA
Maximum Seating	5	6	6	6	6	3	3	3	5	3
Max Cargo Capacity (cu ft.)	81.6	NA	NA	NA	NA	NA	NA	NA	NA	NA
Maximum Payload (lbs.)	82	3985	3540	4620	4655	4305	6595	4030	1550	1650
Number of Cylinders	8	8	8	8	8	8	8	8	4	4
Displacement (liters)	5	5.8	5.8	5.8	7.5	5.8	5.8	5.8	2.3	2.3
Horsepower @ RPM	NA@	210@3600	210@3600	210@3600	245@4000	210@3600	210@3600	210@3600	112@4800	112@4800
Torque @ RPM	NA@	325@2800	325@2800	325@2800	400@2400	325@2800	325@2800	325@2800	135@2400	135@2400
Fuel Capacity	21	37	37	37	37	37	37	37	20	17
Towing Capacity	6500	12500	12500	12500	12500	12500	12500	10000	5800	6000
EPA City (mpg) - Manual	NA	NA	NA	NA	NA	NA	NA	NA	23	23
EPA Hwy (mpg) - Manual	NA	NA	NA	NA	NA	NA	NA	NA	28	28
EPA City (mpg) - Auto	NA	NA	NA	NA	NA	NA	NA	NA	21	21
EPA Hwy (mpg) - Auto	NA	NA	NA	NA	NA	NA	NA	NA	25	25

SPECIFICATIONS & EPA MILEAGE RATINGS

	Ranger 4WD X-cab	Ranger 2WD Reg Cab LB	Ranger 4WD Reg Cab SB	Ranger 4WD Reg Cab LB	Ranger Splash 2WD X-cab	Ranger Splash 4WD X-cab	Ranger Splash 2WD Reg Cab	Ranger Splash 4WD Reg Cab	Windstar GL	Windstar LX
Acceleration (0-60/sec)	9.5	9.5	9.5	9.5	8.8	9.5	8.4	9.5	10.3	10.3
Braking Dist. (60-0/ft)	151	144	NA	NA	140	151	155	NA	139	139
Turning Circle (in.)	41.6	38.3	36.5	38.3	41.6	41.6	36.5	36.5	40.7	40.7
Length (in.)	201.4	196.3	184.3	196.3	201.4	198.2	184.3	184.3	201.2	201.2
Width (in.)	69.4	69.4	69.4	69.4	69.4	69.4	69.4	69.4	74.3	74.3
Height (in.)	64.1	64	67.5	64	64.1	67.5	64	65	68	68
Curb Weight (lbs.)	3650	3010	3430	3050	3460	3740	3130	3470	3800	3800
Wheelbase (in.)	125.2	113.9	107.9	113.9	125.4	125.2	107.9	107.9	120.7	120.7
Front Head Room (in.)	39.3	39.1	39.1	39.1	39.3	39.3	39.1	39.1	39.3	39.3
Rear Head Room (in.)	NA	NA	NA	NA	NA	NA	NA	NA	38.1	38.1
Front Leg Room (in.)	42.4	42.4	42.4	42.4	42.4	42.4	42.4	42.4	41.8	41.8
Rear Leg Room (in.)	NA	NA	NA	NA	NA	NA	NA	NA	35.3	35.3
Maximum Seating	5	3	3	3	5	5	3	3	7	7
Max Cargo Capacity (cu ft.)	NA	NA	NA	NA	NA	NA	NA	NA	144	144
Maximum Payload (lbs.)	1450	1650	1550	1650	1050	1200	1050	1250	1800	1800
Number of Cylinders	6	4	4	4	6	6	4	6	6	6
Displacement (liters)	3	2.3	2.3	2.3	3	3	2.3	3	3	3.8
Horsepower @ RPM	147@5000	112@4800	112@4800	112@4800	147@4800	147@5000	112@4800	147@5000	150@4000	200@4000
Torque @ RPM	162@3000	135@2400	135@2400	135@2400	162@2400	162@3000	135@2400	162@3000	170@3000	230@3000
Fuel Capacity	20.5	17	17	17	20	20	16.3	16.3	20	25
Towing Capacity	5800	6000	4400	6000	2000	2000	2000	2000	3500	3500
EPA City (mpg) - Manual	19	23	23	23	19	19	23	19	NA	NA
EPA Hwy (mpg) - Manual	25	28	28	28	25	25	28	25	NA	NA
EPA City (mpg) - Auto	18	21	21	21	18	18	21	18	NA	NA
EPA Hwy (mpg) - Auto	23	25	25	25	23	23	25	23	NA	24

SPECIFICATIONS & EPA MILEAGE RATINGS	Windstar Cargo Van	**GEO** Tracker 2WD Convertible	Tracker 2WD 4-door	Tracker 4WD Convertible	Tracker 4WD 4-door	**GMC** Jimmy 2WD 2-door	Jimmy 2WD 4-door	Jimmy 4WD 2-door
Acceleration (0-60/sec)	NA	11.6	12.1	13.6	13	NA	NA	9
Braking Dist. (60-0/ft)	139	139	133	153	142	NA	NA	147
Turning Circle (in.)	40.7	32.2	35.4	32.9	35.4	34.8	36.6	36.9
Length (in.)	201.2	143.7	158.7	143.7	158.7	175	181.2	175.1
Width (in.)	74.3	64.2	64.4	64.2	64.4	67.8	67.8	67.8
Height (in.)	68	64.3	65.7	65.1	66.5	66	64.8	66.9
Curb Weight (lbs.)	3800	2339	2619	NA	NA	3535	3692	3814
Wheelbase (in.)	120.7	86.6	97.6	86.6	97.6	100.5	107	100.5
Front Head Room (in.)	39.3	39.5	40.6	39.5	40.6	39.5	39.5	39.5
Rear Head Room (in.)	NA	39	40	39	40	38.1	38.1	38.1
Front Leg Room (in.)	41.8	42.1	42.1	42.1	42.1	42.4	42.4	42.4
Rear Leg Room (in.)	NA	31.7	32.7	31.7	32.7	36.3	36.3	36.3
Maximum Seating	2	4	4	4	4	4	6	4
Max Cargo Capacity (cu ft.)	159.5	32.9	45	32.9	45	66.9	74.1	66.9
Maximum Payload (lbs.)	1800	NA	NA	NA	NA	914	1158	971
Number of Cylinders	6	4	4	4	4	6	6	6
Displacement (liters)	3	1.6	1.6	1.6	1.6	4.3	4.3	4.3
Horsepower @ RPM	150@5000	95@5600	95@5600	95@5600	95@5600	190@4400	190@4400	190@4400
Torque @ RPM	170@3250	98@4000	98@4000	98@4000	98@4000	250@2800	250@2800	250@2800
Fuel Capacity	20	11.1	14.5	11.1	14.5	19	18	19
Towing Capacity	3500	1000	1500	1000	1500	5500	5500	5000
EPA City (mpg) - Manual	NA	24	24	24	24	NA	NA	NA
EPA Hwy (mpg) - Manual	NA	26	26	26	26	NA	NA	NA
EPA City (mpg) - Auto	NA	23	22	23	22	NA	NA	NA
EPA Hwy (mpg) - Auto	NA	24	25	24	25	NA	NA	NA

SPECIFICATIONS & EPA MILEAGE RATINGS

	Jimmy 4WD 4-door	Safari 2WD	Safari AWD	Savana 1500 SWB Cargo	Savana 1500 SWB Passenger	Savana 2500 SWB Cargo	Savana 2500 LWB Cargo	Savana 2500 SWB Passenger	Savana 2500 LWB Passenger	Savana 3500 SWB Cargo
Acceleration (0-60/sec)	9.4	10.3	12.7	NA	NA	NA	NA	NA	NA	NA
Braking Dist. (60-0/ft)	155	151	151	NA	NA	NA	NA	NA	NA	NA
Turning Circle (in.)	41.2	39.5	40.5	45.1	45.1	45.1	53.4	47.4	53.4	47.4
Length (in.)	181.1	189.8	189.8	218.8	218.8	218.8	238.8	218.8	238.8	218.8
Width (in.)	67.8	77.5	77.5	79.2	79.2	79.2	79.2	79.2	79.2	79.2
Height (in.)	64.8	76	76	80.7	80.7	82.7	81.3	82.7	81.3	83.3
Curb Weight (lbs.)	4023	4197	4427	4654	5075	4829	4983	5803	6008	5434
Wheelbase (in.)	107	111	111	135	135	135	155	135	155	135
Front Head Room (in.)	39.5	39.1	39.1	40.6	40.6	40.6	40.6	40.6	40.6	40.6
Rear Head Room (in.)	38.1	38.7	38.7	NA	39.1	NA	NA	39.1	39.1	NA
Front Leg Room (in.)	42.4	41.6	41.6	41.1	41.1	41.1	41.1	41.1	41.1	41.1
Rear Leg Room (in.)	36.3	38.5	38.5	NA	38.6	NA	NA	38.6	38.6	NA
Maximum Seating	6	8	8	2	12	2	2	12	12	2
Max Cargo Capacity (cu ft.)	74.1	170.4	170.4	267.3	267.3	267.3	316.8	267.3	316.8	267.3
Maximum Payload (lbs.)	1277	1753	1673	1446	2025	2471	2317	2798	2592	4066
Number of Cylinders	6	6	6	6	6	6	6	8	8	8
Displacement (liters)	4.3	4.3	4.3	4.3	4.3	4.3	4.3	5.7	5.7	5.7
Horsepower @ RPM	190@4400	190@4400	190@4400	200@4400	200@4400	200@4400	200@4400	250@4600	250@4600	250@4600
Torque @ RPM	250@2800	250@2800	250@2800	250@2800	250@2800	250@2800	250@2800	330@2800	330@2800	330@2800
Fuel Capacity	18	25	25	31	31	31	31	31	31	31
Towing Capacity	5000	5500	5000	6000	6000	8000	8000	8000	8000	10000
EPA City (mpg) - Manual	NA	NA	NA	NA	NA	NA	NA	NA	NA	NA
EPA Hwy (mpg) - Manual	NA	NA	NA	NA	NA	NA	NA	NA	NA	NA
EPA City (mpg) - Auto	NA	NA	NA	NA	NA	NA	NA	NA	NA	NA
EPA Hwy (mpg) - Auto	NA	NA	NA	NA	NA	NA	NA	NA	NA	NA

SPECIFICATIONS & EPA MILEAGE RATINGS

	Savana 3500 LWB Cargo	Savana 3500 SWB Passenger	Savana 3500 LWB Passenger	Sierra 1500 2WD Reg Cab SB	Sierra 1500 2WD Reg Cab LB	Sierra 1500 2WD X-cab SB	Sierra 1500 2WD X-cab LB	Sierra 1500 4WD Reg Cab SB	Sierra 1500 4WD Reg Cab LB	Sierra 1500 4WD X-cab SB
Acceleration (0-60/sec)	NA	NA	NA	NA	NA	9.2	9.2	NA	NA	NA
Braking Dist. (60-0/ft)	NA	NA	NA	144	144	147	147	NA	NA	NA
Turning Circle (in.)	53.4	47.4	53.5	39.8	39.8	46.6	46.6	40.7	40.7	47.6
Length (in.)	238.8	218.8	238.8	194.5	213.4	217.5	236.6	194.5	213.4	218
Width (in.)	79.2	79.2	79.2	76.8	76.8	76.8	76.8	76.8	76.8	76.8
Height (in.)	82.1	83.3	82.1	70.8	70	70.6	70.1	72.7	72.5	72.6
Curb Weight (lbs.)	5609	5937	6142	3869	4021	4160	4407	4275	4426	4533
Wheelbase (in.)	155	135	155	117.5	131.5	141.5	155.5	117.5	131.5	141.5
Front Head Room (in.)	40.6	40.6	40.6	39.9	39.9	39.9	39.9	39.9	39.9	39.9
Rear Head Room (in.)	NA	39.1	38.4	NA	NA	37.5	37.5	NA	NA	37.5
Front Leg Room (in.)	41.1	41.1	41.1	41.7	41.7	41.7	41.7	41.7	41.7	41.7
Rear Leg Room (in.)	NA	38.6	38.4	NA	NA	34.8	34.8	NA	NA	34.8
Maximum Seating	2	12	15	3	3	6	6	3	3	6
Max Cargo Capacity (cu ft.)	316.8	267.3	316.8	NA	NA	NA	NA	NA	NA	NA
Maximum Payload (lbs.)	3891	3563	3358	2231	2079	2040	1793	1825	1674	2067
Number of Cylinders	8	8	8	6	6	6	8	6	6	6
Displacement (liters)	5.7	5.7	5.7	4.3	4.3	4.3	5	4.3	4.3	4.3
Horsepower @ RPM	250@4600	250@4600	250@4600	200@4400	200@4400	200@4400	230@4600	200@4400	200@4400	200@4400
Torque @ RPM	330@2800	330@2800	330@2800	255@2800	255@2800	255@2800	285@2800	255@2800	255@2800	255@2800
Fuel Capacity	31	31	31	25	34	25	34	25	34	25
Towing Capacity	10000	10000	10000	7000	7000	7000	7000	6500	6500	6500
EPA City (mpg) - Manual	NA	NA	NA	NA	NA	NA	NA	NA	NA	NA
EPA Hwy (mpg) - Manual	NA	NA	NA	NA	NA	NA	NA	NA	NA	NA
EPA City (mpg) - Auto	NA	NA	NA	NA	NA	NA	NA	NA	NA	NA
EPA Hwy (mpg) - Auto	NA	NA	NA	NA	NA	NA	NA	NA	NA	NA

SPECIFICATIONS & EPA MILEAGE RATINGS	Sierra 1500 4WD X-cab LB	Sierra 2500 2WD Reg Cab LD	Sierra 2500 2WD Reg Cab HD	Sierra 2500 2WD X-cab SB	Sierra 2500 2WD X-cab LB	Sierra 2500 4WD Reg Cab HD	Sierra 2500 4WD X-cab SB	Sierra 2500 4WD X-cab LB	Sierra 3500 2WD Reg Cab	Sierra 3500 2WD X-cab Dually
Acceleration (0-60/sec)	NA	NA	NA	NA	NA	NA	NA	NA	NA	NA
Braking Dist. (60-0/ft)	NA	NA	144	144	NA	NA	NA	NA	NA	NA
Turning Circle (in.)	47.6	43.4	43.4	NA	51.9	NA	NA	51.9	43.4	NA
Length (in.)	236.6	213.1	213.1	217.9	236.6	213.1	217.9	236.6	213.1	236.6
Width (in.)	76.8	76.8	76.8	76.8	76.8	76.8	76.8	76.8	76.8	94.3
Height (in.)	73.2	NA	NA	NA	71.2	76	NA	NA	NA	NA
Curb Weight (lbs.)	4825	4293	4293	NA	5013	5154	NA	5442	4474	5395
Wheelbase (in.)	155.5	131.5	131.5	141.5	155.5	131.5	141.5	155.5	131.5	155.5
Front Head Room (in.)	39.9	39.9	39.9	39.9	39.9	39.9	39.9	39.9	39.9	39.9
Rear Head Room (in.)	37.5	NA	NA	37.5	37.5	NA	37.5	37.5	NA	37.5
Front Leg Room (in.)	41.7	41.7	41.7	41.7	41.7	41.7	41.7	41.7	41.7	41.7
Rear Leg Room (in.)	34.8	NA	NA	34.8	34.8	NA	34.8	34.8	NA	34.8
Maximum Seating	6	3	3	6	6	3	6	6	3	6
Max Cargo Capacity (cu ft.)	NA	NA	NA	NA	NA	NA	NA	NA	NA	NA
Maximum Payload (lbs.)	1975	2907	4307	NA	3587	3446	NA	3158	4126	3205
Number of Cylinders	8	8	8	8	8	8	8	8	8	8
Displacement (liters)	5	4.3	5.7	5	5.7	5.7	5.7	5.7	5.7	5.7
Horsepower @ RPM	230@4600	230@4600	255@4600	230@4600	255@4600	255@4600	255@4600	255@4600	255@4600	255@4600
Torque @ RPM	285@2800	285@2800	330@2800	285@2800	330@2800	330@2800	330@2800	330@2800	330@2800	330@2800
Fuel Capacity	34	34	34	25	34	34	25	34	34	34
Towing Capacity	6500	8500	8500	8500	8500	8000	8000	8000	10000	10000
EPA City (mpg) - Manual	NA	NA	NA	NA	NA	NA	NA	NA	NA	NA
EPA Hwy (mpg) - Manual	NA	NA	NA	NA	NA	NA	NA	NA	NA	NA
EPA City (mpg) - Auto	NA	NA	NA	NA	NA	NA	NA	NA	NA	NA
EPA Hwy (mpg) - Auto	NA	NA	NA	NA	NA	NA	NA	NA	NA	NA

SPECIFICATIONS & EPA MILEAGE RATINGS

	Sierra 3500 4WD Reg Cab	Sierra 3500 2WD Crew Cab	Sierra 3500 4WD X-cab Duallie	Sierra 3500 4WD Crew Cab	Sonoma 2WD Reg Cab SB	Sonoma 2WD Reg Cab LB	Sonoma 2WD X-cab	Sonoma 4WD Reg Cab SB	Sonoma 4WD Reg Cab LB	Sonoma 4WD X-cab
Acceleration (0-60/sec)	NA	NA	NA	NA	NA	NA	NA	9.4	9.3	9.3	10.1
Braking Dist. (60-0/ft)	NA	173	NA	NA	NA	NA	NA	155	NA	131
Turning Circle (in.)	NA	53.8	51.9	55.7	36.9	36.9	41.3	37.3	37.3	41.6
Length (in.)	213.1	250.9	236.6	250.9	189	205	203.7	189	205	203.7
Width (in.)	76.8	76.8	94.3	76.8	67.9	67.9	67.9	67.4	67.9	67.9
Height (in.)	72.6	73.9	74	74.5	63.2	62.1	63.3	65.4	65.4	63.9
Curb Weight (lbs.)	5201	5169	5778	5527	2930	2983	3168	3469	3565	3717
Wheelbase (in.)	131.5	168.5	155.5	168.5	108.3	117.9	122.9	108.3	117.9	122.9
Front Head Room (in.)	39.9	39.9	39.9	39.9	39.5	39.5	39.5	39.5	39.5	39.5
Rear Head Room (in.)	NA	40.8	37.5	40.8	NA	NA	NA	NA	NA	NA
Front Leg Room (in.)	41.7	41.7	41.7	41.7	42.4	42.4	42.4	42.4	42.4	42.4
Rear Leg Room (in.)	NA	37.9	34.8	37.9	NA	NA	NA	NA	NA	NA
Maximum Seating	3	6	6	6	3	3	5	3	3	5
Max Cargo Capacity (cu ft.)	NA	NA	NA	NA	NA	NA	NA	NA	NA	NA
Maximum Payload (lbs.)	4316	3431	2822	3073	1200	1547	1195	1132	1537	909
Number of Cylinders	8	8	8	8	4	4	4	6	6	6
Displacement (liters)	5.7	5.7	5.7	5.7	2.2	2.2	2.2	4.3	4.3	4.3
Horsepower @ RPM	255@4600	255@4600	255@4600	255@4600	118@5200	118@5200	118@5200	180@4400	180@4400	180@4400
Torque @ RPM	330@2800	330@2800	330@2800	330@2800	130@2800	130@2800	130@2800	240@2400	240@2800	240@2800
Fuel Capacity	34	34	34	34	19	19	19	19	19	19
Towing Capacity	10000	10000	10000	10000	6000	6000	6000	5500	5500	5500
EPA City (mpg) - Manual	NA	NA	NA	NA	NA	NA	NA	NA	NA	NA
EPA Hwy (mpg) - Manual	NA	NA	NA	NA	NA	NA	NA	NA	NA	NA
EPA City (mpg) - Auto	NA	NA	NA	NA	NA	NA	NA	NA	NA	NA
EPA Hwy (mpg) - Auto	NA	NA	NA	NA	NA	NA	NA	NA	NA	NA

SPECIFICATIONS & EPA MILEAGE RATINGS

	Suburban C1500	Suburban C2500	Suburban K1500	Suburban K2500	Yukon 2WD 2-door	Yukon 4WD 2-door	Yukon 2WD 4-door	Yukon 4WD 4-door
Acceleration (0-60/sec)	NA	13.7	10.1	9.9	9.5	NA	8.7	9.6
Braking Dist. (60-0/ft)	150	157	162	157	169	NA	154	159
Turning Circle (in.)	43.7	43.4	44.7	44.7	38.1	39	39.8	40.7
Length (in.)	219.5	219.5	219.5	219.5	188	188	199.6	199.6
Width (in.)	76.7	76.7	76.7	76.7	77.1	77.1	76.8	76.8
Height (in.)	71.3	73	73.6	74.6	71.4	71.4	72.8	75
Curb Weight (lbs.)	4802	5243	5235	5687	4471	4827	4816	5225
Wheelbase (in.)	131.5	131.5	131.5	131.5	111.5	111.5	117.5	117.5
Front Head Room (in.)	39.9	39.9	39.9	39.9	39.9	39.9	39.9	39.9
Rear Head Room (in.)	37.9	37.9	37.9	37.9	37.8	37.8	38.9	38.9
Front Leg Room (in.)	41.3	41.3	41.3	41.3	41.7	41.7	41.7	41.7
Rear Leg Room (in.)	26.2	27.1	27.1	27.1	36.4	36.4	36.7	36.7
Maximum Seating	9	9	9	9	6	6	6	6
Max Cargo Capacity (cu ft.)	149.5	149.5	149.5	149.5	99.4	99.4	118.2	118.2
Maximum Payload (lbs.)	1998	3357	1965	2914	1629	1423	1484	1575
Number of Cylinders	8	8	8	8	8	8	8	8
Displacement (liters)	5.7	5.7	5.7	5.7	5.7	5.7	5.7	5.7
Horsepower @ RPM	255@4600	255@4600	255@4600	255@4600	255@4600	255@4600	255@4600	255@4600
Torque @ RPM	330@2800	330@2800	330@2800	330@2800	330@2800	330@2800	330@2800	330@2800
Fuel Capacity	42	42	42	42	30	30	30	30
Towing Capacity	6500	10000	6000	10000	7000	6500	7000	7000
EPA City (mpg) - Manual	NA	NA	NA	NA	NA	NA	NA	NA
EPA Hwy (mpg) - Manual	NA	NA	NA	NA	NA	NA	NA	NA
EPA City (mpg) - Auto	NA	NA	NA	NA	NA	NA	NA	NA
EPA Hwy (mpg) - Auto	NA	NA	NA	NA	NA	NA	NA	NA

SPECIFICATIONS & EPA MILEAGE RATINGS

	Honda Odyssey LX	Honda Odyssey EX	Honda Passport EX/LX 2WD 5M	Honda Passport EX/LX 2WD AT	Honda Passport EX/LX 4WD 5M	Honda Passport EX/LX 4WD AT	Infiniti QX4
Acceleration (0-60/sec)	11.7	11.2	10	10.9	10	10.9	11.2
Braking Dist. (60-0/ft)	139	141	139	139	139	139	146
Turning Circle (in.)	37.6	37.6	37.7	37.7	37.7	37.7	NA
Length (in.)	187.2	187.2	176.5	176.5	176.5	176.5	178.3
Width (in.)	70.6	70.6	66.5	66.5	66.5	66.5	68.7
Height (in.)	64.6	64.6	66.5	66.5	66.5	66.5	67.1
Curb Weight (lbs.)	3472	3483	3848	3883	4078	4133	NA
Wheelbase (in.)	111.4	111.4	108.5	108.5	108.5	108.5	106.3
Front Head Room (in.)	40.1	38.9	38.5	38.5	38.5	38.5	39.5
Rear Head Room (in.)	39.3	39.3	38	38	38	38	37.5
Front Leg Room (in.)	40.7	40.7	41	41	41	41	41.7
Rear Leg Room (in.)	40.2	40.2	34.5	34.5	34.5	34.5	31.8
Maximum Seating	7	6	5	5	5	5	5
Max Cargo Capacity (cu ft.)	93.5	102.5	74.9	74.9	74.9	74.9	85
Maximum Payload (lbs.)	1257	1257	NA	NA	NA	NA	NA
Number of Cylinders	4	4	6	6	6	6	6
Displacement (liters)	2.2	2.2	3.2	3.2	3.2	3.2	3.3
Horsepower @ RPM	140@5600	140@5600	190@5600	190@5600	190@5600	190@5600	168@4800
Torque @ RPM	145@4500	145@4500	188@4000	188@4000	188@4000	188@4000	196@2800
Fuel Capacity	17.2	17.2	21.9	21.9	21.9	21.9	21.1
Towing Capacity	1000	1000	4500	4500	4500	4500	5000
EPA City (mpg) - Manual	NA	NA	16	NA	16	NA	NA
EPA Hwy (mpg) - Manual	NA	NA	19	NA	19	NA	NA
EPA City (mpg) - Auto	20	20	NA	15	NA	15	15
EPA Hwy (mpg) - Auto	24	24	NA	18	NA	18	19

SPECIFICATIONS & EPA MILEAGE RATINGS — ISUZU

	Hombre S/XS Regular Cab	Hombre XS Spacecab 4 cyl.	Hombre XS Spacecab V-6	Oasis	Oasis LS	Rodeo 2WD S 5M	Rodeo 2WD S V6 5M	Rodeo 2WD S V6 AT	Rodeo 4WD S V6 5M
Acceleration (0-60/sec)	12.6	NA	NA	NA	12.4	12.4	NA	NA	NA	10
Braking Dist. (60-0/ft)	149	NA	NA	141	141	143	143	143	143
Turning Circle (in.)	36.9	41.3	41.3	37.6	37.6	37.7	37.7	37.7	37.7
Length (in.)	188.9	203.5	203.5	187.2	187.2	184	184	184	184
Width (in.)	67.9	67.9	67.9	70.6	70.6	66.5	66.5	66.5	66.5
Height (in.)	62.1	62.2	62.2	64.6	64.6	66.5	66.5	66.5	66.5
Curb Weight (lbs.)	3125	3305	3500	3473	3483	3705	3890	3925	4115
Wheelbase (in.)	108.3	122.9	122.9	111.4	111.4	108.7	108.7	108.7	108.7
Front Head Room (in.)	39.5	39.5	39.5	40.1	38.9	38.6	38.6	38.6	38.6
Rear Head Room (in.)	NA	NA	NA	37.5	37.5	38	38	38	38
Front Leg Room (in.)	42.4	42.4	42.4	40.7	40.7	41.2	41.2	41.2	41.2
Rear Leg Room (in.)	NA	NA	NA	34	34	34.5	34.5	34.5	34.5
Maximum Seating	3	5	5	7	6	6	6	5	5
Max Cargo Capacity (cu ft.)	NA	NA	NA	93.5	102.5	74.9	74.9	74.9	74.9
Maximum Payload (lbs.)	1138	1154	1154	1267	1257	845	860	825	890
Number of Cylinders	4	4	6	4	4	4	5	6	6
Displacement (liters)	2.2	2.2	4.3	2.2	2.2	2.6	3.2	3.2	3.2
Horsepower @ RPM	118@5200	118@5200	175@4400	140@	140@	120@4600	190@5600	190@5600	190@5600
Torque @ RPM	130@2800	130@2800	240@2800	145@	145@	150@2600	188@4000	188@4000	188@4000
Fuel Capacity	18.5	18.5	18.5	17.2	17.2	21.9	21.9	21.9	21.9
Towing Capacity	2000	5500	5500	840	1000	2000	4500	4500	4500
EPA City (mpg) - Manual	23	23	NA	NA	NA	18	16	NA	16
EPA Hwy (mpg) - Manual	30	30	NA	NA	NA	22	19	NA	19
EPA City (mpg) - Auto	NA	NA	20	20	20	NA	NA	15	NA
EPA Hwy (mpg) - Auto	NA	NA	24	24	24	NA	NA	18	NA

SPECIFICATIONS & EPA MILEAGE RATINGS

	Rodeo 4WD S V6 AT	Rodeo 2WD LS V6 AT	Rodeo 4WD LS V6 5M	Rodeo 4WD LS V6 AT	Trooper S 5M	Trooper S AT	Trooper LS	Trooper Limited	JEEP Cherokee SE 2WD 2-Door
Acceleration (0-60/sec)	10.9	10.9	10	10.9	NA	11.2	11.2	11.2	NA
Braking Dist. (60-0/ft)	143	143	143	143	143	143	143	143	146
Turning Circle (in.)	37.7	37.7	37.7	37.7	38.1	38.1	38.1	38.1	35.9
Length (in.)	184	184	184	184	183.5	183.5	183.5	183.5	167.5
Width (in.)	66.5	66.5	66.5	66.5	69.5	69.5	72.2	72.2	67.9
Height (in.)	66.5	66.5	66.5	66.5	72.2	72.2	72.2	72.2	63.9
Curb Weight (lbs.)	4170	3925	4115	4170	4275	4315	4315	4640	2947
Wheelbase (in.)	108.7	108.7	108.7	108.7	108.7	108.7	108.7	108.7	101.4
Front Head Room (in.)	38.6	38.6	38.6	38.6	39.8	39.8	39.8	39.4	37.8
Rear Head Room (in.)	38	38	38	38	39.8	39.8	39.8	37.8	38.5
Front Leg Room (in.)	41.2	41.2	41.2	41.2	40.8	40.8	40.8	40.8	41.4
Rear Leg Room (in.)	34.5	34.5	34.5	34.5	39.1	39.1	39.1	39.1	35
Maximum Seating	5	5	5	5	5	5	5	5	5
Max Cargo Capacity (cu ft.)	74.9	74.9	74.9	74.9	90.2	90.2	90.2	85.3	71
Maximum Payload (lbs.)	830	825	885	830	1235	1195	1195	870	1150
Number of Cylinders	6	6	6	6	6	6	6	6	4
Displacement (liters)	3.2	3.2	3.2	3.2	3.2	3.2	3.2	3.2	2.5
Horsepower @ RPM	190@5600	190@5600	190@5600	190@5600	190@5600	190@5600	190@5600	190@5600	125@5400
Torque @ RPM	188@4000	188@4000	188@4000	188@4000	188@4000	188@4000	188@4000	188@4000	150@3250
Fuel Capacity	21.9	21.9	21.9	21.9	22.5	22.5	22.5	22.5	20
Towing Capacity	4500	4500	4500	4500	5000	5000	5000	5000	5000
EPA City (mpg) - Manual	NA	NA	16	NA	NA	NA	NA	NA	19
EPA Hwy (mpg) - Manual	NA	NA	19	NA	NA	NA	NA	NA	23
EPA City (mpg) - Auto	15	15	NA	15	NA	NA	NA	NA	NA
EPA Hwy (mpg) - Auto	18	18	NA	18	NA	NA	NA	NA	NA

SPECIFICATIONS & EPA MILEAGE RATINGS

	Cherokee SE 2WD 4-Door	Cherokee SE 4WD 2-Door	Cherokee SE 4WD 4-Door	Cherokee Spt/Cntry 2WD 2-Dr	Cherokee Spt/Cntry 2WD 4-Dr	Cherokee Spt/Cntry 4WD 2-Dr	Cherokee Spt/Cntry 4WD 4-Dr	Grand Cherokee 2WD	Grand Cherokee 4WD	Wrangler SE
Acceleration (0-60/sec)	NA	8.4	8.4	NA	NA	8.4	8.4	NA	8.6	NA
Braking Dist. (60-0/ft)	146	146	146	146	146	146	146	138	138	132
Turning Circle (in.)	35.9	35.9	35.9	35.9	35.9	35.9	35.9	37.5	37.5	33.6
Length (in.)	167.5	167.5	167.5	167.5	167.5	167.5	167.5	177.2	177.2	151.8
Width (in.)	67.9	67.9	67.9	67.9	67.9	67.9	67.9	69.3	69.3	66.7
Height (in.)	63.9	64	64	63.9	63.9	64	64	64.9	64.9	70.2
Curb Weight (lbs.)	2993	3111	3153	2947	2993	3111	3153	3609	3785	3092
Wheelbase (in.)	101.4	101.4	101.4	101.4	101.4	101.4	101.4	105.9	105.9	93.4
Front Head Room (in.)	37.8	37.8	37.8	37.8	37.8	37.8	37.8	38.9	38.9	42.3
Rear Head Room (in.)	38.5	38.5	38.5	38.5	38.5	38.5	38.5	39	39	40.6
Front Leg Room (in.)	41.4	41.4	41.4	41.4	41.4	41.4	41.4	40.9	40.9	41.1
Rear Leg Room (in.)	35	35	35	35	35	35	35	35.7	35.7	34.9
Maximum Seating	5	5	5	5	5	5	5	5	5	4
Max Cargo Capacity (cu ft.)	71	71	71	71	71	71	71	79.3	79.3	55.7
Maximum Payload (lbs.)	1150	1150	1150	1150	1150	1150	1150	1150	1150	800
Number of Cylinders	4	4	4	6	6	6	6	6	6	4
Displacement (liters)	2.5	2.5	2.5	4	4	4	4	4	4	2.5
Horsepower @ RPM	125@5400	125@5400	125@5400	190@4600	190@4600	190@4600	190@4600	185@4600	185@4600	120@5400
Torque @ RPM	150@3250	150@3250	150@3250	225@3000	225@3000	225@3000	225@3000	220@2400	220@2400	140@3500
Fuel Capacity	20	20	20	20	20	20	20	23	23	15
Towing Capacity	5000	5000	5000	5000	5000	5000	5000	6700	6500	2000
EPA City (mpg) - Manual	19	19	19	18	18	17	17	NA	NA	19
EPA Hwy (mpg) - Manual	23	22	22	23	23	21	21	NA	NA	21
EPA City (mpg) - Auto	NA	NA	NA	15	15	15	15	15	15	17
EPA Hwy (mpg) - Auto	NA	NA	NA	21	21	19	19	21	20	19

SPECIFICATIONS & EPA MILEAGE RATINGS

	Wrangler Sport/Sahara	KIA Sportage 4-dr 2WD 5M	Sportage 4-dr 2WD AT	Sportage 4-dr 4WD 5M	Sportage 4-dr 4WD AT	LAND ROVER Defender 90 Convertible	Defender 90 Hardtop	Discovery 5M
Acceleration (0-60/sec)	8.8	NA	NA	12	NA	10.5	10.5	11
Braking Dist. (60-0/ft)	132	167	167	167	167	169	169	146
Turning Circle (in.)	33.6	34.8	34.8	34.8	34.8	40	40	39.4
Length (in.)	151.8	167.1	167.1	167.1	167.1	157.1	157.1	178.7
Width (in.)	66.7	68.1	68.1	68.1	68.1	70.5	70.5	70.6
Height (in.)	70.2	65	65	65	65	80.2	80.2	77.4
Curb Weight (lbs.)	3229	3170	3214	3314	3358	3913	3913	4465
Wheelbase (in.)	93.4	104.3	104.3	104.3	104.3	92.9	92.9	100
Front Head Room (in.)	42.3	39.6	39.6	39.6	39.6	57	57	37.4
Rear Head Room (in.)	40.6	37.8	37.8	37.8	37.8	NA	NA	39.2
Front Leg Room (in.)	41.1	44.5	44.5	44.5	44.5	NA	NA	38.5
Rear Leg Room (in.)	34.9	31.1	31.1	31.1	31.1	NA	NA	36.3
Maximum Seating	4	5	5	5	5	4	6	7
Max Cargo Capacity (cu ft.)	55.7	55.4	55.4	55.4	55.4	NA	NA	69.8
Maximum Payload (lbs.)	800	838	838	838	838	NA	NA	NA
Number of Cylinders	6	4	4	4	4	8	8	8
Displacement (liters)	4	2	2	2	2	3.9	3.9	3.9
Horsepower @ RPM	181@4600	130@5500	130@5500	130@5000	130@5000	182@4750	182@4750	182@4750
Torque @ RPM	222@2800	127@4000	127@4000	127@4000	127@4000	233@3000	233@3000	233@3000
Fuel Capacity	15	15.8	15.8	15.8	15.8	15.6	15.6	23.4
Towing Capacity	2000	2000	2000	2000	2000	5000	5000	7700
EPA City (mpg) - Manual	17	19	NA	19	NA	NA	NA	13
EPA Hwy (mpg) - Manual	21	22	NA	23	NA	NA	NA	17
EPA City (mpg) - Auto	15	NA	19	NA	19	NA	NA	NA
EPA Hwy (mpg) - Auto	18	NA	21	NA	22	NA	NA	NA

SPECIFICATIONS & EPA MILEAGE RATINGS

	Discovery AT	Range Rover 4.0 SE	Range Rover 4.6 HSE	LEXUS LX 450	MAZDA B-Series Pickup B2300 2WD SB	B-Series Pickup B4000 4WD SB	B-Series Pickup B2300 2WD X-cab	B-Series Pickup B4000 2WD X-cab
Acceleration (0-60/sec)	11.7	11.2	9.6	11.6	NA	9.5	NA	10
Braking Dist. (60-0/ft)	146	143	141	132	NA	149	NA	145
Turning Circle (in.)	39.4	39	39	40.4	36.5	37.3	41.6	41.6
Length (in.)	178.7	185.5	185.5	189.8	184.5	184.5	202.7	202.7
Width (in.)	70.6	74.4	74.4	76	69.4	69.4	69.4	69.4
Height (in.)	77.4	71.6	71.6	73.6	64	67.5	64.1	64.1
Curb Weight (lbs.)	4465	4960	4960	4971	2989	3242	3355	3355
Wheelbase (in.)	100	108.1	108.1	112.2	107.9	108.2	125.2	125.2
Front Head Room (in.)	37.4	38.1	38.1	40.3	39.1	39.1	39.4	39.4
Rear Head Room (in.)	39.2	38.2	38.2	36.7	NA	NA	35.6	35.6
Front Leg Room (in.)	38.5	42.6	42.6	41.7	42.4	42.4	42.4	42.4
Rear Leg Room (in.)	36.3	36.5	36.5	28.5	NA	NA	41.2	41.2
Maximum Seating	7	5	5	7	3	3	5	5
Max Cargo Capacity (cu ft.)	69.8	58	58	90.9	NA	NA	NA	NA
Maximum Payload (lbs.)	NA	NA	NA	NA	1250	1250	1550	1550
Number of Cylinders	8	8	8	6	4	6	4	6
Displacement (liters)	3.9	4	4.6	4.5	2.3	2.3	2.3	4
Horsepower @ RPM	182@4750	190@4750	225@4750	212@4600	112@4800	160@4200	112@4800	160@4200
Torque @ RPM	233@3000	236@3000	280@3000	275@3200	135@2400	220@3000	135@2400	220@3000
Fuel Capacity	23.4	24.6	24.6	25	17	17	20.5	20.5
Towing Capacity	7700	7700	7700	5000	2300	2000	1300	5800
EPA City (mpg) - Manual	NA	NA	NA	NA	NA	NA	NA	NA
EPA Hwy (mpg) - Manual	NA	NA	NA	NA	NA	NA	NA	NA
EPA City (mpg) - Auto	14	13	12	13	NA	NA	NA	NA
EPA Hwy (mpg) - Auto	17	17	16	15	NA	NA	NA	NA

SPECIFICATIONS & EPA MILEAGE RATINGS

	B-Series Pickup B4000 4WD X-cab	MPV 4WD	**MERCURY** Mountaineer	Villager	**MITSUBISHI** Montero LS	Montero SR	**NISSAN** Pathfinder 2WD 5M
Acceleration (0-60/sec)	NA	12.1	NA	12.3	13.4	10.4	10.4
Braking Dist. (60-0/ft)	NA	158	NA	141	144	137	148
Turning Circle (in.)	42.4	39.6	37.3	39.9	38.7	38.7	35.4
Length (in.)	202.7	183.5	188.5	190.2	185.2	186.6	178.3
Width (in.)	69.4	71.9	70.2	73.8	66.7	70.3	68.7
Height (in.)	67.5	71.5	66.7	65.9	73.8	74.6	67.1
Curb Weight (lbs.)	3637	4105	NA	3990	4300	4465	3675
Wheelbase (in.)	125.4	110.4	111.5	112.2	107.3	107.3	106.3
Front Head Room (in.)	39.4	40	39.8	39.4	40.9	40.9	39.5
Rear Head Room (in.)	35.6	36.9	39.3	39.7	40	40	37.5
Front Leg Room (in.)	42.4	40.4	42.4	39.9	40.3	40.3	41.7
Rear Leg Room (in.)	41.2	32.5	37.7	34.8	37.6	37.6	31.8
Maximum Seating	5	8	5	7	7	7	5
Max Cargo Capacity (cu ft.)	NA	110	81.6	126	72.7	72.7	85
Maximum Payload (lbs.)	1450	NA	NA	1200	1406	1381	NA
Number of Cylinders	6	6	8	6	6	6	6
Displacement (liters)	4	3	5	3	3	3.5	3.3
Horsepower @ RPM	160@4200	155@5000	210@4600	151@4800	177@5500	215@5000	168@4800
Torque @ RPM	220@3000	169@4000	275@3200	174@4400	188@4500	228@3000	196@4000
Fuel Capacity	20.5	19.8	21	20	24.3	24.3	21
Towing Capacity	5600	NA	6500	3500	5000	5000	3500
EPA City (mpg) - Manual	NA	NA	NA	NA	NA	NA	17
EPA Hwy (mpg) - Manual	NA	NA	NA	NA	NA	NA	20
EPA City (mpg) - Auto	NA	15	NA	17	15	14	NA
EPA Hwy (mpg) - Auto	NA	19	NA	23	18	18	NA

SPECIFICATIONS & EPA MILEAGE RATINGS

	Pathfinder 2WD AT	Pathfinder 4WD 5M	Pathfinder 4WD AT	Quest XE/GXE	Truck - 2WD Reg Cab SB 5M	Truck - 2WD Reg Cab SB AT	Truck - 2WD X-cab 5M	Truck - 2WD X-cab AT	Truck - 4WD Reg Cab 5M	Truck - 4WD X-cab AT
Acceleration (0-60/sec)	10.5	11.2	11.3	12.1	NA	NA	NA	NA	NA	NA
Braking Dist. (60-0/ft)	148	148	148	142	NA	NA	NA	NA	151	151
Turning Circle (in.)	35.4	35.4	35.4	39.9	33.5	33.5	36.7	36.7	36.7	36.7
Length (in.)	178.3	178.3	178.3	189.9	174.6	174.6	190	190	190	190
Width (in.)	68.7	68.7	68.7	73.7	65	65	65	65	65	65
Height (in.)	67.1	67.1	67.1	65.6	62	62	62	62	67.1	67.1
Curb Weight (lbs.)	3695	3920	3945	3876	2805	2805	2900	2900	2900	2900
Wheelbase (in.)	106.3	106.3	106.3	112.2	104.3	104.3	116.1	116.1	116.1	116.1
Front Head Room (in.)	39.5	39.5	39.5	39.5	39.3	39.3	39.3	39.3	39.3	39.3
Rear Head Room (in.)	37.5	37.5	37.5	39.7	NA	NA	NA	NA	NA	NA
Front Leg Room (in.)	41.7	41.7	41.7	39.9	42.2	42.2	42.6	42.6	42.6	42.6
Rear Leg Room (in.)	31.8	31.8	31.8	36.3	NA	NA	NA	NA	NA	NA
Maximum Seating	5	5	5	7	3	3	4	4	4	4
Max Cargo Capacity (cu ft.)	85	85	85	114.8	NA	NA	NA	NA	NA	NA
Maximum Payload (lbs.)	1155	NA	NA	NA	1400	1400	1400	1400	1400	1400
Number of Cylinders	6	6	6	6	4	4	4	4	4	4
Displacement (liters)	3.3	3.3	3.3	3	2.4	2.4	2.4	2.4	2.4	2.4
Horsepower @ RPM	168@4800	168@4800	168@4800	151@4800	134@5200	134@5200	134@5200	134@5200	134@5200	134@5200
Torque @ RPM	196@4000	196@4000	196@4000	174@4400	154@3600	154@3600	154@3600	154@3600	154@3600	154@3600
Fuel Capacity	21	21	21	20	15.9	15.9	15.9	15.9	15.9	15.9
Towing Capacity	5000	3500	5000	3500	3500	3500	3500	3500	3500	3500
EPA City (mpg) - Manual	NA	16	NA	NA	22	NA	22	NA	18	18
EPA Hwy (mpg) - Manual	NA	18	NA	NA	26	NA	26	NA	20	20
EPA City (mpg) - Auto	16	NA	15	17	NA	21	NA	21	NA	NA
EPA Hwy (mpg) - Auto	20	NA	19	23	NA	26	NA	25	NA	NA

SPECIFICATIONS & EPA MILEAGE RATINGS	Truck - 4WD X-cab 5M	OLDSMOBILE	Bravada	Silhouette 3-door Reg Length	Silhouette 3-door Ext. Length	Silhouette 4-door Ext Length	PLYMOUTH	Grand Voyager	Voyager	
Acceleration (0-60/sec)	NA		10.2	9.9	10.9	10.9		13.5	NA	
Braking Dist. (60-0/ft)	151		143	143	143	143		140	NA	
Turning Circle (in.)	36.7		39.5	37.4	39.7	39.7		37.6	37.6	
Length (in.)	190		180.9	187.4	201.4	201.4		196.6	186.3	
Width (in.)	65		66.5	72.2	72.2	72.2		76.8	76.8	
Height (in.)	67.1		63.2	67.4	68.1	68.1		68.5	68.5	
Curb Weight (lbs.)	2900		4023	3721	3843	3942		3700	3533	
Wheelbase (in.)	116.1		107	112	120	120		119.3	113.3	
Front Head Room (in.)	39.3		39.7	39.9	39.9	39.9		39.8	39.8	
Rear Head Room (in.)	NA		38.6	38.8	38.8	38.8		40	40.1	
Front Leg Room (in.)	42.6		42.4	39.9	39.9	39.9		41.2	41.2	
Rear Leg Room (in.)	NA		36.1	34	36.7	36.7		39.6	36.6	
Maximum Seating	4		5	7	7	7		7	7	
Max Cargo Capacity (cu ft.)	NA		74.1	126.6	148.3	155.9		168.5	146.2	
Maximum Payload (lbs.)	1400		1277	NA	NA	NA		NA	NA	
Number of Cylinders	4		6	6	6	6		4	4	
Displacement (liters)	2.4		4.3	3.4	3.4	3.4		2.4	2.4	
Horsepower @ RPM	134@5200		190@4400	180@5200	180@5200	180@5200		150@5200	150@4800	
Torque @ RPM	154@3600		250@2800	205@4000	205@4000	205@4000		167@4000	167@2800	
Fuel Capacity	15.9		18	20	25	25		20	20	
Towing Capacity	3500		5000	2000	3500	3500		3500	3500	
EPA City (mpg) - Manual	18		NA	NA	NA	NA		NA	NA	
EPA Hwy (mpg) - Manual	20		NA	NA	NA	NA		NA	NA	
EPA City (mpg) - Auto	NA		16	18	18	18		NA	NA	
EPA Hwy (mpg) - Auto	NA		21	25	25	25		NA	25	

SPECIFICATIONS & EPA MILEAGE RATINGS

PONTIAC / SUZUKI

	Trans Sport SWB 3-door	Trans Sport Ext. 3-door	Trans Sport Ext. 4-door	Sidekick 4WD Sport 4-Dr 5M	Sidekick 4WD Sport 4-Dr AT	X-90 2WD 5M	X-90 4WD 5M	X-90 4WD AT
Acceleration (0-60/sec)	9.9	10.9	10.9	NA	NA	NA	NA	NA
Braking Dist. (60-0/ft)	143	143	143	NA	NA	NA	NA	NA
Turning Circle (in.)	37.4	39.7	39.7	36.1	36.1	32.2	32.2	32.2
Length (in.)	187.3	201.3	201.3	162.4	162.4	146.1	146.1	146.1
Width (in.)	72.7	72.7	72.7	66.7	66.7	66.7	66.7	66.7
Height (in.)	67.4	68.1	68.1	66.3	66.3	60.5	60.5	60.5
Curb Weight (lbs.)	3702	3825	3920	2917	2950	2321	2493	2542
Wheelbase (in.)	112	120	120	97.6	97.6	86.6	86.6	86.6
Front Head Room (in.)	39.9	39.9	39.9	40.6	40.6	34.2	34.2	34.2
Rear Head Room (in.)	38.8	38.9	38.9	38.6	38.6	NA	NA	NA
Front Leg Room (in.)	39.9	39.9	39.9	42.1	42.1	41.5	41.5	41.5
Rear Leg Room (in.)	34	36.7	36.7	32.7	32.7	NA	NA	NA
Maximum Seating	8	8	8	4	4	2	2	2
Max Cargo Capacity (cu ft.)	126.6	155.9	155.9	45	45	8.4	8.4	8.4
Maximum Payload (lbs.)	1655	1532	1437	765	732	413	461	412
Number of Cylinders	6	6	6	4	4	4	4	4
Displacement (liters)	3.4	3.4.	3.4	1.6	1.6	1.6	1.6	1.6
Horsepower @ RPM	180@5200	180@5200	180@5200	120@6500	120@6500	95@5600	95@5600	95@5600
Torque @ RPM	205@4000	205@4000	205@4000	114@3500	114@3500	98@4000	98@4000	98@4000
Fuel Capacity	20	25	25	18.5	18.5	11	11.1	11.1
Towing Capacity	3500	3500	3500	1500	1500	1000	1000	1000
EPA City (mpg) - Manual	NA	NA	NA	23	NA	25	25	NA
EPA Hwy (mpg) - Manual	NA	NA	NA	25	NA	28	28	NA
EPA City (mpg) - Auto	18	18	18	NA	21	NA	NA	23
EPA Hwy (mpg) - Auto	25	25	25	NA	24	NA	NA	27

SPECIFICATIONS & EPA MILEAGE RATINGS — TOYOTA

	4Runner 2WD 5M	4Runner 2WD AT	4Runner 4WD 5M	4Runner 4WD AT	4Runner 2WD V6 AT	4Runner 4WD V6 5M	4Runner 4WD V6 AT	Land Cruiser	Previa 2WD S/C
Acceleration (0-60/sec)	NA	NA	NA	NA	NA	10.1	NA	10.1	11.6	10.6
Braking Dist. (60-0/ft)	NA	NA	NA	NA	NA	NA	NA	131	139
Turning Circle (in.)	37.4	37.4	37.4	37.4	37.4	37.4	37.4	40.4	37.4
Length (in.)	178.7	178.7	178.7	178.7	178.7	178.7	178.7	189.8	187
Width (in.)	66.5	66.5	66.5	66.5	66.5	66.5	66.5	76	70.8
Height (in.)	66.5	66.5	66.5	66.5	66.5	66.5	68.7	93.6	70.1
Curb Weight (lbs.)	3340	3355	3690	3735	3565	3850	3925	4834	3755
Wheelbase (in.)	105.3	105.3	105.3	105.3	105.3	105.3	105.3	112.2	112.8
Front Head Room (in.)	39.2	39.2	39.2	39.2	39.2	39.2	39.2	40.3	39.4
Rear Head Room (in.)	38.7	38.7	38.7	38.7	38.7	38.7	38.7	39.7	38.9
Front Leg Room (in.)	43.1	43.1	43.1	43.1	43.1	43.1	43.1	42.2	40.1
Rear Leg Room (in.)	34.9	34.9	34.9	34.9	34.9	34.9	34.9	33.6	36.6
Maximum Seating	5	5	5	5	5	5	5	7	7
Max Cargo Capacity (cu ft.)	79.7	79.7	79.7	79.7	79.7	79.7	79.7	90.9	157.8
Maximum Payload (lbs.)	1810	1795	1560	1515	1685	1400	1310	1636	1655
Number of Cylinders	4	4	4	4	6	6	6	6	4
Displacement (liters)	2.7	2.7	2.7	2.7	3.4	3.4	3.4	4.5	2.4
Horsepower @ RPM	150@4800	150@4800	150@4800	150@4800	183@4800	183@4800	183@4800	212@4600	161@5000
Torque @ RPM	177@4000	177@4000	177@4000	177@4000	217@3400	217@3400	217@3600	275@3200	201@3600
Fuel Capacity	18.5	18.5	18.5	18.5	18.5	18.5	18.5	25.1	19
Towing Capacity	3500	3500	3500	3500	5000	5000	5000	5000	3500
EPA City (mpg) - Manual	20	NA	17	NA	NA	17	NA	NA	NA
EPA Hwy (mpg) - Manual	25	NA	21	NA	NA	20	NA	NA	NA
EPA City (mpg) - Auto	NA	19	NA	18	17	NA	17	12	18
EPA Hwy (mpg) - Auto	NA	24	NA	22	21	NA	19	15	22

http://edmunds.com — EDMUND'S 1997 NEW TRUCKS

SPECIFICATIONS & EPA MILEAGE RATINGS

	Previa All-Trac S/C	RAV4 2-Door 2WD 5M	RAV4 2-Door 2WD AT	RAV4 4-Door 2WD 5M	RAV4 4-Door 2WD AT	RAV4 2-Door 4WD 5M	RAV4 4-Door 4WD 5M	RAV4 4-Door 4WD AT	T100 2WD Reg Cab 5M	T100 2WD Reg Cab AT
Acceleration (0-60/sec)	NA	9.8	NA	10.1	NA	NA	NA	NA	NA	NA
Braking Dist. (60-0/ft)	145	NA	NA	NA	NA	NA	NA	NA	NA	NA
Turning Circle (in.)	37.4	33.5	33.5	36.1	36.1	33.5	36.1	36.1	37.7	37.7
Length (in.)	187	147.2	147.2	163.4	163.4	147.2	162	162	209.1	209.1
Width (in.)	70.8	66.7	66.7	66.7	66.7	66.7	66.7	66.7	75.2	75.2
Height (in.)	70.5	64.8	64.8	65.2	65.4	65	65.2	65.4	67.2	67.2
Curb Weight (lbs.)	3975	2496	2513	2612	2644	2646	2789	2844	3320	3350
Wheelbase (in.)	112.8	86.6	86.6	94.9	94.9	86.6	94.9	94.9	121.8	121.8
Front Head Room (in.)	39.4	40	40	40.3	40.3	40	40.3	40.3	39.6	39.6
Rear Head Room (in.)	38.9	38.6	38.6	39	39	38.6	39	39	NA	NA
Front Leg Room (in.)	40.1	39.5	39.5	40.4	40.4	40.4	40.4	40.4	42.9	42.9
Rear Leg Room (in.)	36.6	33.9	33.9	30.1	30.1	30.1	30.1	30.1	NA	NA
Maximum Seating	7	4	4	5	5	4	5	5	3	3
Max Cargo Capacity (cu ft.)	152.3	34.3	34.3	57.9	57.9	34.3	57.9	57.9	NA	NA
Maximum Payload (lbs.)	1435	1003	821	1246	1201	859	1102	1036	1680	1650
Number of Cylinders	4	4	4	4	4	4	4	4	4	4
Displacement (liters)	2.4	2	2	2	2	2	2	2	2.7	2.7
Horsepower @ RPM	161@5000	120@5400	120@5400	120@5400	120@5400	120@5400	120@5400	120@5400	150@4800	150@4800
Torque @ RPM	201@3600	125@4600	125@4600	125@4600	125@4600	125@4600	125@4600	125@4600	177@4000	177@4000
Fuel Capacity	19	15	15	15	15	15	15	15	24	24
Towing Capacity	3500	1500	1500	1500	1500	1500	1500	1500	4000	4000
EPA City (mpg) - Manual	NA	24	NA	24	NA	22	22	NA	20	NA
EPA Hwy (mpg) - Manual	NA	30	NA	30	NA	27	27	NA	24	NA
EPA City (mpg) - Auto	17	NA	24	NA	24	NA	NA	22	NA	19
EPA Hwy (mpg) - Auto	20	NA	29	NA	29	NA	NA	27	NA	22

SPECIFICATIONS & EPA MILEAGE RATINGS	T100 2WD Xtracab 5M	T100 2WD Xtracab AT	T100 4WD Xtracab 5M	T100 4WD Xtracab AT	Tacoma 2WD Reg Cab 5M	Tacoma 2WD Xtracab 5M	Tacoma 2WD Reg Cab AT	Tacoma 2WD Xtracab AT	Tacoma 4WD Xtracab 5M	Tacoma 4WD Reg Cab 5M
Acceleration (0-60/sec)	8.6	NA	8.9	NA	8.3	NA	NA	NA	NA	NA
Braking Dist. (60-0/ft)	169	169	143	143	142	133	142	133	144	NA
Turning Circle (in.)	37.7	37.7	43.3	43.3	35.4	41.3	35.4	41.3	41.3	35.4
Length (in.)	209.1	209.1	209.1	209.1	180.5	199	180.5	199	199	180.5
Width (in.)	75.2	75.2	75.2	75.2	66.5	66.5	66.5	66.5	66.5	66.5
Height (in.)	68.6	68.6	71.6	71.6	61.8	62	61.8	62	68.3	68.5
Curb Weight (lbs.)	3580	3600	4040	4110	2560	2745	2580	2765	3345	3190
Wheelbase (in.)	121.8	121.8	121.8	121.8	103.3	121.9	103.3	121.9	121.9	103.3
Front Head Room (in.)	39.6	39.6	39.6	39.6	38.2	38.4	38.2	38.4	38.2	38.2
Rear Head Room (in.)	37.8	37.8	37.8	37.8	NA	35.5	NA	35.5	35.3	NA
Front Leg Room (in.)	42.9	42.9	42.9	42.9	41.7	42.8	41.7	41.7	43.7	41.7
Rear Leg Room (in.)	29.6	29.6	29.6	29.6	NA	NA	NA	NA	NA	NA
Maximum Seating	6	6	6	6	3	5	3	5	5	3
Max Cargo Capacity (cu ft.)	NA	NA	NA	NA	NA	NA	NA	NA	NA	NA
Maximum Payload (lbs.)	2120	2070	1960	2070	1684	1752	1664	1732	1884	1914
Number of Cylinders	6	6	6	6	4	4	4	4	4	4
Displacement (liters)	3.4	3.4	3.4	3.4	2.4	2.4	2.4	2.4	2.7	2.7
Horsepower @ RPM	190@4800	190@4800	190@4800	190@4800	142@5000	142@5000	142@5000	142@5000	150@4800	150@4800
Torque @ RPM	220@3600	220@3600	220@3600	220@3600	160@4000	160@4000	160@4000	160@4000	177@4000	177@4000
Fuel Capacity	24	24	24	24	15	15	15	15	18	15
Towing Capacity	5200	5200	5000	5000	5000	5000	5000	5000	5000	5000
EPA City (mpg) - Manual	17	NA	17	NA	22	22	NA	NA	18	18
EPA Hwy (mpg) - Manual	21	NA	19	NA	28	28	NA	NA	22	22
EPA City (mpg) - Auto	NA	17	NA	16	NA	NA	22	22	NA	NA
EPA Hwy (mpg) - Auto	NA	20	NA	18	NA	NA	25	25	NA	NA

SPECIFICATIONS & EPA MILEAGE RATINGS

	Tacoma 4WD Xtracab AT	Tacoma 4WD Reg Cab AT	Tacoma 4WD Reg Cab V6 5M	Tacoma 2WD Xtracab V6 5M	Tacoma 2WD Xtracab V6 AT	Tacoma 4WD Xtracab V6 5M	Tacoma 4WD Xtracab V6 AT
Acceleration (0-60/sec)	NA	NA	9	7.1	8.5	9.1	9.5
Braking Dist. (60-0/ft)	144	NA	NA	133	133	144	144
Turning Circle (in.)	41.3	35.4	35.4	41.3	41.3	41.3	41.3
Length (in.)	199	180.5	180.5	199	199	199	199
Width (in.)	66.5	66.5	66.5	66.5	66.5	66.5	66.5
Height (in.)	68.3	68.5	68.5	62	62	68.3	68.3
Curb Weight (lbs.)	3375	3220	3245	2895	2915	3410	2740
Wheelbase (in.)	121.9	103.3	103.3	121.9	121.9	121.9	121.9
Front Head Room (in.)	38.4	38.2	38.4	38.4	38.4	38.4	38.4
Rear Head Room (in.)	35.3	NA	NA	35.5	35.5	35.3	35.3
Front Leg Room (in.)	43.7	41.7	41.7	42.8	42.8	42.8	42.8
Rear Leg Room (in.)	NA	NA	NA	NA	NA	NA	NA
Maximum Seating	5	3	3	5	5	5	5
Max Cargo Capacity (cu ft.)	NA	NA	NA	NA	NA	NA	NA
Maximum Payload (lbs.)	1729	1860	1859	1602	1582	1694	1664
Number of Cylinders	4	4	6	6	6	6	6
Displacement (liters)	2.7	2.7	3.4	3.4	3.4	3.4	3.4
Horsepower @ RPM	150@4800	150@4800	190@4800	190@4800	190@4800	190@4800	190@4800
Torque @ RPM	177@4000	177@4000	220@3600	220@3600	220@3600	220@3600	220@3600
Fuel Capacity	18	15	15.1	15	15.1	18	18
Towing Capacity	5000	5000	5000	5000	5000	5000	5000
EPA City (mpg) - Manual	NA	NA	18	19	NA	17	NA
EPA Hwy (mpg) - Manual	NA	NA	22	23	NA	19	NA
EPA City (mpg) - Auto	18	18	NA	NA	19	NA	17
EPA Hwy (mpg) - Auto	21	21	NA	NA	22	NA	19

STEP-BY-STEP COSTING FORM

MAKE: _____ EXTERIOR COLOR: _____
MODEL: _____ INTERIOR COLOR: _____
TRIM LEVEL: _____ ENGINE SIZE/TYPE: _____

ITEMS	MSRP	INVOICE
Basic Vehicle Price:		
Optional Equipment		
1.		
2.		
3.		
4.		
5.		
6.		
7.		
8.		
9.		
10.		
11.		
12.		
13.		
14.		
TOTAL		
SUBTRACT Holdback Amount		
SUBTRACT Rebates and/or Incentives		
ADD 5% Fair Profit to New Total		
ADD Destination Charge		
ADD Advertising Fees (1-3% of MSRP)		
SUBTRACT Trade-In Value or Cash Down Payment		
or		
ADD Difference Between Trade Value and Loan Balance		
FINAL PRICE		
ADD Sales Taxes, Documentation/Prep Fees, and License Plates		
TOTAL COST		

http://edmunds.com

CRASH TEST DATA

Crash Test Data

In 1994, the National Highway and Traffic Safety Adminsitration (NHTSA) changed the way they rate crash test performances of the cars and trucks they run into a concrete barrier at 35 mph. Instead of the confusing numerical scale that had been in place for years, NHTSA decided to make the data more user-friendly for interested consumers by converting to a five star rating system, just like that used by the movie reviewer in your local paper and the lucky folks AAA employs to travel around the world eating and sleeping in the best restaurants and hotels. Boy, they've got it rough, don't they?

The scale is as follows:

1 Star	Better than a 45% chance of life-threatening injury
2 Stars	A 35-45% chance of life-threatening injury
3 Stars	A 20-35% chance of life-threatening injury
4 Stars	A 10-20% chance of life-threatening injury
5 Stars	Less than a 10% chance of life-threatening injury

Listed below are the results from crash testing conducted since 1994. All test results are applicable to the 1997 equivalent of the listed model. In other words, the 1997 model is the same as the listed vehicle with regard to structure and safety equipment.

Crash test data 1994:

Chevrolet Camaro	Driver: 5 Stars	Passenger: 5 Stars
Chrysler LHS	Driver: 4 Stars	Passenger: 4 Stars
Dodge Intrepid	Driver: 4 Stars	Passenger: 4 Stars
Dodge Ram 1500	Driver: 5 Stars	Passenger: No Data
Ford Aerostar	Driver: 4 Stars	Passenger: 3 Stars
Ford Probe	Driver: 5 Stars	Passenger: 4 Stars
Ford Thunderbird	Driver: 5 Stars	Passenger: 5 Stars
Honda Accord	Driver: 4 Stars	Passenger: 3 Stars
Infiniti J30	Driver: 4 Stars	Passenger: 4 Stars
Lexus GS 300	Driver: 3 Stars	Passenger: 3 Stars
Mazda 626	Driver: 4 Stars	Passenger: 5 Stars
Mercedes C-Class	Driver: 4 Stars	Passenger: 4 Stars
Toyota Corolla	Driver: 4 Stars	Passenger: 4 Stars
Toyota Previa	Driver: 4 Stars	Passenger: 3 Stars
Toyota T100	Driver: 4 Stars	Passenger: 4 Stars
Volvo 850	Driver: 5 Stars	Passenger: 4 Stars

CRASH TEST DATA

Crash test data 1995:

Make/Model	Driver	Passenger
Acura Integra	Driver: 4 Stars	Passenger: 3 Stars
Audi A6	Driver: 5 Stars	Passenger: 5 Stars
BMW 3-Series	Driver: 4 Stars	Passenger: 4 Stars
Buick Le Sabre	Driver: 5 Stars	Passenger: 3 Stars
Cadillac Eldorado	Driver: 4 Stars	Passenger: 4 Stars
Cadillac Seville	Driver: 4 Stars	Passenger: 4 Stars
Chevrolet Blazer	Driver: 3 Stars	Passenger: 1 Star
Chevrolet Cavalier	Driver: 3 Stars	Passenger: 3 Stars
Chevrolet Lumina	Driver: 5 Stars	Passenger: 4 Stars
Chrysler Cirrus	Driver: 3 Stars	Passenger: No Data
Chrysler Concorde	Driver: 4 Stars	Passenger: 4 Stars
Chrysler Sebring	Driver: 5 Stars	Passenger: 5 Stars
Dodge Avenger	Driver: 5 Stars	Passenger: 5 Stars
Dodge Intrepid	Driver: 4 Stars	Passenger: 4 Stars
Dodge Neon	Driver: 3 Stars	Passenger: 3 Stars
Dodge Stratus	Driver: 3 Stars	Passenger: No Data
Eagle Vision	Driver: 4 Stars	Passenger: 4 Stars
Ford Explorer	Driver: 4 Stars	Passenger: 4 Stars
Ford Windstar	Driver: 4 Stars	Passenger: 5 Stars
Eagle Talon	Driver: 4 Stars	Passenger: 4 Stars
Geo Prizm	Driver: 4 Stars	Passenger: 4 Stars
GMC Jimmy	Driver: 3 Stars	Passenger: 1 Star
Honda Odyssey	Driver: 4 Stars	Passenger: 4 Stars
Hyundai Sonata	Driver: 3 Stars	Passenger: 4 Stars
Isuzu Trooper	Driver: 3 Stars	Passenger: 3 Stars
Mazda Millenia	Driver: 4 Stars	Passenger: 5 Stars
Mazda MX-6	Driver: 4 Stars	Passenger: 5 Stars
Mercury Cougar XR7	Driver: 5 Stars	Passenger: 5 Stars
Mazda Protege	Driver: 3 Stars	Passenger: No Data
Mitsubishi Eclipse	Driver: 4 Stars	Passenger: 4 Stars
Mitsubishi Montero	Driver: 4 Stars	Passenger: 4 Stars
Nissan Maxima	Driver: 4 Stars	Passenger: 3 Stars
Oldsmobile 88	Driver: 5 Stars	Passenger: 3 Stars
Oldsmobile Aurora	Driver: 3 Stars	Passenger: 3 Stars
Pontiac Bonneville	Driver: 5 Stars	Passenger: 4 Stars
Pontiac Firebird	Driver: 5 Stars	Passenger: 5 Stars
Pontiac Sunfire	Driver: 3 Stars	Passenger: 3 Stars
Saab 900	Driver: 4 Stars	Passenger: 4 Stars
Subaru Legacy	Driver: 4 Stars	Passenger: 4 Stars
Toyota Tercel	Driver: 3 Stars	Passenger: 4 Stars
Volkswagen Jetta	Driver: 3 Stars	Passenger: 3 Stars
Volkswagen Passat	Driver: 4 Stars	Passenger: 4 Stars

CRASH TEST DATA

Crash Test Data 1996:

Vehicle	Driver	Passenger
Acura SLX	Driver: 3 Stars	Passenger: 3 Stars
Acura TL Series	Driver: 4 Stars	Passenger: 4 Stars
Audi A4	Driver: 5 Stars	Passenger: 4 Stars
Chevrolet Astro	Driver: 3 Stars	Passenger: 3 Stars
Chevrolet C/K Pickup	Driver: 5 Stars	Passenger: 5 Stars
Chrysler T&C LWB	Driver: 3 Stars	Passenger: 4 Stars
Dodge Grand Caravan	Driver: 3 Stars	Passenger: 4 Stars
Dodge Neon	Driver: 4 Stars	Passenger: 4 Stars
Dodge Ram Van/Wagon	Driver: 3 Stars	Passenger: 4 Stars
Ford Crown Victoria	Driver: 5 Stars	Passenger: 5 Stars
Ford Mustang	Driver: 5 Stars	Passenger: 5 Stars
Ford Taurus	Driver: 4 Stars	Passenger: 4 Stars
Geo Tracker Convertible	Driver: 2 Stars	Passenger: 3 Stars
GMC Safari	Driver: 3 Stars	Passenger: 3 Stars
GMC Sierra	Driver: 5 Stars	Passenger: 5 Stars
Honda Civic Coupe	Driver: 4 Stars	Passenger: 4 Stars
Honda Civic Sedan	Driver: 4 Stars	Passenger: 5 Stars
Honda Passport	Driver: 4 Stars	Passenger: 3 Stars
Hyundai Accent	Driver: 3 Stars	Passenger: 4 Stars
Hyundai Elantra	Driver: 3 Stars	Passenger: 3 Stars
Isuzu Rodeo	Driver: 4 Stars	Passenger: 3 Stars
Jeep Grand Cherokee	Driver: 3 Stars	Passenger: 4 Stars
Land Rover Discovery	Driver: 3 Stars	Passenger: 3 Stars
Lincoln Town Car	Driver: 4 Stars	Passenger: 5 Stars
Mazda Miata	Driver: 4 Stars	Passenger: 3 Stars
Mazda MPV	Driver: 4 Stars	Passenger: 4 Stars
Mercury Grand Marquis	Driver: 5 Stars	Passenger: 5 Stars
Mercury Sable	Driver: 4 Stars	Passenger: 4 Stars
Mercury Villager	Driver: 4 Stars	Passenger: 3 Stars
Mitsubishi Mirage	Driver: 3 Stars	Passenger: 3 Stars
Nissan 200SX	Driver: 4 Stars	Passenger: 4 Stars
Nissan Altima	Driver: 4 Stars	Passenger: 4 Stars
Nissan Quest	Driver: 4 Stars	Passenger: 3 Stars
Nissan Sentra	Driver: 4 Stars	Passenger: 4 Stars
Nissan Truck	Driver: 2 Stars	Passenger: 4 Stars
Plymouth Neon	Driver: 4 Stars	Passenger: 4 Stars
Plymouth Grand Voyager	Driver: 3 Stars	Passenger: 4 Stars
Subaru Impreza	Driver: 4 Stars	Passenger: 4 Stars
Suzuki Sidekick Conv.	Driver: 2 Stars	Passenger: 3 Stars
Toyota 4Runner	Driver: 3 Stars	Passenger: 3 Stars
Toyota Avalon	Driver: 4 Stars	Passenger: 5 Stars
Toyota Tacoma	Driver: 2 Stars	Passenger: 3 Stars

CRASH TEST DATA

Crash Test Data 1997:

Cadillac DeVille	Driver: 4 Stars	Passenger: 4 Stars
Chevrolet S10 Pickup	Driver: 3 Stars	Passenger: 2 Stars
Chrysler Sebring Conv.	Driver: 4 Stars	Passenger: 4 Stars
Chrysler T&C SWB	Driver: 4 Stars	Passenger: 4 Stars
Dodge Caravan	Driver: 4 Stars	Passenger: 4 Stars
Ford F-150 Pickup	Driver: 4 Stars	Passenger: 5 Stars
Ford Ranger	Driver: 4 Stars	Passenger: 4 Stars
Geo Metro	Driver: 4 Stars	Passenger: 4 Stars
GMC Sonoma	Driver: 3 Stars	Passenger: 2 Stars
Jeep Wrangler	Driver: 4 Stars	Passenger: 5 Stars
Mazda B-Series Pickup	Driver: 4 Stars	Passenger: 4 Stars
Mitsubishi Galant	Driver: 4 Stars	Passenger: 4 Stars
Oldsmobile Regency	Driver: 5 Stars	Passenger: 3 Stars
Plymouth Voyager:	Driver: 4 Stars	Passenger: 4 Stars
Pontiac Grand Am	Driver: 4 Stars	Passenger: 5 Stars
Pontiac Grand Prix	Driver: 4 Stars	Passenger: 4 Stars
Toyota Paseo	Driver: 4 Stars	Passenger: 4 Stars

40 mph offset frontal crash tests (conducted by Insurance Institute for Highway Safety):

1997 Chevrolet Astro	Poor
1996 Chevrolet Blazer	Poor
1995 Chevrolet Cavalier	Poor
1995 Chevrolet Lumina	Good
1997 Chevrolet Venture	Poor
1995 Chrysler Cirrus	Poor
1997 Chrysler Town & Country	Marginal
1997 Dodge Grand Caravan	Marginal
1995 Dodge Stratus	Poor
1997 Ford Aerostar	Poor
1995 Ford Contour	Poor
1996 Ford Explorer	Acceptable
1997 Ford Windstar	Good
1996 GMC Jimmy	Poor
1997 GMC Safari	Poor
1995 Honda Accord	Acceptable
1997 Honda Odyssey	Marginal
1996 Honda Passport	Poor
1996 Infiniti I30	Poor

CRASH TEST DATA

1997 Isuzu Oasis	Marginal
1996 Isuzu Rodeo	Poor
1996 Land Rover Discovery	Acceptable
1995 Mazda Millenia	Acceptable
1997 Mazda MPV	Marginal
1995 Mercury Mystique	Poor
1997 Mercury Mountaineer	Acceptable
1997 Mercury Villager	Marginal
1995 Mitsubishi Galant	Poor
1995 Nissan Maxima	Poor
1997 Nissan Quest	Marginal
1996 Oldsmobile Bravada	Poor
1997 Oldsmobile Silhouette	Poor
1997 Plymouth Grand Voyager	Marginal
1997 Pontiac Trans Sport	Poor
1995 Saab 900	Poor
1995 Subaru Legacy	Acceptable
1996 Toyota 4Runner	Acceptable
1997 Toyota Previa	Poor
1995 Volkswagen Passat	Poor
1995 Volvo 850	Good

1997 Ford Windstar LX

PAYMENT TABLE

Depicts monthly payment per $1,000 borrowed*

		TERM (length of loan)				
		12	24	36	48	60
I	4%	85.15	43.40	29.50	22.55	18.45
N	5%	85.60	43.85	29.95	23.00	18.90
T	6%	86.05	44.30	30.40	23.50	19.35
E	7%	86.55	44.75	30.90	23.95	19.80
R	8%	87.00	45.25	31.35	24.40	20.30
E	9%	87.45	45.70	31.80	24.90	20.75
S	10%	87.90	46.15	32.25	25.35	21.25
T	11%	88.40	46.60	32.75	25.85	21.75
	12%	88.85	47.05	33.20	26.35	22.25
R	13%	89.30	47.55	33.70	26.85	22.75
A	14%	89.80	48.00	34.20	27.35	23.25
T	15%	90.25	48.50	34.65	27.85	23.80
E	16%	90.75	48.95	35.15	28.35	24.30

*rounded to nearest nickel

LEASING TIPS

Like most consumers, you want to know how to buy or lease the car of your choice for the best possible price. Buyers are attracted to leasing by low payments and the prospect of driving a new car every two or three years. Many people figure that a car payment is an unavoidable fact of budgetary life, and they might as well drive 'new' rather than 'old.' True, leasing is an attractive alternative, but there are some things you need to understand about leasing before jumping in feet first without a paddle. Whatever. You know what we mean.

1) Low Payments — You've seen the ads: Mazda Miata for $219 a month. Nissan Altima for $249 a month. Jeep Grand Cherokee for $299 a month. Zowie! Visions of new golf clubs in your trunk, a big-screen TV in your living room and two weeks of prime vacationing in Vail release endorphins at twice the Surgeon General's recommended level. Hold on a sec. Read the fine print. See where it says *"Capitalized Cost Reduction"*? That's lease-speak for down payment. See where it says "30,000 miles over term"? That's lease-speak for 'You're going to the Safeway and back—and that's all folks.' Want the car for zero down? That's gonna cost you. You drive someplace more than twice a month? That's gonna cost you too.

Low payments aren't a fallacy with leasing, when taken in proper context. For example, a hypothetical Ford Ranger XLT stickers at about $14,000, give or take. To lease for two years with no *capitalized cost reduction* (down payment); it'll cost you about $355 per month. To lease for three years; about $280 per month. Generally, Ford allows 15,000 miles per year and charges 11 cents per mile for each one over the term limit. To buy that Ranger, financed for 24 months at 10% APR with no money down, you would pay about $690 per month, including tax and tags. For three years at 10%, the payment would be around $485 per month. So you see, leasing is cheaper on a monthly basis when compared to financing *for the same term*.

There are two flaws here. First, 60 month financing is now the standard. The Ranger will cost right around $300 per month for five years, at 10% APR with zero down, and still be worth a good chunk of change if cared for properly. Second, ownership is far less restrictive, even if the bank holds the title until 2002. You can drive as far as you want, paint the thing glow-in-the-dark orange with magenta stripes, and spill coffee on the seats without sweating a big wear-and-tear bill down the road. Leasing for two years costs about $8,400, and you don't own the truck at lease-end. Financing for two

LEASING TIPS

years costs about $16,560, but you own a truck worth about $8,500 when the payment book is empty, which makes your actual cost a tad over $8,000. Is leasing cheaper? Monthly payments, when compared to financing over the same term, are lower. But in most cases, leasing is actually more expensive in the long run.

2) Restrictions — Leasing severely restricts your use of a vehicle. Mileage allowances are limited, modifications to the vehicle can result in hefty fines at the end of the lease, and if the vehicle is not in top condition when it is returned, excessive wear-and-tear charges may be levied. Many dealers will be more lenient if you buy or lease another vehicle from them at the end of your term, but if you drop off the car and walk, prepare yourself for some lease-end misery.

Be sure to define these limitations at the beginning of the lease so that you know what you're getting yourself into. Find out what will be considered excessive in the wear-and-tear department and try to negotiate a higher mileage limit.

3) How to Lease — Never walk into a dealership and announce that you want to lease a car. Don't talk payment either. Concentrate on finding a car you like, and know before you go into the dealership what you can afford. Lease payments are based on something called a *capitalized cost,* which is the selling price of the car. The *residual value* is the predicted value of the vehicle at the end of the lease term, and can be expressed as a percentage of the MSRP. A *money factor*, which is lease-speak for 'interest rate,' is also involved in the calculation of a lease payment. If the money factor is expressed as a percentage, convert the percentage to the money factor by dividing the number by 24 (yes, it's 24 regardless of the term of the lease). For example, a 7% interest rate converts to a .0029 money factor. Then, of course, there are associated taxes and fees that are added. Accept the fact that if the car you want to lease is not a popular model, your lease may be a bit higher than you anticipated.

Calculating an actual lease payment is nearly impossible, particularly when the lease is subsidized by the automaker, but you can arrive at an approximate ball-park figure by using the following formula, which we will illustrate using a 36-month lease on a 1997 Ford Escort LX as an example. Remember, if

LEASING TIPS

you put any money down, or trade in your old car, you must deduct this amount from the capitalized cost. This deduction is called the *capitalized cost reduction*.

1997 Ford Escort LX (MSRP)	**$12,934**
Capitalized Cost Reduction	**$1,000**
Capitalized Cost	**$11,934**
Destination Charge	**$415**
Residual Value after 3 years	(45% of MSRP in this example) $12,934 x .45 = **$5,820.30**
Term Depreciation	(Capitalized Cost - Residual Value) $11,934 - $5,820.30 = **$6,113.70**
Money Factor	(Interest Rate divided by 24) 6% (.06) divided by 24 = **.0025**
Monthly Depreciation	(Term Depreciation divided by Lease Term) $6,113.70 divided by 36 = **$169.83**
Monthly Lease Rate	(Capitalized Cost + Residual Value) x .0025 $11,934 + $5,820.30 x .0025 = **$44.39**
Monthly Sales Tax	(Monthly Depreciation + Monthly Lease Rate) x Sales Tax Rate [6.5% in this ex.] $169.83 + $44.39 x .065 = **$13.92**
Monthly Payment	(Monthly Depreciation + Monthly Lease Rate + Monthly Sales Tax) $169.83 + $44.39 + $13.92 = **$228.14**

Keep in mind that every vehicle will have a unique residual value, and that the above formula doesn't take into consideration documentation fees, the cost of license plates, or trade-in values. Deduct the trade-in value from the Capitalized Cost before calculating the lease. If you're *upside down* on your trade, which means the car is worth less than you owe on the loan, then you'll need to add the difference between the balance due on the loan and the trade in value to the Capitalized Cost. Also, deduct the amount of any cash down payment from the Capitalized Cost before calculating the lease, as we did in the example above. The example we illustrated is a straight-forward, no factory subsidy lease. This formula will not account for *subsidized leases*. Subsidized leases allow dealers to lower payments by raising residual values or lowering the capitalized cost. You can recognize a subsidized lease easily. Any nationally or regionally advertised lease is generally subsidized by the

LEASING TIPS

manufacturer to keep lease payments low. The $249 per month Nissan Altima and $299 per month Jeep Grand Cherokee are examples of subsidized leases.

Computing a lease payment can be frustrating. Ford Motor Company has developed special calculators for the sole purpose of computing lease payments because the method is not nearly as simplistic as the one above. However, a buyer interested in an Escort LX can use the ball-park figure of $228.14 to find out whether or not the lease fits their budget, with a $1,000 down payment. This figure can also be compared to competing models from manufacturers who may or may not be offering subsidized leases.

Actual lease payments are affected by negotiation of the sticker price on the vehicle, term of the lease, available incentives, residual values, and layers of financial wizardry that even sales managers can't interpret without divine intervention. Once you find a car you can afford, negotiate the sticker price and then explore leasing based on the negotiated price. Ask what the residual value is and subtract any rebates or incentives from the Capitalized Cost. Use the formula above to calculate a ball-park figure, and if the dealer balks at your conclusion, ask them to explain the error of your ways.

Your best bet when leasing is to choose a model with a subsidized lease. Payments are very low, terms are simple to understand, and they are the only true bargain in the world of leasing.

4) Lease-end — Studies show that consumers generally like leases, right up until they end. The reason for their apprehension is rooted in the dark days of *open-end leasing*, when Joe Lessee was dealt a sucker punch by the lessor on the day Joe returned the car to the leasing agent. Back then, residual values were established at the end of the lease, wear-and-tear charges maxxed out credit cards and dealers laughed all the way to the bank.

Leasing has evolved, and with today's *closed-end leases* (the only type of lease you should consider), the lease-end fees are quite minimal, unless the car has 100,000 miles on it, a busted-up grille and melted chocolate smeared into the upholstery. Dealers want you to buy or lease another car from them, and can be rather lenient regarding excess mileage and abnormal wear. After all, if they hit you with a bunch of trumped up charges, you're not going to remain a loyal customer, are you?

Additionally, closed-end leasing establishes the value of the car in advance, at the beginning of the lease. Also, any fees or charges you may incur at the

LEASING TIPS

lease-end are spelled out in detail before you sign the lease. All the worry is removed by the existence of concrete figures.

Another leasing benefit is the myriad of choices you have at the end of the term. Well, maybe not a myriad, but there are four, which is more than you have after two or three years of financing. They are:

• **Return the vehicle to the dealer and walk away from it** after paying any applicable charges like a termination fee, wear-and-tear repairs, or excessive mileage bills. Of course, if you don't plan to buy or lease another car from the dealer, you may get hit for every minor thing, but dem's da risks.

• **Buy the vehicle** from the dealer for the residual value established at the beginning of the lease. If the car is in good shape, the residual value is probably lower than the true value of the car, making it a bargain, and many leasing companies will guarantee financing at the lowest interest rate available at the time your lease ends. We recommend this option if the lease vehicle is trashed just to avoid the lease-end charges such a vehicle would certainly incur.

• **Use any equity in the vehicle as leverage in a new deal** with the dealer. Since residual values are generally set artificially low, the car is likely worth more than the residual value at lease-end. A well-maintained, low mileage lease car should allow the dealer to knock up to a couple of thousand bucks off your next deal.

• **Sell the vehicle yourself** and pay off the residual value, pocketing whatever profit you make.

Closed-end leasing is a win-win situation for everybody. The manufacturer sells more cars, the dealer sells more cars, you get low payments and a new car every couple of years. However, it is important to stress that you never own the car and leasing can be quite restrictive. If you're a low mileage driver who maintains cars in perfect condition, don't like tying up capital in down payments and don't mind never-ending car payments, leasing is probably just right for you. If you're on the road all day every day, beat the stuffing out of your wheels, enjoy a 'customized' look or drive your cars until the wheels fall off, buy whatever it is you're considering

WARRANTIES & ROADSIDE ASSISTANCE

All new vehicles sold in America come with at least two warranties, and many include roadside assistance. Described below are the major types of warranties and assistance provided to consumers.

Basic. Your basic warranty covers everything except items subject to wear and tear, such as oil filters, wiper blades, and the like. Tires and batteries often have their own warranty coverages, which will be outlined in your owner's manual. Emission equipment is required to be covered for five years or 50,000 miles by the federal government.

Drivetrain. Drivetrain coverage takes care of most of the parts that make the car move, like the engine, transmission, drive axles and driveshaft. Like the basic warranty, parts subject to wear and tear like hoses and belts are not covered. However, most of the internal parts of the engine, such as the pistons and bearings, which are subject to wear and tear are covered by the drivetrain warranty. See your owner's manual or local dealer for specific coverages.

Rust. This warranty protects you from rust-through problems with the sheetmetal. Surface rust doesn't count. The rust must make a hole to be covered by the warranty. Keep your car washed and waxed, and rust shouldn't be a problem.

Roadside Assistance. Most manufacturers provide a service that will rescue you if your car leaves you stranded, even if it's your fault. Lock yourself out of the car? Somebody will come and open it up. Run out of gas? Somebody will deliver some fuel. Flat tire? Somebody will change it for you. See your owner's manual for details, or ask the dealer about the specifics, and don't pay for extended coverage if your insurance company already provides this type of assistance.

WARRANTIES & ROADSIDE ASSISTANCE

Make	Basic (yrs/mi)	Drivetrain (yrs/mi)	Rust (yrs/mi)	Roadside Assistance (yrs/mi)
Acura	4/50,000	4/50,000	4/Unlimited	4/50,000
Audi	3/50,000	3/50,000	10/Unlimited	3/Unlimited
BMW	4/50,000	4/50,000	6/Unlimited	4/50,000
Buick	3/36,000	3/36,000	6/100,000	3/36,000
Cadillac	4/50,000	4/50,000	6/100,000	4/50,000
Chevrolet	3/36,000	3/36,000	6/100,000	3/36,000
Chrysler	3/36,000	3/36,000	5/100,000	3/36,000
Dodge	3/36,000	3/36,000	5/100,000	3/36,000
Eagle	3/36,000	3/36,000	5/100,000	3/36,000
Ford	3/36,000	3/36,000	6/100,000	3/36,000
Geo	3/36,000	3/36,000	6/100,000	3/36,000
GMC	3/36,000	3/36,000	6/100,000	3/36,000
Honda	3/36,000	3/36,000	5/60,000	None Available
Hyundai	3/36,000	5/60,000	5/100,000	3/36,000
Infiniti	4/60,000	5/70,000	7/Unlimited	4/60,000
Isuzu	3/50,000	5/60,000	6/100,000	5/60,000
Jaguar	4/50,000	4/50,000	6/Unlimited	4/50,000
Jeep	3/36,000	3/36,000	5/100,000	3/36,000
Kia	3/36,000	5/60,000	5/100,000	3/36,000
Land Rover	3/42,000	3/42,000	6/Unlimited	3/42,000
Lexus	4/50,000	6/70,000	6/Unlimited	4/Unlimited
Lincoln	4/50,000	4/50,000	6/100,000	4/50,000
Mazda	3/50,000	3/50,000	5/Unlimited	3/50,000 (Millenia only)
Mercedes	4/50,000	4/50,000	4/50,000	Unlimited
Mercury	3/36,000	3/36,000	6/100,000	3/36,000
Mitsubishi	3/36,000	5/60,000	7/100,000	5/60,000
Nissan	3/36,000	5/60,000	5/Unlimited	None Available
Oldsmobile	3/36,000	3/36,000	6/100,000	3/36,000
Plymouth	3/36,000	3/36,000	5/100,000	3/36,000
Pontiac	3/36,000	3/36,000	6/100,000	3/36,000
Porsche	2/Unlimited	2/Unlimited	10/Unlimited	2/Unlimited
Saab	4/50,000	None Avail.	6/Unlimited	4/50,000
Saturn	3/36,000	3/36,000	6/100,000	3/36,000
Subaru	3/36,000	5/60,000	5/Unlimited	3/36,000 (SVX only)
Suzuki	3/36,000	3/36,000	3/Unlimited	None Available
Toyota	3/36,000	5/60,000	5/Unlimited	None Available
Volkswagen	2/24,000	10/100,000	6/Unlimited	2/24,000
Volvo	4/50,000	4/50,000	8/Unlimited	4/Unlimited

DEALER HOLDBACKS

What is Dealer Holdback?

Dealer holdback is built-in profit to the dealer. It comes in the form of a quarterly kickback for every vehicle the dealer sold during the previous quarter. Think of it as a dealer credit, paid by the manufacturer as a reward for selling a car.

For example, let's say you're interested in a Ford with a Manufacturer's Suggested Retail Price (MSRP) of $20,000, including optional equipment. Dealer invoice on this hypothetical Ford is $18,000, including optional equipment. The invoice includes a dealer holdback that, in the case of all Ford vehicles, amounts to 3% of the total MSRP. The destination charge should not be included when figuring the holdback. So, on this particular Ford, the true dealer cost is actually $17,400, plus destination charges. Even if the dealer sells you the car for invoice, which is unlikely, he would still be making $600 on the deal when his quarterly check arrived. That $600 is profit to the dealer; the sales staff doesn't see any of it.

Does the dealer need to use holdback money to pay the bills? That depends on how long the car has been sitting on the lot. Holdback money is an incentive from the manufacturer to the dealer to entice the dealer to stock vehicles on the lot. Dealers pay a monthly floorplanning fee for each vehicle in stock. If the Ford used in the example above arrived on the lot in December, and you bought it in July, chances are very good that floorplanning fees for this particular car have eaten up most, if not all, of the holdback money. However, the dealer is more than making up for this loss with sales of cars that have been in stock for only a month or two.

To determine a fair price for the car illustrated above, you would add 5% to the true dealer cost. Edmund's recommends 5% because it will allow the dealer to cover costs involved with selling the car, and it will provide the salesperson, who likely makes a meager commission, with a paycheck. In this example, add a fair profit of $870, for a target price of $18,270. Remember, this price doesn't include destination charges, advertising

DEALER HOLDBACKS

charges, tax, license plates, or any fees associated with processing paperwork.

Dealer holdback allows dealers to advertise big sales. Often, ads promise that your new car will cost you just "$1 over/under invoice!" Additionally, the dealer stands to reap further benefits if there is some sort of dealer incentive or customer rebate on the car. Generally, sale prices stipulate that all rebates and incentives go to the dealer. Using the example above, let's see what happens when there is a rebate.

Suppose the car described above has a $1,000 rebate in effect. You need to subtract that $1,000 rebate (remember, the dealer is keeping the rebate) from the true dealer cost of $17,400, which results in a new dealer cost of just $16,400. Now, you must calculate a fair price. In this example, 5% of true dealer cost of $16,400 is $820, which means that the price you should try to buy the car for is $17,220, plus destination, advertising, tax, and fees.

Domestic manufacturers (Chrysler, Ford, and GM) generally offer dealers a holdback equaling 3% of the total sticker price, or MSRP, of the car. Import manufacturers (Honda, Nissan, Toyota, etc.) provide holdback amounts that are equal to a percentage of total MSRP, base MSRP, or base invoice. Following is a list of makes and the confirmed amount of the dealer holdback.

Make	Holdback
Acura	2% of the Base MSRP
Audi	2% of the Total MSRP
BMW	2% of the Total MSRP
Buick	3% of the Total MSRP
Cadillac	3% of the Total MSRP
Chevrolet	3% of the Total MSRP
Chrysler	3% of the Total MSRP
Dodge	3% of the Total MSRP
Eagle	3% of the Total MSRP

DEALER HOLDBACKS

Ford	3% of the Total MSRP
Geo	3% of the Total MSRP
GMC	3% of the Total MSRP
Honda	2% of the Base MSRP
Hyundai	2% of the Base Invoice
Infiniti	3% of the Total MSRP
Isuzu	3% of the Total MSRP
Jaguar	2% of the Total MSRP
Jeep	3% of the Total MSRP
Kia	Unknown at this time.
Land Rover	2% of the Total MSRP
Lexus	2% of the Base Invoice
Lincoln	3% of the Total MSRP
Mazda	3% of the Total MSRP
Mercedes-Benz	2% of the Total MSRP
Mercury	3% of the Total MSRP
Mitsubishi	2% of the Base MSRP
Nissan	3% of the Total MSRP
Oldsmobile	3% of the Total MSRP
Plymouth	3% of the Total MSRP
Pontiac	3% of the Total MSRP
Porsche	2% of the Total MSRP
Saab	3% of the Total MSRP
Saturn	One-price sales. Customer pays MSRP.
Subaru	3% of the Total MSRP
Suzuki	Unknown at this time.
Toyota	2% of the Base Invoice (Amount may differ in Southeastern U.S.)
Volkswagen	2% of Total MSRP
Volvo	$300 Flat Amount on 850 models $900 Flat Amount on 960 models

FREQUENTLY ASKED QUESTIONS

Edmund's solicits e-mail from consumers who visit our website at http://www.edmund.com. Below are 23 commonly asked questions regarding new cars and the buying process.

1. How soon after a price increase does Edmund's modify its data?

This depends on how soon our sources are notified. Sometimes, it's a matter of days; other times, it can take longer. Rest assured that we painstakingly attempt to maintain the most up-to-date pricing. If a dealer disputes the accuracy of our pricing, ask them to prove it by showing you the invoice so that you can compare. If prices have indeed increased, the amount will not be very substantial, and the new figures should easily be within a few percentage points of those published in this guide.

2. Do factory orders cost more than buying from dealer stock?

All things considered equal, ordered vehicles cost no more than vehicles in dealer stock and, in some cases, may actually cost less. When you buy from dealer stock, you may have to settle for a vehicle with either more or less equipment and your second or third color choice. Moreover, the dealership pays interest on stock vehicles at a predetermined monthly rate to the manufacturer. This interest is called floor plan, and is subsidized by the dealer holdback. When you factory order, you get exactly what you want, in the color you want, and the dealer eliminates the floor plan. In most cases, the dealer passes the savings on to the customer, and the savings could amount to several hundred dollars.

The downside to ordering is that incentives and rebates are only good on the day of delivery. If an incentive or rebate plan was in effect when the vehicle was ordered, but not in effect the day of delivery, the customer is not eligible for the incentive or rebate. If you order a vehicle, and the delivery date is very close to the expiration date of a rebate or incentive program, beware that the dealer may try to delay delivery until after the rebate or incentive has expired.

FREQUENTLY ASKED QUESTIONS

From a negotiation standpoint, dealers may be more likely to offer a better price on a vehicle in stock, particularly if the monthly floor plan payments have exceeded the holdback amount and are now chewing into the dealer's profit.

3. Can I order a car directly from the factory without going through a dealer?

No, you cannot. Direct factory ordering is a hoax concocted by Zeke and Butherus over their nightly Jack Daniels' pow-wow at Hic a Billies. Dealers are franchisees of the manufacturer, and are protected as such.

4. Why is the car I'm looking at on the West Coast priced differently than what's listed in this guide?

California, Oregon, and Washington are the testing grounds for different pricing and option schemes. Because of the popularity of imported makes in this market, domestic manufacturers will often slash dealer profit margins and offer better-equipped cars at lower prices than those available in other parts of the country. This is why some dealer incentives and customer rebates do not apply in California, and why some option packages available in California may not be listed in this guide.

5. When should a car be considered used?

Technically, a vehicle is considered used if it has been titled. However, some dealers can rack up hundreds or thousands of miles on a new car without titling it. In these cases, the ethical definition of a used car should include any car used for extensive demonstration or personal use by dealership staff members. The only miles a new car should have on the odometer when purchased are those put on during previous test drives by prospective buyers (at dealerships where demonstrators are not used), and any miles driven during a dealer trade, within a reasonable limit. If the new car you're considering has more than 300 miles on the odometer, you should question how the car accumulated so many miles, and request a discount for the excessive mileage. We think a discount amounting to a dime a mile is a fair charge for wear and tear inflicted by the dealership.

FREQUENTLY ASKED QUESTIONS

A car should not be considered used if it is a brand-new leftover from a previous model year. However, it should be discounted as much as 5%, because many manufacturers offer dealers a carryover allowance (see question #18 for an explanation of carryover allowance) designed to help the dealer lower prices and clear out old stock. According to our sources, Chrysler Corporation does not offer a carryover allowance program, preferring to use hefty incentives and rebates to clear out old stock.

6. Why doesn't Edmund's list option prices for some makes and models?

Almost all Acura, Honda, and Suzuki options are dealer installed. Some manufacturers, like Nissan, Subaru, and Volvo, will offer both factory- and dealer-installed options. Pricing for these items can vary depending on region and dealer. Therefore, it is impossible for Edmund's to list an accurate price for these items. Our experience shows that these items often carry a 100% mark up in dealer profit. We recommend that you avoid buying dealer-installed options if you can help it.

7. How can a dealer sell a new car for much less than the invoice price Edmund's publishes?

Auto manufacturers will often subsidize volume-sellers to keep sales and production up by offering car dealers hefty cash rewards for meeting monthly or quarterly sales goals. In other words, the dealer will take a slight loss on the car in anticipation of a larger cash reward if sales goals are met. It has been our experience that when a dealer sells a vehicle for less than invoice, the deal is always being subsidized by the manufacturer in one form or another. In print ads, always look for phrases such as "all incentives and/or rebates assigned to dealer."

Also, since profit can be made on other parts of the deal, a dealer may be willing to take a loss on the price of the car in exchange for profit gleaned from a low-ball trade-in value, financing, rustproofing, an extended warranty, and aftermarket or dealer-installed accessories. We once met a Plymouth salesman who bragged that he sold a Neon Sport for invoice, but with the undervalued trade-in, high-interest financing and dealer-installed items factored into the deal, the buyer actually

FREQUENTLY ASKED QUESTIONS

paid more than $20,000 for the car. Keep in mind that there is more to a good deal than a low price.

8. How much does an extended warranty cost the warranty company?

Until the term of the warranty expires, the cost of the warranty cannot be determined. Let's say you bought a $1,000 extended warranty, and never used it. Gross profit on that warranty is $1,000. Now let's say you bought a $1,000 extended warranty, and problems with your car caused the warranty company to pay $1,200 in repair bills. Gross profit on that warranty is non-existent; the warranty cost the company $200. Now, average the two warranties together. The warranty company made $800 on both, or $400 a piece. Warranty companies sell thousands of warranties annually, and are able to make a healthy profit because most modern cars do not require many expensive repairs. By examining a warranty company's profit statement and sales figures, we could calculate average profit per warranty. However, calculating the true cost of an individual extended warranty that you're considering buying is impossible.

Our advice is to negotiate the lowest possible price that you can for warranty coverage.

9. Why won't the dealer accept my offer of 5% over true dealer cost?

The dealer doesn't have to sell you a car. If demand for the model is high, or if supplies are short, or if the dealer enjoys making a healthy profit, you won't be able to buy the car for a fair price. Don't argue the point, just find another dealer.

10. How do I figure a fair deal?

Use this formula: Dealer Invoice of car and options - Dealer Holdback - Rebates/Incentives + 5% Fair Profit + Destination Charge + Advertising Fees + Tax = Fair Deal

11. Why should I pay advertising fees?

The auto manufacturer charges the car dealer an advertising fee roughly equivalent to 1% of the sticker price. The car dealer passes

FREQUENTLY ASKED QUESTIONS

this cost on to the consumer. Additionally, regional and local advertising pools exist in most medium to large metropolitan areas. Participation by the car dealer in these regional and local advertising pools is voluntary, but the auto manufacturer may ensure that a dealer join a local advertising pool by withholding stock, sending less popular rather than hot-selling models to the dealer, and cutting incentive money. Essentially, the factory is blackmailing the dealer, forcing the dealer to join regional and local advertising pools in an effort to make its models more visible to the consumer. Regional advertising fees should never be more than 2% of the sticker price. If you're paying more than 3% of the sticker price in advertising fees, find another dealership.

12. Can I negotiate the price of a new Saturn?

No, you cannot. All Saturn dealers post the same non-negotiable price for identical cars. This way, a buyer cannot shop down the street for a better deal, because the deal will be the same. You can, however, demand top dollar for your trade and/or a lower interest rate to lower the overall cost of the deal.

13. How can I find out what customer rebates or dealer incentives are currently available?

Rebates to customers are clearly announced in advertising. Incentives to dealers, commonly known as "back-end monies," are not. Edmund's publishes current national and large regional rebate and incentive programs online at http://www.edmund.com. Local rebate and incentive programs also exist on occasion, but Edmund's doesn't have access to this information. Ask your dealer if the local automobile dealer association or advertising association is sponsoring any rebates or incentives in your metropolitan area.

14. Why do some dealer incentives on specific models have a range of values?

Sometimes, the manufacturer will tell the dealer that he must sell a certain number of cars to qualify for an incentive. For example, let's say Nissan offered dealers an incentive of $100-1,000 on the Altima. This a quota-based incentive. It means that to get the $100 per car, the

FREQUENTLY ASKED QUESTIONS

dealer might have to sell 10 cars before a certain date. To get $500 per car, the dealer might have to sell 50 cars before a certain date. To get $1,000 per car, the dealer might have to sell 100 cars before a certain date. The more cars the dealer sells, the more money he makes, because quota-based rebates are retroactive.

With these types of quota-based incentives, you have leverage. With your sale, the dealer is one more car closer to clearing the next hurdle and making more money. We recommend that you request half of the maximum quota-based incentive while negotiating your deal, unless the dealer or salesperson bungles and admits that your sale will put them into the next tier of incentive qualification. In this case, demand the maximum incentive.

15. When I use Edmund's formula to calculate a lease, I get a payment that is substantially higher than what the dealer quoted me. Why is this?

Most nationally advertised leases are subsidized by the manufacturer. This means that the manufacturer gives the dealer incentive money to lower the capitalized cost (selling price) listed on the lease, or that the financing institution owned by the manufacturer has artificially inflated the residual value to lower the monthly payment, or both. Dealers may not inform you of these adjustments in the numbers.

Another problem with advertised lease payments seen in newspapers and on television is that consumers don't read the terms of the lease carefully. Sometimes, a substantial capitalized cost reduction (down payment) is required. Sometimes hefty deposits and other drive-off fees are involved. Mileage limits may be ridiculously low. Payments may be required for 48 or 60 months rather than the conventional 24- or 36-month term. Read the fine print carefully!

Also, keep in mind that there are more than 250 different lending institutions across the country, and each one sets its own different residual values for lease contracts. Don't be surprised if you go to three different dealers and get three different lease payments for the same vehicle over the same term.

FREQUENTLY ASKED QUESTIONS

16. Why are destination charges the same for every dealer around the country?

Auto manufacturers will average the cost to ship a car from the factory to the furthest dealership with the cost to ship a car from the factory to the closest dealership. Some manufacturers do this for each model, others average costs across an entire make. Sometimes, shipping costs to Hawaii and Alaska may be higher than the averaged amount for the contiguous 48 states.

17. Can I avoid paying the destination charge by picking up a car at the factory?

Currently, the only North American factories that allow customers to take delivery the minute a car rolls off the assembly line are the Corvette plant in Bowling Green, Kentucky, and the Dodge Viper plant in Detroit. Buyers who opt to travel to the Bluegrass or Great Lakes states to pick up their new Corvette or Viper still pay the dealer they bought it from the destination charge. Edmund's doesn't know if you can avoid paying destination charges on European models by ordering and taking delivery of a car in Europe, but that's an expensive proposition to avoid paying a few hundred bucks.

18. What is a carryover allowance?

At the beginning of a new model year, manufacturers often provide dealers with a carryover allowance in addition to the dealer holdback. The carryover allowance is applied to cars from the previous model year, and is designed to assist dealers in lowering prices and clearing out old stock. Mark Eskeldson, radio talk show host, author, and auto industry veteran, claims that Ford Motor Company and General Motors offer dealers carryover allowances equal to 5% of the sticker price. Other manufacturers aren't mentioned in Eskeldson's book, "What Car Dealers Don't Want You to Know," but Edmund's predicts that import manufacturers provide carryover allowances at least equal to the dealer holdback. Chrysler Corporation, according to an industry source, abolished its carryover allowance program recently in favor of expanded customer rebate and dealer incentive programs.

FREQUENTLY ASKED QUESTIONS

19. Should I buy rustproofing, fabric protection packages, paint sealant, and other dealer-installed items?

Of course not. Most new cars are covered against rust perforation for several years and up to 100,000 miles. Want to protect your fabric? Go to an auto parts store and buy a can or two of Scotchgard. Most new cars have clearcoat paint, which offers protection from the elements. A little elbow grease and a jar of Mother's carnauba wax will keep the finish protected and looking great. By investing a little time and effort into your automobile, you can save hundreds on these highly profitable dealer protection packages.

20. Who sets the residual value for a lease?

The financing institution that is handling the lease for the dealership sets the residual value, which can be affected by market forces and vehicle popularity. When shopping leases, it is important to shop different financing institutions for the highest residual value and the lowest interest rate.

21. I want to pay cash for my new car. Do I have an advantage?

Not necessarily. You must remember that no matter how you pay for your car, it's all cash to the dealer. In the old days when dealers carried your note, you could save money by paying cash because there was no risk to the dealer. Today, dealerships finance through one of several lending institutions (banks, credit unions, or the automaker's captive financing division) who pay them cash when the contract is presented. In fact, if dealerships do the financing on your behalf, they tend to make more money on your contract in the form of a reserve; anywhere from ½ to 1 point spread on the interest. For example, if the published rate is 8.75%, the lender to dealer rate may be discounted to 8%; the .75% being the reserve held by the dealer as additional profit. This may not sound like much, but it adds up to hundreds of thousands of dollars a year at larger dealerships. This is the reason you should always arrange financing before going to the dealership, and then ask the dealer if they can beat your pre-approved rate. In most cases, they cannot, because of the reserve.

FREQUENTLY ASKED QUESTIONS

Paying cash is an advantage if you suffer from poor credit or bankruptcy, because it allows you to avoid the higher interest rates charged on loans to people with past credit problems.

22. When is the best time to purchase a car from a dealer?

The absolute best day to buy a car is December 31, particularly if it is raining or snowing. If you can't wait that long, try the day before Christmas or Thanksgiving. If that doesn't work out for you, any day the last week of any given month is a great time, and the nastier the weather, the better. Make the deal near closing time, when the sales staff is eager to go home for the night, but not so eager that they're willing to throw away a deal that could make them a few bucks. To ensure success, go into the dealership a few days beforehand and make sure they know you want to do the deal, but don't commit on that day. They'll call you back before quota time is up at the end of the month.

Why is this the best time to buy? Sales people are given quotas and incentives to reach X sales for the month. It is not uncommon for a salesperson to let a car go at invoice during the last week of the month to hit their goal, which results in a monetary or other tangible reward.

23. Where is the 1997 Honda CR-V pricing?

At the last minute, the debut of the Honda CR-V in showrooms was delayed until mid-February, 1997. Prices were expected before our deadline, but have been delayed along with the release of this sporty new mini-ute. What we can tell you is this: the CR-V is bigger inside than a Toyota RAV4 and the Geo Tracker/Suzuki Sidekick twins. It is powered by a 2.0-liter, 130-horsepower four-cylinder engine, mated to an automatic transmission. Base price is $19,800, and the only factory options are an alloy wheel/ABS combo that runs $1,000. The drivetrain runs in front-wheel drive until slippage is detected, and then it automatically switches to all-wheel drive. The CR-V is going to be a huge hit for Honda. We predict that demand will far outstrip the measly supply of 60,000 units expected for 1997.

ROAD TEST: Chevrolet K1500

1997 Chevrolet K1500 Extended Cab

Everybody Needs A Truck

by Christian Wardlaw
Managing Editor, Edmund Publications

Vehicle Tested: 1997 Chevrolet K1500 Extended Cab

Base Price of Test Vehicle: $21,451 (including destination charge)

Options on Test Vehicle: Silverado Preferred Equipment Group 1SC (includes air conditioning, color-keyed cloth and carpet trimmed door panels, color-keyed carpeting, rubber floor mats, added sound deadening insulation, AM/FM stereo with cassette player, seek/scan, and clock; leather-wrapped steering wheel, power windows, power door locks, power exterior mirrors, tilt steering wheel, cruise control, chrome front bumper with black rub strip, chrome rear bumper with step pad, deluxe chrome grille, dual composite halogen headlights, chrome wheel opening moldings, rally wheel trim, Silverado badging, remote keyless entry, electrochromic rearview mirror with integrated compass, power driver's seat, split bench seat with leather upholstery), Deep Tinted Glass, Sliding Rear Window, Bedliner, Third Door, Heavy-duty Chassis Equipment, 3.73 Rear Axle Ratio, Vortec 5700 V-8 Engine, 4-speed Automatic Transmission w/overdrive, Electronic Shift Transfer case, Cold Climate package, LT245/75R16C tires, California Emissions, Heavy-duty Trailering Equipment

Price of Test Vehicle: $29,399 (including destination charge)

Everybody needs a truck. Those of you who've got one parked in your driveway right now realize this, partly because you need it, and partly because you've always got a bunch of no-good friends asking you to borrow it. We decided we needed a truck recently, and asked Chevrolet if we could borrow one, because like your no-good friends, we don't own one ourselves.

What we really needed was a Suburban, but beggars can't be choosers. Over the Thanksgiving holiday, we had lots of family visiting Colorado from Massachusetts. We had a big dinner planned. We had several trips to make to Vail and to Estes Park, loaded down with assorted

ROAD TEST: Chevrolet K1500

gear and lots of beer. We had people and luggage to transport to Denver International Airport. We had a big table and 10 folding chairs to pick up. Yes, we really needed a Suburban, but Chevrolet only had a K1500 extended cab pickup available, and in the end, it served us just fine. Fortunately, it came equipped with a third door, also known as the Easy Access Panel.

Until you've lived with the third door, you don't know what you're missing. Now that we've had occasion to use the Easy Access Panel extensively, we can't imagine owning an extended cab pickup of any size without this indispensable feature. Loading the space behind the front seats is so much easier with this extra door that it is quite surprising it took nearly two decades of extended-cab pickup development before somebody thought about adding it. Better yet, the third door on the C/K pickup doesn't rattle like a set of loose dentures when driving over broken pavement, unlike those we've sampled on the smaller S-Series GM pickups.

Yes, the K1500 served us well. We loved the cut-off switch for the passenger airbag, which is a new-for-1997 item on Chevy's full-size pickups. Several small children and pregnant women were able to ride in the K1500's front seat thanks to the ability to shut the airbag off. We piled small adults and kids into the rear seat for a snowy trip to the Rockies, the lined bed full of luggage and skis. No complaints from those rear seat riders, so we put a couple of good-sized guys back there for a jaunt to Colorado Springs. This didn't work as well, and the group decided a Ford Escort would be preferable for the short trip south. Another day found us climbing Loveland Pass in a full-on blizzard with four-wheel drive engaged. I-70 was a mess, with frozen bridges, blinding snow, and snow-covered pavement making for treacherous passage. We were feeling pretty good about the K1500's performance until a rear-drive Ford Club Wagon shuttle van zoomed by on the left, skis jutting from a box on the back, no doubt driven by some young ski bum working for a resort in exchange for meager wages and a free season lift ticket.

At least the heater worked well. The K1500's powerful Vortec 5700 V-8 engine heated up quickly, and wasn't shy about pumping that heat directly to the interior. Despite the leather seats on our test truck and my refusal to wear long pants if the outside temperature is above freezing, the K1500 never turned occupants into popsicles waiting for the heat to

ROAD TEST: Chevrolet K1500

kick in. Chevy improved the climate control system in its line of C/K pickups for 1997, and we think they've done a dandy job.

No full-size pickup is easy to maneuver in urban settings, and this K1500 is no exception. However, it is important to note that Chevrolet has made driving the C/K truck in tight spots easier this year with the addition of Electronic Variable Orifice steering, which makes low-speed steering easier thanks to added boost. Also new for 1997 is a tighter turning diameter for K1500 models. During a brief off-road run in the foothills of the Rockies, we found a narrow trail that dead-ended in a campsite on a ridge. The tighter turning diameter allowed us to make a three-point turn and bounce back down the hill. Previously, we would have spent lots of time at the campsite, figuring out how to get the K1500 flipped around.

While it is true that we prefer the Ford F-150 pickup, the Chevrolet K1500 is no slouch. We found the Chevy imminently comfortable, which was rather unexpected. Usually, we find that in its most upright position, the driver's backrest still feels slightly reclined. In this K1500, we had no problem finding a comfortable seating position. The punch from the 255-horsepower pushrod engine is much more satisfying than Ford can deliver from either of its more advanced overhead cam V-8s. Our test truck wore a new shade of paint called Medium Blue Green Metallic, and while it wasn't the most masculine hue, it offended none of the staffers. Oddly, our $30,000 test vehicle included leather seats, but a CD player and alloy wheels were conspicuously absent. One complaint we have with interior ergonomics concerns the stereo controls. Last year, Chevy trucks came equipped with stereos that featured big light gray buttons and dials covered in large lettering. Not exactly aesthetically pleasing, but they were simple to understand and operate. This year, controls are colored charcoal to match the dashboard bezel, and the buttons for selecting pre-set stations on the stereo in our test truck are much smaller than last year. The 1997 C/K brochure indicates that perhaps we had a more basic head unit installed in our test K1500 than in the past. Again, at $30,000, why is a basic head unit still in the dashboard?

By the end of our week with the K1500, we had driven nearly 1,000 miles in all kinds of weather and over all kinds of road surfaces. The K1500 never put a foot wrong, except for the time we crossed an ice coated, steeply banked C-470 overpass in rush hour traffic without 4WD

ROAD TEST: Chevrolet K1500

engaged. Ha. That was fun. Still, the K1500 emerged unscathed, aside from a healthy coat of road grit. According to industry sources, this is the final full model year for the C/K pickup in current guise. General Motors is readying an all-new pickup for debut during the early part of 1998, and spy photos reveal a four-door extended cab that might actually hold larger adults in back with a minimum of discomfort. Styling is expected to be evolutionary, not as egg-shaped as the current Ford pickup, and not as brash as the Dodge Ram. Also, expect the current model to remain in production as GM ramps up production of the all-new pickup, similar to Ford's launch of the 1997 F-150.

In the meantime, Chevrolet produces a very handsome, very competent full-size pickup. The Vortec 5700 V-8 is one of our favorites, and with a third door and shift-on-the-fly four-wheel drive, the K1500 extended cab easily becomes a necessity rather than a luxury. Everybody needs a truck, and the K1500 is as good as any of them.

ROAD TEST: Mazda B4000 SE

1997 Mazda B4000 SE 2WD Extended Cab Pickup

Hey man, nice truck!

By Christian Wardlaw,
Managing Editor, Edmund Publications

Base Price of Test Vehicle: $16,225 (includes destination charge)

Options on Test Vehicle: Automatic transmission, floor mats, CD changer, SE-5 Plus Group (includes premium AM/FM stereo with cassette player, P225/70R14 outline white-lettered all-season tires, alloy wheels, pivoting quarter windows, privacy glass, sliding rear window, cargo cover, bedliner, passenger-side airbag with deactivation feature, 4-wheel anti-lock brakes, power windows, power door locks, power exterior mirrors, tilt steering wheel, cruise control, air conditioning, remote keyless entry)

Price of Test Vehicle: $21,030 (includes destination charge and package discount)

Howard Stern is nowhere to be found. I'm sitting in a parking lot near LAX, scanning stations in search of the King of all Media, when an attendant approaches saying, "Hey man, nice truck." Shortly thereafter, I find Howard engaging in intellectual discourse with a stripper, and I'm off for Sherman Oaks, laughing all the way.

The first thing I notice accelerating up the Century freeway ramp from Sepulveda is that the 160-horsepower 4.0-liter V-6 engine feels much more lively and capable in the B-Series pickup than it does in the Ford Explorer. For the uninitiated, Ford rebadges Ranger pickups as Mazda B-Series models per an agreement between the two automakers. This is good news for Mazda, because the Ranger is one of the better small trucks on the market today. Under the hood of the crimson B4000 I'm driving is the same powerplant that feels wheezy and overmatched in the Ford Explorer. Zipping onto the 405 northbound is effortless, though I do find the motor somewhat weak at higher speeds.

Jumping off the traffic-snared 405 at Mulholland, I decide to see how the B4000 handles the curves. Riding on somewhat small 14-inch tires and wheels, the B4000 cannot whiz above Bel Air with much alacrity,

ROAD TEST: Mazda B4000 SE

though the jouncy suspension certainly makes the ride seem much faster than it is. Overall, the B4000 is easy to control when hoofing it at speed.

Coldwater Canyon is clogged with cars. Suddenly, traffic comes to a halt. In the rearview mirror, I see two teens in a late-80s Honda Accord fiddling with the stereo just as I had been not long before. Looking up, the driver's face becomes a mask of surprise and horror, and the nose of the Accord dives sharply, right into the B4000's rear bumper. Nobody has the phone number for the Studio City police, and the kid doesn't have collision coverage. The Mazda appears undamaged, though careful inspection reveals that the gap between the right rear corner of the bed and the bumper's edge has shrunk to the point that my index finger no longer fits. We decide to forget about the police report, and exchange information. The kid is worried that Mazda will call his dad, and wonders if he should lie about the extensive damage suffered by the Accord. "Hey, you know your dad better than I do," I reply.

Inside the B4000, occupants are treated to the same interior trimmings found in the Ford Ranger and Explorer. Ergonomics are fantastic, and seat comfort is excellent. Materials are rich in appearance and feel, though the ashtray's ratchety deployment left something to be desired. We also noticed that the rear premium speaker grilles would certainly poke into the backs of passengers uncomfortably ensconced in the Mazda's rear jump seats. The ventilation system emitted a particularly foul odor, with only 1,700 miles on the odometer. Our final gripe involves the lack of a third door. Hoisting a 30-pound duffel bag in and out of the rear quarters was not especially gratifying, but if adding an additional portal meant we'd have to live with the creaks and rattles plaguing 3-door versions of the Chevy S-10 and the GMC Sonoma, we could live without it.

Our test truck was equipped with a passenger airbag that could be switched off when necessary. Excellent solution to the current airbag problem. The premium sound system produces rich sound, and was enhanced by a 6-disc CD changer, which we did not use. Mounted along the rear wall of the cab, the disc changer is out of reach while driving, and hampers operation of the cargo cover. Large exterior mirrors, generous glass area, and a high driving position contribute to excellent visibility. Seats are very comfortable, more so with the height-adjustable seatbelts that come standard. Seat fabric is attractive and feels

ROAD TEST: Mazda B4000 SE

particularly durable. In between the seats of our test truck was a deep console with dual cupholders that could accommodate Super Size Sprites side by side. We do wish that the audio storage slots at the bottom of the console would vanish, however, leaving a smooth console floor.

More than one person admired the B4000 we drove. Dressed in a crimson metallic with silver-painted alloy wheels and a helping of chrome accents, the Mazda turned plenty of heads. We'd dump the bodyside pinstriping, though we realize that graphics are a part of the B4000's heritage. It's a good looking piece, but we still prefer the looks of the Ford Ranger.

Mazda is selling a fun-to-drive, fully-loaded pickup for less than you'd think. Intellichoice calls it "Best Overall Value" in its class. With shrewd bargaining, the truck we drove could be had for a little over $20,000 out the door. Best of all, the B4000 features a more comprehensive warranty than the Ford Ranger and GM's S-10/Sonoma duo. Tight, rattle-free construction, a strong engine, evident resistance to rear collision damage, and a world-class cabin make the Mazda B4000 one truck you ought to be complimenting, and considering.

ROAD TEST: Mercury Mountaineer

1997 Mercury Mountaineer

Where's The Gas Station?

by Christian Wardlaw
Managing Editor, Edmund Publications

Vehicle Tested: 1997 Mercury Mountaineer AWD

Base Price of Test Vehicle: $29,765 (including destination charge)

Options on Test Vehicle: Preferred Equipment Group 655A (includes luggage rack, floor mats, running boards, power bucket seats, overhead console [with compass, outside temperature display, reading lights, and storage bin], electronics group [with remote keyless entry, door keypad, anti-theft system, and automatic lock/relock], retractable cargo cover, high series floor console [with rear heater, rear audio controls, and front/rear cupholders]), Multi-disc CD Changer, Front License Plate Bracket, Electrochromic Rearview Mirror (includes autolamp system), Leather Seats

Price of Test Vehicle: $32,260 (including destination charge)

The night attendant at the Amoco station down the street from my office is beginning to recognize me. A Goodyear tire shop is going up next door to the Amoco, and blowing dust is clogging the credit card slots on the gas pumps, requiring a trip inside to pay for gas. The Mercury Mountaineer we've been driving for over six weeks is about as unable to pass by the Amoco station without stopping as Tommy Lee is a room full of slow-witted female Motley Crue groupies sucking down Bacardi and Coke. In other words, the Mountaineer is never satisfied.

By now, many readers know that the Mercury Mountaineer is a thinly disguised Ford Explorer V-8. The transformation starts with a chrome grille full of fine vertical bars and a Mercury logo in the center. From the side, clues that the SUV is a Mercury are limited to painted wheel ports with Mercury badges on the chrome center caps and a bodyside molding embossed with the word Mountaineer. In back, the Mercury gets a glittery strip of trim connecting the reverse lights, an obnoxiously huge Mercury emblem in the center of the tailgate, and the bumper from the export version of the Explorer, which contains twin red reflectors.

ROAD TEST: Mercury Mountaineer

Inside, the steering wheel hub is embossed with the Mercury emblem. Front and rear bumpers are painted gray to match the lower body paint.

The Mountaineer comes in two different editions: two-wheel drive and all-wheel drive with a 5.0-liter V-8 engine and two-tone paint. You can have cloth or leather seats, but if you want fake wood decorating the interior you'd better look elsewhere. One style of aluminum wheels is available, which is OK, because they look great. Another plus is the lack of Eddie Bauer wheel flares, which we think makes the Explorer look more pudgy than it already does. Choose among several tasteful shades of paint for the upper body, all of which nicely complement the gray lower half of the Mountaineer. Overall, we like the exterior treatment of the Mountaineer much better than that of the Ford Explorer Eddie Bauer or Limited models, the latter seemingly always painted a putrid color patterned after that old, politically-incorrect Crayola shade called Flesh. Aside from the big Mercury emblem on the back, the Mountaineer is quite tastefully finished.

Inside, the familiar dashboard from the Explorer and Ranger greets occupants. All controls are located and sized for ease of operation, with the exception of the secondary stereo controls. Our Mountaineer came with optional power highback bucket front seats dressed in leather, and they proved to be eminently comfortable, except on very cold days. We'd like to see seat heaters made available for sub-freezing temperatures. A JBL sound system is optional on the Mountaineer, but our test vehicle thankfully did not have this uplevel stereo. See, every Explorer or Mountaineer we've driven has been equipped with JBL sound, and the sub-woofer mounted in the right cargo area wall does little but boom into the brains of rear seat passengers. The standard system in this tester offered door panel speakers front and rear, and sounded much better than the JBL unit. Save your money. We did have a six-disc changer slipped into the center console, but the disc magazine was missing, so we didn't get a chance to give it a whirl.

The Mountaineer boasts one of the largest interiors of any compact SUV. There is plenty of room for four large adult occupants, and on our test truck, those in the rear got their own heater and stereo controls, though headphones were required to switch radio stations. The cargo compartment shade pulls forward from a spindle that rests parallel to the rear seatback, and while it easy to use, we prefer one that pulls from the side so that the spindle doesn't require removal each time

ROAD TEST: Mercury Mountaineer

larger cargo is loaded. Much appreciated was a power door lock switch located in the cargo compartment. Our Mountaineer was equipped with running boards that we cannot recall actually using because the truck is easy to climb into without them. We do worry that the unneeded running boards will dirty pants and dresses in foul weather, however.

Visibility forward and rearward is very good, despite darkly tinted windows. Our Mountaineer was equipped with an electrochromic mirror, whose function escapes us. Look at how dark the tint is on those windows! The Autolamp function, which detects the amount of ambient light outside the truck and operates the headlights automatically, is an integral part of the electrochromic mirror, so if you want automatic headlights, you must opt for the mirror. The driving position is very good, and all gauges are clearly marked and easy to see. Thoughtful backlighting makes it easy to find the power window and lock switches at night.

The Mountaineer's pushrod V-8, pilfered from the Mustang GT after that model went modular for 1996, moves the truck with surprising alacrity, but the penalty of a heavy foot is familiarity on a first name basis with the local gas jockey. One afternoon, we drove from the south end of Denver to downtown Colorado Springs and back, averaging about 80 mph on I-25. Half a tank was drained during the drive. You can almost watch the needle sink on the gas gauge. Fuel economy is our single major complaint about the Mountaineer, because everything else works so well. In fact, this vehicle guzzles so much fuel that it would be economically unfeasible for any of our staffers to own one.

Handling feels tippy to the uninitiated, but after six weeks behind the wheel, we could toss the Mountaineer about with little more than severe tire squeal to worry about. In one snow and ice storm that arrived during the same week that we also tested a Subaru Legacy Outback, the Mountaineer felt much more stable and controllable thanks to its more aggressive tires and heavier curb weight. We did not drive faster than 90 mph (where it felt solid as a rock), and we did not mash the brakes to the floor from high speed. In urban settings, the brakes worked well, offering smooth stops, though we discovered that unless you plant your foot flat on the center of the brake pedal, the edge of your shoe can depress the accelerator slightly at the same time. Then again, this editor has gargantuan size 12 feet, and nobody else on staff has found

ROAD TEST: Mercury Mountaneer

pedal placement to be a problem. We also did not take this Mountaineer off-road, but previous experience in a different model indicates that this Mercury will take nearly everybody nearly anyplace they want to go.

We've noticed plenty of drivetrain lash in other V-8 Explorers and Mountaineers we've driven, and this model was no exception. To date, however, we haven't heard from readers that the occasional shudder that makes its way to the passenger cabin has caused any problem. One staff member has an old college buddy who owns an all-wheel drive Explorer and holds a job as an automotive engineer with a firm in Detroit. Old College Buddy seemed unconcerned about the issue, which plagues his Explorer when accelerating out of a right hand turn. Something to worry about? The next few years will tell the tale.

During our time with the Mountaineer, we experienced no mechanical failures. The final week the Mountaineer spent with us, the left headlamp bulb burned out, and some punk(s) decided the rear window wiper would function better if it appeared that Salvador Dali had designed it. After bending the wiper arm back into position, it still required replacement because it wouldn't contact the rear window any longer.

Like its twin, the Explorer, Mercury's Mountaineer is a very capable and comfortable vehicle. In fact, this editor would prefer either small SUV to Ford's hulking new Expedition, but only equipped with the new overhead cam V-6 engine, which feels just as strong as the V-8 but without the horrendous fuel economy suffered by the larger engine. As much as we enjoy the Mountaineer, we are happy to return the vehicle to Ford. Simply put, we're tired of gassing the darn thing up.

QUICK SPIN: Toyota 4Runner

1997 Toyota 4Runner

High Expectations Result in Lukewarm Impressions

By Christian J. Wardlaw
Managing Editor, Edmund Publications

Grant Whitmore, one of Edmund's automotive editors, loves Peanut Buster Parfaits from Dairy Queen, though he finds this phrase to be quite a tounge twister and almost always refers to them as Peanut Puster Barfaits (not exactly appetizing, eh?). Discuss one of these fake ice cream concoctions in front of him, and you'd better have a napkin handy to mop up the drool that is sure to spill on his collar. One day last summer, I decided to skip my usual Mud Pie Breeze in favor of a Peanut Buster Parfait. I mean, the curiosity was killing me. It was good, satisfyingly chocolately and nutty, but not spectacular. Now I know how folks feel when I foist a bottle of Yoo Hoo on them.

When expectations are high, a let down is almost inevitable. Exceptions to this rule include the Mazda Miata, the Demon Drop at Ohio's Cedar Point, Fat Tire beer, and New York cheesecake procured from a Marie Callendar's restaurant. For more than a year, we've been hearing how good the redesigned Toyota 4Runner is from sources ranging from Popular Mechanics to 4-Wheeler to Car and Driver. We finally got a chance to briefly drive the new 4Runner in Chicago recently, and it is quite evident that we expected a supertruck. The loaded Toyota 4Runner Limited we drove did not meet our expectations.

Like the Ford Expedition, the Toyota 4Runner excels off-road but not on. Rural Illinois provides little opportunity for boulder-bashing, so we settled for the next best thing, a gravel road with deep drainage channels on either side. Back and forth across the gravel we went, diving into and out of the muddy drainage channels. The 4Runner laughed at our attempts to overwhelm it, digging in and yanking us back and forth over the crown of the road. We were very impressed with the 4Runner's tight, controlled behavior and the stiffly sprung suspension.

After our jaunt through the mud, we drove the 4Runner mostly on frost-heaved and pockmarked two-lane highways. The ride was barely acceptable. The suspension that performs flawlessly off-road transfers every on-road jiggle, wiggle, and bounce to passengers, and the cargo

QUICK SPIN: Toyota 4Runner

area cover rattled and squeaked ceaselessly until we finally stopped and pulled it into place, an operation that took several attempts to get the plastic retainers lined up properly. The 3.4-liter V-6 engine is strong, but doesn't feel so in the overweight Limited model. Excessive engine noise and vibration are troublesome too, not expected in a vehicle slathered with glossy fake wood trim and leather seats. Our intern, Greg Anderson, said of the motor, "It sounds like it's trying to clear its throat." Travel more than 60 mph, and expect to enjoy lots of wind noise from around the A-pillars and huge, square exterior mirrors.

Think the stereo will clear up the wind noise problem? It will, as long as you can figure out how to use it without pulling over and consulting the owner's manual. Our Limited had an AM/FM stereo with CD player that featured far too many tiny dials, buttons, and words to encourage efficient operation. At least the driver's seat is comfortable, though it features a limited (Ha! Get it?) range of adjustment. Power recliners, however, are a bit much in an SUV. Who really needs them anyway? They're slow and expensive to repair when they break. Rear passengers will find a supportive backrest, but the bottom cushion is mounted too low for comfort, and there is little room under the front chairs for feet or toes.

Gauges are clearly marked and legible, nestled in a sea of ugly fake wood trim. Climate controls are of the slide lever variety, and we prefer rotary dials. However, Toyota has thoughtfully provided rear passengers with heat and air conditioning ducts that can be operated independently to adjust fan speed and temperature. Deep tinted glass makes the narrow 4Runner Limited feel somewhat claustrophobic, and a gaze

QUICK SPIN: Toyota 4Runner

around the interior makes you wonder why the 4Runner Limited costs nearly as much as a loaded Chevrolet Tahoe.

You've heard the phrase "surprise and delight?" Toyota evidently prefers "surprise and upset." The power sunroof doesn't feature one-touch open operation. The front cupholders easily pop out of a slot in the dashboard, but require additional manual manipulation to insert your favorite beverage. The running boards are too skinny to actually rely upon them for entry and exit assistance, but they stick out just far enough to coat the backs of legs and pants with drainage channel mud. Finally, and this one is the real horror, the Limited model doesn't have an illuminated visor vanity mirror! Gasp!

Is the Toyota 4Runner a bad sport/utility? Certainly not. It's tough off-road, great looking, and boasts an excellent reputation for quality and reliability. Is it a bad value? Yes, especially in Limited trim. A Chevrolet Tahoe or Ford Expedition would make much better sense in the mid-$30,000 range where the 4Runner Limited competes, while the less-powerful and less-expensive Nissan Pathfinder is a more refined, user-friendly choice if buying American is simply not an option. From Whitmore's perspective, a Peanut Puster Barfait this truck ain't.

Edmund's SINGLE COPIES / ORDER FORM

Please send me:

☐ **USED CARS: PRICES & RATINGS** *(includes S&H)* $11.99

☐ **NEW CARS**
   —American & Import *(includes S&H)* $11.99

☐ **NEW TRUCKS [PICKUPS, VANS & SPORT UTILITIES]**
   —American & Import *(includes S&H)* $11.99

Name _____
Address _____
City, State, Zip _____
Phone _____

PAYMENT: __ MASTERCARD   __ VISA   __ CHECK or MONEY ORDER $ _____

Make check or money order payable to:
Edmund Publications Corporation P.O.Box 338, Shrub Oaks, NY 10588
For more information or to order by phone, call **(914) 962-6297**

Credit Card # _____ Exp. Date: _____
Cardholder Name: _____
Signature: _____

Prices above include shipping within the U.S. and Canada only. Other countries, please add $6.00 to the price ($11.99 + 6.00) per book (via air mail) and $2.00 to the price ($11.99 + 2.00) per book (surface mail). Please pay through an American Bank or with American Currency. Rates subject to change without notice.

SUBSCRIPTIONS / ORDER FORM

BUYER'S PRICE GUIDES

Please send me a one year subscription for:

☐ **USED CAR PRICES & RATINGS**
AMERICAN & IMPORT (includes S&H) $30.30
Canada $35.30/Foreign Countries $61.30 (includes air mail S&H)
4 issues/yr

☐ **NEW CARS**
AMERICAN & IMPORT (package price includes $6.75 S&H) $22.75
Canada $26.50/Foreign Countries $46.00 (includes air mail S&H)
3 issues/yr

☐ **NEW TRUCKS [PICKUPS, VANS & SPORT UTILITIES]**
AMERICAN & IMPORT (package price includes $6.75 S&H) $22.75
Canada $26.50/Foreign Countries $46.00 (includes air mail S&H)
3 issues/yr

☐ **NEW VEHICLE PRICES**
AMERICAN & IMPORT (package price includes $13.50 S&H) $45.50
Canada $53.00/Foreign Countries $92.00 (includes air mail S&H)
6 issues/yr:
3 NEW CARS [American & Import]
3 NEW TRUCKS [American & Import]

☐ **PREMIUM PLAN**
AMERICAN & IMPORT (package price includes $20.50 S&H) $75.80
Canada $88.35/Foreign Countries $153.35 (includes air mail S&H)
10 issues/yr:
4 USED CARS [American & Import]
3 NEW CARS [American & Import]
3 NEW TRUCKS [American & Import]

Name _____

Address _____

City, State, Zip _____

PAYMENT: __ MC __ VISA __ Check or Money Order-Amount $_____   Rates subject to change without notice

Make check or money order payable to:
Edmund Publications Corporation P.O.Box 338, Shrub Oaks, NY 10588
For more information or to order by phone, call **(914) 962-6297**

Credit Card # _____ Exp. Date: _____
Cardholder Name: _____
Signature _____

Edmund's

BUYER'S DECISION GUIDES SCHEDULED RELEASE DATES FOR 1997/1998*

VOL. 31/32		RELEASE DATE	COVER DATE
U3102	USED CARS: Prices & Ratings	APR 97	SUMMER 97
N3102	NEW CARS: Prices & Reviews [American & Import]	JUN 97	SUMMER/FALL 97
S3102	NEW TRUCKS: Prices & Reviews [American & Import]	JUN 97	SUMMER/FALL 97
U3103	USED CARS: Prices & Ratings	JUL 97	FALL 97
U3104	USED CARS: Prices & Ratings	OCT 97	WINTER 97
N3103	NEW CARS: Prices & Reviews [American & Import]	DEC 97	WINTER 98
S3103	NEW TRUCKS: Prices & Reviews [American & Import]	DEC 97	WINTER 98
U3201	USED CARS: Prices & Ratings	JAN 98	SPRING 98
N3201	NEW CARS: Prices & Reviews [American & Import]	MAR 98	SPRING 98
S3201	NEW TRUCKS: Prices & Reviews [American & Import]	MAR 98	SPRING 98

*Subject to Change